IMPLEMENTING EVIDENCE-BASED ACADEMIC INTERVENTIONS IN SCHOOL SETTINGS

IMPLEMENTING EVIDENCE-BASED ACADEMIC INTERVENTIONS IN SCHOOL SETTINGS

EDITED BY

SYLVIA ROSENFIELD AND VIRGINIA BERNINGER

OXFORD
UNIVERSITY PRESS
2009

OXFORD

UNIVERSITY PRESS

Oxford University Press, Inc., publishes works that further
Oxford University's objective of excellence
in research, scholarship, and education.

Oxford New York
Auckland Cape Town Dar es Salaam Hong Kong Karachi
Kuala Lumpur Madrid Melbourne Mexico City Nairobi
New Delhi Shanghai Taipei Toronto

With offices in
Argentina Austria Brazil Chile Czech Republic France Greece
Guatemala Hungary Italy Japan Poland Portugal Singapore
South Korea Switzerland Thailand Turkey Ukraine Vietnam

Published by Oxford University Press, Inc.
198 Madison Avenue, New York, New York 10016
www.oup.com

Oxford is a registered trademark of Oxford University Press

Library of Congress Cataloging-in-Publication Data
Implementing evidence-based interventions in school settings / edited
by Sylvia Rosenfield and Virginia Berninger.
p. cm.
Includes bibliographical references and index.
ISBN 978-0-19-532535-5 (cloth : alk. paper)   1. Educational psychology.   2. Learning,
Psychology of.   3. Effective teaching.   I. Rosenfield, Sylvia A.   II. Berninger, Virginia Wise.
LB1051.I465 2009
370.15′23—dc22   2008031114

9 8 7 6 5 4 3 2 1

Printed in the United States of America
on acid-free paper

Foreword

In the past decade, we have witnessed an incredible number of developments in what is now called the evidence-based practice movement. The transition from considering "empirically validated" interventions to a broader consideration of practice perimeters using evidence-based strategies is well upon us with the American Psychological Association sponsoring two major task forces devoted to this topic. It is a delight to write the forward for the volume that Sylvia Rosenfield and Virginia (Ginger) Berninger have edited entitled, "*Implementing Evidence-Based Academic Interventions in School Settings.*"

In many ways, the book represents the culmination of a journey that many of us have taken in thinking about how we can promote and sustain the use of evidence-based instructional and mental health interventions in schools. During the early to mid-1990s our colleagues in clinical psychology began to develop lists of "empirically validated" treatments for a variety of childhood disorders. The efforts at the time were controversial but spawned a number of important developments in many divisions and professional groups including, and especially, school psychology. In 1999, I had an opportunity to present on the topic of "empirically-supported treatments" at the Winter Meeting of the Council of Directors of School Psychology Training Programs (CDSPP). On the heels of the CDSPP meeting, I made a recommendation to Dr. Beth Doll that school psychologists take some leadership in moving forward on this important agenda. As the old adage goes, no good deed goes unpunished and for over 10 years I have Co-Chaired the Task Force on Evidence-Based Interventions in School Psychology, first with Karen Callan Stoiber and then with Kimberly Eaton Hoagwood. Sylvia Rosenfield and Virginia Berninger were among a core group of dedicated individuals who participated early on in various activities of the Task Force; and as this volume illustrates, they have continued to make major and significant contributions to the practice of school psychology. In particular, they have taken on a most important responsibility: to share their vision for what some of the next steps in research and practice should be for the implementation of evidence-based interventions.

One of our early agendas for the Task Force was to review the literature in various domains of intervention research and practice. In some of our early deliberations, Virginia Berninger and Edward Shapiro agreed to serve as Co-Chairs of the Academic Intervention domain (several intervention domains were established). One of the agendas for each of the domain chairs was to organize and help individuals review various interventions of relevance to school psychologists in practice. However, in their efforts to examine the number of academic interventions available to educational professionals, they found that many review efforts had already occurred. Yet, many of these reviews were in diverse outlets and not easily retrieved for translation into practice. Thus, rather than designate topics and individuals to conduct systematic literature reviews, they decided that a better strategy would be to summarize the literature and report out to the field what we know in evidence-based instructional interventions. (More details on that history are provided in the introductory chapter of this volume.)

Ed, Sylvia, and Ginger participated in a conference call in which there was consensus that a summary of work was needed but also that some future directions for intervention research needed to be mapped out. Sylvia and Ginger decided to collaborate on this project; their work in this volume and that of the contributors has gone well beyond the early focus of the Task Force and has charted new directions for evidence-based practice in psychology and education. Their vision reflects tremendous advances in thinking about what it will take to support and sustain evidence-based or science-based practice in educational settings.

It is important to examine some of the transitions that have occurred in the evidence-based practice movement. As eluded to above, one of the first transitions was in thinking about how we conceptualize interventions. Interventions are conceptualized as a "work in progress" and not really ever validated; interventions and instructional practices accumulate a certain level of scientific support that is ever changing. In fact, research may call a once supported practice into question or designate a preference for an instructional strategy among alternatives. Yet, as authors in this volume carefully articulate, research to document the effectiveness of an intervention is not enough. It is important to think about how that instructional intervention can be translated into practice.

Designation of an intervention as scientifically supported is a first and important step. Yet, other issues need to be considered in the evidence-based practice journey. To translate research into practice, a much more sophisticated and inherently much more complex system of issues must be considered in research. In addition to conducting research on an intervention through quantitative experimental methods (e.g., a randomized clinical trial or single-case research) to establish efficacy and effectiveness, researchers have begun to examine options for the transportability and evaluation of interventions in the social ecology and context in which they are implemented. This focus is at the heart of evidence-based practice.

The organizational structure of the edited volume that Sylvia and Ginger have outlined in this text is noteworthy and reflects the trend toward taking into account the complexity of systems and issues that we now confront in this translational process of securing the application of evidence-based instruction in our schools. As will be evident in the organizational structure of the volume, the editors characterize the *process* of translating science-supported instruction in practice as a six step series of issues that must be considered.

Step 1 involves knowing the research literature and being a critical consumer. We now have major groups who are supporting that important agenda and there is growing evidence that this information will make a strong database for decision making regarding what interventions are available. The challenges in this area are the diversity of sources of information for educational professionals and locating this information to meet local needs (Kratochwill, 2007).

Step 2 involves a consideration of concepts and mechanisms of implementation that have become a central area of research. Understanding the issues that promote and inhibit the actual implementation of an evidence-based practice is a critical research agenda because many instructional interventions are not possible to implement given the ecology of our school practice settings. Authors in this section review various dimensions of what we know and what we will need to know in order to advance understanding and actual implementation.

Steps 3 and 4 involve the actual implementation process. Transformation of the evidence into professional practice is a complex issue. Authors in this area review work that will guide our efforts in understanding what it will take to ensure that a good program, instructional practice or procedure is implemented with integrity.

Step 5 represents a focus on assessment and evaluation of practices designed to improve student performance. It is perhaps one of the critical issues we have emphasized in psychological practice for the past 60 years. The evaluation of practice through individual analysis of students or evaluation of programs on a large-scale basis is a significant factor because it provides information that can be used to make decisions about program modifications, integrity, system implementation issues, and a host of variables that are outlined earlier in the text.

Step 6 involves a critical aspect that deserves considerable attention in the future; that is, actually acquiring the knowledge base to implement interventions in educational settings. Far too few educational programs are training teachers and other school-based professionals to implement evidence-based interventions and practices. Information in this section provides critical information that will be necessary to move our educational institutions and professional training of preservice and inservice professionals forward. The challenges in this area are great and, for example, range from the diversity in scientific paradigms in our teacher-training programs to logistical barriers to professional development in school settings.

This is a text that is clearly on the cutting edge of science and advances our understanding and the scope of evidence-based practice in educational settings. It is timely and important that we understand the messages that authors are providing in this book to promote effective outcomes for our students and our schools. I congratulate the editors and the authors for their dedication and extraordinary scientific contributions in what has become one of our most important agendas in education and mental health.

Thomas R. Kratochwill, Madison, WI

■ Reference

Kratochwill, T. R. (2007). Preparing psychologists for evidence-based practice: Lessons learned and challenges ahead. *American Psychologist, 62,* 826–843.

PREFACE

Why this book? Why this book now? Both editors, and several of the chapter authors, have been involved in the work of the Task Force on Evidence-based Interventions in School Psychology (Task Force), cosponsored by the American Psychological Association, the APA Division of School Psychology (Division 16), and the Society for the Study of School Psychology; the Task Force was also endorsed by the National Association of School Psychologists. Beginning in 1999, the Task Force set out to "move forward the agenda of defining concepts, terms, and issues that should be considered in formulating a realistic and meaningful framework for identifying effective prevention and intervention programs" based on research (Kratochwill & Stoiber, 2002, p. 342). A major contribution of the Task Force has been the Procedural and Coding Manual, developed by the Manual Subcommittee of the Task Force (Kratochwill & Stoiber, 2002).

In pursuing its goals, the Task Force also designated five domains, each of which was challenged to review the literature in its area. One of the domains was the Academic Skills Domain, co-chaired by Edward Shapiro and Virginia Berninger. In a letter in 2003 from the co-chairs of the Academic Skills Domain to Tom Kratochwill, chair of the Task Force, they listed the various meta-analyses and conference panels that had already reviewed the extensive research in the academic domain and proposed that instead of conducting yet another set of reviews, "the academic skills domain focus on mechanisms for disseminating what is known about effective academic interventions to school practitioners.... In other words, research validates what works in general, but practitioners need to evaluate the *implementation of research-supported practices for individual students* (italics in original) in specific schools and programs to determine if the intervention is working for that student" (Shapiro & Berninger, October, 2003). That is the fundamental question that

ix

this book is designed to address. Sylvia Rosenfield and Virginia Berninger, both members of the Task Force, began a collaboration that included other members of the Task Force, some of whom are chapter authors in this volume, to expand efforts to study the research and implementation process within the academic domain. Our collaboration has culminated in this volume on the implementation of research into school settings.

This book is designed for both researchers and practitioners. We have formulated a stepwise progression from reporting in scientific terms what the current state of evidence is to the extremely complex process of implementing evidence-based academic interventions into the real world of practice. By examining these two sides of the domain together, we believe that a complete state of the field is provided. As we move from the descriptions of research to the exigencies of practice, one conclusion is that there is an urgent need for more and stronger research evidence on the implementation process itself.

The structure of the book is set up as a series of steps or stages, following the introductory chapter: Step 1: a review of the research knowledge base itself; Step 2: concepts and mechanisms of implementation; Step 3: systems issues in implementation; Step 4: teachers and psychologists transforming research into practice in schools; Step 5: assessment issues; and Step 6: preservice preparation of teachers and psychologists for implementation. This combination of the voices of researchers and school-based practitioners is one of the special features of this book. It seems clear that a productive dialogue between these two partners needs to be further developed.

As co-editors, we are truly indebted to the authors of these chapters, who provided us a rich course on academic interventions and their implementation in the world of practice, and the reviewers who gave generously of their time and contributed greatly to the quality of the final products. Their time and responsiveness were much appreciated and are acknowledged below. We also wish to thank Mariclaire Cloutier and Regan Hofmann, our editors at Oxford University Press, for their wisdom and patience during the long incubation period of this project. The co-editors are also grateful for grant support during the preparation of the book from the Institute of Educational Sciences (Rosenfield, Grant No. R305F050051) and the National Institute of Child Health and Human Development (Berninger, Grant No. HD25858); the opinions expressed in this book are those of the authors and editors and not of either of these federal agencies. A final thank you to our ever-patient husbands as this project overflowed into our lives.

■ Reviewers

The co-editors gratefully acknowledge the contributions of the reviewers of the chapters in this volume.

Robert Abbott
Scott Beers
E. Todd Brown
Kate Sutton Burkhouse
Deanna Burney
Joanne Carlisle
Michael Copland
Katura Cramer
Marvin Feuerberg
Barbara Foorman
Steve Graham
Willis Hawley
John Hintze
Maureen Hoskyn
Brinda Jegatheesan
Janine Jones
Mark Jewell
Joseph Jenkins
Malt Joshi
Lauren Kaiser
Michael Knapp
Mary Levinsohn-Klyap
Richard Mayer
Peggy McCardle
Brett Miller
Victoria Molfese
William Nagy
Deborah Nelson
Daniel Newman
Stephen Peverly
Jonathan Sandoval
Ann Schulte
Tim Standall
William Strein
Joanna Uhry

CONTENTS

CONTRIBUTORS

Nicole Alston-Abel, M.Ed., Ph.C.
School Psychology Ph.D. Candidate
University of Washington

Kathleen L. Anderson, M.Ed.
The Clinical Center for the
    Study of Development and
    Learning
The Carolina Institute
    for Developmental Disabilities
University of North Carolina School
    of Medicine

Kathy Aux
Office of Special Education
Prince William County Public
    Schools

Virginia Berninger, Ph.D.
Educational Psychology
Multidisciplinary Learning
    Disability Center
Literacy Trek and Write
    Stuff Intervention
University of Washington

Emily Binks, Ph.D.
Lecturer and Research Co-ordinator

Scarborough School of Education
University of Hull

E. Todd Brown, Ph.D.
Department of Teaching and
    Learning
College of Education and Human
    Development
University of Louisville

Carol A. Christensen
School of Education
The University of Queensland

Maura Crowe, M.A.
Division of Mental Health Services
    and Policy Research
Columbia University

Emily Ocker Dean
Department of Curriculum and
    Instruction
McMurry University

Alnita Dunn, Ph.D.
Psychological Services
    Department
Division of Special Education

Los Angeles Unified School
District

Susan G. Forman, Ph.D.
School Psychology Program
Department of Applied Psychology
Graduate School of Applied and
Professional Psychology
Rutgers University

Nina E. Goodman
The Abraham Joshua Heschel School

Lori Graham, Ph.D.
Department of Teaching, Learning
& Culture
Texas A&M University

Todd A. Gravois
Department of Counseling and
Personnel Services
School of Education
University of Maryland

Kimberly Eaton Hoagwood, Ph.D.
Division of Mental Health Services
and Policy Research
Columbia University

Stephen R. Hooper, Ph.D.
Department of Psychiatry and The
Clinical Center for the Study of
Development and Learning
The Carolina Institute for
Developmental Disabilities
University of North Carolina School
of Medicine

Maureen Hoskyn, Ph.D.
SFU Centre for Research
on Early Child Health and
Education
Simon Fraser University

Martha C. Hougen, Ph.D.
Principal Investigator,
Texas Higher Education
Collaborative
The Meadows Center for Preventing
Educational Risk & The Vaughn
Gross Center for Reading &
Language Arts
The University of Texas
at Austin

R. Malatesha Joshi, Ph.D.
Professor of Reading Education,
ESL, and Educational Psychology
Texas A&M University

Paul Kimmelman, Ed.D.
Learning Point Associates

Kelly Cutler Kirk, M.Ed.
School Psychologist
Norwich, CT Public Schools

Steve Knotek, Ph.D.
School of Education
University of North Carolina,
Chapel Hill

Sean B. Knuth
School of Education
University of North Carolina,
Chapel Hill

Jim Kohlmoos
Knowledge Alliance

Barbara Lowe-Greenlee, Ph.D.
School of Education
University of North Carolina,
Chapel Hill

Peggy McCardle, Ph.D., MPH
Child Development & Behavior
Branch

Center for Research for Mothers
    & Children
Eunice Kennedy Shriver
    National Institute of Child
    Health and Human
    Development
National Institutes of Health

Brett Miller, Ph.D.
Child Development & Behavior
    Branch
Center for Research for Mothers
    and Children
Eunice Kennedy Shriver National
    Institute of Child Health and
    Human Development
National Institutes of Health

Douglas Miller, M.A.
Los Angeles Unified
    School District

Victoria J. Molfese, Ph.D.
Department of Teaching and
    Learning
College of Education and Human
    Development
University of Louisville

William Nagy, Ph.D.
School of Education
Seattle Pacific University

Michael T. Neall
Prince William County Public
    Schools

Deborah Nelson
Department of Counseling and
    Personnel Services
School of Education
University of Maryland
    College Park

S. Serene Olin, Ph.D.
Division of Mental Health Services
    and Policy Research
Columbia University

Erin M. Olson, M.Ed., Ph.C.
School Psychology Ph.D. Canditate
University of Washington

Stephen T. Peverly, Ph.D.
Department of School
    Psychology
Teachers College
Columbia University

Paul Robb
Seattle (WA) Public Schools

Laura Rogan
Learning Remedies

Hilary Rosenfield
Seattle (WA) Public Schools

Sylvia Rosenfield, Ph.D.
Department of Counseling and
    Personnel Services
University of Maryland
    College Park

John Sabatini, Ph.D.
Research and Development
Educational Testing Service

Noa Saka, Ph.D.
Division of Mental Health Services
    and Policy Research
Columbia University
and
Hebrew University of Jerusalem

Andrea Sauer-Lee, Ph.D.
School of Education

University of North Carolina,
  Chapel Hill

Cheryl M. Scott, Ph.D.
Department of Communication
  Disorders and Sciences
Rush University Medical Center

Luann Sessions
Cognitive Science Institute
University of Colorado

Edward S. Shapiro, Ph.D.
Center for Promoting Research
  to Practice
Lehigh University

Elaine R. Silliman, Ph.D.
Communication Sciences &
  Disorders & Cognitive & Neural
  Sciences
University of South Florida

Dennie L. Smith
Professor and Department Head
Claude H. Everett, Jr. Endowed
  Chair
Texas A&M University

Sam Stringfield, Ph.D.
Department of Leadership,
  Foundations, and Human
  Resource Education
School of Education and Human
  Development
University of Louisville

H. Lee Swanson, Ph.D.
Educational Psychology and Special
  Education
Graduate School of Education
University of California-Riverside

Shurita Thomas-Tate, Ph.D.
Department of Communication
  Disorders
College of Communication
Florida State University

Joanna K. Uhry, Ed.D.
Graduate School of Education
Fordham University

Mary C. Wagner
Department of Psychology
University of Notre Dame

Julie A. Washington, Ph.D.
Department of Communicative
  Disorders
College of Letters and Science
University of Wisconsin-Madison

Maria Wauchope
School of Education
The University of Queensland

Owen R. White, Ph.D.
Department of Special Education
College of Education
University of Washington

Barbara Wise, Ph.D.
Center for Spoken Language
  Research
University of Colorado

Donna Carlson Yerby, M.Ed.
The Clinical Center for the Study
  of Development and
  Learning
The Carolina Institute for
  Developmental Disabilities
University of North Carolina School
  of Medicine

IMPLEMENTING EVIDENCE-BASED ACADEMIC INTERVENTIONS IN SCHOOL SETTINGS

Introduction: Implementing Evidence-Based Academic Interventions in School Settings

Sylvia Rosenfield and Virginia Berninger

> Diagnosing practical problems and developing detailed plans to deal with them may or may not be more difficult than solving scientific problems, but it is certainly different. (Miller, 1969)

As the twenty-first century dawned, two lines of thinking about psychology and education were emerging. First, the concept of evidence-based practice had moved from medicine into the applied social sciences including education. Second, it became increasingly clear that issues of implementation, treatment integrity, and sustainability of interventions were fundamentally important. As the research literature emerged in increasing volume, along with critical discussion of what constitutes evidence, an equally powerful question has been gaining ground: how to bridge the gap between the knowledge generated by scientific research and application of that knowledge to educational practice. That question is as demanding for those who apply psychology to education and schooling as is the creation of a solid body of scientific research on learning and teaching.

One goal of the current edited book is to inspire the field to make the evolutionary leap to adopting evidence-based academic practices as the standard of the profession. In this book, the authors look at two sides of the issue with reference to the domain of academic interventions: what do we know and what is involved in translating that knowledge into educational practice. Some attention is also given to mental health interventions because learning and social emotional functions are interrelated.

Before introducing the chapters of this book, we provide the contemporary context, looking at the forces that have propelled psychology and education into an evidence-based world and exploring the research to practice divide.

■ Evidence-Based Practice

The beginning of the evidence-based movement in psychology might well be traced back to the origins of the field, as Wundt, Kraeplin, and other early psychologists separated the field from philosophy, attesting to their "allegiance to the methods and results of scientific research" (Norcross, Beutler, & Levant, 2006, p. 4). A more recent history relates to the increasing societal zeitgeist of accountability that emerged in the early 1990s in various fields, including medicine, psychology, and education, requiring "professionals to base their practice, to whatever extent possible, on evidence" (Norcross et al., p. 6). The concept that science should guide practice has been embedded historically in the scientist-practitioner model of applied psychology, and "prominent in school psychology since the Thayer conference laid the groundwork for a scientific focus of the profession" (Stoiber & Kratochwill, 2000, p. 75).

But the evidence-based intervention (EBI) movement has provoked many questions as well (Norcross et al., 2006). According to Norcross et al., "Defining evidence, deciding what qualifies as evidence, and applying what is privileged as evidence are complicated matters with deep philosophical and huge practice consequences" (p. 7). Debate has emerged, for example, about the focus on randomized experiments over other types of research in the definition of what constitutes evidence. Norcross et al. provide a stimulating discussion of many of these questions within mental health practice.

Within the field of education, the call for evidence-based practice has also increased in volume. The No Child Left Behind (NCLB) (2001) law includes the phrase "scientifically based research" over 100 times. NCLB's requirement that schools disaggregate outcomes for diverse populations, including special education and minority groups, has also increased the pressure for ensuring that all students have access to quality interventions. Clearly, the need for scientific standards in education practice did not begin with the NCLB, and may actually have had some of its origins in the reading debates of the 1990s (Manna & Petrilli, 2008), with their explicit call for "scientifically based research" and data-driven decision making. But, according to Manna and Petrilli, the law was seen as providing an opening for those who wanted to see education more firmly grounded in science. Here, too, multiple questions have emerged about what scientifically based research means (see Manna & Petrilli for an analysis of the concept of SBR in NCLB; see also, McCardle and Miller, this volume, for discussion of the policy context).

Other events also have contributed to the context. The reauthorization of the special education law, the Individuals with Disabilities Education Improvement Act (IDEIA) (2004), mandated an emphasis on documenting how well students respond to intervention before being labeled as handicapped, adding yet another rationale for a science of prevention and intervention becoming a reality in the schools. The need for empirically supported interventions in school psychology grew from several related concerns, including "a gap in the continuum of service delivery between assessment procedures and intervention activities…and fragmented practices for disability determination, intervention planning, and monitoring of outcomes" (Stoiber & Kratochwill, 2000, p. 79—see Stoiber & Krotochwill for a more extensive discussion of the rationale for EBIs in school psychology).

Within organized psychology, multiple groups have been engaged in addressing these questions. School psychologists were among the various clinical, medical, and educational groups and organizations struggling with developing a science of EBIs. With support from the American Psychological Association (APA), the APA Division of School Psychology, and the Society for the Study of School Psychology, along with an endorsement from the National Association of School Psychologists, the Task Force on Evidence-Based Intervention in School Psychology (Task Force) was formed under the leadership of Kratochwill and Stoiber (2002). The Task Force was charged with constructing "a knowledge base on evidence-based interventions (EBIs) that has application for the field of school psychology" (Kratochwill & Stoiber, 2002, p. 342). The Manual Subcommittee of the Task Force produced the *Procedural and Coding Manual for Review of Evidence-Based Interventions* (Manual) (available at www.indiana. edu/~ebi/documents/_workingfiles/EBImanual.pdf), an evolving document that includes procedures for review and coding of intervention studies to determine their quality as EBIs.

Another goal of the Task Force, however, was to identify evidence-based prevention and intervention approaches that met the criteria delineated in the Manual. The Task Force included several domain subgroups that were originally expected to use the Manual for reviews of the literature. These domain groups were (a) Academic Intervention Programs, (b) Comprehensive School Health Care, (c) School-Based Intervention Programs for Social Behavior Problems, and (d) School-Wide and Classroom-Based Programs (a domain group on school-based prevention programs was dissolved and the charge to include these programs became part of the responsibility of the other domains).

However, the emphasis on identifying EBIs was broadened in two ways. First, the Task Force established a subcommittee on research to practice (reported on in this volume in Chapter 9 by Olin, Saka, Crowe, Forman, & Hoagwood). Second, the co-chairs of one of the domains recommended a focus on implementation. In a letter to the Task Force, the Academic Domain co-chairs, Virginia Berninger and Ed Shapiro (2003, October), provided a list of current meta-analyses of the domain literature, and suggested that, instead of conducting literature reviews, the focus of the Academic Domain needed to be on,

> mechanisms for disseminating what is known about effective academic interventions to school practitioners and trainers of school psychologists....research validates what works in general, but practitioners need to evaluate the implementation of research supported practices for individual students in specific schools and programs to determine if the intervention is working for that student. If the implementation phase is not working, the school psychologists' consultation skills are necessary for problem solving alternative approaches. (pp. 3–4)

■ The Research to Practice Gap

The need to address issues of implementation is not new in psychology or education. The research to practice gap has stimulated its own literature (for a variety of perspectives, see, e.g., Kazdin, Kratochwill, & VandenBos, 1986; Sarason, 2001; Snow, Griffin, & Burns, 2005). Miller (1969), in his APA presidential address, stated, "although our scientific base for valid contributions is far from comprehensive, certainly more is known than has been used intelligently" (p. 1063). McClintock (2007), in his critique of the mass of educational research and its limited application to practice, concluded the following:

> In the lexicon of educational researchers,...researchers must start asking to what degree their work can determine the realities of schooling. These realities are imperious, domineering, and imperative. Schools work the same way the world around; they have powerful routines and massive institutional inertia. Tradition, ritual, convention, interest, bureaucratic procedure, folly, the lore of practice, and expedient intelligence determine the actualities of schools. (p. 3)

An APA conference on bringing to scale educational innovation and school reform (American Psychological Association, 1997) concluded that knowledge on promising practices is not enough, and that the criteria for interventions need to be considered as well. Three criteria, presented by Robert Felner, one of the attendees, were included in the proceedings:

- The program should be effective in real-life settings, meaning it's no longer acceptable to say things like, "It's a great program but it doesn't work in schools." Researchers need to define a problem and then measure whether or not it was solved.
- The program should be viable and sustainable. As programs sweep in and out of schools, teachers left holding the bag become disillusioned.
- The program should be ecologically congruent with the setting. Instead of popping programs into schools, innovators should respect the resource limitations, values, and other conditions in schools. (p. 5)

The issues raised here reflect the distinction between efficacy and effectiveness research. Senge (1990) made a similar point in stating that engineers say that new ideas that are invented in the laboratory become an innovation only when replicated "reliably on a meaningful scale at practical costs (pp. 5–6).

■ Implementation

Implementing EBIs in schools is a challenge. No matter how much quality research supports an intervention or a program, if it is not implemented well, the outcomes will not follow. Mihalic, Irwin, Fagan, Ballard, and Elliott (2004), in discussing the implementation of evidence-based violence and drug prevention programs, comment that as "science-based programs become more readily available to practitioners, the need for identifying and overcoming problems associated with the process of implementation become critical" (p. 1). In the implementation of the programs, they found a wide variety of issues and problems even when funding, training, technical assistance, and evaluation were provided. It is that set of issues to which this book is dedicated.

■ Importance of the Academic Domain

The central task of the school is the development of academic competence, and school improvement relies to a great extent on the improvement of teaching and learning. What happens in classrooms is of critical importance to the learning and development of students. The effect of teachers on achievement outcomes has been well documented (see, e.g., Donovan & Cross, 2002; Sanders & Rivers, 1996; Snow et al., 2005), and recent legislation has increased the attention and emphasis placed on the role of the classroom teacher in student achievement. The NCLB (2001) Act requires a "highly qualified teacher in every classroom."

The effects of instructional quality are even more pronounced when students are at-risk. The National Academy of Science report (Donovan & Cross, 2002) on minority representation in special education noted that,

> There is substantial evidence with regard to both behavior and achievement that early identification and intervention is more effective than later identification and intervention. This is true for children of any race or ethnic group, and children with or without an identifiable "within-child" problem. (Donovan & Cross, 2002, p. ES-5)

The Donovan and Cross report concludes that high-quality instruction that carefully puts the prerequisites for learning in place, combined with effective classroom management that minimizes chaos in the classroom, can put students on a path to academic success. The most recent reauthorization of the special education law (IDEIA, 2004) emphasizes that a child must have been provided with effective instruction before being considered for special education services.

Yet Snow et al. (2005), in summarizing the case for the importance of teacher skill in dealing with students at-risk, report that many teachers indicate they do not have the skills to work with students who are not average. Peverly (this volume) addresses the issues of teacher quality in his chapter. The Education Trust (2008, February) reported on how poor teacher quality impacted the academic achievement of low-income and minority students. The implementation of the research on academic interventions has enormous potential to affect the outcomes for students and schools.

■ How This Book Is Organized

The goal of this book is to support the much discussed and needed change to the adoption and implementation of evidence-based academic practices. The domain of academic interventions is the focus, given the critical importance of such interventions to the achievement and development of students, especially those at-risk. Moving from evidence to practice requires both knowledge of the evidence, training that supports both the knowledge and the practice, an understanding of the issues that impact implementation at national, state, local, and classroom levels, and the means to evaluate the implementation of the EBIs.

The book is divided into six sections—one for each of the proposed steps in an implementation model for translating research into practice. Each of these sections is preceded by a summary of the contents of the chapters in the section. The following steps in the academic domain are proposed to stimulate the thinking of researchers and practitioners as they consider the implementation of evidence-based academic interventions.

Step 1 is to become informed about interventions that research has shown are efficacious. This step involves becoming knowledgeable about existing research literature and developing a set of criteria for evaluating research so that a professional remains a critical consumer of future research. The research presented here reflects the state of the field. However, science is an evolving field and the knowledge base that is relevant to educational practitioners in schools will evolve over their professional career. Six domains of existing knowledge relevant to contemporary educational practice are reviewed for Step 1: (a) reading, (b) writing, (c) math, (d) oral language, (e) linguistic diversity with focus on American African dialect, and (f) prevention science in the preschool years with focus on literacy, math, and social competence.

Step 2 is to become more informed about implementation issues. Four chapters in this section address concepts and mechanisms for the translation of research into practice. The first chapter in this section presents a dynamic model for improving the research-practice interface, and provides a national policy perspective. The second chapter describes consultee-centered consultation, a model for knowledge transfer; the author suggests that for implementation efforts to succeed, collaborative and consultation activities need to be in place in local buildings, where change that affects individual students and the professionals charged with their education is most likely to occur. The third chapter in this section examines two key aspects of research to practice, how to decide what is an evidence-based practice and how developers conceptualize the implementation process. Although the domain in the third chapter in this section is social-emotional interventions, the issues addressed here are equally relevant to the academic domain. The fourth chapter in this section takes an alternative approach to the three-tier model currently popular in the field. The author applies a public health model to deciding how to assess the unique needs of a school, from group concerns to individual ones, and considers what those needs might mean for assessment-intervention links.

Step 3 leads us to a group of authors who have been active in implementation at the systems level, providing rich description of the implementation process in real-world settings, ranging from the state to district level implementation projects. The first chapter in this section addresses a statewide scaling up of an evidence-based assessment process for progress monitoring, with an evaluation of the outcomes as well as a description of lessons learned in the scaling up process. In the next chapter in this section, two co-authors address the challenges of redesigning a teacher professional development and evaluation system in a large urban school district.

Two additional chapters close this section, both reflecting implementations that began when local school district staff members became interested in implementing evidence-based programs. The authors describe in detail the implementation process over a series of years. In both cases, projects were initiated by school psychologists in partnerships with other professionals in the local schools as well as district level administrators. In the first case, the implementation of an intervention is described in the voices of the different participants. In the other case, multiple kinds of quantitative and qualitative evidence are collected to evaluate a series of implementations of evidence-based instructional interventions. Collectively, the chapters in this section illustrate the dynamic interactions of top-down and bottom-up influences in implementing research-supported practices.

Step 4 is to take a closer look at how teachers may transform research knowledge to put it into practice. In a June 21, 2001, *New York Review of Books*, V. Nabokov wrote, "There is no science without fancy, no art without facts." Effective implementation benefits from art as well as science. The first of the four chapters in this section focuses on teacher characteristics in implementing artful, evidence-based practices in preschool and early childhood classrooms. The second presents a rich description of how evidence-based principles can be shared with teachers in the field as they design lessons for students at-risk. The third chapter outlines how research on vocabulary can be applied in the classroom through artful, playful, instructional activities. The fourth documents how university researchers and school staff can work together to improve literacy.

Step 5 in implementation turns to how to assess the effectiveness of intervention during and after implementation. Although gathering data in controlled research studies is a necessary first step to evaluate the efficacy of the intervention in general, it is not sufficient. Data must also be gathered to evaluate the effectiveness of the intervention as implemented in specific school settings for specific purposes for specific students. In this way, evidence is gathered on the transformation of science into educational practice. Single subject methods for evaluating whether individual students are making progress are described in the first chapter in this section and program evaluation methods and challenges for evaluating the effect of large-scale program implementation are explained in the following chapter of this section. Both approaches are needed to demonstrate the effectiveness of the implementation of evidence-based practices to the progress of individual students *and* to evaluate program effectiveness for students in general. In the last chapter of this section, the author recommends going beyond simply monitoring individual student progress to a more comprehensive approach, building conceptually validated and functionally integrated links among assessment of curriculum, assessment of instruction and teacher knowledge, and assessment of the student.

Finally, *Step 6* is to consider the role that professional preparation and development play in preparing educational professionals who not only know what the research shows but also how to implement it in practice. This step is illustrated for two professional groups that play important roles in implementing research into practice in schools—teachers and school psychologists. One chapter considers formal coursework preparation and one chapter considers the role of supervised practice in implementing research into practice.

The volume concludes with some reflections on the considerable wisdom presented by the chapter authors and the implications raised. We also provide some cautions and guarded optimism as educators are challenged to create, evaluate, and implement practices that support student academic development.

■ References

American Psychological Association (1997). *Bringing to scale educational innovation and school reform: Partners in urban education.* Conference Proceedings. Washington, DC, American Psychological Association.

Donovan, S., & Cross, C. (2002). *Minority students in special and gifted educa-tion*. Washington, DC, National Academy Press.

Education Trust (2008, February). *Their fair share: How Texas sized gaps in teacher quality shortchange low-income and minority students*. Retrieved, February 2008, from www.edtrust.org.

Individuals with Disabilities Education Improvement Act, 2004. Retrieved from http://idea.ed.gov.

Kazdin, A. E., Kratochwill, T. R., & VandenBos, G. (1986). Beyond clinical trials: Generalizing from research to practice. *Professional Psychology: Research and Practice*, *3*, 391–398.

Kratochwill, T. R., & Stoiber, K. C. (2002). Evidence-based interventions in school psychology: Conceptual foundations of the Procedural and Coding Manual of Division 16 and the Society for the Study of School Psychology Task Force. *School Psychology Quarterly*, *17*, 341–389.

Manna, P., & Petrilli, M. J. (2008). Double standard? "Scientifically based research" and the No Child Left Behind Act. In F. M. Hess (Ed.), *When research matters: How scholarship influences education policy* (pp. 63–88). Cambridge, MA, Harvard Education Press.

McClintock, R. (2007). Educational research. *Teachers College Record Online*, March 28, 2007, pp. 1–4.

Mihalic, S., Irwin, K., Fagan, A., Ballard, D., & Elliott, D. (2004, July). Successful program implementation: Lessons from blueprints. *Juvenile Justice Bulletin*, pp. 1–11. http://www.ojjdp.ncjrs.org/publications/PubResults.asp.

Miller, G. A. (1969). Psychology as a means of promoting human welfare. *American Psychologist*, *24*, 1063–1075.

No Child Left Behind Act of 2001. Pub. L. No. 107–110 (Elementary and Secondary Education Act).

Norcross, J. C., Beutler, L. E., & Levant, R. F. (Eds.) (2006). *Evidence-based prac-tices in mental health: Debate and dialogue on the fundamental questions*. Washington, DC, American Psychological Association.

Sanders, W., & Rivers, J. (1996, November). *Cumulative and residual effects of teachers on future student academic achievement*. Knoxville, TN, University of Tennessee Value-Added Research and Assessment Center.

Sarason, S. (2001). *American psychology and schools: A critique*. NY, Teachers College Press.

Senge, P. M. (1990). *The fifth discipline: The art and practice of the learning orga-nization*. NY, Currency/Doubleday.

Snow, C. E., Griffin, P., & Burns, M. S. (Eds.) (2005). *Knowledge to support the teaching of reading: Preparing teachers for a changing world*. San Francisco, Jossey-Bass.

Stoiber, K. C., & Kratochwill, T. R. (2000). Empirically supported interven-tions and school psychology: Rationale and methodological issues—Part I. *School Psychology Quarterly*, *15*, 75–105.

STEP 1

IN IMPLEMENTATION: KNOWING THE RESEARCH LITERATURE AS A CRITICAL CONSUMER

■ Introduction to Step 1

This section focuses on the current state of research knowledge in domains that are highly related to school learning and performance. The first three chapters focus on the three R's of academic instruction—reading, 'riting, and 'rithmetic—and reach the same conclusion based on meta-analyses of the instructional research (reading, writing, and math): *Explicit instruction and strategy instruction are the most effective instructional approaches for teaching reading, writing, and math.* However, critical consumers of this research should pay careful attention to the characteristics of the samples on which the research has been conducted and to which results can be validly generalized—typically developing students in general education, at-risk students in general education, or special education students (e.g., students with specific or general learning disabilities). Much of the confusion and many of the arguments about effective instruction has involved generalizing research findings for at-risk or learning-disabled students to the general education population or vice versa.

Because more research exists on reading, the first domain covered, and the research has been reviewed by multiple national panels, national policy for implementing evidence-based reading instruction already exists. In the first chapter, Peggy McCardle and Brett Miller provide a comprehensive overview of the historical context in which this policy, based on research, evolved. They make a valuable contribution in covering implementation issues for a variety of student populations, ranging from (a) learning disabled (LD) to (b) English language learners (ELL) whose first language is Spanish, Chinese, or Korean to (c) adolescents, and they also discuss professional issues such as use of coaches. Of great importance, they remind us that the conclusion of the Commission on Excellence in Special Education, before the recent reauthorization, was that too much focus has been on the process of determining whether students are eligible for special services rather than on delivering evidence-based interventions for purposes of prevention. That is, it is important to focus on the nature of the reading intervention that is implemented in response to intervention (RTI) protocols and not just the response to that intervention to determine whether a student qualifies for special education.

In the second chapter, Stephen Hooper and colleagues Sean Knuth, Donna Yerby, Kathleen Anderson, and Cindy Moore provide historical context for research on writing instruction, an overview of empirical studies on evidence-based writing instruction in the primary and upper grades, and a discussion of the recent meta-analysis of effective writing instruction for adolescents (fourth grade and above), *Writing Next*, sponsored by the Carnegie Foundation. They make a valuable contribution in abstracting from the reviewed research a set of evidence-based instructional design and pedagogical principles of effective writing instruction that can be applied across school settings and curriculum materials. Their chapter also addresses for writing instruction the various steps in implementation covered in this volume, including knowing the research as a critical consumer, preservice education issues, systems issues, evaluating school-based implementations and student response to instruction, and the next steps in the evolution of evidence-based practices.

H. Lee Swanson, who has probably conducted the most meta-analyses of the effectiveness of instructional interventions in math (and reading) explains in the third chapter what a meta-analysis is and how to interpret effect sizes. He makes two innovative contributions in (a) comparing explicit instruction only, strategy instruction only, combined explicit and strategy instruction, and neither explicit nor strategy instruction; and (b) going beyond comparison of instructional studies, which draw on cognitive and behavioral paradigms, to the identification of effective instructional components embedded in these instructional studies. He shows that the combined explicit and strategy instruction is most effective *and* identifies efficacious, clearly defined instructional components that can be applied by teachers using different instructional materials in different school settings. These evidence-based instructional components should be useful to educators who wish to design and evaluate math interventions in their particular school settings. Moreover, he reviews research on which individual differences in learners may mediate response to math instruction (e.g., visual spatial working memory and rapid automatic naming).

As an editorial comment (VB), although much of the current implementation of IDEIA has been on measuring response to instruction, cognitive, developmental, neuroscientific, and genetic research findings show that specific kinds of *individual differences among and within learners may mediate response to academic instruction* (e.g., Berninger & Abbott, 1992; Berninger, Raskind, Richards, Abbott, & Stock, 2008). Universal screening for these individual differences may proactively identify students who may benefit from differentiated, modified instruction within the general education program from the beginning. Waiting for them to fail to respond to core curriculum is still a wait-to-fail approach to educating students with learning differences.

A sizable body of research is also pointing to the role of oral language in learning academic skills and self-regulating behavior during the school years. Although many teachers and psychologists believe that only speech and language specialists need to have knowledge of language, that is not the case. As Elaine Silliman and Cheryl Scott explain in the fourth chapter, listening, speaking, reading, and writing are all language embedded and most literacy instruction and instructional activities draw on each of these language systems. Research is showing that children who have oral language delays in the preschool years and who have more subtle metalinguistic problems with oral language during the school years are at-risk for learning written language and using oral and written language to learn and self-regulate their behavior.

Speech and language specialists tend to provide exclusively one-to-one pull-out services for speech (sometimes in language). However, the coauthors of the fifth chapter are leaders in the child language group of the American Association of Speech, Hearing, and Language (ASHA) spearheading the movement to implement oral language instruction more broadly in general and special education programs for students with selective language learning disability (SLI) or language learning disability (LLD). They provide case studies that illustrate the nature of selective language impairment (SLI) and LLD, due to grammatical or inferencing (possibly working memory) problems and practical issues in teaching students with SLI or LLD. They review the limited research currently available on teaching syntax (grammar and morphology) skills to students with SLI and LLD for which more research on efficacy and effectiveness is needed. They also differentiate the oral register and academic register; the latter poses major challenges early and throughout schooling for many students.

Language issues are not restricted to SLI or LLD and may involve cultural and linguistic diversity. Julie Washington and Shurita Tate coauthored the fifth chapter that reviews the extensive research on dialect differences in the school age population and shows that children who speak a dialect other than mainstream English must learn to be code switchers between language spoken at home and school in order to succeed at school. Important research findings for African American English (AAE) dialect users are discussed. Most African Americans, regardless of socioeconomic status, speak this dialect. Table 5.1 provides valuable information for professionals who are not AAE dialect speakers but who teach or assess students who are. Examples in Table 5.1 will help the professionals translate across codes. The authors of the chapter also caution professionals not to underestimate the language ability of AAE dialect users, as reflected in their speech and writing.

In the final (sixth) chapter on Step 1, Maureen Hoskyn, who brings extensive experience as a school psychologist to her current research career, reminds us of the conclusion of the Commission on Excellence in Special Education—to redirect focus to early identification and intervention and prevention. She reviews research currently available for preschool students, primarily from low socioeconomic backgrounds who are also low-achieving in oral language. The review, based on the principles of meta-analysis, covers three domains—literacy, math, and social competence. The results (see Table 6.1 for outcome measures and Table 6.2 for experimental details of studies) supported the conclusion that a combination of explicit, teacher-directed instruction *and* implicit, child-directed unstructured instructional activities involving play and social interaction may be most effective from a prevention perspective in early childhood. This conclusion merges well with a substantial body of research showing that children learn oral language through conversation (social interaction) with adults and other children and play with language (i.e., the oral register), as well as from explicit instruction in the academic registrar (see Chapter 4 by Silliman and Scott). Some preschoolers need more intervention sessions than others, but calling more sessions more intensive, which implies effortful work, may be misleading because children learned the most when they enjoyed the activities. Another important finding is that teachers learned more effectively from video presentation of teaching techniques than verbally oriented mentoring by other professionals.

■ References

Berninger, V., & Abbott, R. (1992). Unit of analysis and constructive processes of the learner: Key concepts for educational neuropsychology. *Educational Psychologist*, *27*, 223–242.

Berninger, V., Raskind, W., Richards, T., Abbott, R., & Stock, P. (2008). A multidisciplinary approach to understanding developmental dyslexia within working-memory architecture: Genotypes, phenotypes, brain, and instruction. *Developmental Neuropsychology*, *33*, 707–744.

1. WHY WE NEED EVIDENCE-BASED PRACTICE IN READING AND WHERE TO FIND THAT EVIDENCE

Peggy McCardle and Brett Miller

■ The Need for Evidence-Based Educational Practice

In the 1990s, the United States began to recognize a crisis in education, demonstrated by a failure of far too many U.S. children to learn to read. This educational challenge was brought to light in part by findings from the National Assessment of Education Progress (NAEP). The NAEP, which was Congressionally mandated in 1969 and reauthorized most recently in 2002 (PL 107–279), allowed the United States to monitor the performance of its nation's students in various content areas, including reading. NAEP data in the 1990s indicated a serious problem in the proportions of children in grades 4, 8, and 12, who were not succeeding in reading. More recent data have borne out that this was an ongoing problem. The NAEP, which has become known as the Nation's Report Card, includes three different parts: the National NAEP, the long-term trend NAEP, and the State NAEP. This chapter focuses on the long-term trend and National NAEP results.

Data from the long-term NAEP are particularly useful to track change over time because the content that is tested has been held relatively stable over time. (Note that this is not longitudinal data; rather, it is a snapshot of performance at specific age levels each year and is reflective of how well each of those age groups reads in that year.) The NAEP long-term assessment tests literacy performance of the students at three age points: 9, 13, and 17 years. For 9-year-old students in the United States, small, but significant, gains in reading were made. Nine-year-old scores had been relatively level overall during the 1990s; however, in the 2004 results for reading, they began to show

The opinions and assertions presented in this chapter are those of the authors and do not purport to represent those of the *Eunice Kennedy Shriver* National Institute of Child Health and Human Development, the National Institutes of Health, or the U.S. Department of Health and Human Services.

consistent gains compared with previous years. Unfortunately, for 13- and 17-year-old students, the long-term picture has not improved, with 2004 performance being roughly equivalent to the performance levels in 1980. This would not necessarily be problematic if all of our students achieved high levels of literacy skills; thus, educational performance would be stable in its success. However, the number of students in eighth and twelfth grades performing at or below the Basic levels makes this ominous news.

The National NAEP data present a current picture with regard to the performance of U.S. students in reading. It regularly tests students' skills in fourth, eighth, and twelfth grade reading and classifies students based on achievement levels (e.g., Basic, Proficient, Advanced). Although it is possible to compare current results with those of previous years, the strength of the National NAEP is that it can present a more in-depth picture with regard to the literacy skills of students than the long-term trend NAEP can, and the assessment is updated regularly to reflect the changes in curricula and instructional practices in the United States. For fourth grade students in the most recent assessment period available (2005), 69% of students taking the NAEP scored at the Basic or Below Basic levels. To put this into context, fourth graders performing at the Basic level "should be able to make relatively obvious connections between the text and their own experiences and extend the ideas in the text by making simple inferences" (National Center for Education Statistics, 2005a). Unfortunately, 36% of all fourth graders tested are not even achieving this Basic level of performance, as they fall in the Below Basic category. Although this picture may appear somewhat grim, the challenges are even greater for Black, American Indian, and Hispanic students. For Black students tested in 2005, 87% of students score at or below the Basic level in reading. The performance is similar for American Indian and Hispanic fourth grade children, with 82% and 84%, respectively, scoring at or below the Basic level in reading. Unfortunately, the overall picture from the data does not really improve when examining the percentage of eighth and twelfth grade students performing at or below the Basic level. Nationwide, 69% of eighth graders performed at or below the Basic level and only 3% of eighth graders scored at the Advanced level in reading in 2005. See Table 1.1 for differential percentages for minority students.

These data show the challenges the nation faces to build and strengthen the literacy skills of all students. There have been some signs of gains for groups: As mentioned earlier, 9 year olds scored higher in 2004 in reading than in any previous year, and white, Black, and Hispanic students scored higher on average in fourth and eighth grades in 2005 than in 1992 (National Center for Education Statistics, 2005b). Nonetheless, NAEP data taken as a whole, along with other data, suggest two main points. First, far too many of the younger readers have not been able to master the basics of reading by fourth grade. Second, problems with readers do not disappear as the readers

TABLE 1.1   *NAEP Reading Data from 2005*

	Below Basic Only (%)	Basic or Below Basic Levels (%)
Fourth Graders Student Performance on 2005 NAEP Reading Results		
All Students	36	69
Black Students	58	87
American Indian Students	50	82
Hispanic Students	54	84
Eighth Graders Student Performance on 2005 NAEP Reading Results		
All Students	27	69
Black Students	48	88
American Indian Students	41	82
Hispanic Students	44	85

This table presents the cumulative percentages for all tested fourth and eighth grade students separately and include the available group means for certain ethnic subgroups within each grade (U.S. Department of Education, 2005).

move on into junior high and high school. In fact, larger proportions of older readers (eighth and twelfth grades) score below Proficient levels in reading.

As clear as it was in the 1990s that a focus on literacy skills was needed and despite subsequent noted improvements, far too many students at all ages continue to read at levels that do not equip them for a bright future. Part of the promise of the recent emphasis on applying evidence-based practices in teaching literacy is not only for current literacy needs of the students but also for future, cumulative gains that could be made over time in all children, not only in reading but also in education.

■ Legislation on Evidence-Based Practice in Reading

Although the need for improved literacy skills has been noted for many decades (e.g., Chall's 1967 call for early systematic instruction in alphabetics[1] to improve reading), the strong push for evidence-based practices in literacy is relatively recent. The term "scientifically based reading research (SBRR)" came into common usage when it was used in the Reading Excellence Act (REA) of 1998 (PL 105–277). President William Clinton, in his 1996 State of the Union Address (The White House, 1996), quoted NAEP data and called for attention to the proportion of fourth graders not reading at grade level. Acting on this cue, the House Committee on Education and the Workforce[2] held hearings and determined that the key to this national problem was ensuring that teachers were aware of, educated about, and had access to the most up-to-date research findings on reading instruction, and urged that they be encouraged to apply them. This led to the legislation—the REA—that was passed with broad support from both parties and provided funds in block grants to states that were used for teacher professional development in SBRR and to purchase materials for its implementation.

The need for evidence-based practice had gained national attention. Thus, it was no accident that the law was passed in the same year that the Departments of Education and Health and Human Services commissioned the National Academy of Sciences to prepare a research-based report on how reading develops and what practices promote optimal reading development. That report, *Preventing Reading Difficulties in Young Children* (PRD; Snow, Burns, & Griffin, 1998) will be discussed briefly later in this chapter. Following and building on that document came the National Reading Panel (NRP) report (NICHD, 2000), which provided specific evidence of the effectiveness of some instructional methods for teaching reading. Armed with that evidence, Congress acted again.

The REA had been funded for three years, and in 2001, with encouragement from President George W. Bush, Congress passed the Reading First and Early Reading First legislation, which was part of the No Child Left Behind Act of 2001 (PL 107–110). This legislation used the definitions of reading and SBRR in REA and incorporated the instructional principles shown to be effective in the NRP report. As in the case of REA, block grants were provided to states that applied and qualified, via a peer review process, for materials and implementation of research-based practices.

At the same time that this legislation was being developed, the research and practice communities were discussing what the term SBRR really meant and how to best ensure that research findings actually were implemented in the classrooms of America. One result of that discussion was a National Research Council report commissioned by the U.S. Department of Education, *Scientific Research in Education* (Shavelson & Towne, 2002). This report called for more rigorous research in education and the development of a "scientific culture" within education research in order to continue to provide reliable, high-quality research on which to base educational practice. When the research arm of the U.S. Department of Education, the Office of Education Research and Improvement (OERI), was considered for reauthorization, the committees in the House and Senate passed the Education Sciences Reform Act of 2002 (PL 107–279). This legislation established, in place of the OERI, a new Institute of Education Sciences (IES), with a director who would serve a 6-year term. (For a more detailed account of the history of these laws, see Sweet (2004).)

A principal goal of the new Institute was to establish the scientific culture called for in the Shavelson and Towne report. Subsequently, the National Academies began work on yet another report to identify ways to improve scientific research in education. That report, *Advancing Scientific Research in Education* (Towne, Wise, & Winters, 2004), funded by the IES, calls for researchers in education to promote research quality and to facilitate the development of an accumulated knowledge base through peer review panels at federal agencies. The report also calls for the encouragement and support of data sharing by federal agencies, professional associations, journal editors, and editorial boards, and the enhancement of professional development for education researchers and practitioners. All these goals aim at increasing the rigor and quality of the research on which educational practice should be and increasingly is based.

Although overall reading instruction in general education classrooms was receiving so much attention from the public, legislators, and researchers, special education was not being ignored. First, the President's Commission on Excellence in Special Education (2002) issued its report. The Commission made certain clear points, one being that there was too much focus on process (specifically the process of identifying students and determining their eligibility for special services) and not enough focus on the delivery of evidence-based instruction. They criticized the "wait to fail" model of identifying students with disabilities and made some major recommendations. First, they recommended early identification and early intervention (using research-based intervention programs) to prevent learning disabilities whenever possible, adding that the identification process for children with disabilities should be simplified. The Commission also recommended the use of response to intervention (RTI) models for the identification and assessment process and for progress monitoring, and the use of universal design in accountability tools to ensure that all assessments are designed to allow for necessary accommodations and modifications. On the basis of the information presented in the report, legislators made significant changes in the Individuals with Disabilities Education Improvement Act (IDEIA) in its 2004 reauthorization.

IDEA (now IDEIA) is the primary federal program that authorizes state and local aid for special education and related services for children with disabilities. Public Law 108–446, a major reauthorization and revision of IDEA, preserves the basic structure and civil rights guarantees of IDEA but now includes new provisions (optional use of RTI rather than the IQ-achievement discrepancy formula) for the identification of learning disabilities.[3] This decision was influenced by evidence that the IQ-discrepancy model is ineffective in identifying all students with learning disabilities (Lyon et al., 2001). There is not as much evidence on how well RTI will work, but there is enough evidence to date that high-quality instruction can reduce the number of children requiring special education (Torgesen, 2004; Torgesen et al., 1999) to warrant confidence in this process and to at least allow it as an alternative to something we know is not effective in successfully identifying all children with learning disabilities.

At present, many schools are implementing or working toward implementing an RTI approach. In fact, some schools have been using a "tiered approach" for a few years already. To gather information to assist schools in considering the implementation of RTI, the International Dyslexia Association (IDA) convened a meeting in December 2004. This jointly sponsored meeting[4] was attended by 33 interested organizations. Participants reviewed information on models of implementation for (a) RTI, (b) tiered models of instruction, (c) adequate teacher preparation, and (d) scaling innovative practices; basic information to inform discussions was presented by researchers and practitioners who had direct experience. The resulting document (Denton, 2006) lays out steps in planning, implementing, and evaluating RTI in schools and classrooms. The keys to understanding and succeeding in implementing RTI are that it begins in the general education classroom, but must involve an ongoing partnership among general and special education teachers and specialists, and that it requires the entire school to support it.

Because RTI is being widely implemented by schools, it quickly became clear that role redefinition was a topic requiring attention. Therefore, the International Reading Association (IRA) convened a working group of professional associations and concerned organizations to create a compendium of role definitions, *New Roles in Response to Intervention: Creating Success for Schools and Children* (International Reading Association, 2006), which is available on the World Wide Web.[5] Clearly not as much information on RTI as is needed is available. It is known that high-quality instruction can significantly reduce the number of children requiring special education, and implementing an RTI approach and strengthening the general education–special education partnership should be very positive steps in the right direction.

■ Bases for Evidence on Effective Instruction—Reading
   in the Elementary Grades

The research community has responded to the need and demand by the public and the educational practice community for effective practices that will change the profile of failure in reading in schools. This response has taken the form of reports or documents that pull together bodies of research evidence that converge to inform and guide instructional practices in reading. Many of these documents are mentioned earlier because of the role that they played in motivating and to some extent influencing legislation. These include both panel reports and research reviews and syntheses by individual or small groups of researchers and/or education practitioners. In this chapter, only the reports of panels that reviewed the research findings are discussed.

It is important to recognize that the value of these panel reports lies in three key factors. First, the panels, by virtue of their makeup of multiple individuals, bring to bear various perspectives and interests, as well as varied expertise. Second, they review the research literature systematically, using specific criteria for what types of work are included or excluded, thus introducing an important element of objectivity to the process. Third, they are looking for convergence of research evidence. Although it is important that teachers and students benefit from research findings, it is equally important that confidence in those findings not be overturned by the next study to be published, considering the precious financial resources expended on changes in practice and the time and energy of the teachers invested in learning, preparing, and implementing new practices. Convergent evidence can take various forms. Replication of studies in slightly different groups of students, under slightly different conditions, with the same essential finding is one such form. Another is multiple studies performed with differing designs and different populations, measures, or conditions that result in the same or highly similar findings. These sorts of evidence give confidence that changing practice based on them will be a worthwhile and productive effort.

There are four major national reports that have specifically addressed convergent evidence that should affect teaching reading in the classroom: *Preventing Reading Difficulties in Young Children* (Snow et al., 1998), a report of the National Research Council; *Teaching Children to Read: The Report of the National Reading Panel* (NICHD, 2000), a report requested by the U.S. Congress and supported by the National Institute of Child Health and Human Development, National Institutes of Health; *Teaching Reading* (Commonwealth of Australia, 2005), a report commissioned by the Australian government; and *Reading for Understanding*, a report commissioned by the U.S. Department of Education and produced by the RAND Corporation (Snow, 2002). Each of these will be discussed briefly.

■ Preventing Reading Difficulties

Preventing Reading Difficulties in Young Children (PRD) (Snow et al., 1998), a report of the National Research Council (NRC) of the National Academy of Sciences, succeeded in bringing national and governmental attention to the issue of reading. In their report, the authors of PRD recommended explicit instruction in the alphabetic principle and decoding, reading fluency, and comprehension strategies (summarizing, predicting, inferencing, and monitoring). The PRD panel made an important point that reading in the primary grades depends heavily on early language abilities and prereading experiences, thus highlighting the importance of high-quality preschool experiences for all children and advocating for improved preschools for poor children. They emphasized the importance of motivation, encouraging independent reading. They also included a strong call for high-quality teacher education and professional development that would ensure that teachers understand how children learn to read and how to instruct them in the component skills of reading. Many of their findings are in agreement with the later findings of the NRP; a key difference is that the NRP, acting on a mandate from Congress for more specific findings, actually performed meta-analyses with effect sizes on the decoding (phonemic awareness and phonics) and fluency instruction studies.

In addition, the NRC produced a companion document, *Starting Out Right: A Guide to Promoting Children's Reading Success* (Burns, Griffin, & Snow, 1999), to assist teachers, parents, and the non-scientist public in both understanding and taking action on the basis of the PRD findings. This useful document was precedent-setting in that subsequent panels on reading have similarly produced or are producing companion documents, many of which are implementation guides to assist teachers in putting into practice research findings on reading instruction and remediation. (These documents are noted with references and information on how to obtain them, as the reports on which they are based are discussed later in this chapter.)[6]

■ Teaching Children to Read: The Report
of the National Reading Panel

Although it had great value and impact, the PRD did not answer the specific question that the U.S. Congress had now been primed by NAEP statistics to ask: What evidence is there that specific reading instructional methods and approaches are effective? To answer this question, Congress directed the National Institute of Child Health and Human Development (NICHD) to convene a panel. This panel, the NRP, released their report in 2000 (NICHD, 2000). Facing a daunting task and limited time and resources, the panel decided to limit their work to addressing the five key components of reading—phonemic awareness, phonics, reading fluency, vocabulary, and reading comprehension. They also commented on teacher preparation and the use of instructional technology, although in a less systematic and thorough manner, as their primary focus was the five components of reading. As outlined in the Methodology section of the NRP report, the panel and their staff thoroughly and systematically searched and surveyed the literature on these domains, based on the criteria established, agreed upon, and published by the panel. The panel's efforts resulted where possible in meta-analyses; where there were not sufficient studies to perform meta-analyses, syntheses of the research literature were performed.

The NRP findings were, very briefly, as follows. Overall, the panel noted that explicit instruction in reading is both important and effective. First, the panel reported that the research on phonemic awareness showed that teaching children to manipulate phonemes in words was highly effective under a variety of teaching conditions with a variety of learners across a range of grade and age levels. In addition, the NRP found that teaching phonemic awareness to children, especially when linked to alphabet letter knowledge, significantly improves their reading more than instruction that does not include phonemic awareness. Teaching one or two phonemic awareness skills appeared to be more effective than teaching multiple skills, and the most powerful combination of skills appeared to be segmenting and blending. Phonics instruction was also found to produce significant benefits for students in kindergarten through sixth grade and for children having difficulty learning to read. Kindergartners who received systematic phonics instruction had enhanced ability to read and spell words; first graders who were taught systematic phonics were better able to decode and spell and showed significant improvement in their ability to comprehend text. Older children who received phonics instruction also benefited in their ability to decode and spell words and to read text orally; however, their comprehension of text was not significantly improved. Although many approaches to teaching systematic phonics were shown to be effective, systematic synthetic phonics instruction in particular had a positive and significant effect with children of various ages, abilities, and socioeconomic backgrounds, and with students with learning disabilities (NICHD, 2000).

The NRP made the important point that skill in alphabetics (phonemic awareness and phonics), while important, is necessary but not a sufficient condition to learning to read. Fluency, the ability to read with speed, accuracy, and expression, is also an important step toward the ultimate goal of reading, comprehension. The panel concluded that guided repeated oral reading that included guidance from teachers, peers, or parents had a significant and positive impact on word recognition, fluency, and comprehension across a range of grade levels. However, examining the research on independent silent reading, the panel found the evidence inconclusive as to whether encouraging students to read independently helped improve reading fluency. Therefore, they recommended that, if silent reading is used in the classroom, then it should be complemented by guided oral reading (NICHD, 2000).

The ultimate goal of reading is to be able to understand what you are reading. The NRP summarized research evidence indicating that vocabulary instruction plays an important role in understanding text. Although vocabulary instruction does lead to gains in comprehension, methods must be appropriate to the age and ability of the reader. The use of computers was found to be more effective than some traditional methods for instruction in vocabulary. The NRP also noted that preteaching of vocabulary and techniques such as task restructuring and repeated exposure to words enhance vocabulary development. Finally, substitution of easy words for more difficult words can assist low-achieving students (NICHD, 2000). However, it is important to realize that this must be carefully planned and used as an assist to bring students to higher levels where they can access the more difficult words.

Comprehension is an active process, and one that requires an intentional and thoughtful interaction between reader and text. In order for students to be able to accomplish this, they must be equipped with reading comprehension strategies. The NRP found that comprehension can be improved by teaching students to use specific cognitive strategies or to reason strategically as they read. They indicated that teaching a combination of reading comprehension strategies is most effective, and listed seven types of comprehension instruction that, when used as part of a multistrategy method, improve comprehension in nonimpaired readers: comprehension monitoring, cooperative learning, use of graphic and semantic organizers (including story maps), question answering, question generation, story structure, and summarization. The use of these strategies in combination was shown to improve student achievement as measured on standardized comprehension tests (NICHD, 2000).

On the basis of the NRP report, the National Institute for Literacy (NIFL), a federal agency whose mission is the dissemination of information on research-based evidence on reading, prepared several documents for teachers. The first of these was a guide to teacher implementation of the NRP findings, called *Put Reading First*, which provides examples and suggestions for classroom implementation (Partnership for Reading, 2001b). A companion document for parents was also produced (Partnership for Reading, 2001a). In addition to the NIFL documents, the IRA also produced a document to assist teachers in implementing the NRP findings, *Evidence-Based Reading Instruction*, IRA's Summary of the National Reading Panel Report (International Reading Association, 2002). All of these documents are available for free download on the World Wide Web.

A book building on the NRP findings and including other background information on the use of research evidence for teachers was produced. McCardle and Chhabra (2004), who had been associated with the NRP, produced an edited volume, *The Voice of Evidence in Reading Research*. There are three major sections of this book that are especially helpful. One section presents evidence for classroom implementation. This includes an update of the NRP evidence, often with new or additional studies, on phonemic awareness and phonics (Ehri, 2004), reading fluency (Stahl, 2004), and vocabulary and comprehension (Kamil, 2004). Another major section includes reading research evidence collected in classroom studies or based on multiple studies and experiences in classrooms. Finally, there is a major section on research that is used in reading research, including research design and methods, meta-analysis, longitudinal research, and clinical trials. This volume was targeted for teachers, to assist them not only in understanding and implementing the research findings but also in recognizing the types of research methods that should be used in addressing various questions, how and why research is done as it is, and the background for current reading research activities.

■ Teaching Reading

A few years after the NRP report was published, the Australian government (Department of Education, Sciences and Training) commissioned a panel similar to the PRD and NRP, which also produced a report. Their report, *Teaching Reading* (Commonwealth of Australia, 2005), citing the NRP findings and other sources of evidence from reading research, specifically targeted teacher preparation and professional development. In this report, the Australian panel called strongly for basing instructional practice on research evidence. The report made 18 recommendations, calling for the key focus of teacher preparation to be reading, including the study of specific topics: how children learn to read, how to best adapt instruction for those who are having difficulties, what evidence-based approaches to instruction are and how to use them, and basic information on child and adolescent development.

This report strongly recommended that elementary reading instruction include systematic, direct, and explicit phonics instruction so that children can break the alphabetic code, and that this instruction include oral language, vocabulary, grammar, fluency, reading comprehension, and use of new technologies. Assessment of every child was recommended at strategic points in their education (entry to school, grades 3, 5, 7, and 9, and twice annually during the first three years of elementary school). Literacy specialists trained in special graduate programs should facilitate whole-school literacy plans, support staff professional development, assist classroom teachers in their own professional development, and help ensure that progress monitoring includes the individual plans for children experiencing reading difficulties.

The panel also called for teacher registration that would include the demonstration of not only knowledge of evidence-based practice but also the ability to use that knowledge instructionally. Teacher preparation and professional development should be supported by teacher training institutions, professional organizations, communities, and schools. National standards should be established and supported by all of these groups and by all levels of government. The report also called for all teachers to be prepared, K-12, to meet the needs of diverse classrooms of children, using native language instruction in the early years where possible for English language learners. Individual unique identifiers for all children were also recommended to track the performance of students who may be geographically mobile. Although the focus of the Australian report is primarily teacher education, it clearly addresses the need for that training to include evidence-based instruction, and reinforces the evidentiary base presented by the other national reports available.

■ Reading for Understanding

Another key report, with funding and oversight by the IES, is the RAND report on reading comprehension, *Reading for Understanding: Toward an R&D Program in Reading Comprehension* (Snow, 2002). This report set out to identify what is known about reading comprehension, which is the ultimate goal and most complex aspect of reading, and to lay out a research agenda for the necessary next steps to understand more fully the nature of comprehension and how best to teach it at various levels. The panel indicated that instruction designed to enhance reading fluency (such as reading practice techniques, e.g., guided repeated oral reading) not only supports gains in reading fluency but also enhances word recognition skills, and produces moderate reading comprehension gains. However, they reiterated the NRP's finding that there is insufficient evidence of a causal connection between sustained silent reading to recommend it as an effective technique to develop fluency. Instructional strategies such as concept and story mapping, question generation, summarizing, identifying the big ideas in stories, and using graphic techniques foster reading comprehension by promoting self-monitoring in reading comprehension. Finally, explicit instruction in comprehension strategies has been shown to enhance student learning, especially for low-achieving students, through providing clear explanations, encouraging sustained attention to task, activating prior knowledge, breaking tasks into smaller steps, and providing opportunities for practice that incorporate frequent feedback. In a follow-up volume, Sweet and Snow (2003), RAND panel members, elaborated on their findings, especially in terms of how these might be used in the classroom.

■ Bases for Evidence on Effective Instruction—Preschool and English Language Learners

There are also panel reports available or soon to be available that offer research evidence that can inform classroom practice for other age groups or populations. These are addressed briefly in this section.

National Early Literacy Panel Report

The National Center for Family Literacy, under contract from the NIFL, established a panel to evaluate and report on the research evidence on reading and prereading abilities and activities in the preschool period. Although the report of the National Early Literacy Panel (NELP) has not yet been published, panel representatives have made presentations on some of the findings, and preliminary results are summarized on the panel's Web site.[7] The panel is addressing these key questions: what skills and abilities in children from birth to age five years predict later reading outcomes, and what programs or interventions, environments and settings, and child characteristics contribute to or inhibit the development of skills and abilities that are later linked to reading outcomes? To date, they have reported preliminary findings on predictors of later decoding, reading comprehension, and spelling: The NELP found strong evidence for the importance of alphabetic knowledge, phonological awareness, rapid naming tasks (letter, digits, objects, or colors), being able to write one's own name, and phonological short-term memory. Global oral language skills and concepts about print were less consistently found to be good predictors after controlling for phonological awareness and alphabet knowledge. The panel also reported that explicit attempts to build alphabetic awareness and oral language, share books with young children, and to use home, preschool, and kindergarten interventions can all be valuable for some later language and literacy skills.

■ Developing Literacy in Second Language Learners

Both the PRD and NRP reports explicitly called for a synthesis of available research on teaching English language learning (ELL) students to read. Previously, the NRC had produced a report on this topic: *Educating Language Minority Children* (August & Hakuta, 1998), calling for additional research and additional reporting on this topic. As a result, under contract from the IES with additional support from the U.S. Department of Education Office of English Language Acquisition and the NICHD, the Center for Applied Linguistics and SRI International established the National Literacy Panel for Language Minority Children and Youth (NLP). Their report, *Developing Literacy in Second-Language Learners* (August & Shanahan, 2006), was edited by one of the authors of the earlier NRC report on the same topic, Diane August, and by NLP chair Timothy Shanahan, who was also a member of the NRP.

The NLP report, which is far too extensive to summarize here in a paragraph, serves as a benchmark for ELL education in the United States. In that report, the panel presented syntheses of various types of research that bear on key topics, and the report consists of four major sections. These sections address literacy development in second language learners, the relation of sociocultural context and literacy development, instructional approaches and professional development, and student assessment. The major findings from the NLP include the importance of focusing reading instruction on the major components of reading identified by the NRP (phonemic awareness, phonics, fluency, vocabulary, and comprehension); explicit work in these areas is particularly beneficial for language minority students. Instruction in these five areas is considered necessary but not sufficient for language minority students learning to read; oral English proficiency is also critical. Oral language and literacy proficiency in the first language can facilitate literacy in English. The extent to which this is true and in which areas will depend in part on the characteristics of the first language, but literacy in one language certainly conveys some advantage to literacy development in the second language. The importance of taking sociocultural context into account is also emphasized.

Although this report is relatively recent, there are already efforts in process to produce the companion documents to promote classroom implementation that both the research and practice communities have come to expect. The IRA is producing a practice guide and the IRA, in partnership with NICHD and other federal agencies and organizations, convened meetings of practitioners and researchers to provide input on a document specific to classroom reading instruction for ELL students, based on parts of the NLP report and with updated information; two documents will be produced from this effort, a classroom instruction document and a research agenda, both informed by contributions from key agencies and organizations that made up the planning group for these activities.

■ What We Know in Adolescent Literacy

As illustrated by the NAEP results presented earlier in this chapter, although the nation is seeing small but important gains in the reading skills for fourth grade students, these gains currently are not being obtained at the eighth and twelfth grade levels. There was also far less research evidence on what instructional methods are effective in improving the literacy of students beyond the early elementary grades, although clearly the challenges to building literacy skills do not stop in elementary school. The need for more research in the area of adolescent literacy is well acknowledged (e.g., Biancarosa & Snow, 2006; Graham & Perin, 2007; MacArthur, Graham, & Fitzgerald, 2006; Perin & Graham, 2006; Snow, 2002); however, there is sufficient information available currently to guide instruction while we await additional evidence.

Upon entering middle school, adolescents face many changes. Not least among these are the diversity and difficulty of the texts they are expected to read, and the demands that will be made on their writing abilities. In addition, they are now being taught by content area teachers, who will expect them to read, comprehend, interpret, and integrate, and then discuss and/or write about information from those texts. In an attempt to present some information drawn from current and ongoing research that might prove useful to teachers of adolescents, Moak, Shuy, and McCardle (2006a) edited a thematic issue of IDA Perspectives. In their introduction to that issue (Moak, Shuy, & McCardle, 2006b), they offer four myths and realities of adolescent literacy, which are later expanded upon by the authors of the four research-based articles in the issue. Myth 1 is that students are not interested in reading; the reality is that motivation plays a key role in reading, and Moje (2006) reports that many students considered lacking in literacy skills actually read well in non-academic settings with materials that are of high interest to them. Both contexts and texts can either motivate or demotivate adolescents. Moje cautions teachers not to forget about individual variation; a given student may be a competent reader in one domain and an effortful processor in another, since not only complexity but also interest level and background knowledge can affect how well a student reads and comprehends a text.

Myth 2 is that all teachers should be reading teachers; in reality, all teachers can include strategy instruction, vocabulary instruction, and techniques that build background knowledge in their content area, but those students who need intensive work in foundational areas such as decoding and reading fluency will need the assistance of a reading specialist or teacher trained specifically in reading instruction. Deshler, Hock, and Catts (2006) present a continuum of literacy instruction with six levels, from the enhancement of content instruction through embedded and intensive strategy instruction to levels of remediation and intervention. These authors recommend screening all adolescents as they enter middle school, monitoring progress at least four times per year, providing access to engaging reading materials at levels appropriate for the particular student, and creating a culture of growth and achievement, with high expectations for all students and high-quality instruction, and coaches whose sole role is assisting teachers in improving the quality of instruction and student outcomes.

Myth 3 is that adolescent students do not need decoding instruction; the reality is that many teens do have problems with decoding. Deshler and colleagues (Deshler, Hock, & Catts, 2006; Hock, Brasseur, Deshler, Catts, & Marquis, 2005) indicate that 57% of adolescents in one sample had reading abilities at or below the 40th percentile and needed intensive word-level intervention in addition to comprehension work. On the basis of this, these authors speculate that large numbers of struggling readers may require both word-level and reading comprehension intervention. Calhoon (2006) offers an example of linguistically based word-level intervention, which she sequences with work on passage comprehension to remediate struggling middle school readers.

Myth 4 is that coaches are the key; the reality is that there is little evidence about how well or under what conditions coaching is effective. Deshler, Hock, and Catts (2006) emphasize that coaches should not be charged with administrative duties and should not be charged with, for example, administering the school's state assessment program. McPartland, Balfanz, and Legters (2006) also highlight the role of coaches. In their research, which compares levels of teacher support in a randomized experimental study, the coaches see every teacher twice weekly and are not part of the evaluation of teacher performance within the school system. In addition, McPartland and colleagues are providing workshops and complete instructional materials to some groups of teachers (with and without coaching). Although results are not all in for these studies, clearly the roles and responsibilities of reading coaches will be crucial to how effective they are in assisting teachers in improving the literacy abilities of adolescent struggling readers.

A number of consensus reports have also been published recently that highlight the aspects of instruction and systemic changes within schools that could be implemented to support greater reading and writing achievement for today's adolescents, and are presented next.

■ Reading Next

Although the research on adolescent and middle grade students was underway, the need to assemble what was known or could reasonably be extrapolated from other research to inform education practices with these students was urgent. In response to this need, the Alliance for Excellent Education and the Carnegie Corporation of New York produced a report with recommendations on elements that could compose an effective adolescent literacy program (Biancarosa & Snow, 2006). This report was based on input from a group of leading researchers in the field and included input from various public and private stakeholders. The strength of this report is the focus on steps that could be taken immediately to benefit adolescents and on future research directions that might benefit the next generation of adolescents as well.

The report listed a series of 15 elements that could be implemented in today's classrooms. The authors suggest that practitioners and literacy program directors could flexibly combine different elements of existing programs to meet the needs of their students. They also emphasize the importance of sustained teacher professional development programs, and the ongoing use of both less formal formative assessments to evaluate the ongoing progress of students and more formal summative assessments that could be used to evaluate not only student performance but also program success.

The elements recommended in the report fall into two general categories: instructional suggestions and infrastructure or institutional suggestions. The instructionally focused suggestions include recommending the use of direct, explicit comprehension instruction; importantly, this instruction could be provided not only in language arts classrooms but also in content area classrooms. The authors of the report also recommended using texts with a range of topics and difficulty levels, using ongoing formative assessments, encouraging and building the motivation of students, and providing the skills necessary for later independent learning. In addition, the report emphasized the importance of providing opportunities to improve writing skills through both intensive writing instruction and tutoring to provide opportunities for individualized instruction. It is worth noting that tutoring here was envisioned as not only building content knowledge, but also skills in "how to learn" (Biancarosa & Snow, 2006, p. 18). Similarly, the authors recommended providing opportunities for text-based collaborative learning, emphasizing rich interpersonal interactions centered around a text or series of texts and the use of technology as a tool to enhance literacy skills. These suggestions provide a range of options for teachers to use to build literacy skills within their classrooms.

Some suggestions were more strategic or systematic, aimed at improving infrastructure support for adolescent literacy. These include providing additional time for literacy instruction, developing teacher teams to help coordinate literacy efforts, emphasizing the importance of strong leadership in the success of a literacy program, and constructing a comprehensive and coordinated literacy program that could include not only individuals within the school but also organizations outside the school and the community at large. Finally, the report suggests the use of ongoing summative assessments of both student progress and success of the literacy program as a whole. These systematic changes can encourage buy-in from various stakeholders, not just teachers and administrators, and emphasize the importance of literacy skills for the success of students in all content area classes.

■   Writing Next

Recently, *Writing Next* (Graham & Perin, 2007), developed as a companion to *Reading Next* (Biancarosa & Snow, 2006) by the same Carnegie Corporation–Alliance for Excellent Education partnership, was released. This document has helped to bring continued attention to the need to develop stronger writing skills in today's adolescents as well as in future cohorts of middle and high school students. The authors of this summary document conducted a meta-analysis of studies that measured the efficacy of various instructional approaches to develop writing skills. The recommendations include 11 instructional elements that have been demonstrated to be effective.

In contrast to *Reading Next*, all of the recommendations are instructional recommendations, and in keeping with the authors' convention, they are mentioned by order of effect size from largest to smallest. However, it is important to note two points. First, although one element may have a larger effect size than a previous element, this does not mean that the difference in effect size is statistically reliable. Equally important, although an element may have a relatively small effect size as interpreted through Cohen's benchmarks[8] (Cohen, 1988), in the context of a classroom setting, the gains may be educationally meaningful.

In *Writing Next*, the authors identified 11 research-based elements that have been shown to be effective and that could be incorporated into classroom writing instruction. These include the use of writing strategies, summarization activities, collaborative writing with peers, and incorporating specific product goals for students' writing activities. Other elements include incorporating the use of word processing, sentence-combining techniques to construct increasingly complex sentences, prewriting activities, and inquiry activities designed to help students build ideas and data to support those ideas for their writing. The three final elements are the use of process writing approaches, the study of models of writing that students could practice emulating to strengthen their own writing styles, and writing as an activity for content area learning.

Within these elements, there are overlapping themes, including the potential for collaborative learning opportunities among peers. Similar to the *Reading Next* document, the elements of *Writing Next* provide concrete suggestions that could be incorporated not only in language arts classrooms, but also in other content area classrooms. Instructors in content area classrooms could strategically incorporate some of these suggestions into their classroom activities to enhance content learning. For example, the use of inquiry activities during the writing process could fit relatively naturally into the context of a science classroom, with some planning by the instructor.

Although these recommendations provide instructional elements or activities that teachers and administrators can incorporate immediately, based on research currently available, this document and others (Graham, 2006; MacArthur, Graham, & Fitzgerald, 2006; Perin & Graham, 2006) point to the need for further research in the development of writing skills. Research is needed to understand more fully the normal development of writing skills in both young children and adolescents and the types and combinations of instructional interventions that support this development, for both normally progressing students and students who struggle to develop strong writing skills.

■ Reading to Achieve: A Governor's Guide to Adolescent Literacy

Although *Reading Next* (Biancarosa & Snow, 2006) and *Writing Next* (Graham & Perin, 2007) focused on what teachers and administrators could do to support literacy activities in the classroom, the National Governors' Association (NGA) released a report entitled *Reading to Achieve: A Governor's Guide to Adolescent Literacy* (Berman & Biancarosa, 2005), which focuses on what can be done at the state level to support adolescent literacy. The recommendations in this document were guided in large part by the NGA's Center for Best Practices' Advisory Panel. The panel was composed of leading researchers in the field and representatives from governmental, nonprofit, and private organizations. Their feedback was solicited in two panel meetings and during the drafting process. The NGA also sought feedback from a wider range of public and private organizations concerned with adolescent education as well.

The NGA guide highlights the need to focus on adolescent literacy, providing five concrete steps that governors and states can take to increase achievement levels. First, governors should work to build support for a statewide focus on adolescent literacy. The report recommends designating a state office or coordinator for adolescent literacy and developing reporting activities such as a state literacy report card that would allow governors to determine the levels of literacy skills in their state.

Second, the report recommends raising literacy expectations across grades and curricula by raising state literacy standards and by making the literacy expectations clear and explicit. This includes taking into consideration how other organizations have defined the literacy demands for adolescents and the real-world demands that will be placed on these students by future employers and post-secondary education. Importantly, the report recognizes the importance of building support among educators and parents, who will ultimately be the implementers of any changes made.

Third, the guide recommends encouraging and supporting school and district literacy plans, which must be based on research evidence wherever possible and must acknowledge the literacy needs of struggling adolescent readers.

Fourth, educator capacity must be built to provide literacy instruction to adolescents. Without the appropriate training and professional development opportunities for new and existing teachers and principals, the changes necessary to address adolescent literacy cannot be undertaken successfully. Teacher preparation and licensure programs and a special certification program are also recommended. Finally, the guide emphasizes the need to be able to measure the progress that students are making.

■ Double the Work: Challenges and Solutions to Acquiring Language and Academic Literacy for Adolescent English Language Learners

The previous reports on adolescents include suggestions that could be incorporated by administrators, teachers, and state officials; however, the unique needs of ELL were not specifically addressed in these reports. *Double the Work: Challenges and Solutions to Acquiring Language and Academic Literacy for Adolescent English Language Learners* specifically addresses this need (Short & Fitzsimmons, 2007). For this report, a panel of researchers, policymakers, and practitioners was convened. The panel defined its focus as being on *academic literacy*, encompassing reading, writing, and oral discourse. The authors emphasized that academic literacy can vary by subject and that knowledge of different styles and purposes of text and text media are necessary; they acknowledge that academic literacy could be influenced by students' personal, social, and cultural experience and their literacy behaviors in settings outside of school.

In their report, the panel identifies six challenges to building better literacy skills in adolescent ELL students. First, they point out that there is no standard definition for ELL and that current assessments do not collect sufficient information that could inform and constrain possible definitions. The standardization of definitions could allow for more appropriate placement of students and could facilitate the collection and comparison of student performance data within and between states. Second, there is a great need for accurate assessment for ELLs to distinguish between challenges faced in learning a second language, in this case English, or possible learning disabilities. Third, it is important to build teachers' knowledge and capacity in the area of second language literacy instruction. With the growing number of ELLs in schools, the need for instructors with training to meet the literacy needs of ELLs will certainly increase. Fourth, the structure of current education programs in high school is not flexible enough to meet the needs of ELL students; these students frequently need additional time to build proficiency in English and to gain necessary content knowledge in the other coursework. The panel argues that one option to address this problem would be greater flexibility in the design of high school programs (including options such as allowing ELLs to remain in high school for more than four years). Fifth, the use of research-based instructional practices appropriate for ELL students is not as widespread as it should be. Finally, the panel argues that currently the adolescent ELL field lacks a "strong and coherent" literacy research agenda, based in large part on the relative paucity of research with ELLs in this age group.

These documents, taken together, emphasize the growing appreciation for the need to address the reading and writing needs for all of today's and future adolescents. As additional research evidence on effective practices becomes available, that information can be translated to practice.

■ Moving Toward Consensus

Even though the various reports and documents described in the previous section vary in their emphasis and foci, there are a number of important converging conclusions and recommendations that one can glean from these documents. For the sake of brevity, just four of the major points are highlighted.

First, there is recognition of the value of explicit instruction in reading (e.g., Commonwealth of Australia, 2005; NICHD, 2000; Snow, 2002). This recognition is particularly noteworthy given the range of topics, populations, and ages covered by these documents.

Second, several of the reports highlight that all teachers can play a role in addressing the literacy needs of their students, including those in content area classrooms (e.g., Biancarosa & Snow, 2006; Deshler, Hock, & Catts, 2006; Graham & Perin, 2007). Although content area teachers will not be literacy teachers per se and provide instruction in decoding for struggling middle grade or adolescent students (e.g., Deshler, Hock, & Catts, 2006; NIFL, 2007), these teachers can support the literacy needs of their students in learning content-specific vocabulary and comprehension of content material. The vision where all teachers play an active role in the development of literacy skills is broadly consistent with recommendations for comprehensive and coordinated literacy programs at schools and potentially within the community at large (e.g., Berman & Biancarosa, 2005; Biancarosa & Snow, 2006).

Third, the authors of various documents recognize the importance of the role of assessments (both summative and formative) and progress monitoring more generally, and the needs of the field to develop more accurate assessments, particularly for ELLs (e.g., Berman & Biancarosa, 2005; Biancarosa & Snow, 2006; Short & Fitzsimmons, 2007). Assessments can be an effective tool to aid teachers' efforts to identify students who may be struggling in reading or in other areas and, importantly, to adapt instruction as needed to ensure that students learn the concepts that are being taught.

Fourth, given the critical importance of teachers providing high-quality, research-based instruction, there is also a growing recognition with regard to the need for high-quality, sustained professional development to support teachers' efforts in the area of literacy and in assessment and progress monitoring in literacy (e.g., Biancarosa & Snow, 2006; Commonwealth of Australia, 2005). Developing and building upon teacher's existing skills in this area will be crucial as the responsibilities for literacy instruction continue to move toward a more systemic approach; teachers must be able to collect and interpret information from both formative and summative assessments to modify instruction as needed. All four of these points of convergence reflect the important role that teachers play in the development of students' literacy skills and the importance of providing adequate tools and professional development opportunities to support their role.

■ New Evidence on the Horizon

The existence of all these reports clearly does not signal that we know all we need to know to be able to teach all children to read efficiently and effectively. There is a continuing need for research both on the fundamental understanding of how children learn, including how they learn to read, and on the sources of learning difficulties, including reading disabilities. The NICHD has funded research on how children learn to read for over 35 years. Both the NICHD and the IES have ongoing studies on reading, reading disabilities, instruction, and remediation/intervention. The IES also funds work on teacher preparation and professional development in reading, and the NICHD supports researchers studying the neural and genetic bases of reading disabilities, as well as the neurobiology of reading, language, and bilingual development both in their own right and as they relate to reading disabilities. Both agencies support the development of new assessment measures and techniques, and both support product-oriented research under their small business research initiatives. Importantly, these and other federal agencies communicate and collaborate in cross-agency partnerships to ensure coordinated efforts across agencies, including working on interagency groups on reading research dissemination convened by the NIFL.

Later progress at the NICHD in specific areas is briefly summarized. Although the Institute is continuously funding new grants, and supports work at universities and research institutions across the country (and internationally) on all aspects of reading, across the lifespan including preschool, elementary school, and adult, three areas are relevant to topics covered in this volume: bilingual literacy, adolescent literacy, and learning disabilities. These three areas of literacy are among those in which NICHD research administrators have established consortia where researchers meet annually to share preliminary results and research challenges, and to discuss and share thoughts on measures and methods. (There are also consortia for preschool learning, adult literacy, and other areas of child development.)

Bilingual literacy. Although there is always more to do, great strides have been made in research to inform practice on reading instruction for ELL students. From 2000 to 2005, the NICHD and the U.S. Department of Education Office of Education Research and Improvement, now the IES, jointly funded a network of research projects. Termed the Development of English Literacy in Spanish-Speaking Children or DELSS, this network of researchers from across the nation conducted research, developed collaborations across projects, and published their findings. A summary of the projects, the assessment instruments they developed, and the publications that continue to emanate from these projects can be found at the DELSS Web site (http://www.cal.org/delss). A consortium of research projects on ELL reading continues to be supported by the NICHD, no longer limited to Spanish-speaking children, but encompassing additional languages such as Chinese and Korean. In addition, the IES continues to fund work on ELL reading and education. Given the responses of the professional associations and government agencies with interest in this topic, it seems clear that, as additional research findings are published and converge in ways that give us confidence that they are sufficiently reliable to serve as a basis for changing practice, companion documents for educators will be produced.

Adolescent literacy. From March through May 2002, a series of workshops cosponsored by multiple federal agencies and professional associations were convened to focus on the under-researched area of adolescent literacy.[9] On the basis of the research agenda that was developed at these workshops, in 2003–2004, the NICHD, together with the Office of Vocational and Adult Education and the Office of Special Education and Rehabilitation Services (OSERS) at the U.S. Department of Education, solicited and funded six research grants to form the Adolescent Literacy Research Consortium. All projects use some experimental methods, as well as descriptive/qualitative research methodologies. Two projects use longitudinal cohorts, whereas three will examine the brain-behavior linkages in reading and reading disabilities to test the effectiveness of reading interventions. One project primarily seeks to study the relations between literacy achievement and student motivation and engagement. Another study examines the impact of providing different levels of teacher support on student achievement and teacher practices in an intensive high school literacy intervention. The NICHD continues to fund work on adolescent literacy through investigator-initiated proposals, and as additional research is funded addressing issues in adolescent literacy, those investigators will join the consortium.

Learning disabilities. In January 1987, a National Conference on Learning Disabilities was held. This meeting was cosponsored by the Interagency Committee on Learning Disabilities (of which the NICHD was designated as the lead agency) and the Foundation for Children with Learning Disabilities, now the National Center for Learning Disabilities. The resulting document, *Learning Disabilities: A Report to the U.S. Congress* called for a systematic effort to conduct research to develop a valid and reliable definition and classification system that could provide a theoretical, conceptual, and empirical framework for the identification of different types of learning disabilities. This research was also targeted at the identification of distinctions and interrelationships (comorbidities) between types of learning disabilities and other childhood disorders, including general academic underachievement, disorders of attention, mental retardation, genetic disorders, and emotional disturbance. The document also called for a systematic effort to develop rigorous research strategies and intervention trials to examine the responses of children with learning disabilities to different forms of treatment.

On the basis of those recommendations, the NICHD funded three multidisciplinary Learning Disability Research Centers (LDRCs) in 1988 to initiate studies on the definition, classification, and etiology of learning disabilities and related disorders. Since that time, the NICHD has supported LDRCs, solicited and selected through open research funding competitions. Studies conducted at these LDRCs, along with the other research projects funded by the NICHD, yielded a number of scientific advances. This research was able to demonstrate the critical cognitive and linguistic factors involved in children's learning to read, and to delve into what goes wrong when children do not learn to read—to describe and define reading disabilities, including a preliminary examination of the genetic and neurological bases of reading disabilities. Prevention and remediation studies addressing deficits in word level reading skills and other aspects of reading produced converging evidence on the importance of phonemic awareness, the development of the alphabetic principle, reading fluency, vocabulary, and reading comprehension strategies in learning to read. Much of this early research is included in the NRP report. NICHD-supported scientists have obtained evidence for specific neural systems related to the development of some componential reading skills and the ability of these systems to respond to well-defined interventions has been impressive (e.g., Gayan & Olson, 2003; Meng et al., 2005; Pugh et al., 1997; Shaywitz et al., 2002; Simos et al., 2005). However, far more information about the neurological and genetic aspects of reading disability is needed, and there is some indication that through this work more about the link between how neural systems respond and learning in general will be discovered.

As a result of the important advances of the LDRC Consortium and the ongoing need for research building on these findings, a third competition was held in 2005, and one existing and three new LDRCs were funded, continuing the research consortium. These four centers, distributed across the country (University of Colorado, University of Houston, Florida State University, and the Kennedy Krieger Institute/Johns Hopkins University) are actively engaged in researching various aspects of reading and reading disabilities, including new work on the neurobiology and genetics of reading and reading disability. In addition, they have been specifically asked to examine the effectiveness of RTI as a means of identifying and remediating students with reading difficulties.

■ Conclusion

Clearly, the importance of basing reading instruction on solid, reliable research evidence cannot be understated. Although few would buy a car without some evidence of its reliability and crash-worthiness, or would trust one's own or a loved one's health to medical treatments for which no scientific basis or evidence of effectiveness existed, these same demands for evidence-based practice in educating children have not always been raised. This may be because there was insufficient evidence available, or that evidence was not being published and disseminated in the outlets read by teachers and/or the public, or the findings were not being tested in large-scale classroom implementations with diverse groups of students where we could have confidence in generalizability of the findings to our own classrooms. But all of these potentially limiting factors have changed and are continuing to change.

Reliable evidence now exists for many instructional practices in reading and reading remediation. While not everything is known, a lot is known! In the new age of accountability in education, better measures for evaluating the effectiveness of the implementation of research-based practices in the classrooms are needed. Efficient and effective ways to prepare new teachers and continue the professional development of already practicing teachers for evidence-based practices are needed. As RTI models are implemented across the nation, research is needed on optimal ways to implement them in various types of schools with a variety of student populations. The promise of RTI is that children at risk for reading failure can be identified and treated at early ages to prevent reading disability with general and special education working together as a team.

The fact that more remains to learn through research does not negate the potential impact of findings to date. Remediating reading problems should be approached with optimism. However, questions remain in various areas and the chapter ends with some of these that serve as a reminder that research in general and on reading in particular is an ongoing, evolving process. Such questions include the following: how best to implement RTI effectively, how different students can best be instructed in reading comprehension, how the interconnections between oral language ability and reading comprehension can be exploited to instruct all students more effectively in the complex area of reading comprehension, how children and adolescents develop reading and writing skills, how best to ensure that learning happens through evidence-based instruction, how best to bring preschoolers to school ready to learn, how to adapt instruction to optimally ensure success for ELL students both in reading English and their first language, and how best to identify and remediate those who have difficulty learning to read and write, regardless of age.

■ References

August, D., & Hakuta, K. (1998). *Educating language-minority children.* Washington, DC, National Academies Press.

August, D., & Shanahan, T. (Eds.) (2006). *Developing literacy in second-language learners: Report of the National Literacy Panel on language-minority children and youth.* Mahwah, NJ, Lawrence Erlbaum Associates.

Berman, I., & Biancarosa, G. (2005) *Reading to achieve: A Governor's guide to adolescent literacy.* Washington, DC, National Governor's Association.

Biancarosa, G., & Snow, C. E. (2006). *Reading next: A vision for action and research in middle and high school literacy: A report to Carnegie Corporation of New York* (2nd ed.). Washington, DC, Alliance for Excellent Education.

Burns, M. S., Griffin, P., & Snow, C. E. (Eds.) (1999). *Starting out right: A guide to promoting children's reading success.* Washington, DC, National Academies Press.

Calhoon, M. (2006). Rethinking adolescent literacy instruction. *Perspectives*, 32(3), 31–35.

Cohen, J. (1988). *Statistical power analysis for the behavioral sciences* (2nd ed.). Hillsdale, NJ, Lawrence Erlbaum Associates.

Commonwealth of Australia. (2005). *Teaching reading: Report and recommendations, national inquiry into the teaching of literacy.* Australia, Department of Education, Science, and Training.

Denton, C. (Ed.) (2006). Theme articles focused on Response to Intervention. *Perspectives, 32*(1).

Deshler, D., Hock, M., & Catts, H. (2006). Enhancing outcomes for struggling adolescent readers. *Perspectives, 32*(3), 21–25.

Education Sciences Reform Act of 2002, PL 107–279, 20 U.S.C. § 9621.

Ehri, L. C. (2004). Teaching phonemic awareness and phonics: An explanation of the National Reading Panel meta-analyses. In P. McCardle & V. Chhabra (Eds.), *The voice of evidence in reading research* (pp. 153–186). Baltimore, MD, Brookes.

Gayan, J., & Olson, R. (2003). Genetic and environmental influences on individual differences in printed word recognition. *Journal of Experimental Child Psychology, 84*, 97–123.

Graham, S. (2006). Strategy instruction and the teaching of writing: A meta-analysis. In C. MacArthur, S. Graham, & J. Fitzgerald (Eds.), *Handbook of writing research* (pp. 187–207). New York, The Guilford Press.

Graham, S., & Perin, D. (2007). *Writing next: Effective strategies to improve writing of adolescents in middle and high schools: A report to Carnegie Corporation of New York.* Washington, DC, Alliance for Excellent Education.

Hock, M., Brasseur, I., Deshler, D., Catts, H., & Marquis, J. (2005). *What is the nature of adolescent struggling readers in urban high schools?* Lawrence, KS, Research Report No. 1, University of Kansas Center for Research on Learning.

International Dyslexia Association. (2006). Theme articles on adolescent. *Perspectives on language and literacy: Special edition, 32.* 1, 7, 10–14, 21–25, 31–35, 39–42.

International Reading Association. (2002). *Evidence-based reading instruction: Putting the National Reading Panel report into practice.* Newark, DE, Author.

International Reading Association. (2006). *New roles in response to intervention: Creating success for schools and children.* Newark, DE, Author.

Kamil, M. L. (2004). Vocabulary and comprehension instruction: Summary and implications of the National Reading Panel findings. In P. McCardle & V. Chhabra (Eds.), *The voice of evidence in reading research* (pp. 213–234). Baltimore, MD, Brookes.

Lyon, G. R., Fletcher, J. M., Shaywitz, S. E., Shaywitz, B. A., Torgesen, J. K., Wood, F. B., Schulte, A., & Olson, R. (2001). Rethinking learning disabilities. In C. E. Finn Jr., A. J. Rotherham, & C. R. Hokanson, Jr. (Eds.), *Rethinking special education for a new century* (pp. 259–287). Washington, DC, Thomas B. Fordham Foundation and the Progressive Policy Institute.

MacArthur, C. A., Graham, S., & Fitzgerald, J. (Eds.) (2006). *Handbook of writing research.* New York, The Guilford Press.

McCardle, P., & Chhabra, V. (Eds.) (2004). *The voice of evidence in reading research.* Baltimore, MD, Brookes.

McPartland, J., Balfanz, R., & Legters, N. (2006). Supporting teachers for adolescent literacy interventions. *Perspectives, 32*(3), 39–42.

Meng, H., Smith, S. D., Hager, K., Held, M., Liu, J., Olson, R. K., Pennington, B. F., DeFries, J. C., Gelernter, J., O'Reilly-Pol, T., Somlo, S., SkudlarskI, P., Shaywitz, S. E., Shaywitz, B. A., Marchione, K., Wang, Y., Paramasivam, M., LoTurco, J. J., Page, G. P., & Gruen, J. R. (2005). DCDC2 is associated with reading disability and modulates neuronal development in the brain. [Erratum in: *Proceedings of the National Academy of Sciences U S A, 102,* 18763.] *Proceedings of the National Academy of Sciences U S A, 102,* 17053–17058.

Moak, R., Shuy, T., & McCardle, P. (Eds.) (2006a). Theme issue on adolescent literacy [Special Issue]. *Perspectives, 32*(3).

Moak, R., Shuy, T., & McCardle, P. (2006b). Myths and realities of adolescent literacy. *Perspectives, 32,* 1, 7.

Moje, E. B. (2006). Motivating texts, motivating contexts, motivating adolescents: An examination of the role of motivation in adolescent literacy practices and development. *Perspectives, 32*(3), 10–14.

National Assessment of Education Progress, PL 107–279, 116 Stat 1983, 20 U.S.C. § 9622.

National Center for Education Statistics. (2005a). *The NAEP reading achievement levels by grade.* Retrieved February 15, 2007, from http://nces.ed.gov/nationsreportcard/reading/achieveall.asp#grade4.

National Center for Education Statistics. (2005b). *The nation's report card: Reading 2005.* Retrieved February 15, 2007, from http://nces.ed.gov/pubsearch/pubsinfo.asp?pubid=2006451.

National Institute of Child Health and Human Development (NICHD). (2000). *Report of the National Reading Panel. Teaching children to read: An evidence-based assessment of the scientific research literature on reading and its implications for reading instruction: Reports of the subgroups (NIH Publication No. 00–4754).* Washington, DC, U.S. Government Printing Office.

National Institute for Literacy (NIFL). (2007). *What content-area teachers should know about adolescent literacy* (ED002624P). Washington, DC, U.S. Government Printing Office.

No Child Left Behind Act of 2001, PL 107–110, 115 Stat. 1452, 20 U.S.C. §§ 6301 *et. seq.*

Partnership for Reading. (2001a). *Put reading first: Helping your child learn to read. A parent guide: Preschool through grade 3.* Washington, DC, Author.

Partnership for Reading. (2001b). *Put reading first: The research building blocks for teaching children to read. Kindergarten through grade 3.* Washington, DC, Author.

Perin, D., & Graham, S. (2006). Teaching writing skills to adolescents: Evidence-based practices. *Perspectives on Language and Literacy, 32,* 10–14.

President's Commission on Excellence in Special Education. (2002). *A new era: Revitalizing special education for children and their families.* Washington, DC, U.S. Department of Education, Office of Special Education and Rehabilitative Services.

Pugh, K., Shaywitz, B., Shaywitz, S. R., Shankweiler, D., Katz, L., Fletcher, J., Constable, R. T., Skudlarski, P., Fulbright, R., Bronen, R., & Gore, J. (1997). Predicting reading performance from neuroimaging profiles: The cerebral basis of phonological effects in printed word identification. *Journal of Experimental Psychology: Human Perception and Performance, 23,* 299–318.

Reading Excellence Act of 1998, PL 105–277, 112 Stat. 2681–337, 2681–393, 20 U.S.C. § 6661a *et. seq.*

Shavelson, R. J., & Towne, L. (Eds.) (2002). *Scientific research in education.* Washington, DC, National Academies Press.

Shaywitz, B. A., Shaywitz, S. E., Pugh, K. R., Mencl, W. E., Fulbright, R. K., Skudlarski, P., Constable, R. T., Marchione, K. E., Fletcher, J. M., Lyon, G. R., & Gore, J. C. (2002). Disruption of posterior brain systems for reading in children with developmental dyslexia. *Biological Psychiatry, 52,* 101–110.

Short, D. J., & Fitzsimmons, S. (2007). *Double the work: Challenges and solutions to acquiring language and academic literacy for adolescent English language learners: A report to Carnegie Corporation of New York.* Washington, DC, Alliance for Excellent Education.

Simos, P., Fletcher, J., Sarkari, S., Billingsley, R., Francis, D., Castillo, E., Pataraia, E., Denton, C., & Papanicolaou, A. (2005). Early development of neurophysiological processes involved in normal reading and reading disability: A magnetic source imaging study. *Neuropsychology, 19,* 787–798.

Snow, C. (Ed.) (2002). *Reading for understanding: Toward an R&D program in reading comprehension.* Washington, DC, The RAND Corporation.

Snow, C., Burns, S., & Griffin, P. (Eds.) (1998). *Preventing reading difficulties in young children.* Washington, DC, National Academies Press.

Stahl, S. A. (2004). What do we know about fluency? Findings of the National Reading Panel. In P. McCardle & V. Chhabra (Eds.), *The voice of evidence in reading research* (pp. 187–211). Baltimore, MD, Brookes.

Sweet, R. (2004). The big picture: Where we are nationally on the reading front and how we got here. In P. McCardle & V. Chhabra (Eds.), *The voice of evidence in reading research* (pp. 13–44). Baltimore, MD, Brookes.

Sweet, A. P., & Snow, C. (Eds.) (2003). *Rethinking reading comprehension.* New York, The Guilford Press.

The White House. (January 23, 1996). *State of the Union address of the President.* Retrieved February 1, 2007, from http://clinton2.nara.gov/WH/New/other/ stateunion-top.html.

Torgesen, J. K. (2004). Lessons learned from research on interventions for students who have difficulty learning to read. In P. McCardle & V. Chhabra (Eds.), *The voice of evidence in reading research* (pp. 355–382). Baltimore, MD, Brookes.

Torgesen, J. K., Wagner, R., Rashotte, C., Rose, E., Lindamood, P., Conway, T., & Garvan, C. (1999). Preventing reading failure in young children with phonological processing disabilities: Group and individual responses to instruction. *Journal of Educational Psychology, 91,* 579–593.

Towne, L., Wise, L., & Winters, T. (Eds.) (2004). *Advancing scientific research in education.* Washington, DC, National Academy Press.

U.S. Department of Education. (2005). *2005 National Assessment of Educational Progress.* Washington, DC, National Center for Education Statistics and U.S. Department of Education. Retrieved using the NAEP Data Explorer on February 15, 2007, from http://nces.ed.gov/nationsreportcard/naepdata/.

Valentine, J. C., & Cooper, H. (2003). *Effect size substantive interpretation guidelines: Issues in the interpretation of effect sizes.* Washington, DC, What Works Clearinghouse.

■ Notes

1. The term alphabetics is used here to refer to phonemic awareness, sound-letter correspondence, and phonics.

2. The House Committee on Education and the Workforce is the Congressional committee that oversees the budgets for the U.S. Departments of Education, Health and Human Services, and Labor.

3. Note that RTI is more than a method for identification; it is a tiered approach to the provision of high-quality instruction and careful progress monitoring for all children. It begins with general education and provides for increasingly intensive service delivery as the tiers increase.

4. Cosponsors were IDA, NICHD, the Office of Special Education and Rehabilitation Services, the American Speech-Language-Hearing Association, the Council for Exceptional Children/Division of Learning Disabilities, the National Center for Learning Disabilities, and the National Research Center on Learning Disabilities.

5. This document is available free at http://www.reading.org/downloads/ resources/rti_role_definitions.pdf.

6. *Starting Out Right* is available online at the National Academies Press Web site (http://www.nap.edu/openbook/0309064104/html/index.html).

7. Preliminary findings of the NELP are summarized at http://www.nifl.gov/ partnershipforreading/family/ncfl/NELP2006Conference.pdf.

8. It is worth noting that Cohen's benchmarks were aimed to reflect the typical range of effect sizes within behavioral science as a whole, and he cautioned against using his benchmarks categories when interpreting effect sizes in a particular domain (e.g., Valentine & Cooper, 2003 for discussion).
9. Summary documents from these workshops are posted at http://www.nifl. gov/partnershipforreading/publications/adolescent.html.

2. A Review of Science-Supported Writing Instruction with Implementation in Mind

Stephen R. Hooper, Sean B. Knuth, Donna Carlson Yerby, and Kathleen L. Anderson

■ Introduction

The teaching of writing dates back centuries with our Greek and Roman ancestors employing a variety of strategies to teach rhetoric in the written form (Bloodgood, 2002). The study of writing has been discussed in the professional literature for decades. Mills (1953) proposed that writing be understood as a "process" rather than the ultimate product and his writings stimulated significant discussion of the writing process and how to teach it. These early roots continue to be present in the National Writing Project and other similar programs that train teachers in specific pedagogical principles for teaching writing as a process (Calkins, 1994). Empirical evidence to support this approach to the teaching of writing, particularly with students with learning differences, disabilities, and challenges, has been lacking, but some is emerging (Pritchard & Honeycutt, 2006).

At the same time, the cognitive basis for written expression can be traced to the Dartmouth Seminar conducted at Dartmouth College in 1966. This multidisciplinary conference included scholars from a variety of different disciplines who were interested in the topic of writing and, as a result of this conference, began to study writing using information emerging from cognitive psychology. This cognitive approach spawned an influential theory of written expression proposed by Hayes and Flower (1980). For example, the

This project was completed with grant support from the Department of Education Institute for Educational Science (R305H06042), Maternal Child Health Bureau (#MCJ379154A), and the Administration on Developmental Disabilities (#90DD043003).

Hayes and Flower (1980) model set the stage for subsequent scientific studies of writing in children (for a review, see Berninger & Amtmann, 2003) and adults (Hayes, 2006). This cognitive perspective of writing as a "problem solving process" opened up writing to investigations from many disciplines, including education, neurology, psychology, neuropsychology, and neuroscience and led to the realization that effective instruction must deal with the complexities of the writing process. Written composition requires that ideas be generated, organized, and expressed in writing, which has to be examined for its relationship to writing goals and evaluated and re-evaluated for clarity. Given this complexity, how should instruction proceed? Bereiter and Scardamalia (1987) noted that even in a good writer, the early onset of writing may be less clear, with increased clarity coming as the recursive processes involved in composing unfold.

From the cognitive perspective, written expression requires ongoing scientific research to increase understanding of the writing process, its development, and effective instructional approaches, especially when writing development is atypical (Wong & Wilson, 1984). Written language problems are highly prevalent in schools across the country. Lerner (2000) speculated that probably the most prevalent communication disability involves the expression of ideas through written language. Using unreferred samples of elementary school students, Berninger and Hart (1992) reported that 1.3–2.7% of 300 primary grade children had problems with handwriting, 3.7–4% had problems with spelling, and 1–3% had problems with written narratives. On the basis of a large epidemiological sample, Hooper et al. (1993) reported significantly higher rates of text generation problems in middle school when writing demands increase, with rates ranging from 6% to 22% depending on region of the country and gender. More recently, the National Center for Education Statistics (NCES, 2003) reported that only about 28% of fourth graders could write at a proficient level or above, 58% wrote at a basic level, and 14% wrote below the basic level. Written language clearly poses unique challenges for teachers, particularly as students move through the educational system and encounter increased demands for writing in all of their classes. The Scholastic Aptitude Test (SAT) has recently added a writing test, but anecdotal evidence indicates that college admission offices are not quite sure how to use this task as part of the college entry process (Chute, 2007), further substantiating the need for more research on writing throughout schooling.

Writing problems may be prevalent because written language is one of the most complex functions in which we engage (Lerner, 2000). Although the "decade of the brain" (the 1990s) and the research stimulated by the Hayes and Flower (1980) model of the cognitive processes in writing increased understanding of brain-behavior relationships in writing and writing development (Berninger & Richards, 2002), writing research continues to lag behind reading research, especially with regard to effective instruction. Nevertheless, some evidence is accumulating and is even being replicated across research groups. This chapter focuses on the cognitive functions of developing writers that are relevant to writing and evidence from the past 20–25 years related to effective writing instruction.

■ Cognitive Functions in Written Expression: An Overview

A number of studies have documented the qualities inherent in "experts" who excel in writing versus "novices" or those who struggle with writing (e.g., Berninger, Fuller, & Whitaker, 1997; Gregg, 1992; Gregg & Mather, 2002; Hayes, 2000; Hayes & Flower, 1980; Houck & Billingsley, 1989; Wong & Wilson, 1984). For example, Wong and Wilson (1984) observed that late elementary and early middle school children with learning disabilities were less aware of passage organization than their typically developing peers, and struggled to a significantly greater degree to impose organizational structure on a disorganized passage. However, both groups focused on other features of a passage to determine its difficulty level (e.g., sentence length, vocabulary, volume of information, etc.), suggesting that providing instruction in organization of writing may be important for all children and especially those with learning problems.

Knowledge of neuropsychological factors (e.g., memory, attention) in writing has expanded over the past decade. Levine et al. (1993) proposed that all of the following are involved in writing: memory, attention, graphomotor output, sequential processing, higher-order cognition, language, and visual-spatial functions. Abbott and Berninger (1993) conducted a cross-sectional study of students in grades 1–6 and found that orthographic coding of written words in memory, phonological coding of spoken words in memory, and finger function (control and planning) contributed to transcription skills (handwriting and spelling), whereas not only these transcription skills but also oral language vocabulary and comprehension contributed to written composition. Berninger and Rutberg (1992) pinpointed graphomotor planning (as assessed by sequential touching of fingers to thumb) as a finger function skill contributing uniquely to handwriting. Hooper and colleagues have since examined the multidimensionality of neuropsychological functions in elementary school students with and without writing problems, with results strongly indicative of multiple subtypes in both the regular (Hooper et al., 2006; Wakely et al., 2006) and special education (Sandler et al., 1992) populations. These studies also showed the importance of specific linguistic factors (e.g., semantics, grammar), along with reading and spelling, in explaining the multiple dimensions involved in written expression.

Another key cognitive function in writing is working memory (Lea & Levy, 1999; McCutchen, 2000). Working memory is important to written expression because it underlies the active maintenance of multiple ideas, the retrieval of grammatical rules from long-term memory, and the recursive self-monitoring that is required while writing (Kellogg, 1999). Working memory contributes to the management of these simultaneous processes, and breakdowns in working memory may lead to problems with written output (Levy & Marek, 1999). McCutchen (1996) noted that poor writers typically have reduced working memory capacity when compared with good writers. Swanson and Berninger (1996) reported that working memory made both general and domain-specific contributions to the writing process. Recent work by Hooper and colleagues compared fourth and fifth grade students with and without writing problems and documented that both working memory deficits and broader memory problems across modalities were related to the writing process (Hooper et al., 2007).

Finally, a number of studies document the importance of executive functions to the writing process. Graham and colleagues were the forerunners in examining this cognitive component of the writing process and its treatment implications (Graham, 1997; Graham et al., 1998). Their Self-Regulated Strategy Development (SRSD) model, supported by many empirical studies, enables students to develop composing skills, develop automatic and reflective writing strategies, understand the parameters of "good" writing, and develop positive attitudes about their abilities to communicate via writing (Graham & Harris, 2000). Good and poor writers differ in executive functions (Hooper et al., 2002). Fourth and fifth grade students with and without writing problems differed in their profile of executive functions, with the poor writers being less proficient at initiating, sustaining, shifting set, and inhibiting; effect sizes were small to moderate (Hooper et al., 2006). Altemeier, Jones, Abbott, and Berninger (2006) showed that executive functions are related to integrating reading and writing during note-taking and report writing in elementary school students. Taken together, these findings indicate the importance of executive functions in the development of written expression, and in the integration of reading and writing skills.

■ Introduction to the Science-Based Literature in Writing Instruction

The evidence base for teaching writing is expanding, from the elementary school to the junior and senior high school, to the adult and college levels (Gregg, 1992). However, what we know about the science of writing instruction for younger children and children with learning differences and disabilities is still in its infancy.

Professional development for teachers in "best practices" (Bradley-Johnson et al., 1989; Kulberg, 1993; Lesiak, 1992) has tended to focus on reading rather than writing (NCES, 2003). As noted earlier, writing is an inherently challenging task for most children and thus requires quality writing instruction, which may not be taking place in many of America's classrooms (Troia, 2002) despite the increased emphasis on accountability demanded by No Child Left Behind standards and other state-driven expectations. Teachers might benefit from professional development in teaching writing while simultaneously attending to the curricular demands of numerous content areas and related high stakes testing required by states (Troia & Graham, 2002).

Specific teaching practices in the regular classroom have been linked to proficient writing achievement: providing frequent opportunities to write, focusing on the writing process (particularly the acts of planning and revising), clarifying criteria for successful writing, and taking a balanced approach that includes an emphasis on mechanical correctness and effective rhetoric (Bromley, 1999; Gersten & Baker, 2001; Gleason & Isaacson, 2001; Troia & Graham, 2004). For students with writing problems, effective interventions have been devoted to the higher-order aspects of composing, such as planning and revising (De La Paz, 1997; Englert, 1990, 1992; MacArthur et al., 1991; Mercer & Mercer, 2001; Schumaker & Sheldon, 1985; Wong et al., 1991, 1994, 1997), organization and self-monitoring (Isaacson, 1995), and metacognition and self-regulation strategies (Harris & Graham, 1992, 1996; Welch & Jensen, 1991), the linguistic/mechanics aspects of composing such as spelling, capitalization, syntax, and grammar (Berninger et al., 2002; Bos & Vaughn, 1988), and genre-specific writing strategies (Berninger et al., 2002; Wong et al., 1997). Consistent with findings for reading (see McCardle & Miller, Chapter 1), explicit instruction is essential to the development of writing skills (Gleason & Isaacson, 2001; Graham & Harris, 1994; Troia, 2002). Explicit writing instruction has been shown to improve the length, organization, and quality of students' compositions (Graham & Harris, 2003).

◾ Intervention Studies Examining the Major Components of Writing: An Overview

The study of writing, which is a complex, multidimensional process, has tended to focus on specific components of the writing process. For example, research on writing instruction often focused on one of the three major related, but dissociable, components of written expression: handwriting, spelling, and composition. Findings for each of these skills, which often involved teaching strategies for learning them, are illustrated by available representative empirical studies.

Evidence-Based Interventions for Handwriting

Handwriting evolves from early sensory-motor movements to scribbles on a page to printing one's name to later cursive narrative output. For students who struggle with this developmental progression, written expression may be significantly challenging and interventions may be necessary. Berninger et al. (1997) investigated the efficacy of five different handwriting instruction treatments for 144 first graders at-risk in handwriting. The five different instructional approaches include (a) imitating motor movements; (b) visual cues—studying numbered arrows for letter formation; (c) memory retrieval—writing letters from memory; (d) visual cues + memory retrieval; and (e) copying. The control group received phonological awareness training. The visual cues + memory retrieval intervention was more effective than the other treatments or control treatment, with respect to legible and automatic manuscript handwriting and transfer to compositional fluency.

Work by Graham and colleagues (e.g., Graham et al., 2001) have examined the execution of handwriting in young elementary school students. Most recently, Graham and Harris (2005) evaluated the handwriting and writing skills of 38 first-grade students. The control group received phonological awareness instruction, and the experimental group received handwriting instruction designed to increase the accuracy and fluency of writing lower-case manuscript letters. The experimental group showed higher levels of accuracy in naming, writing letters, copying connected texts, and constructing sentences, and for the most part maintained skills over a six-month period.

Evidence-Based Interventions for Spelling

Evidence that using specific strategies, mostly involving direct instruction of the sound-symbol associations and/or self-monitoring of the alphabetic principle, improves spelling dates back at least 50 years (Gillingham & Stillman, 1973; Horn & Otto, 1954; Kauffman et al., 1978; Stephens, 1977). Teaching other specific strategies (e.g., Fernald, 1988; Graham & Freeman, 1986; Graham, Harris, & Loynachan, 1994; Graham & Voth, 1990; Greene, 1994; Harp, 1988; Kearney & Drabman, 1993; Mercer & Mercer, 2001; Varnhagen, 1995; Wirtz et al., 1996; Wong, 1986) and/or direct instruction (Berninger et al., 2002; Dixon, 1991; Ehri, 1986; McNaughton et al., 1994; Shanker & Ekwall, 1998; Stein, 1983; Henderson & Templeton, 1986; Treiman, 1993) have/has also improved spelling.

Berninger et al. (1998) examined the efficacy of seven different strategies (saying the word and naming all its letters, onset-rime, and alphabetic principle correspondences between phonemes and one or two letters—alone and in each combination of two or three strategies) and a phonological awareness control in a sample of 128 second graders at-risk in spelling. The interventions, which included modeling, teaching for transfer to word spelling, and composing, were provided in 20-minute sessions twice a week spread across 24 weeks. All seven strategies led to improved spelling of taught words, but whole word plus onset-rime training resulted in better transfer to untrained monosyllabic words and phoneme-grapheme correspondences led to better spelling during independent composing. Multiple strategies facilitated spelling.

In a follow-up study in third grade, Berninger et al. (2000) found that the faster responders in second grade maintained gains at the beginning and end of second grade. The slower responders the previous year were given additional treatment: alphabetic principle instruction or combined alphabetic principle and syllable awareness instruction. After this second dose of treatment, the slower responders reached the average range for their chronological age; adding syllable awareness improved spelling of silent "e" words but otherwise adding syllable awareness training had no advantage in spelling two syllable words. Both groups improved significantly on Wechsler Individual Achievement Test (WIAT) spelling, Woodcock Reading Mastery Test-Revised (WRMT-R) word identification, and on phonological memory.

Graham and Harris (2005) evaluated the efficacy of a 20-minute spelling instruction intervention delivered three times per week over a 16-week period to 60 children who scored below the 25th percentile on the WIAT *and* were identified by their classroom teacher as having difficulties with spelling. Children who received the spelling instruction outperformed a control group in identifying sound-letter combinations and in correctly spelling the words used in the intervention. They also surpassed the control group in tasks consisting of constructing sentences and decoding nonsense words.

Evidence-Based Explicit Instruction in Composition

Most research on teaching written expression has focused on older students (e.g., Calkins, 1994; Phelps-Gunn, 1982). Some studies investigate specific strategies of composition instruction, whereas others investigate explicit composition instruction.

Table 2.1 summarizes the empirical studies devoted to younger children and/or elementary school students (Englert, 1992; Gordon & Braun, 1983; Graham, 1992; Graves, 1994; Isaacson, 1995; Leavell & Ioannides, 1993; MacArthur et al., 1991; Phelps-Terasaki & Phelps-Gunn, 2000; Polloway et al., 1981; Rico, 1983; Strong, 1983; Tompkins & Friend, 1985). Programmatic lines of research on written composition have been conducted at the University of Washington by Berninger and colleagues (e.g., for a review, see Berninger, 2008) and University of Maryland and Vanderbilt University by Graham and colleagues (for reviews, see Graham, 2006; Graham & Perin, 2007a, 2007b).

TABLE 2.1 *An Overview of Writing Intervention Studies using Explicit/Combined Instruction Approaches to Improve Composition for Elementary School Students*

Authors (year)	Sample Description	Interventions	Measures	Findings
Sawyer, Graham, & Harris (1992)	43 students: 23 grade 5 and 20 grade 6. All LD; IQ between 80 and 120 ($M = 93.8$), ≥2 years below grade level on achievement and teacher nominated as having compositional difficulties. Male = 25, Female = 18; 27 were black, 13 were white, 2 were Hispanic, and 1 was Asian	Three intervention groups: Direct Teaching, SRSD w/o explicit self-regulation instruction, and full SRSD. One control group. In addition, a normally achieving (NA) score was reported.	Story Grammar Scale (Scale designed by Graham to assess inclusion and quality of eight common story elements), a holistic rating scale, and a self-efficacy scale for story writing. All scales applied to each of five writing probes (pretest, post-test, generalization, two maintenance).	Grammar scale: All three experimental groups increased notably. Control group stayed the same. SRSD condition increased to above control at post-test stage and then fell to commensurate with the other two experimental groups at generalization and maintenance measures. Quality ratings: All three experimental groups increased notably. Control group stayed the same. No experimental group exceeded NA.
Berninger, Abbott, Whitaker, Sylvester, & Nolen (1995)	39 children with writing problems, mean age of 113 months at pretest, divided into two treatment groups (8 males, 4 females) and a control group (10 males, 5 females). 87% white, 7.7% Hispanic, and 2.6% African American and Native American	Two experimental groups received instruction in handwriting automaticity, spelling strategies, and compositional process. In addition, one received extra practice in composing and one received special training in orthographic and phonological coding.	At the pretest, midtest (half way through), post-test, and follow-up (6 months later) all children completed measures of handwriting, spelling, real word reading, sentence memory, sequential and non-sequential finger movements. Treatment subjects also completed probe measures in each of 14 tutorial sessions.	Treatment groups improved at a faster rate than the control group on handwriting, spelling, and composition measures, and showed if tests related to additional treatment. The treatment group continued to perform at a more favorable level at the 6-month follow-up on some measures of handwriting, spelling, and compositional quality.

Abbott, Reed, Abbott, & Berninger (1997)	16 first grade students referred for severe reading problems	Year-long tutorial from the end of first to the end of second grade	orthographic and phonological coding, word identification of real words, word attack of pseudowords, reading comprehension, letter automaticity, spelling	Gains in all tabled measures on left significantly greater than chance. Marginally significant gains in written composition were found.
Berninger, Vaughan, Abbott, Abbott, Brooks, Rogan, Reed, & Graham (1997)	144 first grade students (103 boys and 41 girls) identified as "at-risk" in handwriting; 86.8% were right-handed; CA mean = 6.72 years (SD = 3.99); Mean WISC-III Vocabulary score = 10.89 (SD = 2.7); Maternal education > high school = 86.6%; 7.0% Asian American, 3.5% African American, 80.3% European American, 3.5% Hispanic, 4.2% Native American, and 1.4% not specified. Of the 144 subjects, 17.4% receiving special services	Random assignment to one out of six groups. Five groups received different kinds of handwriting instruction treatments; the sixth group (control) received phonological awareness training. Treatment delivered to groups of 3 that met twice a week in twenty-four 20-minute sessions	Handedness, pencil grip, alphabet writing task, text copy tasks, handwriting automaticity test, dictation task, WJ-R: writing fluency subtest, finger function (fine motor control) task, orthographic coding task, WISC-III vocabulary subtest, WRMT-R: word attack subtest	Combining numbered arrows and memory retrieval was the most effective treatment for improving both handwriting and compositional fluency.

(continued)

TABLE 2.1 *Continued*

Authors (year)	Sample Description	Interventions	Measures	Findings
Graham (1997)	12 LD students, 3 in grade 5 and 9 in grade 6; 5 Caucasian, 6 African American, 1 Hispanic; 6 male and 6 female; all were noted by teachers as having writing difficulties; WISC-R IQ = 97	Students were instructed on the CDO (compare/diagnose/operate) technique of story revision	Two writing assignments, one before and one after the CDO intervention stage	10 out of 12 students indicated that the CDO process helped them. Effect size of 0.68 favoring CDO was found in the number of nonsurface revisions (surface = spelling, capitalizations). CDO condition students made more nonsurface revisions than non-CDO students (ES = 0.84).
Berninger, Vaughan, Abbott, Brooks, Abbott, Reed, Rogan, & Graham (1998)	128 poor spellers in second grade; 59.4% male; 83.6% right-handed; CA = 7.95 years; verbal IQ = 105; maternal education > high school = 81.2%; 5.5% Asian American, 1.6% African American, 81.3% Caucasian, 3.9% Hispanic, 4.2% Native American; 9.4% had language problems during preschool years; 10.2% received speech/language; 1.6% physical therapy; 14.8% received Chapter I reading; 48.4% had family history of poor spelling	Twenty-four 20-minute sessions including direct alphabetic instruction, modeling different approaches for developing connections between spoken and written monosyllabic words, and practice in composing	Screening battery: WRAT-3: Spelling subtest, WIAT: Spelling subtest, WISC-3: Vocabulary subtest, and orthographic and phonological coding. Progress monitoring battery: WRAT-3 and WIAT spelling subtests, Taught Spelling Words from the intervention, Untrained Spelling Words, Attention Ratings, Handwriting Automaticity, WRMT-R: Word ID subtest, compositional fluency measures	More than one way of developing sound-spelling connections is effective in teaching spelling. After training in the alphabet principle, combining whole word and onset-rime training is most effective in achieving transfer of the alphabet principle across word contexts; teaching grapheme (1- and 2-letters)–phoneme correspondence in alphabetic principle transferred to spelling during composing; spelling training transferred to improved composition and word recognition.

Study	Sample	Design	Measures	Results
Sexton, Harris, & Graham (1998)	6 LD students, grade 5 and 6; 4 males, 2 females; 5 blacks, 1 white. FSIQ ranged from 81 to 117	Self-Regulated Strategy Development (a collaborative approach)	Baseline Probes, Instruction Essay Probes, Post Instruction Essay Probes, Maintenance Essay Probes, Generalization Essay Probes	Positive effect on student's writing. Effects transferred across settings and teachers; maintenance data were mixed
Berninger, Vaughan, Abbott, Brooks, Begay, Curtin, Byrd, & Graham (2000) [follow-up to Berninger et al., 1998]	48 third grade students; CA = 8.8 years; 52.1% male; 85.4% right-handed; VIQ = 109.9; maternal education > high school = 66.7%; 8.3% Asian American, 8.3% African American, 62.5% Caucasian, 4.2% Hispanic, 4.2% Native American; 45.8% had a family history of spelling problems	Two groups, one group receiving alphabetic principle instruction, one receiving combined alphabetic principle and syllable awareness	Handwriting fluency task, WRAT3 and WIAT spelling subtests, inventory of taught words, Rosner test of phoneme and syllable detection, phonological segmentation and memory, letter-cluster coding, orthographic choice, and WRMT-R Word Identification subtest	Only treatment specific effects were a main effect for transfer test and length of composition measure. The slower responders to first dose in grade 2 of spelling treatment now reached average range after a second dose of spelling treatment in third grade.
Berninger, Vaughan, Abbot, Begay, Byrd, Curtin, Minnich, & Graham (2002)	96 third grade students with low compositional fluency (M = −1 SD), VIQ > 80. 61 were male, 35 female; 69.8% Caucasian, 5.2% Asian, 4.2% African American, 4.2% Hispanic, 1% Native American, 15.6% unknown/unspecified; 50% mothers, 55% fathers had college degrees	Four randomly assigned groups. Each group consisted of 24 lessons over 4 months. Groups were Spelling, Composing, Combined Spelling and Composing, and Treated Control	Verbal IQ, Handwriting Automaticity (no. of correctly written sequential letters in 15 seconds), WRAT3 spelling, Spelling inventory for taught structure and content words, WJ-3 Writing fluency, and Writing Quality. Writing prompts WRMT-R Word Identification, and Word Attack	Spelling and Combined Spelling Plus Composing improved on word-specific spelling. Teaching alternations transferred to spelling in composing. Composing and Combined Spelling Plus Composing improved on persuasive essay writing. Combined Spelling Plus Composing improved on both spelling and composing.

(continued)

TABLE 2.1 *Continued*

Authors (year)	Sample Description	Interventions	Measures	Findings
Troia & Graham (2002)	20 LD students, grades 4 and 5; IQ ranged from 85 to 135 and an IQ-achievement discrepancy ≥1 SD in reading or written expression; 80% male; 65% was Caucasian, 25% African American; 30% on free or reduced lunch; 15% ADHD and 20% language impaired	Experimental Group received advance planning strategy instruction (SI). Control Group received modified process writing instruction (PI).	Three writing probes, two prompt-based writing samples	Story Writing Sample—Quality Measure: SI up, PI down; Length Measure: SI up, PI down; Advance Planning Time: SI up, PI up less. Essay Writing Sample—Quality Measure: SI down, PI up; Length Measure: SI up, PI down; Advance Planning Time: SI up, PI up.
Graham & Harris (2005)	38 students, grade 1. 71% black, 48% receiving a free or reduced lunch, 37% had a diagnosed disability, 47% receiving reading recovery instruction	Experimental: extra handwriting instruction; Control: phonological awareness instruction	Measures assessing handwriting and writing skills	Handwriting instruction students were more accurate in naming (ES = 0.86) and writing (ES = 0.94) letters, producing letters (ES = 1.39), and copying connected text (ES = 1.49). Six-month maintenance effect sizes were all greater than 0.65 (except on text copying). Experimental group also showed greater skill at constructing sentences immediately following instruction (ES = 0.76, 0.70 after 6 months). Additional positive impact on writing output (ES = 1.21).

Study	Participants	Intervention	Measures	Results
Graham & Harris (2005)	60 children scoring below the 25th percentile on the WIAT and identified by their classroom teacher as having spelling problems; 65% African American; 65% receiving free or reduced lunch; 38% were diagnosed with a learning disability	20-minute spelling instruction sessions three times per week for 16 weeks	Norm-referenced spelling tests administered upon completion and 6 months later	Spelling-instructed students outperformed control groups in identifying sound-letter combinations (ES = 0.7) and in correctly spelling words used during the intervention (ES = 2.86). In addition, spelling instructed students exceeded control at constructing sentences (ES = 0.78) and decoding nonsense words (ES = 0.82).
Hooper, Wakely, de Kruif, & Swartz (2006)	73 students, 38 fourth and 35 fifth grade; 53% male; CA ranged from 8.95 to 11.92 years; 56% African American, 41% Caucasian, 1.4% Asian American, 1.4% Hispanic American; 40% receiving the school's free/reduced lunch; 35.6% received various special education services (e.g., LD)	Students participated in twenty 40-minute lessons to improve their self-regulation and metacognition about writing. The first 10 days were devoted to improving the students' awareness about planning, translating, and reflecting on written products (15 minutes of direct instruction and modeling). The second 10-day phase stressed the students' independent use of these cognitive processes.	Two narrative writing tasks received holistic ratings and were scored for syntax errors, semantic errors, and spelling errors. Measures for the subtype classification included executive functions (Matching Familiar Figures Test, Tower of Hanoi, Wisconsin Card Sorting Test), attention (Visual Search and Attention Test), and working memory (and a specialized working memory task designed for the study), and language (PPVT-R, Test of Word Finding, CELF-R Sentence Formulation, CELF-R Recalling Sentences)	Cluster analysis procedures yielded seven reliable clusters: four normal variants, Problem Solving Weakness, Problem Solving/Language Weakness, and Problem Solving Strength. The response to the single treatment by these various subtypes revealed positive, but modest findings. Significant group differences were noted for improvement in spelling and use of syntax, with only spelling showing differential improvement in the Problem Solving/ Language Subtype.

(continued)

TABLE 2.1 *Continued*

Authors (year)	Sample Description	Interventions	Measures	Findings
Berninger, Rutberg, Abbott, Garcia, Anderson-Youngstrom, Brooks, & Fulton (2006)	Study 1 (Tier 1): 14 children (2 female, 12 male) in the first grade, all scoring one or more standard deviations below norm on two measures of alphabet letter production and speed of copying text. All were European American.	Subjects were randomly assigned to one of two groups. The Neurodevelopmental Pretreatment group received combined neurodevelopmental and handwriting instruction. The other group received only handwriting instruction. Ten 30-minute instructional sessions.	Each child completed writing probes (writing a letter five times rapidly from memory, writing the alphabet from memory, verbal mediation-verbalizing steps of letter formation, speed of copying text) at each instructional session. Pretest, midtest, and post-test measures were PAL Finger Succession and Receptive Coding and WJ-R Writing Samples and Writing Fluency.	The Neurodevelopmental Pretreatment condition was found to exhibit superior growth curves on accuracy of alphabet writing probe and verbal mediation probe. The Handwriting Only group showed faster individual growth on the probes involving time and on the WJ-R fluency measure.
	Study 2 (Tier 1): 20 first grade students, 14 boys and 6 girls, 18 right-handed and 2 left selected for −1 SD or more on one of three handwriting measures, 17 European American, 2 mixed-ethnic, and 1 unspecified. Mean age > 77.9 months (SD = 4.5).	Subjects were randomly assigned to treatment groups: combined motor training and pencil writing (MOTOR + WRITE), or combined orthographic coding and pencil writing (ORTH + WRITE). Twelve 1-hour sessions of 5 instructional components unique to treatment and 3 common to both treatments	PAL alphabet writing, Copy A, Copy B, Finger Repetition and Succession, RAN letters, and WIAT-II Word Reading, WISC-3 Vocabulary and Block Design subtests were given at pretest.	Both groups improved in tasks of naming letters, copying letters in a sentence, writing letters from memory, and reading real words on a list without context cues.

Study 3 (Tier 1): 13 children (9 male, 4 female, all right-handed, 11 European American, 2 Asian American). Mean age = 87.9 months (SD = 4.1). Mean of Verbal Comprehension Factor = 103.5 (SD = 9.9). WIAT-II Mean word reading = 87.2 (SD = 6.2), Mean pseudoword reading = 89.8 (SD = 4.9), Mean reading comprehension = 83.5 (SD = 8.0)

Subjects were randomly assigned to either a Decoding + Handwriting (n = 7) or Decoding Only (n = 6) treatment group. Each received 20 instructional sessions. The Decoding + Handwriting group received extra practice in letter writing seperate from phonics. Letter writing was embedded in phonics instruction in Decoding only.

WIAT-II Word Reading, Pseudoword Reading, and Reading Comprehension, and PAL RAN Letters, Receptive Coding, Phonemes and Rimes, Alphabet Writing, Copy A, and Copy B given at both pretest and post-test stages. WISC-3 Verbal Comprehension was also given at pretest

The Decoding only group improved significantly more on word reading, decoding, and automatic letter writing. The Decoding and Handwriting improved more on tasks of sustained letter writing in copying from a model sentence. Extra handwriting practice improved handwriting but not automatic letter retrieval from memory or letter-sound associations.

(continued)

TABLE 2.1 *Continued*

Authors (year)	Sample Description	Interventions	Measures	Findings
	Study 4 (Tier 2): 94 students (22 female, 72 male) that did not pass a third grade screening instrument keyed to a fourth grade high-stakes writing assessment. 74.2% were European American, 5.2% were Hispanic American, 7.2 were defined as "other," and 4.1% chose not to report. Of the 94 students, 18 spoke English and another language at home, and 3 spoke no English at home. 19 were identified as Chapter 1, 15 were identified as participating in Special Education, 16 in Speech and Language services, and 2 in Physical Therapy services	Club groups were randomly assigned by school (n = 10) to a group that either received extra writing instruction in the fourth grade (treatment, n = 5) or regular program in the fourth grade (control, n = 5). The treatment groups met either before (n = 3) or after (n = 2) school for sessions, with an approximately even split in the number of students in both conditions (n = 28, n = 25, respectively). The treatment consisted of writing-based warm-up activities, 25 minutes of writing instruction and composing activities, and 10 minutes of word-play activities.	WJ-R Writing Samples, third grade screen to identify at-risk composers, and fourth grade high stakes test in writing. WISC-3 Prorated Verbal IQ was also given at pretest.	Children in the writing treatment groups scored significantly higher than those in the control on the spring-administered fourth grade high stakes test (M = 8, SD = 2.1, vs. M = 7.2, SD = 1.4). 22 of the 52 treatment group children (42.3%) met the state standard, whereas only 8 of the 38 control group children (21.1%) met standard.

Abbott, Reed, Abbott, and Berninger (1997) conducted a year-long reading and writing tutorial (design experiment) for 16 first grade students who had been referred for severe reading problems. Students showed individual differences in response to the same instruction but in general made more progress in reading than in writing. As a group, they improved on measures of orthographic and phonological coding, word identification, word attack, reading comprehension, automatic letter writing, and spelling, but only marginally significant gains were made in written composition for writing tasks that involved writing about texts they read in contrast to creative writing.

Troia and Graham (2002) evaluated the efficacy of an advanced planning strategy compared to a control group receiving modified process writing instruction in 24 fourth and fifth graders with identified learning disabilities. Three writing probes were given throughout the study, each consisting of two writing samples: one story writing and one essay writing. On the story writing, they found increases in measures of quality, length, and planning time for children given advanced planning instruction, whereas children given process writing instruction decreased on measures of quality and length, and did not increase as much as the experimental group on advanced planning. For the probes involving essay writing, the findings were mixed. Advanced strategy instruction resulted in increases in measures of length of writing and advanced planning time, but a decrease in measures of quality. The control group showed an increase in quality and advanced planning, but a decrease in measures of length.

Berninger et al. (2002) compared instruction in spelling alone, composing alone, or both spelling and composing compared to a treated control group in 96 third graders at-risk in compositional fluency. The Spelling and Spelling + Composition treatment groups showed the greatest gains in word-specific spelling tasks. On persuasive essay writing, the Composition and Composition + Spelling intervention groups showed the greatest gains. Only the group receiving the Spelling + Composition intervention showed gains in both spelling and composition.

Some of the published writing instruction at the University of Washington has been translated into lessons teachers can implement in the classroom: *Process Assessment of the Learning (PAL) Research-Supported Reading and Writing Lessons* (Berninger & Abbott, 2003). Tier 1 Lesson Set 3 (handwriting) and Lesson Sets 4 and 5 (spelling) designed to prevent writing problems in the beginning writers. Tier 2 Lesson Sets 7, 8, and 10 (transcription and composition) are based on research designed to help students pass high stakes tests, consistent with recommendations from the National Research Council (Snow et al., 1998) and early writing standards (Edwards, 2003). Tier 3 Lesson Sets 13 and 14 are designed to help students with persistent learning problems integrate writing and reading skills in content area of the curriculum (e.g., children with special education needs). Teachers who use these lessons, previously evaluated for effectiveness in research, still need to evaluate the treatment utility of these lessons for specific implementations in the school settings for specific students or groups of students for specific purposes.

In more recent research, Rutberg's dissertation research showed that neurodevelopmental pretreatment + handwriting instruction improves letter formation accuracy, while handwriting instruction and practice alone for a comparable amount of time improved letter writing automaticity (Berninger, Rutberg et al., 2006, first study). In another study, letter writing interfered with rather than facilitated learning phonics correspondences (Berninger et al., 2006, third study). In a fourth study, 94 students who did not pass a third grade screening for writing were randomly assigned to a treatment group that received writing instruction in before or after school clubs in the fourth grade, or a control group (regular reading and writing instruction program) (Berninger, Rutberg et al., 2006, fourth study). Results indicated that children in the writing treatment group scored significantly higher than those in the control group on the spring-administered fourth grade high stakes test in writing, with 42.3% of this group meeting the state standard and only 21.1% of the control group meeting the standard.

Using a subtype-by-treatment approach, Hooper, Wakely, de Kruif, and Swartz (2006) examined the effectiveness of a metacognitive intervention for written language performance in 73 fourth and fifth grade students. The intervention consisted of twenty 45-minute writing lessons designed to improve the students' awareness of writing as a problem-solving process. Each lesson was conducted within intact classrooms and addressed some aspect of planning, translating, and reflecting on written products, self-regulation of these processes; and actual writing practice. Preintervention and postintervention measures included holistic assessments of writing samples, errors in syntax, semantics, and spelling. Cluster analysis of neurocognitive variables, generated seven reliable clusters: four normal variants, Problem Solving Weakness Subtype, Problem Solving/Language Weakness Subtype, and Problem Solving Strength Subtype. At postintervention, the response of each of the subtypes to this single treatment was positive, but modest in strength. Significant group differences were found for improvement in syntax errors and spelling, but with spelling gains being noted only for the Problem Solving/Language Weakness Subtype.

Evidence-Based Instruction in Specific
Writing Strategies

Wong (2000) described the evolution of educational applications of strategies to the writing process beginning with Alley and Deshler (1979), who encouraged the efforts of Graham and colleagues (e.g., De La Paz, 1997; Graham, 2006), Englert (1990, 1992), Wong and colleagues (Wong, 1997, 2000; Wong, Wong, & Blenkisop, 1989; Wong, Butler, Ficzere, & Kuperis, 1996, 1997), and others (e.g., Sturm & Rankin-Erickson, 2002) to develop and validate the use of writing strategies for children with problems in written expression. Representative examples of this line of research are discussed next.

Graham (1997) instructed 12 students with learning disabilities on the Compare/Diagnose/Operate (CDO) story revision technique. Graham administered two writing assignments before the intervention and two after the intervention. The evaluation consisted of measures of surface and nonsurface revisions at both time points scored for measures of quality and length. Although 10 of the 12 students indicated that the CDO process helped them, the findings were mixed. Although the CDO technique increased the number of nonsurface revisions made by the subjects, CDO-instructed students also made more nonsurface revisions that lowered their quality score than did non-CDO-instructed students.

Sexton, Harris, and Graham (1998) evaluated the effect of a self-regulated strategy approach using a multiple baseline experimental model. They administered their treatment to six fifth and sixth grade students identified as having learning disabilities, and administered probes at five different time points (baseline, instruction, post instruction, maintenance, and generalization). At each of these time points, the students were evaluated on the quantity of functional elements produced. The self-regulated strategy approach was found to have a positive effect on each student's writing, though several of the students returned to baseline levels when probed at the maintenance stage; also see Graham (2006).

Sawyer, Graham, and Harris (1992) divided a sample of 33 fifth and sixth grade students with learning disabilities into three experimental groups given contrasting writing instruction: (a) direct teaching, (b) full self-regulated strategy development (SRSD), and (c) SRSD without explicit self-regulation instruction. In addition, 10 normally achieving students were included as a control group. Pretest, post-test, generalization, and two maintenance probes were administered to each group; each probe was also assessed on a holistic rating scale. The Story Grammar Scale and a self-efficacy scale for story writing were also given. All three experimental groups increased notably over the control group on the Story Grammar Scale. The full SRSD group increased above the control group on the post-test probe, and then dropped to levels commensurate with the other two experimental groups on generalization and maintenance measures. In addition, all three experimental groups increased notably on the holistic rating scale, although none of the experimental group exceeded the normally achieving students on this measure.

Graham (2006) Meta-Analysis

Meta-analyses have proven useful in determining the efficacy across studies of explicit instruction and specific strategies instruction to writing improvement (Graham, 2006; Graham & Harris, 2003). Graham (2006)'s meta-analysis, which included studies dating as far back as 1981, examined 39 total studies: 19 were single subject studies and 20 involved group comparisons.

The studies were coded on seven separate variables: design type, student type, grade, genre, cognitive process, instructor, and instructional model. The subjects in these studies were in grades ranging from second to twelfth, and were writers of all abilities including students with learning disabilities. The strategies taught ranged from planning, revising, editing, to a combination of all three, and a wide variety of types of writing were targeted. The most common compositional strategy taught in these studies was that of planning in advance of writing through the use of brainstorming and organizing ideas. For strategies of revision, participants were most commonly presented with specific criteria with which to evaluate their writing. Across the studies, the strategy employed most, but not always, was the Self-Regulated Strategy Development Instructional Model (SRSD) (Graham & Harris, 1996; Harris & Graham, 1996). SRSD was used in 68% of the single-subject studies and 45% of the group comparison studies, and instruction was provided by research assistants, researchers, and teachers. There was no statistical significance found on the effect of a treatment when parsed by instructor category.

For the meta-analysis proper, two different techniques were used to evaluate the efficacy of each study. For multisubject studies, an effect size (ES) was calculated, with an ES of 0.2 being considered small, 0.5 medium, and ≥ 0.8 large. For single subject experiments, Scruggs and Mastropieri's (2001) percentage of overlapping data (PND) was used (PND = proportion of data points in a treatment condition that exceed the most extreme value in a baseline condition). Specifically, a PND $< 50\%$ designated a treatment as ineffective, a PND between 50% and 70% designates a treatment as questionable, a PND between 70% and 90% represents effective treatment, and a PND $> 90\%$ represents a very effective treatment. Means and standard deviations for each of five composite variables (quality, elements, length, revisions, and mechanics) were computed for three different points (post-test, maintenance, and generalization), and for four different classifications of students (poor writers, average writers, good writers, and students with learning disabilities).

Single-Subject Studies. The primary finding was that the use of strategy instruction techniques is an effective way to improve students' writing performance. For example, for the quality of writing postintervention, the PND was found to range from 78% for students with learning disability to 100% for the other student groups. Similarly high PNDs were generated for the elements of a composition (PND = 92%), length (88%), and revisions (87%) for all students. At the maintenance time point, PNDs ranged from 85% on revisions for the students with learning disability to 100% for each of the other groups. Generalization to different persons and settings also produced high PNDs in the meta-analysis, ranging from 70% in the quality of the written expression for students with learning disability to 100% for the Good and Average writer groups. The deployment of strategies, as derived from the single-subject studies, ranges from effective to very effective in modifying various aspects of the written product in all students.

Group Comparison Studies. These effect sizes were generally medium to large across all of the writing elements examined, across the different writers represented in the studies examined, and across different time points. For example, at post-test, the ES for the quality of written expression ranged from 0.82 for average writers to 1.88 for poor writers. Similarly, at post-test, the effects sizes for the elements of a composition for all four student types ranged from 0.60 for the good writers to 2.18 for the poor writers. On the quality of writing, the effect sizes at the maintenance (ES = 0.90 for students with learning disability to 1.24 for poor writers) and generalization (ES = 0.47 for students with learning disability to 1.88 for poor writers) stages for the group comparison studies were medium to large. The latter findings are important in that they suggest that strategies, once learned, generalize across different persons and settings. The meta-analysis also produced impressive effect sizes for the impact of strategy use on the length of a writing sample (ES = 0.73 for average writers to 1.39 for students with learning disability) and revisions (ES = 0.90 for all students), but it was small for mechanics (ES = 0.30) for all students. The effect size for the post-test gains for good writers also was quite small (ES = −0.02), but it was based on only two studies.

Graham and Perin (2007) Research Synthesis

Most recently, Graham and Perin (2007a, 2007b) completed one of the most comprehensive research syntheses of the writing intervention literature for older children and adolescents (grades 4 and above). Using meta-analytic procedures, Graham and Perin examined nearly 125 studies that provided quantitative findings reflecting the effectiveness of various intervention approaches for students in grades 4 through 12. These intervention approaches included strategy instruction, summarization, peer assistance, setting product goals, word processing, sentence combining, inquiry, prewriting activities, process writing, study of models, and grammar instruction. These approaches were grouped into four broad categories: Process Approach, Explicit Teaching, Scaffolding Students' Writing, and Alternative Approaches to Composing. Graham and Perin also examined the quality of each study used in the meta-analysis (e.g., assignment of subjects to treatment, mortality, ceiling and floor effects at post-test, pretest equivalence, instructor training, control condition, Hawthorne effect, treatment fidelity controls, teacher effects) so as to gauge the impact of each study in the overall results. Only about one-third of the studies contained within this meta-analysis involved random assignment of students to designated treatment conditions.

The findings from the extensive meta-analytic review showed that for studies that generated four or more effect sizes, the approaches using process writing (21 studies), strategy instruction (20 studies), and word processing (18 studies) clearly were the most examined. More importantly, the average weighted effect size was the highest for strategy instruction, summarization, peer assistance, and setting product goals, with effect sizes ranging from moderate (0.70 for setting product goals) to large (0.82 for summarization and peer assistance). Effect sizes were lowest for grammar instruction (−0.32), study of models (0.25), inquiry (0.32), prewriting activities (0.32), and process writing without explicit instruction (0.32).

From this comprehensive and meticulous meta-analysis, Graham and Perin generated 10 recommendations for evidence-based writing instruction, rank-ordered by the strength of the mean weighted effect size. Their first recommendation involved teaching students various strategies for planning, revising, and editing their written text. The Self-Regulated Strategy Development model noted above proved to be particularly powerful in this regard. Their second recommendation involved the reading-writing connection; they found that teaching students reading summarization improved their ability to present this information in written format. Their third recommendation was using peer assistance instructional models for the planning, drafting, revising, and editing components of written expression. Their fourth and fifth recommendations involved setting clear and specific goals for writing and using word processing as a method. The last five recommendations involved sentence combining instruction, the use of the process writing approach, inquiry, prewriting tasks, and the use of good models; these were generally less effective than the other approaches.

The meta-analysis supported using explicit instruction to teach adolescents the strategies necessary for planning and organizing, constructing narrative, revising, and editing their written work. The importance of structured peer work groups also seemed important so that students can receive immediate constructive feedback on their written efforts. Assisting with the output aspects of writing (e.g., word processing) also was deemed to be particularly important to improving student's writing. Finally, Graham and Perin noted the importance of good professional development for teachers to implement the above recommendations (e.g., National Writing Project, Nagin, 2003). Although this meta-analysis is a tremendous contribution to the writing instruction literature for adolescent students, the application of these findings and recommendations to different special education populations as well as to younger, developing writers remains to be seen. Also see McCardle and Miller (Chapter 1) for discussion of the implications of the meta-analyses in *Writing Next*.

■ Summary of Evidence of Effective Writing Instruction

In general, the scientific basis of writing instruction and intervention clearly is moving forward. Table 2.1 summarizes many of the effective instructional approaches, including those with younger children in the primary grades. Evidence-based findings to date indicate the importance of strategy use as an effective way to improve the writing performance of all students, and especially adolescents (grades 4 and above). The various strategies appear to be important to the maintenance and generalization of their use over time. In addition, explicit instruction of targeted writing components appears to be effective and, perhaps in combination with strategy use and alternative methods for output (e.g., word processing), may serve to address many of the needs of students struggling with written output. Positive evidence also has begun to surface highlighting the importance of including selected executive functions (e.g., problem solving, metacognition) in writing interventions, perhaps via either explicit instruction or strategy applications as part of the intervention program.

■ Implementation of Evidence-Based Writing Instruction Research

On the basis of the available research, Wong and Berninger (2004) described a series of instructional design principles that should facilitate the movement of research findings in writing into effective classroom practice. These proposed design principles are both general and developmentally specific, and require the teacher or other intervention specialist to have general knowledge of teaching strategies and domain-specific knowledge about the different aspects of writing so that they can be implemented in a productive manner. The general instructional design principles are listed in Table 2.2, and should provide initial guidance in implementing evidence-based writing instruction research into classroom instruction in both regular and special education settings. Reference to Wong and Berninger (2004) provides additional details for implementing these instructional design principles.

Wong and Berninger (2004) also proposed 10 field-tested pedagogical principles that can facilitate translation of research findings in writing instruction into the classroom setting (see Table 2.3). The first four principles are based on Hayes' theoretical model of written expression (Hayes, 2006) and involve the constructs of working memory, reading, long-term memory, and motivation/affect. The next three principles address the demands from the external social and physical environment on writing activities. The eighth principle pertains to increasing self-awareness with respect to linguistic demands in writing, whereas the ninth principle relates to teachers providing specific prompts to encourage student prompting for each subcomponent of the writing process. The final principle involves increased collaboration between regular and special education teachers for students with writing problems so as to move a particular student forward in a unified manner. These 10 pedagogical principles

TABLE 2.2   *Instructional Design Principles for Translating Scientific-Based Written Instruction to the Classroom Setting*

1	Give careful consideration to the timing of the instructional components
2	Provide explicit instruction within an interactive dialogue mode of instruction
3	Design writing activities so that children succeed but move along their zone of proximal development
4	Design writing activities so that students develop self-efficacy as a writer, that is, the belief that they can communicate effectively with others through written language
5	Teach for transfer—Both near transfer to taught knowledge/skills over time and far transfer to generalize knowledge/skills to novel contexts
6	Evaluate specific writing skills on a daily basis so that writers receive feedback as to what they are doing well and what they need to try to improve
7	Be patient and do not expect instant mastery of writing skills
8	Do not expect computers alone to transform poor writers into good writers

Adapted from Wong, B. Y. L., & Berninger, V. W. (2004). Instructional principles for composition in elementary, middle, and high school: Merging process writing instruction with cognitive processes of the writer and teacher. In B. S. Schulman, K. Apel, B. Ehren, E. R. Silliman, & A. Stone (Eds.), *Handbook of language and literacy development and disorders* (pp. 600–624). New York, The Guilford Press.

provide a framework for how teachers can implement research-based instructional findings in their day-to-day teaching activities. Additional information pertaining to each of these principles is detailed in Wong and Berninger (2004). Research within the field of written language instruction and intervention clearly has moved issues of classroom implementation to being as important as increasing scientific knowledge base.

In general, "best practices" tend to drive what pre-service training programs in any area of study teach to students as well as what practitioners in the field use in their day-to-day efforts. Although not always the case, it is hoped that these "best practices" are driven by research-based findings. Although research can produce results about a specific application, the important next step is translating or moving that information into practical application. In fact, the major sections of this book are devoted to the various aspects of moving evidence-based instruction into the classroom setting via several key steps: (a) Knowing the research as a critical consumer; (b) preservice education of professionals in education, (c) consideration of system issues; (d) school based implementations, (e) evaluation of response to instruction, and (f) consideration of the next steps in the evolution of evidence-based practices. Although this chapter is positioned in the "knowledge" section of

TABLE 2.3 *Pedagogical Principles for Implementing Scientific-Based Written Instruction in the Classroom Setting*

1	Because working memory is a limited resource, use procedural facilitators
2	Help students understand the relationship between reading and writing and teach a specific kind of reading related to reviewing and revising writing
3	Teach well-honed schema for paragraph structure and genre-specific text structures to facilitate the text-generation component of composing
4	Motivate students to write by teaching (a) self-regulation strategies (Harris & Graham, 1996) and (b) self-efficacy in writing
5	Create an optimal social environment for the composing process
6	Adapt writing instruction to the physical environment in which writing naturally occurs, which includes the physical tools used to generate text
7	Organize the classroom for an optimal physical layout for large group, small group, and independent activities
8	Teach metalinguistic awareness of the difference between the oral and literate language styles or registrars and strategies for achieving the oral-literate shift
9	Provide verbal self-prompting cues or questions to guide each subprocess in writing
10	Implement strategy instruction for low achieving writers in the context of a systems model that includes a partnership between general education and special education

Adapted from Wong, B. Y. L., & Berninger, V. W. (2004). Instructional principles for composition in elementary, middle, and high school: Merging process writing instruction with cognitive processes of the writer and teacher. In B. S. Schulman, K. Apel, B. Ehren, E. R. Silliman, & A. Stone (Eds.), *Handbook of language and literacy development and disorders* (pp. 600–624). New York, The Guilford Press.

this book, future research would benefit from discussion of these implementation issues in determining some of the important issues to address in future research.

Implementation issues are not new and other fields have devoted attention to them for years. For example, business has a long-standing focus on developing efficient research-to-practice methods. Computer industry corporations, such as Microsoft, have developed research facilities that focus on long-range research, but also have product groups that focus on translating the research into products that are quickly available to the public (e.g., conferences showcasing new products, media events at retail stores, press releases). Similarly, in the broad area of health and medicine, The National Institutes of Health (NIH) have taken a strong position on the importance of translating medical research to clinical practice, and view this translational process as core to their mission. In fact, recent NIH funding initiatives (e.g., Roadmap for Medical Research, the Clinical and Translational Science Awards) have the clear objective of changing the way clinical and translational research is conducted.

In the field of education, *professional development* and *staff development* encompass a continuum of instructional models and a diverse assortment of methods (e.g., Dede, 2006); *continuing education* might consist of attending a brief workshop, an extended conference, graduate level coursework or degree acquisition, or specific programs such as National Board certification; *comprehensive school reforms* provide a school or entire school district with specific principles and materials to bring about systemic change; and *learning communities* consist of ongoing teams that meet on a regular basis with a commitment to continuous improvement of daily work to advance the achievement of a school or district. Although it follows that teachers could benefit from evidence-based training, research suggests that many teachers do not receive these experiences, and a master teacher must seek out the information that informs best practices and effective learning experiences for students (Scarborough, Ehri, Olson, & Fowler, 1998).

The process of translating any new learning on the part of a teacher into changes in classroom instruction remains a significant challenge. What works for teachers? Educators are generally site-oriented and site-bound. Their professional roles reflect the policies and expectations of a particular school or system. The optimal model of professional development is one that is easily accessible, supported by their administration, and consistent with school mission. Theoretically, Guskey (2002) has argued that professional development programs alone do not bring about teacher change, but it is the change in classroom practices that lead to positive student outcomes which, in turn, produces a lasting impact on teachers' beliefs; that is, teachers may try new teaching strategies and approaches, but only those practices which result in positive student outcomes lead to enduring changes in teachers' beliefs and attitudes. Guskey also noted that this process is not linear but, rather, cyclical in nature, and that one alteration in practice can lead to other alterations— especially if one of the outcomes is positive student change. Strategies such as teacher-researcher partnerships (Pressley et al., 2001) and site-based delivery models of evidence-based findings (Walpole & McKenna, 2006) may be vehicles that could facilitate this process more generally.

■ Conclusions

Although lagging behind the research in reading, the available research on writing—its cognitive and neurodevelopment underpinnings, component processes, and effective instruction—is increasing. Evidence in support of explicit writing instruction and instruction that teaches specific writing strategies and self-regulated writing is clear. Although it is important that writing instruction represent not just "best practices" but, rather, "evidence-based best practices," evidence-based writing assessment and instruction awaits further research, especially in applications of response to intervention (RTI) (Fuchs & Deshler, 2007) to students with special needs in writing.

■ References

Abbott, R. D., & Berninger, V. W. (1993). Structural equation modeling of relationships among developmental skills and writing skills in primary- and intermediate-grade writers. *Journal of Educational Psychology, 85,* 478–508.

Abbott, S., Reed, E., Abbott, R., & Berninger, V. (1997). Year-long balanced reading/writing tutorial: A design experiment used for dynamic assessment. *Learning Disability Quarterly, 20,* 249–263.

Alley, G., & Deshler, D. D. (1979). *Teaching the learning disabled adolescent: Strategies and methods.* Denver, CO, Love Publishing Company.

Altemeier, L., Jones, J., Abbott, R. D., & Berninger, V. W. (2006). Executive functions in becoming writing readers and reading writers: Note taking and report writing in third and fifth graders. *Developmental Neuropsychology, 29,* 161–173.

Bereiter, C., & Scardamalia, M. (1987). *The psychology of written composition.* Hillsdale, NJ, Lawrence Erlbaum Associates.

Berninger, V. (2008). Evidence-based written language instruction during early and middle childhood. In R. Morris & N. Mather (Eds.), *Evidence-based interventions for students with learning and behavioral challenges* (pp. 215–235). Mahwah, NJ: Lawrence Erlbaum Associates.

Berninger, V., & Amtmann, D. (2003). Preventing written expression disabilities through early and continuing assessment and intervention for handwriting and/or spelling problems: Research into practice. In H. L. Swanson, K. R. Harris, & S. Graham (Eds.), *Handbook of learning disabilities* (pp. 345–363). New York, The Guilford Press.

Berninger, V., Vaughan, K., Abbott, R., Abbott, S., Brooks, A., Rogan, L., et al. (1997). Treatment of handwriting fluency problems in beginning writing: Transfer from handwriting to composition. *Journal of Educational Psychology, 89,* 652–666.

Berninger, V., Vaughan, K., Abbott, R., Begay, K., Byrd, K., Curtin, G., et al. (2002). Teaching spelling and composition alone and together: Implications for the simple view of writing. *Journal of Educational Psychology, 94,* 291–304.

Berninger, V., Vaughan, K., Abbott, R., Brooks, A., Abbott, S., Reed, E., et al. (1998). Early intervention for spelling problems: Teaching spelling units of varying size within a multiple connections framework. *Journal of Educational Psychology, 90,* 587–605.

Berninger, V., Vaughan, K., Abbott, R., Brooks, A., Begay, K., Curtin, G., et al. (2000). Language-based spelling instruction: Teaching children to make multiple connections between spoken and written words. *Learning Disability Quarterly, 23,* 117–135.

Berninger, V. W., Abbott, R. D., Whitaker, D., Sylvester, L., & Nolen, B. (1995). Integrating low- and high-level skills in instructional protocols for writing disabilities. *Learning Disability Quarterly, 18,* 293–309.

Berninger, V. W., & Abbott, S. P. (2003). *Process Assessment of the Learning (PAL): Research-based reading and writing lessons.* San Antonio, TX, Harcourt Assessments.

Berninger, V. W., Fuller, F., & Whitaker, D. (1996). A process model of writing development across the life span. *Educational Psychology Review, 8,* 193–218.

Berninger, V. W., & Hart, T. (1992). A developmental neuropsychological perspective for reading and writing acquisition. *Educational Psychology, 27,* 415–434.

Berninger, V. W., & Richards, T. L. (2002). *Brain literacy for educators and psychologists.* New York, Academic Press.

Berninger, V. W., & Rutberg, J. (1992). Relationship of finger function to beginning writing: Application to diagnosis of writing disabilities. *Developmental Medicine and Child Neurology, 34,* 155–172.

Berninger, V. W., Rutberg, J. E., Abbott, R. D., Garcia, N., Anderson-Youngstrom, M., Brooks, A., et al. (2006). Tier 1 and tier 2 early intervention for handwriting and composing. *Journal of School Psychology, 44,* 3–30.

Bloodgood, J. W. (2002). Quintillion: A classical educator speaks to the writing process. *Reading Research and Instruction, 42,* 30–43.

Bos, C. S., & Vaughn, S. (1998). *Strategies for teaching students with learning and behavior problems* (4th ed.). Needham Heights, MA, Allyn & Bacon.

Bradley-Johnson, S., & Lesiak, J. L. (1989). *Problems in written expression: Assessment and remediation.* New York, The Guilford Press.

Bromley, K. (1999). Key components of sound writing instruction. In L. B. Gambrell, L. M. Morrow, S. B. Neuman, & M. Pressley (Eds.), *Best practices in literacy instruction* (pp. 152–174). New York, The Guilford Press.

Calkins, L. (1994). *The art of teaching writing.* New York, Heinemann Publications.

Chute, E. (February 25, 2007). *Colleges still unsure how to use new SAT. Many schools waiting to see how writing scores correspond with performance.* Pittsburgh Post-Gazette. Retrieved August 28, 2007, from http://www.post-gazette.com/pg/07056/764841-298.stm.

Dede, C. (2006). *Online professional development for teachers: Emerging models and methods.* Cambridge, MA, Harvard Education Publishing.

De La Paz, S. (1997). Strategy instruction in planning: Teaching students with learning and writing disabilities to compose persuasive and expository essays. *Learning Disability Quarterly, 20,* 227–248.

Dixon, R. C. (1991). The application of sameness analysis to spelling. *Journal of Learning Disabilities, 24,* 285–291, 310.

Edwards, L. (2003). Writing instruction in kindergarten: Examining an emerging area of research for children with writing and reading difficulties. *Journal of Learning Disabilities, 36,* 136–148.

Ehri, L. C. (1986). Sources of difficulty in learning to spell and read. In M. L. Wolraich, & D. Routh (Eds.), *Advances in developmental and behavioral pediatrics, Volume 7* (pp. 121–195). Greenwich, CT, JAI Press.

Englert, C. S. (1990). Unraveling the mysteries of writing through strategy instruction. In T. E. Scruggs & B. Y. L. Wong (Eds.), *Intervention research in learning disabilities* (pp. 186–223). New York, Springer-Verlag.

Englert, C. S. (1992). Writing instruction from a sociocultural perspective: The holistic, dialogic, and social enterprise. *Journal of Learning Disabilities, 25,* 153–172.

Fernald, G. M. (1988). *Remedial techniques in basic school subjects.* Austin, TX, PRO-ED.

Fuchs, D., & Deshler, D. D. (2007). What we need to know about responsiveness to intervention (and shouldn't be afraid to ask). *Learning Disabilities Research & Practice, 22,* 129–136.

Gersten, R., & Baker, S. (2001). Teaching expressive writing to students with learning disabilities: A meta-analysis. *The Elementary School Journal, 101,* 251–272.

Gillingham, A., & Stillman, B. W. (1973). *Remedial training for children with specific disability in reading, spelling, and penmanship.* Cambridge, MA, Educators Publishing Service.

Gleason, M. M., & Isaacson, S. (2001). Using the new basals to teach the writing process: Modifications for students with learning problems. *Reading & Writing Quarterly, 17,* 75–92.

Gordon, C., & Braun, C. (1983). Using story schema as an aid to reading and writing. *Reading Teacher, 37,* 116–121.

Graham, S. (1992). Helping students with LD progress as writers. *Intervention in School and Clinic, 27,* 133–144.

Graham, S. (1997). Executive control in the revising of students with learning and writing difficulties. *Journal of Educational Psychology, 89,* 223–234.

Graham, S. (2006). Strategy instruction and the teaching of writing. In C. MacArthur, S. Graham, & J. Fitzgerald (Eds.), *Handbook of writing research* (pp. 187–207). New York, The Guilford Press.

Graham, S., Berninger, V., & Weintraub, N. (1998). But they use both manuscript and cursive letters—A study of the relationship of handwriting style with speed and quality. *Journal of Educational Psychology, 91,* 290–296.

Graham, S., & Freeman, S. (1986). Strategy training and teacher- vs. student-controlled study conditions: Effects on LD students' spelling performance. *Learning Disability Quarterly, 9,* 15–22.

Graham, S., & Harris, K. R. (1994). Implications of constructivism for teaching writing to students with special needs. *Journal of Special Education, 28,* 275–289.

Graham, S., & Harris, K. R. (1996). Self-regulation and strategy instruction for students who find writing and learning challenging. In M. Levy & S. Ransdell (Eds.), *The science of writing: Theories, methods, individual differences, and applications* (pp. 347–360). Mahwah, NJ, Lawrence Erlbaum Associates.

Graham, S., & Harris, K. R. (2000). The role of self-regulation and transcription skills in writing and writing development. *Educational Psychologist, 35,* 3–12.

Graham, S., & Harris, K. R. (2003). Students with learning disabilities and the process of writing: A meta-analysis of SRSD studies. In H. L. Swanson, K. R. Harris, & S. Graham (Eds.), *Handbook of learning disabilities* (pp. 323–344). New York, The Guilford Press.

Graham, S., & Harris, K. R. (2005). Improving the writing performance of young struggling writers: Theoretical and programmatic research from the Center on Accelerating Student Learning. *Journal of Special Education, 39,* 19–33.

Graham, S., Harris, K. R., & Loynachan, C. (1994). The spelling for writing list. *Journal of Learning Disabilities, 27,* 210–214.

Graham, S., & Perin, D. (2007a). *Writing Next: Effective strategies to improve writing of adolescents in middle and high schools—A report to Carnegie Corporation of New York.* Washington, DC, Alliance for Excellent Education.

Graham, S., & Perin, D. (2007b). A meta-analysis of writing instruction for adolescent students. *Journal of Educational Psychology, 99,* 445–476.

Graham, S., & Voth, V. P. (1990). Spelling instruction: Making modifications for students with learning disabilities. *Academic Therapy, 25,* 447–457.

Graham, S., Weintraub, N., & Berninger, V. (2001). Which manuscript letters do primary grade children write legibly? *Journal of Educational Psychology, 93,* 488–497.

Graves, D. H. (1994). *A fresh new look at writing.* Portsmouth, NH, Heinemann.

Greene, G. (1994). The magic of mnemonics. *LD Forum, 19,* 34–37.

Gregg, N. (1992). Expressive writing. In S. R. Hooper, G. W. Hynd, & R. E. Mattison (Eds.), *Developmental disorders: Diagnostic criteria and clinical assessment* (pp. 127–172). Hillsdale, NJ, Lawrence Erlbaum Associates.

Gregg, N., & Mather, N. (2002). School is fun at recess: Informal analyses of written language for students with learning disabilities. *Journal of Learning Disabilities, 35,* 7–22.

Guskey, T. R. (2002). Professional development and teacher change. *Teachers and Teaching: Theory and Practice, 8,* 381–391.

Harp, B. (1988). When the principal asks: "Why are your kids giving each other spelling tests?" *Reading Teacher, 41,* 702–704.

Harris, K. R., & Graham, S. (1992). *Helping young writers master the craft: Strategy instruction and self-regulation in the writing process.* Cambridge, MA, Brookline Books.

Harris, K. R., & Graham, S. (1996). *Making the writing process work: Strategies for composition and self-regulation.* Cambridge, MA, Brookline Books.

Hayes, J. R. (2000). A new framework for understanding cognition and affect in writing. In R. Indrisano & J. R. Squire (Eds.), *Perspectives on writing* (pp. 6–44). Newark, DE, International Reading Association.

Hayes, J. R. (2006). New directions in writing theory. In C. A. MacArthur, S. Graham, & J. Fitzgerald (Eds.), *Handbook of writing research* (pp. 28–40). New York, The Guilford Press.

Hayes, J. R., & Flower, L. S. (1980). Identifying the organization of writing processes. In L. Gregg & E. Steinberg (Eds.), *Cognitive processes in writing: An interdisciplinary approach* (pp. 3–30). Hillsdale, NJ, Lawrence Erlbaum Associates.

Henderson, E. H., & Templeton, S. (1986). A developmental perspective of formal spelling instruction through alphabet, pattern, and meaning. *Elementary School Journal, 86,* 304–316.

Hooper, S. R., Swartz, C., Montgomery, J., Reed, M. S., Brown, T., Wasileski, T., & Levine, M. D. (1993). Prevalence of writing problems across three middle school samples. *School Psychology Review, 22,* 608–620.

Hooper, S. R., Swartz, C. W., Wakely, M. B., & de Kruif, R. E. L. (2007). Memory profiles of good and poor writers: The importance of short-term and long-term memory to the writing process. Manuscript submitted for review.

Hooper, S. R., Swartz, C. W., Wakely, M. B., de Kruif, R. E. L., & Montgomery, J. W. (2002). Executive functions in elementary school children with and without problems in written expression. *Journal of Learning Disabilities, 35,* 37–68.

Hooper, S. R., Wakely, M. B., de Kruif, R. E. L., & Swartz, C. W. (2006). Aptitude-treatment interactions revisited: Effect of metacognitive intervention on subtypes of written expression in elementary school students. *Developmental Neuropsychology, 29,* 217–241.

Horn, T., & Otto, H. J. (1954). *Spelling instruction: A curriculum-wide approach.* Austin, TX, University of Texas.

Houck, C. K., & Billingsley, B. S. (1989). Written expression of students with and without learning disabilities: Differences across the grades. *Journal of Learning Disabilities, 22,* 561–567, 572.

Isaacson, S. (1995). Written language. In P. J. Schloss, M. A. Smith, & C. N. Schloss (Eds.), *Instructional methods for adolescents with learning and behavioral problems* (2nd ed., pp. 200–234). Boston, Allyn & Bacon.

Kauffman, J. M., Hallahan, D. P., Haas, K., Brame, T., & Boren, R. (1978). Imitating children's errors to improve their spelling performance. *Journal of Learning Disabilities, 11,* 217–222.

Kearney, C. A., & Drabman, R. S. (1993). The write-say method for improving spelling accuracy in children with learning disabilities. *Journal of Learning Disabilities, 26,* 52–56.

Kellogg, R. T. (1999). Components of working memory in text production. In M. Torrance & G. Jeffery (Eds.), *The cognitive demands of writing* (pp. 143–161). Amsterdam, Amsterdam University Press.

Kulberg, J. M. (1993). What school psychologists need to know about writing disabilities. *School Psychology Review, 22,* 685–686.

Lea, J., & Levy, C. M. (1999). Working memory as a resource in the writing process. In M. Torrance & G. Jeffery (Eds.), *The cognitive demands of writing* (pp. 63–82). Amsterdam, Amsterdam University Press.

Leavell, A., & Ioannides, A. (1993). Using character development to improve story writing. *Teaching Exceptional Children, 25*, 41–45.

Lerner, J. W. (2000). *Children with learning disabilities: Theories, diagnosis, teaching strategies* (8th ed.). Boston, Houghton Mifflin.

Lesiak, J. (1992). The remediation of written expression problems: "Best" practices for teaching composition skills. *Reading and Writing Quarterly: Overcoming Learning Difficulties, 8*, 5–24.

Levine, M. D., Hooper, S. R., Montgomery, J. W., Reed, M., Sandler, A., Swartz, C., et al. (1993). Learning disabilities. An interactive developmental paradigm. In G. R. Lyon, D. B. Gray, J. F. Kavanaugh, & N. A. Krasnegor (Eds.), *Better understanding learning disabilities. New views from research and their implications for educational and public policies* (pp. 229–250). Baltimore, MD, Brookes.

Levy, C. M., & Marek, P. (1999). Testing components of Kellogg's multicomponent model of working memory in writing: The role of the phonological loop. In M. Torrance & G. Jeffery (Eds.), *The cognitive demands of writing* (pp. 25–41). Amsterdam, Amsterdam University Press.

MacArthur, C., Schwartz, S., & Graham, S. (1991). Effects of reciprocal peer revision strategy in special education classrooms. *Learning Disability Research and Practice, 6*, 201–210.

McCutchen, D. (1996). A capacity theory of writing: Working memory in composition. *Educational Psychology Review, 8*, 299–325.

McCutchen, D. (2000). Knowledge, processing, and working memory: Implications for a theory of writing. *Educational Psychologist, 35*, 13–23.

McNaughton, D., Hughes, C. A., & Clark, K. (1994). Spelling instruction for students with learning disabilities: Implications for research and practice. *Learning Disability Quarterly, 17*, 169–185.

Mercer, C. D., & Mercer, A. R. (2001). *Teaching students with learning problems* (6th ed.). Upper Saddle River, NJ, Merrill/Prentice-Hall.

Mills, B. (1953). Writing as process. *College English, 15*, 19–56.

Nagin, C. (2003). *Because writing matters: Improving student writing in our schools.* San Francisco, Jossey-Bass.

National Center for Educational Statistics (NCES). (2003). *National Assessment of Educational Progress (NAEP), 1998 and 2002 Writing Assessments.* Washington, DC, U.S. Department of Education, Institute of Education Sciences, National Center for Education Statistics.

Phelps-Gunn, T. (1982). *Written language instruction: Theory and remediation.* Aspen, CO, Aspen Publishers.

Phelps-Terasaki, D., & Phelps-Gunn, T. (2000). *Teaching competence in written language* (2nd ed.). Austin, TX, PRO-ED.

Polloway, E. A., Patton, J., & Cohen, S. (1981). Written language for mildly handicapped children. *Focus on Exceptional Children, 14*, 1–16.

Pressley, M., Wharton-McDonald, R., Allington, R., Clock, C. C., Morrow, L., Tracey, D., et al. (2001). Strategy instruction for elementary students searching informational text. *Scientific Studies of Reading, 5*, 35–58.

Pritchard, R. J., & Honeycutt, R. L. (2006). The process approach to writing instruction. Examining its effectiveness. In C. A. MacArthur, S. Graham, & J. Fitzgerald (Eds.), *Handbook of writing research* (pp. 275–290). New York, The Guilford Press.

Rico, G. L. (1983). *Writing the natural way.* Boston, Houghton Mifflin.

Sandler, A. D., Watson, T. E., Footo, M., Levine, M. D., Coleman, W. L., & Hooper, S. R. (1992). Neurodevelopmental study of writing disorders in middle childhood. *Journal of Developmental and Behavioral Pediatrics, 13,* 17–23.

Sawyer, R., Graham, S., & Harris, K. (1992). Direct teaching, strategy instruction, and strategy instruction with explicit self-regulation: Effects on the composition skills and self-efficacy of students with learning disabilities. *Journal of Educational Psychology, 84,* 340–352.

Scarborough, H. S., Ehri, L. C., Olson, R. K., & Fowler, A. E. (1998). The fate of phonemic awareness beyond the elementary years. *Scientific Studies of Reading, 2,* 115–142.

Schumaker, J. B., & Sheldon, J. (1985). *The sentence writing strategy.* Lawrence, University of Kansas, Center for Research on Learning.

Scruggs, T., & Mastriopieri, M. (2001). How to summarize single-participant research: Ideas and applications. *Exceptionality, 9,* 227–244.

Sexton, M., Harris, K., & Graham, S. (1998). Self-regulated strategy development and the writing process: Effects on essay writing and attributions. *Exceptional Children, 64,* 295–311.

Shanker, J. L., & Ekwall, E. E. (1998). *Locating and correcting reading disabilities* (7th ed.). Upper Saddle River, NJ, Pearson Education.

Snow, C. E., Burns, M. S., & Griffin, P. (Eds.). *Preventing reading difficulties in young children.* Washington, DC, National Academy Press.

Stein, M. (1983). Finger spelling: A kinesthetic and to phonetic spelling. *Instruction in School and Clinic, 18,* 305–313.

Stephens, T. M. (1977). *Teaching skills to children with learning and behavior disorders.* Columbus, OH, Merrill.

Strong, W. (1983). *Sentence combining: A composing book* (2nd ed.). New York, Random House.

Sturm, J. M., & Rankin-Erickson, J. L. (2002). Effects of hand-drawn and computer-generated concept mapping on the expository writing of middle school students with learning disabilities. *Learning Disabilities Research and Practice, 17,* 124–139.

Swanson, H. L., & Berninger, V. W. (1996). Individual differences in children's working memory and writing skills. *Journal of Experimental Child Psychology, 63,* 358–385.

Tompkins, G. E., & Friend, M. (1985). On your mark, get set, write! *Teaching Exceptional Children, 18,* 82–89.

Treiman, R. (1993). *Beginning to spell.* New York, Oxford University Press.

Troia, G., & Graham, S. (2002). The effectiveness of a highly explicit, teacher-directed strategy instruction routine: Changing the writing performance of students with learning disabilities. *Journal of Learning Disabilities, 35,* 290–305.

Troia, G. A. (2002). Teaching writing strategies to children with disabilities: Setting generalization as the goal. *Exceptionality, 10,* 249–269.

Troia, G. A., & Graham, S. (2004). Students who are exceptional and writing disabilities: Prevention, practice, intervention, and assessment. *Exceptionality, 12,* 1–2.

Varnhagen, C. K. (1995). Children's writing strategies. In V. W. Berninger (Ed.), *The varieties of orthographic knowledge: II. Relations to phonology, reading, and writing* (pp. 251–290). Dordrecht, The Netherlands, Kluwer.

Wakely, M. B., Hooper, S. R., de Kruif, R. E. L., & Swartz, C. W. (2006). Subtypes of written expression in elementary school children: A linguistic-based model. *Developmental Neuropsychology, 29,* 125–159.

Walpole, S., & McKenna, M. C. (2004). *The literacy coaches' handbook: A guide to research-based practice.* New York, The Guilford Press.

Welch, M., & Jensen, J. B. (1991). Write, P.L.E.A.S.E: A video-assisted strategic intervention to improve written expression of inefficient learners. *Remedial and Special Education, 12,* 37–47.

Wirtz, C. L., Gardner, R., Weber, K., & Bullara, D. (1996). Using self-correction to improve the spelling performance of low-achieving third graders. *Remedial and Special Education, 17,* 48–58.

Wong, B. Y. L. (1986). A cognitive approach to teaching spelling. *Exceptional Children, 53,* 169–173.

Wong, B. Y. L. (1997). Research on genre-specific strategies for enhancing writing in adolescents with learning disabilities. *Learning Disability Quarterly, 20,* 140–159.

Wong, B. Y. L. (2000). Writing strategies instruction for expository essays for adolescents with and without learning disabilities. *Topics in Language Disorders, 20,* 29–44.

Wong, B. Y. L., & Berninger, V. W. (2004). Instructional principles for composition in elementary, middle, and high school: Merging process writing instruction with cognitive processes of the writer and teacher. In B. S. Schulman, K. Apel, B. Ehren, E. R. Silliman, & A. Stone (Eds.), *Handbook of language and literacy development and disorders* (pp. 600–624). New York, The Guilford Press.

Wong, B. Y. L., Butler, D. L., Ficzere, S. A., & Kuperis, S. (1996). Teaching low achievers and students with learning disabilities to plan, write, and revise opinion essays. *Journal of Learning Disabilities, 29,* 197–212.

Wong, B. Y. L., Butler, D. L., Ficzere, S. A., & Kuperis, S. (1997). Teaching adolescents with learning disabilities and low achievers to plan, write, and revise compare-and-contrast essays. *Learning Disabilities Research and Practice, 12,* 2–15.

Wong, B. Y. L., Butler, D. L., Ficzere, S. A., Kuperis, S., Corden, M., & Zelmer, J. (1994). Teaching problem learners revision skills and sensitivity to audience through two instructional modes: Student-teacher versus student-student interactive dialogues. *Learning Disabilities Research and Practice, 9*, 78–90.

Wong, B. Y. L., & Wilson, M. (1984). Investigating awareness of and teaching passage organization in learning disabled children. *Journal of Learning Disabilities, 17*, 477–482.

Wong, B. Y. L., Wong, R., & Blenkisop, J. (1989). Cognitive and metacognitive aspects of composing problems in learning-disabled adolescents. *Learning Disability Quarterly, 12*, 300–322.

Wong, B. Y. L., Wong, R., Darlington, D., & Jones, W. (1991). Interactive teaching: An effective way to teach revision skills to adolescents with learning disabilities. *Learning Disabilities Research and Practice, 6*, 117–127.

3. Science-Supported Math Instruction for Children with Math Difficulties

Converting a Meta-Analysis to Practice

H. Lee Swanson

Children with math difficulties (MD) are a heterogeneous group, and therefore, no general instructional model can be recommended for all of them. However, some common general principles for teaching children with learning difficulties in math have emerged in the scientific literature and effective programs capitalize on these principles. Although these principles often operate in different ways with different students, in different content areas of math, and different settings, nevertheless, these principles underlie effective remediation programs for such students. In this chapter, findings related to a meta-analysis of the literature (Swanson, Hoskyn, & Lee, 1999) are summarized and compared with findings from other more recent meta-analyses that focus on math. Few systematic syntheses of the experimental instructional literature for children with MD are available. The goal is to consider how findings that are available might be translated into instructional practice. Before the review of instructional practices, a short description of the characteristics of children with MD is necessary.

■ Characteristics of Children with Math Difficulties

Several studies (Badian, 1983; Gross-Tsur, Manor, & Shalev, 1996) estimate that approximately 6–7% of the school age population have MD. Although this figure may be inflated because of variations in definition (e.g., Desoete, Roeyers, & De Clercq, 2004, suggest that the figure varies between 3% and 8%), consensus exists that a significant number of children demonstrate poor achievement in mathematics and the incidence of MD may be as common as reading disabilities. A defining characteristic of these sample of children is that they have memory deficits related to the accessing of number facts. Although the causes related to these deficits are still under investigation, there is some consensus that arithmetic facts in children with MD are not retrieved accurately and/or quickly. Thus, the ability to utilize memory resources to store numbers temporarily when attempting to reach an answer is of significant importance in learning math. Poor recall of arithmetic facts, for example, leads to difficulties in executing calculation procedures and immature problem-solving strategies. Many children with MD may have difficulties keeping information in working memory (WM). Early in math development, they may have trouble monitoring the counting process and thus make errors in their counting.

Current research supports three subtypes of math disabilities (see Geary, 1993, 2003, for a review). One subtype characterizes children with MD as deficient in semantic memory. These children are characterized as having weak fact retrieval and high error rates in recall. The slow retrieval deficits suggest that their problems may not be specific to math and may reflect a cognitive disorder that is pervasive across other domains as well (similar to word retrieval) and persistent across a broad age span. Another subtype of math disability is procedural and involves the algorithms of arithmetic calculation. Children in this category generally use developmentally immature procedures in numerical calculations and have difficulties in sequencing the multiple steps in complex procedures. A third subtype of math disability is referred to as a visual/spatial math disorder. These children are characterized as having difficulties representing numerical information spatially. For example, they may have difficulties representing the alignment of numerals in multicolumn arithmetic problems or may rotate numbers. Further, they have difficulties in areas that require spatial ability such as geometry and place value.

■ Meta-Analysis

Reviews of the instructional literature that have been influential in providing an understanding of treatment outcomes use a procedure called meta-analysis, which is a statistical reviewing technique that provides a quantitative summary of findings across an entire body of research (Cooper & Hedges, 1994). The results of individual studies are converted into a standardized metric or effect size. The scores are then aggregated across the sample of studies to yield an overall effect size. Particular attention is given to the magnitude of the effect size estimate. According to Cohen (1988), 0.80 is considered a large effect size, 0.50 a moderate effect size, and 0.20 a small effect size.

The content of this chapter comes primarily from a major meta-analysis funded by the U.S. Department of Education that focused on experimental intervention research for children with learning disabilities (LD) that covered a 35-year period (Swanson et al., 1999). The instructional conclusions of this earlier meta-analysis closely match more recently published meta-analyses on math instruction with more diverse samples of children. In general, Swanson and colleagues (e.g., Swanson, 1999; Swanson & Deshler, 2003; Swanson & Hoskyn, 1998; Swanson & Sachse-Lee, 2000) assembled published studies and doctoral dissertations that included single subject designs (85) and group designs (180) published between the years of 1963 and 2000 on participants with LD (defined by reading and/or math scores). The sample included public school children (chronological age: $M = 11.16$, SD $= 3.22$; IQ scores: $M = 93.51$, SD $= 16.85$; norm-referenced reading scores: $M = 71.44$, SD $= 26.65$; and norm-referenced math scores: $M = 75.36$, SD $= 12$). Eighty-two (82) percent of the intervention studies included children of elementary age (grades 1–6). They reported over 3,000 effect sizes including a mean effect size of 0.79 for treatment versus control conditions for group design studies (Swanson & Hoskyn, 1998) and 1.00 for single subject design studies (Swanson & Sachse-Lee, 2000). Using Cohen's (1988) threshold of 0.80 for large effects, the earlier meta-analysis suggested that various instructional approaches have a significant beneficial effect for participants with LD. However, effect sizes varied by instructional domain, with higher effect sizes in some areas (e.g., reading comprehension, 0.84, when compared to math, 0.59). More specifically, outcomes related to math measures for group design studies (number of studies = 21) were 0.33 for standardized measures and 0.42 for experimental measures (see p. 83) and 0.91 for single subject design studies (number of studies =14; Swanson et al., 1999, p. 174). The synthesis showed that the majority of interventions were in reading (>70% of the studies) and relatively few studies were in math (<10%).

Two important findings emerged from this synthesis as applied to evidence-based instruction. First, the synthesis suggested that *not all* forms of intervention work equally well. In this synthesis, studies were classified into one out of eight general instructional orientations across instructional domains (see Swanson, 2000). Several instructional models were considered: direct instruction, explicit strategy training, monitoring, individualized remedial training, small interactive group instruction, teacher-indirect instruction, verbal questioning/attribution instruction, and technology-mediated instruction. Overall, the analysis showed that combined direct and explicit strategy instruction (explicit practice, elaboration, strategy cuing) and small group interactive settings best predicted the size of treatment outcomes across various academic domains. The implication of this finding is that a combination of direct instruction and strategy instruction provided a general evidence-based instructional heuristic for improving academic performance (effect sizes >0.80) in children with learning difficulties. In addition, many of the same instructional components (to be discussed) that significantly predicted increases in effect sizes for reading were comparable to those in math (see Swanson et al., 1999). This finding held when the analysis included controls for methodology, age, and type of research design. In addition, regression analyses found no main effects for chronological age (see Tables 13 and 31 of Swanson et al., 1999) for either group or single subject designs, suggesting that the instructional procedures were robust across chronological age.

Second, the results of best evidence studies cannot be taken at face value. That is, in the just described synthesis, all studies had well-defined control groups and/or baseline conditions before their inclusion in the synthesis. The selection of these studies reflected what is considered best evidence-based instructional practices because studies of poor methodological quality were eliminated from the analysis (Cook & Campbell, 1979). Selecting only studies that meet a certain standard of internal validity is a defensible basis for meta-analysis (Valentine & Cooper, 2005; Wortman, 1994, for a review). For example, one group pretest and post-test only designs were excluded from the meta-analysis because they are subject to numerous threats to internal validity (e.g., Valentine & Cooper, 2005).

However, even best evidence studies must be carefully scrutinized (Levin, 2005). More specifically, Simmerman and Swanson (2001) analyzed studies in the Swanson et al. (1999) synthesis and found that slight variations in the internal and external validity moderated magnitude of treatment outcomes for students with LD. Violations that were significantly related to treatment outcomes included the following:

- Teacher effects (studies that used the very same experimenter for treatment and control in administrating treatments yield smaller effect sizes than those studies that used different experimenters in administering treatments).
- Establishment of a criterion level of instructional performance before moving to the next level (studies that specified performance criteria yield significantly larger weighted effect sizes than those that did not).
- Reliance on experimental measures (studies that did not use standardized measures had much larger effect sizes than those that reported using standardized measures) and different measures between pretest and post-test (larger effect sizes emerge for studies that used alternative forms when compared to those that used the same test).
- Use of a heterogeneous sample in age (studies that included both elementary and secondary students yielded larger effect sizes than the other age level conditions).
- Use of the correct unit of analysis (studies that applied the appropriate unit of analysis yield smaller effect sizes than those that used the incorrect unit of analysis; when small groups receive the interventions, the appropriate unit of analysis is groups instead of individuals).

Furthermore, studies that left out critical information inflated treatment outcomes in a positive direction. The under-reporting of information related to the following yielded larger effect sizes than those that provided the information: ethnicity (studies that reported ethnicity yielded smaller effect sizes than those that did not report ethnicity), locale of the study (larger effect sizes occurred when no information was provided about the locale of the study), psychometric data (larger effect sizes occurred when no psychometric information was reported when compared to the other conditions), and teacher application (studies that provide minimal information in terms of teacher implications and recommendations yielded larger effect sizes than those that provide more information). The magnitude of effect sizes was also influenced by whether studies relied on federal definitions (studies that did not report using the federal definition yielded the larger weighted effect score than those that did) or reported using multiple definitional criteria (studies that included multiple criteria in defining their sample yielded smaller effect sizes than those that did not report using multiple criteria in selecting their sample). In addition, they found that some methodological variables that influenced the magnitude of effect sizes were not violations of internal or external validity, but rather were moderating variables that appear to maximize the effects of treatment. These variables relate to the instructional setting (small instructional groups yield larger effect sizes than individual or large group instruction), direct teaching of transfer (studies that trained for transfer to different abstract skills yield larger effect sizes than those that do not), and the degree to which treatments were implemented as intended (studies that indicated the specific sessions in which treatment integrity was assessed yielded larger effect sizes than those that did not). In summary, studies considered as "best evidence" must be carefully scrutinized.

■ Previous Meta-Analyses

Before discussing the instructional implication of the current findings as they apply to math instruction, three other major meta-analyses focusing on other children at-risk for MD are considered. A recent meta-analysis of the literature by Baker, Gersten, and Dae-Sik (2002) focused on teaching mathematics to low-achieving students. As indicated by the authors, their synthesis built upon Swanson and colleagues' earlier synthesis (Swanson et al., 1999) but was broadened to investigate directly the effects of instruction on mathematics achievement in low SES children. Baker et al. indicated that Swanson et al.'s previous meta-analysis did not include children with MD unless they also fit the LD category. Further they noted that only 18 instructional intervention studies that addressed mathematics were included. Most of these studies had a mean effect size of 0.40 on mathematics performance, which is considered only a moderate effect. This effect size contrasts with reading comprehension, word recognition, and writing for which effect sizes were 0.72, 0.57, and 0.63 respectively.

The Baker et al. (2002) synthesis was also an extension of the National Research Council (NRC) report (Kilpatrick, Swafford, & Findell, 2001) that synthesized diversity studies on mathematics in the elementary and middle school years. The NRC report focused on students experiencing serious difficulties learning mathematics. The report argued for a blend of focused explicit instruction with more open-ended problem solving, consistent with the notions about direct instruction and strategy instruction. However, the NRC panel examined all types of experimental interventions, including qualitative research and therefore many of the studies could not be put on a common metric.

The Baker et al. meta-analysis focused on math intervention studies published between 1971 and 1999. To be included in the analysis, math instruction had to have lasted over a minimum of 90 minutes and the study had to include a group design with a control group. By using very broad classification criteria to solicit articles, they found that of 599 studies only 194 actually included interventions and of those only 15 studies met their criteria. They eliminated studies where there was insufficient information to document that the students were low achieving in mathematics and/or did not use control groups. The primary criteria for studies that defined a low-achieving group were teacher-based nomination or a measure of math performance. Some studies determined at-risk children as those below the 50th percentile whereas others selected children at-risk below the criteria of the 34th percentile. Students with LD were included in one-third of the studies in their analysis.

In four of the studies in their synthesis, students were provided computer-generated feedback. These studies involved providing students with information on their effort or performance in solving mathematics problems. Some of these studies utilized curriculum-based measurements (CBM) to monitor student progress. General effect size for this computer-generated feedback or CBM on achievement measures was in the range of 0.50. In general, these studies support a common practice of providing feedback to students. Another set of studies (six) addressed the issue of peer-assisted learning. These studies were based on the assumptions that teachers cannot always be available to help an individual student and therefore peers are necessary to provide the answer or help to teach or solve the problem. The idea here is that working together with peers facilitates persistence and encouragement to low achievers. The effect size for this condition was also moderate (0.66). It is important to note that the magnitude of effect size was greater on computation than on general math ability (e.g., problem solving). The average effect size on computation problems was 0.62 but on general math achievement the effect sizes varied from 0.06 to 0.40, producing an average mean effect size of

0.29. Thus, it is unclear how helpful peer tutoring might be in other areas of mathematics beyond computation.

Some studies addressed the effects of providing problems in terms of a context. In this situation, instruction focused on teaching or emphasizing real-world applications of mathematical principles. Those studies that used direct instruction had an aggregated effect size weight of around 0.58, and studies that focused on mathematical thinking without direct instruction (those influenced by a framework for mathematics instruction developed by the National Council in Teaching Mathematics, 1989) had an overall effect size of 0.01 (essentially 0). Thus, it appears that strategy instruction void of direct instruction of specific skills is not supported by the literature.

In general, Baker et al.'s conclusions from 15 study results were similar to those of Swanson et al. (1999). First, providing feedback to students on how they are performing enhances mathematics achievement (the average effect size is 0.68 standard deviation units). Second, using small groups of peers positively influences math computation. Third, principles of direct or explicit instruction coupled with strategy instruction are critical in teaching mathematical concepts and procedures. Both found very few well-controlled studies that address some of the intricate issues in terms of teaching mathematics. Although the NRC argues for "high quality research in playing a central role in the effort to improve mathematics learning ..." (Kilpatrick et al., 2001, p. 26), it is difficult to draw sound conclusions with so few studies.

Another synthesis by Xin and Jitendra (1999) focused on word problem solving intervention research with samples of students with learning problems broadly defined. This synthesis provided an overview of research with word problem solving interventions in samples of students with learning problems, those with mild disabilities, and those at-risk for mathematics failure. IQ scores of the sample varied from 84 to 99, but minimal information on the range of scores related to reading and mathematical skills is reported. The effectiveness of word problem solving instruction was examined in 14 group design studies and 12 single subject design studies. The synthesis considered variations in outcomes as a function of student characteristics, instructional focus, and length of instruction. In general, the synthesis concluded that strategy instruction and procedures that emphasize "problem representation" techniques produced larger effect sizes than other more general approaches. Four categories were considered in analyzing interventions. One category of intervention focused on the "representation of ideas" or information given in a word problem. These procedures included ways of diagramming (e.g., pictorially diagramming) or using manipulatives to solve a problem. Another category included problem-solving heuristics that involved both direct instruction and cognitive strategies (e.g., explicit teaching and self-monitoring strategy) about how to solve the problem. A third intervention was a computer-aided instruction in which there was an interactive video or disc program. Of the intervention categories, the most frequently used for problem solving was strategy training. Overall, the effect size was 1.05 for representation instruction, 1.01 for strategy instruction, and 2.46 for computer-assisted instruction. There was a general category of instruction that was nonspecific to mathematics and had an overall effect size of essentially 0.

A final meta-analysis of interventions is reported by Kroesberger and Van Luit (2003). This meta-analysis investigated studies on math interventions from 1985 to 2000. The samples in the studies included low-achieving populations, such as underachieving, below average, and related disability categories. The search yielded about 220 articles concerned with elementary mathematics. On the basis of the final selection criteria, 55 studies were included in the synthesis. Unfortunately, the meta-analysis combined single subject design scores and repeated analysis scores (which greatly inflates the effect size) with group design comparisons. In addition, the sample was not described that well, although age and type of disability was indicated. An effect size was found for direct instruction versus the control situation of 0.91, and self-instruction or strategy instruction versus a control situation of 1.45. Unfortunately, it is very difficult to generalize from this synthesis because neither the description of the instructional conditions nor the instructional components were taken into account.

Although a combination of group and single subject studies is questionable, the authors drew some conclusions. One conclusion was that the sample characteristics did not matter in terms of the magnitude of the effect size. There were some studies, however; in which problem-solving interventions for children with mild retardation were more effective than those with students with LD. The authors argued that the reason for this is that children with mild retardation probably receive more intensive training over extended periods of time. They also found that in terms of treatment interventions that self-instruction (not clearly defined) is more effective than general instruction.

However, in the learning of basic skills, direct instruction appeared to be more effective whereas strategy instruction was more effective when applied toward problem solving. In general, the results of these three syntheses on children with low achievement profiles are highly consistent with the findings of the larger meta-analysis of Swanson and colleagues that included learning-disabled samples. Thus, the studies that include math measures from the Swanson et al. (1999) meta-analysis are relevant to instruction and are now reviewed.

■ Separating Studies into Strategy
   and Direct Instruction Models

Across the four syntheses, studies that include elements of direct or strategy instruction are more effective than control conditions. Thus, the questions emerge: What does direct and/or strategy instruction entail? How can it be operationalized for practice?

To answer these questions, it is important for the reader to keep in mind that the distinctions between these two approaches in math studies are sometimes subtle, creating difficulties in clearly analyzing the two approaches. Both approaches include a graduated sequence of steps with multiple opportunities for overlearning the content and skills in a math program. Let us consider word problems. Both instructional models include cumulative review routines, mass practice, and teaching of all component skills to mastery criterion. For the strategy model, the students learn word problem solving strategies with additional discussion given to metacognitive issues, such as strategy implementation, strategy choice, and self-monitoring. Clear discussion is given to students about (a) *why* a strategy facilitates word problem solving, (b) *how to apply* the strategy, and (c) *how to check* whether the strategy is working. Students systematically practice these strategies with various problems. There is a compare and contrast activity that explicitly trains the students on what they need to know to help them solve a problem.

The direct instruction condition follows the same procedures as strategy instruction except for two variations: (a) direct instruction focuses on subskills ($9 \times 9 = 81$) and (b) discussion of processes and use of general rules is minimized. Thus, what appears to separate the two instructional models is focus. The strategy program focuses on processes or global skills for a general approach to problems, whereas a direct instruction model focuses on the algorithm. A further contrast between the two models is that the strategy model focuses on teaching a few problems to mastery, whereas the direct instruction model focuses on the level of calculation skills.

Although direct and strategy instructional treatments may be distinguished by the unit of information (i.e., direct instruction focuses primarily on isolated skills, whereas strategy instruction focuses primarily on rules) and processing perspective (direct instruction is characterized as a bottom-up processing approach and strategy instruction as a top-down processing approach), there are, of course, other distinctions that are less subtle. For example, direct instruction emphasizes fast-paced, well-sequenced, and highly focused lessons. The lessons occur usually in small groups of students who are given several opportunities to respond and receive feedback about accuracy and responses (see Adams & Carnine, 2003; Kaméenui, Jitendra, & Darch, 1995, for a review of model variations).

Components related to effective strategy instructional programs have been reviewed elsewhere (see Graham, Harris, & Zito, 2005; Sternberg, 1998; Swanson, 1993; Wong, Harris, Graham, & Butler, 2003). Some of these components include the following: Advance organizers (providing students with a type of mental scaffolding on which to build new understanding), organization (directing students to stop from time to time to assess their understanding), elaboration (thinking about the material to be learned in a way that connects the material to information or ideas already in their mind), generative learning strategies (making sense of what they are learning by summarizing the information), general study strategies (working in pairs to summarize sections of materials), metacognitive strategies (thinking about and controlling one's thinking process), and attributions (evaluating the effectiveness of a strategy).

Given the distinctions between the two major kinds of instruction, how might they overlap? An answer to this question is important because it may account for some of the confusion in differentiating between the two instructional models. Strategy instruction and direct instruction models overlap in at least two ways. First, both models (in one form or another) assume that effective *methods* of instruction include (a) daily reviews, (b) statements of an instructional objective, (c) teacher presentation of new material, (d) guided practice, (e) independent practice, and (f) formative evaluations (see Rosenshine, 1995; Shuell, 1996, for a review). Second, both direct instruction and strategy instruction follow a *sequence of events*, such as the following:

1. State the learning objectives and orient the students to what they will be learning and what performance will be expected of them.
2. Review the skills necessary to understand the concept.
3. Present the information, give examples, and demonstrate the concepts/materials.
4. Pose questions (probes) to students and assess their level of understanding and correct misconceptions.
5. Provide group instruction and independent practice. Give students an opportunity to demonstrate new skills and learn the new information on their own.
6. Assess performance and provide feedback. Review the independent work and give a quiz. Give feedback for correct answers and reteach skills if answers are incorrect.
7. Provide distributed practice and review.

No doubt, the above sequence has variations within a strategy or direct instruction model for math instruction (e.g., Fuchs & Fuchs, 2003).

In summary, points of distinction and commonality exist in the instructional components that make up the two orientations. Thus, the two models must be operationalized. In our synthesis, treatments were coded as reflecting *direct instruction* if four of the following criteria were present: (a) breaking down a task into small steps, (b) administering probes, (c) administering feedback repeatedly, (d) providing a pictorial or diagram presentation, (e) allowing for independent practice and individually paced instruction, (f) breaking the instruction down into simpler phases, (g) instructing in a small group, (h) teacher modeling a skill, (i) providing set materials at a rapid pace, (j) providing individual instruction, (k) teacher asking directed questions, and (l) teacher presenting the new (novel) materials (e.g., experimental materials that supplement existing classroom materials).

Studies were categorized as strategy instruction if they included at least three of the following instructional components: (a) problem-solving explanations (systematic explanations, elaborations, and/or plan to direct task performance), (b) teacher modeling (verbal modeling, questioning, and demonstration from teachers), (c) reminders to use certain strategies or procedures (cues to use taught strategies, tactics, or procedures), (d) step-by-step prompts or multiprocess instructions, (e) dialogue (teacher and student talk back and forth), (g) teacher-generated questions, and (g) teacher provided necessary assistance.

On the basis of the operational criteria, some studies could be expected to share *both* strategy instruction and direct instruction criteria. Therefore, studies were further separated into those that included only strategy components (SI-only model), those that included only direct instruction components (DI-only), those that included both strategy and direct instruction components (combined model includes a minimum of three strategy and four direct instruction components), and those studies that did not include the minimum number of components for either direct or strategy instruction (nondirect instruction and nonstrategy instruction model). Thus, the latter studies may have included some components of either model, but none of these studies met a critical threshold of strategy and/or direct instruction components.

On the basis of these classifications of instructional models and methodological rigor, what were the results related to math as the dependent variable? Answering this question first requires emphasizing that although all studies included in the present synthesis met all of the selection criteria in Simmerman and Swanson (2001), not all studies were of equal methodological sophistication, and controls for the variation in methodological rigor had to be added to the analyses. To address this issue, we coded each study on a number of methodological variables. Methodological composite scores related to both internal validity and methodological sophistication were created. Studies were assigned a positive score on the following methodological dimensions: (a) instructional sessions greater than 10 (selection of this variable was based on the assumption that the intensity of instruction as reflected by the number of sessions yields more reliable and stable outcomes than shorter intervention sessions), (b) random assignment to treatment, (c) multiple measures of treatment integrity (treatment was carried out as intended), (d) use of standardized tests (higher reliability than experimental measures), (e) internal validity scores of 11 (number reflects the best possible ratings on items, see above), and (f) high control and treatment condition overlap in terms of steps and procedures (at least three steps and/or procedures overlap). The amount of standardized test information reported was also included in the methodological composite score if additional psychometric information beyond an IQ score was reported (e.g., reading scores). For each study, the composite score across the seven variables varied from 0 to 14, with 14 reflecting methodologically superior studies. The mean methodological composite score for 28 studies that included math measures was 7.25, suggesting that on average studies fell in the middle of our methodological continuum.

The following results that address the question above of what the results showed for math are based on analyses that partialed out variations related to the methodological score. The mean effect sizes, and the total number of studies for group design studies were 0.58 ($N = 9$), 0.48 ($N = 7$), 0.32 ($N = 3$), and 0.26 ($N = 9$) for the Combined, DI-alone, SI-alone, and Nondirect instruction and Nonstrategy instruction models, respectively. Thus, the Combined model yielded higher effect sizes than the other models.

■ Instructional Components

The above analysis, of course, may be unsatisfactory for teachers because the instructional models appear rather general in description. On the basis of the comprehensive reviews that have identified instructional components that influenced student outcomes (e.g., Shuell, 1996), we reclustered (or reconfigured) the 45 instructional activities shown in Appendix A into 18 clusters of components. We coded the occurrence of the following instructional components (also provided are the numbers related to the coding sheet provided in Appendix A):

1. *Sequencing.* Statements in the treatment description related to breaking down the task, and/or sequencing short activities (activity numbers 12 and 29).
2. *Explicit practice.* Statements in the treatment description related to distributed review and practice, repeated practice, sequenced reviews, daily feedback, and/or weekly reviews (activity numbers 23, 26, 27, 39, and 45).
3. *Novelty.* Statements in the treatment description about a new curriculum that was implemented, and/or emphasis on teacher presenting new material from the previous lesson (activity numbers 20 and 38).
4. *Attributions.* Statements in the treatment description about the teacher presenting the benefits of taught strategies (activity number 41).
5. *Reinforcement.* Statements in the treatment description about intermittent or consistent use of rewards and reinforcers (activity number 28).

6. *Peer modeling.* Statements in the treatment description about peers presenting or modeling instruction (activity number 18).

7. *Task reduction.* Statements in the treatment description about breaking down the targeted skill into smaller units, mastery criteria, and/or task analysis (activity numbers 1, 17, and 34).

8. *Advance organizers.* Statements in the treatment description about directing children to look over material before instruction, directing children to focus on particular information, providing prior information about task, and/or the teacher stating objectives of instruction (activity numbers 2, 3, 11, and 40).

9. *Questioning.* Treatment description related to directing students to ask questions, the teacher and student or students engaging in dialogue, and/or the teacher asking questions (activity numbers 33, 35, and 36).

10. *One-to-one instruction.* Statements in the treatment description about activities related to independent practice, tutoring, instruction that is individually paced, and/or instruction that is individually tailored (activity numbers 9, 10, and 13).

11. *Control difficulty or processing demands of a task.* Treatment statements about probing learning, fading probes or prompts, short activities so the level of difficulty is controlled, and/or teacher providing necessary assistance (activity numbers 4, 7, 16, and 42).

12. *Technology.* Statements in the treatment description about developing pictorial representations, using specific material or computers, and/or using media to facilitate presentation and feedback (activity numbers 5, 31, and 44).

13. *Elaboration.* Statements in the treatment description about additional information or explanation provided about concepts, and/or redundant text or repetition within text (activity numbers 6, 24, and 30).

14. *Skill modeling.* Statements or activities in the treatment description that involve modeling from teacher in terms of skills (activity number 19).

15. *Small group instruction.* Statements in the treatment description about instruction in a small group, and/or verbal interaction occurring in a small group with students and/or teacher (activity number 14).

16. *A supplement to teacher involvement.* Statements in the treatment description about homework and/or parents helping reinforce instruction (activity numbers 8, 21, and 22).

17. *Strategy cues.* Statements in the treatment description about reminders to use strategies or multisteps, the teacher verbalizing steps or procedures to solve problems, and/or use of "think aloud models" (activity numbers 25, 32, and 43).

18. *Large group learning.* Statements in the treatment description about instruction in large groups and/or teacher only demonstration (activity numbers 15 and 37).

Those components most often associated with strategy instruction programs are best reflected in component numbers 4, 8, 9, 11, 13, 15, and 17. For example, the *advanced organizer* component (no. 8) characterizes treatment approaches that activate prior knowledge or provide a precursor to the main instructional activity. The component that reflected the *control of difficulty or processing demands of a task* addressed the variations in teacher support of the student (e.g., the teacher provided necessary assistance on tasks sequenced from easy to difficult and help was provided to the student that covaries with the learner's ability) and reflected activities such as mediated scaffolding. Following an explicit set of steps and prompting the use of these steps *as a strategy cue* are considered important activities that underlie strategy instruction.

Although the coding of instructional activities was based on reviews of instructional literature, no attempt was made to code the treatment by *what* aspect of instruction was addressed (e.g., word problems, etc.), but instead the present synthesis focused on *how* it was taught. A focus was placed on "how" the treatments were delivered because one cannot adequately assess the "what" of instruction unless the "how" is clearly identified. As shown in a previous synthesis (Swanson & Hoskyn, 1998), there are tremendous differences in instructional activities, as well as a host of other methodological variables that inflate treatment outcomes. Unless instructional activities are identified and their influence on outcomes clearly delineated, testing the subtle aspects of content becomes a moot point.

Table 3.1 shows the percentage of studies that used various criteria that measured math outcomes. Column 1 shows the percentage of studies that included math as a dependent measure in the synthesis ($N = 28$) that reported a particular component of instruction. For example, 13 studies of the 28 (46%) reported using a sequencing procedure. The next column shows studies that included math as a dependent measure that yielded effect sizes >0.50 and had high methodological scores (see above) on measures of internal and external validity. Thus, sequencing procedures were reported in five studies with high methodology ratings and effect sizes >0.50. Thus, out of the 13 studies, 5 reported using sequencing procedures (39%). Overall, column 2 in Table 3.1 shows that percentile scores above 30% were related to the instructional components of sequencing, peer modeling control of task difficulty, and strategy cues.

As an additional comparison, components of 180 empirical instructional design studies (Swanson & Hoskyn, 1998) were coded that included a large array of reading and related dependent measures. The percentage of instruction components for these studies shown in column 3 was in the same range as those for column 1. Thus, components of good teaching in general do not differ substantially from those observed in this meta-analysis for math.

TABLE 3.1 *Percent of Instructional Components Reported in Group Design Studies with (a) Math as the Dependent Measure (N = 28 studies), (b) Math as a Dependent Measure but Studies Yielded High Methods Score and High Effect Sizes (>0.50), and (c) Comparison of Studies across Various Domains (N = 180)*

	Total-Math	High Method/ High Effect Sizes	Compared to Other Domains (N = 180)
Sequencing	46 (13)	39 (5)	46.7
Explicit practice	25 (7)	29 (2)	32.8
Novelty	25 (7)	14 (1)	39.4
Attributions	0	—	1.0
Reinforcement	15 (4)	25 (1)	
Peer modeling	7 (2)	50 (1)	3.3
Task reduction	31 (11)	18 (2)	41.1
Advanced organ	21 (6)	16 (1)	28.3
Questioning	4 (1)	0	15.0
One-to-one instruction	71 (20)	25 (5)	68.3
Control difficulty	32 (9)	33 (3)	38.9
Technology	32 (9)	22 (2)	50
Elaboration	7 (2)	0	5
Skill modeling	28 (8)	25 (2)	26.1
Small group instruction	21 (6)	17 (1)	22.8
Supplemental instruction	0	0	6.1
Strategy cues	18 (5)	40 (2)	19.4
Large group learning	32 (9)	22 (2)	38.3

Note: Numerals within parentheses represent total number of studies reported using the instructional component.

■ Processes that Underlie Math Difficulties

Although the focus has been on the instructional implications for children at-risk for MD, the processes that may be helped (or compensated for) when effective instruction is implemented were not identified. Thus, given that methodologically rigorous studies implement a combined strategy and direct instruction approach, what processing may they be compensating for in terms of individual differences in responding? Only speculation on these issues is possible. However, a recent meta-analysis that synthesized published studies comparing children with MD to other children on various cognitive variables (Swanson & Jerman, 2006) may shed light on this issue.

The important findings yielding the highest magnitude of differences include the following. Average achievers outperformed children with MD on measures of verbal problem solving ($M = -0.58$), naming speed ($M = -0.70$), verbal WM ($M = -0.70$), visual-spatial WM ($M = -0.63$), and long-term memory (LTM; $M = -0.72$). Children with MD outperformed children with comorbid disabilities (math disabilities-MD + reading disabilities-RD) on measures of literacy ($M = 0.75$), visual-spatial problem solving ($M = 0.51$), LTM ($M = 0.44$), STM for words ($M = 0.71$), and verbal WM ($M = 0.30$). Interestingly, children with MD could only be differentiated (although weakly) from children with RD on measures of naming speed (-0.23) and visual-spatial WM (-0.30). More important, the analysis showed that the magnitude of effect sizes in overall cognitive functioning between MD and average achievers was primarily related to verbal WM deficits when the effects of all other variables (e.g., age, IQ, reading level, other cognitive domain categories) were partialed out. In general, the results are in line with Geary (2003) suggesting MD can be partly attributed to WM deficits. This variable accounted for most of the overall cognitive functioning of MD participants relative to average achievers. Thus, assuming that children receive good instruction, it is possible that WM deficits may contribute to MD.

■ Application: What Is the Big Idea?

Although the combined model that included components of direct and strategy instruction (ES = 0.58) superseded the other models in the magnitude of the effect size, the magnitude of the effect sizes for direct instruction alone was in the same effect size range (0.48). These moderate effects emerged even when the analysis took into account methodological and age variations between studies. However, a more fine grain analysis indicated that some components of instruction were more important than others. What are those instructional components?

As shown in Table 3.1, greater than 30% of the studies that measured math performance included instructional components related to sequencing, one-to-one instruction, task reduction in processing demand, some form of technology, strategy instruction, and large group learning. Infrequently reported instructional components were related to attribution training, direct reinforcement, elaboration, peer modeling, and supplements to teacher instruction. The analysis also determined whether studies that yielded high effect sizes as well as high methodological scores were more likely to use specific instructional components. Table 3.1, column 2, lists those studies that achieved a high method composite score (>5, with 14 as the highest) and yielded effect sizes at or above 0.50. As shown in Table 3.1, these comparisons showed that *no* one instructional component, except strategy instruction and peer modeling, was reported in more than 40% of the studies. The component included in 30% of the studies was sequencing, control of task difficulty (task reduction), and strategy cuing.

What can be concluded from this synthesis and the others reported related to evidence-based instructional models for children with MD? Two important findings emerged related to designing effective instruction.

First, an effective general model of instruction that combines the components of direct and strategy instruction supercedes other models for remediating math problems. More specifically, the effect size ($M = 0.55$) of the combined strategy instruction and direct instruction model meets Cohen's (1988) criterion of 0.50 for a moderate finding. Because direct instruction and strategy instruction are complex combinations of components, however, these results do not support the conclusion that strategy instruction has better support than direct instruction for treatment outcomes. The reason is many commonalities are shared between a strategy instruction program and direct instruction. Both approaches involve the active presentation of information, clear organization, step-by-step progression from subtopic to subtopic, use of many examples, demonstrations, and visual prompts. All emphasize conscious assessing of student understanding and altering the pace of instruction according to this information. That is, focus is on independent performance. Instruction is criterion-based rather than time-based. A particular stage is mastered before moving on to the next stage. Clear differences also exist in focus. As stated in the introduction, strategy interventions focus on routines and planful action and/or general principles of handling information, whereas direct instruction focuses on isolated skill acquisition to support higher-order processing. However, much of the teaching in both approaches occurs in an explicit manner, relying on oral presentation by the teacher and oral responses by the students. Thus, although direct instruction has been associated with the behavioral paradigms, cognitive paradigms use some of the same procedures. This point is illustrated by Swanson (1988) who suggests that, in practice, both cognitive and behavioral models use many of the same procedures (e.g., feedback, monitoring, and repetition).

Second, although the results show that at a general level a combined direct and strategy instruction model is critical, at the instructional level it appears that sequencing, controlling task demands, and explicit strategy training are important in designing programs that yield high effect sizes. Evidence available suggests that these components should be (a) integrated throughout the intervention package, (b) constitute major features of each instructional program, and (c) designed into the interventions in such a way as to move from a heavy reliance on teacher mediation in the early stages of instruction to a position of ultimately having students mediate the learning process.

Significant advances in devising programs for children at-risk may depend on including both components—direct instruction and explicit strategy instruction—in the remediation program. Determining the most robust treatments for children at-risk may require that both control and treatment conditions include these components. In this way, the unique aspects of the novel treatment program can be more adequately assessed. Sample interventions are those of Bottge and Hasselbring (1999), Fuchs and Fuchs (2003), and others. For example, Fuchs' research program on mathematical problem solving focuses on the student's mastery of solution methods so they can allocate less WM capacity to the details of the solution. Their work shows that explicit instruction is necessary for transfer. They optimize the quality of instruction by providing effective explanation and feedback. Their research program places a heavy reliance on curriculum-based procedures. They use repeated measurements where teachers assess the student's mastery of a single skill, and after this mastery they move the student on to different or more difficult skills. Because information is collected on students in a time series format, the teacher is able to provide explicit practice and feedback to the student. Another example is the intervention program of Scruggs and Masteropieri's (2003), which focuses on content learning in science and social studies. Their procedure makes use of text processing strategies, mnemonic strategies, elaborative integration, and inquiry-oriented or activities-oriented instruction. However, enhancing student performance in the instructional model is related to specifying instructional objectives and maximizing opportunities to respond. They view students with learning difficulties as typically having difficulty in both the creation and application of effective learning strategies, and therefore tasks must be explicitly taught and repeatedly demonstrated.

■ Summary and Conclusion

The chapter selectively reviewed evidence-based models of instruction for students who struggle with math. Overall, the analysis of the experimental intervention literature indicated that direct instruction and explicit strategy instruction (strategy cuing, sequencing, and controlling for task difficulty) positively influence the magnitude of treatment outcomes. The potential for making significant advances in devising programs will partially come about if particular components (sequencing, control of task difficulty, feedback, strategy instruction) are included in various remediation programs for MD. An in-depth meta-analysis of the literature, with controls for methodological rigor, strongly suggested that a combination of strategy and direct instruction provided the best general "evidence-based instructional heuristic" for improving math performance in children with learning difficulties in math. A better chance of determining more robust treatments is possible if both control and treatment conditions include these components. In this way, the unique aspects of novel treatment programs in terms of the "nature of the content" can be more adequately assessed.

Limits must be placed on the generalizability of the findings reported in this chapter. They apply to at-risk, low achieving, or learning-disabled students, to basic math skills, and to pedagogical approaches to teaching these populations basic math skills. The findings do not necessarily apply to evidence-based comparison of alternative math curricula (sets of instructional materials), to other kinds of math skills (e.g., not basic ones but rather advanced ability to do algebra, trigonometry, geometry, or calculus), or to other populations (average or talented in math). Insufficient research exists to evaluate evidence relative to those issues and populations. To reiterate the theme of this chapter, practitioners need to be critical and thoughtful consumers of the research literature that provides the evidence on which they base their practices.

■ References

Adams, G., & Carnine, D. (2003). Direct instruction. In H. L. Swanson, K. Harris, & S. Graham (Eds.), *Handbook of learning disabilities* (pp. 323–344). New York, The Guilford Press.

Badian, N. A. (1983). Arithmetic and nonverbal learning, In H. R. Myklebust (Ed.), *Progress in learning disabilities* (Vol. 5, pp. 235–264). New York, Grune and Stratton.

Baker, S., Gersten, R., & Dae-Sik, L. (2002). A synthesis of empirical research on teaching mathematics to low achieving students. *The Elementary School Journal, 103*, 51–73.

Bottge, B. A., & Hasselbring, T. S. (1999). Teaching mathematics to adolescents with disabilities in a multimedia environment. *Intervention in School and Clinic, 35,* 113–116.

Cohen, J. (1988). *Statistical power analysis for the behavioral sciences* (2nd ed.). Hillsdale, NJ, Lawrence Erlbaum Associates.

Cook, T. D., & Campbell, D. T. (1979). *Quasi-experimentation: Design & analysis issues for field settings.* Boston, Houghton Mifflin.

Cooper, H., & Hedges, L. (Eds.) (1994). *The handbook of research synthesis.* NY, Sage.

Desoete, A., Roeyers, H., & De Clercq, A. (2004). Children with mathematical learning disabilities in Belgium. *Journal of Learning Disabilities, 37*, 50–61.

Fuchs, L., & Fuchs, D. (2003). Enhancing the mathematical problem solving of students with math difficulties. In H. L. Swanson, K. Harris, & S. Graham (Eds.), *Handbook of learning disabilities* (pp. 306–322). New York, The Guilford Press.

Geary, D. C. (1993). Mathematical disabilities: Cognitive, neuropsychological and genetic components. *Psychological Bulletin, 114*, 345–362.

Geary, D. C. (2003). Math disabilities. In H. L. Swanson, K. Harris, & S. Graham (Eds.), *Handbook of learning disabilities.* New York, The Guilford Press.

Graham, S., Harris, K. R., & Zito, J. (2005). Promoting internal and external validity: A synergism of laboratory-like experiments and classroom-based self-regulated strategy development research. In G. Phye, D. Robinson, & J. Levin (Eds.), *Empirical methods for evaluating interventions.* (pp. 85–112). San Diego, CA, Elsevier Academic Press.

Gross-Tsur, V., Manor, O., & Shalev, R. S. (1996). Developmental dyscalculia: Prevalence and demographic features. *Developmental Medicine and Child Neurology, 38,* 25–33.

Kaméenui, E. J., Jitendra, A. K., & Darch, C. B. (1995). Direct instruction reading as contronym and eonomine. *Reading & Writing Quarterly: Overcoming Learning Difficulties, 11,* 3–17.

Kilpatrick, J., Swafford, J., & Findell, B. (Eds.) (2001). *Adding it up: Helping children learn mathematics.* Washington, DC, National Academy Press.

Kroesberger, E., & Van Luit, J. (2003). Mathematics interventions for children with special educational needs: A meta-analysis. *Remedial and Special Education, 24,* 97–114.

Levin, J. R. (2005). Randomized classroom trials on trial. In G. Phye, D. Robinson, & J. Levin (Eds.), *Empirical methods for evaluating interventions* (pp. 3–28). San Diego, CA, Elsevier Academic Press.

National Council of Teachers of Mathematics. (1989). *Curriculum and evaluation standards for school mathematics.* Reston, VA, Author.

Rosenshine, B. (1995). Advances in research on instruction. *Journal of Educational Research, 88,* 262–268.

Scruggs, T. & Mastropieri, M. (2003). Science and social studies. In H. L. Swanson, K. Harris, & S. Graham (Eds.), *Handbook of learning disabilities* (pp. 364–379). New York, The Guilford Press.

Shuell, T. (1996). Teaching and learning in a classroom context. In D. Berliner & R. C. Calfee (Eds.), *Handbook of educational psychology* (pp. 726–764). New York, Simon & Schuster Macmillan.

Simmerman, S., & Swanson, H. L. (2001). Treatment outcomes for students with learning disabilities: How important are internal and external validity? *Journal of Learning Disabilities, 34,* 221–236.

Sternberg, R. (1998). Principles of teaching successful intelligence. *Educational Psychologist, 33,* 65–72.

Swanson, H. L. (1988). Toward a metatheory of learning disabilities. *Journal of Learning Disabilities, 21,* 196–209.

Swanson, H. L. (1993). Principles and procedures in strategy use. In L. Meltzer (Ed.), *Strategy assessment and instruction for students with learning disabilities: From theory to practice* (pp. 61–92). Austin, Pro-Ed.

Swanson, H. L. (1999). Instructional components that predict treatment outcomes for students with learning disabilities: Support for a combined strategy and direct instruction model. *Learning Disabilities Research and Practice, 14,* 129–140.

Swanson, H. L. (2000). Searching for the best model for instructing students with learning disabilities: A component and composite analysis. *Educational and Child Psychology, 17,* 330–347.

Swanson, H. L., & Deshler, D. D. (2003). Instructing adolescents with learning disabilities: Converting meta-analysis to practice. *Journal of Learning Disabilities*, *36*, 124–135.

Swanson, H. L., & Hoskyn, M. (1998). A synthesis of experimental intervention literature for students with learning disabilities: A meta-analysis of treatment outcomes. *Review of Educational Research*, *68*, 277–322.

Swanson, H. L., Hoskyn, M., & Lee, C. M. (1999). *Interventions for students with learning disabilities*. New York, The Guilford Press.

Swanson, H. L., & Jerman, O. (2006). Math disabilities: A selective meta-analysis. *Review of Education Research*, *76*, 249–274.

Swanson, H. L., & Sachse-Lee, C. M. (2000). A meta-analysis of single-subject-design intervention research for students with LD. *Journal of Learning Disabilities*, *33*, 114–136.

Valentine, J. C., & Cooper, H. M. (2005). Can we measure the quality of causal research in education. In G. Phye, D. Robinson, & J. Levin (Eds.), *Empirical methods for evaluating interventions* (pp. 85–112). San Diego, CA, Elsevier Academic Press.

Wong, B., Harris, K., Graham, S., & Butler, D. (2003). Cognitive strategies instruction research in learning disabilities. In H. L. Swanson, K. Harris, & S. Graham (Eds.), *Handbook of learning disabilities* (pp. 383–402). New York, The Guildford Press.

Wortman, P. M. (1994). Judging research quality. In H. Cooper & L. V. Hedges (Eds.), *The handbook of research synthesis* (pp. 97–109). New York, Russell Sage Foundation.

Xin, Y. P., & Jitendra, A. K. (1999). The effects of instruction in solving mathematical word problems for students with learning problems: A meta-analysis. *Journal of Special Education*, *32*, 207–225.

■ Appendix A

Intervention activities were coded based on key words and phrases (descriptions are abbreviated here). (* reflects strategy instruction activities, ** reflects direct instruction activities)

1. —— Breaking down task by skills**
2. —— Child is asked to look over material before instruction
3. —— Children are directed to focus on material presented
4. —— Conduct probes of learning (intermittent test)**
5. —— Diagram or pictorial presentation**
6. —— Elaborate explanations*
7. —— Fading of prompts or cues
8. —— Homework
9. —— Independent practice (e.g., complete worksheet on own)

10. —— Individually paced**
11. —— Information is provided before student discussion
12. —— Instruction broken down into steps**
13. —— Instruction individually**
14. —— Instruction small group (2–5)**
15. —— Instruction large group (>5)
16. —— Level of difficulty applied to each student
17. —— Mastery Criteria
18. —— Modeling—from peers
19. —— Modeling of skill—from teachers**
20. —— New curriculum
21. —— Parent provides instruction
22. —— Peer provides daily feedback on student performance
23. —— Provide distributed practice (pacing) and review (weekly and monthly reviews)**
24. —— Redundant text or materials
25. —— Reminders to use certain strategies or procedures*
26. —— Repeated practice (e.g., drill and repetition)
27. —— Review of material on each session
28. —— Reward and reinforcers
29. —— Short activities sequenced by teacher
30. —— Simplified demonstration
31. —— Specialized film or video tape/audio tape
32. —— Step-by-step prompts or process, multistep process directions*
33. —— Student asks questions
34. —— Task analysis
35. —— Teacher and student talk back and forth (e.g., Socratic dialogue)*
36. —— Teacher asks process-related questions*
37. —— Teacher demonstrates
38. —— Teacher (or experimenter) presents new material**
39. —— Teacher (or experimenter) provides daily feedback on student performance**
40. —— Teacher (or experimenter) states learning objectives
41. —— Teacher presents benefits of instruction
42. —— Teacher provides only necessary assistance*
43. —— Think aloud models (modeling aloud by teacher)*
44. —— Using media (e.g., computer) for elaboration or repetition
45. —— Weekly review

4. Research-Based Oral Language Intervention Routes to the Academic Language of Literacy

Finding the Right Road

Elaine R. Silliman and Cheryl M. Scott

In a world with little consensus, there is general agreement that students must have a strong base of oral language knowledge to attain proficiency in reading, spelling, and composing. Given the central role of oral language in literacy learning, a group of students often not well understood are those with spoken language impairments. Oral language impairment may first become noticeable in the preschool years when a child is described with a "language delay." On the other hand, difficulties with spoken language comprehension and expression may not become visible until the child enters school and is confronted with literacy demands. Sometimes, only the reading disability and not the oral language impairment is acknowledged during the school years. Oral language impairment occurs in all racial, ethnic, home language, dialect, and socioeconomic groups.

The purpose of this chapter is to acquaint other professionals with an understanding of oral language impairment, its implications for literacy learning, and the nature of the evidence base for approaches to oral language intervention. We first address the goal of all students achieving academic language proficiency relative to the academic language demands of schooling. In the second part of the chapter, based on research, two patterns of language impairment are described and illustrated with cases: (a) Specific language impairment (SLI or LI; also referred to as language learning disability, LLD, in the literature), which is a grammatically based language impairment that impacts both language production and comprehension, and (b) an inferencing impairment that affects comprehension. Longitudinal research tracking oral and written language is used to explain how literacy problems related to oral language are likely to evolve. Each pattern is discussed, with focus on its links to literacy, followed by a summary of available evidence on interventions geared to the core deficits in each pattern and discussion of which interventions might help each of the example cases. Educators, speech-language pathologists, and school psychologists have not made maximum use of this type of information when designing intervention protocols that integrate instruction in oral and written language for students struggling with reading, spelling, and composing. In the final segment, language-literacy interventions are featured with special emphasis on integrated approaches to support students' development of academic language proficiency.

■ Academic Language Proficiency and Academic Discourse Demands

Both spoken language and written language are inherently social (Gee, 1999).[1] For communication to take place, speakers or writers must influence the minds of their conversational partners or audience through the process of sense making. Often in the written medium, the audience is hypothetical (non-present) and not necessarily homogeneous. This means that writers must think about readers' presumed knowledge of the topic to adopt a style of communication that will make sense to readers. Furthermore, variations in social language use, whether casual spoken conversation or formal academic written language, are associated with different grammatical patterns (Gee, 1999).

Variations in the social uses of language are referred to as *registers*, which are linguistically distinct ways of communicating as a function of social contexts. Examples of specialized register variations include the "baby talk" register (often called "motherese"), and the "teacher talk" register. Contexts and registers are built dynamically from five interacting features (Silliman & Wilkinson, 1994): (a) The medium of communication; (b) the extent to which the physical setting is shared or displaced in time and space; (c) role relationships and the degree of cultural, social, and world knowledge that participants have in common; (d) the activities and goals participants share; and (e) the familiarity or novelty of the topics.

The Everyday Oral Language Register Compared to the Academic Language Register

The academic language register is the language of schooling that all students must acquire to meet academic discourse expectations. In their first five years of life, children acquire a "first language" that allows them to become competent and cooperative conversationalists in their social interactions with family, peers, and others in accord with the language socialization practices of a child's culture. When children enter school, they must learn the academic language register, which represents a new tool for thinking and communicating in more literate ways. This register is often misunderstood by teachers and researchers as limited to the use of content area vocabulary, for example, *revolution*, *satire*, and *equation* (Zwiers, 2007). However, much more than vocabulary distinguishes the two registers. For example, there is a major difference between producing words in natural conversation and the metalinguistic ability to talk about word units, such as "What is the root word in *equation*?" On the basis of cross-linguistic evidence (Berman & Verhoeven, 2002) and longitudinal studies in the United States (Snow, Porche, Tabors, & Harris, 2007), this protracted learning of a new language register involving proficiency in academic language continues through adolescence and even across the life span (Berman, 2007).

From a cognitive perspective, children deploy attentional resources in a flexible manner to acquire new literacy forms and functions that, in turn, will serve to advance academic language knowledge (Berman, 2007; Ravid & Tolchinsky, 2002). From a social point of view, children must have access to meaningful participation in the specialized oral and written registers of schooling (Cummins, 2000; Gee, 1999). Absolute differences do not distinguish the academic language register, whether spoken or written, from the everyday oral language register (Scott, 1994). Rather, the two registers exist along a continuum of language complexity, but they may be differentiated by a collection of core linguistic features that co-occur in sufficient frequency to establish a functional pattern with systematic variation (Berman, 2007; Biber & Conrad, 2001). This pattern results in enhanced density of lexical and grammatical constructions as displayed in Table 4.1.

Although it would be difficult to identify all oral language contributors to academic language, one strong contender is vocabulary diversity (the amount of *different* familiar meanings in a lexicon), which is associated initially with ease in decoding and then with skill in reading comprehension (Foorman, Anthony, Seals, & Mouzaki, 2002). A related candidate is the *breadth* of lexical knowledge (how many familiar meanings are stored in a lexicon) in grade 1 for middle-class children as assessed by a standardized vocabulary measure. Vocabulary breadth at grade 1 predicted children's level of reading comprehension in grade 11, when measured by standardized instruments (Cunningham & Stanovich, 1997). However, it remains unknown whether vocabulary diversity, breadth, or the *density* (i.e., the elaborated semantic knowledge that words can have multiple meanings) in the early grades (Foorman et al., 2002) is a better predictor of reading comprehension in the later grades (Berman, 2007; Snow & Kim, 2007).

Outcomes from a longitudinal study by the National Institute of Child Health and Human Development Study of Early Child Care and Youth Development (NICHD Early Child Care Research Network, 2005) in a representative sample of 1,137 children from age 3 years through grade 3 offer another perspective on the oral language foundations of the academic

TABLE 4.1   *Comparison of the Oral and Academic Language Registers in Both the Oral and Written Domains**

Lexical/Grammatical System	Oral Register Example	Written Register Example
Clauses conjoined by *and* (oral) are combined in one sentence with subordinate conjunctions (written)	*And then one day he was walking his sheep through the mountains.* *And one of the goats got away.*	*One day, when Yanis was walking his sheep through the mountains, one of the goats got loose.*
Nominalization: Information encoded as a clause (oral) is recoded in noun phrases, allowing for more nominal density within sentences (written)	*And once cactuses die, animals move into the cactus to live.* *So then his mother talked to his father. And they let him go down there.* *And he told him that he wanted to be a fisherman.*	*Animals make homes out of dead plants.* *After a discussion they agree to let him go down there.* *Yanis explained his dream to his father.*
Theme/focus as grammatical subjects (oral) is moved to the end of the sentence (written). Adverbial fronting may be used to accomplish this (written)	*And there's lots of animal and plant life in the desert.* *And the hawk is on top of the food chain.* *There are rainstorms every summer and winter.*	*The desert is a community of plant and animal life.* *The top of the food chain is the hawk.* *Every summer and winter there are big rainstorms.*

* Examples are from Scott (2002). Participants (ages 9–12 years) spoke and wrote the same summaries of a video. The oral and written version was produced by the same student in each case.

language register. One finding was that a broad-based, everyday, oral language register in preschool, and not just phonological awareness, directly related to alphabetic knowledge in grade 1 and reading comprehension in grade 3. A second finding was that oral language capability played a central role in how children learned the academic languages of instruction (e.g., for math, science, language arts). Children who had acquired a rich, everyday oral language register were more likely to be successful in acquiring the more specialized academic language register that then allowed them to meet academic discourse demands in grades 1–3.

Academic Discourse Demands in the Elementary Grades

Snow et al. (2007) propose that the way to think about the academic discourse demands of instruction is to think about them as a jigsaw puzzle that must be continuously reassembled and coordinated on a more complex scale as students progress through the grades. The "glue" holding the puzzle pieces together is the expanding ability to "distance" multiple uses of language from specific social contexts. This distancing is often called *decontextualization* because academic language is used outside the context of informal conversation, but that term is misleading because language use cannot make sense "out-of-context." Instead, to *create new contexts* and *merge them with academic language*, students must be able to draw simultaneously on their knowledge of academic content and language to recreate in their minds the situations (the contexts) that textbook authors or teachers frame through language. For example, by the upper elementary grades, "Students need good basic literacy skills, but they also need familiarity with the academic language of texts, access to the knowledge presupposed by the texts and curriculum, (and) motivation to succeed joined with an understanding of what it takes" (Snow et al., 2007, p. 4). As shown in Table 4.1, the register of written texts differs from the everyday oral language register (e.g., in informal conversation) along a number of linguistic and discourse dimensions. A main characteristic of the written register is the distancing created through the specificity of the words chosen.

The Language Expectations of Science

One content area receiving increased attention relative to academic discourse expectations is science, which has informational or expository text rather than narrative text. Science books are valuable in the lower elementary grades for two reasons. The first reason is that familiarity with this genre affords children with opportunities to experience the academic language register that characterizes "science as a discipline" (Varelas & Pappas, 2006). A second reason is that, when science instruction is contextualized through hands-on experience, it can serve as a bridge between the early forms of literate language and the later forms of academic language required in the upper grades (Westby, Dezale, Fradd, & Lee, 1999). One linguistic property of science books that differentiates them from narrative books (Varelas & Pappas, 2006; Westby et al., 1999) is that verb marking in science books tends to be the present tense versus past tense in narrative books (with the exception of dialogue). A grade 1 teacher's read-aloud on the transformation of states of matter (specifically, the water cycle) illustrates this grammatical pattern:

> So, like all gases, the water vapor gradually spreads throughout the room you are in. If the door is open, it will keep on spreading out the door. You cannot see it, but the water vapor is there all around you. The bubbles say, the water vapor is in that room too! It is! (Varelas & Pappas, 2006, p. 235)

A second linguistic property of science books is related to semantic categories. In contrast to narrative texts in which mental state verbs tend to predominate (i.e., *think*, *feel*, *know*, *remember*), the proportion of verbs that refer
to physical processes and classifications is greater in science texts (Varelas &
Pappas, 2006). Acquiring scientific thinking requires a new, more literate oral
register, the language of analysis, synthesis, and evaluation for talking about
physical phenomena (Pappas, Varelas, Barry, & Rife, 2002; Westby et al.,
1999).

Academic Language Expectations in Content Areas for Grades 4 and 5

Few studies are available on the language expectations of content instruction beyond the lower elementary grades. However, one study examined the
nature of teacher academic discourse demands in five grade 4 and 5 classrooms that were ethnically diverse (Bailey, Butler, Stevens, & Lord, 2007).
The aims were to compare frequency distributions of teacher academic language functions, teacher expectations for students' use of more academic
vocabulary (both general and specific), and the linguistic demands and
vocabulary complexity of grade 5 science, math, and social science textbooks. Three sets of findings from Bailey et al. (2007) are summarized and
illustrated.

1. Four categories of academic language functions in science classrooms
   were identified:
   (a) *Explanations* included (1) demonstration of scientific information,
       (2) elaboration of scientific concepts to enhance student understand-
       ing (see the following example), and (3) reasons for scientific theories
       and explanations:

   The roots of the plants. Its job is to deliver water. Running up the stem,
   it only goes one way. It always goes up. (Bailey et al., 2007, p. 119)

   (b) *Descriptions* helped students construct a visual image (analogy) that
       also incorporated their prior experience to understand, for example,
       how plants take in light through their leaves:

   It moves. The plant has leaves like a dish, a satellite dish, to get light.
   (Bailey et al., 2007, p. 120)

   (c) *Comparisons* integrated new information into existing schemas by
       using two discourse strategies: (1) Relating familiar scientific the-
       ories, concepts, or facts to new theories, concepts, or facts (see the

following example); or (2) classifying multiple scientific concepts into a category:

Flowers have *mechanisms of attraction* like whales have *echolocation* (authors' italics) (Bailey et al., 2007, p. 122).

(d) *Assessment* served to evaluate students' retention of previously taught content, for example:

What did we learn in our last unit on water properties? What does the ocean have besides salt that makes it different? (Bailey et al., 2007, p. 122).

2. Regarding *specialized academic vocabulary*, Bailey et al. (2007) noted that teachers often introduced these scientific items without giving students sufficient contextual support to infer their meanings. Supports offered are typically definitions, synonyms, examples, and repetitions that do not necessarily inform students' knowledge of the scientific content or effective use of the linguistic context. The failure to utilize context well in figuring out meaning may be due to a combination of metalinguistic factors in the syntactic, semantic, and pragmatic domains that include insufficient attention to subtle syntactic clues in more complex sentence constructions (see Table 4.1), insensitivity to relationships between the context of sentence meaning and one's prior situational knowledge, and confusion between the meaning of the vocabulary item and the entire sentence construction (Nagy, 2007). For example, a child might be trying to figure out the meaning of an unfamiliar meaning, such as *antics*, in the sentence "People want to talk about the *antics* of others and don't like to talk about their own" and conclude that the interpretation of *antics* is people like to talk about other people and not themselves (Nagy, 2007). "The metalinguistic *demands* of vocabulary instruction and the metalinguistic *abilities* of students (author's italics) may differ" (Nagy, 2007, p. 67).

3. *Academic language demands of typical textbooks* in science, social studies, and mathematics were analyzed based on typical grade 5 textbooks, which averaged 567 pages in length. Findings indicated, first, that the academic language demands of mathematics textbooks differed from the science and social studies textbooks and, second, that the science and social studies textbooks were generally comparable in their academic language demands. Some characteristic features of these demands follow. Specialized, domain-specific, academic vocabulary (Beck & McKeown, 2007) was common to math, science, and social studies texts, but the science textbook had the greatest proportion. Unique adverbial clause connectors that indicated semantic relationships between clauses, such as *if* and *after*, were more frequent in science and social studies. Derivational

suffixes, for example, *atomic*, *historical*, and *geometric*, were uncommon across the three content areas studied, which was surprising given the role of derivational morphology in building more literate vocabulary meanings beginning in grade 4 (Nagy, Berninger, & Abbott, 2006).

In general, the predominant sentence structure across the three content area texts consisted of a single (main) clause in which grammatical elements (subjects, adverbials, objects) were expanded via prepositional phrases. An example is *The ice on the river melts quickly under the warm sun* (Bailey et al., 2007). More complex clausal structures that consisted of a main clause and a dependent (embedded) clause were most likely to be found in the science text followed by the social studies text, for example, *Although human beings don't notice the noises of nature* (dependent clause), *a lot of animals react to the sounds around them* (main clause).

A chief distinction between science and social studies texts centered on organizational structure. Grade 5 science texts tended to be written in the expository mode, whereas social studies texts were more narrative-like in their organization. The discourse organization of mathematics texts was more problematic to identify. The emphasis on solving word problems within a formulaic structure limited text length. However, all three content area texts shared core organizational features comparable to teachers' academic language use that included comparison, description, enumeration, paraphrase, and sequencing.

Teacher Beliefs and Academic Discourse Expectations

At the level of the individual classroom, features of academic discourse demands interact with features of the academic work students and teachers do together. In other words, the meaning of this academic work is shaped by teachers' beliefs and attitudes about that work (Edelsky, Smith, & Wolfe, 2002). If, for example, a grade 5 teacher values a belief inspired framework about a deep appreciation of literature (the academic work), the academic discourse expectations might be constructed around learning how to do literary analysis and discussion of the fictional universes that authors symbolically create. In this framework, students are being asked to assume the identity of "lover of literature" (Edelsky et al., 2002) and, in the process, are challenged to deploy academic language, such as *from the perspective of, similarities between, differences between, the reason for*, that supports higher-order thinking (Zwiers, 2007). On the other hand, another grade 5 teacher might value a more didactic approach, believing that reading assigned stories (the academic work) teaches students about independent responsibility for completion in the form of a book report (the academic discourse medium). Here, students are being asked to assume a different, and perhaps narrower, identity, that of a "reader and writer." In this situation, the teacher might provide only written prescriptive feedback on the book reports, a procedure that does not inherently advance students' academic language or higher-order thinking (Zwiers, 2007). These two illustrations exemplify how individual teacher beliefs mediate students' understanding of academic discourse expectations, especially how students are to participate verbally and nonverbally in the language of instruction across the curriculum and the roles they are to assume in literacy-building work (Hofer, 2001).

These types of adult expectations also hold for students with oral language impairment and, typically, are not considered as a variable in evidence-based intervention studies on language impairment. For example, consider an intervention study on the effects of sentence repetition on sentence complexity. The researcher, who believes strongly in the experimental paradigm as the only way to do science, tells children that they are to repeat sentences exactly as they hear them and thus conveys how children are to participate in the activity. A few children might refuse to comply because the participation requirements violate their understanding of how to talk. These children might then be erroneously referred to as "nonresponders" with the result that their data are treated as experimentally nonsignificant (Kovarsky & Curran, 2007).

In summary, the language of schooling is a register with distinct words, sentence structures, and discourse structures. In many ways, these new forms and meanings are challenging to children and the challenges continue through adolescence. The familiar "life's a story" schemas that underlie the personal experiences children tell about themselves and others in a conversation, or even in more formal story telling (or retelling) contexts, are very different from the language encountered in science or social studies textbooks. In these texts, as illustrated with numerous examples in this section, long/complex noun phrases occupy grammatical subject slots rather than a simple character name as in a story. Language is more tightly packed into multiclausal constructions and clauses are tied together with logical connectives (e.g., *unless, whereas, likewise*) rather than simple additive or temporal connectives (e.g., *and, then*). It is not unusual to find sentences in textbooks that are four or five clauses in length. When we add to the language challenge the fact that these forms and meanings are *the vehicle for learning new information*, the task can be daunting especially for children who have a language impairment. Within this broad group, there are children whose individual profiles of impairment make it particularly difficult to comprehend and/or produce the more decontexualized and complex language of the academic register. These are the types of impairments that concern us in the next section.

■ Two Patterns of Specific Language Impairment and Evidence-Based Interventions

Two patterns of oral language impairment are described for which there is a reasonable amount of converging evidence in terms of the basic construct of the pattern as well as how the pattern interacts with the development of literacy. Some qualifications are in order: (1) Phonological awareness and decoding are not addressed because this topic has been covered extensively elsewhere (e.g., Berninger et al., 2003; Case, Speece, & Molloy, 2003; Foorman & Torgesen, 2001; Torgesen et al., 2001; Vellutino, Scanlon, Small, & Fanuele, 2006); (2) the patterns are not mutually exclusive but for our purposes, we separate them here; and (3) strict boundaries between language modalities—speaking, writing, listening, and reading—are not assumed because they are intertwined in many academic tasks. In addition, recent longitudinal analyses of a large group of children with and without language impairment call into question whether separate domains of comprehension and production are defensible (Tomblin & Zhang, 2006).

Pattern 1: Grammatically Based Language Impairment

Grammatically based language impairment (LI) is often referred to as a specific language impairment (SLI), because it is not due to impaired cognitive, social-emotional, or medical/neurological function. Although children with SLI as a group are described as linguistically heterogeneous, with various patterns of strengths and weaknesses across lexical, syntactic, and social-pragmatic domains, the "signature" problem is often described as a grammatical (or syntactic) one (Leonard, 1998). Thus, sentence comprehension and production pose significant difficulties for children with SLI, and the more complex the sentence, the greater the difficulty. Thompson and Shapiro (2007, p. 31) outlined four variables that contribute to sentence complexity: (a) The number of verbs, (b) the number of embeddings, (c) the order in which major elements appear in the sentence (e.g., canonical/SVO *John (S) kicked (V) the ball (O)* versus noncanonical *The ball was kicked by John; It was the ball that John kicked*), and (d) the distance between crucial elements in the sentence (e.g., in the following sentence, nine words interrupt the main clause subject and verb: *The Union troops (S) that had just marched across the state of Virginia were (V) tired and sore*).

Research documents that SLI is frequently characterized by difficulty with complex mapping and dependency relations. These include tense and agreement marking (Rice & Warren, 2005) and sentences in which canonical SVO order is altered via movement operations (e.g., questions, passives, object relative clauses) (van der Lely, 2003; see also, Silliman & Scott, 2006). Older children and adolescents who meet SLI criteria have consistently shown lower rates of production of complex sentences when compared with age peers (Marinellie, 2004; Scott & Windsor, 2000), especially sentences that combine various types of subordination and coordination (Gillam & Johnston, 1992; Scott, 2003), which are prominent in academic texts. Grammatical error rates for children with SLI are higher than age or language-matched controls in oral language samples and are greatly exacerbated in written samples (Windsor, Scott, & Street, 2000). However, in contrast to oral production, grammatically based comprehension problems in young children are less transparent and may go unrecognized.

Longitudinal data on SLI show that these problems are often noticeable from the earliest stages of language learning (Moyle, Ellis Weismer, Evans, & Lindstrom, 2007), persist into preschool and school-age years and beyond, and place the child at considerable risk in reading, spelling, and writing. Children with this pattern include those who, during the preschool years, were late talkers (LT). Although many LT turn into late bloomers who resolve their language difficulties at least partially (Ellis Weismer, 2007), a large proportion, approximately 17–25%, may not be identified until age 6 as also having SLI (Rice, 2007). Also, they may have had an associated speech sound disorder; some estimates obtained from clinical samples are that 60% of LT did have a speech sound disorder (Stothard, Snowling, Bishop, Chipchase, & Kaplan, 1998).

Grammatically based language impairments and reading. Following a large number of kindergarten-age children with SLI, Catts and his colleagues documented that 42% at the second grade level and 36% at the fourth grade level would be classified as reading impaired, using a criterion of at least one standard deviation below the mean on a standardized test of reading comprehension (Catts, Fey, Tomblin, & Zhang, 2002). Percentages rose to 67% and 64% (second and fourth grades, respectively) when the researchers broadened the definition of language impairment to include children who did not meet a strict nonverbal IQ cut-off of −1 SD. The prevalence of reading disability among children with SLI has varied from over 50% to under 25%. Interpretations of the documented overlap between SLI and phonological processing deficits also vary. Some cite a core phonological processing deficit, with SLI as a more severe variation, while others (see Catts, Adlof, Hogan, & Ellis Weismer, 2005) consider SLI and dyslexia as separable disorders, that is, a child may have one but not the other, or they may be comorbid conditions. Catts and colleagues (2005) defined dyslexia operationally as difficulty with word recognition. The absence of consensus is not surprising given the variability in research designs, selection criteria for participants, the index disorder chosen (e.g., reading disability or SLI), and the actual measures of language and reading used.

SLI and reading comprehension. Because a major symptom of SLI is difficulty comprehending and producing sentences, it is not surprising that many children with SLI have reading comprehension problems. With poor reading comprehension as the index condition (the children had normal word accuracy), Nation, Clarke, Marshall, and Durand (2004) found that 8-year-olds had significant difficulties in oral semantics, morphosyntax, figurative language, and inferencing. Many of the children met clinical criteria for SLI. Studying an older cohort of poor comprehenders identified in the eighth grade, Catts et al. (2006) compared them to poor decoders and normal readers. Weaknesses were documented in vocabulary recognition, grammatical understanding, and distant inferencing ability. As these students had been followed continuously since kindergarten, findings showed that only one-third of the poor comprehenders had met criteria for SLI as kindergarteners. Thus, SLI may be only one source of reading comprehension problems.

Therefore, it is important to emphasize that reading comprehension problems may not be identified until grades 3 or 4 when academic texts become more taxing in ways described previously. Results of longitudinal studies show that starting at grades 3–4 children with SLI may demonstrate multiple problems with oral language listening comprehension, including vocabulary, sentence processing, and discourse processing (Catts, Adlof, & Weismer, 2006) as well as problems with reading comprehension (Bishop & Snowling, 2004; Cain & Oakhill, 2006; Catts et al., 2006; Catts, Hogan, & Adlof, 2005; Leach, Scarborough, & Rescorla, 2003; Nation et al., 2004; Scarborough, 2005; Snowling & Hayiou-Thomas, 2006). Identification of specific comprehension impairment may increase through grade 8 (Catts et al., 2006), but it cannot be assumed that all students with a specific comprehension problem have the same underlying problem or set of problems (Bishop, 1997).

SLI and writing. Children with grammatically based language impairments may also have difficulty with writing when their compositions require higher-level sentence syntax involving multiple levels of coordination and subordination, more complex noun phrase elaborations, and derivational morphology, which is the basis of new vocabulary learning after grades 3–4 (Nagy et al., 2006). They may also develop problems with fluent word recognition and spelling, which they previously did not have, because of diminished reading comprehension abilities (Cain & Oakhill, 2007).

Taken together, studies on the co-occurrence of SLI and reading suggest that the more common literacy complication for children with grammatically based LI is reading comprehension. These children may or may not have word recognition problems depending on whether there are comorbid word recognition (and underlying phonological processing) difficulties. Given the heterogeneity of both reading and oral language impairments, the varying presentations of both impairments that depend on time of testing, and the many ways of testing both domains, it is not surprising many questions remain unanswered.

Case Studies for SLI Grammatically Based Language Impairment: Shannon and John

Shannon (Box 4.1) and John (Box 4.2) represent two individuals with the first pattern.[2]

BOX 4.1   *Shannon, a Grammatically Based Language Impairment*

Shannon, a first grader who repeated kindergarten, was seen for a speech and language evaluation at the age of 7;6. Testing was suggested by her teacher who reasoned that underlying language problems might explain Shannon's difficulties with reading and spelling. Receptive and expressive language quotients on a comprehensive test of oral language placed her at the 9th percentile in each area. Shannon was also asked to make up a story to go along with a wordless picture book. Although the overall structure and organization of the story was adequate (there were setting, initiating event, action, consequence, and resolution components), her average utterance length of 5.66 words was 2 SD below the mean when compared with normative data for age peers on the same task, indicating an overall reduced level of semantic/syntactic complexity. Eleven (of 31) utterances had one or more grammatical errors; the majority of these were omissions of obligatory tense markers (e.g., *he never move* for *moved*). In 31 utterances, only two were complex (i.e., they contained more than one clause). Although on her own Shannon did not communicate information from the mental realm of character reactions, emotions, or plans, examiner probes (*why do you think the big frog acted like that?*) revealed she knew more than she put in her story (*because the boy like the little frog better*). Shannon was basically a nonreader and nonwriter. She was able to read only half of the words on a pre-primer passage correctly. On a dictated spelling task of one syllable words with singleton consonants and short vowels, Shannon spelled about half the consonants correctly but none of the vowels.

Shannon is a first grader at the beginning of her formal schooling. Her parents worried about her language development as a toddler. Now in the first grade, her difficulties with early decoding and spelling were the catalyst for language evaluation. She appears to be a case where SLI and reading disability are comorbid problems (Catts, Adlof, Hogan, & Ellis Weismer, 2005). Shannon does not yet read well enough to document reading comprehension difficulties but she is clearly at-risk in light of oral language difficulties that include problems with morphosyntactic and complex sentence comprehension and production tasks. In contrast, John reads well enough for us to see that his problems comprehending sentences occur not only in listening but also in reading. On the production side, John no longer makes ostensible morphosyntactic errors and uses some complex sentence structures when he talks casually in a conversational framework, but his grammar problems are all-too-evident when he writes and, on his own, he cannot correct these perhaps because of lingering metalinguistic weaknesses. What be done to help Shannon and John?

BOX 4.2   *John, a Grammatically Based Language Impairment*

John is a seventh grader, age 12;8. John's mother could not recall much about his schedule of learning language as a toddler and preschooler. He entered formal schooling without calling attention to his oral language or beginning reading performance. His grades were not good, however (C's and D's), and his teacher complained that she frequently had to repeat instructions for him. In the third grade, the school agreed to test John for a language learning disability. Testing revealed reading accuracy and fluency within normal limits, but listening and reading comprehension scores that were more than 1 SD below normative comparisons for age peers. In spite of reasonable spelling, John hated to write. When asked to write in testing situations, he rarely produced more than two or three sentences. As a fourth grader, John worked on strategic reading, using a reciprocal teaching approach (Palincsar & Brown, 1984). In one therapy session, he was practicing the strategy of generating questions while reading a social studies textbook passage on the settlement of the territories. After reading the sentence *The land to the west of the Appalachian Mountains was divided into two territories*, John wrote out the question (preserving his own spelling and punctuation) *Why was the appleation mountains divided into two parts*. His question revealed that he had attached the verb *was divided* to the immediately preceding noun *mountains* rather than the true head noun (*land*). In other words, he could not derive the correct underlying phrase structure of the sentence he had read. Several years later, as a seventh grader, John had made some strides in reading comprehension and in writing composition, but generating grammatically correct written sentences was still a laborious task. After reading an article in the paper about insurance companies refusing claims and dropping clients after a busy hurricane season, John wrote a summary of 12 sentences. Six of the 12 sentences had one or more morphosyntactic errors (marking of tense, aspect, number, agreement, and possession), and another 7 had other serious problems that included omission of clausal verbs and obligatory arguments, as shown in the following three examples (spelling has not been corrected).

1. They were losing there policy because of global warming that cause hurricane.
2. Every time a hurricane or a natural disaster and the insurance company had to pay they would lose money.
3. Then they should never deiced to do this if they wasn't go to pay they for damaged that the hole purpose of home owners insurance.

Evidence-Based Intervention for Grammatically Based
Specific Language Impairment

Grammatically based interventions should be carried out *in the service of* broader outcomes of better listening, speaking, reading, and writing rather than the narrow outcomes of improvement on isolated grammar tasks. Facility with syntax serves the higher purpose of effective communication, particularly in academic settings where grammar can be very complex as is the case with the language of science described earlier. If a child or adolescent is unable to comprehend a text that contains object relative clauses (e.g., *the reaction that the oil spill caused locally echoed across the country*) or writes text with so many grammatical errors that the reader never "gets to" the content, interventions that alleviate both situations are needed.

Focused stimulation. Unfortunately for both Shannon and John, the bulk of the intervention research available for grammatically based impairments has been conducted with younger children with a narrow focus of correcting morphosyntactic errors in oral language production. Evidence supports focused stimulation (FS) that provides language models of target forms at higher-than-normal frequencies within meaningful communicative contexts (for reviews, see Fey, Long, & Finestack, 2003; Ellis Weismer & Robertson, 2006). Although outcome measures usually involve tallying target forms used in production, the emphasis in a FS approach is on *input*; the child may or may not be asked to produce the target via direct imitation (*say, he walked*) or some other cuing format (e.g., a cloze cue: *yesterday he* _____ (target: past tense form of verb *walk*). Most investigations of FS are efficacy studies (well-controlled experimental studies conducted under ideal conditions that measure short-term outcomes) as opposed to effectiveness studies (intervention carried out under more "everyday" conditions with broader outcome measures). Variables receiving attention include whether or not the child is prompted to say the target, stimulus parameters such as stress or linguistic context (e.g., moving the target copula BE form to the front of the sentence in a question), and parent or clinician-delivered protocols. Generalization pathways have also received attention. For example, if one exemplar of a grammatical category is stimulated, do other forms in that category change (e.g., if the target is auxiliary *is*, does auxiliary *are* change as well) (Leonard, Camarata, Pawtowska, & Camarata, 2006). Ample evidence exists that FS intervention brings about increased rates of correctly produced syntactic target forms in preschool children.

Several investigators have adapted FS principles in paradigms designed to bring about higher rates of the oral production of complex sentences in older children with SLI. These studies may have more applicability to Shannon and John. Johnson and colleagues (1999) targeted increased use of modal verbs (e.g., *might, should*), verb complement clauses (*I wish she would …*), and relative clauses (*I want the tape recorder that has its own microphone*) in a small group of school-age children with SLI. Clinicians embedded target forms in a conversational context (about pictures) at a rate of 2–5 times/ minute over an 8-session program. Compared with baseline rates, at posttesting children more than doubled their rate of production of targets, and higher rates were maintained in 75% of the comparisons one month posttreatment. In another study (Gummersall & Strong, 1999), children with SLI, ages 8–19 years, were randomly assigned two narrative retell conditions. In the maximum support condition, between listening to the story and retelling it, participants heard each sentence of the story again and repeated it. The sentences were constructed to contain a variety of subordinate clauses characteristic of higher-level language. Compared with those who did not have this type of support, children in the maximum support condition produced twice as many subordinate clauses when retelling the story. Both of these studies could be considered feasibility studies, showing that when children hear (or hear and repeat) these types of advanced structures as part of an interactive activity with an adult, they subsequently produce the same structures at a higher rate.

Explicit teaching of grammatical targets. Several studies have adopted a more direct approach to teaching syntax in older children with SLI. The four investigations summarized in this section all used a "meta" approach that incorporated explicit teaching of how the grammatical targets "work." Structures were "called by their names" (e.g., *in this relative clause...*), written out, color-coded, illustrated with arrows and movables. Children responded in written as well as spoken modalities.

The first study was conducted classroom-wide rather than under laboratory conditions. Hirschman (2000) targeted the increased use of subordinate clauses (adverbial, relative, nominal, and nonfinite clauses) in LI children. Participants were third and fourth grade classrooms in two state-funded specialized schools in Israel that admitted children with specific learning disabilities, the vast majority meeting criteria for SLI. Four classrooms received the intervention and four (control) classrooms did not. Intervention (55 sessions in 9 months) was directed to the entire class (10–15 students) and consisted of teaching a basic framework of what constitutes a sentence, basic elements of sentences (SVO), simple versus complex sentences, and identification of subordinate conjunctions. Then, using Aesop's Fables, students practiced identifying complex sentences, decomposing them into simple sentences, and the opposite, sentence combining (SC). The outcome measure was a tally of subordinate clauses in narrative language samples, oral and written. Results at post-testing, conducted three months after the conclusion of intervention, confirmed significantly higher frequencies of subordinate clauses for treated students. Untreated students showed virtually no change.

SLI students with the poorest use of complex sentences pretreatment made the most gains.

The next two studies, also "meta" in approach, were tied to a specific theoretical perspective. Each investigation was designed to bolster complex grammatical structures symptomatic of a domain-specific (representational) view of a subset of children with SLI. Ebbels and van der Lely (2001) taught comprehension and production of passives (e.g., *the cat was chased by the dog*) and wh-questions (e.g., *which pig is the cow following?*) to four children with severe SLI, ages 11–14 years, using visual cues in the form of shapes, colors, and arrows. For example, when teaching comprehension with these visual enhancements, the participants were taught to (a) identify gaps in the sentence, (b) find the moved constituent (i.e., wh-word), and (c) assign a syntactic/thematic role (e.g., subject or object) to that word. As needed, intervention was individualized according to session-by-session data. Three out of four children improved significantly, based on pre-post comparisons. Ebbels, van der Lely, and Dockrell (2007) continued with "meta" teaching methods in a larger study of 27 adolescents ($M = 13$; 4 years) with SLI. The instructional target was verb argument structure. Argument structure refers to the number and type of "arguments" (e.g., subject, object) obligated by a particular verb. In this study, participants were randomly assigned to three treatment groups. Two groups were variations on a teaching protocol constructed to test two competing theories about how argument structure develops, and the third was a control group that received no treatment. Participants in both treatment groups made significant gains. Progress, however, was defined narrowly as generalization to sentences with verbs not explicitly used in the treatment; the authors did not test more general language effects.

In the fourth study, Levy and Friedmann (in press) worked with a 12-year-old adolescent with SLI to explicitly teach structures predicted to be problematic due to their grammatical complexity. This sixth grade boy was a native speaker of Hebrew. An extensive set of tests encompassing comprehension, repetition, and production (oral and written responses) was devised as pre-post measures of relative clauses (subject and object), object wh-questions, focalization (OVS structures in Hebrew), and verb movement (also a Hebrew-specific structure). Building upon the boy's strengths in understanding argument structure (i.e., various obligatory roles assumed by categories of verbs), he was taught how target structures "worked" using explicit terminology and visual symbols. Post-testing confirmed significant improvements after 16 sessions of treatment spanning 6 months; indeed, performance matched that of controls (adolescents without impairments) for some structures, and training generalized to untreated structures predicted by linguistic theory. Performance was maintained at

10 months post-treatment testing. Neither of the last two treatment studies summarized attempted to determine whether or how these newly acquired oral grammatical skills impacted broader academic performance.

Returning to the cases of Shannon and John, how might intervention approaches advance their knowledge of morphosyntax (Shannon), and the complex language structures that they are encountering in their classrooms and textbooks (both cases)? Shannon's difficulties with morphosyntax, specifically tense marking on verbs, could be treated by a FS approach that is altered to take advantage of the fact that she is a beginning reader and writer. She could sort written words into marked/unmarked verb groups, advancing to identification work in real texts as soon as possible. Of course, she could be asked to repeat/"read" these words (and the sentences) as well, eventually advancing to story generation tasks that call for past tense forms of verbs, with cues faded over time. Both Shannon and John could benefit from explicit teaching of complex sentence forms similar to the paradigms cited in these studies. As shown in John's question example (Box 4.2), he incorrectly parsed sentences with postmodifying phrases or relative clauses that interrupted the main clause subject and verb. For him, an explicit explanation, training, and testing strategy applied to relative clauses (Levy & Friedmann, in press) would seem to have potential.

Pattern 2: Inferencing and Comprehension Impairment

In general, children with a comprehension-specific impairment have inferencing and perspective-taking problems (Cain & Oakhill, 1998, 2007; Cain, Oakhill, Barnes, & Bryant, 2001). "Getting the gist" of what is spoken or read requires continuous cycles of monitoring comprehension, inferencing shifts, and the coordination and integration of the multiple perspectives that authors express in a text, which may differ from one's own beliefs. Perspective-taking is also implicated in syntactic development as "Grammar emerges from conversation as a method for supporting accurate tracking and switching of perspective" (MacWhinney, 2005, p. 125). The outcome of this continual interface between the discourse and syntactic systems is active construction of text that has adequate, appropriate, and coherent representation (Cain & Oakhill, 2007), whether spoken or written (Caccamise & Snyder, 2005). No study has explicitly examined perspective-taking (often referred to as theory of mind) and language impairment in students with a specific comprehension deficit. In fact, only two studies have explored different aspects of perspective-taking in small samples of preschool-age (Miller, 2001) or school-age children (Farmer, 2000) with SLI. Although reciprocal relationships seem to hold between the development of perspective-taking and the growth of the oral language register (Miller, 2006; Milligan, Astington, & Dack, 2007), the focus here is not perspective-taking but rather inferencing in LI.

Inferencing in language impairment

Inferencing is a far from easy concept to define. In its broadest meaning, inferencing is a process for drawing conclusions. It entails relational comparison
of concepts (Keane & Costello, 2001). Something already known (the source
domain) is linked to something to be known (the target domain) and then
combined into a shared schema (Baldwin & Saylor, 2005). This integrated
representation then permits comprehending what is unstated (or "reading
between the lines"). When inferencing has been assessed in children with
known LI, the design is usually cross-sectional with the medium of assessment typically oral story (narrative) comprehension. Results have been mixed
(Bishop & Adams, 1992; Botting & Adams, 2005), perhaps due to variations
in sample size, methodology, or the nature of group comparisons (e.g., LI
versus high functioning autism) (Norbury & Bishop, 2002).

The strongest evidence to date on potential links among reading comprehension, inferencing, and an underlying LI comes from a longitudinal investigation by Catts et al. (2006) that began in kindergarten with reassessments
in grades 2, 4, and 8. In grade 8, two measures of oral discourse comprehension were administered in addition to the assessment of other aspects of oral
language. Readers were then classified into three groups: (a) A specific comprehension deficit ($n = 57$; performance below the 25th percentile in reading
comprehension and above the 40th percentile in word recognition); (b) poor
decoders ($n = 27$; performance below the 25th percentile on word recognition and above the 40th percentile in reading comprehension); and (c) typical reading comprehension ($n = 98$; performance between the 40th and 84th
percentiles). Compared with the poor decoders and typical readers, the group
with a specific comprehension deficit scored less well on standardized measures of vocabulary breadth (scoring near the 20th percentile on single word
meaning) and grammatical understanding (scoring at the 30th percentile).

Although vocabulary breadth and grammatical processing were factors
influencing inferencing ability, Catts et al. (2006) found that the greater barrier to oral and reading comprehension for the participants with a specific
comprehension deficit involved discourse comprehension where inferences
had to be deduced from information separated by four or more sentences.
Less difficulty occurred when the inference was supported by information
contained within the same sentence or an adjacent sentence. Whether this
long distance dependency problem in inferencing (see also John, Box 4.2)
emanates from working memory or sentence processing constraints or a
combination of multiple factors remains a difficult issue to disentangle. How
inferencing functions as one of several possible causal agents for the break-
down of text comprehension, as well as more literate oral comprehension,
also remains elusive. One speculation is that children with oral processing
limitations may be either less efficient at suppressing irrelevant information

and/or engage in more shallow processing than typical readers when content is less interesting or less familiar to them (Bishop, 1997).

Case study for impairment in inferencing
and comprehension: Bettina

As she completed grade 10, Bettina, who represents the second pattern of language impairment, was sufficiently frustrated by the academic discourse demands of high school that she wanted to drop out (Box 4.3).

BOX 4.3   *Bettina, an Inferencing and Comprehension-Based Language Impairment*

Bettina is a 15-year-old finishing her sophomore year in high school. Bettina had a history of oral language impairment, which was initially manifested by delayed language development and unintelligible speech. Bettina's mother was sufficiently concerned about her daughter's late talking at age 3 years that she sought a speech-language evaluation. The speech-language pathologist identified a severe articulation problem. Bettina then received intervention for her speech problem until age 5 years when she entered kindergarten. By that time, Bettina's speech had significantly increased in intelligibility, but in grade 2 she was referred by her teacher for a language evaluation because of her problems with understanding new concepts, retaining what she had just seen or heard, and expressing her ideas easily. In spite of this profile, by the end of grade 2, Bettina had acquired above-average word recognition skills (she remained in the general education classroom, but received "pull-out" services that focused on oral language components only until grade 5, when she was discharged). On the state administered achievement test first taken at the end of grade 3, Bettina tested in the 90th percentile for grammar knowledge, the 68th percentile for reading comprehension, the 53rd percentile for spelling, and the 34th percentile for vocabulary knowledge. By grade 6, Bettina's reading comprehension score was below the 20th percentile and her spelling score, which primarily assessed knowledge of derivational morphology, was at the 7th percentile. Bettina just got by until grade 10 when the academic discourse demands of science and social studies were more than she could cope with. According to Bettina, "It's just so slow to read my science or social studies textbooks. I read it once and it's just words. I have to read it again and again just to get the pictures because I'm afraid I'll get it mixed up." She also encountered significant difficulties in understanding class lectures, taking notes, and composing

(*continued*)

BOX 4.3   *Continued*

---

expository texts. On the state writing assessment in grade 10, she scored a 2.5 (on a 1–5 scale) on expository writing. A salient fact was that Bettina choose writing as medium for expressing her identity outside of school. Since age 8 years, she had enjoyed writing stories and by age 13 years she was writing relatively complex poetry. Analysis of these written narratives and poems indicated that neither did she have difficulty with generating well-formed themes or more complex sentences nor did she evidence unusual spelling problems; however, in her poetry writing there was limited use of derivations beyond simpler forms, such as –*er* and –*ly*. Unfortunately, by tenth grade Bettina had given up on her writing and on school and simply wanted to drop out at the end of the academic year.

A LT who also had a severe speech problem during her preschool years, she was deemed eligible for special education services for a learning disability and language impairment in grade 2 even though she was not having problems with word recognition. Of note, her intellectual abilities, both verbal and nonverbal, were above +1 SD based on a psychological assessment at the end of grade 1. From grades 2 through 5, Bettina managed to keep her head above water in the general educational classroom. A language reassessment at age 12 years when she entered middle school after 5½ years of special education services found that, whereas vocabulary recognition fell within normal variation, Bettina had significant difficulties inferring semantic relationships (e.g., synonyms) and in resolving sentence ambiguities, which is also dependent on inferencing to some extent. However, Bettina had fewer difficulties with pragmatic inferencing, which is related to the social uses of language, because for social situations she could draw on her situational knowledge. But the discourse demands of middle and high school content areas required more than situational knowledge. What should be done to help Bettina regain her sense of competence and succeed academically?

Evidence-based Intervention for Impairments of Inferencing

Minimal intervention research exists on enhancing the inferencing and oral comprehension abilities of students with this kind of language impairment. Three approaches, all employing small samples offer some insights: book sharing practices, explicit instruction in inferencing, and think-aloud practices.

Book sharing conversational practices. The only randomized control trial (RCT) conducted with the explicit aim of enhancing inferential comprehension in children with LI involved book sharing (van Kleeck, Vander Woude, & Hammett, 2006). A total of 30 preschool-age children identified with SLI from low socioeconomic backgrounds (*M* age = 4;2) were randomly assigned either to a treatment group or to a control group. All participants attended Head Start preschool programs and were administered the same pretest and post-test measures to assess their literal and inferential comprehension. Children in the treatment group individually participated twice weekly for 15 minutes over 8 weeks in scripted book sharing conversations with trained research assistants (the readers) whereas the control group did not receive this intervention. Three sets of 25 scripted questions were developed for the two books comprising the intervention. The scripted questions and their related prompts solicited either literal responses (70% of questions), for example, *"What's Bear doing here?"* or inferential responses (30% of questions), e.g., *"What do you think Bear's gonna do with his arrow with the spoon on it?"* (van Kleeck et al., 2006). The treatment group was significantly better than the control group on the pretest to post-test measures of literal and inferential comprehension and the effect sizes were large. However, the magnitude of treatment gains for inferential comprehension was considerably less than for literal comprehension, possibly because there were fewer opportunities for systematic experience with inferential questions (30%) than for literal questions (70%).

Direct instruction of inferencing strategies. Explicit instruction in when and how to make inferences may be a beneficial practice for school-age children. Using a RCT design, McGee and Johnson (2003) explicitly taught three inferencing strategies for narrative text comprehension to 20 less skilled comprehenders and 20 skilled comprehenders, ages 6½ years to 9 years, 11 months. Because oral language measures were not administered, it is unknown whether any of the members of the less skilled readers' group may have met criteria for a specific comprehension deficit. However, on the basis of preintervention measures, children were cross-matched for word accuracy and reading comprehension levels, randomly assigned to either an inferencing or a comprehension intervention group, and seen in groups of five for 20 minutes twice a week over three weeks. The same text passages were used for each group. The inferencing group was taught three strategies: (a) Lexical inferencing (how to search for key words that would allow them to understand the text better and the kinds of inferences that could be made from these words), (b) Wh-question generation (who, where, when, and why) to generate their own queries about the text, and (c) predictive inferences about sentence meaning based on a search of key words surrounding covered sentences. An example of this task is inferring that "Simon had hit the ball (the hidden sentence)" from the surrounding sentences, "It was Simon's turn to bat" and "It was a good hit" (McGee & Johnson, 2003). The comprehension group answered questions about texts after they read them to determine whether they would engage in predictive inferencing without specific instruction. Results indicated two patterns. First, direct instruction in the three inferencing strategies, as well as implicit instruction in predictive inferencing, benefited both the less and more skilled comprehenders. Second, the direct instruction approach influenced the rate of progress more for less skilled readers on a post-intervention standardized measure of comprehension.

Think-alouds. Think-alouds were used in an exploratory study on inferencing in 40 grade 3 children with average and below-average reading comprehension and normal word-level accuracy (Laing & Kamhi, 2002). Two "listening comprehension" procedures were compared to determine which one enhanced inference generation in story comprehension. One condition was listen-through in which children listened to two stories in their entirety. In the second condition, an on-line think-aloud procedure, children were asked to tell about what they understood about the story now after each sentence was orally read to them. Literal and text-based inferential questions followed each story. A measure of verbal working memory was also administered. Performance for both the average and below-average readers was better in the think-aloud condition than in the listen-through-condition, and the average readers produced more explanatory inferences than the below-average readers. Explanatory inferences provide causal connections between motivations and actions, and their outcomes, for example, "Why did John (who wanted to be king) kill William (his brother, who was king)?" (Laing & Kamhi, 2002, p. 445). In some sense, the think-aloud procedure, as used in this study, might allow differentiation between children who have more pervasive problems in language and literacy learning, such as oral inferencing and comprehension, versus those whose difficulties appear confined to word recognition and fluency only (Catts et al., 2006).

Think-alouds can also be used as an instructional strategy for improving inferencing in the classroom (Brown, Pressley, Van Meter, & Schuder, 1996). The text passage below referred to a fox who was a good dancer because he could waltz, boogie, and stomp. Note that the strategy the second grade teacher models applies prior knowledge (source domain) to figuring out a less familiar meaning (the target domain) by creating an analogy that is presented in a child-friendly way (Beck, McKeown, & Kucan, 2005).

> You know what? I'm thinking waltzing, boogieing, doing the stomp. I don't really know what the stomp is. But I'm thinking to myself that the stomp must be a dance because I do know that the waltz is a dance. That's when two people dance together.... And the boogie, well I know that was a dance when I was in high school and that's when you move real fast. So, I'm thinking the word *stomp* (authors' italics)...well, you can stomp your foot, and maybe that's what people do when they do the stomp. But I still think it's a dance. So that's what I'm gonna think, that.... He could do the stomp, so that's a dance. (Brown et al., 1996, p. 21)

How might one or more of these approaches to the support of inferencing ability assist Bettina? From preschool through the early elementary grades,

Bettina would have profited from sustained and challenging engagement in interactive story and informational book-sharing activities that emphasized drawing inferences about the stories. Children with this kind of language impairment seem to need repeated experience with new meanings in order to encode, elaborate on, and store them in their mental lexicon (van Kleeck & Norlander, 2008). As Bettina progressed to the middle and upper elementary grades, she would have benefited from opportunities to make predictive inferences varying in complexity from texts by identifying key word meanings in different grammatical structures (McGee & Johnson, 2003). Finally, a multiple strategies approach across the curriculum, as in science, math, and social studies (see Box 4.3), would be a vital component of an integrated intervention plan.

■ Integrated Language-Based Approaches for Developing Academic Language Proficiency

Finally, evidence is presented for two different instructional approaches that hold promise for improving both oral and written language for students like Shannon, John, and Bettina. Because these children's difficulties in comprehending and producing language material at the sentence and discourse levels have been emphasized, two programs that target semantic/syntactic features of language for which there is a reasonably sized body of evidence are now reviewed.

Fast ForWord-Language and Computer-Assisted Instruction

Although computer-assisted instruction (CAI) software for oral language intervention has been marketed for several decades, the debut of outcome data on Fast ForWord (FFW) in *Science* (Merzenich et al., 1996; Tallal et al., 1996) caught the attention of many researchers and clinicians in language intervention. Part of the excitement stemmed from the fact that the FFW protocol was directly linked to a specific underlying theoretical account of SLI. FFW was developed on the basis of research showing that children with language impairments have difficulty with auditory tasks in which crucial acoustic information is encoded in very short time frames, on the order of a few tens of milliseconds (Tallal, 1976). The solution was to stretch out in time and amplify the acoustic signal at these critical points (e.g., formant transitions of stop consonants). Then, as the child's accuracy on auditory tasks increased, the auditory enhancement was gradually cut back. The FFW regimen is delivered at an intense dosage (100 minutes/day for 4 weeks) as the child progresses through seven computer games requiring decisions on input that range from nonverbal tones (frequency decisions) in early games to minimal phonemic contrasts (in nonsense syllables and words) to morphosyntactic and grammatical distinctions at the sentence level.

Fast ForWord-Language (FFW-L), one of four current versions of FFW, is described by its developer Scientific Learning Corporation as a program to develop cognitive skills required to read and learn effectively, including phonological awareness, language structure, working memory, and listening accuracy (Scientific Learning Corporation, 2007). Because the child is listening but the long range goal is improved reading, FFW-L would seem to be a good intervention fit for the types of children that are the subject of this chapter. Indeed, as reported by Troia and Whitney (2003), over 2,000 school districts and 60,000 children have received training with the FFW software products. On the Scientific Learning Corporation web site, developers report impressive field study results of improvements in domains of oral language, reading, auditory perceptual skills, and behavior for children and adolescents who are either at-risk for academic difficulties or who have diagnosed conditions that impact school success (e.g., language impairment, learning disability, reading disability, autism, attention deficit, etc.).

Outcome measures in computer-delivered interventions. Several years after the initial publication of FFW gains for language impaired children in *Science*, Gillam, Frome Loeb, and Friel-Patti (2001) summarized a series of small-N studies on FFW outcomes. The concern motivating these studies was a perceived disconnect between behaviors trained in the FFW program and actual language outcome measures. The seven games of FFW train very different domains, some that are lower-level processing behaviors (e.g., discrimination and sequencing of tones), some that are metaphonological tasks (e.g., counting syllables in words, phoneme categorization tasks), and still others that tap sentence level linguistic knowledge (e.g., comprehension of morphosyntactic contrasts or relative clauses). Perhaps only two of the games are the critical ones. Alternatively, it could be that what is really important is an intense listening experience with a high rate of responding. Studies in this series offered further evidence that it is difficult to predict outcomes, whether the measures are norm-referenced test results or more naturalistic samples of language (e.g., conversation or narration). A case in point is inflectional morphology or morphosyntax. Even though FFW specifically trains morphosyntax, only one of nine children in these studies posted clinically relevant gains in that domain (Gillam et al., 2001).

Comparison of FFW and other CAI protocols. In spite of lingering questions about which specific language domains should improve after FFW training, researchers have pursued several broad questions about FFW outcomes. A central question is whether FFW offers any comparative advantage over other CAI protocols, also designed to teach language, but lacking the acoustic modification piece, which is the central feature of FFW. A case series study (Gillam, Crofford, Gale, & Hoffman, 2001) compared FFW and Laureate Learning Systems (LLS) software treatments for four children with language impairments (ages 6;11–7:6). All children made clinically significant gains on a broad-based language test; three children increased utterance length on a language sample (2 LLS and 1 FFW), but only one child (LLS) produced utterances with fewer grammatical errors.

Since then, two national RCT investigations have asked the same question. Cohen et al. (2005) compared FFW with a CAI package (six commercially available language-based programs) and a no-treatment condition. Participants were 77 children (mean age 7;4) with significant language impairments who met exclusionary criteria for SLI; on average, children scored more than two standard deviations below age peers in both comprehension and production domains of a comprehensive language test. All children were receiving services for language impairment in their school. Comparisons of 12 pre- and post-treatment (9 weeks and 6 months) scores revealed significant gains on comprehension and production language tests, phonological awareness tasks, and the amount of information encoded on a narrative task, for all three groups, but no additional effect of either computer-based intervention. In contrast, scores for word reading accuracy, and sentence length and complexity on oral narration did not change (Cohen et al., 2005).

The same question about the rapid auditory processing deficit explanation of language impairment motivated a second RCT study that compared the effects of three intervention strategies and one control condition (Gillam et al., 2008). In this project, 216 children (mean age 7;4) were randomly assigned to (a) FFW-L; (b) CAI, a mix of 6 phonological awareness and listening games from two commercial companies; (c) individual language intervention (ILI) with a focus on vocabulary, morphology, sentence structure, narration, and phonological awareness; and (d) a control condition consisting of academic enrichment (AE) via computer programs in math, geography, and science. Outcome measures included comprehensive language test results, language sample analyses, and auditory processing data (speech and nonspeech). Similar to the results of Cohen et al. (2005), children in this study made clinically significant changes in language as measured by pre/post-test comparisons, but there was no effect of intervention (including the control (AE) condition). Likewise, although children made gains in auditory processing skills, there was no effect for intervention.

Another computer-delivered intervention study asked the same question about the necessity of acoustically modified speech and at the same time had a more specific grammatical focus with matched outcome measures (Bishop, Adams, & Rosen, 2006). Specifically, the protocol targeted more consistent and rapid responses on a small set of grammatical constructions known to be difficult for children with language impairments of comprehension. Targets included reversible sentence constructions such as passives and comparatives. Children with specific and nonspecific language impairments between the ages of 6 and 13 ($N = 36$) were randomly assigned to one of the three groups: A computer-presented comprehension task using acoustically modified speech as in FFW-L, an identical computer-presented comprehension task without modified speech, or a no-treatment group. Outcome measures included tests that targeted these same types of constructions. Children assigned to the computer groups made some changes in speed of response, but there was no advantage in accuracy over the untrained group, nor did acoustic modification influence the results. The authors concluded that the computer-presented comprehension approach was not a viable way to train grammatical impairments in this population of children and actually halted recruitment for a second arm of the investigation.

In summary, children with oral language impairments who meet criteria for SLI make significant change on language tests when subjected to intense treatment protocols directed to a variety of language skills, whether delivered via computer games or by language clinicians. Caveats include the fact that untreated children (Cohen et al., 2005) and children who spent comparable time with more general educational computer games, rather than language games per se, also made gains (Gillam et al., 2008). It is important to reiterate that two major RCT studies have found no treatment advantage for FFW-L and its acoustic modification centerpiece, which calls into question a simple temporal auditory processing explanation for primary language impairment. In a recent study with a more focused intervention target (Bishop et al., 2006), children did not make gains under either of the computer-delivered protocols. The review of computer-delivered intervention studies has been limited to those using mainly oral language outcome measures, but there is also a literature more concerned with reading outcomes (e.g., Agnew, Dorn, & Eden, 2004; Hook, Macaruso, & Jones, 2001).

Broad Grammar Instruction for Sentence
Accuracy and Complexity

Not only is grammar a core feature of language impairment, but also it is one with considerable "staying power" (Leonard, 1998) that continues well into the school-age years where effects are often displayed even more prominently in writing (Scott, 1994). Two kinds of grammar studies have been conducted with general educational students to determine whether (a) broadly based traditional school grammar (TSG) instruction actually improves children's writing, and (b) writing outcomes improve following sentence combining (SC) training.

Traditional school grammar. TSG is the study of clause and phrase structure, parts of speech and larger units (nouns, verbs, adjectives, adverbs, predicates, clauses), and other common structures and systems (e.g., pronouns, noun-verb agreement). Controversy surrounding the effects of TSG instruction has raged for decades and has resulted in the appointment of many professional and governmental study panels. In a recent discussion, Smith, Cheville, and Hillocks (2006) identified several consensus points that are critical of TSG. At its core, TSG is an inadequate description of the way language works. Even seemingly straightforward definitions (e.g., a noun is a person, place, or thing; a sentence is a complete thought) quickly become unmanageable because elements of grammar are defined in relation to other units rather than in absolute terms. To illustrate the circularity involved, Noguchi (1991, p. 42) proposed "Isn't it much like looking up the word *structure* in a dictionary and finding the definition 'form' and under the entry for *form* finding the definition 'structure'." Another issue is that students, even good ones, have trouble learning it. TSG has no impact on students' writing (Graham & Perin, 2007).

In a recent systematic review of 11 data-based studies on the effect of TSG on writing, Andrews and colleagues (2006) asked a question about the effect of grammar teaching in English on 5–16 year olds' accuracy and quality in written composition. Although there was some variation in findings depending on the particular grammar (e.g., a transformational grammar) underlying the instructional protocol, they concluded that syntax teaching does not impact sentence level measures of the writing of secondary students. More recently, Graham and Perin (2007) published results of a more formal meta-analysis of the effects of grammar instruction on the quality of writing. They calculated 11 effect sizes. Compared with 10 other interventions, the average effect size for grammar instruction was the lowest of any writing intervention. Several caveats are in order however. The grammar instruction treatment was the control condition for 10 of the 11 effect sizes, leaving one to wonder what kind of resources were assembled for teaching grammar. Further, the one grammar intervention described as grammar *in context* posted a very high effect size. Taken together, these findings have lead professionals active in the teaching of English in regular education to propose other grammar-teaching paradigms that better situate grammar within its true discourse purpose and genre and, in addition, teach material that counteracts high-frequency writing "demons" such as fragments, run-ons, and noun-verb agreement errors (Noguchi, 1991; Weaver, 1996).

Sentence combining. In this approach students are asked to combine short kernel (one-clause) sentences into longer, more syntactically complex sentence, as illustrated:

1. Kernel: The girl was a great pianist.
2. Kernel: The girl was very young.
3. Kernel: The girl took lessons from a famous teacher.
4. Combined: The very young girl, who took lessons from a famous teacher, was a great pianist.

Depending on the structure and content of the kernel sentences, a combined sentence "forces" application of several syntactic operations including deletion, insertion, replacement, embedding, coordination, and subordination. In this example, three simple clauses are combined into one complex sentence with two clauses via operations that insert an attributive adjective (*young*) before the head noun (*girl*) and embed a relative clause. The combination of these operations eliminates two kernel sentences (the second and third kernels).

In their review of 18 studies on SC research that met their evidence criteria, Andrews and colleagues (2006) cited the 1973 study of O'Hare as the best study to date on SC outcomes. O'Hare (1973) randomly assigned 83 seventh graders to SC and control classes and measured six aspects of syntactic maturity pre- and post-test in three types of writing: narration, description, and exposition. Experimental participants obtained significantly higher scores on all measures and matched twelfth grade maturity on most measures. Quality ratings were also higher for the experimental participants. In the recent Graham and Perin (2007) analysis of writing instruction, SC was among the 11 writing interventions analyzed and fared much better than TSG, showing an average effect size (across five studies) of 0.50.

In a recent study with more and less skilled writers, Saddler and Graham (2005) extended SC intervention studies by measuring whether students actually used learned SC skills in real writing revision tasks. Combining SC with peer-assisted learning strategies (PALS), the researchers randomly assigned fourth graders ($N = 44$) to SC and control conditions. Students assigned to the SG condition scored significantly higher on pre- and post-comparisons of SG tasks (a large effect size) and on their ability to improve writing via revisions (a moderate effect size), although there was no treatment effect for quality ratings of first drafts. The less skilled writers benefited more from SC practice.

Scott and colleagues (2006) investigated the development of SC in second, fourth, sixth, and ninth graders ($N = 104$). Students saw a short story written in kernel sentence form, and were shown examples of how to combine sentences to "make it more interesting" and then set about the task of rewriting the story. To the extent that a writer combined sentences, the kernel sentence index (KSI) increased (number of stimulus kernel sentences/number of T-units). The researchers also analyzed the type of syntactic operations used to combine sentences. Results demonstrated that SC is a robust developmental grammatical skill. Floor effects for second graders who routinely rewrote kernel sentences verbatim, changed significantly by the sixth and ninth grades, when students averaged close to two kernels per T-unit. In addition, older students used a more evenly distributed mix of syntactic operations compared to younger students. SC ability was significantly associated with a detailed index of sentence complexity in a naturalistic story-writing task.

Application to practice. John, a seventh grader, has obviously had many years of TSG, but continues to write grammatically flawed sentences like those in Box 4.2. He needs to develop fluency when generating written sentences, and he needs explicit awareness when units he writes do not qualify as sentences. SC may be a good strategy to address both goals. Further, he needs to be able to edit his work on his own. Saddler and Graham's work (2005) reported that less skilled writers trained in SC successfully applied what they learned in editing. SC may also be a treatment of choice in helping Shannon to begin to combine clauses in even simple, additive ways with the appropriate coordinate or subordinate conjunction (e.g., *He wanted to play soccer, but he still had homework to do*).

■ Summary and Conclusions

During the preschool years children learn oral language in informal conversational contexts. When they enter school, they need to learn formal academic language that differs in many ways from conversation. Learning to read and write in this academic register can be challenging for children with typical development. Because reading and writing are language-based activities, the challenges multiply for children with LI whose oral language development lags behind when they are given the added tasking of learning written language. Vocabulary is less familiar, sentences are longer and harder to process semantically and syntactically, and logical connections and inferences are required across long stretches of language. Challenges for regular and special educators are compounded because different types of SLI interact in complex ways with reading and writing at different developmental periods. Finding the road that a child is on and then re-routing that child to a better literacy outcome can be difficult. And, given the protracted length of time required for any person to achieve linguistic literacy, the road is a long one.

Two patterns of oral language impairment were described, a grammatically based impairment (SLI) and an impairment in inferencing, and the research on treating these impairments was reviewed. Overall, little research has focused on treating these language impairments in school-age children, and it is rare to find studies that measure both oral and written language outcomes over time. Nevertheless, some preliminary conclusions can be drawn cautiously. Children seem to benefit from experiences that increase the frequency and saliency of problematic grammatical structures and text-level features. A better match of targeted language goals and outcome measures with academic language would advance this research. Also, children benefit from experiences that require the engagement of production processes that can be operationalized and measured (e.g., articulating implicit information in a text and using this as a basis for making predictions about additional content;

combining short sentences into longer ones; and editing written sentences). Intervention exercises devoid of connections to real texts, whether oral and/ or written should be avoided. Still, it will be necessary to give language targets and processes "names," and practice manipulating them in somewhat decontextualized formats, but *at the same time* drawing connections to "real" texts in a concurrent, flexible manner.

This exposure to real texts would ideally include the same content-specific academic language registers that students with oral language and reading impairments find difficult. Thus, a continuum of strategy instruction (Gaskins, 2005) must be tailored to the linguistic and discourse requirements of the content areas that students must master: "If interventions do not teach academic content, little transfer occurs...(and) if academic content in one domain is learned, it does not lead to improvement in another domain unless that domain is explicitly taught" (Fletcher, Lyon, Fuchs, & Barnes, 2007, p. 273). Further, the achievement of academic language proficiency for all students with grammar-based or inferencing-based oral language impairment likely depends on intervention programs that are integrated across the curriculum. For this integration to be successful, there must be collaborative diagnostic and intervention practices among school psychologists, speech-language pathologists, and regular and special education teachers. As Berninger (2008) points out, only with collaborative expertise we will be able to implement scientifically validated assessment and intervention protocols to determine *who* needs assistance, *why* they need assistance, and *what* assistance will bring them the greatest academic success.

■ References

Agnew, J. A., Dorn, C., & Eden, G. F. (2004). Effect of intensive training on auditory processing and reading skills. *Brain and Language, 88*, 21–25.

Andrews, R., Torgerson, C., Beverton, S., Freeman, A., Locke, T., et al. (2006). The effect of grammar teaching on writing development. *British Educational Research Journal, 32*, 39–55.

Bailey, A. L., Butler, F. A., Stevens, R., & Lord, C. (2007). Further specifying the language demands of school. In A. L. Bailey (Ed.), *The language demands of school: Putting academic English to the test* (pp. 103–156). New Haven, CT, Yale University Press.

Baldwin, D. A., & Saylor, M. M. (2005). Language promotes structural alignment in the acquisition of mentalistic concepts. In J. W. Astington & J. A. Baird (Eds.), *Why language matters for theory of mind* (pp. 123–143). New York, Oxford University Press.

Beck, I. L., & McKeown, M. G. (2007). Different ways for different goals, but keep your eye on the higher verbal goals. In R. K. Wagner, A. E. Muse, &

K. R. Tannenbaum (Eds.), *Vocabulary acquisition: Implications for reading comprehension* (pp. 182–204). New York, The Guilford Press.

Beck, I. L., McKeown, M. G., & Kucan, L. (2005). Choosing words to teach. In E. H. Hiebert & M. L. Kamil (Eds.), *Teaching and learning vocabulary: Bringing research to practice* (pp. 209–222). Mahwah, NJ, Lawrence Erlbaum Associates.

Berman, R. A. (2007). Developing linguistic knowledge and language use across adolescence. In E. Hoff & M. Shatz (Eds.), *Blackwell handbook of language development* (pp. 347–367). Malden, MA, Blackwell.

Berman, R. A., & Verhoeven, L. (2002). Cross-linguistic perspectives on the development of text-production abilities: Speech and writing. *Written Language and Literacy, 5*, 1–43.

Berninger, V. W. (2008). Defining and differentiating dysgraphia, reading disability, and language learning disability within a working memory model. In M. Mody & E. R. Silliman (Eds.), *Brain, behavior, and learning in language and reading disorders* (pp. 103–134). New York, The Guilford Press.

Berninger, V. W., Vermeulen, K., Abbot, R. D., McCutchen, D., Cotton, S., Cude, J., et al. (2003). Comparison of three approaches to supplementary reading instruction for low-achieving second grade readers. *Language, Speech, and Hearing Services in Schools, 34*, 101–116.

Biber, D., & Conrad, S. (2001). Introduction: Multi-dimensional analysis and the study of register variation. In S. Conrad & D. Biber (Eds.), *Variation in English: Multi-dimensional studies* (pp. 3–65). Harlow, Essex, UK, Longman.

Bishop, D. V. M. (1997). *Uncommon understanding: Development and disorders of language comprehension in children*. East Sussex, UK, Psychology Press.

Bishop, D. V. M., & Adams, C. (1992). Comprehension problems in children with specific language impairment: Literal and inferential meaning. *Journal of Speech and Hearing Research, 35*, 119–129.

Bishop, D. V. M., Adams, C. V., & Rosen, S. (2006). Resistance of grammatical impairment to computerized comprehension training in children with specific and non-specific language impairments. *International Journal of Language and Communication Disorders, 41*, 19–40.

Bishop, D. V. M., & Snowling, M. J. (2004). Developmental reading disability and specific language impairment: Same or different? *Psychological Bulletin, 130*, 858–886.

Botting, N., & Adams, C. (2005). Semantic and inferencing abilities in children with communication disorders. *International Journal of Language and Communication Disorders, 40*, 49–66.

Brown, R., Pressley, M., Van Meter, P., & Schuder, T. (1996). A quasi-experimental validation of transactional strategies instruction with low-achieving second-grade readers. *Journal of Educational Psychology, 88*, 18–37.

Caccamise, D., & Snyder, L. (2005). Theory and pedagogical practices of text comprehension. *Topics in Language Disorders, 25*, 5–20.

Cain, K., & Oakhill, J. (1998). Comprehension skill and inference-making ability. In C. Hulme & R. M. Joshi (Eds.), *Reading and spelling: Development and disorders* (pp. 329–342). Mahwah, NJ, Lawrence Erlbaum Associates.

Cain, K., & Oakhill, J. (2006). Profiles of children with specific reading comprehension difficulties. *British Journal of Educational Psychology, 76,* 683–696.

Cain, K., & Oakhill, J. (2007). Reading comprehension difficulties: Correlates, causes, and consequences. In K. Cain & J. Oakhill (Eds.), *Children's comprehension problems in oral and written language: A cognitive perspective* (pp. 41–75). New York, The Guilford Press.

Cain, K., Oakhill, J., Barnes, M. A., & Bryant, P. E. (2001). Comprehension skill, inference-making ability, and their relation to knowledge. *Memory & Cognition, 29,* 850–859.

Case, L. P., Speece, D. L., & Molloy, D. E. (2003). The validity of a response-to-instruction paradigm to identify reading disabilities: A longitudinal analysis of individual differences and contextual factors. *School Psychology Review, 32,* 557–582.

Catts, H., Adlof, S., Hogan, T., & Ellis Weismer, S. (2005). Are specific language impairment and reading disability distinct disorders? *Journal of Speech, Language, and Hearing Research, 48,* 1378–1396.

Catts, H. W., Adlof, S., & Weismer, S. E. (2006). Language deficits in poor comprehenders: A case for the simple view of reading. *Journal of Speech, Language, and Hearing Research, 49,* 278–293.

Catts, H. W., Fey, M. E., Tomblin, J. B., & Zhang, X. (2002). A longitudinal investigation of reading outcomes in children with language impairments. *Journal of Speech, Language, and Hearing Research, 45,* 1142–1157.

Catts, H. W., Hogan, T. P., & Adlof, S. M. (2005). Developmental changes in language and reading. In H. W. Catts & A. G. Kamhi (Eds.), *The connections between language and reading abilities* (pp. 25–40). Mahwah, NJ, Lawrence Erlbaum Associates.

Cohen, W., Hodson, A., O'Hare, A., Boyle, J., Durrani, T., McCartney, E., et al. (2005). Effects of computer-based intervention through acoustically modified speech (fast ForWord) in severe mixed receptive-expressive language impairment: Outcomes from a randomized controlled trial. *Journal of Speech, Language, and Hearing Research, 48,* 715–729.

Cummins, J. (2000). *Language, power and pedagogy: Bilingual children in the crossfire.* Buffalo, NY, Multilingual Matters.

Cunningham, A. E., & Stanovich, K. E. (1997). Early reading acquisition and its relation to reading experience and ability 10 years later. *Developmental Psychology, 33,* 934–945.

Ebbels, S., & van der Lely, H. (2001). Metasyntactic therapy using visual coding for children with severe persistent SLI. *International Journal of Language and Communication Disorders, 36*(Suppl), 345–350.

Ebbels, S., van der Lely, H., & Dockrell, J. (2007). Intervention for verb argument structure in children with persistent SLI: A randomized control trial. *Journal of Speech, Language, and Hearing Research, 50*, 1330–1349.

Edelsky, C., Smith, K., & Wolfe, P. (2002). A discourse on academic discourse. *Linguistics and Education, 13*, 1–38.

Ellis Weismer, S. (2007). Typical talkers, late talkers, and children with specific language impairment: A language endowment spectrum? In R. Paul (Ed.), *Language disorders from a developmental perspective: Essays in honor of Robin S. Chapman* (pp. 83–101). Mahwah, NJ, Lawrence Erlbaum Associates.

Ellis Weismer, S., & Robertson, S. (2006). Focused stimulation approach to language intervention. In R. McCauley & M. Fey (Eds.), *Treatment of language disorders in children* (pp. 175–201). Baltimore, MD, Brookes.

Farmer, M. (2000). Language and social cognition in children with specific language impairment. *Journal of Child Psychology & Psychiatry & Allied Disciplines, 41*, 627.

Fey, M., Long, S., & Finestack, L. (2003). Ten principles of grammatical intervention for children with specific language impairments. *American Journal of Speech-Language Pathology, 12*, 3–15.

Fletcher, J. M., Lyon, G. R., Fuchs, L. S., & Barnes, M. A. (2007). *Learning disabilities: From identification to intervention.* New York, The Guilford Press.

Foorman, B. R., Anthony, J., Seals, L., & Mouzaki, A. (2002). Language development and emergent literacy in preschool. *Seminars in Pediatric Neurology, 9*, 173–184.

Foorman, B. R., & Torgesen, J. (2001). Critical elements of classroom and small-group instruction promote reading success in all children. *Learning Disabilities Research and Practice, 16*, 203–212.

Gaskins, I. W. (2005). *Success with struggling readers: The Benchmark school approach.* New York, The Guilford Press.

Gee, J. G. (1999). *An introduction to discourse analysis.* New York, Routledge.

Gillam, R., & Johnston, J. (1992). Spoken and written language relationships in language/learning impaired and normally achieving school-age children. *Journal of Speech, Language, and Hearing Research, 35*, 1303–1315.

Gillam, R., Loeb, D., Hoffman, L. O., Bohman, T., Champlin, C., Thiboedeau, L, Widen, J., Brandel, J., & Friel-Patti, S. (2008). The efficacy of Fast ForWord language intervention in school-age children with language impairment: A randomized controlled trial. *Journal of Speech, Language, and Hearing Research, 31*, 97–119.

Gillam, R. B., Crofford, J. A., Gale, M. A., & Hoffman, L. M. (2001). Language change following computer-assisted language instruction with FastForWord or laureate learning systems software. *American Journal of Speech-Language Pathology, 10*, 231–247.

Gillam, R. B., Frome Loeb, D., & Friel-Patti, S. (2001). Looking back: A summary of five exploratory studies of FastForWord. *American Journal of Speech-Language Pathology, 10*, 269–273.

Graham, S., & Perin, D. (2007). A meta-analysis of writing instruction for adolescent students. *Journal of Educational Psychology, 99,* 445–476.

Gummersall, D., & Strong, C. (1999). Assessment of complex sentence production in a narrative context. *Language, Speech, and Hearing Services in Schools, 30,* 152–164.

Hirschman, M. (2000). Language repair via metalinguistic means. *International Journal of Language and Communication Disorders, 35,* 251–268.

Hofer, B. K. (2001). Personal epistemology research: Implications for learning and teaching. *Journal of Educational Psychology Review, 13,* 353–383.

Hook, P. E., Macaruso, P., & Jones, S. (2001). Efficacy of fast ForWord training on facilitating acquisition of reading skills by children with reading difficulties-a longitudinal study. *Annals of Reading disability, 51,* 75–96.

Johnson, C., Marinellie, S., Cetin, P., Marassa, L., & Correll, K. (1999, November). *Facilitating a child's syntactic style during conversational language intervention.* A paper presented at the annual meeting of the American Speech Language Hearing Association, San Francisco, CA.

Keane, M. T., & Costello, F. (2001). Setting limits on analogy: Why conceptual combination is not structural alignment. In D. Gentner, K. J. Holyoak, & B. N. Kokinov (Eds.), *The analogical mind: Perspectives from cognitive science* (pp. 287–312). Cambridge, MA, The MIT Press.

Kovarsky, D., & Curran, M. (2007). A missing voice in the discourse of evidence-based practices. *Topics in Language Disorders, 27,* 50–61.

Laing, S. P., & Kamhi, A. G. (2002). The use of think-aloud protocols to compare inferencing abilities in average and below-average readers. *Journal of Learning Disabilities, 35,* 436–447.

Leach, J. M., Scarborough, H. S., & Rescorla, L. (2003). Late-emerging reading disabilities. *Journal of Educational Psychology, 95,* 211–224.

Leonard, L. (1998). *Children with specific language impairment.* Cambridge, MA, The MIT Press.

Leonard, L., Camarata, S., Pawtowska, M., & Camarata, M. (2006). Tense and agreement morphemes in the speech of children with specific language impairment during intervention: Phase 2. *Journal of Speech, Language, & Hearing Research, 49,* 749–770.

Levy, H., & Friedmann, N. (in press). Treatment of syntactic movement in syntactic SLI: A case study. *First Language.*

MacWhinney, B. (2005). The emergence of grammar from perspective. In D. Pecher & R. A. Zwaan (Eds.), *Grounding cognition: The role of perception and action in memory, language, and thinking* (pp. 198–223). New York, Cambridge University Press.

Marinellie, S. (2004). Complex syntax used by school-age children with specific language impairment (SLI) in child-adult conversation. *Journal of Communication Disorders, 37,* 517–533.

McGee, A., & Johnson, H. (2003). The effect of inference training on skilled and less skilled comprehenders. *Educational Psychology, 23,* 49.

Merzenich, M. M., Jenkins, W. M., Johnston, P., Schreiner, C., Miller, S. L., & Tallal, P. (1996). Temporal processing deficits of language-learning impaired children ameliorated by training. *Science, 271*, 77–81.

Miller, C. A. (2001). False belief understanding in children with specific language impairment. *Journal of Communication Disorders, 34*, 73–86.

Miller, C. A. (2006). Developmental relationships between language and theory of mind. *American Journal of Speech-Language Pathology, 15*, 142–154.

Milligan, K., Astington, J. W., & Dack, L. A. (2007). Language and theory of mind: Meta-analysis of the relation between language ability and false-belief understanding. *Child Development, 78*, 622–646.

Nagy, W. (2007). Metalinguistic awareness and the vocabulary-comprehension connection. In R. K. Wagner, A. E. Muse, & K. R. Tannenbaum (Eds.), *Vocabulary acquisition: Implications for reading comprehension* (pp. 52–77). New York, The Guilford Press.

Nagy, W., Berninger, V. W., & Abbott, R. D. (2006). Contributions of morphology beyond phonology to literacy outcomes of upper elementary and middle-school students. *Journal of Educational Psychology, 98*, 134–147.

Moyle, M. J., Ellis Weismer, S., Evans, J. L., & Lindstrom, M. J. (2007). Longitudinal relationships between lexical and grammatical development in typical and late-talking children. *Journal of Speech, Language, and Hearing Research, 50*, 508–528.

Nation, K., Adams, J. W., Bowyer-Crane, C. A., & Snowling, M. J. (1999). Working memory deficits in poor comprehenders reflect underlying language impairments. *Journal of Experimental Child Psychology, 73*, 139–158.

Nation, K., Clarke, P., Marshall, C. M., & Durand, M. (2004). Hidden language impairments in children: Parallels between poor reading comprehension and specific language impairment? *Journal of Speech, Language, and Hearing Research, 47*, 199–211.

National Institute of Child Health and Human Development Early Child Care Research Network. (2005). Pathways to reading: The role of oral language in the transition to reading. *Developmental Psychology, 41*, 428–442.

Noguchi, R. R. (1991). *Grammar and the teaching of writing: Limit and possibilities*. Urbana, IL, National Council of Teachers of English.

Norbury, C. F., & Bishop, D. V. M. (2002). Inferential processing and story recall in children with communication problems: A comparison of specific language impairment, pragmatic language impairment, and high-functioning autism. *International Journal of Language & Communication Disorders, 37*, 227–251.

O'Hare, F. (1973). *Sentence combining: Improving student writing without formal grammar instruction*. Research Report No. 15. Urbana, IL, National Council of Teachers of English.

Palinscar, A. S., & Brown, A. L. (1984). Reciprocal teaching of comprehension fostering and comprehension-monitoring activities. *Cognition and Instruction, 1*, 117–175.

Pappas, C. C., Varelas, M., Barry, A., & Rife, A. (2002). Dialogic inquiry around information texts: The role of intertextuality in constructing scientific understandings in urban primary classrooms. *Linguistics and Education, 13*, 435–482.

Ravid, D., & Tolchinsky, L. (2002). Developing linguistic literacy: A comprehensive model. *Journal of Child Language, 29*, 417–447.

Rice, M. L. (2007). Children with specific language impairment: Bridging the genetic and developmental perspectives. In E. Hoff & M. Shatz (Eds.), *Blackwell handbook of language development* (pp. 411–431). Malden, MA, Blackwell Publishing.

Rice, M. L., & Warren, S. F. (2005). Moving toward a unified effort to understand the nature and causes of language disorders. *Applied Psycholinguistics, 26*, 3–6.

Saddler, B., & Graham, S. (2005). The effects of peer-assisted sentence-combining instruction on the writing performance of more and less skilled young writers. *Journal of Educational Psychology, 97*, 43–54.

Scarborough, H. S. (2005). Developmental relationships between language and reading: Reconciling a beautiful hypothesis with some ugly facts. In H. W. Catts & A. G. Kamhi (Eds.), *The connections between language and reading abilities* (pp. 3–24). Mahwah, NJ, Lawrence Erlbaum Associates.

Scientific Learning Corporation. (2007). *Fast forward-language: Product overview.* Retrieved April 19, 2007, from http:www.scilearn.com/products/language-series/index.php.

Scott, C. (2002, August). *Speaking and writing the same texts: Comparison of school children with and without language learning disabilities.* Paper presented at the annual meeting of the Society for Text and Discourse, Chicago, IL.

Scott, C. (2003, June). *Language as variety: An analysis of clausal connectivity in spoken and written language of children with language learning disabilities.* Paper presented at the annual meeting of the Society for Research in Child Language Disorders. Madison, WI.

Scott, C., Nelson, N., Andersen, S., & Zielinski, K. (2006, November). *Development of written sentence combining skills in school-age children.* Paper presented at the annual meeting of the American Speech-Language-Hearing Association, Miami, FL.

Scott, C., & Windsor, J. (2000). General language performance measures in spoken and written narrative and expository discourse of school-age children with language learning disabilities. *Journal of Speech, Language, Hearing Research, 43*, 324–339.

Scott, C. M. (1994). A discourse continuum for school-age students. In G. P. Wallach & K. G. Butler (Eds.), *Language learning disabilities in school-age children and adolescents: Some principles and applications* (pp. 219–252). New York, Merrill.

Silliman, E. R., & Scott, C. M. (2006). Language impairment and reading disability: Connections and complexities. *Learning Disabilities Research & Practice, 21*, 1–7.

Silliman, E. R., & Wilkinson, L. C. (1994). Observation is more than looking. In G. P. Wallach & K. G. Butler (Eds.), *Language learning disabilities in school-age children and adolescents: Some principles and applications* (pp. 145–173). New York, Merrill.

Smith, M., Cheville, J., & Hillocks, G. (2006). "I guess I'd better watch my English." In C. MacArthur, S. Graham, & J. Fitzgerald (Eds.), *Handbook of writing research* (pp. 263–274). New York, The Guilford Press.

Snow, C. E., & Kim, Y. (2007). Large problem spaces: The challenge of vocabulary for English language learners. In R. K. Wagner, A. E. Muse, & K. R. Tannenbaum (Eds.), *Vocabulary acquisition: Implications for reading comprehension* (pp. 123–129). New York, The Guilford Press.

Snow, C. E., Porche, M. V., Tabors, P. O., & Harris, S. R. (2007). *Is literacy enough? Pathways to academic success for adolescents.* Baltimore, MD, Brookes.

Snowling, M. J., & Hayiou-Thomas, M. E. (2006). The reading disability spectrum: Continuities between reading, speech, and language impairments. *Topics in Language Disorders, 26,* 110–126.

Stothard, S. E., Snowling, M. J., Bishop, D. V. M., Chipchase, B. B., & Kaplan, C. A. (1998). Language impaired preschoolers: A follow-up into adolescence. *Journal of Speech, Language, and Hearing Research, 41,* 407–418.

Tallal, P. (1976). Rapid auditory processing in normal and speech disordered language development. *Journal of Speech and Hearing Research, 19,* 561–571.

Tallal, P., Miller, S. I., Bedi, G., Byma, G., Wang, X., Nagarajan, S. S., et al. (1996). Language comprehension in language-learning impaired children improved with acoustically modified speech. *Science, 271,* 81–84.

Thompson, C., & Shapiro, L. (2007). Complexity in treatment of syntactic deficits. *American Journal of Speech-Language Pathology, 16,* 30–42.

Tomblin, J. B., & Zhang, X. (2006). The dimensionality of language ability in school-age children. *Journal of Speech, Language, and Hearing Research, 49,* 1193–1208.

Torgesen, J. K., Alexander, A. W., Wagner, R. K., Rashotte, C. A., Voeller, K. K. S., & Conway, T. (2001). Intensive remedial instruction for children with severe reading disabilities: Immediate and long-term outcomes from two instructional approaches. *Journal of Learning Disabilities, 34,* 33–58.

Troia, G. A., & Whitney, S. D. (2003). A close look at the efficacy of fast ForWord language for children with academic weaknesses. *Contemporary Educational Psychology, 28,* 465–494.

van der Lely, H. (2003). Evidence for and implications of a domain-specific grammatical deficit. In L. Jenkins (Ed.), *The genetics of language* (pp. 117–145). Oxford, Elsevier.

van Kleeck, A., & Norlander, E. (2008). Fostering form and meaning in emerging literacy using evidence-based practices. In M. Mody & E. R. Silliman (Eds.), *Brain, behavior, and learning in language and reading disorders* (pp. 275–314). New York, The Guilford Press.

van Kleeck, A., Vander Woude, J., & Hammett, L. (2006). Fostering literal and inferential language skills in head start preschoolers with language impairment using scripted book-sharing discussions. *American Journal of Speech-Language Pathology, 15*, 85–95.

Varelas, M., & Pappas, C. C. (2006). Intertextuality in read-alouds of integrated science-literacy units in urban primary classrooms: Opportunities for the development of thought and language. *Cognition and Instruction, 24*, 211–259.

Vellutino, F. R., Scanlon, D. M., Small, S., & Fanuele, D. P. (2006). Response to intervention as a vehicle for distinguishing between children with and without reading disabilities: Evidence for the role of kindergarten and first grade interventions. *Journal of Learning Disabilities, 39*, 157–169.

Weaver, C. (1996). *Teaching grammar in context*. Portsmouth, NH, Heinemann.

Westby, C., Dezale, J., Fradd, S. H., & Lee, O. (1999). Learning to do science: Influences of culture and language. *Communication Disorders Quarterly, 21*, 50–94.

Windsor, J., Scott, C., & Street, C. (2000). Verb and noun morphology in the spoken and written language of children with language learning disabilities. *Journal of Speech, Language, and Hearing Research, 43*, 1322–1336.

Zwiers, J. (2007). Teacher practices and perspectives for developing academic language. *International Journal of Applied Linguistics, 17*, 93–116.

■ Notes

1. Although not all authors would agree, the terms *language* and *discourse* are used interchangeably throughout the chapter to mean how people actually use language across an infinite variety of situations "to enact activities and identities" (Gee, 1999, p. 7).

2. The students who represent the oral language impairment patterns in this chapter are fictional; however, each has been constructed from the authors' and others' research, as well as clinical datasets.

5. HOW RESEARCH INFORMS CULTURAL-LINGUISTIC DIFFERENCES IN THE CLASSROOM

The Bi-Dialectal African American Child

Julie A. Washington and Shurita Thomas-Tate

> When my mama went to the store with my auntie I stayed over to my Big Mama house with my cousin and my baby brother. We was watchin' t.v. and eatin' cookies. We was playin' with our toys and ridin' bikes too. My mama came home and she said "this a really fun day." I laughed. 'Cause I was thinkin' the same thing.
>
> Story told by a 5-year-old African American girl

The dialectal variations evident in this young girl's story do not influence either the clarity or the completeness of her narrative. However, they do influence listener judgments of grammaticality and appropriateness. There are notable structural differences between her oral language and the language that she will encounter in her classroom and in storybooks and textbooks.

The morphology and syntax of her utterances are substantially influenced by the dialect known as African American English (AAE). Although they are not all evident in the passage above, this child's phonology and the pragmatics of her language are undoubtedly influenced by dialect as well. The impact of these differences on teaching, learning, and reading is receiving increased attention among researchers concerned with the reading development and overall achievement of minority children from different cultural and linguistic backgrounds. This chapter focuses on the cultural and linguistic differences apparent for both preschool and older school-aged African American children and the potential impact of these differences in the classroom context.

■ African American English

African American English (AAE) is a systematic, rule-governed dialect used by most African American people in the United States. The dialectal variations evident for AAE are well documented for both children and adults (Craig & Washington, 2006; Seymour, Bland-Stewart et al., 1998; Washington & Craig, 1994, 2002; Wolfram, Temple Adger et al., 1999). In fact AAE currently is the most widely studied dialect of English (Wolfram & Thomas, 2002). Table 5.1

TABLE 5.1 *Morphosyntactic and Phonological Features of AAE with Examples*

AAE Features	Example
Morphosyntactic	
Zero Copula/Auxiliary	*She mad/We goin' to the store*
Subject-Verb Agreement	*They was lookin' for the little one.*
Fitna/Sposeta/Bouta	*We fitna play outside/They bouta ride bikes*
Undifferentiated Pronoun Case	*Him callin' him brother.*
Multiple Negation	*He don't never wanna buy no candy.*
Zero Possessive	*I went to my Big Mama house.*
Zero Past Tense	*He said he already call his Mama.*
Invariant "be"	*He be tryin' to write all neat.*
Zero "to"	*He wanted his dog __run*
Zero Plural	*His hand fit in his gloves.*
Double Modal	*I'm am going to look for another one.*
Regularized Reflexive	*They went to the store by theyself.*
Indefinite Article	*I want a apple with my lunch.*
Appositive Pronoun	*My daddy he like to go fishin'.*
Remote Past "been"	*We been knowin' how to put that together*
Preterite "had"	*for a long time.*
Completive "done"	*We had got his bike fixed already.*
Existential "it"	*You done broke that one.*
	It was two cars parked in front of my house.
Phonological	*'cause/because*
Syllable Deletion	*ar/our*
Monopthongization of Dipthongs	*hiss/his*
Voiceless/Voiced Final Consonants	*sa-/sat*
Postvocalic Consonant Reduction	*jumpin'/jumping*
"g" Dropping	*wif/with, baved/bathed and wit/with*
f/θ, v/ð, and t/θ in Intervocalic	*Dere/there*
and Postvocalic Positions	*Pos/post*
d/ð in Prevocalic Positions	*aks/ask*
consonant cluster reduction	*pin/pen*
Consonant Cluster Movement	
I/ɛ	

presents the morphosyntactic and phonological features that have been documented for child AAE. Many, but not all, of these forms are used by adult
speakers of dialect as well.

The roots of AAE are the subject of continuing debate. According to
Wolfram and Thomas (2002), the widely held creolist hypothesis, which
asserted that the roots of AAE could be found in the languages of the African
diaspora, has been challenged as new corpora have emerged. These new data
support the neo-Anglicist hypothesis. Similar to earlier held positions, this
hypothesis asserts that early African American speech is very similar to early
British dialects that were brought to North America. AAE as currently known
is believed to have diverged considerably from its early British roots and is
now quite distinct from vernaculars used by White speakers (Wolfram &
Thomas, 2002).

What is not debated is the low status of AAE among American dialects.
African American English has been defined throughout its history by the ways
in which it is either different from or similar to Standard American English
(SAE). Unfortunately, these comparisons often have resulted in characteriza-
tions of AAE as a series of subtractions from the "standard" language form,
in this case SAE. Using this subtractive approach, the legitimacy of AAE as
a separate dialect of English was questioned by many linguists. Accordingly,
research in the mid-twentieth century focused largely on debating its legitimacy (Baratz & Shuy, 1969; Bereiter & Engelmann, 1966; Fasold & Shuy, 1970;
Labov, 1972; McDavid & McDavid, 1971; Wolfram, 1971).

Two opposing hypotheses emerged from this early research. The *deficit
hypothesis* asserted that AAE was a deficient form of English spoken by those
living in poverty (Bereiter & Engelmann, 1966). According to deficit theo-
rists, dialectal variations that characterize AAE represent substandard forms
of English that distort the morphology, syntax, and phonology of English.
Consistent with this viewpoint, the focus educationally would be to use methods designed to "correct" or eliminate the child's use of AAE forms, replacing them with SAE. Alternatively, the *difference hypothesis* demonstrated that
AAE is an equivalent system that is as complex and rule governed as SAE
(Baratz & Shuy, 1969; Fasold & Shuy, 1970; Labov, 1972; Wolfram, 1971) and
that it is used by both low- and middle-income African American children
and their families (Washington & Craig, 1994, 1998, 2002). Currently, the
difference hypothesis is widely accepted by linguists and other researchers.
In spite of its acceptance in scholarly writings, however, AAE continues to
be misunderstood and undervalued in many social and educational contexts
(Adger, 2005; Delpit, 2006).

In bilingual research, the term diglossia is used to refer to the phenomenon where a single community uses two or more languages with one language considered superior to the other (Yu Cho, 2002). In an informative

discussion of the sociolinguistic history of diglossia in Korea, Yu Cho (2002, p. 3) provides the following definition:

> Diglossia refers to a sociolinguistic situation in which a community uses two or more languages, one of which is often considered superior to the other(s). The "high" language is perceived as more prestigious, more beautiful, more logical, and more advanced. Hence, this language is exclusively reserved for education, ... and other formal public functions. In contrast, the "low" language is devalued as vulgar, informal, ... even though it is often the native language of the population for all colloquial purpose.

Germane to this chapter is the use of diglossia to refer to intralanguage differences that are governed by distinct social and cultural factors. In this context, diglossia is defined as the presence of a high and low style or standard *within* a language, where one variety is used for writing and in formal speech situations and the other in more colloquial contexts (Saiegh-Haddad, 2003). Saiegh-Haddad described the case of Arabic where children are introduced to *Literary* or *Classical Arabic* when they first enter school. Prior to school entry and outside of school, children are exposed to this "high" form primarily through television programs and news broadcasts. Consequently, the discourse and word level linguistic knowledge that children bring to reading upon school entry is distinctly different from the linguistic knowledge required to read. The linguistic distance between "high" and "low" Arabic is increasing (Saiegh-Haddad, 2003), and this is true for AAE and SAE as well (Wolfram & Thomas, 2002).

Although these authors (Saiegh-Haddad, 2003; Yu Cho, 2002) are referring to languages other than English, the issues and concerns they raise are remarkably similar to the long-standing debates about the use and relative merits of AAE versus SAE. The concerns raised by Yu Cho and Saiegh-Haddad for Korean and Arabic, respectively, provide crosslinguistic validation of this controversy and the potential impact that these linguistic differences may have on children who must become proficient users of both the "high (SAE)" and "low (AAE)" forms of English.

Of further note, Saiegh-Haddad's discussion of the impact of diglossic language use on reading achievement in Arabic children mirrors concerns raised about the impact of linguistic differences on academic achievement in school-age African American children. Importantly, in both cases, the "high" language is the language that children encounter when they go to school, and the "low" language is that which they bring to school from their home communities. This disparity creates from the outset a tension between the language valued in the child's community and the one the child will encounter in the classroom. There should be room for validation of all languages and forms of language. However, our perception of these dialects and the people who use them are frequently heavily value-laden (Delpit, 2001, 2006), manifesting in negative perceptions and low expectations (Farkas, 2003) in the mainstream culture, and unfortunately in schools. Within the cultural context of the community, however, the ability to adapt to both dialects and cultures is often viewed as an indicator of potential.

■ AAE, Children, and Reading

School Entry

At the time of school entry, most African American children, regardless of socioeconomic status (SES), are speakers of AAE (Craig & Washington, 2002, 2004, 2006; Washington & Craig, 1994, 1998). Table 5.1 presents the phonological and morphosyntactic features documented for African American children at these young ages. These features were identified using traditional naturalistic methods, primarily spontaneous language samples collected during freeplay interactions with an African American female adult, who was also a dialect speaker. In addition, all of the children resided in a midwestern urban center. Thus these AAE features are characteristic of northern AAE speakers. Oetting and her colleagues have identified additional AAE features used by young African American children who reside in the southern region of the United States (Oetting & McDonald, 2001, 2002).

The use of AAE by young children is significantly influenced by sociodemographic variables such as gender, SES, and community of residence (Horton-Ikard & Miller, 2004; Washington & Craig, 1998). Washington and Craig (1998) examined the use of AAE in a sample of African American preschool boys and girls from low- and middle-SES households. The results indicated that boys used significantly more dialect than did girls, and low-income children used more dialect than middle-income children. For all children the types of dialect features were comparable despite differences in the amount of use for each type.

The degree to which dialect is spoken by children varies widely even when children come from the same neighborhoods. In an early study, Washington and Craig (1994) found that the dialect used by their low-income, preschool-aged subjects clustered into three distinct groups based upon the density of dialect evident in their spontaneous language. Specifically, children could be reliably characterized as low users, middle users, and high users of dialect. Children in each of these three groups were found to use essentially the same AAE types, but the number of tokens differed considerably with fewer than 10% of utterances affected by dialect for children in the low user group, and more than half affected for high dialect users. In later research, the density of dialect use was identified as a significant predictor of classroom performance, and this was particularly true of reading outcomes (Craig & Washington, 2004, 2006; Craig, Washington et al., 2004).

The notion that reading outcomes may be affected by dialect use is not a new one in literature focused on African American children. It has been hypothesized that the distance between the AAE spoken by children and their families and the SAE that these children will encounter in school results in a mismatch that has a negative effect on early attempts of these children to learn to read (Cecil, 1988; Delpit, 1996; Washington & Craig, 2001). Recent tests of this hypothesis have resulted in mixed results that appear to be influenced by the child's age and schooling history. In an investigation of the relationship between African American children's knowledge of SAE and their reading achievement, Charity, Scarborough, and Griffin (2004) examined the performance of low-income African American kindergarten, first, and second grade students enrolled in public schools in three large urban centers. All of the children were confirmed speakers of AAE who also showed evidence of use of SAE utterances. Results indicated that familiarity with SAE was strongly related to reading achievement. Students who had more knowledge and use of SAE had fewer mismatches between their oral language and the language encountered in text. The authors determined further that the children's knowledge of SAE had a significant influence on teacher perceptions and expectations, both of which significantly affect student achievement (Farkas, 2003).

Connor and Craig (2006) examined the relationship between dialect and emergent literacy skills in a sample of African American preschoolers who had limited experience with formal schooling and written text. The mismatch hypothesis would predict that these children's use of AAE would serve as a barrier to development of early emergent literacy skills (Cecil, 1988). On the contrary, Craig and Connor's 4-year-old subjects exhibited stronger phonological awareness, letter-word recognition, and sentence imitation skills with increased dialect use. That is, the children who used the most dialect also had the best emergent literacy skills. Although this finding seems counterintuitive, it is not without precedent. Craig and Washington (1994) examined the complex syntax skills of low-income African American preschoolers and achieved similar outcomes. Those preschoolers whose dialect use was heaviest were also the most sophisticated language users. The findings of Connor and Craig (2006) and Craig and Washington (2004) suggest that, like young bilingual children who are proficient speakers of their native language, low-income African American children who are proficient users of their community dialect have strong language skills generally.

Thus, it appears that use of AAE may be an advantage at the time of school entry, but later in the child's schooling, use of AAE may become problematic (Charity, Scarborough et al., 2004). Indeed, in a cross-sectional investigation of dialect use in African American children in first through fifth grades Craig, Washington et al. (2005) determined that as children got older, use of dialect was a significant, negative predictor of reading proficiency. Children who continued to use dialect at moderate to heavy levels were also more likely to be reading below grade level. As the African American child moves from using language in primarily oral language contexts to trying to bridge to written language in literary contexts, use of dialect may lose its advantage and become a distinct disadvantage.

Later Schooling

Fourth through twelfth grades are important periods in language and literacy development as students move beyond the emergent stages of development and are involved in more complex uses of written and spoken language. For African American students, this development is compounded by the need to perfect a written code that many of them have yet to gain a secure grasp on orally. Regardless of the level of oral language proficiency, however, African American students who do not master important written language skills such as correct spelling and writing grammatical sentences will be at a significant disadvantage in academic settings.

Current literature recognizes the reciprocal relationship between oral and written language skills. Oral language skills provide the foundation for development of written language skills, which in turn contribute to continued oral language growth. In the early grades, differences in AAE have been noted across oracy and literacy tasks. Thompson, Craig, and Washington (2004) examined African American third grade students' use of AAE across three contexts: picture description, oral reading, and a spontaneous writing task. The results demonstrated that most third grade African American students produced a wide variety of AAE forms within spoken discourse. Although students produced more AAE in the oral tasks than they did on the written task, morphosyntactic and phonological features of AAE were present in writing samples as well. This was significant, as it is expected in English as in other languages (Saiegh-Haddad, 2003), that writing is a context within which only standard language forms are expected and/or accepted. Students whose writing samples contained the most AAE produced similar levels of AAE in their spoken language.

In a related study, Brimo (2005) examined the relationship between oral and written language use in a group of high and low AAE users. She found that fourth grade African American students used several of the most common features of AAE in their writing (see Oetting & Horohov, 1997). These AAE features included zero copula, zero regular past, zero plural, and subject-verb agreement. In addition, high dialect speakers were found to use a wider range of AAE features and at a higher frequency than did low dialect speakers in written responses.

Morphological awareness is particularly important for older students who are at- risk for reading failure because of its relationship to literacy tasks.

Phonological awareness, which is very important for young emerging readers, focuses on the smallest unit of **sound**, the phoneme, as decoding is the major task of reading for these young readers. Morphological awareness, on the other hand, is the explicit understanding of the smallest units of **meaning** in the language, including inflectional (e.g., -ing, -ed) and derivational (e.g., -ly, -tion) markers. This linguistic ability is an especially important skill to develop as researchers have shown that an increase in morphological awareness aids reading comprehension and spelling accuracy (e.g., Carlisle, 1996; Hauerwas & Walker, 2003). Morphological awareness abilities also account for significant and unique variance in reading, writing, and spelling performance above and beyond other linguistic skills (such as phonemic awareness in younger students) (Mahony, Singson, & Mann, 2000). An awareness of the meaning of specific inflectional and derivational markers, then, predicts performance on norm-referenced measures of reading and spelling.

Little is known currently about the direct impact of the morphological transformations that characterize AAE on development of morphological awareness in AAE students. It is perhaps at the level of the morpheme that the mismatch between AAE and SAE occurs for these students. Despite the presence of phonological variants in AAE speakers, investigations with younger children indicate that the development of phonemic awareness among young AAE-speaking children likely occurs as expected, unfettered by phonological variations (Connor & Craig, 2006; Thomas-Tate, Washington et al., 2004). This is not the case for development of comprehension skills. Perhaps these skills, which depend upon intact morphological awareness, are more affected by the morphosyntactic variations that characterize AAE. For speakers of SAE, written morphological skills (use of morphological markers when writing) mirror spoken morphological abilities (e.g., Green, McCutchen, Schwiebert, Quinlan, Eva-Wood, & Juelis, 2003). There is no evidence to support such a relationship among speakers of AAE, but also no reason to believe that the relationship is not valid for these speakers as well.

■ Classroom Performance

The bi-dialectal child in the classroom presents many challenges for teachers and administrators in schools. The rich and varied nature of the dialect that the African American child brings to school is well documented and is currently widely accepted for its cultural and historical importance. This acceptance is tempered by the realization that continued use of AAE once a child has entered school can have significant negative consequences for achievement. African American children who do not learn to code-switch by third grade are very likely to be lagging behind their SAE-speaking peers academically (Craig & Washington, 2006).

Breaking the Classroom Code

Code-switching involves shifting from one language or dialect to another. Code-switching is rule governed, systematic, and influenced by varied aspects of the situational and grammatical contexts (Sprott & Kemper, 1987). Variables influencing the age at which code-switching occurs and the contexts that support code-switching are much better understood for children who are bilingual than for those who are bi-dialectal, such as African American children who use AAE. The stakes are high for African American children who do not learn to code-switch. As children, their reading development may be compromised, and as adults, underemployment and job discrimination have been linked to use of AAE.

Research conducted with African American children at younger and younger ages has clarified the age at which code-switching probably emerges, although much work remains to be done on this issue. For example, Connor and Craig (2006) reported strong evidence of code-switching within a group of low-income African American preschoolers. The children in their sample who appeared sensitive to the change in language expectations at school compared to the expectations in the home/community were also the most prolific AAE users who demonstrated beginning code-switching skills.

In an earlier investigation, Craig and Washington (2004) found grade-related changes in AAE use with a significant drop in the use of AAE between kindergarten and first grade. Together with the findings of Connor and Craig (2006), these data suggest that children with the most flexible language skills present evidence of code-switching in preschool. This is the first wave of code-switchers. Between kindergarten and first grade there is a second wave of code-switching that occurs as those children who attended preschool now have had two full years of exposure to school language, or Standard Classroom English (SCE) in the classroom setting (see Silliman & Scott, this volume). For Craig and Washington's subjects, this pattern of downward shifting of AAE usage continued through third grade and then abated. Children who had not made this spontaneous shift by fourth grade continued to use AAE to a significant degree through fifth grade. It is this group of children who ultimately might be considered *code-resistant*. These children demonstrated below grade level reading performance as fourth and fifth graders (Craig, Washington et al., 2004).

One of the major challenges faced by African American children entering school is to master school language, or SCE (Craig & Washington, 2006). As discussed in the previous section most, but not all, African American children will learn to code-switch spontaneously. Those who will not are likely to be low-income, and comprise approximately one-third of school-age, low-income African American children (Craig & Washington, 2006). This persistent use of AAE even in contexts where SAE is pragmatically most appropriate certainly has some social basis, likely reflecting the isolation documented for children growing up in poverty (Vondra, 1999). Children living in poverty often do not have as many opportunities outside of school to have contact with or exposure to contexts where they might encounter AAE. Similar to the process described for Arabic by Saiegh-Haddad (2003), this lack of exposure results in compartmentalization rather than generalization of SAE.

In addition to social variables, however, those children whose use of dialect does not shift with changes in the physical or linguistic context appear also to have language skills that are less flexible from the outset than their low-income African American peers who learn to code-switch spontaneously. For these code-resistant children, the limited exposure to SAE represented by the school day may not be sufficient to facilitate code-switching. A more explicit approach may be necessary.

In apparent recognition of this pattern for a subset of children, several school districts in the United States have developed programs designed to address this issue directly. The gap in reading and mathematics achievement for African American children compared to their Caucasian American peers is the impetus for many of these programs. One of the oldest and most extensive programs is offered by the Los Angeles Unified School District (LAUSD). The Academic English Mastery Program (AEMP), originally called the Language Development Program for African American Students (LDPAAS), was started in 1990 in an effort to provide "… appropriate language instruction for students who did not speak Mainstream American English" (LAUSD, 2003). Since its inception, the program has been expanded to include children who are English Language Learners. The AEMP describes its focus as incorporating into the curriculum instructional strategies that facilitate learning both standard American English and academic English and increased literacy and academic achievement. This curriculum is to be implemented into an instructional environment that is accepting, affirming, and accommodating of the home language and culture of the students.

Offering programs such as the AEMP is often politically charged, as demonstrated by the visceral response nationally during the Ebonics controversy (Wolfram, 1997). The low status of AAE among English dialects is frequently at the root of these controversies. The sensitive nature of such program offerings aside, the importance of these programs to code-resistant children is undeniable. More research is needed to evaluate the success of these programs, but the wisdom of providing explicit attention to code-switching for children who do not code-switch spontaneously seems clear. As the AEMP statement above highlights, however, teaching these skills in an affirming respectful way is as important as providing the skills themselves.

Teacher Perceptions and Expectations

Some African American children start preschool and kindergarten with poor school readiness skills, including deficits in oral language, emergent literacy, and other academic skill areas (Farkas, 2003). In a landmark study of vocabulary growth in Caucasian American middle-income and African American low-income children, Hart and Risley (1995) demonstrated a significant and intractable gap in vocabulary growth between these two populations, but the differences may be related to income level and dialect differences. The African American children began school with vocabularies that were significantly smaller than their Caucasian American counterparts, and this was influenced to a large extent by the amount of talk in their homes. African American children reportedly begin elementary school one year behind their White peers and graduate approximately four years behind these students (Phillips, Crouse et al., 1998). African American children enter fourth grade with less knowledge than their peers and show lower academic achievement in all grade levels.

Unfortunately for African American children these poor performances and poor preparation have a direct impact on the classroom teachers' perception of their ability. By implication, these perceptions negatively impact teacher expectations (Farkas, 2003; Ferguson, 1998). In schools where low-income African American children predominate, a less demanding curriculum is often taught, thus reducing the opportunity to learn. Ferguson (1998) concluded that the expectations and perceptions of teachers have helped sustain the achievement gap, and in some cases have worked to expand it.

For children who are bi-dialectal these low expectations are compounded by the presence of dialect forms that are often perceived to represent poor English, and reflect badly on the child's academic potential (Washington & Craig, 2001). Combined with the gap in world knowledge and early learning, the presence of dialect creates a seemingly daunting task for the classroom teacher. Washington and Craig (2006) surveyed teachers of African American children using a questionnaire format to determine their beliefs about the potential of their first through fifth grade African American students. Teachers overwhelmingly equated students' potential with their current school performance. This is not good news for African American students who enter school with poor knowledge and below average skills. If teachers believe that the child's current performance level is the extent of their abilities, then African American students have little chance of improving to the levels of their more privileged peers. It is unlikely that teachers will challenge them.

All children are more successful when they have warm relationships with their teachers. Boys, minorities, and children from low-income families are least likely to have these kinds of relationships with their teachers (Vondra, 1999). Getting teachers to see beyond the low-income African American child's current level of low functioning is the first step toward improving performance in the classroom for many of these students. These students frequently come from homes with low educational levels, high mobility, and poor organization. Accordingly, teachers must engage parents in the educational process if they are to be successful in reaching students whose skill levels are below age expectations.

■ Classroom Intervention

Although low teacher expectations and low acceptance of dialectal variations have been identified in this chapter and elsewhere as contributing to
poor outcomes for African American students, the actions (or inactions) of
most teachers more likely reflect few options and poor knowledge than any
specific intent to undermine achievement. Despite all that has been written
about AAE, there is little guidance in the literature for teachers with regard
to reading and writing instruction, code-switching, and African American
children in classrooms. Programs such as AEMP have been initiated with
some success, but have not had the impact that was hoped when they were
designed. Educational programs that succeed with children from diverse language backgrounds have some general characteristics that are widely agreed
to be successful. Ladson-Billings (1995) referred to these teaching methods as
"*culturally relevant pedagogy*." These teaching methods are generally agreed
to involve acknowledgment and inclusion of the child's cultural language in
the classroom (Sheets, 1995). Culturally relevant methods move away from
compensatory and remedial approaches, toward approaches that are academically rigorous and challenging (Ladson-Billings, 1995; Sheets, 1995), These
approaches also identify gaps in learning and fill those gaps in the context
of teaching rather than decontextualizing these concepts as separate lessons
in the curriculum (Sheets, 1995). These principles apply as well to language
programs focused on developing strong literacy and language skills.

In the case of AAE, Fogel and Ehri (2006) demonstrated that the first
important step before initiating intervention is to institute a teacher education program focused on familiarizing classroom teachers with the features
of dialect. Often teachers who use SAE and teach many African American
children are aware that there are systematic, identifiable differences in the
spoken language of their students. Nonetheless, these teachers benefit from
being introduced to the specific features of AAE and the impact that these
may have on reading and writing skills for their students. This teacher education step is of increased importance for teachers who have very few African
American students in their school or classroom. For these teachers the fact
that there are differences may be obvious, but the patterns in those differences
may be less clear and difficult to identify. In such cases, AAE may be viewed
as poor English and attempts to change it less sensitive to the cultural differences represented by these linguistic forms. Fogel and Ehri (2006) found that
teacher education significantly increases sensitivity.

In an investigation of code-switching instruction with 89 third and fourth
grade African American children (Fogel & Ehri, 2000), three approaches to
teaching AAE-speaking children to use SAE in their writing were examined.
Six common AAE forms were targeted: possessive 's,' past tense 'ed,' third
person singular 's,' plural 's,' indefinite article 'a,' and subject/verb agreement.

Results indicated that the teaching condition involving integration of exposure to story structure, instruction on the rules of SAE, and guided practice changing sentences from AAE to SAE was most effective for teaching code-switching in writing. Eighty-one percent of students achieved mastery ($\geq$ 65% use of SAE in obligatory contexts) using this teaching approach.

These outcomes support the findings of others that demonstrate that the most effective methods for achieving language and academic change with African American children are methods that

1. challenge students and accept that they are competent, sophisticated language users who will benefit from being taught language change strategies;
2. start with the students' community language and teach students to contrast their typical language use with the forms being introduced in the classroom. It is not always clear which features are most important to target. It is often helpful to examine students' writing to determine which AAE forms are most prevalent across the group;
3. provide opportunities for active, repeated practice transforming AAE sentences to SAE. Practice increases the saliency and rule-learning of students;
4. use written language as a bridging context for teaching SAE in oral language (Craig & Washington, 2006). That is, teaching code-switching in writing provides a natural "bridge" for explicit teaching of SAE in oral language contexts;
5. provide instruction in use of SAE in ecologically valid, contextualized classroom contexts rather than in separate, decontextualized supplemental instructional contexts; and,
6. above all else, affirm rather than devalue the language of the African American child.

■ Summary

African American children who speak AAE encounter many challenges when they enter school and are faced with negotiating the language of the school. Some of these challenges are directly related to learning school language, while others relate more indirectly to overcoming the misperceptions about dialect use imposed by society and schools. Children who learn to code-switch will be at a tremendous advantage when learning to read and are more likely to be successful academically. Most children will code-switch spontaneously, whereas others will require either more frequent exposure to SAE to learn to code-switch, or they will need direct code-switching instruction. Future research is important for determining the appropriate timing for introduction of explicit teaching of code-switching. Would all African American students benefit from dialect instruction? Can dialect be taught at young ages, before reading instruction is initiated? What approach works best, for which students, and at what age? These are all important questions to address.

AAE is largely devalued in schools. Children who use dialect, particularly those who are heavier users, may experience negative responses from teachers who do not understand this community language form and who may believe that it limits a child's potential. Although there is evidence that AAE may have a negative impact on reading, the dialect itself does not limit overall potential. Instead it should influence the way that we approach reading instruction. Training future teachers to see and to nurture the potential of all students is critical. In addition, teaching teachers to recognize and appreciate AAE is important for changing teacher attitudes (Fogel & Ehri 2006). Fogel and Ehri (2006) found that teacher responses to students' use of AAE were more positive when they were more familiar with the forms that AAE could take. Improving teacher awareness should have a positive impact on both perceptions of dialect and expectations for the students who use it.

■ References

Adger, C. T. (2005). Language varieties in the school curriculum: Where do they belong and how will they get there? In D. J. Ramirez (Ed.), *New perspectives on language and education*. Buffalo, NY, Multilingual Matters.

Baratz, J., & Shuy, R. (1969). *Teaching black children to read*. Washington, DC, Center for Applied Linguistics.

Bereiter, C., & Engelmann, S. (1966). *Teaching disadvantaged children to read*. Englewood Hills, NJ, Prentice Hall.

Brimo (2005). Relationship between African American English and Writing Expositions by 4th grade students. Unpublished honor's thesis, Florida State University, Tallahassee, Florida.

Carlisle, J. F. (1996). An exploratory study of morphological errors in children's written stories. *Reading and Writing, 8*, 61–72.

Cecil, N. L. (1988). Black dialect and academic success: A study of teacher expectations. *Reading Improvement, 25*, 34–38.

Charity, A. H., & Scarborough, H. et al. (2004). Familiarity with school English in African American children and its relation to early reading achievement. *Child Development, 75*, 1340–1356.

Connor, C. M., & Craig, H. K. (2006). African American preschoolers' language, emergent literacy skills, and use of African American English: A complex relation. *Journal of Speech, Language, and Hearing Research, 49*, 771–792.

Craig, H. K., & Washington, J. A. (1994). The complex syntax skills of poor, urban, African American preschoolers at school entry. *Language, Speech, and Hearing Services in Schools, 25,* 171–180.

Craig, H. K., & Washington, J. A. (2002). Oral language expectations for African American preschoolers and kindergartners. *American Journal of Speech-Language Pathology, 11,* 59–70.

Craig, H. K., & Washington, J. A. (2004). Grade-related changes in the production of African American English. *Journal of Speech, Language and Hearing Research, 47,* 450–463.

Craig, H. K., & Washington, J. A. (2006). Malik goes to school: Examining the language skills of African American students from preschool—5th grade. Mahwah, NJ, Lawrence Erlbaum Associates.

Craig, H. K., & Washington, J. A. et al. (2004). Performances of elementary grade African American students on the gray oral reading tests. *Language, Speech, and Hearing Services in Schools, 35,* 141–154.

Craig, H. K., & Washington, J. A. et al. (2005). Oral language expectations for African American children: Grades 1–5. *American Journal of Speech-Language Pathology, 14,* 119–130.

Delpit, L. (2001). The politics of teaching literate discourse. In E. Cushman, E. R. Kintgen, B. M. Kroll, & M. Rose (Eds.), *Literacy: A critical sourcebook* (pp. 545–554). Boston, Bedford/St. Martin's.

Delpit, L. (2006). *Other people's children: Cultural conflict in the classroom (revised).* New York, New Press.

Delpit, L. D. (1996). *Other people's children: Cultural conflict in the classroom.* New York, W.W. Norton.

Farkas, G. (2003). Racial disparities and discrimination in education: What do we know, how do we know it, and what do we need to know? *Teachers College Record, 105,* 1119–1146.

Fasold, R., & Shuy, R. (1970). *Teaching standard English in the inner city.* Washington, DC, Center for Applied Linguistics.

Ferguson, R. (1998). Teachers' perceptions and expectations and the black-white test score gap. In J. Christopher & M. Phillips (Eds.), *The black-white test score gap* (pp. 273–317). Washington, DC, The Brookings Institution.

Fogel, H., & Ehri, L. (2000). Teaching elementary students who speak black English vernacular to write in standard English: Effects of dialect transformation practice. *Contemporary Educational Psychology, 25,* 212–235.

Fogel, H., & Ehri, L. (2006). Teaching African American English forms to standard American English-speaking teachers: Effects on acquisition, attitudes and responses to student use. *Journal of Teacher Education, 57,* 1–17.

Hart, B., & Risley, T. (1995). *Meaningful differences in the everyday experience of young American children.* Baltimore, MD, Brookes.

Hauerwas, L. B., & Walker, J. (2003). Spelling of inflected verb morphology in children with spelling deficits. *Learning Disabilities Research and Practice, 18,* 25–35.

Horton-Ikard, R., & Miller, J. (2004). It is not just the poor kids: The use of AAE forms by African-American school-aged children from middle SES communities. *Journal of Communication Disorders, 37*, 467–487.

Labov, W. (1972). *Language in the inner city: Studies in the black English vernacular.* Philadelphia, University of Pennsylvania Press.

Ladson-Billings, G. (1995). But that's just good teaching: The case for culturally relevant pedagogy. *Theory into Practice, 34*, 159–165.

LAUSD. (2003). Academic English mastery program (AEMP). Retrieved, September 27, 2007, from http://www.learnmedia.com/aemp/index.html.

Mahony, D., Singson, M., & Mann, V. (2000). Reading ability and sensitivity to morphological relations. *Reading and Writing, 12*, 191–218.

McDavid, R. I. , & McDavid, V. G. (1971). The relationship of the speech of American negroes to the speech of whites. In W. Wolfram, N. Clarke, & H. Nona (Eds.), *Black-white speech relationships* (pp. xiii, 161). Oxford, England IED linguistics.

Oetting, J. B., & Horohov, J. E. (1997). Past-tense marking by children with and without specific language impairment. *Journal of Speech, Language and Hearing Research, 40*, 62–74.

Oetting, J. B., & McDonald, J. L. (2001). Nonmainstream dialect use and specific language impairment. *Journal of Speech, Language and Hearing Research, 44*, 207–223.

Oetting, J. B., & McDonald, J. L. (2002). Methods for characterizing participants' nonmainstream dialect use in child language research. *Journal of Speech, Language and Hearing Research, 45*, 505–518.

Phillips, M., & J. Crouse et al. (1998). Does the black-white test score gap widen after children enter school. In C. Jencks & M. Phillips (Eds.), *The black-white test score gap* (pp. 229–272). Washington, DC, Brookings Institution Press.

Saiegh-Haddad, E. (2003). Linguistic distance and initial reading acquisition: The case of Arabic diglossia. *Applied Psycholinguistics, 24*, 431–451.

Seymour, H. N., & Bland-Stewart, L. et al. (1998). Difference versus deficit in child African American English. *Language, Speech, and Hearing Services in Schools, 29*, 96–108.

Sheets, R. H. (1995). From remedial to gifted: Effects of culturally centered pedagogy. *Theory into Practice, 34*, 186–193.

Sprott, R. A., & Kemper, S. (1987). The development of children's code-switching: A study of six bilingual children across two situations. In E. R. Pemberton, M. A. Sell, & G. B. Simpson (Eds.), *Working papers in language development, 2* (pp. 116–134). Lawrence, KS, The University of Kansas Press.

Thomas-Tate, S., & Washington, J. A. et al. (2004). Standardized assessment of phonological awareness skills in low-income African American first graders. *American Journal of Speech-Language Pathology, 13*, 182–190.

Vondra, J. I. (1999). Commentary for schooling and high-risk populations: The Chicago longitudinal study. *Journal of School Psychology, 37*, 471–479.

Washington, J. A., & Craig, H. K. (1994). Dialectal forms during discourse of urban, African American preschoolers living in poverty. *Journal of Speech and Hearing Research, 37*, 816–823.

Washington, J. A., & Craig, H. K. (1998). Socioeconomic status and gender influences on children's dialectal variations. *Journal of Speech and Hearing Research, 41*, 618–626.

Washington, J. A., & Craig, H. K. (2001). Reading performance and dialectal variation. In J. L. Harris, A. G. Kahmi, & K. G. Pollock (Eds.), *Literacy in African American communities* (pp. 147–168). Mahwah, NJ, Lawrence Erlbaum Associates.

Washington, J. A., & Craig, H. K. (2002). Morphosyntactic forms of African American English used by young children and their caregivers. *Applied Psycholinguistics, 23*, 209–231.

Wolfram, W. (1971). Black-white speech differences revisited. In W. Wolfram, N. Clarke, & H. Nona (Eds.), *Black-white speech relationships* (pp. xiii, 161). Oxford, England, IED Linguistics.

Wolfram, W. (1997). Ebonics and linguistic science: Clarifying the issues. Retrieved, October 1, 2007, from http://www.cal.org/topics/dialects/wolfram.html.

Wolfram, W., Temple Adger, C. et al. (1999). *Dialects in schools and communities*. Mahwah, NJ, Lawrence Erlbaum Associates.

Wolfram, W., & Thomas, E. R. (2002). *The development of African American English*. Oxford, Blackwell Publishing.

Yu Cho, Y.-M. (2002). Diglossia in Korean language and literature: A historical perspective. *East Asia: An International Quarterly, 20*, 3–24.

6. THE PREVENTION SCIENCE PERSPECTIVE

Early Intervention Research on Literacy, Mathematics, and Social Competence

Maureen Hoskyn

During their early years, children rapidly develop the foundational capabilities on which future academic and social learning depends. By the time they reach school age, the majority of children will have acquired proficiency in the language of their community (Bates, 1976; Tomasello, 2003). They will also have increased capacities to read the intentions of others, self-regulate their emotions, and problem solve and plan when presented with social or academic challenges. This system of skills and abilities expands in a rhythm unique to the individual and along multiple trajectories defined by interactions among genes, experience, and culture. Given this complexity, it is not surprising that teasing apart biological, cultural, and ontological factors that contribute to the ebb and flow of children's development over time has been difficult (Sameroff & Fiese, 2000). Nevertheless, one of the more robust findings from child development research suggests that the quality of children's early experiences predicts developmental outcomes. In the words of Meisels and Shonkoff (2000, p. 6):

> The scientific evidence on the significant developmental impacts of early experiences, caregiving relationships, and environmental threats is incontrovertible. Virtually every aspect of early human development, from the brain's evolving circuitry to the child's capacity for empathy, is affected by the environments and experiences that are encountered in a cumulative fashion, beginning in the prenatal period and extending throughout the early childhood years…the question of today is not whether early experience matters, but rather how early experiences shape individual development and contribute to children's continued movement along positive pathways.

To further develop understandings of the interaction between early childhood experience and development, researchers turn to early prevention science. That is, by experimentally controlling children's early experience on a variable of interest (e.g., instruction to increase vocabulary) and evaluating outcomes, much is learned about developmental change and whether certain capacities (e.g., vocabulary) are modifiable by experience early in children's lives. This knowledge lays the foundation upon which approaches to increase young children's school readiness and to prevent later academic and/or behavioral problems are built.

Despite having considerable potential to facilitate positive change in children's lives, prevention science is a relatively new field of inquiry. The limited work to date focuses primarily on the effects of model prevention programs on children's general development and cognitive growth and family wellness. These large-scale, early childhood prevention programs were first implemented in the United States and Canada during the 1960s and 1970s in response to growing societal attention to complex social issues and the will of governing bodies to provide funds and services to address these concerns. The most enduring of the prevention programs initiated during this period is *Head Start*, an ambitious project that began with the aim of overcoming the deleterious effects of poverty on children's lives (for a discussion on the effects of poor health and nutrition, household crowding, and birth complications on children's learning outcomes, see Wagmiller et al., 2006). Since its inception, *Head Start* has been envisioned as a comprehensive program of health, education, and social services for young children and their families. Unfortunately, the achievements of *Head Start* during the 1960s and 1970s fell well short of those necessary to eradicate the need for special education and social welfare programs; school completion rates were pervasively low and the prevalence of crime and delinquency remained a concern (Farran, 2000; Meissels & Shonkoff, 2000). In recent years, the aims of *Head Start* have been reconceptualized more realistically as a means to promote children's well-being and development, and to maximize human capital and the long-term sustainability of healthy societies (for a review of current early learning and childcare policy and practices in North America and other countries, see Neuman, 2005; OECD, 2001).

When viewed from this perspective, prevention programs early in development have clearly met with measurable success. A number of narrative (e.g., Barnett, 1995; Brooks-Gunn, 2003; Halpern, 1990, 2000; McCain & Mustard, 1999; Mrazek & Brown, 2002; Nelson, Benner, & Gonzalez, 2003; Nelson, Westhues, & MacLeod, 2003) and meta-analytic (Gilliam & Zigler, 2000; Nelson, Westhues, & MacLeod, 2003) reviews report that well-designed and carefully implemented comprehensive programs, beginning either prenatally or very early in childhood, can have lasting effects on children's cognitive growth well into the adolescent years (Campbell & Ramsey, 1995); on their academic performance into middle childhood (Johnson & Walker, 1991), early adolescence (Campbell & Ramsey, 1995), and young adulthood (Campbell et al., 2001); and their social competence into adolescence (Brotman et al., 2005; Lally et al., 1988; Reynolds, Temple, Robertson, & Mann, 2001; Seitz, Rosenbaum, & Apfel, 1985).

Furthermore, knowledge about factors that mediate program effectiveness is growing. In a meta-analytic review of 34 studies of early prevention programs, Nelson, Westhues, and MacLeod (2003) coded 38 potential mediators, including program characteristics (e.g., type of program, program components, length of intervention, participants in the intervention), child characteristics (e.g., age of child, SES), and study characteristics (e.g., source of publication, methodological quality). Two findings from the Nelson et al. synthesis have significance for educational policy and curriculum design. First, effect sizes for programs that had either a child-focused, direct teaching component, or a centre-based educational component were larger compared with parent-centered programs without these components. Second, the magnitude of effects was stronger for longer and more intense programs compared with shorter, less intense programs. Thus, children at-risk for poor academic or social outcomes benefit from early educational activities before school entry when these activities are part of a larger early intervention initiative.

Less is known about what instructional activities within these comprehensive early education programs optimize positive learning and social outcomes for children at-risk due to biological and/or economic disadvantage. Most studies have focused on evaluating the quality of early childhood programs in a broad sense, such as the extent to which children and parents feel understood, respected, and supported, and the degree to which children have access to safe, play-based environments (Friendly, Doherty, & Beach, 2006). When program quality is defined in this way, factors such as early childhood educator training, salary reimbursement, child-caregiver ratios, and the clarity of organizational structure matter (Layzer & Goodson, 2006); but which characteristics of early educational activities within these programs prevent poor academic and/or social outcomes for young children of different ages and abilities? Also, furthering understandings about the influences that mediate children's responsiveness to educational activities would be helpful to reliably identify children most in need of further targeted support.

This chapter presents an overview of findings from selected studies of early learning that have potential to facilitate learning and social development of young children before school entry. First, an operational definition of early prevention is provided from which to view study findings. Then the procedures used to locate the studies for review and to estimate intervention effects are described. Next, findings from selected studies are organized and discussed according to three outcome domains: pre-literacy, mathematics, and social competence. The chapter concludes with a discussion of the important findings and possible directions for early prevention science in the future.

A Definition of Early Prevention

Early prevention is narrowly defined for the purposes of this chapter as a set of educational activities that facilitate children's early learning before school entry and that prevent poor academic or social outcomes. Although services to support families can positively influence children's well-being, the focus here is on educational approaches for young children in home or early learning and childcare settings. When viewed from this perspective, primary prevention can be either universal and accessible to all children or selective and targeted for individual children who require additional support to facilitate their learning and/or social development. Other forms of early prevention aim at intervening early to alter the uneven and uncharacteristic course of development for children with severe, diagnosed disabilities due to genetic anomalies (e.g., Down's syndrome, fragile-X syndrome), physical insults (e.g., cerebral palsy), or infectious agents (e.g., fetal alcohol syndrome). However, discussion in this chapter is limited to early prevention for children without severe or complex disabilities, although the instructional approaches reviewed may also benefit these children. Throughout the chapter, the words "instruction," "intervention," "treatment," "learning activity," and "educational activity" are used interchangeably to refer to planned alterations to young children's experience to improve later academic or social outcomes. Also, the term "early learning and childcare" is broadly conceived in Canadian usage to mean activities that take place in preschool, nursery school, child-care, and early intervention settings.

Selection of Studies for Review

Several different search strategies were used to find studies to review. First, keywords such as *intervention* and child**, *prevention* and child**, *early literacy* and child** were submitted to these databases: *PsychInfo, ERIC, MEDLINE, Dissertations Abstracts International*. Second, reference lists from the studies, chapters, and books located in this search were reviewed to locate additional studies. Finally, hand searches were conducted of articles published between 2000 and 2006 in *Child Development, Journal of Educational Psychology, Developmental Psychology, Language, Speech and Hearing Services in the Schools, Journal of Experimental Psychology, Journal of Learning Disabilities, Learning Disability Quarterly*, and *Early Childhood Research Quarterly*. Criteria for including a study in this review were as follows: (a) The intervention directly involved the individual child, (b) measures of child outcomes were included in the study, (c) sample children were aged 5 years or younger and had not entered Kindergarten or the first year of formal schooling, and (d) children in the sample described as "at-risk" had not received a formal diagnosis of severe social, cognitive, or physical disability. Of the 178 studies located, only 42 have sufficient data for calculating effect sizes; 36 of these studies targeted approaches to maximize children's skill development in academic domains, and 6 studies investigated activities to improve children's social competence. Notably, the most common reason for a study's rejection (i.e., 74% of rejected studies) was that the research involved children of school age (i.e., kindergarten to grade 3).

Identification of Children Vulnerable to Poor Developmental Outcomes

Children in the majority of studies reviewed were considered vulnerable to poor developmental outcomes on the basis of living in poverty or poor performance on a single or composite language measure. However, not all children living in low socioeconomic conditions struggle in school and false positives (i.e., children identified as at-risk who have good social and academic outcomes) can be expected when such broad-based criteria are used. Also, selection criteria that use cut-off scores on standardized measures of language or cognition may not be sensitive to the developmental differences that have the most impact on the academic learning of young children. Clearly, more research in this area is required to identify evidence-based identification of at-risk children early in development.

Intervention Effects

As shown in Table 6.1, an array of measures was used to evaluate the efficacy of the instructional activities in the studies reviewed. With the exception of the Peabody Picture Vocabulary Test (3rd ed.) that evaluated outcomes in 12 out of the 41 studies, use of specific standardized and experimental measures varied. Effect sizes were calculated using *Cohen's d*. When means and standard deviations were provided, the following formula was used: $d = (M_{\text{txpost}} - M_{\text{conpst}})/\sigma_{\text{pooled}}$; $\sigma_{\text{pooled}} = \sqrt{[(\sigma_{\text{tx}}^2 + \sigma_{\text{con}}^2)/2]}$ where M = mean; txpost = post-test scores of the intervention group; conpst = post-test scores of the control group; and σ = standard deviation. When no means and standard deviations on outcome measures were reported, effect sizes were calculated from *F*-tests or *T*-tests. For purposes of interpretation, an effect size of 0.20 is small, 0.50 is medium, and 0.80 is large (Cohen, 1988, 1992). As shown in Table 6.2, the effect sizes for individual outcome measures within each study reflect diversity. For each study, possible mediators of intervention effects are reported: (a) Child characteristics (e.g., age, at-risk status), (b) intervention components, (c) intensity of intervention, and (d) duration of the intervention. Findings from intervention studies to improve children's pre-literacy skills, mathematics abilities, and social competence are reviewed in reference to the possible effects of these mediating influences and previous research in the field.

TABLE 6.1 *Outcome Measures*

Measure (Author)	Description	Studies that Use Measure
Cognition		
Weschler preschool and primary scale of intelligence—revised (Wechsler, 1989)	General knowledge questions	Aram & Biron, 2004
Cooperative Preschool Inventory (Caldwell, 1974)	Knowledge of colors, shapes, letters, and numbers	Baker, Piotrkowski, & Brooks-Gunn, 1998
Language		
Book vocabulary	Receptive vocabulary: Children hear words selected from texts read and selects one of four pictures to represent the word	Aram, 2006 Hargrave & Sénéchal, 2000 Roberts, 2003 Fletcher et al., 2005
Boehm Test of Basic Concepts—Preschool Version (Boehm, 1986)	Understanding of relational concepts (right/left, widest/narrowest, same/different)	Siefert & Schwarz, 1991
Bracken Basic Concept Scale (Bracken, 1984)	School readiness; direction/position	Connor-Kuntz & Dummer, 1996
Clinical Evaluation of Language Fundamentals—Primary (Wiig et al., 1992)	Linguistic concepts	Lonigan et al., 2003
Concepts about Narrative (Neuman, 1999)	Children are asked to tell a story about a wordless picture book. Ratings and event components and overall plot are made	Nancollis et al., 2005 Neuman, 1999
Expressive One Word Vocabulary Test (Gardner, 1981)	Expressive vocabulary: Children label pictures	Arnold et al., 1994 Hargrave & Sénéchal 2000 Lonigan & Whitehurst, 1998 Lonigan et al., 2003 Whitehurst et al., 1994a

(*continued*)

TABLE 6.1   *Continued*

Measure (Author)	Description	Studies that Use Measure
Illinois Test of Psycholinguistic Abilities (Kirk, McCarthy, & Kirk, 1968)	Verbal fluency of object names: Rapid naming of pictures; phonological awareness	Arnold et al., 1994 Lonigan & Whitehurst, 1998 Whitehurst et al., 1994a Whitehurst et al., 1994b
Individual Growth and Development Indicator (McConnell & McEvoy, 2001)	Vocabulary knowledge	Jackson et al., 2006
Our Word (Whitehurst et al., 1994a)	Expressive vocabulary	Whitehurst et al., 1994a
Peabody Picture Vocabulary Test (3rd ed.) (Dunn & Dunn, 1997) --------*English Picture Vocabulary Test* (EPV; Brimer & Dunn, 1973)	Receptive vocabulary: Children hear a word and select one of four pictures to represent the word	Aram, 2006; Aram & Biron, 2004; Arnold et al., 1994; Hargrave & Sénéchal, 2000; Hatcher et al., 2004 (EPV); Hindson et al., 2005; Lonigan & Whitehurst, 1998; Lonigan et al., 2003; Neuman, 1996, 1999; Van Kleek et al., 2006; Wasik & Bond, 2001; Whitehurst et al., 1994a, 1994b
Pre-Idea Proficiency Test (Williams & Dalton, 1989)	Oral responses to questions about a picture	Roberts, 2003
Preschool Language Assessment Instrument (Blank et al., 2003)	Literal comprehension of language/inferential comprehension of language	Van Kleek et al., 2006
Preschool Language Scale-Revised (Zimmerman, Steiner, & Evatt Pond, 2002)	Expressive communication and auditory comprehension Expressive vocabulary	Bernhard et al., 2006
Story comprehension (Shatil, Share, & Levin, 2000)	Children listen to a story and are asked questions about the story	Aram & Biron, 2004
Woodcock-Munoz Language Survey (Woodcock & Munoz-Sandoval, 2001)	Picture naming, verbal analogies, letter-word identification, and writing	Jackson et al., 2006

(continued)

TABLE 6.1   *Continued*

Measure (Author)	Description	Studies that Use Measure
Phonological awareness		
Phonological Abilities Test (Muter, Hulme, Snowling, & Taylor, 1997)	Rhyme detection; rhyme production; phoneme deletion	Hatcher et al., 2004
Preschool and Primary Inventory of Phonological Awareness (Dodd et al., 2000)	Letter reproduction, nonword reading, spelling, rhyme detection, nonword spelling, phoneme segmentation	Nancollis et al., 2005
Alliteration (Aram, 2006)	Children were asked whether the first syllable of two spoken words was the same or not	Aram, 2006 Aram & Biron, 2004
Phoneme Identity a. Byrne & Fielding-Barnsley, 1991 b. Gillon, 2005 c. Rvachew et al., 2004	a. Objects are drawn and children are asked to nominate which object began with the same sound as a target sound b. Children hear a target phoneme (/m/) and are asked which word starts with the sound (dog, milk, bear) c. Children point to a picture (in an array) that represents a word/children point to a card that represents a sound when they hear that sound/children point to a card with a letter when they hear a word that starts with the sound	a. Byrne & Fielding-Barnsley, 1995; Hindson et al., 2005 b. Gillon, 2005 c. Rvachew et al., 2004
Rhyming a. Aram, 2006 b. Gillon, 2005 c. Byrne & Fielding-Barnsley, 1991 d. MacLean et al., 1987	a. Children were asked whether two spoken words rhymed or not b. Children sort from three pictures the one that does not rhyme c. Children were asked to indicate which of three orally presented words rhymed with a target word	a. Aram, 2006; Aram & Biron, 2004 b. Gillon, 2005 c. Hindson et al., 2005; Roberts, 2003 d. Lonigan et al., 2003

(continued)

TABLE 6.1   *Continued*

Measure (Author)	Description	Studies that Use Measure
	d. Children were asked whether a target picture rhymed with, did not sound the same as, or was different from two other sounds	
Print-related abilities		
Concepts About Print (Clay, 1975)	Understandings of book orientation, left to right reading practices, letter knowledge	Hindson et al., 2005; Neuman, 1996, 1999
Developing Skills Checklist (CTB, 1990)	Various questions in each domain of assessment administered to children	Whitehurst et al., 1994b
Early Word Recognition Test (Hatcher, 1992)	Pronouncing 42 words common to first book stage (of 7)	Hatcher et al., 2004
British Ability Scales, Word Recognition (Elliot, Murray, & Pearson, 1983)	Pronouncing 90 regular and exception words in isolation	Hatcher et al., 2004
Graded Nonword Reading Test (Snowling, Stothard, & McLean, 2006)	Pronouncing 20 pseudowords	Hatcher et al., 2004
Name-writing/word writing (Levin & Bus, 2003)	Written name/words ranked on a scale 1–3 to indicate the degree of graphic representation, writing like, and symbolic	Aram, 2006 Aram & Biron, 2004
Initial letter retrieval (Aram, 2006)	Children name first letter in spoken word (2–3 syllables)	Aram, 2006
Letter knowledge (Bradley & Bryant, 1983)	Children name printed letters presented on a card	Aram, 2006 Aram & Biron, 2004 Gillon, 2005 Hatcher et al., 2004 Hindson et al., 2005 Neuman, 1999 Roberts, 2003 Rvachew et al., 2004

(continued)

TABLE 6.1 *Continued*

Measure (Author)	Description	Studies that Use Measure
Pre-Literacy Skills Screening Test (Crumrine & Lonegan, 1999)	Phonological awareness, letter recognition, and word retrieval	Podhajski & Nathan, 2005
Teacher rating of Oral Language and Literacy (*TROLL*; Dickinson, McCabe, & Sprague, 2001)	Teacher ratings of child's language use (oral), reading, and writing	Jackson et al., 2006
Test of Early Reading Ability (*TERA*; Reid, Hresko, & Hammill, 2001)	Letter identification, awareness of print conventions, using print for meaning	Jackson et al., 2006
The Brief Reading Interest Scale (Oritz et al., 2001)	Parent ranking of children's interest in 11 reading activities	Oritz et al., 2001
Orthographic awareness (Aram & Biron, 2004)	Children are shown letters	Aram & Biron, 2004
Word choice (Byrne & Fielding-Barnsley, 1991)	Children are shown a word (e.g., sat) and asked whether the written word means either the correct choice or an alternative (e.g., does it say bat or sat?)	Byrne & Fielding-Barnsley, 1991 Hindson et al., 2005
Math		
Test of Early Mathematics Ability (standardized) (Ginsburg & Baroody 1990)	Concepts of relative magnitude, counting, calculation, number facts	Arnold et al., 2002
Child Math Interest Self-report (experimental) (Arnold et al., 2002)	Children's self reported interest in math toys and in numbers	Arnold et al., 2002
Social competence		
Child Behavior Checklist (Achenbach, 1992)	Internalizing problem behavior, externalizing problem behavior, total problems	Han et al., 2005 Velderman et al., 2006 Webster-Stratton et al., 2001

(*continued*)

TABLE 6.1 *Continued*

Measure (Author)	Description	Studies that Use Measure
Classroom Adaptation Inventory (Halpern, Baker & Piotrkowski, 1993)	Teacher ratings of child's enjoyment of books, reading, listening, paying attention, task orientation, self-direction in learning, seeking, and using assistance	Baker, Piotrkowski, & Brooks-Gunn, 1998
DPICS-R (Robinson, Eyberg, & Ross, 1981; revised Webster-Stratton et al., 1989)	Observational measure for recording behaviors of children and their parents in the home	Webster-Stratton et al., 2001
Eyberg Child Behavior Inventory (Robinson, Eyberg, & Ross, 1980)	36 item behavioral inventory for children 2–6 year olds	Webster-Stratton et al., 2001
MOOSES—Independent observations of teacher-child in classroom (Tapp, Wehby, & Ellis, 2001)	Classroom observation system to code children's interactions with teachers and peers	Webster-Stratton et al., 2001
Peer Play Scale (Howes, 1980)	Parent ratings of children's social competence and cognitive competence of children during play activities	Rhodes & Hennessey, 2000
Social skills rating system (Gresham & Elliot, 1990)	Problem behaviors/social skills	Han, 2005
Social Competence Behavior Evaluation (LaFreniere & Dumas, 1995)	Parent and teacher ratings of social competence, internalizing behavior problems and externalizing behavior problems	Lobo & Winsler, 2006 Webster-Stratton et al., 2001
Teacher Observation of Classroom Adaptation—Revised (Werthamer-Larsson, Kellam, & Oveson-McGregor, 1990; adapted by Webster-Stratton et al., 2001)	Social health profile—School readiness (fighting, breaking rules, harming others, refusing to accept authority, friendliness, staying on task, completing assignments, self-reliance)	Webster-Stratton et al., 2001

TABLE 6.2 *Instructional Activities to Improve Academic and Social Outcomes in Studies in this Review*

Author	N	Sample Characteristics	Treatment (T)/ Control (C) Groups	Ratio Children:Adult	Activity Length	Developmental Measure	Tx	Effect Size (*Cohen's d*)
Pre-Literacy Cognitive and Language								
Baker, Piotrkowski, & Brooks-Gunn (1998)	182 Coh1 T = 37 C = 32 Coh2 T = 47 C = 66	MN = 56.25 mo. SD = 3.9 mo.	T1: HIPPY C1: No tx control	1:1	12 months	Cognitive skills (gr. 1) Classroom adaptation (gr. 1)	Cohort 1 Cohort 2 Cohort 1 Cohort 2	0.58 0.17 0.48 nsig
Bernhard et al. (2006)	454 T = 280 C = 87	MN = 37.3 mo. SD = 13.3 mo. ELL children Low income	T1: Authoring, reading, storytelling of books + rhymes and poems + alphabet letters in children's names 2: No tx control	No info	12 mo.	Language (general)		0.45
Byrne & Fielding-Barnsley (1991)	T = 64 C = 62	MN = 55.4 mo. SD = 3.3 mo.	T1: Sound Foundations: Phoneme identity training C: language activities	4–6:1	12 weeks 12 sessions 25–30 min/session	Word choice		1.66

Study	N	Participants	Treatment	Ratio	Duration	Outcome	Comparison	Effect size
Byrne & Fielding-Barnsley (1995)	93	MN = 53.9 SD = no info	T1: Sound Foundations: Phoneme identity training (class) C1: No tx control C2: Small group (C1 and C2 from Byrne & Fielding-Barnsley, 1991)	20:1	6–12 weeks	Initial phoneme identity	C1 C2	1.10 2.75
Connor-Kuntz & Dummer (1996)	43	G1: Developing language: MN = 57.92 mo. SD = 9.54 G2: Typical language: MN = 54.7 mo. SD = 7.39 Head start C1: Developing language: MN = 59.0 SD = 7.09 C2: Typical language: MN = 50.61 SD = 4.97	Language within the context of physical activity/education	1:4, 1:6, and 1:11	24 sessions 8 weeks 30 min/ session	School-readiness Language labels/ direction and position	G1:C1 G2:C2 G1:C1 G2:C2	−0.17 0.48 0.83 1.02

(*continued*)

TABLE 6.2 *Continued*

Author	N	Sample Characteristics	Treatment (T)/ Control (C) Groups	Ratio Children:Adult	Activity Length	Developmental Measure	Tx	Effect Size (*Cohen's d*)
Crawley et al. (1999)	108	36 MN = 43 mo. 39 MN = 54 mo. 34 MN = 63 mo.	T1: View Blues Clues episode one time T2: View Blues Clues episode five times C2: View alternative program one time		T1: 1 session T2: 5 sessions C: 1 session	Comprehension of episode Entertainment questions Educational questions	T1:C1 T2:C1 T1:C1 T2:C1	0.86 1.61 0.15 0.67
Gillon (2005)	31 G1 = 12 G2 = 19	MN = 41.16 mo. SD = 3.78 mo. G1: Speech difficulties G2: Control: Not at-risk	Speech intelligibility + Phonological awareness training + Letter-name and letter-sound	3:1 and 1:1	4–6 week blocks 25 sessions (45 min/ session)	Rhyme (oddity) Phoneme matching Letter-name recognition	G1/G2 G1/G2 G1/G2	0.41 0.53 0.08
Hatcher, Hulme, & Snowling (2004)	137 T1 = 42 T2 = 36 T3 = 31 C1 = 28	M = 54 mo. SD = 3.6 mo. At-risk for reading delay	T1: Print skills with rhyme + phoneme awareness training T2: Print skills + rhyme awareness training T3: Print skills + phoneme awareness training C1: Reading alone	10–15:1	3 sessions/ week 40.82 weeks 10 min/ session	Phoneme awareness Rhyme awareness Word reading Nonword reading	T1 T2 T3 T1 T2 T3 T1 T2 T3 T1 T2 T3	0.62 0.65 0.76 0.33 0.00 −0.54 0.59 0.41 0.53 0.77 0.56 1.06

Study	N / Groups	Participants	Intervention	Format	Duration	Outcome measure	Time	ES
Jackson et al. (2006)	143 T1 = 54 T2 = 28 C1 = 32	MN = 52 mo. Low income	T1: Professional development literacy workshop (satellite broadcast) T2: Professional development literacy workshop (satellite broadcast) + mentoring C1: No tx control	Centre-based	15 weeks 44 hours	Oral language Early reading Vocabulary	T1 T2 T1 T2 T1 T2	0.43 nsig 0.30 nsig 0.18 nsig
Lohmann & Tomasello (2003)	138	4 year olds	T1: False belief training (mental verbs) T2: False belief training (communication verbs)	1:1	2 weeks 4 sessions 20–30 min/session	Sentential complement task 1 Sentential complement task 2	T1:T2 T1:T2	0.07 0.23
Lonigan et al. (2003)	45 T1: 22 C1: 23	MN = 55.1 mo. SD = 6.07 mo. Low income	T1: Computer-assisted instruction in phonological sensitivity C1: Head Start	1:1	8 weeks 4–5 sessions/week 15–20 min/session	Rhyme oddity Rhyme matching Word blending Syllable/phoneme blending Multiple-choice blending Word elision Syllable/phoneme elision Multiple-choice elision		0.65 0.36 0.31 0.26 0.55 0.45 0.80 −0.06

(continued)

TABLE 6.2 *Continued*

Author	N	Sample Characteristics	Treatment (T)/ Control (C) Groups	Ratio Children:Adult	Activity Length	Developmental Measure	Tx	Effect Size (*Cohen's d*)
Nancollis, Lawrie, & Dodd (2005)	T1 = 99 C1 = 114	MN = 54 mo. SD = 3.5 mo. Low income	T1: Phoneme awareness training C1: No tx control	No info	9 sessions 9 weeks 45 min/ session	Letter reproduction (K) Nonword reading (K) Spelling (K) Rhyme awareness (K) Nonword spelling (K) Phoneme segmentation (K)		−0.04 0.17 0.12 0.91 0.61 −0.94
Podhajski & Nathan (2005)	101 T1 = 88 C1 = 13	MN = 50.2 mo. SD = 8.8 mo.	T1: Professional development of Building Blocks for Literacy C1:	No info	1 year	Pre-literacy skills		0.21
Roberts (2003)	33 T1 = 16 C1 = 17	MN = 52.82 mo. ELL children Low income	T1: Letter naming C1: Vocabulary + book reading	10–11:1	48 sessions 16 weeks	Book vocabulary English oral proficiency Rhyming		−0.87 0.03 0.56

Study	N / Groups	Participant characteristics	Treatment conditions	Ratio	Duration	Outcome measure	Time	Effect size
Rvachew, Nowak, & Cloutier (2004)	34 T1: 17 C1: 17	MN = 52.88 mo. SD = 3.3 mo.	T1: Phoneme perception training C1: Computer-assisted story reading	1:1	4.75 months Session/week 12.47 sessions 15 min/session	Phoneme perception		0.57
						Articulation (single words)		0.09
						Articulation (conversation)		0.83
						Phonological awareness		0.25
Tyler et al. (2002)	27 T1 = 10 T2 = 10 C1 = 7	MN = 50 mo. Weak phonological awareness and morphosyntactic skills	T1: Phonological awareness first and then morphosyntactic awareness activities T2: Reverse order of T1 C1: No tx control	3:1	24 sessions 12 weeks 30–45 min/session	Phonology	T1 T2	0.93 1.36
						Morphosyntax	T1 T2	0.41 1.03

Shared Book Reading Activities

Study	N / Groups	Participant characteristics	Treatment conditions	Ratio	Duration	Outcome measure	Time	Effect size
Arnold et. al. (1994)	64 T1 = 23 T2 = 14 C = 27	MN = 28.61 mo. SD = 2.88 mo.	T1: Dialogic reading (direct training) T2: Dialogic reading (video) C1: No tx control	Mother child dyads	4 weeks 4 sessions	Receptive vocabulary	T1 T2	nsig 0.45
						Expressive vocabulary	T1 T2	nsig 0.71
						Verbal expression	T1 T2	0.60 0.68

(continued)

TABLE 6.2 *Continued*

Author	N	Sample Characteristics	Treatment (T)/ Control (C) Groups	Ratio Children:Adult	Activity Length	Developmental Measure	Tx	Effect Size (*Cohen's d*)
Aram (2006)	168	MN =	T1: Storybook reading	4–6:1	100 weeks	Name writing	T1	0.81
	T1 = 42	46.12–48.48 mo.	T2: Alphabetic skills		50 sessions	Word writing	T2	1.23
	T2 = 42	SD = 5.73–7.28	T3: Combined story		20–20 min/	Letter knowledge	T3	0.72
	T3 = 42	mo.	reading and alphabet		session	Letter retrieval	T1	0.42
	C = 42	Low income	skills			Phonological	T2	1.32
			C1: No tx control			awareness	T3	0.24
						Receptive	T1	0.77
						vocabulary	T2	2.02
						Book vocabulary	T3	0.79
							T1	0.36
							T2	1.15
							T3	0.62
							T1	1.01
							T2	1.38
							T3	1.17
							T1	0.33
							T2	0.36
							T3	0.57
							T1	0.15
							T2	0.30
							T3	0.61

Study	N	Sample	Intervention	Ratio	Dosage	Measure	Time	Effect size
Aram & Biron (2004)	76 T1 = 38 T2 = 35 C = 24	MN = 46 mo. SD = 4.78 mo. Low income	T1: Alphabet skills + writing T2: Language + storybook reading C: No tx control	4–6:1	33 weeks 66 sessions 20–30 min/session	Phonological awareness	T1 T2	1.21 0.39
						Word writing	T1 T2	0.82 −0.11
						orthographic Awareness	T1 T2	1.54 0.95
						Listening comprehension	T1 T2	−0.42 −0.37
Fletcher et al. (2005)	25 T1 = 12 C1 = 13	18 mo.	T1: Shared picture book reading C1: Play	1:1	27–41 sessions Twice/week 5 min/session	Responsiveness		ns
						Joint attention		ns
						Specific vocabulary		0.91
Hargrave & Sénéchal (2000)	27 T1 = 12 C1 = 15	MN = 49 mo. SD = 7 mo. Poor expressive vocabulary	T1: Dialogic Reading + home reading C1: Reading control	8:1	20 sessions 4 weeks 20–30 min/session	Book vocabulary		0.07
						Expressive vocabulary		0.16
						Receptive vocabulary		−0.12
Hindson et al. (2005)	169 G1 = 101 G2 = 68 G3 = 17	MN = 54.6 mo. G1: Familial risk for dyslexia G2: Not at-risk G3: At-risk waitlist control	Structured Book reading + phonemic awareness training	1:1	12–13 sessions (on average)	Phoneme segmenting	G1/G2 G1/G3	−0.55 1.35
						Letter knowledge	G1/G2 G1/G3	−0.71 0.61
						Rhyme	G1/G2 G1/G3	−0.21 0.57
						Receptive Vocabulary	G1/G2 G1/G3	−0.71 0.49
						Confrontation naming	G1/G2 G1/G3	−0.72 0.49
						Concepts about print	G1/G2 G1/G3	−0.65 1.19

(continued)

TABLE 6.2 Continued

Author	N	Sample Characteristics	Treatment (T)/ Control (C) Groups	Ratio Children:Adult	Activity Length	Developmental Measure	Tx	Effect Size (Cohen's d)
Justice & Ezell (2000)	28 T1 = 14 C1 = 14	MN = 55 mo. SD = 3.5 mo.	T1: Print-focus parent storybook reading (video training) C1: Parent storybook reading (no print focus)	1:1	4 weeks	Words in print alphabet knowledge Oral word segmentation Print recognition Print knowledge		1.09 0.20 0.47 0.38 1.33
Justice & Ezell (2002)	30 T1 = 15 C1 = 15	MN = 53 mo. SD = 6.3 mo. Low income PPVT III and EOWPRT-R ≥85 Adequate hearing	T1: Print-focus storybook reading C1: Picture-focus storybook reading	Small group	24 sessions 8 weeks 5–7 min/ session	Print concepts Print recognition Words in print Orientation Alphabet knowledge Literacy terms Phoneme awareness		0.27 1.81 1.20 0.87 0.47 1.09 1.08
Lonigan & Whitehurst (1998)	91	MN = 44.68 mo. SD = 5.83 mo. Low income High tx compliance centers	T1: Dialogic reading (DR) with teacher T2: DR with parents T3: DR with parents + teachers C1: No tx control	5:1 Teacher + 1:1 parents	30 sessions 6 weeks	Receptive vocabulary Expressive vocabulary Verbal fluency	T1 T2 T3 T1 T2 T3 T1 T2 T3	0.02 −0.20 −0.36 0.35 0.38 0.09 0.34 −0.01 1.31

Study	N		Sample	Intervention	Setting	Duration	Outcome measures	Comparison	Effect size
Neuman (1996)	41	G1 = 18	MN = 50.7 mo. Head Start Preschoolers G1: Parents with low reading proficiency G2: Proficient parent readers	Book club	No info	12 sessions 12 weeks 60 min/ session	Receptive vocabulary	G1:G2	0.08
		G2 = 23					Print awareness	G1:G2	0.42
Neuman (1999)	71	T1 = 71	3–4 year olds	T1: Story book reading aloud	Centre-based	8 months	Receptive vocabulary		0.09
		C1 = 57		C1: No tx control			Print awareness		0.28
							Environmental print awareness		0.19
							Alphabet knowledge		0.67
							Narrative structure		0.34
							Local		0.47
							Global		0.63
							Writing awareness		
Oritz, Stowe, & Arnold (2001)	25	T1 = 13	MN = 31 mo. SD = 3.4 mo.	T1: Shared picture book reading	Parent child dyads	3 sessions 4 weeks	Child interest (direct observation)		0.08
		C = 12		C1: Attention control			Daily reading log-child interest		0.73
							Parent report— Child asks to be read to		0.50
							Child interest scale		0.01

(continued)

TABLE 6.2 *Continued*

Author	N	Sample Characteristics	Treatment (T)/ Control (C) Groups	Ratio Children:Adult	Activity Length	Developmental Measure	Tx	Effect Size (*Cohen's d*)
Van Kleeck, Vander Woude, & Hammett (2006)	30 T1 = 15 C1 = 15	MN = 50 mo. Language delayed	T1: Book sharing scripts C1: No tx control	1:1	16 sessions 8 weeks	Receptive vocabulary		1.20
Vasilyeva, Huttenlocher, & Waterfall (2006)	72	MN = 52 mo. SD = 4 mo.	T1: Stories with active constructions C1: Stories with passive constructions	7–11:1	10 sessions 2 weeks 25 min/ session	Listening comprehension		1.15
Wasik & Bond (2001)	124 T = 63 C = 61	MN = 52 mo. Low income	T1: Interactive book reading C1: Book reading	Whole group	15 weeks	Receptive vocabulary Expressive vocabulary		1.59 2.06
Whitehurst et al. (1994a)	73 T1 = 26 T2 = 24 C = 20	MN = 41.5 mo. SD = 0.36 mo. Low income	T1: Dialogic reading (DR) with teacher T2: DR with parents + teachers C1: No tx control	5:1	30 sessions 6 weeks 5–10 min/ session	Expressive vocabulary Receptive vocabulary Book vocabulary Verbal fluency	T1 T2 T1 T2 T1 T2 T1 T2	0.21 0.43 0.15 0.24 0.07 0.37 −0.03 0.03
Whitehurst et al. (1994b)	280	Preschoolers PPVT ≤105 Head Start Low income	T1: Dialogic reading (DR) with teacher + parents + phoneme awareness training C1: No tx control	4:1	12 months	Language Linguistic awareness Print concepts Writing		ns ns 0.62 0.52

(continued)

Mathematics

Study	N	Age	Conditions	Setting	Duration	Outcome	ES
Arnold et al. (2002)	112	MN = 53.18 mo. SD = 7.32	T1: Math activities C1: No tx control	Small group and classroom	6 weeks 1–5 activities/day	Early math skills	0.44
						Child math interest	0.12

Social Competence

Study	N	Age	Conditions	Setting	Duration	Outcome	ES
Han et al. (2005)	149 T1 = 83 C1 = 66	MN = 52 mo. SD = 4 mo.	T1: Class-based behavior management + social skills training C1: No tx control	Classroom	10 months	Total problems (parent rating)	−0.03
						Internalizing problems (parent rating)	−0.01
						Externalizing problems (parent rating)	0.04
						Total social skills (parent rating)	−0.02
						Total problems (teacher rating)	0.28
						Internalizing problems (teacher rating)	0.32
						Externalizing problems (teacher rating)	0.26
						Total social skills (teacher rating)	0.11

TABLE 6.2 *Continued*

Author	N	Sample Characteristics	Treatment (T)/ Control (C) Groups	Ratio Children:Adult	Activity Length	Developmental Measure	Tx	Effect Size (*Cohen's d*)
Lobo & Winsler (2006)	40 T1 = 21 C1 = 19	MN = 50 mo. SD = 7.39 mo. Head Start Low income	T1: Dance program C1: Attention	10:1	16 sessions 8 weeks 35 min/ session	Social competence (parent rating)		0.24
						Social competence (teacher rating)		0.59
						Internalizing behavior (parent rating)		−0.05
						Internalizing behavior (teacher rating)		0.42
						Externalizing (parent rating)		−0.11
						Externalizing (teacher rating)		
McKinney & Rust (1998)	29 T = 19 C = 10	MN = 49 mo. SD = 7.2 mo.	T1: Social skills training C1: No tx control	No info	30 sessions 15 weeks 45–60 min/ session	Problem behavior Social skills		0.01 0.55
Rhodes & Hennessy (2000)	29 T1 = 16 C1 = 13	MN = 43.32 mo. SD = 2.04 mo.	T1: Foundations in playgroup practice (caregiver training) C1: No tx control	10–15:1	48 sessions 24 weeks 2 hour/ session	Social play Complex Cognitive play		0.95 0.86

Study	N	Age	Conditions	Ratio	Dosage	Outcome measure	Comparison	Effect size
Velderman et al. (2006)	81 T1 = 28 T2 = 26 C1 = 27	MN = 6.83 mo. SD = 1.03 mo.	T1: Video feedback and brochures T2: Video feedback, brochures, and discussion C1: No tx control	1:1	5 sessions 1 ½ hours/session	Oppositional behavior (parent rating)	T1:C1	−0.41
							T2:C1	0.13
						Withdrawn behavior (parent rating)	T1:C1	0.00
							T2:C1	0.06
						Aggressive behavior (parent rating)	T1:C1	−0.21
							T2:C1	0.26
						Anxious (parent rating)	T1:C1	0.14
							T2:C1	0.24
						Overactive (parent rating)	T1:C1	−0.07
							T2:C1	0.52
						Sleep disturbance (parent rating)	T1:C1	−0.29
							T2:C1	0.29
						Somatic complaints (parent rating)	T1:C1	−0.02
							T2:C1	0.27
						Internalizing behavior (parent rating)	T1:C1	0.09
							T2:C1	0.20
						Externalizing behavior (parent rating)	T1:C1	−0.33
							T2:C1	0.28
						Problem behavior (parent rating)	T1:C1	−0.30
							T2:C1	0.37

(continued)

TABLE 6.2 *Continued*

Author	N	Sample Characteristics	Treatment (T)/ Control (C) Groups	Ratio Children:Adult	Activity Length	Developmental Measure	Tx	Effect Size (*Cohen's d*)
Webster-Stratton, Reid, & Hammond (2001)	328 families T1 = 191 C1 = 81	MN = 55.1 mo. SD = 4.33 mo. Head Start Low income	T1: Parent and teacher training C1: No tx control			Child conduct problems (home)		−0.22
						Intensity (home)		−0.17
						Behavior problems (home)		0.09
						Inappropriate behavior (home)		−0.36
						Child deviance (home)		−0.14
						Child conduct problems (school)		0.57
						Child negative to peers or teacher		0.03
						Total score (ADHD)		−0.67
						Externalizing behavior (school)		0.36
						Social competence (school)		0.52
						Antisocial behavior (school)		−0.42

■ Pre-Literacy Skills and Abilities

When designing an educational program to support young children's acquisition of pre-literacy concepts, it is essential to ensure that the skills emphasized are those that are most critical for later reading and writing success (Scarborough, 1998). The research evidence shows that general language abilities, phonological awareness, print concepts, and alphabet knowledge predict children's later reading development (Catts, Fey, Zhang, & Tolmblin, 2002). However, a long-standing debate has not resolved the issue of whether children should be taught pre-literacy skills *explicitly*, as in skill-orientated, small-group instruction or whether children acquire these abilities *implicitly* through their participation in self-initiated literacy practices at home and preschool/childcare day. In the *explicit* model, instruction is skill-orientated and the early childhood educator plays a significant role both in sequencing the content of the curriculum and implementing instructional activities. In the *implicit* model, developmentally appropriate practices rather than skills are the focus, and adults are facilitators creating stimulating environments rather than teachers directing learning activities (Bredekamp, 1987).

Developmentally appropriate practices are conceptually linked to the constructivist theories of Piaget (1952) and Vygotsky (1962), in which children are viewed as active learners in their environments. According to this view, the same set of fundamental abilities (i.e., symbolic thought and representational structures) underlies child learning across domains of literacy, mathematics, and social competence; therefore, the purpose of models of early education is to facilitate growth of these capacities; for a comparative review of *High Scope, Tools of the Mind*, and *Reggio Emilia*, three well-known models of early childhood education, see Copple (2003). Policy statements from the National Association for the Education of Young Children in the United States (NAEYC, 1998) and in position papers of advocacy groups in Canada (e.g., Coalition of Child Care Advocates of British Columbia, 2008) articulate principles of developmentally appropriate practice. Early childhood educators who adhere to these principles create pre-literacy curriculums based on their understandings of child development, the specific abilities of children in their classes, and the social context in which they are situated (Huffman & Speer, 2000). Critics of this implicit approach claim that a focus on developmental theory exists without adequate consideration of the sociohistorical or cultural contexts in which children live and grow (Huffman & Speer, 2000; Nsanamang, 2007). Rather than focus on the provision of developmentally appropriate literacy practices, explicit instruction in the pre-literacy skills that are common to all cultures with alphabetic orthographies may benefit those children who are vulnerable to poor reading outcomes (Stipek & Byler, 1997). However, explicit, structured approaches have also been criticized, primarily for a lack of attention to children's interest and motivation to learn and for promoting a narrow, skill-orientated view of literacy (Huffman & Speer, 2000).

Although debates concerning the efficacy of explicit versus implicit approaches to instruction are far from resolved, a middle ground on the issue may be emerging. The NAEYC has recently initiated a call to its members for input to review critically an earlier position statement (1997) on developmentally appropriate practice. The most recent adaptation of a joint position statement on learning to read and write from the International Reading Association and the NAEYC (2005, p. 1) concluded that no one teaching method or approach is likely to be effective for all children at all times: "*Programs can incorporate a focus on reading and writing into play as well as structured activities, including but not limited to direct teaching of key literacy skills*" (author's emphasis in italics).

The majority of studies located for review in this chapter investigated the efficacy of one or a combination of the following activities on children's pre-literacy skill development:

- Shared book reading (Mean $d = 0.42$, SD $= 0.49$ N studies $= 18$)
- Phonological awareness training (Mean $d = 0.35$, SD $= 0.61$ N studies $= 8$)
- Alphabet instruction (Mean $d = 0.99$, SD $= 0.68$ N studies $= 5$).

The average effect size for each instructional approach to improve pre-literacy skills is moderate; however, there was considerable variability in the magnitude of effect size estimates. Moreover, caution must be exercised when interpreting these findings because the number of studies used to calculate mean effects for each instructional approach was relatively small. In the following sections, we review findings from studies of each of these intervention approaches in more detail.

Shared Book Reading

Dialogic book reading (Whitehurst et al., 1988) is one of the most extensively researched developmentally appropriate literacy practices in early prevention science. As with all shared reading approaches, dialogic book reading emphasizes the importance of triadic communication, a form of social exchange that occurs when a caregiver and a child interact together and share a common focus on an object or event (Tomasello, 2003). Print-referencing (i.e., sharing a common focus on features of the text) during shared story-book reading has been shown to improve the pre-literacy skills of children, including those with language delays (Lovelace & Stewart, 2007). Dialogic book reading represents a variation of this approach, where the child, instead of the adult, assumes the role of a storyteller. In both approaches, children actively communicate with the person with whom they are sharing the book by interpreting the communicative intentions of their book-sharing partner and using the linguistic symbols of their culture to meet their own communicative goals.

Shared book reading is thought to contribute to children's language acquisition, but the research evidence on this assumption is mixed. As shown in Table 6.2, the magnitude of effect sizes on vocabulary measures for shared book reading activities are uniformly positive, but highly variable and range from weak (Arnold et al., 1994; Hargrave & Sénéchal, 2000; Lonigan & Whitehurst, 1998; Whitehurst et al., 1994a, 1994b) to moderate (Aram, 2006; Aram & Biron, 2004; Hindson et al., 2005; Roberts, 2003) to strong (Van Kleck, Vander Woude, & Hammett, 2006; Wasik & Bond, 2001). Overall, the magnitude of shared book reading intervention effects on measures of expressive vocabulary are uniformly positive and on average, slightly larger (mean $d = 0.25$, SD $= 0.15$, range $= 0.07$ to 0.43) than effects found on measures of receptive vocabulary (mean $d = 0.15$, SD $= 0.38$, range $= -0.71$ to 0.57).

This heterogeneity in treatment effects suggests that additional factors are mediating intervention outcomes on vocabulary measures. One possibility is that the *duration* of the intervention may be influencing outcomes. Hindson and his colleagues (2005) found that children's rate of growth after participating in structured book sharing and phoneme awareness training in the familial at-risk group was slower than that of controls not at-risk; however, with additional sessions, the at-risk group met the specific criterion. Another possibility is that the *intensity* of the intervention may be important to obtain meaningful outcomes. For example, Whitehurst et al. (1994a) found that the magnitude of effect sizes on measures of receptive, expressive, and book vocabulary was higher when children read with their parents at home and with their teachers at preschool (ES $= 0.43$, 0.24, and 0.37, respectively) than when they read only with their teachers at preschool alone (ES $= 0.21$, 0.15, and 0.07, respectively). These findings suggest that children benefit when the *same* dialogic book reading strategies are used in different communicative contexts and with different adults.

Also, the *developmental appropriateness* of the texts being shared may mediate treatment effects. Support comes from Vasilyeva, Huttenlocher, and Waterfall's (2006) study that showed young children processed stories with active constructions more effectively than stories with passive constructions (ES $= 1.15$). Children may benefit more from shared book reading experiences when they hear new vocabulary within syntactic structures that are relatively easy for them to process.

Compared to the number of studies that have investigated the effects of shared book reading on vocabulary development, relatively fewer studies have evaluated the impact on other pre-literacy skills such as phonological awareness, letter knowledge, and/or print awareness. As shown in Table 6.2, three studies directly compared the effects of shared book activities with more direct instruction in pre-literacy skills (e.g., alphabet instruction) on a number of pre-literacy measures (i.e., Aram, 2006; Aram & Biron, 2004; Roberts, 2003). Aram (2006) reports that although both instruction in alphabet skills and shared book reading improve children's pre-literacy abilities, the magnitude of positive effects for alphabet instruction were superior to those for shared book reading on measures of name writing ($d = 1.23$ vs. $d = 0.81$), word writing ($d = 1.32$ vs. $d = 0.42$), letter knowledge ($d = 2.02$ vs. $d = 0.77$), letter retrieval ($d = 1.15$ vs. $d = 0.36$), phonological awareness ($d = 1.38$ vs. $d = 1.01$), and book vocabulary ($d = 0.30$ vs. $d = 0.15$). Children's knowledge of letter names at Kindergarten entry is a well-known predictor of reading performance (Adams, 1990; Stevenson & Newman, 1986). Therefore, the finding that young children, regardless of their at-risk status and long before they reach school age, benefit from explicit instruction in letter names has important implications for prevention science.

Alphabet Instruction

How does children's knowledge of letter names prevent later reading difficulties? Roberts (2003) argues that children associate sounds within spoken letter names and these sound relations are foundational to learning the alphabetic principle; that is, as children learn letter names, they associate sounds with letters. For example, studies have shown that letter sounds appearing at the beginning of a letter name (e.g., /b/, /k/, /p/) are easier for children to learn than letter sounds appearing at the end of a letter name (e.g., /l/, /m/, /f/). Roberts showed that children who were taught letter names used these sound associations as strategies to recognize words with simplified phonetic spellings using the letters taught (e.g., *BL* for *ball*; *KND* for *candy*) over words (a) composed of letters that were spelled phonetically, but with letters not taught (e.g., *RYS* for *rice*; *ZR* for *zipper*) and (b) spelled with letter combinations that were visually distinct but not sound related (*cN* for *ball*; *sT* for *lunch*). Alternatively, children who participated in a shared book reading control group recognized words spelled with visually distinct letters better than the words spelled phonetically. Roberts concludes that children who were taught letter names were in the partial alphabetic phase of word learning (Ehri, 1998) and drew upon their partial understandings of letter-sound relationships to identify words; whereas children who participated in the shared book reading intervention were processing words at an earlier phase, using pre-alphabetic, logographic strategies. Roberts speculates that during shared book reading, children point to words in text and this may orientate their attention more to the visual characteristics of words rather than their phonetic structures. Instruction in letter names assisted children to move beyond these visual strategies to the phonetic processing that is characteristic of word reading during the primary grades.

Phonological Awareness Training

It is now well established that phonological awareness training during the early school years is preventative of later reading difficulties for many, but not all, children at-risk for reading failure (Berninger et al., 1999; Torgesen et al., 1999). Support for this conclusion is summarized in comprehensive meta-analytic reviews of selected studies (Ehri, Nunes, Willows, Schuster, Yaghoub-Zadeh, & Shanahan, 2001; National Reading Panel). Average effects of phonological awareness training on reading outcomes for school-aged children are reportedly moderate (i.e., $d = 0.52$, Ehri et al., 2001; $d = 0.38$, National Reading Panel) and the magnitude of effects is increased when phonological awareness training is combined with instruction in print-related skills (i.e., $d = 0.67$, National Reading Panel). Although many studies show that phonological awareness training benefits later word recognition of school-aged children (see Cavanaugh et al., 2004, for a review), few studies document the effects of interventions to improve phonological awareness for children before school entry. As shown in Table 6.2, eight studies located for this review included a phonological awareness training component and on average, short-term effects of phonological awareness training on pre-literacy skills for studies in this review were modest (Mean $d = 0.35$, SD $= 0.61$).

Although phonological awareness of preschool-aged children can be increased through structured educational activities, only three of the eight studies reviewed evaluate the association between children's early growth in phonological awareness and later word identification. The first of these three longitudinal studies was conducted by Byrne and Fielding-Barnsley (1991, 1993, 1995) with typically developing preschoolers. Findings showed that activities to identify phonemes at the beginning and end of words improved children's phonological awareness (i.e., with sounds not directly taught) and their ability to detect sounds on a structured printed word decoding task, but the long-term impact of this intervention on children's reading was less stable. A year after intervention, when children were enrolled in Kindergarten, the intervention group continued to outperform controls on a measure of pseudoword reading, but not on real word reading and spelling tasks. This pattern of results was replicated when the children were in grades 1 and 2 (Byrne & Fielding-Barnsley, 1993). In third grade, children in the treatment group performed better on average than controls on measures of pseudoword reading, but not word identification, listening, or reading comprehension (Byrne & Fielding-Barnsley, 1995). When in fifth grade, children in the treatment group outperformed the control group on measures of reading irregularly spelled words ($d = 0.39$), decoding nonwords ($d = 0.34$) and broad word identification (i.e., reading regular, irregular, and nonwords; $d = 0.33$) (Byrne, Fielding-Barnsley, & Ashley, 2000). Because children received ongoing reading instruction between preschool and fifth grade factors in addition to phonological awareness training may have mediated fifth grade reading outcomes.

Hatcher, Hulme, and Snowling (2004) expanded on the work of Bryne and Fielding-Barnsley in a second study to test the hypothesis that phonological awareness training would better predict long-term reading outcomes if it was combined with other reading-related activities (i.e., concepts about print, letter identification, word reading, writing and spelling, and text reading). Three variations of phonological awareness training in combination with reading-related skills were evaluated for their long-term effect on children's ability to identify irregularly and regularly spelled words. Sample children were vulnerable due to economic disadvantage and therefore, their language skills were expected to be lower, relative to the general population (Riley, Burrell, & McCallum, 2004). However, within this group a subset of children was identified as at greater risk than the others for reading failure due to depressed performance on vocabulary, letter identification, rhyme, and phoneme deletion measures. Children in the control group and all three intervention groups (randomly assigned to additional training in phoneme and rhyme skills together, phoneme awareness alone, or rhyme skills alone) received instruction in reading-related activities.

Two findings are relevant to this chapter. First, children identified as at-high-risk for reading failure based on language measures responded differently to intervention than children not at-risk. Specifically, positive intervention effects across all three conditions were found for children not at-risk; however, in the at-risk group, children were slower to respond when instruction was targeted at the level of the phoneme. This finding is consistent with those from a number of studies of older children that show children who fail to respond to early literacy interventions have phonological awareness deficits (Al Otaiba & Fuchs, 2006). Second, increases in children's phoneme awareness, but not rhyme skills predicted word reading at the end of first and second grades. The authors interpret these findings to mean that preschool-aged children at double-risk (low socioeconomic status and low language scores) (a) can be reliably identified as at-risk for reading failure on the basis of language and pre-literacy skill measures; and (b) benefit from additional training in phoneme awareness and in linking phonemes with letters to prevent later reading problems.

Nancollis, Lawrie, and Dodd's (2005) longitudinal study of an intervention to improve rhyme and syllable awareness among children at-risk for reading failure due to economic disadvantage showed that growth in awareness of rhyme and syllables in speech had limited effect on their long-term reading outcomes. Two years after intervention, the intervention and the control groups performed similarly and below national norms on measures of literacy skills.

Taken together, the findings from these three longitudinal intervention studies indicate young children living in economic disadvantaged settings respond to phonological awareness activities at the level of the rhyme, syllable, and phoneme, but it is training at the level of the phoneme that has the most impact on later reading for this group of children. These findings are generally consistent with those found in studies of older children at-risk for reading failure. What these studies also show is that most children at the age of 4 years can increase their capacities to identify phonemes (i.e., at the beginning and end of spoken words, or segment phonemes in a spoken word) an ability that is foundational to later reading. Early phonemic training that is relatively brief (i.e., 10–30 minute sessions) accounted for a small portion of the early childhood education curriculum (i.e., 30 minutes of training per week).

Instruction at higher levels of language (i.e., morpheme, syntax) may also benefit young children's development of phonological abilities, including phoneme awareness. Tyler et al. (2002) reported that for children at-risk due to depressed phonological and morphosyntactic abilities, the magnitude of intervention effects was greater for young children who participated in phonological awareness activities *after* they had participated in activities targeted at morphosyntactic level of language than when the order of these components were reversed. Morphosyntactic activities, as described by Tyler et al., were intended to increase children's auditory awareness of third person singular regular and irregular past tense and possessive forms of the copula verb BE. The morphosyntactic awareness intervention combined auditory awareness activities (e.g., songs), forced stimulation activities during which the speech-language pathologist recast and expanded upon children's utterances to include intervention targets, and forced choice activities that required children to choose or construct the targeted constructions. The phonological awareness intervention included auditory awareness (e.g., songs) and phonological awareness activities (at the level of the rhyme, onset rime, and phoneme segmentation), in which children were asked to reflect upon contrasting classes of sounds and to classify their own as well as the speech-language pathologist's productions. Intensive intervention such as the one described here may be most appropriate for children who have language problems and are from economically disadvantaged backgrounds.

Teacher/Parent Training

As shown in Table 6.2, three studies in this review investigated the effects of training parents (Baker, Piotrkowski, & Brooks-Gunn, 1998; Lonigan & Whitehurst, 1998) and teachers (Jackson et al., 2006) to deliver pre-literacy interventions to young, preschool-aged children. One approach involved parents in the delivery of instructional activities that complement the curriculums available to children through early learning and childcare programs. HIPPY (Home Instruction for Parents of Preschool Youngsters) is an example. HIPPY coordinators and/or home visitors met with parents in their home once a week and through role-play, modeled activities with children. Parents were provided with 30 packets of instructional materials to use with their children over a 30-week period. The HIPPY curriculum aims to increase children's cognitive problem solving, language, and perceptual development; however, instruction in phonological awareness, letter recognition, book knowledge, and early writing was also given. Although HIPPY has been operational in North America since 1984, there have been few long-term, controlled studies of its effects on children's later academic achievement or social competence. The single controlled study conducted by Baker et al. (1998) reported mixed results: Children in one, but not the second, cohort benefited from participation with their parents in the program as indicated on measures of cognitive growth. Although early pre-literacy skills were taught, children's performance on related measures was not reported.

Jackson et al. (2006) is the only study located for this review that evaluated the effects of teacher professional development on children's early literacy outcomes. Although teacher training is considered an important component of *Head Start* and other comprehensive early prevention programs, most studies evaluate the effects of training on teacher behavior without consideration of direct benefits to the child. This study shows that children benefited more when their teachers received professional development by way of satellite alone ($d = 0.18–0.43$) than when mentoring was included with the satellite delivery (all d's ≤ .00).

Studies of dialogic reading also report greater effects when delivered in video format than when training involves direct mentoring from professionals (Arnold et al., 1994). Further, the effects of dialogic reading were greater when parents and teachers collaborated during training than when parents or teachers delivered the intervention alone (Lonigan & Whitehurst, 1988). Children appear to benefit most from curricula that are designed to promote generalization across settings and people; that is, when similar strategies are used in the home by parents and in early learning and childcare settings by teachers.

■ Mathematics Skills and Abilities

Only one study of a mathematics intervention for young children during the preschool years was found that met criteria for inclusion in this review (i.e., Arnold et al., 2002). Although studies show that children's participation in comprehensive early intervention programs can have lasting effects on their mathematics achievement (Campbell et al., 2001; Reynolds & Temple, 1998), it is not entirely clear which components of the programs accounted for these positive outcomes. The intervention by Arnold and his colleagues for children attending *Head Start* is both explicit (i.e., activities are structured) and designed to be developmentally appropriate (i.e., activities are incorporated into regular classroom routines). Four principles guided instruction: (a) Adults provided encouragement and praise; (b) activities were fun; (c) adults followed the lead of children and adapted activities to meet children's interests; and (d) adults labeled children's behaviors to provide feedback and scaffolding support. Findings showed that children in the experimental group outperformed children in the control group on a measure of general math skills ($d = 0.44$); however, within the experimental group, the response to intervention was greater for boys than for girls, and greater for African American and Puerto Rican children than for Anglo-American children. The authors argue that children of preschool age are developmentally ready to learn math through structured activities that are incorporated into a preschool curriculum. However, longitudinal studies are needed to evaluate the effects of mathematics instruction in preschool on children's later mathematics achievement.

■ Social Competence

Prevention efforts to reduce the prevalence of behavior and/or emotional disorders and to promote social competence of young children have long been a focus of child development research. Much is known about the family factors that place school-aged children at-risk (e.g., harsh or rejecting parenting practices, maternal depression, quality of care-giving, and economic stress) as well as those that protect them (e.g., positive attachments with adults) from poor social outcomes (Shaw et al., 2003). For a review, see Webster-Stratton and Hammond (1998). For the most part, family-centered prevention activities have focused on reducing stress, tension, and aggression in the home by improving parenting practices and strengthening child-caregiver attachments from infancy onward (e.g., Ammaniti et al., 2006; Bates, 2005; Shaw et al., 2006). Findings from a meta-analytic review of 70 studies of sensitivity and attachment interventions in early childhood suggest that stimulating maternal sensitivity through clear-cut behavioral interventions also enhanced children's attachment security (Bakermans-Kranenburg, van IJzendoorn, & Juffer, 2003).

Many studies in the clinical literature using single or multiple case designs to evaluate the effects of therapeutic approaches on parent and child behavior are also relevant. For example, parent-child interaction therapy has been successfully used to decrease anxious behaviors in children (e.g., Choate et al., 2005) and to increase young children's sense of security (e.g., Hoffman et al., 2006). Multicomponent approaches to intervention for children at-risk for behavior disorders such as Attention-Deficit/Hyperactivity have been proposed; however, studies report mixed effects on children's behavior and academic outcomes (McGoey et al., 2005). This chapter focuses only on studies that are directly associated with educational programs within early learning and childcare settings.

The essence of an early childhood center is embedded in the quality of child-adult attachments and the abilities of adults to create learning and social environments that are positive, consistent, and responsive for children with challenging behaviors (Webster-Stratton, Reid, & Hammond, 2001). Despite this recognized need for well-designed activities to promote children's social competence in early learning and childcare settings; there are few controlled studies available to guide implementation of these activities: Four studies were located for this review targeted to development of children's social competence in preschools. As shown in Table 6.2, one investigation focused on developing children's social competence through dance activities (Lobo & Winsler, 2006); the remaining studies targeted management and social skills training in the school (Jackson et al., 2006) and in the home and school together (Webster-Stratton, Reid, & Hammond, 2001).

Together, the findings suggest that children's response to intervention may differ between home and early learning and childcare settings. For example, parent, but not teacher ratings of change in child behavior and social competence increased after dance activities were incorporated into the preschool day; on the other hand, teacher, but not parent ratings, were positive after teachers adapted their classroom management strategies and after they included social skill training activities in the curriculum. When change in management strategies of both parents and teachers was targeted, ratings of child behavior and social competence were positive and robust across home and school settings (Webster-Stratton, Reid, & Hammond, 2001). Parents in the intervention became more positive in their parenting styles, they formed strong associations with the school, and they reduced harsh discipline practices relative to controls who did not participate in the intervention. When parents attended six or more sessions, child behavior in the home improved. Also, teachers in the intervention group used fewer negative management strategies than teachers in the control group. Overall, the high-risk behavior (i.e., aggression, poor social skills, noncompliance) of children in the intervention group were reduced to within normal limits and these gains were maintained over time at the 1-year follow-up. Positive effects of early prevention strategies to improve children's social competence may be greater when teachers and parents are working together to create positive behavioral change.

■ Implications for Practice

The aim of this chapter was to review findings from prevention science on instructional activities to improve pre-literacy, mathematics, and social competence of young children. Overall, findings suggest that carefully implemented, early education activities have potential to reduce the likelihood of poor learning and social outcomes for children at-risk due to biological or economic disadvantage. Of the three domains reviewed, considerably more studies of activities to facilitate children's pre-literacy development were located than of activities to promote growth in mathematics or social competence. Of course, much of the previous intervention work to improve children's developmental and social outcomes has focused on family wellness and parenting practices. However, as more parents enter the paid workforce and seek childcare options, there is a need to ensure that children have universal access to high-quality educational activities in early learning and childcare environments. For children who do not respond well to these activities, additional, targeted support is required.

Who are the children who should receive this targeted intervention? Findings from this review suggest that although all children living in poverty are considered at-risk for poor developmental outcomes, a subset of children with depressed language and phonological abilities appear to be more at-risk for reading failure than children with relatively better language skills. Three main approaches to assessment have been discussed in the literature to identify children most vulnerable to poor academic outcomes. A *critical skills mastery approach* measures children's growth in discrete skills that are assumed to be linked to each other in a developmental hierarchy (Phaneuf & Silberglitt, 2003). A *general outcomes approach* estimates outcomes on curriculum-based measures or on more distal measures of developmental outcomes (e.g., memory and general language). A *responsiveness to intervention approach* evaluates children's *rate* of response to intervention by using several repeated measures of situational and curriculum-based learning.

There are clear benefits to viewing outcomes from several perspectives. For example, Hindson et al. (2005) found after participating in a structured book reading and phoneme awareness intervention, children at-familial-risk for dyslexia outperformed children not at-risk on several discrete as well as general measures of phonological and print awareness. That is, the intervention had high instructional validity. At the same time, the average rate of responsiveness to intervention (i.e., the number of sessions required to meet a criterion) for the at-risk intervention group was slower than that of the control not at-risk group and this slow rate of response was associated with depressed performances on more general measures of verbal memory and vocabulary. The authors concluded that young children at-risk due to familial dyslexia benefit from early instruction in phoneme awareness and shared book reading in much the same way as children not at-risk, but they require more sessions and more sustained teaching. As this study shows, evaluating intervention effects with diverse measurement approaches can lead to valuable insights that may not emerge from an analysis of intervention effects on a single outcome measure.

The use of an array of outcome measures to assess children's response to intervention is also beneficial because children's responses may vary, with improvements seen on some measures, but not on others. For example, findings from Whitehurst et al.'s (1994a) study of Dialogic Reading showed that children's average performance on all language measures increased after intervention; however, the magnitude of effects on measures of expressive vocabulary was greater than on measures of receptive vocabulary and verbal fluency. Ortiz, Stowe, and Arnold (2001) also found that different measures of the same construct (i.e., children's interest in reading) resulted in divergent outcomes. That is, children's interest in reading was rated higher by their parents after they participated in a shared book reading intervention; however, direct observations of children's interest during reading activities as well as children's self-reported levels of interest revealed no treatment effects.

There also appears to be general agreement among researchers in this review that for children to reap long-term benefits of early education activities, they must enjoy participating in the activities. To this end, structured activities to improve children's learning and social outcomes were incorporated by researchers into the regular routines and play within early learning and childcare programs. Although some activities involved only the child and an adult (e.g., dialogic book reading), other, equally effective approaches involved instruction in small groups.

Finally, intervention approaches that involved children, parents, and teachers together appeared to be more effective and long-lasting than intervention approaches that focused solely on teacher or parent training alone. Refocusing intervention efforts to educational approaches that directly influence the child across home and school settings appeared more beneficial for children than when only one context was highlighted.

Prevention science in early childhood is a field of inquiry that has potential to provide policy makers, professionals, and parents with the theoretical and empirical rationale to support early education approaches. However, the field is developing, and there is a pressing need for more controlled studies that investigate children's responsiveness to early education activities in early learning and childcare settings. The challenge for researchers in the next decade is to address this issue within the context of a balanced curriculum—one in which structured, explicit activities are offset with opportunities for children to learn implicitly through unstructured play and social interaction.

■ References

Achenbach, T. (1992). *Manual for the child behavior checklist*. Burlington, VT, Department of Psychiatry, University of Vermont.

Adams, M. J. (1990). *Beginning to read*. Cambridge, MA, MIT Press.

Al Otaiba, S., & Fuchs, D. (2006). Who are the young children for whom best practices in reading are ineffective? *Journal of Learning Disabilities, 39,* 414–431.

Ammaniti, M., Speranza, A. M., Tambelli, R., Muscetta, S., Lucarelli, L., Vismara, L., Odorisio, F., & Cimino, S. (2006). A prevention and promotion intervention program in the field of mother-infant relationship. *Infant Mental Health Journal, 27,* 70–90.

Aram, D. (2006). Early literacy interventions: The relative roles of storybook reading, alphabetic activities, and their combination. *Reading and Writing, 19,* 489–515.

Aram, D., & Biron, S. (2004). Joint storybook reading and joint writing interventions among low SES preschoolers: Differential contributions to early literacy. *Early Childhood Research Quarterly, 19,* 588–610.

Arnold, D., Fisher, P., Doctoroff, G., & Dobbs, J. (2002). Accelerating math development in Head Start classrooms. *Journal of Educational Psychology, 94,* 762–770.

Arnold, D., Lonigan, C., Whitehurst, G., & Epstein, J. (1994). Accelerating language development through picture book reading: Replication and extension to a videotape training format. *Journal of Educational Psychology, 86,* 235–243.

Baker, A. J. L., Piotrkowski, C. S., & Brooks-Gunn, J. (1998). The effects of the Home Instruction Program for Preschool Youngsters (HIPPY) on children's school performance at the end of the program and one year later. *Early Childhood Research Quarterly, 13,* 571–588.

Bakermans-Kranenburg, M. J., van IJzendoorn, M. H., & Juffer, F. (2003). Less is more: Meta-analyses of sensitivity and attachment interventions in early childhood. *Psychological Bulletin, 129,* 195–215.

Barnett, S. W. (1995). Long-term effects of early childhood programs on cognitive and school outcomes. *The Future of Children, 5,* 25–45.

Bates, E. (1976). *Language and context: The acquisition of pragmatics.* New York, Academic Press.

Bates, S. L. (2005). Evidence-based family-school interventions with preschool children. *School Psychology Quarterly, 20,* 352–370.

Bernhard, J., Cummins, J., Campoy, F. I., Flor Ada, A., Winsler, A., & Bleiker, C. (2006). Identity texts and literacy development among preschool English language learners: Enhancing learning opportunities for children at-risk for learning disabilities. *Teachers College Record, 108,* 2380–2405.

Berninger, V. W., Abbott, R. D., Zook, D., Ogier, S., Lemos-Britton, Z., & Brooksher, R. (1999). Early intervention for reading disabilities: Teaching the alphabetic principle in a connectionist framework. *Journal of Learning Disabilities, 32,* 491–503.

Blank, M., Rose, S. A., & Berlin, L. J. (1978). *Preschool language assessment instrument: The language of learning in practice.* New York, Grune & Stratton.

Boehm, A. (1986). *The Boehm test of basic concepts-revised.* New York, The Psychological Corporation.

Bracken, B. A. (1984). *Bracken basic concept scale.* San Antonio, TX, The Psychological Corporation.

Bradley, L., & Bryant, P. (1983). Categorizing sounds and learning to read—a causal connection. *Nature, 301,* 419–421.

Bredekamp, S. (1987). *Developmentally appropriate practice in early childhood programs serving children from birth to age eight.* Washington, DC, National Association for the Education of Young Children.

Brimer, M. A., & Dunn, L. M. (1973). *English Picture Vocabulary Test.* Awre, Glouchestershire, Education Evaluation Enterprises.

Brooks-Gunn, J. (2003). Do you believe in magic?: What we can expect from early childhood intervention programs. *Social policy report: Giving child and youth development knowledge away, 17,* 3–14.

Brotman, L., Gouley, K., Chesir-Teran, D., Dennis, T., Klein, R., & Shrout, P. (2005). Prevention for preschoolers at high risk for conduct problems: Immediate outcomes on parenting practices and child social competence. *Journal of Clinical Child and Adolescent Psychology, 34,* 724–734.

Byrne, B., & Fielding-Barnsley, R. (1991). *Sound foundations: An introduction to prereading skills.* Sydney, Australia, Peter Leyden Educational.

Byrne, B., & Fielding-Barnsley, R. E. (1991). Evaluation of a program to teach phonemic awareness to young children. *Journal of Educational Psychology, 83,* 451–453.

Byrne, B., & Fielding-Barnsley, R. E. (1993). Evaluation of a program to teach phonemic awareness to young children: A 1 year follow-up. *Journal of Educational Psychology, 85,* 104–111.

Byrne, B., & Fielding-Barnsley, R. E. (1995). Evaluation of a program to teach phonemic awareness to young children: A 2 and 3 year follow-up and a new preschool trial. *Journal of Educational Psychology, 87,* 488–503.

Byrne, B., Fielding-Barnsley, R. E., & Ashley, L. (2000). Effects of phoneme identity training after six years: Outcome level distinguished from rate of response. *Journal of Educational Psychology, 92,* 659–667.

Caldwell, B. (1974). *Cooperative preschool inventory—Revised.* Cooperative Tests and Services.

Campbell, F., Pungello, E., Miller-Johnson, S., Burchinal, M., & Ramey, C. (2001). The development of cognitive and academic abilities: Growth curves from an early childhood educational experiment. *Developmental Psychology, 37,* 231–242.

Campbell, F. A., & Ramsey, C. T. (1995). Cognitive and school outcomes for high-risk African American students at middle adolescence: Positive effects of early intervention. *American Educational Research Journal, 32,* 743–772.

Catts, H. W., Fey, M. E., Zhang, X., & Tomblin, J. B. (2002). A longitudinal investigation of reading outcomes in children with language impairments. *Journal of Speech, Language, & Hearing Research, 45,* 1142–1157.

Cavanaugh, C. L., Kim, A., Wanzek, J., & Vaughn, S. (2004). Kindergarten reading interventions for at-risk students: Twenty years of research. *Learning Disabilities: A Contemporary Journal, 2*, 9–21.

Choate, M. L., Pincus, D. B., Eyberg, S. M., & Barlow, D. H. (2005). Parent-child interaction therapy for the treatment of separation anxiety disorder in young children: A pilot study. *Cognitive and Behavioral Practice, 12*, 126–135.

Clay, M. (1975). *The early detection of reading difficulties: A diagnostic survey.* Auckland, New Zealand, Heinemann.

Coalition of Child Care Advocates of British Columbia. (2008). You can't have early learning without care: CCCABC's response to the Early Childhood Learning Agency consultation Paper "Expanding Early Learning in British Columbia for Children Aged 3-5." Retrieved from www.cccabc.bc.ca/cccabcdocs/papers.html.

Cohen, J. (1988). *Statistical power analysis of the behavioral sciences* (2nd ed.). New York, Academic Press.

Cohen, J. (1992). A power primer. *Psychological Bulletin, 112*, 155–159.

Connor-Kuntz, F. J., & Dummer, G. M. (1996). Teaching across the curriculum: Language enriched physical education for preschool children. *Adapted Physical Activity Quarterly, 13*, 302–315.

Copple, C. (2003). Fostering young children's representation, planning and reflection: A focus in three current early childhood models. *Applied Developmental Psychology, 24*, 763–771.

Crawley, A. M., Anderson, D. R., Wilder, A., Williams, M., & Santomero, A. (1999). Effects of repeated exposures to a single episode of the television program *Blue's Clues* on the viewing behaviors and comprehension of preschool children. *Journal of Educational Psychology, 91*, 630–637.

Crumrine, L., & Lonegan, H. (1999). *Pre-literacy skills screening (PLSS).* Baltimore, MD, Brookes.

CTB. (1990). *Developing skills checklist.* Monterey, CA, CTB/McGraw-Hill.

Dickinson, D., McCabe, A., & Sprague, K. (2001). *Teacher rating of oral language and literacy.* Ann Arbor, MI, Center for the Improvement in Early Reading Achievement.

Dodd, B., Crosbie, S., MacIntosh, B., Teitzel, T., & Ozanne, A. (2000). *Preschool and primary inventory of phonological awareness.* London, The Psychological Association.

Dunn, L. M., & Dunn, L. M. (1997). *Peabody picture vocabulary test—revised* (3rd ed.). Circle Pines, MN, American Guidance Service.

Ehri, L. C. (1998). Research on learning to read and spell: A personal-historical perspective. *Scientific Studies of Reading, 2*, 97–114.

Ehri, L. C., Nunes, S. R., Willows, D., Schuster, B. V., Yaghoub-Zadeh, Z., & Shanahan, T. (2001). Phonemic awareness instruction helps children learn to read: Evidence from the National Reading Panel's meta-analysis. *Reading Research Quarterly, 36*, 250–287.

Elliot, C. D., Murray, D., & Pearson, L. S. (1983). *British ability scales.* Windsor, NFER-Nelson.

Farran, D. C. (2000). Another decade of intervention for children who are low income or disabled: What do we know now? In J. P. Shonkoff & S. J. Meisels (Eds.), *Handbook of early childhood intervention* (2nd ed., pp. 510–539). New York, Cambridge University Press.

Fletcher, K. L., Perez, A., Hooper, C., & Claussen, A. H. (2005). Responsiveness and attention during picture-book reading in 18-month-old to 24-month-old toddlers at risk. *Early Child Development and Care, 175,* 63–83.

Friendly, M., Doherty, G. D., & Beach, J. B. (2006). *Quality by design: What do we know about quality in early learning and childcare, and what do we think?* Childcare Resource and Research Unit, University of Toronto.

Gardner, M. F. (1981). *Expressive one-word picture vocabulary test.* Novata, CA, Academic Therapy Publications.

Gilliam, W. S., & Zigler, E. F. (2000). A critical meta-analysis of all evaluations of State-funded preschool from 1977 to 1998: Implications for policy, service delivery and program evaluation. *Early Childhood Research Quarterly, 15,* 441–473.

Gillon, G. (2000). The efficacy of phonological awareness intervention for children with spoken language impairment. *Language, Speech, and Hearing Services in Schools, 31,* 126–141.

Ginsberg, H. P., & Baroody, A. J. (1990). *Test of early mathematics ability* (2nd ed.). Austin, TX, Pro-Ed.

Gresham, F., & Elliot, S. (1990). *Social skills rating system.* Circle Pines, MN, American Guidance Service.

Halpern, R. (1990). Community-based early intervention. In J. P. Shonkoff & S. J. Meisels (Eds.), *Handbook of early childhood intervention* (pp. 469–498). New York, Cambridge University Press.

Halpern, R. (2000). Early intervention for low-income children and families. In J. P. Shonkoff & S. J. Meisels (Eds.), *Handbook of Early Childhood Intervention* (2nd ed., pp. 361–386). New York, Cambridge University Press.

Halpern, R., Baker, A. J. L., & Piotrkowski, C. S. (1993). *The classroom adaptation inventory.* New York, National Council of Jewish Women.

Han, S., Catron, T., Weiss, B., & Marciel, K. (2005). A teacher-consultation approach to social skills training for pre-kindergarten children: Treatment model and short-term outcome effects. *Journal of Abnormal Child Psychology, 33,* 681–693.

Hargrave, A. C., & Sénéchal, M. (2000). A book reading intervention with preschool children who have limited vocabularies: The benefits of regular reading and dialogic reading. *Early Childhood Research Quarterly, 15,* 75–90.

Hatcher, P. J. (1992). *Learning to read: The value of linking phonological training with reading.* Unpublished doctoral thesis, University of York, UK.

Hatcher, P. J., Hulme, C., & Snowling, M. (2004). Explicit phoneme training combined with phonic reading instruction helps young children at risk of reading failure. *Journal of Child Psychology and Psychiatry, 45,* 338–358.

Hindson, B., Byrne, B., Fielding-Barnsley, R., Newman, C., Hine, D., & Shankweiler, D. (2005). Assessment and early instruction of preschool children at risk for reading disability. *Journal of Educational Psychology, 97,* 687–704.

Hoffman, K. T., Marvin, R. S., Cooper, G., & Powell, B. (2006). Changing toddlers' and preschoolers' attachment classifications: the Circle of Security intervention. *Journal of Consulting and Clinical Psychology, 74,* 1017–1026.

Howes, C. (1980). Peer play scale as an index of complexity of peer interaction. *Developmental Psychology, 4,* 99–107.

Huffman, L. R., & Speer, P. W. (2000). Academic performance among at-risk children: The role of developmentally appropriate practices. *Early Childhood Research Quarterly, 15,* 167–184.

Jackson, B., Larzelere, R., Clair, L., Corr, M., Fichter, C., & Egertson, H. (2006). The impact of HeadsUp! Reading on early childhood educators' literacy practices and preschool children's literacy skills. *Early Childhood Research Quarterly, 21,* 213–226.

Johnson, D. L., & Walker, T. (1991). A follow-up evaluation of the Houston Parent-Child Development Center: School performance. *Journal of Early Intervention, 15,* 226–236.

Justice, L. M., & Ezell, H. K. (2000). Enhancing children's print and word awareness through home-based parent intervention. *American Journal of Speech-Language Pathology, 9,* 257–269.

Justice, L. M., & Ezell, H. K. (2002). Use of storybook reading to increase print awareness in at-risk children. *American Journal of Speech-Language Pathology, 11,* 17–29.

Kirk, S. A., McCarthy, J. J., & Kirk, W. D. (1968). *Illinois test of psycholinguistic abilities.* Urbana, IL, University of Illinois Press.

LaFreniere, P. J., & Dumas, J. E. (1995). *Social competence and behavior evaluation: Preschool edition.* Los Angeles, CA, Western Psychological Services.

Lally, J. R., Mangione, P. L., & Honig, A. S. (1988). The Syracuse University family development research program: Long range impact on an early intervention with low-income children and their families. In D. Powell (Ed.), *Parent education as early childhood intervention: Emerging directions in theory, research, and practice* (pp. 79–104). Norwood, NJ, Ablex Publishing.

Layzer, J. I., & Goodson, B. D. (2006). The quality of early care and educational settings: Definitional and measurement issues. *Evaluation Review, 30,* 556–576.

Levin, I., & Bus, A. (2003). How is emergent writing based on drawing? Analyses of children's products and their sorting by children and mothers. *Developmental Psychology, 39,* 891–905.

Lobo, Y., & Winsler, A. (2006). The effects of a creative dance and movement program on the social competence of head start preschoolers. *Social Development, 15,* 501–519.

Lohmann, H., & Tomasello, T. (2003). The role of language in the development of false belief understanding: A training study. *Child Development, 74,* 1130–1144.

Lonigan, C. J., Driscoll, K., Phillips, B. M., Cantor, B. G., Anthony, J. L., & Goldstein, H. (2003). A computer-assisted instruction phonological sensitivity program for preschool children at-risk for reading problems. *Journal of Early Intervention, 25*, 248–262.

Lonigan, C. J., & Whitehurst, G. J. (1998). Relative efficacy of parent and teacher involvement in a shared-reading intervention for preschool children from low-income backgrounds. *Early Childhood Research Quarterly, 13*, 263–290.

Lovelace, S., & Stewart, S. R. (2007). Increasing print awareness in preschoolers with language impairment using non-evocative print referencing. *Language, Speech, and Hearing Services in Schools, 38*, 16–30.

MacLean, M., Bryant, P., & Bradley, L. (1987). Rhymes, nursery rhymes, and reading in early childhood. *Merrill-Palmer Quarterly, 33*, 255–282.

Martin, J., & Sugarman, J. (2003). A theory of personhood for psychology. In D. B. Hill & M. J. Krall (Eds.), *Essays at the crossroads of history, theory, and philosophy* (pp. 73–85). Albany, NY, State University of New York Press.

McCain, M. N., & Mustard, J. F. (1999). *Early years study: Reversing the real brain drain*. Toronto, Ont., Canada, Ontario Productions.

McConnell, S., & McEvoy, M. (2001). *Individual growth and development indicators*. St. Paul, MN, Early Childhood Research Institute, University of Minnesota.

McGoey, K. E., DuPaul, G. J., Eckert, T. L., Volpe, R. J., & van Brakle, J. (2005). Outcomes of a multi-component intervention for preschool children at-risk for Attention-Deficit/Hyperactivity Disorder. *Child and Family Behavior Therapy, 27*, 33–56.

McKinney, E., & Rust, J. (1998). Enhancing preschool African American children's social skills. *Journal of Instructional Psychology, 25*, 235–241.

Meissels, S. J., & Shonkoff, J. P. (2000). Early childhood intervention: A continuing evolution. In J. P. Shonkoff & S. J. Meisels (Eds.), *Handbook of early childhood intervention* (2nd ed., pp. 3–34). New York, Cambridge University Press.

Mrazek, P. J., & Brown, C. H. (2002). Final report: An evidence-based literature review regarding outcomes in psychosocial prevention and early intervention in young children. In C. C. Russell (Ed.), *The state of knowledge about prevention/early intervention* (pp. 42–166). Toronto, Ont., Canada, Invest in Kids Foundation.

Muter, V., Hulme, C., Snowling, M., & Taylor, S. (1997). *Phonological abilities test*. London, Psychological Corporation.

NAEYC. (1997, 1998, 2005). Retrieved from www.naeyc.org/about/positions.asp.

Nancollis, A., Lawrie, B., & Dodd, B. (2005). Phonological awareness intervention and the acquisition of literacy skills in children from deprived social backgrounds. *Language, Speech, and Hearing Services in the Schools, 36*, 325–335.

National Reading Panel. (2000). *Report of the National Reading Panel: Reports of the subgroups*. Washington, DC, National Institute of Child Health and Human Development Clearing House.

Nelson, G., Westhues, A., & MacLeod, J. (2003). A meta-analysis of longitudinal research on preschool prevention programs for children. *Prevention & Treatment*, 6.

Nelson, J. R., Benner, G. J., & Gonzalez, J. (2003). Learner characteristics that influence the treatment effectiveness of early literacy interventions: A meta-analytic review. *Learning Disabilities Research & Practice*, *18*, 255–267.

Neuman, M. J. (2005). Governance of early childhood education and care: Recent developments in OECD countries. *Early Years*, *25*, 129–141.

Neuman, S. B. (1996). Children engaging in storybook reading: The influence of access to print resources, opportunity, and parental interaction. *Early Childhood Research Quarterly*, *11*, 495–513.

Neuman, S. B. (1999). Books make a difference: A study of access to literacy. *Reading Research Quarterly*, *34*, 286–311.

Nsanamang, A. B. (2007). A critical peek at early childhood care and education in Africa. *Child Health and Education: An Interdisciplinary Journal*, *1*, 1–12.

OECD (2001). *Starting strong: Early childhood education and care*. Paris, France, OECD.

Oritz, C., Stowe, R. M., & Arnold, D. (2001). Parental influence on child interest in shared picture book readings. *Early Childhood Research Quarterly*, *16*, 263–281.

Phaneuf, R., & Silberglitt, B. (2003). Tracking preschoolers' language and preliteracy development using a general outcome measurement system: One education district's experience. *Topics in Early Childhood Special Education*, *23*, 114–123.

Piaget. (1952). *The origins of intelligence in children*. New York, International Universities Press.

Podhajski, B., & Nathan, J. (2005). Promoting early literacy through professional development for childcare providers. *Early Education & Development*, *16*, 23–41.

Reid, D., Hresko, W., & Hammill, D. (2001). *Test of early reading ability* (3rd ed.). Austin, TX, Pro-Ed Inc.

Reynolds, A. J., & Temple, J. A. (1998). Extended early childhood intervention and school achievement: Age thirteen findings from the Chicago Longitudinal Study. *Child Development*, *69*, 231–246.

Reynolds, A. J., Temple, J. A., Robertson, D. L., & Mann, E. A. (2001). Long-term effects of an early childhood intervention on educational achievement and juvenile arrest. *Journal of the American Medical Association*, *285*, 2339–2346.

Rhodes, S., & Hennessey, E. (2000). The effects of specialized training on caregivers and children in early-years settings: An evaluation of the foundation course in playgroup practice. *Early Childhood Research Quarterly*, *15*, 559–576.

Riley, J., Bureel, A., & McCallum, B. (2004). Developing the spoken language skills of reception class children in two multicultural, inner-city primary schools. *British Educational Research Journal*, *30*, 657–672.

Roberts, T. (2003). Effects of alphabet-letter instruction on young children's word recognition. *Journal of Educational Psychology, 95*, 41–51.

Robinson, E. A., Eyberg, S. M., & Ross, A. W. (1980). The standardization of an invention of child conduct problem behaviors. *Journal of Clinical Child Psychology, 9*, 22–28.

Robinson, E. A., Eyberg, S. M., & Ross, A. W. (1981). The dyadic parent-child interaction coding system: Standardization and validation. *Journal of Consulting and Clinical Psychology, 49*, 245–250.

Rvachew, S., Nowak, M., & Cloutier, G. (2004). Effect of phonemic perception training on the speech production and phonological awareness skills of children with expressive phonological delay. *American Journal of Speech-Language Pathology, 13*, 250–263.

Sameroff, A. J., & Fiese, B. H. (2000). Transactional regulation: The developmental ecology of early intervention. In J. P. Shonkoff & S. J. Meisels (Eds.), *Handbook of Early Childhood Intervention* (2nd ed., pp. 135–159). New York, Cambridge University Press.

Scarborough, H. S. (1998). Early identification of children at risk for reading difficulties: Phonological awareness and some other promising predictors. In B. K. Shapiro, P. J. Accardo, & A. J. Capute (Eds.), *Specific reading disability: A view of the spectrum* (pp. 75–199). Timonium, MD, York Press.

Seitz, V., Rosenbaum, L. K., & Apfel, N. H. (1985). Effects of a family support intervention: A 10-year follow-up. *Child Development, 56*, 376–391.

Shatil, E., Share, D. C., & Levin, I. (2000). On the contribution of kindergarten writing to grade 1 literacy: A longitudinal study in Hebrew. *Applied Psycholinguistics, 21*, 1–21.

Shaw, D. S., Dishion, T. J., Supplee, L., Gardner, F., & Arnds, K. (2006). Randomized trial of a family-centred approach to the prevention of early conduct problems: 2-year effects of the family check-up in early childhood. *Journal of Consulting and Clinical Psychology, 74*, 1–9.

Shaw, D. S., Gillion, M., Ingoldsby, E. M., & Nagin, D. (2003). Trajectories learning to school-age conduct problems. *Developmental Psychology, 39*, 189–200.

Siefert, H., & Schwarz, I. (1991). Treatment effectiveness of large group basic concept instruction with Head Start students. *Language, Speech, and Hearing Services in the Schools, 22*, 60–64.

Snowling, M. J., Stothard, S. E., & McLean, J. (1996). *The graded nonword reading test.* Reading, Thames Valley Test Company.

Stevenson, H. W., & Newman, R. S. (1986). Long-term predictions of achievement and attitudes in mathematics and reading. *Child Development, 57*, 646–659.

Stipek, D. J., & Byler, P. (1997). Early childhood education teachers: Do they practice what they preach? *Early Childhood Research Quarterly, 12*, 305–325.

Tapp, J. T., Wehby, J. H., & Ellis, D. N. (2001). MOOSES: A multiple option observation system for experimental studies. *Behavior Research Methods, Instruments and Computers, 25,* 53–56.

Tomasello, M. (2003). *A usage-based theory of language acquisition.* Cambridge, Mass., Harvard University Press.

Torgesen, J. K., Wagner, R. K., Rashotte, C. A., Rose, E., Lindamood, P., Conway, T., & Garvan, C. (1999). Preventing reading failure in young children with phonological processing disabilities: Group and individual responses to instruction. *Journal of Educational Psychology, 91,* 579–593.

Tyler, A. A., Lewis, K. E., Haskill, A., & Tolbert, L. C. (2002). Efficacy and cross-domain effects of a morphosyntax and a phonology intervention. *Language, Speech, and Hearing Services in the Schools, 33,* 52–66.

van Kleeck, A., Vander Woude, J., & Hammett, L. (2006). Fostering literal and inferential language skills in Head Start preschoolers with language impairment using scripted book-sharing discussions. *American Journal of Speech-Language Pathology, 15,* 85–95.

Vasilyeva, M., Huttenlocher, J., & Waterfall, H. (2006). Effects of language intervention on syntactic skill levels in preschoolers. *Developmental Psychology, 42,* 164–174.

Velderman, M., Bakermans-Kranenburg, M., Juffer, F., Van Ijzendoorn, M., Mangelsdorf, S., & Zevalkink, J. (2006). Preventing preschool externalizing behavior problems through video-feedback intervention in infancy. *Infant Mental Health Journal, 27,* 466–493.

Vygotsky, L. S. (1962). *Thought and language.* Cambridge, MA, MIT Press.

Wagmiller, R. L., Lennon, M. C., Kuang, L, Alberti, P. M., & Aber, J. L. (2006). The dynamics of economic disadvantage and children's life chances. *American Sociological Review, 71,* 847–866.

Wasik, B., & Bond, M. (2001). Beyond the pages of a book: Interactive book reading and language development in preschool classrooms. *Journal of Educational Psychology, 93,* 243–250.

Webster-Stratton, C., & Hammond, M. (1998). Conduct problems and level of social competence in Head Start children: Prevalence, pervasiveness and associated risk factors. *Clinical Child Psychology and Family Psychology Review, 1,* 101–124.

Webster-Stratton, C., Hollinsworth, T., & Kolpacoff, M. (1989). The long term effectiveness and clinical significance of three cost-effective training programs for families with conduct-problem children. *Journal of Consulting and Clinical Psychology, 57,* 550–553.

Webster-Stratton, C., Reid, M. J., & Hammond, M. (2001). Preventing conduct problems, promoting social competence: A parent and teacher training partnership in Head Start. *Journal of Clinical Child Psychology, 30,* 283–302.

Wechsler, D. (1989). *The preschool and primary scale for intelligence—revised.* Cleveland, OH, The Psychological Corporation.

Werthhamer-Larsson, L., Kellam, S. G., & Oveson-McGregor, K. E. (1990). Teacher interview: Teacher observation of classroom adaptation—revised. In S. G. Kellam (Ed.), *John Hopkins Prevention Center training manual.* Baltimore, MD, John Hopkins University.

Whitehurst, G. J., Arnold, D. S., Epstein, J. N., Angell, A. L., Smith, M., & Fischel, J. E. (1994a). A picture book reading intervention in day care and home for children from low-income families. *Developmental Psychology, 30,* 679–689.

Whitehurst, G. J., Epstein, J. N., Angell, A. L., Payne, A. C., Crone, D. A., & Fischel, J. E. (1994b). Outcomes of an emergent literacy intervention in Head Start. *Journal of Educational Psychology, 86,* 542–555.

Whitehurst, G. J., Falco, F. L., Lonigan, C., Fischel, J. E., DeBaryshe, B. D., Valdez-Menchaca, M. C., & Caufield, M. (1988). Accelerating language development through picture-book reading. *Developmental Psychology, 24,* 552–558.

Wiig, E. H., Secord, W., & Semesl, E. (1992). *Clinical evaluations of language fundamentals-preschool UK.* London, The Psychological Corporation.

Williams, C., & Dalton, E. F. (1989). *The preschool idea proficiency test.* Brea, CA, Ballard & Tighe.

Woodcock, R., & Munoz-Sandoval, A. (2001). *Woodcock-Munoz language survey normative update, English and Spanish forms.* Itasca, IL, Riverside Publishing.

Zimmerman, I. L., Steiner, V. G., & Evatt Pond, R. (2002). *Preschool language scale-revised* (4th ed.). San Antonio, TX, The Psychological Corporation.

STEP 2

IN IMPLEMENTATION: CONSIDERATION OF CONCEPTS AND MECHANISMS FOR TRANSLATION OF RESEARCH INTO PRACTICE

■ Introduction to Step 2

As Forman (this volume) so eloquently states,

> In the recent past, implementation was thought to be an event that would happen automatically when information was made available about a practice or program of good quality. However, literature now informs us that implementation is a complex process in which a practice or program is put into use within a particular context for a particular population.

In this section, the authors provide us a first look at the complex implementation process.

Jim Kohlmoos and Paul Kimmelman ask the critical question as to why evidence-based interventions (EBIs) have not effectively penetrated the public education system in America. They provide an overview of the challenges to knowledge use that are inherent in a decentralized system, and urge that a national model for building organizational capacity for knowledge use be established. An important element in their dynamic model is the focus on the interplay between researchers and practitioners, moving away from the linear model of transfer from research to practice. Their respect for the importance of practitioner engagement in the development and application of research fits well with the implementation cases to come in Steps 3 and 4 of this volume. They discuss the connection between research and education policy at the national level, an issue that has recently received increasing attention (see, e.g., Hess, 2008), and describe the Knowledge Alliance as an advocate agency for knowledge use.

Although Kohlmoos and Kimmelman view the implementation process from the national and policy level, Steve Knotek and his co-authors, Andrea Sauer-Lee and Barbara Lowe-Greenlee take the issue to the local level, focusing on the individual change process. Berninger and Shapiro, in their letter to the Task Force on Evidence-Based Interventions in School Psychology described in the Preface to this volume, note the importance of school psychologists' *consultation skills* (italics in original) in the implementation process. Knotek and his colleagues describes the model of consultee-centered consultation (CCC) as a dissemination vehicle for knowledge diffusion and utilization in supporting teachers to use EBIs as part of a problem-solving process and also to facilitate change in professional practice. They tie the CCC process to Roger's well-recognized model of diffusion of innovation and to professional development, and then demonstrates how CCC might be applied to the response to intervention problem-solving approach, with Instructional Consultation Teams as an example. The focus on teacher conceptual change and understanding is congruent with how implementation is seen by the co-editors of this book.

Serene Olin and her colleagues, Noa Saka, Maura Crowe, Susan Forman, and Kimberly Hoagwood, provide a different perspective on implementation. They present a project of the Task Force on Evidence-Based Interventions in School Psychology, specifically the work of the Committee on Research to Practice, which is studying how researchers of EBIs think about the implementation process. Although their chapter addresses this question from the perspective of social emotional learning (SEL) and mental health related school-based programs, they provide a model for how this question should be studied with developers of academic interventions. They illuminate the vetting process for EBIs, providing a useful table of interventions that have been declared as EBIs by different groups, and then examine the implementation supports available to users. They present research documenting the poor quality of implementation of programs, and the paucity of information about implementation in intervention studies. The emphasis on the teachers as implementers of these nonacademic programs raises important questions for professional development and school psychology consultation practices (see Knotek et al., Chapter 8, this volume). If EBIs are to become standard practice and achieve their outcomes, developers need to become more involved in the implementation issues that their programs demand rather than expect that passive dissemination of information to consumers will suffice.

John Sabatini, the author of the last chapter in this section, proposes a comprehensive model for bringing empirical evidence from the research literature to a problem such as adolescent literacy. He takes a public health approach, suggesting that this model be modified for the unique needs and limited resources of schools. He reminds us of the importance of the unit of analysis in generalizing research findings to educational practice—both the assessment of individuals and the prevalence, scope, and nature of the problem(s) in the student population are relevant. He applies his modified model to a hypothetical middle school where there are substantial literacy needs, but knowing at which level to address those needs is unclear until the assessment is concluded. The importance of linking assessment of instructional needs to intervention in a feasible way is the important message of this chapter.

■ Reference

Hess, F. M. (Ed.) (2008). *When research matters: How scholarship influences education policy.* Cambridge, MA, Harvard Education Press.

7. TOWARD A NEW ERA OF KNOWLEDGE USE IN EDUCATION

National Challenges and Opportunities

Jim Kohlmoos and Paul Kimmelman

In the past 30 years, the U.S. public education system has been the setting for a range of improvement initiatives, from standards-based reform to increased accountability for performance. Smaller schools, longer schedules, and an increased emphasis on instructional leadership (to name just a few) are now facets of many comprehensive reform strategies. One of the least understood or embraced, however, is the use of scientifically based research to improve teaching and learning. To an observer outside the field of education, this would seem strange. The mandate that educational practices be grounded in scientific evidence is found throughout No Child Left Behind (NCLB), the principal federal education law affecting education. And for decades, other professions such as medicine and agriculture have achieved remarkable, widespread success in the generation of knowledge through scientific research. It seems intuitive that the public education system should as well.

Why is it that, on the one hand, the educational literature on effective schools (let alone federal law) regularly cites the importance of using research to improve policies and practices to improve student learning (Supovitz & Klein, 2003), while on the other hand there is ample evidence that the field of education has yet to use scientifically based research systemically or effectively (Hood, 2003)? Indeed, why is it that other professions, such as medicine, have long ago embraced the notion that the systemic generation of knowledge can produce groundbreaking discoveries and fuel innovation, whereas the education profession has not?

The authors wish to acknowledge the contribution of Scott Joftus of Cross & Joftus LLC to this article.

In responding to these important questions, we believe that there are dynamics in play that are particularly unique to the U.S. public education system. These dynamics, which we will describe here, make the effective application of research-based knowledge in education an especially complex and challenging task. Yet despite these obstacles, we will argue that the education profession must continue to advance a "knowledge-use" agenda if it wants to effectively empower teachers and schools with the expertise they need to raise student achievement on a large scale.

■ Navigating a Decentralized System

In fields such as medicine, there is a process by which treatments for major illnesses or surgical techniques are thoroughly researched, field-tested, and peer-reviewed to ensure that they are effective under most conditions. And, despite the many specialties and subfields within the medical profession, its members use a common language, draw from a common knowledge base. The system as a whole is extremely efficient in disseminating information about effective practices. As a result, the level of consensus and coherence among medical researchers and practitioners builds confidence about what works both internally and externally.

The American public education system, in contrast, is not particularly coherent or efficient. Educational research, policy, and practice tend to function independently of one another. There is often little consensus regarding what works, even among experts within the same specialization. Further, there is no uniform mechanism or process by which promising practices are evaluated or disseminated to a field that consists of 50 state education agencies, approximately 15,000 local school districts, and a myriad of schools. Parents, policymakers, and educators receive conflicting messages about what "the research says" on a given topic, which undermines confidence in the system.

At the national level, the need for centralized collection and dissemination of educational innovations has been known for some time. In the 1970s, the United States began experimenting with a number of dissemination and knowledge utilization projects that were designed to help schools improve and innovate. A federally managed infrastructure was developed—modeled similarly on the one created for the agriculture industry—to identify and disseminate research-based practices.

However, this "technocratic" approach was unsuccessful for several reasons. First, the federal government was extremely hesitant to promote some practices over others, instead ceding this decision to states and local school districts. Second, the varied contexts in which educational reforms were implemented made it extremely difficult for researchers and policymakers to identify whether the effects of an educational innovation were due to the reform itself, or the conditions under which it was implemented. Third, although there have been significant attempts to improve the use of knowledge over the past two decades, these attempts have focused more on disseminating research findings rather than on transferring, applying, and using knowledge, resulting in a series of uncoordinated activities (Seashore Louis, 2003).

■ Translating Research to Practice

Criticism of the federal government's management of the Reading First grant program has prompted many observers to note that policymakers have continued to underestimate what it takes to transfer, apply, and manage scientifically based knowledge in specific circumstances and contexts. Kimmelman (2006) argues that resolving these problems requires knowledge acquisition, knowledge management, and knowledge implementation. Simply stated, knowledge acquisition is the ability to acquire and analyze relevant data using credible research or evidence-based information from reliable sources. Knowledge management is the process of using data warehousing technologies that assist in the access and interpretation of data. Finally, knowledge implementation is the ability to offer research and/or evidence-based professional development to those charged with implementing school improvement initiatives.

In other words, effective knowledge utilization is not a simple linear process of "translating research to practice." Mandating the use of scientific evidence, as is the case with Reading First, will not by itself foster the adoption of practices that lead to sustained improvement. Because scientific evidence is highly dependent on the contexts in which educational innovations are implemented, more attention should be given as to how local educators might acquire the competencies associated with knowledge acquisition, management, and implementation. And this capacity must be built both from the bottom up and from the top down, so that local educators, researchers, and other intermediaries are meaningfully involved.

As described in Figure 7.1, knowledge utilization is often viewed as essentially a linear process, in which research generates information; educators implement policies, programs, and practices that are based on that information; and student achievement improves. However, it is the one-way nature of this model that prevents research from benefiting student learning to the extent that it should. What is missing is the substantive collaboration between researchers, on the one hand, and educators and policymakers, on the other, that would allow research to be better prepared to meet educators' and, ultimately, students' needs.

As the process currently works, private and government sponsors support research or evaluations that are proposed by scholars, perhaps in response to

External research

Knowledge

Policies, programs, practices

School/classroom implementation

Increased student achievement   FIGURE 7.1 Linear Model of Knowledge Utilization.

requests for proposals targeted at particular research topics. Unfortunately, these projects rarely address actual problems identified by teachers and school administrators. Although researchers frequently reach out to practitioners to gain access to data and information, to conduct interviews with and observations of practitioners, and to collect data in other ways, it is rare for teachers, administrators, or even policymakers to shape studies in ways that improve school quality or educational practice. This is a critically important consideration for future education research.

Practitioners do have access to research findings. Although they can adapt them for improving policies, programs, and practices, this happens only sporadically. Few systems are in place to encourage practitioners to use research, and those that exist are often fractured and poorly developed. Most practitioners are exposed to some research in their training to become teachers or principals, but rarely see the connection between understanding and implementing it in practice.

How practitioners access research also varies. Some teachers and administrators read about applicable research in the popular press or a trade journal such as *Education Week*. Others learn about research that can be adapted to the classroom or school setting through continuing education, recertification programs, and professional development activities. Yet others learn about research that could inform their practice through informal networks of colleagues. But the incidence of research acquisition in a systemic attempt to improve programs and practices is extremely infrequent. Moreover, there is little incentive for local educators to do so except when it is explicitly required by state and federal accountability systems (Hemsley-Brown & Sharp, 2003).

A more common way for research to influence practice is through programs developed by external service providers, such as software developers, textbook publishers, or district and state administrators. Vendors or school system staffs often use available research to create products or programs intended for use by teachers and principals. They may draw on available research in developing curricula, professional development activities, or plans for turning around schools identified as needing improvement. These products and programs might benefit schools and their students, but the intermediary—whether a commercial vendor or district/state staff—places a barrier between the knowledge producer and the knowledge user. Consequently, practitioners are typically passive and indirect recipients of knowledge, and are therefore less likely to internalize the knowledge and make effective use of the research-based programs and practices (Cross City Campaign for Urban School Education, 2005). As a result, students are less likely to benefit significantly or for any sustained period of time.

A close look at the way the linear model for using knowledge to improve student performance operates reveals that it fails to accommodate two important and related factors. First, the linear model focuses exclusively on what is called explicit knowledge—formalized, systematic, and usually quantifiable—and completely ignores the critical role played by tacit knowledge. According to Nonaka (1998):

> Tacit knowledge consists partly of technical skills—the kind of informal, hard-to-pin-down skills captured in the term "know-how." At the same time, tacit knowledge has an important cognitive dimension. It consists of mental models, beliefs, and perspectives so ingrained that we take them for granted, and therefore cannot easily articulate them. For this very reason, these implicit models profoundly shape how we perceive the world around us. (p. 28)

Second, the linear model fails to acknowledge the important role played by the intellectual communities in which practitioners do their work. Senge (1990) described the importance of "learning communities," places "where people continually expand their capacity to create the results they truly desire, where new and expansive patterns of thinking are nurtured, where collective aspiration is set free, and where people are continually learning how to learn together" (cited in Garvin, 1998, p. 49). Senge's focus on learning communities is an important part of the knowledge building process, but the emphasis needs to be placed both on the knowledge needed for improvement as well as the process of building a learning community.

■ Building More Effective Approaches through Communities of Knowledge

Senge was not the first to stress that practitioners cannot accomplish all that is asked of them on their own. Ideally, it is at the school level that the primary learning community is constituted and where practitioners can be provided the stimulation and support they need to constantly improve their practice.

To foster success, schools as organizations must constantly find new ways to have a continuous and significant impact on student achievement. But, before schools can improve their capacity to help students learn, they first must become "learning organizations"—"skilled at creating, acquiring, and transferring knowledge, and at modifying [their] behavior to reflect new knowledge and insights" (Garvin, 1998, p. 51).

For research to have a significant and long-lasting impact on student achievement, an alternative to the linear model is needed. If the plan for knowledge utilization encompasses both the site level (schools and district administration) as well as the policy level (district school boards of education and the state and federal governments), then the results should be more relevant research and a more direct impact on student learning. The model depicted in Figure 7.2 represents a system by which research and practice

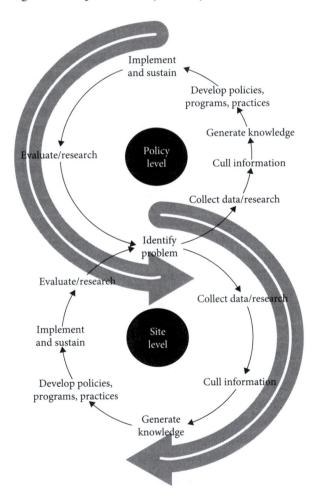

FIGURE 7.2 A Dynamic Model for Knowledge Utilization: Educators, Administrators, and Policymakers Working Collaboratively to Identify Problems and Develop and Implement Solutions.

are integrated. As the model illustrates, the relationship between the two is dynamic; each influences the other and delineates roles and means of interactions for each participant in the system.

The model begins with the notion that practitioners at the site level must be engaged actively and continuously in the development and application of research. Specifically, practitioners can contribute by

- working collaboratively in networks to identify the barriers to higher student achievement;
- collecting and analyzing data and external research that helps them effectively define the barriers and generate strategies for overcoming them;
- generating the knowledge for doing so;
- implementing the strategies and evaluating their effectiveness; and, when appropriate
- bringing to "scale" the strategies shown to improve student outcomes.

Throughout the process, practitioners should be engaged in evaluating the impact of their policies, programs, and practices as well as the process for creating and implementing them (Brown, 1998). At the same time, districts, state education agencies, and the federal government—charged with supporting schools and holding them accountable—would go through a similar process. Under this model, schools and the policymaking organizations would also be contributing to the research base by disseminating and implementing the results of the evaluations of their own efforts.

This dynamic model for developing and applying knowledge has at least three advantages over the linear model of knowledge utilization. First, it empowers teachers and principals, as well as policymakers and administrators, to identify and solve problems in a way that draws on external research. It requires them to engage actively in generating an understanding of the problems as well as considering alternative solutions.

Second, the model recognizes and accommodates the importance of tacit knowledge. High-quality research is critical for helping practitioners and policymakers understand the problems they have identified and generate solutions to those problems.

Application of the dynamic model will create demand for research that is both practical and of high quality. Teachers, administrators, and policymakers will be encouraged to look to the literature for guidance in understanding and ultimately solving problems they have identified as important for them to be more successful. The model will also need to create incentives for researchers to work more closely with schools to ensure the relevance of their work.

Having access to and using external research, however, is a necessary but not sufficient condition for practitioners and policymakers to improve the quality of schools. Although it provides knowledge about the experiences and outcomes of others and a theoretical base for the difficult work of school reform, research rarely can address the tacit knowledge that is critical for successful school reform. Effective application of the "explicit knowledge" derived from external research also requires tacit knowledge. Moreover, this process is not automatic: "sharing tacit knowledge requires interaction and informal learning processes such as storytelling, conversation, coaching, and apprenticeship of the kind that communities of practice provide" (Wenger, McDermott, & Snyder, 2002).

Finally, the model accounts for the dynamic nature of school systems— and of knowledge itself. The interconnected circles in Figure 7.2 represent the idea that problems are never completely solved: Once an apparently effective policy, program, or practice has been implemented to address an identified problem, additional "problems"—such as imperfect implementation, unintended consequences, and sustainability—can be expected. A new process to identify and address the new problems is therefore needed.

The fact that the circles in Figure 7.2 are interconnected represents also the notion that the site and policy levels are dependent on and supportive of one another. As solutions to problems are implemented, teachers, administrators, and policymakers will find ways in which the new policy, program, or practice can be improved or integrated more effectively with others already in existence. As a school learns from its successes and ongoing challenges, it should be disseminating information to its district and state, which in turn can learn from the school's experience and build its capacity to support other schools.

However, there is little chance that research can address all the problems faced by educators and policymakers. Even if it could, there are insufficient incentives or opportunities for teachers and administrators to keep up-to-date on new research and consistently apply it to increasing student achievement (Hemsley-Brown & Sharp, 2003), creating a role for intermediaries. Intermediaries, such as professional researchers and technical assistance providers, play a critical role in the dynamic model of knowledge utilization. First, professional researchers can provide input to both the site and policy levels by providing data and information on the effectiveness of strategies of schools, districts, and states from across the country (see, e.g., Dunn and Miller, Chapter 14, this book). In addition, technical assistance providers provide input by helping to facilitate the community of knowledge process. Such assistance might include working with the organization (school, district or state or federal government) to (a) create the communities of practice, (b) develop their processes, (c) offer advice about managing them, and (d) help to gather and analyze information and data (see Shapiro, Chapter 11, this book).

Perhaps the most consistent and ubiquitous finding in the literature on knowledge use and application is the importance of practitioners having frequent and direct contact with a respected and knowledgeable support person.

Thus, another important potential role for the technical assistance provider is to support the implementation of policies, programs, and practices developed or identified by a community of knowledge (see, e.g., Nelson, Aux, Neall, & Gravois, Chapter 13, this book). To use knowledge to improve educational practice and student outcomes, schools and districts might decide to hire instructional coaches or an individual responsible for facilitating the school or district change process.

Intermediaries generally, and researchers in particular, can also help the site and policy levels with the "output" functions of communities of knowledge. As noted previously, one of the main distinctions between a community of knowledge and community of practice is the responsibility held by the community of knowledge to not only evaluate the implementation and impact of their policies, programs, and practices as communities of practice must do, but also to do so in a way that potentially builds the capacity of other communities across the world. To do so, communities of knowledge must publish and disseminate significant findings and lessons learned. These are tasks that most schools, districts, and state agencies are not accustomed to doing.

To help communities of knowledge fulfill this important responsibility, researchers must change the way they operate. Specifically, researchers need to (a) focus greater attention on helping practitioners and policymakers evaluate the effectiveness of their policies, programs, and practices; (b) determine whether existing research findings are replicable; and (c) work closely with practitioners and policymakers to ensure that the research conducted is rigorous, relevant, and responsive to critical problems.

■ Building Capacity

Although NCLB clearly emphasizes the use of instructional practices and innovations derived from scientifically based research, the capacity of the U.S. Department of Education's research and development enterprise to support NCLB is seriously hindered by inadequate funding. On the basis of the recent on-line report from the American Association for the Advancement of Science (http://www.aaas.org/spp/rd/upd1207t1.pdf), funding for R&D for the U.S. Department of Education is the lowest of any major federal executive agency with a level representing less than one percent of the Department's discretionary budget. Without an increased investment in developing and testing research-based practices, schools and districts will continue to have serious difficulty in fulfilling NCLB's mandate for using such practices.

What is needed are more funds, or a redeployment of extant funding. Although calls for increased funding are nothing new, and typically invoke renewed criticism of the educational establishment as a whole, directing those funds in a targeted way for research and development can greatly improve the efficiency and effectiveness of the system—and by extension, America's competitive advantage on the global stage.

A more systematic process for knowledge acquisition, management, and implementation will likewise build the capacity of state education agencies to assist schools with the most pressing learning needs. A 2005 assessment by the nonpartisan Center on Education Policy emphasizes that "the Department and the Congress should (provide) more funding and...other types of support to help strengthen states' and districts' capacity to assist schools identified for improvement. Many states and districts lack sufficient funds, staff, or expertise to help improve all identified schools...." (p. 29)

Essentially, the knowledge marketplace is seriously underdeveloped in education. In simplified market terms, NCLB stimulates and shapes demand for research-based solutions through its accountability and sanctioning provisions, whereas the Education Sciences Reform Act (ESRA) represents the supply side through its investments in research and development. Although there are numerous provisions in NCLB for scientific-based research and in ESRA for school improvement, the links between supply and demand have not been able to fully mature and they remain functionally weak. We attribute part of the problem to bureaucratic and implementation inertia. But the problem is also exacerbated by a lack of incentives to build capacity and create stronger linkages among policy, research, and practice.

■ Advancing a Knowledge Agenda in Federal Policy

There are three promising reasons to be optimistic that the federal education policy is progressing toward a new era of knowledge-driven reform, where effective knowledge utilization takes its rightful place as a central organizing concept for improvement and innovation. First, the standards-based reform framework on which the past three reauthorizations of Elementary and Secondary Education Act (ESEA)—including No Child Left Behind Act—have been based continues to receive fundamental support from most policymakers and education groups. It should be noted here that most of the criticisms directed at NCLB have centered on more specific issues relating to ineffective implementation, jurisdictional questions, technical accountability problems, and insufficient capacity in terms of funding and expertise. Although these issues are important, the standards-based framework remains intact, creating common ground for fundamental policy agreement on both sides of the congressional aisle. We expect the concept of standards-based reform to again be an integral part of the future reauthorizations of ESEA. Although ESEA was not reauthorized in 2007 as some had expected, it is unlikely that the core concepts will be changed in the future.

In fact, one could assume that it is the knowledge gained from the process of implementing the law that will ultimately lead to making changes that will improve it. For example, few will argue that the current "Adequate Yearly Progress" provisions are the only or best way to measure school success. The Department of Education with the blessing of Congress experimented with several alternative growth models that will likely be considered in the next reauthorization. The use of knowledge and evidence should play an even greater role the longer it takes for Congress to take up the law again.

Second, in keeping with this standards-based construct, we believe that federal education policy is headed toward a new era characterized by a more collaborative approach to school improvement. Ever since the launch of a national standards-based reform effort by President George H. Bush in Charlottesville, VA, in 1989, education policy has evolved in progressive phases in concert with the implementation of the elements of standards-based reform:

Standards: In the spring of 1991 the Bush administration announced *America 2000 with* two important but controversial provisions dealing with standards. One provision called for the development of "voluntary national standards" in core subjects. Another provision called for states either to embrace the National Education Goals and adopt voluntary national standards or to develop their own. While Bush's 1992
election defeat effectively ended *America 2000*, the Clinton administration maintained the national focus on standards through its *Goals 2000* education initiative.

Alignment: Spurred by Goals 2000 and Clinton's Improving America's Schools Act of 1994—the precursor to NCLB—most states moved forward in developing standards and assessments. The goal was to establish equitable and unified state systems for identifying problems and directing resources and solutions to those schools in greatest need. The alignment process proved to be far more complex than some initially anticipated and was somewhat slowed by weak accountability systems.

Accountability: Passing the *No Child Left Behind Act* (NCLB) was a third element in the standards-based reform process, tying federal sanctions and awards to school progress. State standards and tests continued to serve as the foundation for instruction and assessment, but under NCLB's accountability provisions they became a federal matter. The law further extended the use of evidence in education by mandating the use of scientifically based research in NCLB programs, effectively mandating the use of evidence in making basic decisions about K-12 education.

Solutions: NCLB and the often overlooked Education Sciences Reform Act (ESRA) provide the impetus for what should logically be the next phase of the standards-based reform process—the development and implementation of solutions to the problems identified by the NCLB accountability measures. The question is whether standards-based reform can emerge from an accountability phase and move on to real classroom solutions for improving teaching and student achievement.

In summary, the focus on standards and assessments in the late 1980s and early 1990s spawned a major focus on the alignment of standards, curriculum, and assessments that, in turn, resulted in the current emphasis on accountability and real reform initiatives. The next logical step in this standards-based continuum is a more comprehensive and vigorous focus on school improvement—when significant new resources and expertise would be targeted both to turning around low performing schools and to building a knowledge capacity and infrastructure in all schools for sustained improvement. We believe this is where the federal education policy in general and the future reauthorizations of ESEA are headed.

And third, should future reauthorizations of ESEA focus on school improvement as expected, the time will be ripe for the emergence of education's research and development as a key catalyst for improvement and innovation, particularly through the reauthorization of the Education Sciences Reform Act. Current law undervalues and underestimates what it takes to produce, transfer, apply, and manage scientifically based knowledge in specific circumstances and contexts. If various advocacy efforts are effective, knowledge transfer and utilization can and should become an essential component in the next phase of federal reform efforts.

There are a number of promising examples of the effective use of knowledge. One excellent case is the productive working relationship between researchers at Johns Hopkins University and teachers and administrators at the Talent Development High School in Baltimore. Another noteworthy development is the groundbreaking work of the Strategic Education Research Program (SERP) that was initiated in the 1990s by the National Research Council with support from the U.S. Department of Education. SERP developed a powerful conceptual framework for knowledge development and utilization and is now in the process of building an infrastructure in such locations as Boston.

■ Advocating for Effective Knowledge Use

Of course, federal education policy will not simply evolve to a new knowledge emphasis on the strength of its own validity. Strong advocacy efforts are needed to advance the knowledge agenda and mobilize the political will for substantive change. With the impending reauthorizations of ESEA and

ESRA, the knowledge sector in education needs to work as a community and mobilize its efforts as is commonly performed by the knowledge industries in health, defense, energy, and agriculture. In this context, we propose a comprehensive, national knowledge utilization initiative based on the following guiding principles:

1. *Accelerating and Sustaining Improvement*—Effective use of education knowledge can significantly enhance, accelerate, and sustain the nationwide efforts to improve academic performance and close achievement gaps in K-12 education.

2. *Applying Useable Knowledge to School Improvement*—Knowledge that is used to shape policy and practice should be derived from the best available empirical evidence as well as informed by sound professional judgment.

3. *Collaborating among Key Stakeholders*—The effective use of knowledge in school improvement requires the active participation of and the ongoing collaboration among five key stakeholder groups: practitioners, policymakers, researchers, developers and providers, and intermediaries/facilitators who help to broker and sustain the collaborations.

4. *Building a Dynamic Knowledge Base*—Effective knowledge use for school improvement depends on dynamic ongoing exchanges of data and information among the stakeholders and involves a continuous process of research, application, and adaptation. As knowledge is used and adapted, new knowledge is created and applied in a cumulative, iterative fashion.

5. *Focusing School Improvement Policies*—School improvement policies at the federal, state, and local levels should focus priority attention on the effective use of knowledge and create incentives to stimulate greater demand for and increased supply of knowledge-based solutions.

■ Building a Knowledge Alliance

In the spring of 2007, the National Education Knowledge Industry Association (the trade association for R&D organizations in education with which we have been closely affiliated) officially changed its name to Knowledge Alliance. The term is intended to reflect a new, dynamic view of the future of the K-12 education market place. The Alliance foresees a new knowledge era in education reform in which the escalating demand for school improvement solutions is matched by a growing supply of research-based innovation. The Alliance participants envision a robust, responsive, and rigorous R&D infrastructure where researchers, developers, practitioners, and policymakers work together to develop and apply research-based knowledge to critical education problems.

The idea of a knowledge alliance is not only compelling from a policy point of view, but also essential for mobilizing a strategic advocacy effort making practical progress through advocacy. For all the reasons mentioned above, the time is uniquely ripe for a strong and comprehensive effort in shaping federal policy that brings together the research enterprise and the school improvement community. The Alliance has already been actively involved in the process for the next reauthorization of Elementary and Secondary Education Act and will be opportunistic in advancing a knowledge agenda in other relevant statues as well as in the annual appropriations process in Congress. Building the capacity of a knowledge infrastructure and culture will be a key part of the Knowledge Alliance's advocacy agenda in the years ahead.

In addition to mobilizing a strong advocacy effort for knowledge-driven education reform, the Knowledge Alliance has a leadership role to play in examining dynamic societal forces affecting education in the future and probing knowledge-based entrepreneurial innovations to anticipate the future. To complement its advocacy efforts, the Alliance plans to convene policy forums, executive retreats, and big ideas symposia. There is much excitement among Alliance members for future prospects.

■ Conclusions

The very nature of the title of this chapter identifies the daunting challenge confronting policymakers and those with vested interests in improving student achievement and the quality of teaching in U.S. schools through knowledge use, as in the medical and agricultural models. The critical key to improving American schools is to use a systemic plan based on proven practices that would be implemented with integrity. In medicine, for example, most treatments for major illnesses or surgical techniques are similar after having been thoroughly researched and tested to ensure they are effective under most conditions. The reason for the uniform application of treatments and procedures in medicine is because there is a system in place. Using high-quality standards for education practices, aligning them to interventions, holding practitioners collaboratively as well as individually accountable for their implementation, and assessing results to ensure the interventions are working could lead to greater student achievement and higher quality teaching in schools.

Most people, when thinking of a system, visualize a number of interacting parts that form a functional whole object. The American school system, however, does not conform to what most people would visualize as an efficient system. Rather, the American school system is a collection of parts that work independently of one another with no uniform application of interventions. Therefore, focusing on translating science-supported instruction for evidence-based practices will require new ways of thinking about how 50 different state education agencies, approximately 15,000 local school districts and a myriad of hybrid schools in the United States could be encouraged to accept new methods of educating their students.

Since 1965, the federal government through the ESEA and other federal funding policies has made an effort to achieve some form of national systemic school improvement efforts, but the results have not been very promising. Until the reauthorization of ESEA known as the NCLB, most of the nearly 50 years of reauthorizations passed without much fanfare. Not until Congress reauthorized NCLB in 2001 and included serious sanctions and accountability provisions for schools not meeting benchmarks did educators give much serious thought to a national level role for school improvement planning.

Though subject to considerable debate, there needs to be a national model for building organizational capacity in schools through the use of a knowledge framework. The framework includes knowledge acquisition, knowledge management, knowledge production, and knowledge implementation. Using the knowledge framework and "pushing the envelope" suggest that federal funding would be an incentive for schools to apply the principles of science-supported instruction and evidence-based programs. A clear and identifiable pattern of improvement in the quality of instruction and student achievement in American schools has the potential to emerge.

■ References

Brown, J. (1998). Research that reinvents the corporation. In *Harvard business review on knowledge management* (pp. 153–180). Boston, Harvard Business School Press.

Center on Education Policy. (2005, March). *From the capital to the classroom: Year 3 of the No Child Left Behind Act*. Washington, DC, Author.

Cross City Campaign for Urban School Education. (2005). *A delicate balance: District policies and classroom practice*. Chicago, Author.

Garvin, D. (1998). Building a learning organization. In *Harvard business review on knowledge management* (pp. 47–80). Boston, Harvard Business School Press.

Hemsley-Brown, J., & Sharp, C. (2003). The use of research to improve professional practice: A systematic review of the literature. *Oxford Review of Education*, *29*, 449–470.

Hood, P. (2003, July 1). *Scientific research and evidence-based practice*. San Francisco, WestEd. Retrieved from www.wested.org/online_scientific. research.pdf.

Kimmelman, P. (2006). *Implementing NCLB: Creating a knowledge framework to support school improvement*. Thousand Oaks, CA, Corwin Press.

Nonaka, I. (1998). The knowledge-creating company. In *Harvard business review on knowledge management* (pp. 21–46). Boston, Harvard Business School Press.

Petrides, L., & Guiney, S. (2002). Knowledge management for school leaders: An ecological framework for thinking schools. *Teachers College Record*, *104*, 1702–1717.

Seashore Louis, K. (2005). Knowledge producers and policymakers: Kissing kin or squabbling siblings? In Kenneth Leithwood (Section Ed.), *International handbook of education* policy (pp. 219–238). Springer, London.

Senge, P. (1990). *The fifth discipline*. New York, Doubleday.

Supovitz, J., & Klein, V. (2003, November). *Mapping a course for improved student learning: How innovative schools systematically use student performance data to guide improvement*. Philadelphia, Consortium for Policy Research in Education.

8. Consultee-Centered Consultation as a Vehicle for Knowledge Diffusion and Utilization

Steve Knotek, Andrea Sauer-Lee, and Barbara Lowe-Greenlee

The purpose of this chapter is to demonstrate how consultee-centered consultation (CCC) can facilitate the diffusion and use of innovations in education. As schools attempt to meet their ever widening mandate to realize the academic, social, and psychological potential of all students, they are increasingly looking to implement proven innovations to attain these goals. However, to successfully foster the diffusion of innovations schools must have a systematic approach to support the effectiveness, transportability, and dissemination of new programs (Knotek, 2007). Programmatic content cannot simply be downloaded into schools via single session workshops or through administrative mandate. Transportability of innovation requires an embedded diffusion process that takes into account professional development needs, adaptation to the school's unique ecological context, a workable evaluation process, and a means to encourage system acceptance of the model (Glisson, 2002).

One movement that would potentially benefit from CCC is the utilization of evidence-based interventions such as the problem-solving approaches found in response to intervention (RTI), an innovation in supporting students at-risk for academic failure. The chapter begins with a description of CCC and how it can be utilized to support knowledge diffusion and utilization. The chapter moves on to describe how it can support problem-solving methods utilized in RTI. Next, there is an acknowledgment of the difficulties and obstacles of diffusing and using innovations in schools. Finally, the chapter concludes with a look at the application of CCC in one existing approach to RTI, the problem-solving model, to demonstrate how schools and systems can use a well-established, well-researched form of consultation to meet student, faculty, and staff needs.

■ Consultation as a Vehicle for Knowledge Diffusion and Utilization

Consultation is generally defined as an indirect service through which a consultee (i.e., a teacher) gains support for a client (i.e., a student) by engaging in a problem-solving process with a consultant (Bergan & Kratochwill, 1990; Caplan, 1970). This core attribute of consultation leads it to be directly useful in supporting problem-solving innovations in schools. For instance, in a school setting a teacher may initiate consultation with a school psychologist in order to problem-solve about ways to provide classroom support for a child who is a frequent target of bullies. In this case, the consultation's goal will be to enhance the teacher's acquisition of new perspectives and skills that she may use in creating new solutions to the work problem (classroom interventions to stop bullying).

Consultee-Centered Consultation

This type of consultation evolved out of Caplan's original model and has developed to the point that it is in many ways distinct from the form of consultation traditionally known as Caplanian Mental Health Consultation (Lambert, 2004). The contemporary definition of consultee-centered consultation was developed over three international seminars in the past 10 years and contains the following key elements (Knotek & Sandoval, 2003):

1. Consultee-centered consultation emphasizes a nonhierarchical helping role relationship between a resource (consultant) and a person or group (consultee) who seeks professional help with a work problem involving a third party (client).
2. This work problem is a topic of concern for the consultee who has a direct responsibility for the learning, development, or productivity of the client.
3. The primary task of the consultant is to help the consultee pinpoint critical information and then consider multiple views about well-being, development, intrapersonal, interpersonal, and organizational effectiveness appropriate to the consultee's work setting. Ultimately, the consultee may reframe his/her prior conceptualization of the work problem.
4. The goal of the consultation process is the joint development of a new way of conceptualizing the work problem so that the repertoire of the consultee is expanded and the professional relationship between the consultee and the client is restored or improved. As the problem is jointly reconsidered, new ways of approaching the problem may lead to acquiring new means to address the work dilemma.

The name "consultee-centered" consultation itself reflects the core focus of the consultation relationship, which is predicated on facilitating change in the conceptual understandings of the consultee. Although the expectation exists that clients will ultimately be better served through consultation, the prime goal is to reframe consultees' knowledge and reconceptualize their understanding of the work problem. CCC seeks to facilitate change through the interpersonal process of the relationship, and can be considered as open with respect to the content discussed during consultation.

Consultee-Centered Consultation as a Support for Knowledge Use and Diffusion

CCC may be used in both a direct and indirect manner to support the utilization and diffusion of innovations. Consultation can be used as a direct intervention to help a consultee problem solve and gain a new perspective on a work problem by focusing only on the consultee's prior knowledge and guiding her through an in-depth problem identification process to support a focused concern with a limited number of students (Knotek, 2003). Indirectly, CCC can also be used in a manner analogous to Caplan's program-centered and consultee-centered administrative consultation (Caplan & Caplan, 1993). In this case, consultation can be used at a system and/or classroom level to support consultees' (e.g., superintendents, principals, and teachers) implementation of a range of problem-solving innovations within the distinctive climate of a school district, school building, or a particular classroom.

For example, innovative reading interventions often come with their own set of assumptions about students' skill level and academic ability. However, if a student does not have the prior knowledge or skill (e.g., vocabulary knowledge) assumed in the innovation and the student falls below the presupposed norm, the innovation may not initially be effective with that student. At the classroom level, CCC can help a teacher consultee consider how to effectively adapt and implement a reading program within the context of her classroom composed of "below grade level" readers. These direct and indirect qualities of consultation, as a stand-alone problem-solving process and as an innovation utilization tool, give it promise as a means to support the utilization and diffusion of prevention programs into the complex ecological environments of schools.

Diffusion and Utilization of Innovation

The art of diffusing knowledge is based on a large body of literature across many disciplines. Interestingly, research indicates that the way information is diffused and linked to current practice is strikingly similar across disciplines, such that research on knowledge diffusion from any discipline could instruct an educational system on the know-how of diffusion of an educational initiative or innovation (Thayer & Wolf, 1984). For an innovation to find an existence in real-world practice, information about the new idea or technology must be disseminated within an organization in a process of interactive learning (Morone & Taylor, 2004), and then become embedded into the system through unreserved acceptance of the need and use for this new innovation. Rogers uses four elements (in italics) to define diffusion, "as the process by which (1) an *innovation* (2) is *communicated* through certain channels (3) over *time* (4) among members of *a social system*" (Rogers, 2003).

Innovation Characteristics

Advances can be thought of as ideas and practices that are "perceived as new by an individual or other unit of adoption" (Rogers, 2003, p. 11). However, all innovations are not the same and their diffusion will be impacted by their unique qualities. Five characteristics are used by Rogers to describe important dimensions of innovations: (a) relative advantage, (b) compatibility, (c) complexity, (d) trialability, and (e) observability. Relative advantage refers to the added value an innovation brings to a situation. Compatibility describes the fit of the innovation with the past, present and future values and needs of the adopters. Complexity is "the degree to which an innovation is perceived as difficult to understand and use" (Rogers, 2003, p. 16). Trialability refers to the ability of an innovation to be piloted in a limited manner. Finally, observability describes the visibility of the innovation to others.

Communication Channels

Rogers (2003) places such importance on communication that he refers to it as the "essence" of the diffusion process. Communication is how diffusion happens. The facilitation of diffusion occurs through a communication channel in which a person who understands the innovation assists another person's adoption of it. Traditionally in schools such channels have taken the form of dyadic presentations, manuals, and limited supervision (Gravois, Knotek, & Babinski, 2002). Consultation's parallel focus on communication in the service of problem-solving makes it an ideal channel with which to support innovation dissemination. After all, the ultimate goal of CCC is to facilitate the consultee's acquisition of new means to address work dilemmas.

Time

Adoption of complex innovations occurs across such dimensions of time as the speed of the decision process and the rate of adoption. Dissemination requires the buy-in of personnel across numerous levels of system and its diffusion will impact the capacity of a system to respond to the changes necessary to successfully implement the paradigm.

Social System

Diffusion within any given school system has to occur across numerous inter-related levels and social boundaries. District, school, and classroom level units of the social system are involved, and each unit has its own norms, decision-making, and change agents. Diffusion is complex and successful implementation and sustainability will need to be managed and facilitated. An effective social process will need to be in place to support the behavioral change of the targeted adopters—superintendents, principals, teachers, and parents. School personnel will need to take on the role of facilitating communication and supporting professional development to successfully consider an innovation into a district and its classrooms.

Knowledge Utilization

Utilization of an intervention is a tremendous undertaking that requires considerable thought, planning, and hard work. Kratochwill and Stoiber (2002), writing on EBI research protocols, discuss how interventions are not necessarily ready for utilization or diffusion simply by the virtue of statistical significance in studies of effectiveness. If an innovation is to have impact, then it needs to systematically account for factors related to utilization and dissemination, and the research-to-practice gap between laboratory efficacy and real-world effectiveness will have to be bridged (Hoagwood, 2001).

For example, systemic problem-solving approaches such as RTI are notable because of the breadth and depth of their reach across the population of schools' general education staff and students, and for the complexity of their multilayered structure. Guided by a prevention perspective that reframes students' functioning from a point of view of deficit to one of potential, the RTI innovation changes how teachers and school psychologists should conduct important aspects of their professional business. Innovations of such scope are complex and therefore are challenging to implement and utilize with fidelity. How will the knowledge and skill necessary for implementation of RTI be acquired by working professionals? One piece of the answer may be to focus on the process of professional development that is tied to innovation implementation.

CCC is well suited to support the diffusion of the problem-solving innovations because it offers an effective communication channel that can be utilized within the various units of a school's social system. In addition, CCC can be used to help adopters think through the relative advantages, compatibility, and complexity of implementing a problem-solving innovation such as RTI in their site. This chapter continues with an overview of RTI and includes examples of how CCC can be used to enhance teachers' delivery of instruction within the RTI problem-solving innovation.

■ Problem Solving in Response to Intervention

Education has seen its fair share of "innovations" and "new movements" arrive backed by enthusiasm and good intentions, only to see them soon fade away. Reasons for implementation failure are many and include a lack of success because they are difficult to implement, they do not meet the needs of students or teachers, or they are not adequately supported through effective professional development (Hoagwood, 2001). Given the checkered history of innovation implementation, it is understandable how educators may experience "innovation fatigue." Feelings of resistance to new educational innovations may be expected given the realities of today's high-stakes testing educational environment, where there is little time, money, or desire for a new innovation even if it is evidence-based.

One such new movement currently impacting schools is RTI, written into the reauthorization of IDEA in 2004. RTI has created interest among lawmakers, researchers, and educational innovators because of its goals of serving children with instructional and behavioral needs, with the potential to benefit both general education and special education populations (Gresham, 2002). However, RTI is a complex intervention that requires change in the tools, goals, and methods used by school personnel.

RTI is characterized by three core concepts: (a) The application of high-quality instruction, (b) systematic and ongoing measurement of students' response to interventions, and (c) the use of data to inform instruction (NASDSE, 2006; NJCLD, 2005). It is distinguished by a tiered, data-driven process that includes early intervention for students who are at-risk for academic difficulty and who are served with evidence-based interventions. RTI is designed to work within the regular education setting with the aid of support staff and problem-solving teams, with labels such as Student Support Teams. Most importantly, the RTI process has the potential to address the need for a research-based approach to academic interventions and classroom assessment. It may be conceptualized as an innovation whose interventions (i.e., academic skill building tasks) are embedded within interventions (i.e., data-driven assessment), within interventions (i.e., a problem-solving team). The diffusion and utilization of such a multifaceted innovation requires an effective delivery mechanism.

RTI and Problem Solving

One of the major models of RTI is the problem-solving approach (RTI PS) (Christ, Burns, & Ysseldyke, 2005). It is thought to be favored by practitioners who like it because of its flexibility and usefulness with individual students (Fuchs & Fuchs, 2006). RTI PS involves collaboration between service providers and classroom teachers, is flexible in that it emphasizes teachers' development of individualized interventions, derives interventions from the analysis of instructional/environmental conditions unique to a child in a specific classroom, customizes teacher training and support to meet individual teacher's needs, and increases the capacity of teachers to meet their own professional development needs (Christ, Burns, & Ysseldyke, 2005).

RTI as an Innovation

This chapter broadly discusses the use of CCC to support the diffusion and utilization of innovations, and has focused on RTI as an innovation to illustrate potential linkages. However, for the sake of clarity it is important to specify how RTI merits the designation of innovation. In an overarching sense it is argued that the organizing RTI framework, with its general emphasis on assessment-for-intervention and focus on instruction within the general education environment, is an innovation. Luecke and Katz (2003) view innovation, "generally understood as the successful introduction of a new thing or method...Innovation is the embodiment, combination, or synthesis of knowledge in original, relevant, valued new products, processes, or services" (p. 2). One of the innovative elements of RTI is the synthesis of the characteristics highlighted in the RTI problem-solving model in a relevant and valued way to improve instruction for all children.

RTI PS has the potential to change how many schools address their problem-solving business and has qualities of being both evolutionary and revolutionary across different dimensions. Given that RTI consists of an integration of theoretical orientations in combination with specific practices, confusion may result when discussing RTI as an innovation. For example, it is possible to be talking about Instructional Assessment problem-solving steps (an innovation) or the fact that they are embedded within a programmatic structure (e.g., Instructional Consultation), which is a larger synthesis type of innovation. In this chapter, the discussion of innovation will at times be focused on the use of specific components of the problem-solving process, such as data-driven assessment for intervention, and at other times it will focus on the larger conception of RTI as a systemic and integrated problem-solving program.

■ Integrating Diffusion and Utilization in Problem Solving

RTI is a multifaceted innovation that will require attention to the process by which it is diffused and ultimately utilized in schools. Although highly regarded because of its ability to target problems and solutions and with specific students, RTI PS is also very difficult to implement. The innovation's very adaptability to unique contexts requires adopters to have deep knowledge and skill to implement it effectively. The promise and complexity of RTI PS as an innovation therefore makes it an exemplar with which to illustrate how CCC can be used as a vehicle of dissemination and implementation of innovations. The next section of the chapter will discuss how CCC can be used as the vehicle to integrate the elements and processes needed for knowledge diffusion and utilization within this problem-solving innovation.

Roger's four elements of diffusion and the basic tenets of utilization need to be explicitly and adequately addressed in an innovation's implementation. Adopters must attend to an innovation's characteristics, communication channels, time, social system dynamic, and the gap between an innovation's idealized state and the reality of the context of implementation.

Characteristics

CCC can facilitate the diffusion of a problem-solving innovation by supporting the diffusion process along its critical dimensions. A consultant can help adopters attend to the innovation's relative advantage, its compatibility with the organization's past, present and future practices, and the relative complexity of its implementation.

Relative Advantage

One of the first questions that adopters and other end users should, and often do, ask about an innovation is "Why bother?" The utility and superiority of a new problem-solving innovation may not be readily apparent to teachers, students, parents, administrators, and tax payers. Innovations that do not pass the basic "why bother" criterion are unlikely to be diffused in any appreciable manner. Therefore, a process should be in place to enhance users' understanding and appreciation of the added value of a problem-solving innovation. A consultant using CCC can help a principal or superintendent address this dimension.

At times superintendents and school boards do not agree on the need for innovation; for example, a superintendent who recognized the need for a more effective and equitable academic problem-solving process in her district may face a board completely at home with the status quo. To help a frustrated superintendent/consultee, a consultant would work with her to understand and clarify the board's concerns so that the board's sense of "why bother" could be ameliorated and a more collaborative stance struck. The consultant would help the consultee pinpoint critical information about the situation, by asking questions such as "What are board members' understandings of the current problem solving process?," "What do they see as the goals of problem solving?," and "What incentive would the board need to seriously consider and embrace a change?" The consultee would be challenged to consider multiple views about sources of concern or disinterest on the part of board members. Eventually, the superintendent might reconsider her view of the board as resistant and instead arrive at a more flexible and workable conceptualization of the problem.

Compatability

Educational innovations are not implemented in a vacuum; districts, schools, and classrooms all have sanctioned means to problem solve and meet students' needs. The compatibility and goodness-of-fit of an innovative problem-solving program within a school needs to be considered during diffusion. Federal and state guidelines ensure that most schools currently have some kind of formalized problem-solving process in place. An innovation, no matter how spectacular, must be integrated into a school's existing process.

CCC can be used to help staff undertake a "gap analysis" (Vail, Gravois, & Rosenfield, 2005) to see what problem-solving needs the school currently possesses and to think through how a problem-solving innovation might fit in the school's emerging future. Consultation would begin with helping the stakeholders put into words a vision of how the innovation would fit with the school's goals. Questions such as "How do we want the school's problem solving to function?" and "What are the school's problem-solving goals?" would be posed to the staff. They would then assess current problem-solving needs and functions. The consultant would ask questions about how problem solving currently worked and how teachers currently received support for problems. Next, the consultation would center on a discussion and exploration of "the gap" that existed between the vision and the present state of affairs. Personnel would consider changes necessary to narrow or close the identified gap and think through the kinds of resources that would be necessary to bring about change. Finally, the consultant would support the staff's consideration of how the innovation would support and/or enhance their newly instantiated problem-solving goals. Specific issues and concerns would vary by site and individual; however, consultation would support the exploration and hopeful resolution of a potential roadblock to implementation.

Complexity

Schools are incredibly dynamic and complex environments. A problem-solving process that involves the cooperation and coordination of efforts of individual teachers, experts, teams, administrators, families, and students may be perceived at best as challenging and at worst impossible to understand and make use of. Stakeholders may resist participating in a process that appears to be ungainly or unresponsive to their needs. In such a circumstance, consultation could be used to help stakeholders develop policies that would facilitate communication, buy-in, and ease of use.

First, the consultant would help establish a process and structure in which representative viewpoints are expressed individually and in groups. Because of her role the consultant would be free to move up and down and across levels of the school's structure so that the voices of a diverse set of participants would be heard. Relevant personnel would be engaged in discussion and an environment in which individuals could safely express both concerns and hopes about the innovation and its effects would be established. Group discussions would be mediated and effective and supportive communication strategies modeled. Consultation strategies such as addressing a lack of self-confidence to foster hope in the potential of the innovation would be used. Buy-in would be facilitated by the consultant as the groups exchanged ideas, explored multiple views of the issues, and worked toward developing a common vision. Ultimately, she would work with the consultees to help them formulate coherent and reasonable structures that would mesh with the resources available in the building. Consultees would be encouraged to consider issues such as training needs, staffing, and coordination of efforts.

If schools are to provide more than a band-aid approach to problem solving and if they wish to be systemic and comprehensive, then the issue of complexity must be dealt with. Emerging innovations to foster improved and efficacious approaches to problem solving will benefit from having a process such as CCC to attend to dimensions critical to successful diffusion.

Communication Channels

Communication is defined as "an act or instance of transmitting" (In Merriam-Webster Online Dictionary 2008) and the intransitive verb *diffusing* (from diffusion) is defined as "to spread out or become transmitted especially by contact" (Webster Online Dictionary, 2008). Conceptually, then communication and diffusion are linked through the process of transmission, in which communication is the contact by which something is spread out. From this perspective, diffusion of an innovation may be framed as what happens when a person with knowledge of the innovation contacts another person to assist in its dispersal and its adoption. How might CCC buttress communication or serve to enhance the contact between the person diffusing an innovation and the person who is adopting it?

Essential characteristics of CCC that support communication are as follows: (a) Consultation will support orderly reflection, (b) challenges may be viewed through multiple perspectives, and (c) hypotheses to explain and solve challenges will be generated (Knotek & Sandoval, 2003). CCC may be a potent addition to the innovation diffusion process because it will provide structure to the contact, encourage a thoughtful examination of challenges to implementation such as complexity and compatibility, and result in the generation of hypotheses related to an action plan for implementation. Most importantly, CCC may support the collaborative potential between the person responsible for disseminating the innovation and the person who will adopt and utilize it. This can occur through fostering mutual construction of a shared reality about the challenges in implementing the innovation (Rosenfield, 2000).

Successful Implementation and Utilization of New Processes

Bringing a problem-solving innovation into a school and implementing the process will require existing school personnel to develop and acquire new skills or use existing skills in new ways in order to be successful diffusion agents, assessors, interveners, and problem-solvers. This process will vary according to staff members' existing skills and the requisite skills associated with individuals' new roles. The skills themselves will vary widely, as well, from proper screening and formative assessment administration to data collection, presentation, and interpretation. School personnel will need to be consumers of research, able to match problem-solving needs with appropriate research-based strategies while setting goals and implementing class-wide, group, and individualized interventions at the same time (Burns & Coolong-Chaffin, 2006). The challenge of utilizing problem-solving highlights a need to provide for skill acquisition and integration.

Meeting the Demand for Skill Acquisition

Acquisition of the skills needed to utilize a comprehensive problem-solving innovation must be planned for and integrated into the diffusion process. To successfully impact the students whom an innovation is intended to profit, school staff may need to learn a myriad of new skills. Effective problem solving may require that teachers acquire the ability to undertake tasks such as curriculum-based assessment, data charting, and single subject design. Although these components of problem solving may be familiar to specialists such as school psychologists, other school professionals may not be well versed in them. How will other professionals acquire proficiency in these skills? How will this acquisition of knowledge occur in these professionals' school-based work setting? Preservice training for most teachers focuses on grade level content, curriculum, and instruction. If problem solving actually rests at the feet of teachers, then some vehicle must be found to embed professional development in the school setting. Successful diffusion and utilization of problem-solving needs to be systematically presented to teachers. The model of professional development offered by Showers and Joyce (1996), and utilized in some consultation models (Rosenfield & Gravois, 1996), offers a comprehensive means to support school-based professionals' acquisition of skills.

What Does Effective Professional Development Look Like?

Higher-order skills and problem-solving abilities will not be acquired by sitting through a single session "drive by" training. Roy (1998) encourages schools to consider the bottom line for professional development to be whether or not a training program makes a measurable impact on the achievement of students in classrooms. Showers and Joyce (1996) suggest that four major levels of impact are needed to ensure that education professionals can adequately implement a new intervention: Awareness, conceptual understanding, skill acquisition, and application of skills. The levels are as follows:

> Level One: An awareness of the problem is heightened through didactic presentations that result in a person's ability to cite the general ideas and principles associated with the intervention. In problem solving, a teacher would be able to cite important features of the innovation such as scientifically based interventions and data-based decision making.

> Level Two: An individual's deepening conceptual understanding of an intervention is facilitated through modeling and demonstration. For example, in problem solving a teacher who had acquired conceptual understanding would be able to articulate the difference between assessment for referral and assessment for intervention.

> Level Three: Skill acquisition occurs when a teacher engages in simulated practices that are observed and commented on by a knowledgeable observer. An individual leaning how to operationally define her goals for a student's sight word vocabulary would practice the process on several different examples.

> Level Four: This level of professional development is reached when a person is able to demonstrate a successful application of the new innovation within the actual context of his or her school site. For instance, when a teacher is able to implement instructional problem solving with fidelity with a number of students she will be considered to have reached the level of skill application.

Problem-solving innovations are varied in their complexity and depth of impact, and it is reasonable to expect that the form and process of programs would vary immensely. On the top of this variance between innovations, there will likely be disparities in the capacity and willingness of districts and schools to support professional development. Some districts commit time and other resources to attain the levels of professional development suggested by Showers and Joyce (1996), whereas other districts do little to enhance diffusion and utilization of problem-solving innovations. A well-designed and executed professional development program is invaluable and can serve to enhance and improve teachers' acquisition of problem-solving skills through Showers and Joyce's levels.

Using CCC to support Utilization of
Problem-Solving Innovation

Awareness

Problem solving is such a ubiquitous term that without context and elabo-ration it has no real meaning. An innovation designed to support problem solving would need to have components specified and be differentiated from the existing process and structure embedded in a school or district. A further confounding variable is that systemic problem-solving innovations require the collaboration, participation, and expertise of individuals across professions. Classroom teachers, school psychologists, special educators, and administra-tors are among the roles commonly drafted to engage in cross-disciplinary problem solving. The specialization of knowledge inherent in disciplines sug-gests that what is evident and well known about problem solving to one set of educational professionals may seem foreign and abstract to others (Knotek, 2003). Innovation diffusion, let alone utilization, will not occur with any kind of fidelity or validity if practitioners are not first made aware of the specific components, belief systems, issues and concepts that underlie a particular problem-solving innovation (English & Hill, 1994).

For example, a problem-solving innovation that featured an assessment for intervention approach may be unknown to a school that has had a long tradition of problem solving as assessment for special education labeling, and staff may not be clear about the difference (see, e.g., Benn & Rosenfield, 2005). Personnel must be explicitly aware of the aims and goals of prob-lem solving before they can be expected to acquire and correctly utilize an innovative program. Conceptual change can be facilitated as CCC is used to foster consultee's understanding of the issues and processes embedded in problem solving.

Conceptual Understanding

A true innovation in problem solving is likely to entail evolutionary if not rev-olutionary shifts in the conceptualizations of the goals, aims, and causal forces at work in effecting positive changes in students' academic and/or behavioral functioning. For example, as problem solving shifts toward early intervention and an ecological understanding of student's functioning, and away from an emphasis on tertiary intervention and a deficit model, new skills will need to be acquired to implement the innovation. The practice of using assessments that are standardized on national norms to find deficits and that are divorced from a child's curriculum is being supplanted in problem solving by an early intervention focus on teacher-invented assessment and interventions cus-tomized to fit individual children in unique classrooms. Successful problem solving using the early intervention approach would require, in reading, for example, that the teacher have an understanding of diagnostic assessment based on a scientifically supported model of critical reading domains. If teachers have previously conceptualized successful problem solving as assess for diagnosis and placement, then the early intervention innovation of effective problem solving may be a conceptual mismatch.

Through the contracting stage of CCC, a consultant would be able to assist the teacher to pinpoint critical information that would help her consider a new view of the problem-solving process. First, the consultant would work to understand the teacher's current conceptualization of issues relevant to problem solving (e.g., Who is responsible for change?). Using questioning and other communication skills, the consultant might ask "How do you see the problem? How is your view of problem solving different from the view of early intervention? What are the similarities between the two views?" After the consultant and teacher have jointly explored alternative ways to see the problem, the consultant will then help the consultee consider alternative ways and means to address the problem.

Skill Acquisition

Innovation in problem solving will require school personnel to not only have a different perspective on issues, but also to acquire new means to effect changes that are congruent with a new guiding philosophy. If a district does not provide teachers and other specialists with more than lectures or one day seminars, then it is reasonable to expect that not many will move to the level of actual skill acquisition. Given that diffusion and utilization of new forms of problem solving require a means for skills acquisition, some process must be in place to support embedded professional development. CCC can be used to provide teachers with feedback and a structured plan to practice and utilize the new skills.

The time and energy required for teachers to acquire new skills can be substantial; if administrators do not provide adequate time and other resources, problem solving may fail. For example, in one instance a facilitator who was trying to implement a team problem-solving innovation was met with resistance by her principal. The administrator would not allow the facilitator to schedule training meetings during the work week, instead insisting that the team meet over the weekend at a local restaurant. As a result, the facilitator became concerned that her staff was not acquiring any of the skills associated with the innovation. The facilitator and her project consultant met and initially the problem was framed by the facilitator as being about the personal interactions between herself and the principal. In the facilitator's perception of the situation, neither she nor the administrator was going to shift stance. The consultation task was to first explore the facilitator's current view of the problem, and then work together to reconceptualize the issue. The facilitator and her team had in fact developed a cohesive and collaborative process. The problem was instead about the compatibility of the innovation with the existing processes in the building, and the task was about how to integrate it into the structures already in place, freeing up time for training. The CCC process was used to reconceptualize and resolve the issue.

Application of Skills

Use of a problem-solving innovation will occur when personnel have acquired an understanding of its conceptual underpinnings, practiced the skill, and then begin to use it in their actual school environment. Effective problem solving must not remain an abstraction; rather, it must be used and integrated into ongoing professional practice. Unpacking an idea and figuring out the best way to implement it requires support. CCC can be used to help a teacher think about issues related to the compatibility of problem solving in her classroom. Consultation could focus on questions such as "What do I need to change in my weekly schedule to make this fit? How can I arrange my instruction to make better use of the skills I have acquired? How do I engage parents to support early intervention?" The goal of consultation will be to jointly develop new ways of understanding how the consultee can utilize her new skills within her classroom. Across each level of professional development, CCC can be used to foster consultees' successful utilization of newly acquired skills and concepts.

So far, the chapter has focused on the use of CCC as a vehicle to support the diffusion and utilization of generic problem solving. Next, the use of CCC to support a specific and widely implemented problem-solving innovation, RTI PS (Christ, Burns, & Ysseldyke, 2005) will be briefly discussed.

How Does Problem-Solving RTI Happen?

The RTI problem-solving model is currently being implemented in school districts across the country and it is being heralded as having the potential to greatly impact issues such as disproportionality, the provision of high-quality instruction, and early intervention with students at-risk for school failure (Gresham, 2007; Newell & Kratochwill, 2007). However, the overarching challenge that is being targeted by this innovation is nothing less than changing the *instructional* landscape of classrooms (Bender, 2002; Swanson, 1999). As Dickman writes, "it is the instruction that is actually being delivered that is the critical foundation on which the success of RTI depends" (2006, p. 5). Instruction permeates RTI (NJCLD, 2005); its goal is to improve the instructional environment through the regular education teacher's "implementation of research-supported teaching strategies and approaches;" and to promote "intensive, systematic, specialized instruction" (p. 5). RTI rests on the capacity of teachers to enhance their instructional abilities to better meet the needs of the range of the learners in their classrooms. How will the promise of this problem-solving innovation, which aspires to no less a goal than changing the quality of instruction in our nation's schools, be delivered? One RTI PS model, called Instructional Consultation (Rosenfield & Gravois, 1996), has embedded CCC in its design, and the consultation acts as a vehicle for its service delivery and professional development related to quality instruction.

Instructional Consultation Teams

Instructional Consultation Teams (IC Teams) (Rosenfield & Gravois, 1996) incorporate CCC within a model that is based on an ecologically grounded approach. IC Teams are designed to bridge the gap between a student's instructional assessment, curricular challenges, and instructional delivery. This structured, systematic, and data-driven problem-solving consultation process focuses on improving the instructional ecology of schools by enhancing the ability of teachers to meet students' academic needs.

Diffusion and Utilization of IC

The range of skills that IC Teams demand teachers acquire is daunting, and the list includes (a) stepwise problem solving, (b) instructional assessment, (c) single subject design, and (d) the creation of individualized intervention protocols. Knowledge is diffused to teachers through embedded professional development that is based on CCC. In the tradition of CCC, the consultant assumes responsibility for fostering the teacher's new conceptualization of the work problem and for developing new skills, whereas the teacher assumes responsibility for figuring out how to carry out the results of the problem-solving steps within the context of her classroom. Teachers are supported throughout the implementation of the IC problem-solving process. The consultant establishes an effective communication channel (Rogers, 2006) that allows the consultee to pinpoint critical information and operationalize an aspect of student's academic functioning.

For example, a nebulous presenting problem of "Johnny will not ever pay attention during reading" would first be narrowed down through the use of a jointly constructed problem-solving protocol. Then, data would be gathered through instructional assessment. Because many teachers have not previously learned how to conduct these diagnostic assessments, the consultant, mindful of the tenets of Showers and Joyce (1996), will support the teacher's engagement in the task of assessment. First, the consultant will model the process with the student, and then the teacher will take charge of the assessment. Through a structured and guided process, the consultant will facilitate the teacher's engagement in the instructional assessment.

In addition, a reflective communication strategy is used during which the consultant helps the teacher monitor her fidelity of implementation of each step in the problem-solving process. For instance, sometimes teachers are not familiar with the emphasis on data-driven decisions, and this is problematic because each successive step of the IC protocol relies on outcome data from the previous one. Teachers who are new to the problem-solving RTI process have occasionally struggled with allowing data to disconfirm their initial hypothesis, and consultation may be used to increase the teacher's awareness of her inconsistent use of data. The result is to expand the teacher's problem-solving repertoire to include an increased fidelity to data-driven decision-making. After the initial data were collected, the consultant would then support the teacher's creation of an intervention protocol that was uniquely and specifically targeted to the student. Consultation would continue through the assumption of agreed upon goals or until the teacher was able to undertake the problem-solving process independently.

■ Conclusion

Effective and purposeful problem solving will not happen in schools without a vehicle in place to support the diffusion and utilization of innovations designed to improve upon the systems that currently exist. If teachers and other school personnel are to enhance and improve their capacity to effectively understand and foster the learning environment so that it better serves all children, they must have access to a professional development process that is based on the known conditions of adult learning. CCC offers a means to collectively improve problem solving and professional development. Through consultation a consultee can pinpoint critical information, consider multiple views of the work issue, and ultimately reframe his or her conceptualization of and approach to the work problem. Problem solving can become less problematic if professionals are provided the means and support to adopt new innovations.

■ References

Bender, W. N. (2002). *Differentiating instruction for students with learning disabilities: Best teaching practices for general and special educators.* Thousand Oaks, CA, Corwin Press, Inc.

Benn, A. E., & Rosenfield, S. (2005, August). *Analysis of problem-solving teams as communities of practice.* Poster presented at the American Psychological Association Meeting, Washington, DC.

Bergan, J. R., & Kratochwill, T. R. (1990). *Behavioral consultation and therapy.* New York, Plenum Press.

Burns, M. K., & Coolong-Chaffin, M. (2006). Response to intervention: The role and effect of school psychology. *School Psychology Forum: Research into Practice, 1,* 3–15.

Caplan, G. (1970). *The theory and practice of mental health consultation.* New York, Plenum.

Caplan, G., & Caplan, R. B. (1993). *Mental health consultation and collaboration.* San Francisco, Josey-Bass.

Christ, T. J., Burns, M. K., & Ysseldyke, J. (2005). Conceptual confusion within response-to-intervention vernacular: Clarifying meaningful differences. *Communique, 34,* 1–7.

Communication. (2008). In Merriam-Webster Online Dictionary. Retrieved March 3, 2008, from http://www.merriam-webster.com/dictionary/hacker.

Dickman, G. E. (2006). RTI: A promise that relies on the capacity to teach. *Perspectives on Language and Literacy, Special Edition,* p. 5.

English, F., & Hill, J. C. (1994). *Total quality education: Transforming schools into learning places.* Thousand Oaks, CA, Corwin Press.

Fuchs, L. S., & Fuchs, D. (2006). Implementing responsiveness-to-intervention to identify learning disabilities. *Perspectives on Dyslexia, 32,* 39–43.

Glisson, C. (2002). The organizational context of children's mental health services. *Clinical Child and Family Psychology Review, 5,* 233–253.

Gravois, T. A., Knotek, S., Babinski, L. M. (2002). Educating practitioners as consultants: Development and implementation of the Instructional Consultation Team Consortium. *Journal of Educational & Psychological Consultation, 13,* 113–132.

Gravois, T. A., & Rosenfield, S. (2002). A multi-dimensional framework for the evaluation of instructional consultation teams. *Journal of Applied School Psychology, 19,* 5–29.

Gresham, F. M. (2002). Responsiveness-to-intervention: An alternative approach to the identification of learning disabilities. In R. Bradley, L. Danielson, & D. P. Hallahan (Eds.), *Identification of learning disabilities: Research to practice* (pp. 467–519). Mahwah, NJ, Lawrence Erlbaum Associates.

Gresham, F. M. (2007). Evolution of the response-to-intervention concept: Empirical foundations and recent developments. In S. Jimerson, M. Burns, & A. VanDerHeyden (Eds.), *Handbook of response to intervention: The science and practice of assessment and intervention* (pp. 10–24). New York, Springer.

Hoagwood, K. (2001). Evidence-based practice in children's mental health services: What do we know? Why aren't we putting it to use? *Emotional & Behavioral Disorders in Youth, 1,* 84–87.

Knotek, S. E. (2003). Bias in problem solving and the social process of student study teams: A qualitative investigation of two SSTs. *Journal of Special Education, 37,* 2–14.

Knotek, S. E. (2007). Consultation within response to intervention models. In: S. R. Jimerson, M. K. Burns, & A. M. VanDerHeyden (Eds.), *The Handbook of Response to Intervention: The Science and Practice of Assessment and Intervention* (pp. 53–64). New York, Springer Inc.

Knotek, S. E., & Sandoval, J. (2003). Introduction to the special issue: Consultee centered consultation as a constructivistic process. *Journal of Educational and Psychological Consultation, 14,* 243–250.

Kratochwill, T. R., & Stoiber, K. C. (2002). Evidence-based interventions in school psychology: The state of the art and future directions. *School Psychology Quarterly (Special issue), 17,* 341–389.

Kurns, S., Morrison, D., & Batsche, G. (2006) *Response to Intervention (RTI): Blueprints for Implementation at the State, District and Local Levels.* NASDSE. file:///C:/Documents%20and%20Settings/Owner/Local%20Settings/Temporary%20Internet%20Files/Content.IE5/P4JGFIVH/nasdse---rti-dec-6%5B1%5D.ppt#256,1.

Lambert, N. M. (2004). Consultee-centered consultation: An international perspective on goals, process, and theory. In N. Lambert, I. Hylander, & J. Sandoval (Eds.), *Consultee-centered consultation: Improving the quality of professional services in schools and community organizations* (pp. 3–20). Mahwah, NJ, Lawrence Erlbaum Associates.

Luecke, R., & Ralph Katz (2003). *Managing creativity and innovation.* Boston, Harvard Business School Press.

MERRIAM-WEBSTER ONLINE (www.Merriam-Webster.com). Copyright 2005 by Merriam-Webster, Incorporated.

Morone, P., & Taylor, R. (2004). *A laboratory experiment of knowledge diffusion dynamics.* Retrieved December 17, 2006, from EconWPA, http://129.3.20.41.

NASDSE (2006). Response to Intervention. A Joint Paper by the National Association of state Directors of Special Education and the Council of Administrators of Special Edicatuio. Available at: www.nasde.org/projects.cfm?pageprojectid=23.

National Joint Committee on Learning Disabilities (NJCLD). (2005). *Responsiveness to Intervention and learning disabilities.* Retrieved November 2, 2007, from http://www.ldonline.org/about/partners/njcld#reports.

National Research Center on Learning Disabilities. (2005). *Responsiveness to intervention in the SLD determination process.* Retrieved November 2, 2007, from http://www.osepideasthatwork.org/toolkit/pdf/RTI_SLD.pdf.

Newell, M., & Kratochwill, T. R. (2007). The integration of response to intervention and critical race theory-disability studies: A robust approach to reducing racial discrimination in evaluation decisions. In S. Jimerson, M. Burns, & A. VanDerHeyden (Eds.), *Handbook of response to intervention: The science and practice of assessment and intervention* (pp. 65–79). New York, Springer.

Rogers, E. M. (2003). *The diffusion of innovations* (5th ed.). New York, The Free Press.

Rogers, E. M. (2006). *Diffusion of innovations* (6th ed.). New York, The Free Press.

Rosenfield, S. (2000). Crafting usable knowledge. *American Psychologist, 55,* 1347–1355.

Rosenfield, S. A., & Gravois, T. A. (1996). *Instructional consultation teams: Collaborating for change.* New York, The Guilford Press.

Roy, P. (1998). Staff development that makes a difference. In C. M. Brody & N. Davidson (Eds.), *Professional development for cooperative learning: Issues and approaches* (pp. 79–99). Albany, NY, SUNY Press.

Sandoval, J. (2004). Constructivism, consultee-centered consultation, and conceptual change. In N. Lambert, I. Hylander, & J. Sandoval (Eds.), *Consultee-centered consultation: Improving the quality of professional services in schools and community organizations* (pp. 37–44). Mahwah, NJ, Lawrence Erlbaum Associates.

Showers, B., & Joyce, B. (1996). The evolution of peer coaching. *Educational Leadership, 53,* 12–16.

Stolz, S. (1981). Adoptions of innovations from applied behavioral research: "Does."

Swanson, H. L. (1999). Instructional components that predict treatment outcomes for students with learning disabilities: Support for a combined strategy and direct instructional model. *Learning Disability Research & Practice, 14,* 129–140.

Thayer, W. R., & Wolf, W. C. (1984). The generalizability of selected knowledge diffusion/utilization know-how. *Science Communication, 5,* 447–467.

Vail, L., Gravois, T. A., & Rosenfield, S. A. (2005). *Instructional Consultation Teams: Team Facilitator Training Manual.* Authors.

9. Implementation of Evidence-Based Interventions in Schools

Issues and Challenges in Social-Emotional Learning and Mental Health Programs

S. Serene Olin, Noa Saka, Maura Crowe,
Susan G. Forman, and Kimberly Eaton Hoagwood

This chapter describes the efforts of a subgroup of the Task Force on evidence-based interventions (EBI) in School Psychology, supported by a coalition of school psychology organizations, to better understand factors that influence the implementation of EBIs in schools. Using preliminary data from a study focused on social-emotional learning (SEL) and mental health related school-based programs, this chapter discusses the issues and challenges of implementing EBI, highlighting implications for schools as adopters and implementers of such programs, as well as for program developers as facilitators of high-quality program implementation.

■ What is Evidence-Based Intervention?

Over the past decade, increased emphasis on accountability has placed pressures on schools to adopt and implement evidence-based practices. The term *evidence-based practice*, within a school framework, refers to the use of current scientific evidence for the selection and implementation of interventions in schools (Kratochwill, Albers, & Shernoff, 2004). The U.S. Department of Education specifies that instructional curricula provided by schools,

The authors would like to acknowledge the support of the American Psychological Association (APA) Division 16 Task Force on Evidence-Based Interventions in School Psychology, the Society for the Study of School Psychology, and the National Association of School Psychologists.

encompassing both core academic content areas and prevention interventions should be "guided by theory; rigorously evaluated so as to determine that it actually does what it is set out to do; replicable; and validated or supported by researchers in the field" (National Training and Technical Assistance Center for Drug Prevention and School Safety Program Coordinators, 2003, as cited in Greenberg et al., 2003). For example, the Department of Education policy for substance use prevention requires school districts to follow "Principles of Effectiveness," or risk losing their funding (Hallfors & Godette, 2002). This policy requires schools to conduct needs assessments, set measurable objectives, choose and implement research-based programs, and evaluate progress and outcomes (No Child Left Behind Act, 2001; U.S. Department of Education, 1998a, 1998b).

Recently, there has been a plethora of books, monographs, and special issues of journals devoted to the topic of EBI and evidence-based practices (e.g., Norcross, Beutler, & Levant, 2006). Evidence-based practice has been described as a "movement" within the specialty of school psychology and other fields, resulting in organized efforts to identify, disseminate, and promote the adoption of practices with demonstrated efficacy and effectiveness. It has been embraced by a variety of political and legal institutions, and has been codified in ethical codes and principles of practice governing the delivery of services in schools (Kratochwill, Hoagwood, Frank, Levitt, Romanelli, & Saka, in press).

■ The Challenge of Implementing Evidence-Based Interventions in Schools

Schools increasingly operate under severe fiscal and policy constraints. These issues, along with the significant administrative and operational challenges associated with the adoption of any new program, constrain the ability of schools to implement many effective interventions, even if the research base suggests that their impact is robust. In addition, even when resources are available, it can be challenging for school personnel to select from among the diversity of available interventions. Schools tend to select heavily marketed curricula that have not been evaluated, have been evaluated inadequately, or have not been shown to produce the desired positive outcomes (Ennett et al., 2003; Hallfors & Godette, 2002; Rohrbach, D'Onofrio, Backer, & Montgomery, 1996; Swisher, 2000; Tobler & Stratton, 1997). In many cases, schools prefer programs that are similar to already existing curricula, or use untested "homegrown" prevention programs (Hansen & McNeal, 1999). For example, Hallfors and Godette's (2002) findings indicated that although schools recognized the advantages of using evidence-based programs, they were either implementing them with low quality or they selected research-based programs along with several additional untested programs. These authors also found that heavily marketed programs that were most compatible with past practices were much more likely to be selected for implementation by the schools, despite their lack of scientific support or poor outcomes. In contrast, programs that have been rigorously tested and found to be effective, but have not been marketed to the same extent, were much less likely to be adopted by the schools.

To bridge the gap between research and practice, several federal agencies and private organizations took the initiative of vetting the large number of programs available to consumers. Within the mental health and substance abuse field, federal agencies, community support organizations, and various professional groups have undertaken systematic reviews and developed evidentiary guidelines for vetting. The goal for such efforts is to provide potential consumers, such as schools, some guidance on the selection and use of EBIs based on the quality of research evidence available.

Within the educational arena, similar efforts have been made to identify educational interventions that have an evidence base. For example, the U.S. government convened the National Reading Panel (National Institute of Child Health and Development, 2000) to summarize the available evidence on interventions and instruction supporting five areas in reading: Vocabulary, fluency, phonemic awareness, comprehension, and phonics. Although this report remains controversial, the resulting document provides an important resource for educators when selecting interventions to support reading in students. More recently, the U.S. Department of Education's Institute of Education Sciences (IES) established the "What Works Clearinghouse" (http://ies.ed.gov/ncee/wwc/) to provide educators, policymakers, researchers, and the public with a centralized source of research evidence on educational interventions, including programs, products, practices, and policies. Because school policy and decision makers and potential implementers of EBIs have limited access to scientific literature, the resources, guidelines, or registries created and distributed by these various agencies and organizations constitute an important source of information regarding EBIs, despite their various shortcomings.

Yet, the selection of an appropriate intervention that matches the schools' population, mission, needs, and resources is only the first step in a lengthy process of implementation. A significant challenge associated with using any new program in schools is creating an ongoing support system that will enable the program to be implemented with quality and sustained at that level over time. The quality of the implementation process itself (i.e., the degree to which an intervention is installed, monitored, and supported successfully in a new setting) has until recently, received relatively limited attention in the literature. There is no evidence to support that using an evidence-based program will *necessarily* produce the desired outcomes previously demonstrated in rigorous trials. Indeed, there is evidence to suggest that factors related to implementation may be as important as the scientific merits of an EBI in influencing the desired outcome.

When implementation processes have been monitored, implementation quality has been documented to influence positive student outcomes (Battistich, Schaps, Watson, & Solomon, 1996; Botvin, Baker, Dusenbury, Botvin, & Diaz, 1995; Derzon, Sale, Springer, & Brounstein, 2005; Gottfredson, Gottfredson, & Hybl, 1993; Rohrbach, Graham, & Hansen, 1993; Skroban, Gottfredson, & Gottfredson, 1999). Meta-analyses support the importance of understanding implementation factors because programs that monitor implementation or that were better implemented produce more change (DuBois, Holloway, Valentine, & Cooper, 2002; Gresham, Gansle, & Noell, 1993; Wilson & Lipsey, 2007). More significantly, poorly implemented programs can unintentionally lead to adverse outcomes. For example, in a meta-analysis of 55 evaluations of mentoring programs for youth, at-risk youths with personal vulnerabilities were found to be particularly susceptible to the impact of poorly implemented programs in that they were adversely affected by program participation (Dubois et al., 2002).

Data from a recent national survey indicate good cause for concerns about the state of program implementation in schools. In general, school prevention programs are poorly implemented (Gottfredson & Gottfredson, 2002; Gottfredson et al., 2000; Hallfors & Godette, 2002). For example, Gottfredson and Gottfredson (2002) found that among a nationally representative sample of schools, depending on the type of intervention activity, only a quarter to half of the programs were implemented at a dosage comparable to research-based programs (i.e., number of sessions), with only 47–78% of programs being implemented for more than a month. This study found that school-wide activities such as those involving planning and climate changes were better implemented than interventions targeted at individual students. Taken together, the evidence reinforces the fact that poor implementation quality can undermine the expected positive impact of an intervention or worse yet, create potentially deleterious effects.

■ Task Force on EBI in School Psychology Study

As part of a larger effort to promote the use of EBIs, a subgroup of the Task Force on EBIs in School Psychology developed a qualitative research project to better understand the challenges associated with the implementation of EBIs in schools. Although substantial efforts have been made in establishing a scientific knowledge base on interventions and practices, relatively less attention has been made to understand implementation processes and factors, particularly in schools. For example, only 5% of over 1,200 published studies of prevention provide data on implementation (Durlak, 1998). Similarly, Dane and Schneider (1998) reported that only 39 out of 162 programs they reviewed contained information on program integrity, and only 13 examined the impact of fidelity on outcomes. Because of the emphasis on outcome, consumers are left with lists of model, promising, or best-practice programs that have demonstrated desirable outcomes in research trials, but are provided with very little information on how to implement them in natural settings.

To create new knowledge to facilitate the successful adoption, implementation, and sustainability of EBIs in schools, this Task Force subgroup chose to interview developers of EBIs that have been widely advocated for school adoption. The first part of this effort involved developing a systematic way for selecting a number of school evidence-based programs on which to focus this project. The second part of this effort involved the development of a semi-structured interview protocol on implementation and sustainability issues in schools. Developers of the selected school-based EBIs were then contacted via email and/or by phone and formally invited to be a part of this qualitative research study. Data from these interviews are presented in a separate paper (Forman, Olin, Hoagwood, Crowe, & Saka, in press). For the purposes of this chapter, we will focus on the first aspect of this project. Thus, we will

1. Describe this Task Force effort to identify the most commonly advocated EBIs in schools.
2. Describe common characteristics among these most frequently advocated evidence-based programs.
3. Discuss potential issues and challenges for schools to consider in implementing EBIs.
4. Discuss potential issues and challenges for developers or disseminators to consider in promoting the uptake of EBIs in schools.

■ Identifying EBIs for Review

As an initial step, evidence-based programs were identified using lists and registries that are readily available to school consumers. Lists of EBIs put together by major agencies and organizations were located through web-searches, literature reviews, and snowball sampling during 2004–2005. All federal agencies involved in health, education, or mental health for children or youth were included in the original list. For the purposes of this project, the Task Force chose to focus on EBIs in schools that targeted primarily SEL or mental health–related programs. Although the National Reading Panel (NICHD, 2000) and the IES's "What Works Clearinghouse" provide information on evidence-based educational interventions, they do not provide listings of programs. For example, the National Reading Panel used meta-analysis to identify types of evidence-based instructional methods (e.g., phonics instruction). "What Works Clearinghouse" summarizes findings for educational interventions by topic area and has only begun to put out lists of "advocated" programs. Because the SEL and mental health–related programs were identified and listed by various designating agencies and organizations using similar strategies, a focus on these programs provided a more coherent way of selecting school-based EBIs. Although educational interventions are not included as the focus of this review, we believe that the knowledge gleaned is likely applicable to the implementation of other types of EBIs in schools. In fact, issues schools face in implementing SEL and mental health–related programs are likely to be more complex because social and emotional issues are not the primary mission of schools, and thus more vulnerable when schools need to prioritize limited resources.

A total of 11 designating agencies and organizations were identified for inclusion in this project. Table 9.1 lists these agencies, together with their main mission, key program ratings, and selection criteria. These designating agencies and organizations endorsed 455 programs. These programs were screened by the authors according to three criteria: (a) School-based or had school-based components; (b) tested in studies utilizing either a randomized control or a quasi-experimental research design (quasi-experimental was defined as matched control or comparison group without random assignment; usually with equivalence of groups or statistical adjustment); and (c) outcome data show clear evidence of the program's effectiveness (e.g., significant effect on targeted variables). Using this procedure, 357 programs were screened out, leaving 98 programs that met the above criteria.

To create a shortlist of programs, the Task Force chose to select ones that were the most frequently advocated. Out of the 98 programs, 58 were endorsed by more than a single designating agency; a natural cut-point of four endorsements was identified, with 29 programs being endorsed by four or more agencies or organizations. The rationale for focusing on the most frequently advocated programs is that these programs are likely to receive a higher level of exposure and hence have a greater potential of being implemented. The 29 programs included in this chapter are listed in Table 9.2.

■ Coding of Programs

General information on each of the 29 programs was abstracted from published literature or on-line sources. A coding system was developed to summarize the common features of these widely advocated programs. Program characteristics were coded along several dimensions: Intervention Target, Intervention Context, Program Characteristics, Dosage, Implementation Support, and Outcomes. Table 9.3 details what is captured under each dimension, and provides information on the proportion of programs that have that specific characteristic.

TABLE 9.1 *Agency and Organizational Rating Categories and Criteria for Evidence-Based Programs*

Organization	Key Source	Mission	Rating Categories	Focus and Criteria
American Youth Policy Forum	Washington, DC, American Youth Policy Forum (www.aypf.org)	Reducing juvenile crime	Effective	Programs are described based on a review of the scientific literature; however, *no specific criteria for the inclusion of programs are provided*
Blueprints for Violence Prevention	www.colorado.edu/cspv/blueprints	Violence prevention in children and adolescents from birth to age 19. Programs focus on violence, delinquency, aggression, and substance abuse	Model Promising	*Promising programs:* Show evidence of deterrent effect with a strong research design (experimental or quasi-experimental) on one of the targeted outcomes *Model programs:* (a) Meet above criteria and include (b) sustained effects for at least one year post-treatment and (c) replication at more than one site with demonstrated effects
Center for Mental Health Services, U.S. Department of Health and Human Services	Greenberg, M. T., Domitrovich, C. & Bumbarger, B. (1999). *Preventing mental disorders in school-aged children: A review of the effectiveness of prevention programs.* State College, PA, Prevention Research Center for the Promotion of Human Development, College of Health and Human Development, Pennsylvania State University (http://prevention.psu.edu/projects/ChildMentalHealth.html)	Reduction of risks or effects of psychopathology in school-aged children, from ages 5 to 18	Effective Promising	*Effective Programs:* (a) Evaluated using an adequate comparison group with either randomized or quasi-experimental design, (b) pretest and post-test data and preferably follow-up data, (c) written implementation manual, (d) produced improvements in specific psychological symptoms, psychiatric symptoms, or factors directly associated with increased risk for child mental disorders *Promising Programs:* Programs that seem promising but do not meet the above criteria (lack a controlled design, have a very small sample or the findings are only indirectly related to mental health outcomes)

(continued)

TABLE 9.1 *Continued*

Organization	Key Source	Mission	Rating Categories	Focus and Criteria
Center for Substance Abuse Prevention (CSAP), National Registry of Effective Prevention Programs(NREPP)[a]	Substance Abuse and Mental Health Services Administration (www.modelprograms.samhsa.gov)	Substance abuse prevention	Model Effective Promising	Programs are scored 1 to 5, with 1 being the lowest and 5 being the highest score, relative to 15 criteria. *Model programs* are well implemented and evaluated according to rigorous standards of research, scoring at least 4.0 on the five-point scale. *Promising programs* have been implemented and evaluated sufficiently and are considered to be scientifically defensible, but have not yet been shown to have sufficient rigor and/or consistently positive outcomes required for Model status. Promising programs must score at least 3.33 on the five-point scale. *Effective programs* meet all the criteria as the Model programs, but for a variety of reasons, these programs are not currently available to be widely disseminated to the general public
Department of Education, Safe and Drug-free Schools	www.ed.gov (Visit U.S. Department of Education and search for Office of Safe and Drug Free School)	Making schools safe, disciplined, and drug-free: Reducing substance use, violence, and other conduct problems	Exemplary Promising	*Both Exemplary and Promising programs meet the following criteria:* (a) Evidence of efficacy/effectiveness based on a methodologically sound evaluation that adequately *controls for threats to internal validity,* including attrition; (b) Clear and appropriate program goals with respect to changing behavior and/or risk and protective factors for the intended population and

Source	Reference	Focus	Rating	Criteria
Communities That Care, Developmental Research and Programs	Posey, Robin, Wong, Sherry, Catalano, Richard, Hawkins, David, Dusenbury, Linda, Chappell, & Patricia (2000). *Communities That Care prevention strategies: A research guide to what works.* Seattle, WA, Developmental Research and Programs, Inc. (www.preventionscience.com/ctc/CTC.html)	Preventing adolescent substance abuse, delinquency, teen pregnancy, school dropout, and violence as well as promoting the positive development of youth and children. Programs focus on the family, school, and community	Effective	setting; (c) Clearly stated rationale underlying the program, and the program's content and processes are aligned with its goals; (d) Program's content takes into consideration the characteristics of the intended population and setting; (e) Program implementation process effectively engages the intended population; (f) Application describes how the program is integrated into schools' educational missions; and (g) the program provides necessary information and guidance for replication in other appropriate settings *Effective programs:* (a) Address research-based risk factors for substance abuse, delinquency, teen pregnancy, school dropout, and violence; (b) Increase protective factors; (c) Intervene at developmentally appropriate age; and (5) Show significant effects on risk and protective factors in controlled studies or community trials
Mihalic and Aultman-Bettridge (2004)	Mihalic, Sharon, Aultman-Bettridge, & Tonya (2004). *A guide to effective school-based prevention programs.*	School-based, prevention programs	Exemplary Promising Favorable	*Model and Promising programs* utilize Blueprints criteria and outcomes (see above). *Favorable programs* broaden the outcomes to include

(continued)

TABLE 9.1 *Continued*

Organization	Key Source	Mission	Rating Categories	Focus and Criteria
	In William L. Tulk (Ed.), *Policing and school crime.* Englewood Cliffs, NJ, Prentice Hall Publishers			factors relevant for school safety and success, such as school disciplinary problems, suspensions, truancy, dropout, and academic achievement. These programs may also have weaker research designs; however, there is "reasonable" scientific evidence that behavioral effects are due to the intervention and not other factors. These programs all have experimental or matched control group designs
National Institute of Drug Abuse	National Clearing House for Alcohol and Drug Information, Preventing drug use among children and adolescents: A research-based guide, #734 at 1-800-729-6686	Drug prevention and reduction	Effective	Each program was developed as part of a research protocol in which an intervention group and a comparison group were matched on important characteristics, such as age, grade in school, parents' level of education, family income, community size, and risk and protective factors. The interventions were tested in a family, school, or community setting, all with positive results
Strengthening America's Families	www.strengtheningfamilies.org	Family therapy, family skills training, in-home family support, and parenting programs	Exemplary I Exemplary II Model Promising	Each program was rated on theory, fidelity, sampling strategy, implementation, attrition, measures, data collection, missing data, analysis, replications, dissemination capability, cultural and age appropriateness, integrity, and program utility and placed into the following categories: *Exemplary I:* Program has experimental design with randomized sample and replication by an independent investigator. Outcome data show clear evidence of program effectiveness

				Exemplary II: Program has experimental design with randomized sample. Outcome data show clear evidence of program effectiveness *Model*: Program has experimental or quasi-experimental design with few or no replications. Data may not be as strong in demonstrating program effectiveness *Promising*: Program has limited research and/or employs nonexperimental designs. Data appear promising but requires confirmation using scientific techniques
Surgeon General's Report (2001)	U.S. Department of Health and Human Services. (2001). *Youth violence. A report of the Surgeon General.* Rockville, MD (www.surgeongeneral.gov/library/youthviolence)	Violence prevention and intervention	Model Promising: Level 1—Violence Prevention Level 2—Risk Factor Prevention	*Model programs*: (a) Have rigorous experimental design (experimental or quasi-experimental); (b) Significant effects on violence or serious delinquency (Level 1) or any risk factor for violence with a large effect size of 0.30 or greater (Level 2); (c) Replication with demonstrated effects; and (d) Sustainability of effect *Promising program*: Meet the first two criteria (although effect sizes of 0.10 or greater are acceptable), but programs may have either replication or sustainability of effects (both not necessary)
Title V (OJJDP)	Title V *Training and technical assistance programs for state and local governments: Effective & promising programs guide.*	Delinquency Prevention	Exemplary Effective Promising	*Exemplary*: The program required evidence of statistical deterrent effect using randomized treatment and control groups *Effective*: The program had evidence obtained with a control or matched comparison group but without randomization

(continued)

TABLE 9.1   *Continued*

Organization	Key Source	Mission	Rating Categories	Focus and Criteria
	Washington, DC, Office of Juvenile Justice and Delinquency Prevention, Office of Justice Programs, U.S. Dept. of Justice (www.dsgonline.com)			*Promising:* The program had evidence of a correlation between the prevention program (generally pre/post) and a measure of crime
Promising Practices Network	http://www.promisingpractices.net/	What works to improve the lives of children, youth, and families	Proven Promising	*Proven programs:* (a) Affect relevant variables, with substantial effect size (at least one outcome changes by 20% or 0.25 standard deviation). Statistically significant at 0.05. (b) Design: Randomized control trial (experimental design) or quasi-experimental design. Sample size exceeds 30 in each group. (c) Program Evaluation Documentation is publicly available *Promising programs:* (a) May impact an intermediary outcome for which there is evidence that it is associated with one of the PPN indicators. Change in outcome is more than 1%. Outcome change is significant at the 10% level. (b) Study has a comparison group, but it may exhibit some weaknesses, e.g., the groups lack comparability on pre-existing variables or the analysis does not employ appropriate statistical controls. Sample size exceeds 10 in each group. (c) Program evaluation documentation is publicly available

Hamilton Fish Institute	http://www.hamfish.org/programs	Violence prevention	Demonstrated Promising	*Demonstrated programs*: (a) Design: A control group (does not have to be randomized), No replication needed. (b) Outcomes: The intervention group demonstrated a larger change in target variables over time than control group *Promising programs*: (a) Positive trends but not consistent significant outcomes. (b) Designs were too weak to be sure that the programs caused the positive effect. (c) Some programs were not evaluated but merely be theoretically designed to achieve objectives outlined in the "comprehensive framework"
Center for Disease Control	http://www.cdc.gov/hiv/resources/reports/hiv_compendium/index.htm	AIDS prevention	Effective	*Effective programs*: (a) Random assignment to intervention and control groups, with at least post-intervention data, or quasi-experimental designs with equivalence of groups or statistical adjustment, with pre and post data. (b) Statistically significant positive results on target variables. (c) Conducted in the US
CASEL	http://www.casel.org/programs/selecting.php	SEL skill areas	Select Safe and Sound	*Safe and Sound programs* are school-based programs that (a) Have at least eight lessons in one of the years. (b) Have either lessons for at least two consecutive grades or grads spans, or a structure that promotes lessons reinforcement beyond the first program year. (c) The program is nationally available *Select programs*: (a) Cover five essential SEL skills areas; (b) Have at least one well-designed evaluation study demonstrating their effectiveness; and (c) offer high-quality professional development supports beyond the initial training

a This refers to the original NREPP, and not the current one that was launched in March 2007. The current registry was redesigned and expanded to improve the transparency of the rating system.

TABLE 9.2 *Evidence-Based School Prevention and Intervention Programs*

Program	Developer	Content
Adolescent transitions program (ATP)	Thomas Dishion, Ph.D. Kathryn Kavanaugh	Family-centered intervention targeting students at-risk for behavior problems or substance use
All stars	William B. Hansen, Ph.D. http://www.allstarsprevention.com/	Preventing risk behaviors: Alcohol, tobacco, and drug use, postpone sexual activity and reduce fighting and bullying
Athletes training and learning to avoid steroids (ATLAS)	Linn Goldberg, M.D. http://www.ohsu.edu/hpsm/atlas.cfm	Prevention of alcohol, illicit and performance enhancing drugs
Olweus' Bullying Prevention Program	Dan Olweus, Ph.D. In U.S.: Marlene Snyder, Ph.D. Susan Limber, Ph.D. http://www.clemson.edu/olweus/	Reduce and prevent bullying and improve peer relations at school
CASASTART (Striving Together to Achieve Rewarding Tomorrows)	Lawrence F. Murray, CSW http://www.casacolumbia.org/absolutenm/templates/Home.aspx?articleid=287&zoneid=32	Prevent substance abuse, delinquent behavior; improve school performance and attendance; improve youth and family communication, and family involvement with school and social service agencies; reduce drug sales and related crime in community
Child development project	Eric Schaps, Ph.D. http://www.devstu.org/cdp/	School change program to foster students' sense of belonging and school connection, with emphasis on literacy development
Creating lasting family connections (COPES)	Ted Strader, Ph.D. http://copes.org	Reduce substance use, increase communication and bonding between parents and children, foster use of community services to resolve family and personal problems, reduce violence

(continued)

TABLE 9.2   *Continued*

Program	Developer	Content
FAST track	Mark T. Greenberg, Ph.D. www.fasttrackproject.org	Prevent serious and chronic antisocial behavior
Good behavior game	Sheppard G. Kellam, Ph.D.	Reduce aggressive behavior
I can problem solve	Myrna Shure, Ph.D. www.thinkingchild.com/icps.htm	Develop interpersonal cognitive problem solving skills to prevent more serious behavior problems
Life skill training	Gilbert Botvin, Ph.D. www.lifeskillstraining.com	Prevent substance use and violence
Linking the interests of families and teachers (LIFT)	John B. Reid, Ph.D. http://www.oslc.org	Prevent conduct problems
Behavior monitoring and reinforcement program (BMRP)	Brenna Bry, Ph.D. http://gsappweb.rutgers.edu/facstaff/faculty/bry.php	Prevent juvenile delinquency, substance use, and school failure
Preventive treatment program (Montreal longitudinal experimental study)	Richard E. Tremblay, Ph.D.	Delinquency prevention
Project ALERT	Phyllis L. Ellickson, Ph.D. www.projectalert.com	Prevent substance use
Project Northland	Cheryl Perry, Ph.D. www.hazelden.org/web/go/projectnorthland	Reduce alcohol use
Project PATHE (Positive Action Through Holistic Education)	Denise Gottfredson, Ph.D. www.gottfredson.com	Reduce school disorder and improve school environment to enhance students' experiences and attitudes about school
Project STAR (Midwestern prevention project)	Mary Ann Pentz, Ph.D. www.colorado.edu/cspv/blueprints	Substance abuse prevention

(continued)

TABLE 9.2 *Continued*

Program	Developer	Content
Project toward no drug use (TND)	Steve Sussman, Ph.D. FAAHB www.cceanet.org/Research/Sussman/tnd.htm	Substance use prevention
Project toward no tobacco use	Steve Sussman, Ph.D. FAAHB	Smoking prevention
Promoting alternative thinking strategies (PATH)	Mark T. Greenberg, Ph.D. http://www.channing-bete.com/prevention-programs/paths/	Promote social and emotional learning, character development, bully prevention and problem solving
Quantum opportunities program (QOP)	C. Benjamin Lattimore www.oicworld.org	Prevent high school drop out Promote positive behavior to deter teen pregnancy and criminal behavior
Reconnecting youth	Leona L. Eggert, Ph.D., RN, FAAN http://www.son.washington.edu/departments/pch/ry/curriculum.asp	Prevent drug abuse, school dropout, depression and suicide behavior
Responding in positive and peaceful ways (RIPP)	Wendy Northup, M.A. Aleta Lynn Meyer, Ph.D. http://www.has.vcu.edu/RIPP/	Reduce youth violence
School transitional environmental program (STEP)	Robert D. Felner, Ph.D. http://www.ncset.org/publications/essentialtools/dropout/part3.3.09.asp	Ease school transitions and enhance healthy adjustment
Second step	Claudia Glaze www.cfchildren.org	Reduce negative and violent behaviors
Seattle Social Development Project	J. David Hawkins, Ph.D. http://depts.washington.edu/sdrg/page4.html#SSDP	Reduce school failure, drug abuse, and delinquency
The incredible years	Carolyn Webster-Stratton, Ph.D. www.incredibleyears.com	Reduce conduct problems and promote social, emotional, and academic competence
Cognitive Behavioral Intervention for Trauma in Schools (CBITS)	Lisa H. Jaycox, Ph.D. http://www.hsrcenter.ucla.edu/research/cbits.shtml	Early trauma intervention for students exposed to violence

TABLE 9.3 *Program Coding: Characteristics of the 29 Most
Widely Advocated Programs*

	% (*n*) Programs
I. Intervention Target	
Target Population	
Students	100 (29)
Parents (targeted or involved)	69.0 (20)
Teachers/School Staff	17.2 (5)
Grades: Elementary School (8 ES only)	48.3 (14)
Middle School (6 MS only)	58.6 (17)
High School (4 HS only)	41.4 (12)
Population Demographics	
Minority	72.4 (21)
Setting: Urban	69.0 (20)
Suburban	48.3 (14)
Rural	58.6 (17)
Id based on Risk Factors	41.4 (12)
II. Intervention Context	
Domains	
School-wide	20.7 (6)
Classroom	79.3 (23)
Targeted Students	34.5 (10)
Community	20.7 (6)
Home/Family	65.5(19)
Prevention Level	
Multiple	27.6 (8)
Universal (14 universal only)	75.9 (22)
Selected (2 selected only)	34.5 (10)
Indicated (5 indicated only)	37.9 (11)
III. Program Characteristics	
Primary Target Skills or Problems	
Multiple Targets	51.7 (15)
Externalizing Behaviors	58.6 (17)
Substance Use	55.2 (16)
School Failure	13.8 (4)
School Bonding (e.g., attitudes)/Climate (e.g., safety)	20.7 (6)
Prosocial behavior	27.6 (9)
Sexual Activity	6.9 (2)
Trauma	3.4 (1)
Academics	6.9 (2)
Program Components	
Multiple	93.1 (27)
Social Skills	41.4 (12)
Self-regulation	31.0 (9)

(continued)

TABLE 9.3 *Continued*

	% (*n*) Programs
Drug resistance	20.7 (6)
Stress management	10.3 (3)
Personal management	27.6 (8)
Motivational concepts (attitudes/beliefs)	24.1 (7)
Health habits	6.9 (2)
Mentoring	20.7 (6)
Monitoring w/feedback	6.9 (2)
Discipline/classroom management	24.1 (7)
Cooperative learning	10.3 (3)
Academic skill	24.1 (7)
Parent Training	34.5 (10)
Parent-child	31.0 (9)
Home-School Coordination	20.7 (6)
School Policy/Norms/Structure	20.7 (6)
Community Policy/Norms/Involvement	24.1 (7)
Approach	
Psychoeducational	75.9 (22)
Behavioral, Cognitive, CBT	82.8 (24)
Service Provision	17.2 (5)
Organizational Change	20.7 (6)
Dosage	
Not time limited	13.8 (4)
Variable/Flexible	13.8 (4)
Less than one year	20.7 (6)
1 year	6.9 (2)
2 years	13.8 (4)
3 or more	31.0 (9)
Variable number of sessions (>10) per year	13.8 (4)
<10 sessions per year	3.4 (1)
10 or more sessions per year	41.4 (12)
20 or more sessions per year	41.4 (12)
IV. Implementation Support/Requirements	
Delivery methods	
Curriculum or Manual	93.1 (27)
Training (required)	86.2 (25)
Training (Optional/Recommended)	10.3 (3)
Training time: 1 day or less	10.3 (3)
2 days	24.1 (7)
3 or more days	27.6 (8)
TA support	69.0 (20)
TA (Optional)	20.7 (6)
Primary Implementer	
Out of school staff	17.2 (5)

(*continued*)

TABLE 9.3   *Continued*

	% (*n*) Programs
School Staff (any)	86.2 (25)
Teacher	65.5 (19)
Other (e.g., GC, prevention specialist, coach, peer leaders)	37.9 (11)
V. Outcomes	
Externalizing Behaviors	65.5 (19)
Internalizing Behaviors (e.g., Depression/ Suicidal behavior/Anxiety	13.8 (4)
Social skills	27.6 (8)
Problem Solving/Conflict resolution	24.1 (7)
Substance use reduction/onset	62.1 (18)
Reduced Unemployment	3.4 (1)
Health habits	3.4 (1)
Parent behavior	20.7 (6)
Community Service Use	3.4 (1)
School functioning (any)	65.5 (19)
Attendance/Truancy/Tardiness	17.2 (5)
Suspension	13.8 (4)
Grade promotion	10.3 (3)
Special Education Services	6.9 (2)
Interpersonal Classroom Behavior	27.6 (8)
School Bonding/climate	20.7 (6)
Grades/Test scores	13.8 (4)
Graduation/Drop out	17.2 (5)
College attendance	3.4 (1)

Intervention Target

This dimension captures the population being targeted for an intervention, as well as the demographics for which the intervention might be appropriate. As seen in Table 9.3, all 29 programs target students. Over two thirds (69%) of these school-based programs either involve parents (e.g., require parent involvement in homework assignments, or as part of committees) or directly target parents (e.g., through parent trainings) as part of their intervention. Less than one-fifth (17%) of them directly target teachers or other school staff as part of the intervention. These 29 programs cover a range of schools, with programs well spread across the different levels (elementary, 48%; middle, 59%; and high, 41%) and types of settings (urban, 72%; suburban, 69%; and rural, 59%). Over two thirds of these programs were considered to be appropriate for or have been tested with minority populations; among those that did not provide information on population demographics, participants were identified based on specific risk factors such as academic problems, truancy, and poverty (e.g., CASASTART, COPES, QOP).

Intervention Context

By selection, all 29 programs are school-based or have a school component. The vast majority (79%) have a classroom-based component. One-fifth (21%) target the whole school in their intervention efforts (e.g., PATHE, STEP, Child Development Project, Olweus' Bullying Prevention, Project STAR, Reconnecting Youth). Approximately two thirds (69%) of the programs had a component that reached out to parents in their homes (e.g., through homework assignments, calls, home visits) or through parent trainings. Only six (21%) of the programs involved a community component, through outreach to raise awareness, community task forces, multiagency activities or collaboration (e.g., Project STAR, COPES, Project Northland, Reconnecting Youth), or are community based but school-centered programs (e.g., Quantum Opportunity Program, CASASTART). The majority of the programs (76%) contained universal level prevention efforts, targeting all students in a school. About one-quarter (28%) of the programs were comprehensive programs that contained prevention efforts at multiple levels (e.g., universal, selected, and indicated). Far fewer programs targeted schools solely at the selected level (e.g., QOP, ATLAS—involving members of a subgroup with higher than average risk of developing a problem) or indicated level (e.g., CBITS, CASASTART, Reconnecting Youth, Montreal Longitudinal Study, Behavior Monitoring, and Reinforcement—involving individual students who manifest risk factors or conditions that puts them at high risk for developing a problem).

Program Characteristics

The most frequently targeted problem behaviors were externalizing (e.g., aggression; delinquency, 59%; and substance use, 55%). At least half the programs (52%) targeted more than one problem or skill area. Other target areas included school failure (14%), school bonding (e.g., attitudes toward schools) or climate (21%), and prosocial behaviors (28%). Sexual activity, trauma, and academics were the primary focus of only a few of the EBI programs. For the most part, these programs target individual level skills or problems.

Almost all the programs consist of multiple components, targeting various skill or problem areas. Common components include social skills training (41%), training in self-regulation (31%), personal management (e.g., goal setting, decision making, 28%), mentoring (21%), motivational concepts (e.g., attitudes and beliefs, 24%), academic skill (24%), and classroom management (24%). Only six programs took a school-wide approach and had components targeting school climate change or involved a school planning structure or process to manage change. Community involvement was as also a feature of seven programs (24%), with six programs having community-based components (e.g., case management, community task forces, multiagency activities, etc.) and one involving community participation in revising school policies, designing, and managing school change (PATHE). As noted previously, more than two thirds of the programs involve or target parents as part of the intervention. Of the 29 programs, 34% utilize parent training, 31% include parent-child communication or bonding training, and 21% include home-school coordination components.

The majority of the programs use a psychoeducational (76%) and/or cognitive, behavioral, or cognitive-behavioral (83%) approach in addressing target problems. Five of the 29 programs (17%) provide services such as case management, job skill training, and family assessment or therapy (CASASTART, QOP, PATHE, ATP, COPES). Six programs take an organizational change approach, targeting school-wide changes through activities involving student, school staff, parents, and/or community (PATHE, STEP, Child Development Project, Olweus' Bullying Prevention, Project STAR, Reconnecting Youth) to address the target problem. For example, the Olweus' Bullying Prevention program involves the establishment of school policies or norms about bullying, which involves the formation of a Bullying Prevention Coordinating Committee, the development of school-wide rules against bullying and a coordinated system of supervision.

Program Intensity

Program intensity is captured by looking at the duration of the entire program, as well as the number of sessions/lessons that must be implemented per year. Only one-fifth of the programs (21%) took less than a year to complete. Over half of the programs took at least a year or more to complete. Approximately, one-third (31%) of the programs are highly intensive programs, lasting three or more years. Four programs are not time limited, and are supposed to be implemented continuously (PATHE, GBG, Bullying Prevention, STEP). The majority of the programs are implemented over at least 10 sessions each year, with about half consisting of more than 20 sessions per year. The only program that had fewer than 10 sessions per year (Project Northland) is completed over 3 years, so that students are exposed to a total of 24 sessions. Taken together, these data indicate that these most frequently advocated programs are quite intensive to implement, and require significant commitment of time.

Implementation Support/Requirements

For the majority of the programs (86%), the primary implementer involves a school staff member, often a teacher (65%) and/or occasionally a school counselor, prevention specialist, coach, or peer leaders. In 17% of the programs, an out-of-school staff person is necessary (e.g., such as a project or program manager, case manager, parent consultant, or other community-based person).

Among these 29 programs, several were research studies that are not being disseminated or that do not have a product available to consumers (Fast Track, PATHE, LIFT, Montreal Longitudinal Study, Project STAR). For all but two of the programs (PATHE and STEP), a manual or a curriculum was developed or is available to guide the delivery of the various program components. For both PATHE and STEP, a key goal is organizational change and neither relies on a curriculum or packaged product for program delivery. Training is required to implement the program for all but three of the programs (Behavior Monitoring and Reinforcement, ATLAS, Project Northland) where training is recommended or optional. Of those programs that provided details about training requirements, the modal number of training days was three or more. Over two thirds (69%) of the programs provide technical assistance during the implementation phase; for one-fifth (21%) of the programs, technical assistance during the implementation phase is optional.

Other implementation supports and requirements including training and technical assistance were also examined as part of this project. However, due to the significant variation in program training and technical assistance requirements and costs (e.g., variation by school size, onsite vs. offsite trainings, etc.), these could not be meaningfully summarized in Table 9.3. It should be noted, however, that implementation costs may include personnel training, training material, curriculum, or workbook costs. For some programs, technical assistance may be free or included as part of training costs, but when not, these costs may run up to several thousand to tens of thousands of dollars, on top of training costs. Limited grant writing support is sometimes offered by programs and can be helpful for schools trying to obtain outside support for such programs. For example, COPES provides free grant writing assistance.

Outcomes

The majority of the programs positively affected school-based outcomes, even when such outcomes were not the primary target of the program. Most significantly, although only eight programs (PATHE, Behavior Monitoring and Reinforcement, Child Development Program, All Stars, QOP, Reconnecting Youth, STEP, SOAR) identify primary target areas that are directly related to school functioning (i.e., school failure, school bonding/climate, academics), 19 programs (66%) demonstrated positive outcomes for school behavior functioning. This indicates that many of these SEL programs have positive benefits for school functioning even if they do not directly target these areas.

Thus, as an example, even though the Bullying Prevention program focused on externalizing behaviors, this school-wide bullying prevention effort led to positive changes in school climate, increased school attendance, and improved interpersonal classroom behavior.

■ Implications for Schools: Issues and Challenges in Implementing EBIs

The findings outlined in the previous section have important implications for the implementation of EBIs in schools. For many years, the fundamental mission of schools has been broadened from the primary purpose of educating children by fostering knowledge and academic skills to an expanded educational agenda that involves enhancing students' social-emotional competence, prosocial behaviors, health, and civic engagement (Greenberg et al., 2003; Metlife, 2002; Public Agenda, 1994, 1997, 2002; Rose & Gallup, 2000). In addition to producing students who are culturally literate, intellectually reflective, and who pursue lifelong learning, high-quality education should provide students with the skills and means required for interacting in socially acceptable and respectful ways, practicing positive, safe and healthy behaviors, refraining from risk behaviors, and contributing responsively and enthusiastically to their peers, families, and communities (Greenberg et al., 2003). This new broader agenda has greatly increased the demands on schools to implement effective educational approaches that promote academic success, enhance health, and prevent problem behaviors (Greenberg et al., 2003; Kolbe, Collins, & Cortese, 1997).

To meet the increasing demands for accountability and to address the broader educational agenda, schools logically need to pay attention to programs that demonstrate outcomes in areas that line up with goals they set up in order to meet district, state, and federal levels of required competencies. Schools prefer prevention programs that target multiple behaviors and academic failure, and programs that demonstrate an impact beyond the target nonacademic problem area (National Institute of Drug Abuse, 2003). Not surprisingly, many of the most widely advocated school EBIs examined in this chapter have demonstrated program impact that extends beyond their primary target area to show favorable outcomes on school functioning.

Beyond selecting programs that meet such requirements, schools also need to pay attention to the implementation requirements and costs of the programs they select. As illustrated earlier, many of the widely advocated programs are highly intensive, multicomponent programs that often involve implementation over many months, and often years, to demonstrate program effects. Further, the 29 EBIs examined in this project vary in terms of the degree to which schools need to change existing ways of operation, with some programs utilizing peripheral staff (e.g., case managers in CASASTART, clinicians in CBITS) to target solely a small subset of high-risk students, to those requiring significant coordination, mobilization, or restructuring of resources throughout the school (e.g., PATHE, STEP). The majority of these EBI programs utilize teachers as primary implementers, which has important implications for staff buy-in, professional development needs, staff support, and how the EBI curriculum is integrated into the overall school curricula. Many of these programs also require schools to reach out to parents in new or different ways, whereas a handful involves community level participation for successful implementation. To pave the path for smoother implementation of such programs, schools need to establish a structure for home-school coordination, family involvement, and community outreach before adopting such programs.

Data from a nationally representative sample of 544 schools support the need to pay attention to implementation factors. In their survey of these 544 schools, Payne, Gottfredson, and Gottfredson (2006) suggested that schools should take into consideration a number of guidelines to improve the quality or intensity of implementation. These suggestions include engagement in a local planning process, selecting a program that is standardized (i.e., with clearly specified intervention material and procedures for delivery), eliciting principal support for the program, increasing organizational capacity, and integrating the program into normal school activities. These guidelines are consistent with lessons learned through large-scale studies of educational reform efforts (Nunnery, 1998).

■ Implications for Developers: Issues and Challenges in Promoting the Uptake of School EBIs

To meet the broader demands placed on the education system, schools need to be efficient in allocating finite resources. Thus, it is not surprising that almost unanimously the most widely advocated SEL or mental health–related programs contain components that address multiple areas and demonstrate effects beyond their primary targets. Compared to findings from a recent review where only a third of methodologically rigorous school-based mental health interventions examined both mental health and academic outcomes (Hoagwood et al., 2007), two thirds of this pool of widely advocated programs actually demonstrated impact on both SEL status and school functioning. Still, this means that a third of these widely advocated school programs either fail to measure or to demonstrate outcomes directly relevant to the school mission. To facilitate the uptake of school EBIs, program developers need to establish or demonstrate program effects on academic achievement, or minimally, show how program effects support schools' academic mission. In this climate of academic accountability in schools, such data have the potential to impact a school's ability to sustain effective EBIs.

Because the positive results demonstrated by these widely advocated EBIs are derived from rigorous research or evaluation efforts, a much higher degree of attention is paid to implementation quality than would occur in most school settings. Given the evidence (described earlier) that lower quality implementation leads to poorer or even adverse outcomes, program developers must pay attention to ways they can facilitate quality implementation in schools. For example, Gottfredson and Gottfredson (2002) found that one of the most important program characteristics associated with high-quality implementation is the availability of program materials that are clear and explicit, including implementation manuals, prepared handouts, overheads, and videotapes. Further, programs with standardized material, delivery procedures with clear guidelines, greater monitoring, and supervision, ease implementations and decrease the likelihood of program deviation. The development of such tools is clearly critical to support implementation efforts that will yield desired outcomes.

For schools to better understand the type of resources or supports that are needed to achieve the effects established in rigorous evaluation efforts, program developers need to go beyond the provision of curriculum or manuals for various components of interventions and provide essential information for proper implementation and maintenance of the effective programs over time. Because programs, regardless of complexity, tend to be heavily modified by schools and individual teachers during implementation (Dusenbury, Brannigan, Hansen, Walsh, & Falco, 2005; Hallfors & Godette, 2002), program developers must help implementers understand what features or components of their programs need to be preserved, and what aspects may be adapted to fit local conditions. Because many EBIs require months and sometimes years to fully implement, outcome data may not be immediately evident, making it difficult for schools to adhere to programs in the face of competing demands. Program developers should consider developing simple quality assurance measures that can help schools monitor how well they are implementing a program so that additional consultation or course corrections are possible to maximize the likelihood of program benefits. Such steps may be critical to avoid disappointment and to ensure that school resources are not wasted.

As illustrated from examining the most widely advocated school EBIs, almost all require or recommend some level of training as well as a support system (i.e., ongoing coaching, supervision, and support) for effective implementation. This requirement is supported by studies indicating that quality of training and ongoing support are related to higher intensity of program implementation (e.g., Aber, Brown, & Jones, 2003; Payne et al., 2006). This type of support facilitates the implementation process by helping implementers such as teachers understand the intervention, the mechanics of program delivery, and appropriate ways to tailor, adapt, and integrate the intervention with existing practices. The importance of technical assistance and coaching/consultation has been demonstrated in a meta-analysis of research on training and coaching among public school teachers. Joyce and Showers (2002) found that training consisting of theory, discussion with demonstration, practice, and feedback, resulted in only 5% of teachers using new skills in the classroom. However, when this training was accompanied by on-the-job coaching, 95% of the teachers used the new skills in the classroom. Further, the authors noted that such training and coaching is only possible with the full support and participation of school administrators and works best with teachers who are motivated. These data suggest important ways that developers can facilitate the high-quality implementation of EBIs in schools.

To date, limited research has been conducted to understand the influence of community or school factors on the implementation of EBIs in schools. At the school level, organizational capacity and support have been linked to the quality of program implementation (Joyce & Showers, 2002; Payne et al., 2006). Thus, as a part of implementation efforts, program developers must pay attention to such contextual factors to increase the likelihood of successful implementation. For example, Payne et al. (2006) found that how well a program is integrated into normal school operations influences the level of enthusiasm and the degree to which the program is adopted in the school. Yet, only about one-fifth of these 29 widely advocated school EBI programs have a school level component that addresses organizational level factors. More attention to these contextual factors is needed.

■ Conclusion

In a comprehensive review of the implementation literature, it has become clear that in order to bridge the research to practice gap, a much more active process or set of activities is required than passively disseminating or diffusing research information to consumers (Fixen, Naoom, Blasé, Friedman, & Wallace, 2005; Fixen, Naoom, Blasé, & Wallace, 2007). The need to pay attention to implementation factors is underscored by the failure of EBIs to demonstrate beneficial effects in natural settings. Although the federal governments spends over $95 billion a year in research to help create new interventions, and over $1.6 trillion a year to support services (Clancy, 2006), this research has had little impact on human services. Part of the lack of impact is due to the fact that high-quality research is not being applied, or is not being applied well enough, to have a measurable impact, thus failing to provide the intended benefits. Although the research field has begun to identify and outline key factors or processes that influence successful implementation, the relative importance of such factors and how they influence one another is as yet poorly understood (Mihalic & Irwin, 2003). Indeed, the discrepancy between research-based outcomes and outcomes obtained in natural settings has captured the attention of the scientific community, and efforts to study such implementation issues are now considered a research priority. Towards this end, a multilevel framework for considering factors that influence the implementation quality of school-based interventions was recently proposed to guide research on implementation quality (Domitrovitch et al., 2008). This comprehensive framework, which includes macro level (e.g., state policies), school level (e.g., school climate, resources), and individual level (e.g., implementer attitudes) factors, can also provide a useful starting point for both program developers and schools as they address the challenges of implementing EBIs effectively in schools.

As schools are increasingly pressed to address the broader social and emotional needs of their students, many of them choose to do so by adopting and implementing preventive intervention programs. Despite the availability of lists and registries to guide school selection of such programs, our knowledge about the implementation of such programs in schools to ensure desired outcomes that can be sustained over time is very limited. The examination of the characteristics of the most widely advocated SEL or mental health–related EBI school programs shed some light on the range of programs, the scope of their interventions and impact, as well as potential challenges that face both schools as adopters and implementers of EBIs and program developers as facilitators of program uptake.

Although this chapter highlights some of the issues schools need to consider as they take on new programs and what program developers could do to facilitate the successful uptake of EBIs, clearly challenges in implementation are also influenced by system levels factors. For example, at the system level, attention needs to be paid to the preservice training teachers receive. Behavioral and cognitive behavioral approaches are the most commonly used techniques in EBIs and training in basic behavioral and cognitive behavioral concepts during teacher preservice education would increase schools' capacity to implement EBIs. System efforts are also necessary because schools are constantly bombarded by new programs, new initiatives, and reforms, and they are under tremendous pressure to meet ever changing demands that are at times conflicting. Uncoordinated efforts to meet various mandates can be disruptive because they are typically introduced as a series of fragmented initiatives that come and go (Greenberg et al., 2003). Many SEL and mental health preventive programs address target problems that are not adequately tied to the central mission of schools or to the issues for which schools are held accountable that are primarily, academic. To help schools reap the benefits of EBIs and institutionalize such programs, systemic changes (state-level, district-level, and school-level) are just as critical to ensure that these programs are better coordinated, monitored, evaluated, and improved over time.

Furthermore, systemic changes are necessary to ensure that financial, organizational, and human resources are made available over a sustained period of time to provide the necessary supports for EBIs to achieve their intended benefits.

■ References

Aber, J. L., Brown, J. L., & Jones, S. M. (2003). Developmental trajectories toward violence in middle childhood: Course, demographic differences, and response to school-based intervention. *Developmental Psychology, 39,* 324–348.

Battistich, V., Schaps, E., Watson, M., & Solomon, D. (1996). Prevention effects of the child development project: Early findings from an ongoing multi-site demonstration trial. *Journal of Adolescent Research, 11,* 12–35.

Botvin, G. J., Baker, E., Dusenbury, L., Botvin, E. M., & Diaz, T. (1995). Long-term follow-up results of a randomized drug abuse prevention trial in a white middle-class population. *Journal of the American Medical Association, 273,* 1106–1112.

Clancy, C. (2006). The $1.6 trillion question: If we're spending so much on healthcare, why so little improvement in quality? *MedGenMed, 8.* Retrieved from www.medscape.com/viewarticle/532247.

Dane, A. V., & Schneider, B. H. (1998). Program integrity in primary and early secondary prevention: Are implementation effects out of control? *Clinical Psychology Review, 18,* 23–45.

Derzon, J. H., Sale, E., Springer, J. F., & Brounstein, P. (2005). Estimating intervention effectiveness: Synthetic projection of field evaluation results. *Journal of Primary Prevention, 26,* 321–343.

Domitrovich, C. E., Bradshaw, C. P., Poduska, J., Hoagwood, K. E., Buckley, J., Olin, S., Hunter-Romanelli, L., Leaf, P. J., Greenberg, M. T., & Ialongo, N. S. (2008). Maximizing the implementation quality of evidence-based preventive interventions in schools: A conceptual framework. *Advances in School Mental Health Promotion, 1,* 6–28.

DuBois, D. L., Holloway, B. E., Valentine, J. C., & Cooper, H. (2002). Effectiveness of mentoring programs for youth: A meta-analytic review. *American Journal of Community Psychology, 30,* 157–197.

Durlak, J. A. (1998). Common risk and protective factors in successful prevention programs. *American Journal of Orthopsychiatry, 68,* 512–520.

Dusenbury, L., Brannigan, R., Hansen, W. B., Walsh, J., & Falco, M. (2005). Quality of implementation: Developing measures crucial to understanding the diffusion of preventive interventions. *Health Education Research, 20,* 308–313.

Ennett, S. T., Ringwalt, C. L., Thorne, J., Rohrbach, L. A., Vincus, A., Simons-Rudolph, A., & Jones, S. (2003). A comparison of current practice in school-based substance use prevention programs with meta-analysis findings. *Prevention Science, 4,* 1–14.

Fixen, D., Naoom, S., Blase, K., Friedman, R., & Wallace, F. (2005). *Implementation research: A synthesis of the literature.* Tampa, University of South Florida. Retrieved from www.nirn.fmhi.usf.edu/resources/publications/Monograph.

Fixen, D., Naoom, S., Blase, K., & Wallace, F. (2007). Implementation: The missing link between research and practice. *The APSAC Advisor, Winter/Spring,* 4–7.

Forman, S. G., Olin, S. S., Hoagwood, K. E., Crowe, M., & Saka, N. (in press). Evidence-based interventions in schools: Developers' views of implementation barriers and facilitators. *School Mental Health.*

Gottfredson, D. C., & Gottfredson, G. D. (2002). Quality of school-based prevention programs: Results from a national survey. *Journal of Research in Crime and Delinquency, 39,* 3–36.

Gottfredson, D. C., Gottfredson, G. D., & Hybl, L. G. (1993). Managing adolescent behavior: A multi-year, multi-school study. *American Educational Research Journal, 30,* 179–215.

Gottfredson, G. D., Gottfredson, D. C., Czeh, E., Cantor, D., Crosse, S., & Hantman, I. (2000). *A national study of delinquency prevention in school final report.* Ellicott City, MD, Gottfredson Associates, Inc.

Greenberg, M. T., Weissberg, R. P., O'Brien, M. U., Zins, J. E., Fredericks, L., Resnik, H., & Elias, M. J. (2003). Enhancing school-based prevention and youth development through coordinated social, emotional, and academic learning. *American Psychologist, 58,* 466–474.

Gresham, F. M., Gansle, K. A., & Noell, G. H. (1993). Treatment integrity in applied behavior analysis with children. *Journal of Applied Behavior Analysis, 26,* 257–263.

Hallfors, D., & Godette, D. (2002). Will the 'Principles of Effectiveness' improve prevention practice? Early findings from a diffusion study. *Health Education Research: Theory & Practice, 17,* 461–470.

Hansen, W. B., & McNeal, R. B., Jr. (1999). Drug education practice: Results of an observational study. *Health Education Research, 14,* 85–97.

Hoagwood, K. E., Olin, S. S., Kerker, B. D., Kratochwill, T. R., Crowe, M., & Saka, N. (2007). Empirically based school interventions targeted at academic and mental health functioning. *Journal of Emotional and Behavioral Disorders, 15,* 66–92.

Joyce, B., & Showers, B. (2002). *Student achievement through staff development* (3rd ed.). Alexandria, VA, Association for Supervision and Curriculum Development.

Kolbe, L. J., Collins, J., & Cortese, P. (1997). Building the capacity for schools to improve the health of the nation: A call for assistance from psychologists. *American Psychologist, 52,* 256–265.

Kratochwill, T. R., Albers, C. A., & Shernoff, E. S. (2004). School-based interventions. *Child & Adolescent Psychiatric Clinics of North America, 13,* 885–903.

Kratochwill, T. R., Hoagwood, K. E., Frank, J., Levitt, J. M., Romanelli, L. H., & Saka, N. (in press). Evidence-based interventions and practices in school psychology: Challenges and opportunities for the profession.

In T. B. Gutkin & C. R. Reynolds (Eds.), *Handbook of School Psychology* (4th ed.). New York, Wiley.

Metlife. (2002). *The Metlife Survey of the American Teacher 2002—Student life: School, home, and community* (pp. 275–337). New York, Author.

Mihalic, S. F., & Irwin, K. (2003). Blueprints for violence prevention: From research to real-world settings-factors influencing the successful replication of model programs. *Youth Violence and Juvenile Justice, 1,* 307–329.

National Institute of Child Health and Human Development (NICHD). (2000). *Report of the National Reading Panel. Teaching children to read: An evidence-based assessment of the scientific research literature on reading and its implications for reading instruction* (NIH Publication No. 00-4769). Washington, DC, U.S. Government Printing Office.

National Institute on Drug Abuse. (2003). *What do schools really think about prevention research? Blending research and reality.* Bethesda, MD, Author.

Norcross, J. C., Beutler, L. E., & Levant, R. F. (Eds.) (2006). *Evidence-based practices in mental health: Debate and dialogue on the fundamental questions.* Washington, DC, American Psychological Association.

No Child Left Behind Act 2001, Public Law No.107-110.

Nunnery, J. A. (1998). Reform ideology and the locus of development problem in educational restructuring: Enduring lessons from studies of educational reform. *Education and Urban Society, 30,* 277–295.

Payne, A., Gottfredson, D. C., & Gottfredson, G. D. (2006). School predictors of the intensity of implementation of school-based prevention programs: Results from a national study. *Prevention Science, 7,* 225–237.

Public Agenda. (1994). *First things first: What Americans expect from the public schools.* New York, Author.

Public Agenda. (1997). *Getting by: What American teenagers really think about their schools.* New York, Author.

Public Agenda. (2002). *A lot easier said than done: Parents talk about raising children in today's America.* New York, Author.

Rohrbach, L. A., D'Onofrio, C. N., Backer, T. E., & Montgomery, S. B. (1996). Diffusion of school based substance abuse prevention programs. *American Behavioral Scientist, 39,* 919–934.

Rohrbach, L. A., Graham, J. W., & Hansen, W. B. (1993). Diffusion of a school-based substance abuse prevention program: Predictors of program implementation. *Prevention Medicine, 22,* 237–260.

Rose, L. C., & Gallup, A. M. (2000). *The 32nd Annual Phi Delta Kappa/Gallup poll of the public's attitudes towards the public schools.* Retrieved, July 7, 2002, from http://www.pdkintl.org/kappan/kpol0009.htm.

Skroban, S. B., Gottfredson, D. C., & Gottfredson, G. D. (1999). A school-based social competency promotion demonstration. *Evaluation Review, 23,* 3–27.

Swisher, J. D. (2000). Sustainability of prevention. *Addictive Behaviors, 25,* 865–873.

Tobler, N. S., & Stratton, H. H. (1997). Effectiveness of school-based drug prevention programs: A metaanalysis of the research. *Journal of Primary Prevention, 18,* 71–128.

U.S. Department of Education (1998a). *Nonregulatory guidance for implementing the SDFSCA principles of effectiveness.* Washington, DC, U.S. Department of Education, Office of Elementary and Secondary Education, Safe and Drug-Free Schools Program.

U.S. Department of Education (1998b). Notice of final principles of effectiveness. *Federal Register, 63,* 29902–29906.

U.S. Department of Education (2002). Institute of Education Science, What Works Clearing House. Retrieved from http://ies.ed.gov/ncee/wwc/.

Wilson, S. J., & Lipsey, M. W. (2007). School-based interventions for aggressive and disruptive behavior: Update of a meta-analysis. *American Journal of Preventive Medicine, 33* (*Suppl. 2*), S130–S143.

10. FROM HEALTH/MEDICAL ANALOGIES TO HELPING STRUGGLING MIDDLE SCHOOL READERS

Issues in Applying Research to Practice

John Sabatini

■ Overview of Chapter

This chapter discusses the transfer of scientific research and evidence-based practices to application settings. In a 2006 article in the *Educational Researcher*, Riehl (2006) put a kinder, gentler face on the "medical model" of research as applied in the field of education. She and others (e.g., Holland, 1986, 1993; Holland and Rubin, 1982) discussed the particular kinds of causal inference that stem from experimental designs. In the first part of this chapter, those ideas are expanded by modeling the reasoning one can/should and cannot/should not make from experimental research trials. In the second part, I work through a case example of how to reason through the application of research findings to address reading difficulties in middle school settings. Throughout, the role of assessments in guiding decision-making at different levels (school, teacher, clinician) is highlighted to supplement the gaps in the current evidence-based research on adolescent reading. A fundamental theme addressed is the seeming contradiction between experimental studies that validate effectiveness of treatment programs and the fact that particular individuals in these studies may fail to respond to those treatments.

■ Health/Medicine as Metaphors for Educational Research to Practice

In moving from a statistical science that has its origins in agriculture and crop rotations (Fisher, 1970) to applications concerned with helping individuals achieve their learning potential in classrooms, issues surface. In creating statistical models of effective agricultural practices, no one was particularly concerned whether a particular wheat seed did or did not germinate and become fertilized and thrive. The same cannot be said about the sentiment behind *No Child Left Behind Act (NCLB) of 2001*, which is that every effort will be made to ensure that every single child will reach an adequate or proficient achievement level. The concern is not so much about sacrificing some crops (or children) to the practice of randomization, but rather coming to terms with the fundamental uncertainty of causal inferences based on randomized trial designs when applied to the individual case.

■ Promoting Public Health versus Diagnosing and Treating Individual Cases

Much of the current terminology (e.g., treatment, intervention, dosage level) used in educational research is borrowed from the health/medical context. In doing so, a central point to consider is the distinction between (public) health and individual medical models of applying scientific research. Addressing public health issues often requires applying research findings to groups with the aim of raising or lowering the prevalence or incidence of a health-related condition—for example, the goal is to lower the incidence of asthma, obesity, or high blood pressure in a population. In applying such public health research, one seeks to implement the program that benefits the greatest number of individuals with a reasonable investment of resources. Nevertheless, not all medical problems can be solved through public health models. Individuals still need treatment for medical problems that cannot be prevented by a single treatment applied on a large scale.

The distinction between diagnostic medical practice for the individual and promoting (public) health deserves closer consideration. The former is typically a clinical or one-on-one activity. An individual visits a doctor's office or health clinic, either because some symptoms have affected the individual's health or for a routine checkup to maintain one's health. From the health provider's point of view, the individual has or will accumulate a medical history that includes the results of various descriptive tests (e.g., weight, height, blood pressure, results of blood tests), previous ailments, responses to various treatments, and so forth. Some tests are repeated each visit (temperature, pulse, blood pressure)—a screening/monitoring function—and not all tests are given all the time to all people. Some tests are conducted at particular periodic or benchmark points, sometimes because independent research suggests that various risk factors increase when the individual has other correlated characteristics such as reaching a certain age, or a certain weight to height ratio, cholesterol count, and so on. Over time, the tests are adapted to the individual histories, except when new symptoms or risk factors arise that warrant specialized testing.

The model for promoting or maintaining public health, on the other hand, has a different focus. The mantra is something like—the greatest good for the largest group, with the least individual risk, at the most feasible cost in effort and resources—making it the near polar opposite of the clinical, diagnostic model. Why? Because the clinical model has a capacity limit that makes individual, adaptive treatment prohibitively expensive and inefficient at dealing with problems of scale. It works best when there is an opportunity for individualization. The individual may benefit from the same treatment recommended to the general public, but that individual may fail to heed or may neglect receiving the public offering, only to find that a personal doctor ends up delivering the same treatment, most probably at greater cost.

In addressing public health issues, one basic research issue concerns the prevalence of the problem or risk. Prevalence estimates help prioritize the need for active remedies and the feasibility of different approaches. Another issue concerns prevention—it is better to prevent an epidemic before its outbreak or spread or reduce the prevalence of cancers or heart disease by promoting healthy behavior and reducing risk factors in the environment. Reduced prevalence ensures adequate capacity for individualized treatment of those who still contract the ailment and/or are perhaps resistant to the publicly provided treatment. Prevalence also defines the nature and scope of resources necessary to address the larger health/medical issue. Prevalence can be measured with survey-style, population sampling techniques that allow the researcher to predict what proportion of the population has the particular health issue, such that the scale of the solution required can be planned. Every individual need not be definitively diagnosed; no blood need be drawn and sent to the lab. This keeps costs down. Anonymous self-report surveys or periodic examination of existing health records, can be used to determine current prevalence and rises and declines in levels over time, with statisticians correcting for error in these less reliable data collection techniques. Applied educational and psychological assessments mirror these models of large-scale and individual testing in medicine.

The interaction of individual differences and environments also influences health/illness as it does educational outcomes. Individuals come with a full array of genetically based differences that interact with his or her environment to promote health or raise the risk of illness—height, weight, bone structure, metabolism, allergies, and specific propensities for contracting particular conditions. Individuals will or will not respond to some treatments based on factors quite unique to them. However, and this is another key point, some groups of people are identifiable as having a higher prevalence of risk or adverse reactions, though it may still be probabilistic whether any particular individual of that group has this unique characteristic. What can be said is that an individual has a higher risk, and that risk probability can be quantified, but it cannot be said for certain whether the risk will result in the condition. This group identification can be gender or ethnic background or any number of characteristics that are shared across individuals in the population. The practice of obtaining a family history is a way of estimating individual probabilities of risk from group membership. Overall population prevalence will vary with the proportion and size of various groups in the population, such that localities with higher proportions of high-risk groups will experience higher prevalence of the condition (Ialongo, Kellam, & Poduska, 2000).

Finally, environments influence the health/illness equation. This is one of the oldest addressable public health issues known to medical professionals. Think of how polluted air raises the prevalence of tuberculosis or asthma; mosquitos spread malaria; fleas spread the bubonic plague; and nonflourinated water increases the prevalence of tooth decay. Not only have widespread public solutions reduced the prevalence and in some cases all but eliminated some diseases, but the techniques used in these cases are often replicable—inoculations, vaccinations, policies to reduce environmental risk factors, and so forth. Once the prevalence is reduced to a manageable number of individual cases, individual diagnostic care is feasible. This is the great success story of the public health model.

One contrast between public health solutions and individual care is that when a doctor treats a patient with an ailment, the treatments continue until a remedy is found. If one treatment does not work, another one is tried, then another, until all researched treatments are exhausted, which then may be followed by experimental treatments, that is, treatments with no evidentiary support as of yet of their effectiveness. Hopefully, a sound medical system does not give up on the individual until all viable options are exhausted. The doctor will probably move through treatments in a sequence based on the probability of success given research evidence. With the exception of prevention or maintenance purposes, one does not continue to treat a person who is not sick or is cured, though one may continue to monitor the recovery with periodic tests to ensure no relapse. In public health situations, as noted earlier, one chooses the treatment that has the highest probability of remedying the largest number of people given resource limitations. That may result in treatments for the least, moderate, or most severe cases, and by definition, the treatment will work for some and not others.

Now, there are many notable differences to consider in comparing health/medicine to education, both in research and practice. With respect to research, the curing of disease/illness has a more definitive outcome as a dependent variable—the individual gets better or not; lives or dies. In contrast, education and learning are the positive accrual of knowledge and skill, often closer in analogy to fitness as a result of exercise; a definitive outcome criterion is not so much the case as continua of skilled performance and behavior. Many other complexities unique to education with respect to curriculum, learning, development, teaching practice, and social environment may not be explained by the health/medicine metaphor. Perhaps, the clinical, diagnostic, medical model is relevant only when the trajectory of healthy educational developments goes awry. That is when the application of the research and science to the individual comes to bear.

From Practice to Research in Practice

One might wonder why not simply apply the wisdom and experience of clinical field–based results as effective practices. Insights and techniques from practical experience are foundational sources of effective treatment, whether it is in the field of medicine or education. However, the practical reality of clinical practice weakens the generalizability and scientific inferences one can draw beyond each case. Why? Because when a treatment is successful in the individual case, the treatment ceases (so one cannot infer much about alternative treatments except when unsuccessful). The clinician only sees that select, biased set of patients that visit him/her, and there is no way to know that they are representative of patients that see other practitioners or the general population. This makes the clinician highly susceptible to biases when trying to generalize clinical insights beyond a specific setting. Clinicians may be seeing a particular community group that shares a particular set of characteristics that interact with treatments differently than the general population. They may not realize how their biases influence their beliefs about what works.

The solution to this problem, such that we can make causal inferences about interventions, is the randomized experiment. The randomized trial is designed to distribute differences *randomly* across the treatment levels, maximizing the generalization for the group. Researchers have generally found that their best judgment and theories about what characteristic differences matter most are as often wrong as right and as often introduce biases into the design that result in nongeneralizable outcomes. More often than not, the evidence shows that many differences do not make a difference, at least in isolation. In fact, it is one of the most disconcerting elements of educational research to find out how many times differences that one hypothesizes would make a difference, in fact, do not! Practitioners are likewise not immune to having well-reasoned, but ultimately biased assumptions about what will work for whom. Together, however, there is a chance of creating a scientific foundation that actually can be applied to improve the reading prospects of future learners.

Randomized Clinical Trials: What They Can and Cannot Tell Us

In this section, the logic, strengths, and limitations of causal inference based on controlled experiments are reviewed. The *gold standard* design, a randomized clinical trial (RCT), whether in health/medicine or education, can lead to the inference that the probability of a successful outcome is higher for Treatment A than Treatment B across each unit of the population. Treatment A may work well for some, but Treatment B works better for more. As Holland (1986, 1988, 1993) makes clear, the causal inference is with respect to the causal effect—that is, to the outcome, not to causal mechanisms. A randomized study does not necessarily tell us why Treatment B is working better to cause the desired outcome, only that it is more effective in comparison with Treatment A. Even if subjects are assigned randomly, unless the study is designed to test theory-driven hypotheses, it may not yield insight into mechanisms that cause an effect.

Importantly, it is also not telling us whether it is optimal for each and every person in the population. There may be a set of individuals for which Treatment A was optimal. There just may be fewer of them in the population than those who responded to Treatment B. And it is difficult and impossible to know who is who from conducting a basic randomized trial, because each individual really only receives one treatment (or one treatment at a time) and the randomization intentionally attempted to balance all the various characteristics across the different groups.

Holland (1986) emphasizes that an RCT is measuring "the effects of causes," not "the causes of effects." This type of causal inference, he argues, is greatly assisted by randomized, controlled experimental methods. He contrasts this with research that is interested in deducing the causes of a given effect or the details of causal mechanisms. The latter are "why" questions. Both of these are legitimate and necessary areas of study. However, "why" questions are often more subtle and difficult scientific questions that require years of study and sometimes theoretical breakthroughs. We may want to know why penicillin is a remedy for bacterial infections or why an instructional program helps a child to learn to read better. However, "why does penicillin remedy infections" is a very different type of question than "does penicillin remedy infections better than aspirin?" Experimental designs that address the "what question" yield information that is relevant to the prevention and general programs for the population at large, whereas designs that address the "why question" may yield breakthrough information that permits design of solutions readily tailored to diverse individuals.

The randomized trial alone, thus, does not isolate causal mechanisms. The researcher may have hypotheses about what those mechanisms are and may manipulate them in the design. However, not all educational research is designed to tease apart causes of effects and may focus instead only on effects. The effect of reducing class size on achievement is a good example of a reasonably well-established effect without a well-proscribed description of the causes or active ingredients. Is the effect attributable to teachers having more time for individualization, or to the teacher being better able to manage behavior, or to less disruptive group dynamics among students or other factors? Similarly, a reading intervention program designed to teach systematic phonics may include a package of curriculum materials, readings, teacher's guides, lesson plans, activity sheets, professional development, and assessments (NRP, 2000). Which of these many elements are necessary or sufficient causal ingredients to the effect? Are they all necessary, in equal proportions? One can draw inferences about causal mechanisms from the entire body of educational research literature on professional development, teacher change, reading models, classroom practices, motivation, and so forth; however, no single RCT study will have definitively isolated which set of these valid causal mechanisms was at play in the particular intervention study.

Therefore, an RCT study does not necessarily tell us why a particular intervention or instructional strategy works at this fine-grained causal level. However, as noted, the body of research literature, such as this volume, is designed to provide guidance and expertise to educational professionals in the form of instructional strategies, models of reading development, and so forth, such that practitioners can reason through their own problems of practice.

However, there is another shortfall in applying the results of an RCT that must be considered. The question we may ask is whether a particular cause, that is, a treatment or intervention (these terms are used interchangeably), will work in a particular, individual case. To this question of applying scientific research, there remains a fundamental uncertainty. In technical terms, Holland and Rubin (1988) wrote:

> Although this notion of a causal effect can be *defined* for each unit
> in U, in general we are not able to directly *measure* a causal effect for
> a single unit because having exposed unit to: *treatment*, we cannot
> return in time to expose the same unit to *control*, instead. This is the
> Fundamental Problem of Causal Inference... (p. 205)

Riehl (2006) makes the same point:

> Even the most highly regarded randomized trials in medicine do not
> guarantee results in individual cases; in the end, medical care is about
> the health and well being of individual patients. In the statistical
> parlance of the health sciences, RCTs are designed to generate
> population-level estimates of the absolute and relative likelihoods for
> having particular outcomes, both positive and negative (Bluhm, 2005).
> Even the seemingly most determinant causal association in medicine
> (such as the relationship between smoking and lung cancer) is really just
> a probability. (p. 26)

"Just a probability" perhaps underestimates the value of knowing the odds and conditions under which any treatment or intervention might prove effective, but it is a statement worth reckoning with nonetheless. In the end, the level of uncertainty about the individual case is often driving our decision-making, not only for that individual, but also for various group levels.[1]

If the outcome of a series of randomized trials were such that an intervention worked well for everybody each time, then one would be in a strong position to conclude that individuals were homogeneous with respect to the intervention. In this case, for all practical purposes, individual differences across learners do not make a difference in the effectiveness of the treatment. It does not matter whether you have high or low ability in related cognitive or language skills, your background, your school or community, your motivational profile. This is the magic bullet, the holy grail of instructional interventions. One size truly does fit all! In reality, what one *sometimes* can say is that a particular intervention type is likely to work well with most kids. Perhaps, one will be able to say there is no evidence that it works better or worse with kids from high- or low-income schools and it works no differently with kids who are black, white, or other. One might even be able to say it works better in some settings than others.

The problem is that often one does not really know what differences make a difference. Not enough is known about the specific learners in those settings for which the treatment was successful, enough about those for whom it failed, or why. Less is known about causes of effects and more about effects of causes![2]

Instead, inferences are made based on correlated factors and left to the human judgment of the practitioner as to how much weight to give to these correlated, covariate factors. For example, suppose instructional intervention A worked much better for boys than girls, but there was a small advantage for B over A for girls. Based only on this evidence, a teacher might choose to use A for boys and B for girls, or A for everybody (on the argument that A worked almost as well for girls and it was difficult to implement both in classroom at the same time). Both decisions are consistent with the available evidence. But a closer look at the instruction, background histories of the students, and his or her own hypotheses about why the interaction might have occurred, might lead the teacher to one of the other options. So, having said that practitioners are not immune to biases about what will work for whom, nonetheless, they are at the front line of making that decision.

■ Summary and Implications of Medical/Health
Model Applied to Educational Contexts

In summary, a randomized trial is a methodology that allows conclusions about the "effects of causes," that is, which treatments or interventions are relatively better than the alternative for most of the individuals in the population sampled. It is a powerful technique for providing causal inferences about effectiveness, for winnowing out effective from ineffective treatments, and for providing supporting evidence for plausible causal explanations. Results are often extremely helpful (a) when there is a significant *prevalence* of the condition, and therefore (b) broadscale *prevention* or *remediation* of the prevalent condition is warranted, (c) when there are relatively obvious *environmental influences* that can be manipulated, and (d) there is reason to believe that results generalize and do no harm across identifiable *individual differences*. However, the causal inference does not provide certainty about effectiveness in each individual case and it does not confirm causal mechanisms regarding why any given treatment might be more effective. Judgments at the local level are still required, such that individualized care is provided for each case/child that requires it.

The implication is that the application of evidence and research in practical settings will require the reasoned judgment of well-informed professionals adjudicated between what is known and what is not. One drawback of the randomized control trial in education is that the research trajectory from field trial to practical application is slow with respect to all the potential covarying individual differences in response to treatment. Large, well-designed studies can generalize the main effect—Treatment A works better for more individuals, on average, than Treatment B—but say less about what worked for whom under what conditions. However, the overall research process does move the science continuously toward understanding *why* questions—the causes of effects that may, some day, lead to even more efficient and effective instruction that may be tailored to individuals.

Following are some recommendations about how to apply this general health/medicine model metaphor in the problem setting of raising proficiency levels of struggling adolescent readers. The point is that the administration of health care or education involves more than identifying the problem and following the research findings to recommend treatments. There are individual and environmental differences that may mediate response to scientifically validated treatments. There are so many simultaneous variables to consider, many that go beyond what is known based on research, that the practitioner must make reasoned judgments to help solve each case. How might researchers gather and validate the evidence that is generalizable and replicable such that practitioners and public officials can use them to make judgments about individual cases and groups?

■ Applying the Analogy to Struggling Adolescent Readers at the Middle School Level

The reason for this extended, elaborated discussion of the health/medical model and RCTs is to set a context for thinking about whether and how to apply it to educational problems. The problem concerns struggling adolescent readers (Biancarosa & Snow, 2004; Leach, Scarborough, & Rescorla, 2003). That is, all learners who leave elementary school with less than proficient reading skills such that their entire, future academic learning potential is at-risk. These are students who may not have been identified for special educational services because of reading difficulties, but still read well below grade level expectations. Evidence is presented that the prevalence of this problem is of sufficient scale to warrant considering it as analogous to a health risk, not rationally addressed on a case by case, diagnostic model. Consequentially, although it may be helpful and necessary for individual education providers to be equipped with the latest knowledge and skills of the empirical base of effective instructional strategies for improving reading prospects for learners, approaching this as a clinical problem is an insufficient solution. The focus is on middle school years but most of the discussion would apply to secondary school as well where curriculum and instruction is subject-area-specific, and teachers are expected and trained to teach their content, not reading.

A few recommendations are provided that constitute a basic framework or starter kit for assessing the scope of the problem at the middle school level and preparing a plan to address it using the empirical research base. A few caveats are in order. This approach does not try to address the myriad institutional, historical, and sociological issues that may interfere with implementing school reform that might improve reading outcomes in schools (e.g., Plaut & Sharkey, 1996). The focus instead is on the relationship between assessment data and decision-making about reading curriculum, interventions, and individual differences at the school and classroom levels. The goal is to provide models of how one could apply scientific research results to improve student performance over time.

■ Recommendations for Addressing Struggling Reader at the Middle School Level

The position argued for here is that the effective application of empirical evidence from the research literature is contingent on understanding the prevalence, nature, and scope of the problem. It may be misleading to talk as if the focal point of a solution is simply for individual, middle school classroom teachers to learn research-based effective reading strategy techniques and apply them. Imagine that a classroom teacher is a sixth grade language arts teacher, with no prior training in reading, still responsible for literacy content standards, and facing perhaps ten or more struggling readers (per class of which he/she may teach five per day) with different profiles of component reading strengths and weaknesses. Which students are struggling? What are their profiles? How does one integrate reading instruction with content learning that is targeted to subgroup needs? The analogy is the health clinic staff facing an epidemic of some new strain of ailment without medicine and resources.

The first question to ask is whether adolescent reading proficiency fits the health/medicine model just sketched. Is there really a struggling reader epidemic? One way to address that question is to determine whether there is a high prevalence of reading difficulties in the nation. The National Assessment of Educational Progress (NAEP) is designed to provide population estimates of the reading proficiencies of the nation's youth at grade levels 4, 8, and 12. The fourth grade NAEP (Lee, Grigg, & Donahue, 2007) results for reading show 33% of fourth graders read at a benchmark scale level deemed Below Basic and 34% at Basic levels. At eighth grade, 27% read Below Basic and 43% at Basic levels. Given a goal of nearly 100% readers at the Proficient level, this constitutes a high prevalence. The prevalence of readers Below Basic at fourth and eighth grades recommend a more public health approach to reading, both at the primary level and beyond (see McCardle and Miller, Chapter 1, this volume).

One might ask whether there are foundational skill difficulties at the root of some of these poor comprehension performances. One index of foundational skills difficulties is inaccurate word reading or slow oral reading rates. In two special studies conducted by NAEP to examine the oral reading performance of fourth graders, a very strong association between Basic and Below Basic comprehension performance and slow, inaccurate, and dysfluent oral reading was demonstrated (Daane, Campbell, Grigg, Goodman, & Oranje, 2005; Pinnell, Pikulski, Wikxson, Campbell, Gough, & Beatty, 1995). This association between low reading comprehension and slow, inaccurate reading rate and accuracy is being documented repeatedly in middle school populations as well (Deno & Marsten, 2006).

Estimates of specific reading disabilities or dyslexia tend to range from 5% to 17.5%, suggesting that many, if not most, of these fourth graders have the potential to become more skilled readers (Shaywitz, 1998). As a reasonable goal, we suggest that 75–90% of those students should be expected to respond to quality reading instruction, resulting in fourth grade NAEP estimates with 75–90% of students at Proficient or above levels. Then more intensive, individualized resources could be directed toward the remaining 10–25% to improve their prospects.

Perhaps this was a somewhat unexpected historical circumstance that significant numbers of adolescents were still in need of basic reading proficiencies. Certainly, teachers or schools have not been prepared for a quarter to third of middle school students to be in need of direct reading instruction— whether at the basic skills or comprehension strategy level. Nonetheless, the evidence suggests that this is the case. But it is also true that the population of struggling readers is not evenly distributed across the country. Some states, districts, and schools have relatively higher or lower concentrations of learners in need. In some places, it is only a handful of students to be identified and treated individually. In others, it may be nearly half or more of a school population. Knowing the concentration (i.e., prevalence) is a necessary first step in shaping a reasonable approach to a solution.

A sensible local unit to address the problem systematically is the school level. A middle school has the opportunity to work with an incoming adolescent with reading difficulties across grades 6–8 or more. They can allocate resources for literacy coaches and reading specialists. Schools can plan elective classes and after-school programs. Schools can implement professional development for subject area teachers and launch school-wide programs within subject area courses to enhance a focus on reading improvement. Schools can implement an assessment plan for monitoring the prevalence of incoming cohorts as well as the effectiveness of various strategies designed to address the problems. The individual classroom teacher simply does not have the resources to address the problem in this systematic matter. With this in mind, the following recommendations are made.

1. *Identify a school-wide goal for reading proficiency, a benchmark target, then estimate the prevalence of the struggling reader population at the school level*. It would be best to have a criterion-referenced standard by which to judge whether a student was proficient in reading. At the middle school level, one might define proficiency as the ability to comprehend and learn independently and with appropriate fluency from grade level, subject area texts (Science, Social Studies, Literature, Mathematics). That is, subject area teachers should be able to assume that proficient readers may struggle with learning the conceptual content of coursework, but not struggle unduly with reading the assigned texts. Sufficient vocabulary and background knowledge are also prerequisite both to reading and learning content, but it is also a fact that the learning of new vocabulary and knowledge from text is a major reason why reading is taught in the first place.

What might be an indicator or benchmark standard of reading proficiency against which to assess students' reading proficiency. Under NCLB (2001), schools increasingly have available a grade level snapshot, taken in the Spring, of the proportions of students above and below three to four threshold points, typically characterized as Below Basic, Basic, Proficient, and Advanced Proficient. The distribution of students across these levels sets a baseline prevalence of the problem space. If state test scores are unavailable, a benchmark such as the 50th percentile on a standardized, norm-referenced test could be chosen. This assumes that students scoring at the 50th percentile or better are proficient readers, that is, able to benefit and learn from typical grade level content readings.

Why is prevalence important? First, the sensible allocation of resources is highly dependent on the scope and prospective longevity of the problem.

In Figure 10.1, three different distributions of student levels on the same hypothetical state reading test are shown. The Ideal situation school (third bar) has about 5% of students reading Below Basic and about 10% at Basic levels, the remainder distributed among Proficient and Advanced. The Challenge school (first bar) has about the reverse distribution, 5% Advanced Proficient, 15% Proficient, the remainder Basic and Below Basic. The intermediate school (middle bar) occupies an intermediate level distribution. Given an incoming class of about 200 students, the Ideal school still has about 10 students with reading difficulties and another 30 who might be considered at-risk of reading failure, but who are also potentially proficient readers with the appropriate instructional attention. Addressing their needs could take as little as one or two reading resource specialists and a small investment in intervention programs. The Challenge school, on the other hand, may require a school-wide program of professional development, intervention programs, and specialists to address the multiple needs of some 160 students.

One immediate problem is that any given school is not as likely to have a snapshot of the incoming class (e.g., Grade 6, 7, or 8) on day 1, as these students most probably arrive from a number of feeder schools. A snapshot could be assembled, assuming most students arrive from feeder schools within the district or state and therefore have comparable state test scores from the previous spring. However, if many students are arriving from elsewhere or many kinds of intervention services may have taken place between the last testing point and the new school year, then prevalence estimates may be considerably off. Thus, it is worthwhile for schools to consider administering some screener battery of assessments to incoming students in the first semester at the school.

Despite the inordinate number of standardized comprehension tests administered to students, educators remain suspicious or confused about

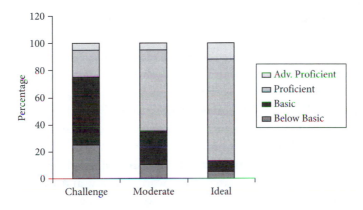

FIGURE 10.1 Distributions of Student Levels on the Same Hypothetical State Reading Test.

their reliability and validity in identifying specifically who has what kind of reading problem. It seems safe to conclude that it is highly probable that any individual who consistently gets high scores across years on a variety of different comprehension tests is likely a skilled reader. The reading constructs are not likely that far off for reading proficiency and it is very diffi-cult, short of cheating, to score well on these tests without strong underlying proficiencies. Such test scores are likely corroborated by teacher observations and grades in classrooms that routinely require reading and writing of grade level content. Therefore, one has a fair amount of confidence that relatively skilled readers can be identified.

On the other end of the distribution, consistently scoring poorly can stem from a number of reasons that are not necessarily poor reading skills. Assuming lack of interest, anxiety, or just a bad testing day can be ruled out as the cause of the poor test performance, diagnostic assessments are a next step to develop a pro-file of reading needs. Here, individual histories collected from teachers, parents, across years and settings can corroborate the judgment of difficulty in reading.

It is toward the middle to low middle of the distribution (25th to 50th percentile or so) where predictions based on standard reading tests are pre-carious. In this range, individuals may move from year to year upward in the distribution to appear as if they are developing adequately and therefore responsive to routine classroom instruction, or fall into risk and failure cate-gories. Regardless of low or middle, the traditional standardized, high stakes reading achievement tests reveals scant component profile information about individual students, which leads to the second recommendation.

2. *Do not assume a single profile of difficulties for all the struggling readers.* In some ideal, future world, by sixth grade every learner would be securely into Chall's (1967) *reading to learn* and *reading to do* stages, not still *learning to read*. Then instruction might simply focus on refreshing or enhancing read-ing comprehension strategies (McNamara, 2007). However, the reality is that many middle school learners struggle with the foundational skills of reading and command of academic language as it appears in adolescent and adult learning materials. At present, most of the empirical base for this conclu-sion must be inferred from the presence in fourth graders (Buly & Valencia, 2002; Deane, Sheehan, Sabatini, Futagi, & Kostin, 2006; Pinnell et al., 1995) and low literate adults (Kutner, Greenberg, & Baer, 2007; Sabatini, 2003) of component skill difficulties in individuals that are not classified as read-ing disabled, though a few studies have targeted adolescents (Leach et al., 2003; Scarborough, 1998; Scarborough, Ehri, Olson, & Fowler, 1998). In the authors' ongoing, collaborative projects, a significant number of adolescents with component skill weaknesses at the word, fluency, and vocabulary level are being identified (see Christensen and Wauchope, Chapter 18, this vol-ume, for a similar finding in Australia). For example, in a sample of 300 sixth and seventh graders in several middle schools who took the Tests of Word

Reading Efficiency (Torgesen, Wagner, & Rashotte, 1999), from 25% to 33% of students in schools had scale scores that placed them more than two grade levels behind the mean for their grade and reading rates well below grade level expectations (Rasinski, 2001).

What kinds of problems may these adolescents face? Novel words may require effort to decode, recognize, learn their meaning(s), and usage. Complex sentence and discourse structures that are prevalent in academic texts may also require considerable cognitive effort to extract the basic meaning units necessary to build a memory representation that can be integrated with existing background knowledge. Weakness in processing text can easily result in diminished rate of growth in the numbers and variety of morphologically diverse vocabulary words that appear primarily in written versus oral text discourse. As a consequence, students will fail to learn from reading. They will fail in understanding and comprehending the richer, conceptual content and themes of text not necessarily out of a failure of the ability to think and reason about the content, but out of a more fundamental weakness in the prerequisite skills that provide efficient, robust access to that content via the printed perceptual channel of processing language. In summary, the postelementary struggling readers also struggle with text.

In addition to the differences that arise from learners of different ages and instructional exposure in schools, several other group differences stand out as fundamental. These include identifying students with disabilities that include physical, behavioral, emotional, cognitive, mental, learning, and various comorbid conditions. It also includes English language learners—including, for example, children whose non-English speaking parents migrate to the United States and who, similar to their parents, may have no or minimal English language or reading skills. These are often group differences that make a difference (see August & Shanahan, 2006; NRC, 1998; RAND, 2002).

3. *Estimate the prevalence of a few key profile clusters.* Our basic assessment approach applies a modified Simple View framework to all struggling readers. As described by Hoover & Tunmer (1993), "the simple view makes two claims: First, that reading consists of word recognition and linguistic comprehension; and second, that each of these components is necessary for reading, neither being sufficient in itself" (p. 3). Word recognition and decoding are stronger predictors of reading level in the early grades because reading comprehension test performance is highly dependent on recognizing the words in the passages. As word recognition becomes more fluent and automatized, listening/language comprehension becomes a stronger predictor of reading ability, though word recognition continues to contribute significant variance even in skilled readers (see also Carver 1997, 2003; Carver & David, 2001; Catts, Adlof, & Weismer, 2006; Gough, 1996).

What is meant by language comprehension is an array of cognitive and linguistic skills including background knowledge, vocabulary, language structure (e.g., syntax/grammar), verbal reasoning ability, and literacy knowledge (e.g., genre and discourse knowledge) (Perfetti, 2007; Perfetti, Landi, & Oakhill, 2005). Across development, these component skills become more and more entwined, reinforcing, and/or compensating for each other as necessary during the reading process (Scarborough, 2001). One reason that there is a greater load on the language skills at higher grade levels is that we are demanding more application of higher level skills and reasoning applied to texts and tests at these levels (Keenan, Betjemann, & Olson, 2006). (See Christensen and Wauchope, Chapter 18, this volume, who also found the importance of including cognitive and metacognitive strategies in secondary reading instruction.) Tests tend to focus more on literal and basic inferential processing in forming a mental model of texts in grades K to 3 or 4, but increasingly ask for complex interpretations, evaluations, and syntheses in higher grades (Cain, Oakhill, & Byrant, 2004; Lee et al., 2007; Rapp, van den Broek, McMaster, Kendeou, & Espin, 2007). At the same time, the structural complexity of text is increasing as well (Deane et al., 2006).

The author's team attempts to capture a four-pronged profile relative to this more complex reading model—basic decoding/word recognition ability, fluency/reading rate, vocabulary, and sentence and discourse text processing. The basic premise is that difficulty in decoding novel words when initially encountered in a text, or in easily recognizing a large percentage of one's listening vocabulary as printed words, will impede the efficiency of reading proficiency, especially at the middle school level and beyond (Perfetti, 2007). Typically, explicit word or lexical code level instruction ends around second or third grade. Middle school classroom teachers are not typically trained in explicit reading comprehension instruction, much less in basic reading skills instruction. However, the alarming number of fourth graders, adolescents, and adults who demonstrate profound difficulties in basic and efficient decoding and word recognition skills, strongly suggests that we cannot take for granted that a focus on the code is unfounded (e.g., Sabatini, 2002, 2003).

Even for those with adequate skills, the middle school years are a good time to re-emphasize the morpho-phonemic structure of the English language (Venezky, 1999; Verhoeven & Perfetti, 2003). Latin and Greek roots and the influence of derivational affixes on meaning and grammatical sentence structure are central to reading, vocabulary growth, and learning in the content areas such as social studies (e.g., monarchy, oligarchy, senatorial) and sciences (e.g., osteoporosis, metabolize, antihistamine). The good news is that the greatest percentage of students in most middle schools will show proficiency at this level of commanding the language code in print and need not be repeatedly tested to confirm this accomplishment, that is, if one maintains a longitudinal student history of component proficiency. For those with distinct word level problems, some targeted intervention using outside classroom resources (e.g., tutors, pull-out programs, resource staff, etc.) may be required, and monitoring of progress strongly recommended (see Shapiro, Chapter 11, this volume).

As noted, evidence continues to accrue for a consistent, large correlation between reading rate and comprehension in empirical data sets (Deno & Marsten, 2006). For example, in analyses conducted based on the NAEP special study of oral reading (Daane et al., 2005), a 0.68 correlation between basic reading rate and overall performance on the NAEP reading proficiency scale is reported. Returning to the medical analogy, reading rate is a candidate task for monitoring as an initial indicator of potential reading difficulties, such as temperature or blood pressure, consistent with the current progress monitoring literature (Deno, Fuchs, Marston, & Shin, 2001; Fuchs, Fuchs, Hosp, & Jenkins, 2001; Wayman, Wallace, Wiley, Ticha, & Espin, 2007). Strong "print skills" as indexed by rapid, fluent, accurate, automatized word recognition and continuous text reading rule out a whole host of potential underlying problems (Torgesen, Wagner, & Rashotte, 1999).

There are any number of instruments with acceptable psychometric properties that do an adequate job of screening for decoding, efficient word recognition, or appropriate grade level reading rates. Readers who are strong on these print skills, but still weak in comprehension performance on standardized tests, are likely to have difficulties with the composite of language skills or comprehension strategies. Readers with weak print skills, however, may and in fact are likely to still have weak comprehension skills. The weak print skills confound direct measurement of the comprehension skills. It is conceivable that bright students might be very strong reasoners and inferencers or possess strong general verbal ability, but not be able to apply those skills because they cannot read words. Highly educated foreign-born students who are still learning to speak and read English often have this profile. Students with specific reading-based disabilities, who are identified early in their school career and provided appropriate alternate exposure to educational programs (i.e., not channeled through their weak print reading skills), may also show this profile. However, the vast majority of slow, inaccurate readers of print will also show concomitant weaknesses in vocabulary development, knowledge of print genres, and various comprehension strategies.

In summary, we are recommending that a school level profile of the prevalence of reading difficulties be undertaken. Screening and initial profiling could estimate the size of groups who are clearly proficient, severely struggling, and potentially at-risk. For the latter two groups, component tests are recommended that identify specific difficulties with (a) accurate word recognition/decoding, (b) word and text reading rate/fluency, (c) vocabulary knowledge, and (d) sentence and discourse processing. At this point in the process, the goal is not to obtain incontrovertible profile evidence for each individual tested. Any given student may be mismeasured for a variety of reasons ranging from low motivation, instrument unreliability, or just a bad testing day. However, the proportion of students in each category should be precise enough to make a school-wide plan that addresses larger-scale remedies (e.g., professional development or classroom interventions; pull-out small group interventions; investments in intervention programs, etc.) versus individualized, diagnostic attention (e.g., more complete diagnostic testing by a specialist, highly individualized and tailored interventions targeting specific needs, and plans for alternate approaches should the initial program prove insufficient).

4. *Make a plan for resources that is aligned with the prevalence and profile clusters.* With this information, the school and teachers are now in a better position to address the needs of learners. The need and nature for literacy coaches and reading specialists can be determined. If there is a strong need for direct comprehension strategy instruction (McNamara, 2007), reading in the content areas (e.g., Romance & Vitale, 2001), fluency (Samuels & Farstrup, 2006), or vocabulary (Beck & McKeown, 2001) for an identifiable subgroup of students, elective classes and after-school programs can be organized. If it is a school-wide concern, then professional development for subject area teachers and school-wide program can be launched. With baseline information, the school can implement an assessment plan for monitoring the prevalence or improvements in reading, as well as the effectiveness of various strategies that are implemented to address the problems.

The point here is that the solutions are relevant to the scope and nature of the problems. *Given the expense of different solutions and limited resources of time and funding to implement them, it is not prudent to jump directly from research findings to broad changes in policy and practice, without a closer assessment of needs.* At the middle school level, where the curriculum standards primarily assume reading proficiency as a prerequisite to other achievement goals, and teachers organize their instruction based on these standards, a data-based plan is essential. Clusters of students may have weaknesses in any or all of the varied component skills that comprise reading proficiency. Remediating different levels of problems will likely have different time lines and resource demands. Intensive, foundational reading skill programs for adolescents may range from 6-weeks, to an entire year, to multiyear supplements to the existing curriculum. Raising vocabulary levels of students is another aim that may require a sustained duration of treatment before strong effects are detectable with measures.

This issue underscores the need for estimating the prevalence of general difficulties and some estimation of whether they are widespread, shared difficulties. It may be necessary to make some difficult choices about how to best help the greatest number at the most reasonable cost, as a first step in the plan. For example, if all struggling readers have difficulty in comprehension strategies, then a school-wide program falls into the category of generally helpful and doing no harm to those few who may already have some command of such strategies. Just because there is potential for a wide variety of unique individual profiles does not mean there will not be shared needs that can be broadly administered.

5. *Start with evidence-based programs and practices, and implement as if your school is a clinical research trial site.* The next step should be to apply the resea-rch findings on effective interventions for struggling readers at the middle school level. However, at the time of writing this chapter, the RCT evidence is thin about what works for whom under what conditions, though there is a wealth of sound instructional advice built on the foundational empirical work in the component skills of reading in younger students. The "clinical" practitioner, whether it is teacher or reading specialist at the middle school level, will have to make his or her best judgments of how to adapt and apply techniques that may have worked with younger or special populations to their own students. That is the approach taken to helping low literate adults improve their reading and currently being implemented with a cohort of adolescents (Sabatini, Scarborough, Shore, Bruce, & Sawaki, 2007). These learners had word reading skills between the second and sixth grades and profiles that suggested the need for a combination of direct phonics and fluency instruction to supplement ongoing vocabulary and comprehension classroom instruction. The team adapted programs proven effective, yet designed for young populations, making the content and activities appropriate for adult learners, but attempting to maintain the active ingredients of instruction that led to their empirical effectiveness (Shore, Bruce, & Korber, 2005). In general, the adaptations have been successful in that adult students consistently report satisfaction and interest in the content of the programs, though data are still being collected as to the relative effectiveness of the programs in improving component reading skills (Bruce, Shore, & Sabatini, 2006; Sabatini et al., 2007; Sabatini & Shore, 2005, 2006). As the scientific community collects evidence of what works for adolescents, it will be on the shoulders of the practice community to adapt and apply the best of what the current evidence base suggests.

Therefore, a strategy that allows schools to learn how to improve the prospects for each cohort of entering students to leave three years later as proficient readers, applying new findings as they emerge, seems warranted. So, another logical step is to align progress and outcome assessments to the goals one seeks for students so as to inform school administrators as to whether alternate programs or strategies are helping students to achieve their learning goals. If the four-pronged approach above is adopted, then there should be outcome measures that show whether adequate progress is made for each prong. If the school invests in an intervention program, then students who take that program should show appropriate progress on targeted skills, as well as the integration of those skills toward comprehension outcome proficiency.

The research literature can provide guidance regarding how to set and temper expectations. Even when provided with the best of our science and instructional approaches, studies continue to find resister groups who simply show slow or no progress (NRP, 2000). Studies also indicate the varying rates of progress that students achieve given the level of intensity and duration of the instructional treatment provided. Typically, they describe methods used to ensure fidelity of treatment. Interventions are expected to have effectiveness to the extent to which the key elements are actually administered; so researchers try to ensure that there is consistency in implementation. In the author's studies (e.g., Shore, Sabatini, & Bruce, 2006), that process has been reversed to support professional development, using rubrics based on program designers' identification of key aspects of each program. Teacher logs and observational evidence (audio CDs of sessions) were collected and feedback was provided to teachers to improve their practice. Focus was then on identifying which of those features of a program were easily detected and mastered, which often required individual coaching, and those that were more generally difficult, which required additional teacher training workshops and materials (see also Darling-Hammond, Chung, & Frelow, 2002; Flowers, Dawson, & Hancock, 2003).

Schools might govern themselves as if they were their own clinical trial site in which data are rigorously collected, managed, analyzed, and applied to ensure optimal results. Regular classroom teachers and/or school level reading specialists are analogous to general practitioners in this model, as they must apply their knowledge to individuals. One of the most important decisions a general practitioner may make is when to refer to a specialist, which itself is based on a judgment about the limits of one's own expertise or knowledge in helping a student in a particular case.

In some cases, the individualization of a program based on teacher expertise and craft knowledge of their students can equal or improve on expected outcomes. In other cases, teacher's best intentions to modify aspects based on their personal experiences may actually decrease the effectiveness for students. As always, there's no research formula for knowing precisely which is which. Schools might initially implement a program by following the guidelines recommended by the authors and researchers, and then consider systematically varying aspects that might improve the fit to specific groups of students or school conditions. This approach mimics the research process and allows schools to make inferences about whether changing the program improves or reduces outcomes.

■ Limitations of Empirical Research and What the School Can Do about It

The manner of reporting results in RCT studies does not always lend itself well to judging the impact on students. Effect sizes help researchers understand relative effectiveness, but do not help schools to know how many students would benefit and how much growth to expect. *Research studies should provide frequency distributions of the amount of change in individual students, rather than reporting only mean gains for a group or effect sizes.* Although means and effect sizes can be helpful when researchers are reporting results to each other, they do not directly translate into expectations concerning student progress. Figure 10.2 shows a chart produced for a study of the relative effectiveness of adult reading supplemental programs (Sabatini et al., 2007). In this chart, students who gained on multiple outcome measures were identified based on the assumption that any single score gain may be the result of a chance score, but students who are gaining on multiple measures are likely to experience a more robust instructional effect. The chart shows that less than 10% of the students in any treatment showed no gains at all; about 75–80% made gains on at least two tests; and about 15–30% made gains on four tests. In another analysis, the size of gains was charted on key measures that were above the threshold of chance gains, showing the percentage of students who made reliable individual gains that appeared to move them back into grade level achievement range. Using percentile scales with chosen cutpoints, such as below 25th percentile, between 25th and 50th percentile, and above 50th percentile, is another way of setting benchmarks and estimates.

A second difficulty in using the research literature is in setting expectations because most studies do not really do population sampling. Consequently, it is not always clear whether any particular school can expect equivalent percentages of students to respond. However, if a school

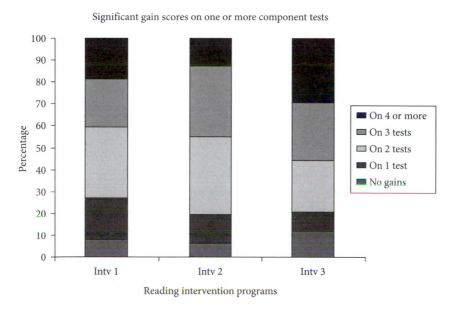

FIGURE 10.2 Low Literate Adult Students Who Gained on Multiple Outcome Measures after Intervention.

sets initial expectations based on the literature and conducts the program for a few cohorts of students, then the more the local empirical findings can become the new baseline for expectations and comparisons of new intervention programs. School personnel should be cautioned against presuming that "my" school is so different that research results are irrelevant or would not work. Individual studies cannot make claims of generalization beyond their particular samples; however, schools should consider themselves no better at judging their nonrepresentativeness in predicting how well a program will work. It very well may be true that the school context or student population is so different that nothing generalizes, but as noted earlier, individual differences that make a difference are remarkably slippery. Better to run a trial, measure whether the program is working better or worse in one's school than in the study, and then make predictions about why. In this way, the school accumulates wisdom and expertise regardless of initial results.

Another key weakness of educational experimental research is the paucity of longitudinal intervention trials (for an exception, see O'Connor, Fulmer, Harry, & Bell, 2005). Although there are a great number of studies interested in so-called resistors (i.e., students who do not respond to available treatments), researchers can rarely implement multiyear treatments that vary in intensity and duration limitlessly. Most intervention studies in the literature provide from 50 to 100 hours of intervention. Many times that appears to be insufficient for some students, especially those further behind in skills. They may show some progress, albeit on a slower trajectory. There are no guarantees about whether progress will continue to be linear beyond the end point of a research study versus the student experiencing a period of accelerated growth or a final plateau that is below proficiency expectations. In many complex skill domains, such as learning a musical instrument, there may be long periods in which progress appears to be slow if not halted, followed by a period of consolidation and apparent rapid growth.

For struggling readers, the goal should be achieving high levels of proficiency, and varying the type, intensity, and duration of instruction are key tools the educator has for supporting attainment of that goal. Middle schools should factor in that they have multiple years to effect solutions for each entering student. They can try various approaches and continue to administer treatments until the student reaches proficiency or they must move on. Collecting better evidence of when a student is truly nonresponsive to a treatment versus mired in a temporary plateau is a function that schools could help researchers to ascertain. Data from various monitoring assessments used to map such nonlinear growth trajectories would serve such purpose. In general, schools may need to be patient and persistent in their efforts to help each child improve in reading proficiency. Implementing a systematic program of trials and documenting their relative success and failure is a credible strategy in the face of uncertain scientific guidance.

■ Comenius Middle School: A Hypothetical Case

Comenius Middle School is an urban school with a largely minority population, 75% black, African American, 20% Latino, and 5% other. Reading/Literacy scores on the state's language arts/reading test last year showed 55% Below Basic, 25% Basic, 15% Proficient, and 5% Advanced at sixth, seventh, and eighth grades and these proportions have remained basically stable for the past two years.

As a first step at addressing the school-wide literacy problems, the principal decides to implement a school-wide screening battery for all returning sixth and seventh graders at the following school year. In the Fall they will administer the test to the incoming sixth graders and any new students entering at seventh or eighth grades. The battery takes about one class period to administer and includes brief measures of decoding/word reading, reading fluency, vocabulary, and sentence level comprehension skills. The measure is computerized, and includes both multiple choice responses and constructed response items (i.e., written and spoken responses captured and stored by the software). The multiple choice responses allow quick turnaround for basic scores for students that can be used by school administrators for estimating prevalence of struggling readers at different levels and estimates of specific component difficulties of subgroups. The constructed responses provide more individual detail, but require more resources to score and interpret and, therefore, are only scored on an as needed basis. That is, the subset of students whose score profiles are low or mixed are targeted for further scoring and interpretation. This conserves school resources by putting effort into understanding assessments of students with individual needs, rather than students who are already progressing normally.

In the initial year of implementation, the administration uses the classification categories (i.e., Basic, Below Basic, Proficient) to construct student group levels on component screener measures. Assume that a standard score of 90 is the 25th percentile (or up to two grade-level equivalents below average) and, of course, 100 is the 50th percentile. Thus, any student with a score above 100 is above the 50th percentile on that skill, between 100 and 90 they may have some difficulty on the skill, while below 90 they have significant difficulties. As shown in Table 10.1, the mean performances on the component scores reflect the general classifications based on the state proficiency scores, that is, Proficient/Advanced students score higher than the 50th percentile, Basic students a little below, and Below Basic well below the 50th percentile.

A further confirmatory/descriptive step is to create a contingency table of proficiency level by component test scores. An example of such a table for Decoding is provided as Table 10.2. One would not expect perfect alignment between the component scores and the overall proficiency scores. Not all students have the same profile underlying their global comprehension performance.

TABLE 10.1   *Average Scores on Individual Tests by Skill Group for Comenius Middle School (Groupings Based on State Total Test Standard Score (SS) of 192 Sixth Graders)*

Grade (SS)	Proficient/Advanced	Basic	Below Basic	Total
	Means			
Sample size	$n = 40$	$n = 50$	$n = 110$	$n = 200$
Decoding/word recognition	110	95	80	90
Vocabulary	105	90	79	87
Sentence	110	95	80	90
Reading fluency (words per minute)	140	120	95	110

Assuming perfectly reliable and valid measures, Table 10.2 can be interpreted as saying that not all students who score Below Basic also have significant decoding/word recognition problems. Although 50 students have scores less than 90, 50 are between 90 and 100, and 10 are above 100. Not all students have significant decoding problems underlying their poor comprehension performances.

Of course, individual test scores are not perfectly reliable and valid. A student may have had a bad test day, or anxiety, or unfamiliarity with a task type, resulting in an anomalous score. Furthermore, the cells in Table 10.2 are based on ranges of scores. A student with a score of 99 may be more like another student with a score of 100 than one with a score of 90; yet the 99 and 90 are in the same cell in Table 10.2. That is why we have described this as a screening assessment. Any decision about an individual student such as placement into an intervention program should be based on a more than one test score in one test session. Instead, the table permits an estimate of prevalence for aligning resources and diagnostic testing. In this sixth grade, some 60 or more students would appear to have significant decoding difficulties underlying poor comprehension scores and may need interventions to support growth. Another 55 students appear to have decoding competency or proficiency, whereas another 85 may need further diagnostic testing or careful monitoring to determine whether decoding/word recognition ability is an authentic difficulty that should be addressed. If the school has limited resources, this kind of table (and associated individual scores) suggests those with most need.

In Comenius Middle School, the screening data show that about 50–60 students have scores less than 90 on the decoding test, and therefore may benefit from an intervention that focuses on more basic decoding/word recognition skills. A similar contingency table based on vocabulary data, however, shows that more than three quarters of all students show weakness (SS less than 100) in vocabulary. Thus, the administration decides that a

TABLE 10.2 *Classification of Word Skill Groups by Proficiency level (Groupings Based on State Total Test Standard Score (SS) of 200 Sixth Graders)*

	Proficient/ Advanced	Basic	Below Basic	Total
	Means			
Sample size	*n* = 40	*n* = 50	*n* = 110	*n* = 200
Decoding/Word Recognition				
Greater than 100	35	10	10	55
Between 99 and 90	5	30	50	85
Less than 90	0	10	50	60
Total	40	50	110	200
Vocabulary				
Greater than 100	25	5	0	30
Between 99 and 90	13	30	55	98
Less than 90	2	15	55	67
Total	40	50	110	200

school-wide program to improve vocabulary skills is a sound resource investment. Enhancing students' vocabulary will benefit more than reading performance; vocabulary knowledge and learning skills are a necessary foundation to all content area learning. Consequently, all content area teachers might benefit from professional development to enhance their repertoire of instructional strategies with respect to evidence-based vocabulary learning (see Nagy, Chapter 17, this volume). Even proficient students may benefit from a review and focus on vocabulary learning, so no harm is perceived in implementing such a program. As part of their training, teachers learn how to interpret student reading profiles and assessments relative to vocabulary skills. They learn formative assessment techniques for monitoring individual and group vocabulary learning.

Thus, when teachers are assigned a roster of students, they also receive the screening and profile information, along with access to the test information. Constructed response data in the screening battery can now be used to enhance the quality of interpretations to help teachers better understand individual and subgroup difficulties. For example, teachers can listen to oral reading samples of struggling students assigned to their class to get a sense of their reading fluency and rate with respect to grade level, content-based passages. Do students have difficulty sounding out simple or complex subject-specific content words at grade level? Is their prosody and expression fluent when reading complex, expository sentences? Will they struggle with the typically assigned text of the course? Similarly, there may be a set of pre-requisite science content vocabulary (e.g., genetics, biodiversity) that nonproficient students consistently erred on in component vocabulary tests. These results may be predictive of the students' ability to know and learn course content. Of course, this level of information is only useful if instructors have some training or background in understanding reading difficulties and remedies. If content level teachers do not understand the relation of fluency or vocabulary to reading and learning, or do not have training or resources to implement instructional strategies at the classroom level, then this assessment information is of little use to them.

In contrast to the school-wide vocabulary solution, the administration determines that intensive decoding interventions are best handled as a pull-out program for students with specific decoding skill needs. Many of these students were already assigned to after-school tutoring programs because of their below basic reading comprehension scores. The administration decides to invest more in published programs that have an evidence base supporting their effectiveness. The district has approved and invested in a small set of published intervention programs that are available to schools. However, when the curriculum specialist examines the existing programs approved by the district, they note that the research does not address whether the programs were effective with linguistic minorities or nonnative speakers of English. A significant percentage of the students with decoding problems come from families in which the first language spoken in the home is not English and the students, while proficient in conversational English, may still have English language learning needs. They decide to apply the intervention program as is for the first semester. However, their English Language Learning specialist is assigned to monitor the response of language minority students in the program, and should they fail to respond as expected, to offer recommendations of modifications that might better fit this subgroup's needs. They can compare in subsequent cycles the value in learning gains of adapting the program based on these recommendations.

The school organizes an assessment plan and longitudinal database to monitor and track the progress of struggling readers across their years at Comenius Middle School. Their goal, of course, is to move the distribution of student reading achievement toward Proficient levels or above on state exams. They are able to examine achievement of students who were assigned to various intervention programs relative to instructional aims of those programs (e.g., decoding, fluency). If a particular student does not show gains relative to other students in the same program after a sufficient duration of exposure to the intervention, then they schedule a meeting with a reading specialist to identify alternate or additional resources.

They also establish a plan for examining whether their school-wide program in vocabulary is effective. They use the initial year of the program to establish a baseline performance level of students on vocabulary measures by proficiency level, whereas teachers are just being trained in strategies. In the next year, as teachers begin to implement what they have learned in their classrooms, they will look for a significant group mean gains, with the greatest gains among Basic and Below Basic students. If gains do not materialize or are uneven, they will look first to issues of fidelity of implementation and effectiveness of training, as well as re-examining evidence-based vocabulary instructional approaches in the research literature that might lead to new or enhanced approaches. Thus, the outcome information on students becomes formative to improvement of the vocabulary program as a whole. If gains are significant, administrators may still move to enhance teacher skills consistent with the current implemented approaches. Or they may move to address other priority issues related to reading difficulties such as comprehension strategies or fluency. Each year, they monitor the incoming freshman class, hopefully seeing a trend of less reading difficulties stemming from prior student preparation. They can then adjust resource allocation to better target new student needs.

■ Summary and Conclusions

How the health/medical model of promoting public health and treating individual cases could be applied to the problem of struggling adolescent readers in educational settings was examined. In doing so, the logic, strengths, and weaknesses of RCTs as a means of establishing a scientific basis for practice and potential applications in schools were examined. Conclusions point to a fundamental uncertainty as to whether any inference of causal effectiveness for a group would also work for particular individuals and highlight the generalizability problem of whether results would better fit unique local settings and populations. This led to five recommendations for addressing reading difficulties of struggling readers at the middle school level, with recognition that in many problem contexts middle school teachers will not have all the resources and expertise to address the problems of adolescent reading by themselves. That is, the analogy of a public health problem is the more apt metaphor than the individual diagnostic case. In settings with a low prevalence of struggling readers, the skillful, well-informed language arts or content teacher can directly read and apply insights from the research literature or volumes such as these to improve the prospects for those at-risk readers. In many schools and districts, however, literacy problems are more prevalent and therefore more complex. There will be clusters of readers with different profiles and different instructional needs, and classroom teachers will be pressed to find the resources, time, and expertise to address the problems on their own. Rather, in these cases, a school level plan, as illustrated in the hypothetical example of Comenius Middle School, will be necessary.

■ Acknowledgments

This research is funded in part by grants from the Institute of Education Sciences (R305G04065) and from the National Institute for Literacy, the Office of Vocational and Adult Education, and the National Institute of Child Health and Human Development (NICHD) (HD 043774), NICHD (HD 046130 & P50 HD052121–02). I would also like to acknowledge collaborations with Strategic Educational Research Partnership (SERP) Institute, Harvard University, Boston University, University of Michigan, Haskins Laboratories, and Kennedy-Krieger Institute for working with our ETS team to help develop, collect, and apply assessment information in support of struggling readers. Thanks to Drew Gitomer, Tenaha O'Reilly, Dan Eigner, and anonymous reviewers for helpful comments. Variations of the ideas and recommendations presented here are being implemented in collaboration with these partners in actual settings. Thus, they deserve credit and acknowledgement for recommendations deemed useful, but no blame for the opinions expressed by this author. Any opinions expressed in this chapter are those of the author and not necessarily of Educational Testing Service.

■ References

August, D., & Shanahan, T. (2006). *Report of the national literacy panel on language minority children and youth*. Mahwah, NJ, Lawrence Erlbaum Associates.

Beck, I. L., & McKeown, M. G. (2001). Inviting students into the pursuit of meaning. *Educational Psychology Review, 13*, 225–241.

Biancarosa, G., & Snow, C. E. (2004). *Reading Next—A vision for action and research in middle and high school literacy: A report from Carnegie Corporation of New York*. Washington, DC, Alliance for Excellent Education.

Bruce, K., Shore, J., & Sabatini, J. P. (2006, February). *Teaching low literate learners with fluency and phonics approaches*. Paper presented at the Annual Meeting for the Learning Disabilities Association, Jacksonville, FL.

Buly, M. R., & Valencia, S. W. (2002). Below the bar: Profiles of students who fail state reading assessments. *Educational Evaluation and Policy Analysis, 24*, 219–239.

Cain, K., Oakhill, J., & Byrant, P. (2004). Children's reading comprehension ability: Concurrent prediction by working memory, verbal ability, and component skills. *Journal of Educational Psychology, 96*, 31–42.

Carver, R. P. (1997). Reading for one second, one minute, or one year from the perspective of rauding theory. *Scientific Studies of Reading, 1*, 3–43.

Carver, R. P. (2003). The highly lawful relationships among pseudoword decoding, word identification, spelling, listening, and reading. *Scientific Studies of Reading, 7*, 127–154.

Carver, R. P., & David, A. H. (2001). Investigating reading achievement using a causal model. *Scientific Studies of Reading, 5,* 107–140.

Catts, H. W., Adlof, S. M., & Weismer, S. E. (2006). Language deficits in poor comprehenders: A case for the simple view of reading. *Journal of Speech, Language & Hearing Research, 49,* 278–293.

Chall, J. S. (1967). *Stages of reading development.* New York, McGraw-Hill.

Daane, M. C., Campbell, J. R., Grigg, W. S., Goodman, M. J., & Oranje, A. (2005). *Fourth-grade students reading aloud: NAEP 2002 special study of oral reading* (No. NCES 2006–469). Washington, DC, U.S. Department of Education, Institution of Education Sciences, National Center for Educational Statistics.

Darling-Hammond, L., Chung, R., & Frelow, F. (2002). Variation in teacher preparation: How well do pathways prepare teachers to teach? *Journal of Teacher Education, 53,* 286–302.

Deane, P., Sheehan, K. M., Sabatini, J., Futagi, Y., & Kostin, I. (2006). Differences in text structure and its implications for assessment of struggling readers. *Scientific Studies of Reading, 10,* 257–275.

Deno, S. L., Fuchs, L. S., Marston, D., & Shin, J. (2001). Using curriculum-based measurements to establish growth standards for students with learning disabilities. *School Psychology Review, 30,* 507–524.

Deno, S. L., & Marsten, D. (2006). Curriculum-based measurement of oral reading: An indicator of growth in fluency. In S. J. Samuels & A. E. Farstrup (Eds.), *What research has to say about fluency instruction* (pp. 179–203). Newark, DE, International Reading Association.

Fisher, R. (1970). *Statistical methods for research workers* (14th ed.). Edinburgh, Oliver and Boyd.

Flowers, C., Dawson, R., & Hancock, A. (2003). An interview protocol and scoring rubric for evaluating teacher performance. *Assessment in Education: Principles, Policy & Practice, 10,* 161–168.

Fuchs, L. S., Fuchs, D., Hosp, M. K., & Jenkins, J. R. (2001). Oral reading fluency as an indicator of reading competence: A theoretical, empirical, and historical analysis. *Scientific Studies of Reading, 5,* 239–256.

Gough, P. B. (1996). How children learn to read and why they fail. *Annals of Dyslexia, 46,* 3–20.

Holland, P. W. (1986). Statistics and causal inference. *Journal of the American Statistical Association, 81,* 945–966.

Holland, P. W. (1988). *Causal inference, path analysis and resursive structural equations* (No. PSRTR-88–81). Princeton, NJ, Educational Testing Service.

Holland, P. W. (1993). *Probabilistic causation without probability* (No. 93–29). Princeton, NJ, Educational Testing Service.

Holland, P. W., & Rubin, D. B. (1982). *On Lord's paradox* (No. 82–34). Princeton, NJ, Educational Testing Service.

Holland, P. W., & Rubin, D. B. (1988). Causal inference in retrospective studies. *Evaluation Review, 12,* 203–231.

Hoover, W. A., & Tunmer, W. E. (1993). The components of reading. In G. B. Thompson, W. E. Tunmer, & T. Nicholson (Eds.), *Reading acquisition processes* (pp. 1–19). Philadelphia, Multilingual Matters.

Ialongo, N. S., Kellam, S. G., & Poduska, J. (2000). A developmental epidemiological framework for clinical child and pediatric psychology research. In D. Drotar (Ed.), *Handbook of research in pediatric and clinical child psychology* (pp. 21–49). New York, Kluwer Academic.

Keenan, R. M., Betjemann, R. S., & Olson, R. K. (2006). Reading comprehension tests vary in the skills they assess: Differential dependence on decoding and oral comprehension. *Scientific Study of Reading, 10*, 363–380.

Kutner, M., Greenberg, E., & Baer, J. (2007). *National Assessment of Adult Literacy (NAAL). A first look at the literacy of American adults in the 21st century.* Washington, DC, National Center for Educational Statistics, Institute of Educational Sciences, U.S. Department of Education.

Leach, J. M., Scarborough, H. S., & Rescorla, L. (2003). Late-emerging reading disabilities. *Journal of Educational Psychology, 95*, 211.

Lee, J., Grigg, W. S., & Donahue, P. L. (2007). *The Nation's Report Card: Reading 2007* (NCES 2007–496). Washington, DC, National Center for Educational Statistics, Institute of Educational Sciences, U.S. Department of Education.

McNamara, D. S. (Ed.) (2007). *Reading comprehension strategies: Theories, interventions, and technologies.* Mahwah, NJ, Lawrence Erlbaum Associates.

National Reading Panel, National Institute of Child Health and Human Development (NRP). (2000). *Report of the National Reading Panel: Teaching children to read.* Bethesda, MD, National Institute of Child Health and Human Development.

National Research Council Committee on the Prevention of Reading Difficulties in Young Children (NRC). (1998). *Preventing reading difficulties in young children.* Washington, DC, National Academy Press.

No Child Left Behind Act of 2001, Pub. L. No. 107–110, 115 Stat. 1425 (2002).

O'Connor, R. E., Fulmer, D., Harty, K. R., & Bell, K. M. (2005). Layers of reading intervention in kindergarten through third grade: Changes in teaching and student outcomes. *Journal of Learning Disabilities, 38*, 440–455.

Perfetti, C. (2007). Reading ability: Lexical quality to comprehension. *Scientific Study of Reading, 11*, 357–385.

Perfetti, C., Landi, N., & Oakhill, J. (2005). The acquisition of reading skill. In M. J. Snowling & C. Hulme (Eds.), *The science of reading: A handbook* (pp. 227–253). Oxford, UK, Blackwell.

Pinnell, G. S., Pikulski, J. J., Wikxson, K. K., Campbell, J. R., Gough, P. B., & Beatty, A. S. (1995). *Listening to children read aloud: Data from NAEP's Integrated Reading Performance Record (IRPR) at Grade 4* (No. NAEP-23-FR-04; NCES-95-726). Princeton, NJ, Educational Testing Service.

Plaut, S., & Sharkey, N. S. (Eds.) (1996). *Education policy and practice: Bridging the divide.* Cambridge, MA, Harvard Education Press.

RAND. (2002). *Reading for understanding: Toward an R&D program in reading comprehension.* Santa Monica, CA, RAND Corporation.

Rapp, D. N., van den Broek, P., McMaster, K. L., Kendeou, P., & Espin, C. A. (2007). Higher-order comprehension processes in struggling readers: A perspective for research and intervention. *Scientific Study of Reading, 11,* 289–312.

Rasinski, T. (2001). *Revisiting reading rate as a diagnostic tool for reading difficulties.* Seattle, WA, Annual Meeting of the American Educational Research Association.

Riehl, C. (2006). Feeling better: A comparison of medical research and education research. *Educational Researcher, 35,* 24–29.

Romance, N. R., & Vitale, M. R. (2001). Implementing an in-depth expanded science model in elementary schools: Multi-year findings, research issues, and policy implications. *International Journal of Science Education, 23,* 373–404.

Sabatini, J. P. (2002). Efficiency in word reading of adults: Ability group comparisons. *Scientific Studies of Reading, 6,* 267–298.

Sabatini, J. P. (2003). Word reading processes in adult learners. In E. Assink & D. Sandra (Eds.), *Reading complex words: Cross-language studies.* London, Kluwer Academic.

Sabatini, J. P., Scarborough, H. S., Shore, J. S., Bruce, K., & Sawaki, Y. (2007, July). *Preliminary results for low literacy adults receiving decoding and fluency interventions.* Paper presented at the Annual Meeting of the Society for the Scientific Study of Reading, Prague, Czech Republic.

Sabatini, J. P., & Shore, J. S. (2005). *Developing reading interventions for adult literacy learners based on research driven practices.* Paper presented at Proliteracy Conference, Anaheim, CA.

Sabatini, J. P., & Shore, J. S. (2006). *The relative effectiveness of adult literacy interventions study.* Paper presented at Proliteracy Conference, Atlanta, GA.

Samuels, S., & Farstrup, A. E. (2006). *What research has to say about fluency instruction.* Newark, DE, International Reading Association.

Scarborough, H. S. (1998). Predicting the future achievement of second graders with reading disabilities: Contributions of phonemic awareness, verbal memory, rapid naming, and IQ. *Annals of Dyslexia, 48,* 115–136.

Scarborough, H. S. (2001). Connecting early language and literacy to later reading (dis)abilities: Evidence, theory, and practice. In S. Neuman & D. Dickinson (Eds.), *Handbook for research in early literacy* (pp. 97–110). New York, The Guilford Press.

Scarborough, H. S., Ehri, L. C., Olson, R. K., & Fowler, A. E. (1998). The fate of phonemic awareness beyond the elementary school years. *Scientific Studies of Reading, 2,* 115.

Shaywitz, S. E. (1998). Dyslexia. *New England Journal of Medicine, 338,* 307–312.

Shore, J., Bruce, K., & Korber, S. (2005, February). *Using profiles of adult learners to create classroom activities.* Paper presented at the annual Pennsylvania Association for Adult Continuing Education Conference, Hershey, PA.

Shore, J., Sabatini, J., & Bruce, K. (April, 2006). *Fidelity rubrics as a means for mentoring and training educators of adolescent and adult struggling readers: A professional development model.* Annual Meeting for the American Educational Research Association, San Francisco, CA.

Torgesen, J. K., Wagner, R. K., & Rashotte, C. A. (1999). *Test of Word Reading Efficiency (TOWRE)*. Austin, TX, Pro-Ed.

Venezky, R. L. (1999). *The American way of spelling*. New York, The Guilford Press.

Verhoeven, L., & Perfetti, C. (2003). Introduction to this special issue: The role of morphology in learning to read. *Scientific Studies of Reading, 7*, 209–217.

Wayman, M. M., Wallace, T., Wiley, H. I., Ticha, R., & Espin, C. A. (2007). Literature synthesis on curriculum-based measurement in reading. *The Journal of Special Education, 41*, 85–120.

■ Notes

1. There is a special case in which this is only a modest problem. The results of a randomized trial will generalize better when the units are homogeneous, that is, they are all identical! This is generally not true for snowflakes, or even chemical samples in an industrial laboratory, so it is not likely to hold true for humans.

2. In conducting research, there are various ways to improve on this state of affairs. If the researcher can identify characteristics specific to individuals who consistently did not respond to Treatment B, but consistently responded positively to Treatment A, then we may be on the way to improving our ability to predict which treatment is optimal for which individuals, that is, what works for whom under what conditions. Such scientific knowledge, however, is a long, grueling, and complicated endeavor. To make the same causal inference of a main effect of treatment, except conditioned on other variables (e.g., demographics, ability levels, component cognitive or linguistic skills, school or instructional contexts, etc.), each set of variables that might make a difference needs to be isolated and then randomly assigned to treatments (so as to balance out all the covarying variables) in subsequent randomized trial studies, with enough individuals in each cell to carry out the statistical tests. However, studies are expensive and time consuming, so repeating this procedure over and over is not typically feasible.

   It should also be noted that replications of studies under varying conditions also strengthen the causal inferences of generalizability, as for example, when studies try the same basic treatment with different age groups, in different settings, compared against different treatments and controls, or by varying elements of the treatment itself. These individual studies can be compiled in research meta-analyses and more generalized, robust conclusions can be synthesized. In such cases, there is higher confidence in acting on the evidence. Absent that, there is a fair level of necessary educated guessing at the delivery level about whether particular treatments might generalize to untested subgroups.

STEP 3

IN IMPLEMENTATION: SYSTEMS ISSUES IN IMPLEMENTATION AT STATE, DISTRICT, AND LOCAL LEVELS

◼ Introduction to Step 3

In this step, the chapters begin to look at actual implementation of innovations in real-world settings. These chapters represent state and district level implementation projects.

Edward Shapiro has been an active, widely published researcher in the academic assessment arena. In his chapter, he describes a model of progress monitoring, a critical skill for teachers in determining whether the intervention has been successful in increasing student performance. However, the focus of the chapter is on how a progress monitoring system was scaled up statewide. He presents the training processes used to reach this widespread implementation, and presents the outcomes of the process at each phase of the implementation. The project is noteworthy for both its large-scale goal and the emphasis on evaluating progress at each point along the way. Shapiro also provides some important lessons that were learned in this implementation.

In the next chapter, Paul Robb and Hilary Rosenfield, working in the district office of a large urban school district, describe the challenges of introducing an ambitious initiative to change how teachers would be evaluated. The reform in processes and policy was designed to improve the quality of instruction rather than focus on evaluating the current competence of the teaching staff. Because of the recognition of how critical teacher quality is, written now into the NCLB law and supported by Peverly's (Chapter 21, this volume) review of the teacher effectiveness literature, this type of project has high potential to improve outcomes for students. They describe how the project implementation became stalled, and use an economic lens in theorizing what happened. They conclude with recommendations for those in the future who attempt to make such a systems level change.

The final two chapters in this step continue the description of attempts to implement research into schools from the district office level. These implementations of research by a team of professionals in schools are both informed by research and evaluated for effectiveness on the basis of data gathered by the professionals. The goal of the data gathering is in one case both to implement instructional consultation teams and to generate new research knowledge; and in the second, to evaluate effectiveness of a particular evidence-based instructional implementation in a specific school setting for a specific purpose. This kind of professional practice is what is needed to transform the practice from where the experts tell those in the field what works to an evidence-based field in which informed and autonomous professionals design and evaluate their own implementations. Most of all, these last two chapters serve as an inspiration that school professionals, such as school psychologists, can be leaders and change agents (see Chapter 24 by Forman in this volume) and bridge the gap between general and special education.

Deborah Nelson, Kathy Aux, Michael Neal, and Todd Gravois present a systems level model for the implementation of an innovation, Instructional Consultation Teams (IC Teams), which are designed to facilitate and support the development of collaborative, problem-solving school cultures. Although the model of IC Teams has been evaluated in multiple contexts, its implementation in this district is unique in that it includes an outcome study in which randomization occurred at the school level. They describe a working partnership both for implementation and research, and the process is presented from the various voices of the participants at the university, district, and school levels. In addition, they identify the key elements essential for successful program implementation and institutionalization of a complex change process.

Alnita Dunn, Director of School Psychology for the Los Angeles School District (LASU), and her colleague, Douglas Miller, coauthored the final chapter in Step 3. They tell the story of a field-initiated partnership between general education and special education launched by school psychologists in one of the largest, most ethnically and linguistically diverse urban school districts in the country. These professionals first did their homework in investigating what research had been carried out that was both efficacious and relevant to the population they served, and made a commitment to collecting evidence about the effectiveness of the implementation. In a series of ongoing implementations, they collected data to evaluate the effectiveness of the research-supported interventions they implemented. Just as importantly, they share the many challenges they faced in implementing the early intervention and prevention projects they have attempted, providing practical suggestions for dealing with the complexities of implementation and creating cooperative working relationships at many levels of the system—from top level administrators to classroom teachers and building principals.

11. Statewide Scaling Up of Progress Monitoring Practices

Edward S. Shapiro

◼ Statewide Scaling Up of Progress Monitoring

The National Center on Student Progress Monitoring defines progress monitoring as "a scientifically based practice that is used to assess students' academic performance and evaluate the effectiveness of instruction" (National Center on Student Progress Monitoring, 2004). Progress monitoring, that is, the ongoing evaluation of student progress over time, has become a substantial component of the process of measuring student outcomes in the implementation of school change. Progress monitoring has many uses that impact students in both general and special education such as creating instructional groups (e.g., Fuchs, Fuchs, & Bishop, 1992), identifying specific skill deficits (e.g., Fuchs, Fuchs, Hamlett, & Allinder, 1991; Whinnery & Fuchs, 1992), screening students for potential early school failure (e.g., Speece & Case, 2001), assisting in eligibility decision-making (e.g., Shinn, Habedank, Rossen-Nord, & Knutson, 1993), and evaluating the reintegration process for students moving from special to general education settings (e.g., Shinn, Powell-Smith, & Good, 1996). Applications of progress monitoring are usually focused on the progress of individual students who are defined as at-risk through the implementation of screening of an entire class, school, or district and for whom some form of intervention plan has been put in place (Elliott, Huai, & Roach, 2007; Glover & Albers, 2007). However, progress monitoring can also involve all students in an entire class, grade, or school.

As a function of the strong national interest and importance in the application of progress monitoring, two large centers funded by the U.S. Department of Education have been established. The National Center on Student Progress

Special thanks to Fran Warkomski, Ed.D., Director, Pennsylvania Training and Technical Assistance Network; Dan Thompson, PaTTAN Consultant; and all PaTTAN and Intermediate Unit staff who provided tremendous support and direction for the development, implementation, and evaluation of the Pennsylvania Progress Monitoring Initiative. Also, thanks to Naomi Zigmond, Ph.D., Professor, Special Education, University of Pittsburgh, and Lana Edwards Santoro, Ph.D., who jointly served with myself as University consultants to the initiative.

Monitoring (http://www.studentprogress.org) and the Research Institute on Progress Monitoring (http://www.progressmonitoring.net) provide technical assistance, dissemination, and research development for the use of progress monitoring.

Effective use of progress monitoring involves establishing a goal against which student progress will be measured. Performance is measured on a specified basis over time (e.g., biweekly, weekly, bimonthly, monthly, quarterly), and comparisons are made between the students' expected rate of progress and their attained rate of progress. When students' rates of progress are not on target to reach their goals, education professionals initiate conversations about potential changes in interventions to get students back on target. Likewise, for those students whose rates of progress are substantially above their targets, conversations can be initiated about the need to increase goals. Overall, the progress monitoring process provides ongoing feedback to teachers and school professionals about the impact of the interventions on student performance. Progress monitoring offers immediate indications about the effectiveness of teaching practices and allows for adjustments in teaching practices to be made quickly if students are not on track to meet their objectives (Shinn, Shinn, Hamilton, & Clarke, 2002). In addition, the direct connection made by progress monitoring for teachers between instruction and its outcomes often initiates broader discussion among teachers about effective and ineffective teaching practices. Further, progress monitoring can provide a framework for data-driven discussions about instruction among multiple educational professionals within a team process (Foegen, 2006; Tindal, Duesbery, & Ketterlin-Geller, 2006).

The use of progress monitoring has become widespread over the past decade (Shapiro, Angello, & Eckert, 2004; Wallace, Espin, McMaster, Deno, & Foegen, 2007; Wayman, Wallace, Wiley, Tichá, & Espin, 2007). In the passage of IDEA 2004, the law required that student progress be monitored in making determinations regarding student eligibility for special education. Specifically, in the identification of students with specific learning disabilities, the law states in 34 CFR 300.309 that:

> (b) To ensure that underachievement in a child suspected of having a specific learning disability is not due to lack of appropriate instruction in reading or math, the group must consider, as part of the evaluation described in Sec. 300.304 through 300.306 ... (2) Data-based documentation of repeated assessments of achievement at reasonable intervals, reflecting formal assessment of student progress during instruction, which was provided to the child's parents (34 CFR 300.309, IDEA 2004).

In addition, progress monitoring was viewed as a key component to the ongoing evaluation of students who are already identified as those with special education needs.

Types of Progress Monitoring

Fuchs and Deno (1991) identified two broad classes of progress monitoring procedures—General Outcomes Measurement (GOM) and Specific Subskill mastery measurement (SS). GOMs represent standardized measures that are designed to index the overall progress of students across curriculum objectives. Measures are brief and designed to be repeated frequently (as equivalent alternate forms) so that change over time would reflect attainment of proficiency across the expected range of the curriculum. All measures are standardized so that measurement error due to differences in test construction is minimized. The measures are focused on assessing the long-term effect of instruction and indicate to teachers whether the instructional process improves student performance. One of the most well-developed types of GOM has been curriculum-based measurement (CBM) developed by Deno and his colleagues (e.g., Deno, 1985, 2003a, 2003b; Fuchs, 2004).

Specific subskill mastery measurement (SS) involves measuring the performance of students on identified skill objectives. These objectives are built on skill hierarchies that define the particular skills that are being instructed within the curriculum. Each skill requires a measurement system built only on the assessment of that individual skill. As students show competency on the skill, a new measurement tool must be built to reflect attainment of that particular skill. SS measurement focuses on the short-term attainment of specific skill objectives and is especially valuable for assessing students who have low-incidence disabilities (e.g., severe cognitive impairment, autism, sensory disabilities) and whose Individual Education Plans (IEPs) often focus on the development of functional skills. However, the measures can be used across all academic areas and have been applied to problem-solving models providing instructional support (Brown-Chidsey, 2005; Shapiro, 2004).

The measures are usually teacher-made and not standardized, and shifts in the nature of the measure reflecting competency are required as teachers move from assessing one skill to the next. SS measurement is the common method that most teachers use in their instructional process, that is, testing specifically the student's attainment of the skills as an *evaluation* of what was learned from what students were taught. Some of the developed models of SS monitoring are Curriculum-Based Evaluation as described by Howell and colleagues (e.g., Howell & Nolet, 2000) and Curriculum-Based Assessment as described by Gickling and colleagues (Gickling & Thompson, 1985; Gravois & Gickling, 2002).

■ Plan for Statewide Implementation of Progress Monitoring

The importance of progress monitoring for instructional decision-making in special education was clearly recognized by administrators and educators throughout the Commonwealth of Pennsylvania. The research had established the importance of both GOM and SS models for decision-making when working with students with identified special education needs, as well as a means to identify students who may be at-risk for academic failure. In addition, with the passage of IDEA 2004, increased interest in the use of a Response-to-Intervention methodology as an alternative to the ability/achievement discrepancy for identifying students with specific learning disabilities made achieving widespread use and competency in progress monitoring processes extremely important (e.g., Fuchs & Fuchs, 2006; Stoner, Scarpati, Phaneuf, & Hintze, 2002). However, policy makers recognized that the challenges of bringing the implementation of progress monitoring to the scale of statewide adoption among the special education community would require a careful planning and stepwise process (Grimes, Kurns, & Tilly, 2006).

The Context

The Commonwealth of Pennsylvania consists of 501 individual school districts, which range in size from a total of 267 students with one elementary, middle, and high school to over 214,000 students. The diversity of the state is very widespread consisting of the fifth largest city in the United States (Philadelphia) to many rural and isolated communities. In addition to individual districts, the state is also divided into 29 Intermediate Units. These are regionally based groupings, usually by single or multiple counties, providing both direct and indirect support as well as technical assistance services to districts for special as well as general education that are within the boundaries of the Intermediate Units. Further, the state has three regionally based technical assistance and training centers (Pennsylvania Training and Technical Assistance Network, PaTTAN) whose primary mission is to provide professional development in support of special education, Early Intervention, student assessment, and tutoring in partnership with all schools designed to help all students succeed.

The challenge presented in implementing progress monitoring statewide was to develop a strong model based in documented scientific practice, develop and evaluate the effectiveness of training, and scale the training up to a level that could be implemented across the state. The key to implementation was to maintain the evaluation of outcomes on a statewide basis as training was implemented at such a large scale. The process was focused on bringing progress monitoring processes to the routine instructional practices of all special education teachers statewide, with clear implications that such practice would also filter to teachers of students at some risk for becoming identified as having special education needs.

The Plan

To accomplish such a large-scale implementation, the progress monitoring training initiative began with a mini-pilot, moved to a statewide pilot that incorporated a trainer-of-trainers model, and finally a full trainer-of-trainers model with phased implementation over a 2-year period to provide the same levels of training proficiency across all 501 school districts. The process is illustrated in Figure 11.1. The PaTTAN partnered with three university consultants, all located within the state, recognized as national experts in progress monitoring. These consultants played a very active role in developing the training materials, delivering the training in the mini-pilot and statewide pilot, and conducting the evaluation of outcomes of both the statewide pilot as well as the statewide implementation.

At the level of the mini-pilot, the feasibility of training and development of training materials on the scale of a limited number of teachers in selected locations were the objectives. At the level of the statewide pilot, the objectives were to provide training within all three major regions of the state (east, central, west), deliver and evaluate impact on a larger number of teachers and students, and establish and evaluate extensive training materials to be subsequently used statewide. In addition, during the statewide pilot, key individuals who would become the trainer-of-trainers were incorporated in the process of providing direct training by university consultants to the pilot sites. In the final phase of implementation, the trainers selected at the statewide pilots established a network of trained professionals through

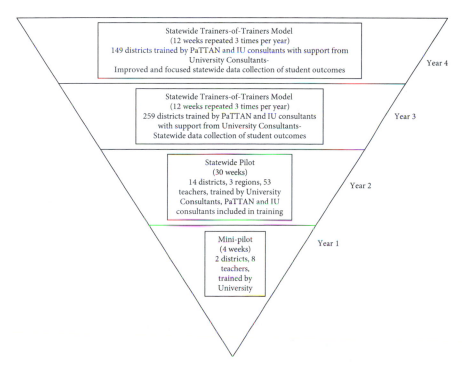

FIGURE 11.1 Statewide Model of Progress Model Training across Four Years.

the Intermediate Units who could deliver training in progress monitoring statewide at the level of the local district.

To maintain statewide evaluation of outcomes, a data collection process was established to determine student progress and to reflect the impact of the progress monitoring process across the Commonwealth. The process of evaluation was maintained for a 2-year period as the effect of the progress monitoring effort reached every district in the state. Figure 11.1 shows the 4-year planning process to move from the mini-pilot through the statewide rollout of training.

The purpose of this chapter is to describe the process and outcomes of the statewide scaling up of progress monitoring. Emphasis is on describing the training processes that were used to reach such widespread implementation. Another goal is to present the outcome data that were used at each phase of the process to reflect outcome. Many of the specific tools and materials developed for progress monitoring training are available on the PaTTAN Web site (http://www.pattan.k12.pa.us/teachlead/ProgressMonitoring.aspx).

■ The Mini-Pilot

In the spring of 2002, an effort to train and implement a small number of elementary teachers (total of eight) in progress monitoring processes for reading and math computation was implemented in two small school districts. The primary objective of this first phase of implementation was to provide a demonstration of the feasibility of training special education as well as general education teachers to conduct progress monitoring of academic skills for students with disabilities and students at-risk. Although the main focus of the statewide training effort was to bring progress monitoring into routine use by special education teachers, a collateral anticipated outcome was that progress monitoring would begin to gain acceptance and use by general education teachers. They were working with students who were at-risk for academic problems that could potentially result in identification as a student in need of special education services. The mini-pilot also was used as an opportunity to begin to develop training materials that could be used for future training. Use of technology-enhanced and not-technology-enhanced progress monitoring was compared.

Across the staff implementing progress monitoring were four learning support (Learning Disabilities) special education teachers (one K-second grade, one second-third grade, one third-fourth grade, one sixth grade), one emotional support (Emotional/Behavior disorders) special education teacher, two regular education teachers (one third grade, one fourth grade), and one elementary reading/instructional support specialist (K-sixth grade). Teachers each monitored at least two students in their classrooms in reading (oral reading fluency) and math (computation only) for a total of 22 students (some teachers chose to monitor more than two students). Teachers were permitted to select the level of monitoring that they felt was appropriate for their students. All identified special education students were monitored below their enrolled grade level, whereas students in the general education classrooms were monitored at their enrolled grade level. Although special education teachers did not conduct a formal survey level assessment to determine instructional level, teachers were asked to select the grade level for monitoring that they viewed as consistent with the student's instructional level.

An important question was the potential use of technology to enhance the progress monitoring process. Teachers were divided into two groups, with one group using technology-based data collection and recording process for reading developed by AIMSweb (www.aimsweb.com), which was a new product for progress monitoring on the market at that time. The low-tech group used paper-and-pencil data collection and graphing processes. All teachers used paper-and-pencil methods for monitoring math computation.

Materials used by all teachers for reading were the passages developed by AIMSweb (www.aimsweb.com) and the "black line masters" included in *Monitoring Basic Skills Progress, Second Edition: Basic Math Computation* (MBSP; Fuchs, Hamlett, & Fuchs, 1998) available through ProEd. Monitoring in reading was conducted twice each week, with at least one day between all monitoring sessions. Monitoring in math was done weekly.

All teachers received training on the reading and math progress monitoring at a one-day session held in late April of 2002. The training program consisted of the following components: (a) Introduction; (b) Overview, rationale, and framework; (c) Administration procedures; (d) Practice on scoring passages/math problems; (e) Setting goals and determining trend lines based on baseline data; and (f) Graphing data. All teachers were trained on how to access and use the AIMSweb product as well as the low-tech graphing methods, even though some teachers would not be given access to the AIMSweb product during the mini-pilot implementation. Follow-up classroom visits were made by the trainers during the first week of monitoring to answer questions and make sure that teachers were accurately implementing the monitoring process. A second set of classroom visits were made during the third week of implementation when teachers were observed for purposes of determining integrity of conducting the progress monitoring process. During the observations of integrity, a brief checklist of the essential components of progress monitoring was used (i.e., select passage for assessment, administer according to instructions provided during training, scored passage correctly, entered scores into the appropriate database, and graphed student scores if they were in the low-tech group). All teachers achieved over 90% of the steps, and for those few steps not correctly implemented, corrective feedback to teachers was provided. Monitoring began the first week of May and continued until

May 31. A final wrap-up session was held the first week of June when teachers provided all their progress monitoring data, provided feedback to the trainers about successes and challenges to the progress monitoring process, and helped to generate a list of specific questions that needed to be addressed for future training. Finally, the AIMSweb product was provided to all teachers who had been in the low-tech group.

The outcomes of the mini-pilot provided many lessons for future training. During both the in-class visits and discussions during the final wrap-up session, teachers reported the positive impact of progress monitoring on students, the motivational value of progress monitoring, and the surprising amount of information that they learned from administering, scoring, and graphing data collected twice weekly. None of the teachers had difficulty finding the time in their busy daily schedules to do reading and math probes. Even the general education teachers found that they could use time during independent seat work to pull the two students being monitored to a quiet spot in the room and complete the assessments. In classrooms where only some of the students present were monitored, teachers had no difficulty with the students who were not participating in the pilot. Teachers reported that they enjoyed the opportunity for more one-to-one contact with struggling students and the increased contact with these struggling students did not have an adverse effect on the rest of the class. All eight teachers believed that the progress monitoring data provided useful information for planning their instruction.

Although all reading probe and scoring materials were provided for the teachers in a usable fashion, each teacher devised her own organizational scheme that made administration and scoring move more smoothly for her. In particular, teachers reported a countdown timer was more useful in conducting progress monitoring than a standard stopwatch. Teachers reported that even the youngest students could learn to graph and interpret their own data and that not only did students learn graphing skills, but also they were very motivated to demonstrate increasing scores so the graphs would show upward trends. There were no differences in the level of enthusiasm about progress monitoring in reading from the hi-tech and the low-tech teachers as reported during the June session. Nevertheless, there was general agreement by the four teachers in the hi-tech condition that the AIMSweb product produced readable and effective graphs, as well as notes to the teacher useful in reporting back to parents or in setting IEP goals. Although the pilot lasted only a month, all eight teachers believed that they could (and would) sustain progress monitoring over the course of an entire school year, monitoring reading twice weekly and math once each week. The teachers found it very helpful that more than one teacher in the school was part of the pilot so that they could support each other in implementing the procedures. Finally, teachers generated a long list of important questions that should be answered in any future training. They also strongly recommended that teacher-to-teacher training would lend significant credibility to the training process.

Clearly, the mini-pilot's success demonstrated that teachers could easily be trained to conduct progress monitoring, and that the process was viewed by teachers as acceptable and valuable to teachers, beneficial to instruction, and motivating to students. The use of technology-enhanced monitoring, which was a new product on the market at the time, was viewed as beneficial to the process. Most important, teachers provided a rich context for the development of subsequent training.

■ The Statewide Pilot

The successful mini-pilot in spring 2002 lead the state of Pennsylvania to begin an effort to move to statewide implementation of progress monitoring within special education settings. The first step in the process was to initiate a statewide pilot project in 2002–2003 to demonstrate and evaluate the training process, the potential effect of training on teacher behavior, and the effect on student outcomes of progress monitoring. Leading this effort were the PaTTAN in collaboration with university partners at Lehigh University and the University of Pittsburgh, who had been the developers of training for the mini-pilot. Table 11.1 shows the training plan that was developed to effectively implement the statewide pilot.

Invitations were extended to interested districts statewide to participate. A total of 14 districts were selected on a first-come, first-served basis, 5 from the eastern region, 4 from the central, and 5 from the west. In order for districts to participate, they were required to send teams consisting of a site coordinator (e.g., Principal, Special Education supervisor) and up to five teachers of classrooms for students needing Learning Support and/or Emotional Support. Across the 14 districts, a total of 56 teachers and 14 coordinators participated in the training. All members of the team were required to attend all scheduled trainings provided by the university consultants. Teams had to agree to do weekly progress monitoring in reading and/or bimonthly (every two weeks) monitoring in math computation and applications. Teachers had to collect the data, enter the data into the appropriate database or data collection forms, make instructional adjustments as appropriate, and report the data in formats required by the trainers. Also attending all sessions were consultants from PaTTAN and the Intermediate Units who would become subsequent trainers the following year when training would be extended statewide.

As developed through the mini-pilot, a total of five training sessions were offered to the teams. The content of these sessions involved the following: (a) Introduction to progress monitoring in reading and math computation and concepts; (b) instructional decision-making from progress monitoring

TABLE 11.1 *Progress Monitoring—2003–2004 Statewide Initiative Training Plan*

Date/Location	Content
Trainers—IU CSPD Staff and PaTTAN Consultants	
August 15 Central location	Overview of training content and process Big picture as well as details More background information than teachers will get; preparation for troubleshooting teachers' questions
Late September–Early October Regional	Attend Workshop 1 given by University consultants; participate in post-workshop debriefing and review of workshop notes and handouts to prepare for training presentations at each IU
Visits to schools, October–November	Review with each teacher the implementation of PM procedures
Early December	Attend Workshop 2 given by University consultants; participate in post-workshop debriefing and review of workshop notes and handouts to prepare for training presentations at each IU
Visits to schools, December–February	Review with each teacher the implementation of PM procedures
January 22 Regional	Review of Project to date; intensive workshop on making instructional changes in reading and mathematics instruction on the basis of progress monitoring data
Late February, early March	Attend Workshop 3 given by University consultants; participate in post-workshop debriefing and review of workshop notes and handouts to prepare for training presentations at each IU
Visits to schools, March–April	Review with each teacher the implementation of PM procedures
Early May	Attend Workshop 4 given by University consultants; participate in post-workshop debriefing and review of workshop notes and handouts to prepare for training presentations at each IU
May 12 Central location	Final review of project implementation; evaluation of implementation; planning and revision for Year 2 implementation

data; (c) on-site visitation to facilitate progress monitoring and address questions; (d) using data to inform instructional change; and (e) on-site visitation to facilitate progress monitoring and address questions. A final sixth session was held with key representatives from all 14 sites, Intermediate Units, all three PaTTAN training groups in the east, central, and western parts of the state, and the University consultants to discuss findings and outcomes from the statewide progress monitoring pilot. Although direct integrity of progress monitoring implementation data were not collected, all teachers were observed at least twice in their classrooms by University and PaTTAN consultants, and given informal feedback about the integrity of implementation of progress monitoring; teachers were required to provide the graphed data collected during progress monitoring on a monthly basis to the consultants. These processes provided indirect evidence that the teachers were indeed actually implementing the progress monitoring process.

Data reflecting change in teacher perceptions and use of progress monitoring were collected as well as student performance through the progress monitoring process. Teachers were asked to complete a self-report measure at the end of the late February, early March, 2003 training session. Specifically, questions were asked regarding the teacher's experience with progress monitoring, the degree of confidence that they had with the data generated by the procedure, the degree to which the measures reflected accurately student achievement, and the importance of doing routine progress monitoring. For each item, teachers were asked to retrospectively respond where they viewed themselves at the start of the project and their current perspectives at the time the measures were completed. Informal discussions about teacher satisfaction with the progress monitoring process were held in May through meetings among teachers, trainers, and PaTTAN consultants.

All 56 teachers completed the measure across the three regions (25 east, 12 central, 19 west). Some teachers assessed only one academic area so those items pertaining to areas not assessed were not answered. Table 11.2 reflects the overall outcomes of teacher self-report across summarized items. Data for each individual item are provided in Figure 11.2. All items showed changes in the desired direction comparing before and during the project. Some items showed substantial change. In particular, confidence in the data obtained through GOM monitoring increased in all academic areas. The strongest confidence in data appeared in the oral reading fluency and math computation data. Progress monitoring was noted as an important part of the instructional process by teachers before beginning the project but was viewed as even more critical following the project implementation.

Beyond survey data on self-reported changes in behavior or attitude, data were reported on each student by calculating an ordinary least squares (OLS) regression line across the academic subject of progress monitoring. The OLS represented the slope or rate of change in behavior across the assessment

TABLE 11.2   *Summary of Teacher Self-Reported Data on Progress Monitoring Feedback Form*

	Prior to Project	As of March 2003
Previous experience w/progress monitoring	2.90	4.06
Confidence in using data	3.41	4.07
Reading	3.19	3.92
Math computation	3.39	4.01
Math concepts	3.08	3.62
Importance of progress monitoring	3.88	4.73

Note: Items scored on a five-point Likert scale (1: Very Rarely; 2: Rarely; 3: Sometimes; 4: Often; 5: Very Often).

sessions. As part of the progress monitoring process, teachers established goals for student performance. Goals for performance were established uniformly across students in reading and math based on the expected outcomes for CBM measures reported by Fuchs, Fuchs, Hamlett, Walz, and Germann (1993). An aimline established the expected rate of change between baseline and the goal. To determine the degree to which students matched, exceeded, or fell below their aimline, a goal score was calculated by subtracting the slope of the student's attained performance minus the slope of the aimline. A goal score of zero indicated that the student's performance matched exactly the expected level of performance. The greater than zero the goal score, the more the student exceeded the established goal. The more the goal score was below zero, the more the student underperformed against the established goal. These calculations were performed for each academic area monitored. For example, if a student had an oral reading fluency baseline of 50 words correct per minute, and the teacher set a goal of 2 word improvement per minute per week across 25 remaining weeks, the student would be expected to gain at a rate of +2.00 words per minute per week. If the student attained an actual performance of +2.50 words per minute per week, the goal score calculation would be equal to +0.50. Thus, in this case, the student's performance exceeded the expected performance.

Student outcome data were reflected in the average slopes across reading, math computation, and math concepts as reported by each of the teachers. Given that students varied across grades 1 through 8, and that all monitoring was at the grade level identified by teachers where students were being instructed, the data were examined to determine the degree to which progress monitoring would reflect student achievement in these subject areas. In

Background Information

Teacher ID #:	(Place an ID number you will remember, not your name)
Position (e.g., learning support, inclusion, emotional support):	
Grade level of students monitored:	Indicate range:
Instructional level of students monitored:	Indicate range:
Number of students monitored for the pilot project:	
Core curriculum used in Reading:	
Core curriculum used in Math:	
Years of classroom teaching experience:	

Progress Monitoring

Consider your experience with progress monitoring assessment in the progress monitoring pilot project. Rate your experience on the following scale both before the project began and currently:

[--]

1 – Very Rarely   2 – Rarely   3 – Sometimes   4 – Often   5 – Very Often

Previous Experience with Progress Monitoring Assessment	Before the Project						Currently				
	1	2	3	4	5		1	2	3	4	5
I used/use progress monitoring assessment in my classroom.			3.04							4.38	
I used/use progress monitoring assessment data to make instructional decisions.			2.81							4.15	
I used/use progress monitoring data to communicate progress with parents and students.			2.85						3.73		
Progress monitoring data directly impacted changes in my instruction.			2.83						3.90		
I used/use progress monitoring assessment as part of my regular instructional routine.			2.94							4.13	
OVERALL			2.90							4.06	

FIGURE 11.2 Continued

How confident are you that the data you are collecting reflects student achievement and the instructional process? How confident are you in using data to make instructional decisions?

[---]

1 – Very Uncertain   2 – Somewhat Uncertain   3 – Moderately Confident   4 – Somewhat Confident   5 – Very Confident

Is Data an Accurate Reflection of Student Achievement ? Your confidence using the data?

	Before the Project	Currently
Student oral reading fluency data accurately reflects my general impression of student reading performance.	3.35	3.96
Student oral reading fluency data accurately reflects the instructional process.	3.02	3.87
Student math computation data accurately reflects my general impression of student math performance.	3.40	3.99
Student math computation data accurately reflects the instructional process.	3.38	4.04
Student concepts and applications data accurately reflects my general impression of student math performance.	3.06	3.58
Student concepts and applications data accurately reflects the instructional process.	3.10	3.65
I can read and interpret graphed data.	3.98	4.56
I can use data to make specific instructional decisions.	3.46	4.43
When examining student data, I know whento implement instructional changes.	3.46	4.28
When I need to make "a change," I know a variety of intervention or instructional strategies to consider.	3.63	4.28
OVERALL	3.41	4.07
READING (ORF, 1 & 2) CLUSTER	3.19	3.92
MATH COMP (3 & 4) CLUST ER	3.39	4.01
MATH CONCEPST (5 & 6) CLUSTER	3.08	3.62

FIGURE 11.2 Continued

Is data collection and progress monitoring important? Rate the following items using the scale below:

[--]

1 – Definitely NotImportant   2 – Probably Not Important   3 – Maybe/Maybe NotImportant   4 – ProbablyImportant   5 – Definitely Important

Importance	Before the Project						Currently				
	1	2	3	4	5		1	2	3	4	5
Progress monitoring data's use to make instructional decisions			3.63						4.72		
Assessment regularly used ininstructional routines			4.12						4.73		
Progress monitoring data collected frequently (e.g., at least 1x a week or every other week)			3.56						4.66		
Assessment as integral to the instruction process			4.19						4.81		
OVERALL			3.88						4.73		

OTHER:

Please provide any additional comments and feedback about the progress monitoring project and the data collection/instructional decision-making process that you would like the project coordinators and PaTTAN consultants to consider.

FIGURE 11.2 Progress Monitoring Feedback Form.

TABLE 11.3   *Overall Rate of Improvement in Reading, Math Computation, and Math Concepts across Students in the Statewide Pilot Project*

	Mean (SD) Rate of Improvement	Mean Aimline for Goal Set by Teachers	Mean Goal Score
Reading (words correct/min per week) ($n = 223$)	1.05 (0.19)	1.38	−0.33
Math Compute (digits correct/min per week) ($n = 129$)	0.19 (0.24)	0.33	−0.14
Math Concepts (total points correct per week) ($n = 109$)	0.41 (0.33)	0.36	+0.05

addition, although teachers were only asked to monitor a total of two students per class, many teachers chose to monitor their entire class or a large subset. Thus, across the 56 teachers, a total of 223 students were monitored in reading, 129 in math computation, and 109 in math concepts across the 14 districts. Table 11.3 reflects the overall rates of improvement across these students.

Examination of the data across students and districts reflected that average rates of gain in reading, math computation, and math concepts were quite strong. However, it was clear from the pilot data that far fewer students were achieving the goals that were set for them through the progress monitoring process. Goals were initially selected on a "best guess" basis in conjunction with teachers and examination of existing data on expected levels of progress for students in special education (Deno, Fuchs, Marston, & Shin, 2001; Fuchs, et al., 1993; Hosp & Hosp, 2001). Teachers were instructed to set reading goals equivalent to improvement of 2 words per week across the monitoring period and 0.5 digits or 0.5 points per week for math computation and concepts/application.

Data from the pilots showed that students did not in all cases reach their recommended goals, and the goals may have been too challenging for this group of largely special education students. Data from a normative study in a small urban school district within the eastern region of the state found that the average rate of change from a fall to spring period among average elementary students in math was no better than 1 digit per minute per month in computation and 1 point per month in concepts. Thus, recommended goals during the pilot (0.5 digit or point per week, or 2 digits or points per month) doubled what would have been expected for students without disabilities

(Shapiro, Edwards, & Zigmond, 2005). Further, data reported by Hasbrouck and Tindal (2005) and normative data reported by AIMSweb confirmed that the rates of improvement set were far beyond what one would have expected for typical performing students at these grade levels. Considering the students in the pilot were all identified as in special education, the goals established were clearly too challenging.

Overall, the impact of the statewide pilot demonstrated that teachers were capable of implementing progress monitoring, of using the data to make instructional decisions, and of being able to use the technology enhanced products; also they felt the process was beneficial to both their instruction as well as student performance. Also, because progress monitoring in reading has been often suggested in the literature to be done twice per week, we asked teachers whether monitoring more than once per week would have been possible. Teachers provided us strong indications that monitoring on more than a once per week basis would have been difficult to place into their busy instructional routines. The nature of interventions selected by teachers was primarily related to motivation and simple modifications of instructional processes. The pilots demonstrated a real need to enhance the knowledge base of teachers in terms of quality of instructional interventions in both reading and math.

■ Statewide Rollout of Training

As a function of the successful mini-pilot and statewide pilot, the decision was made to bring progress monitoring training for special education teachers to the scale of full implementation across all 501 school districts in the Commonwealth of Pennsylvania. The challenge of scaling progress monitoring training to all school districts throughout the state was addressed by recognizing the potential power of a trainer-of-trainer model. During the 2002–2003 statewide pilot year, consultants from PaTTAN and consultants who serviced the districts within their Intermediate Units attended all training sessions offered by the university consultants. In addition, specific PaTTAN personnel in each region of the state were paired with the University consultants when on-site visitations were made. As a result, during the 2003–2004 year, these PaTTAN and IU consultants served as the primary training resource for school district personnel. The University consultants faded their direct involvement and served in an advisory capacity to the PaTTAN and IU consultants on an as needed basis. Training modules developed during the initial pilot year were revised and streamlined to meet the specific needs of teachers at the level of districts and classrooms. Additional training on developing specific interventions was also provided by the PaTTAN and IU consultants who had extensive expertise in instructional strategies.

One of the major decisions in moving to statewide implementation was the requirement that the training that was delivered across the year of the statewide pilot be condensed into a shorter time frame. By collapsing the time period of training from the 6 to 8 months of the original pilot to approximately a 12-week period, consultants were able to deliver the training in three sessions which were repeated three times during the year, thus delivering the training to more districts in the same amount of time.

Of course, a concern that would naturally be raised with the collapsing of the training was that the impact of the original training, which was designed to last over a 6- to 9-month period and included multiple on-site visits to support teachers through the implementation process, would be diminished. To move the training to scale, it was decided that the same content would be covered in training sessions. However, the amount of follow-up and on-site visitation would be lessened. At the same time, to maintain the high quality of the training, districts would be given the opportunity to attend repeated trainings to ensure that the implementation of the process was maintained as districts were trained. The objective of the statewide training initiative was to impact all 501 school districts within a 2-year period.

Invitations to attend what was labeled as "Level 1 Progress Monitoring Training," were offered to all 501 school districts in the state at the start of the 2003–2004 school year. Any district that agreed to attend a training session was required to then train identified special education teachers in their district. These trained teachers were required to conduct progress monitoring on at least one student in reading or math, and to report the resulting data to PaTTAN at the end of the year. In the first year of the statewide rollout, teachers were given the option to monitor a student using either General Outcome Measurement or Specific Skills monitoring processes, both of which were included in the Level 1 training in the initial year of the statewide rollout.

The first year of statewide training resulted in progress monitoring training being delivered to 1,232 special education teachers across 259 school districts representing all 29 Intermediate Units in the state. Data on students were reported on 2,690 special education students by 1,049 special education teachers. Keeping in mind that many teachers were collecting progress monitoring data on multiple students in their classes but were only asked to report data on a single student, the data reported on the students represented a minimum number of progress monitoring implementations. Because there were no requirements related to the nature of the type of disabilities for those students selected for progress monitoring, data were reported across all categories of identified special education students. However, the largest number of students for whom progress monitoring data were reported were those identified as having a specific learning disability (1,745; 64.9%), followed by those with emotional/behavior disability (271; 10.1%), and those with mental retardation (244; 9.1%). In addition, the type of progress monitoring (GOM or SS) to be conducted was not specified to teachers. A total of 1,967 (73.1%) reported that they were using GOM methods, while 211 (7.8%) reported conducting SS monitoring. Unfortunately, the data collection process in the initial year of statewide rollout produced some confusion in the nature of the data reported with the result that for 346 students (12.9%), the nature of the progress monitoring process could not be clearly determined.

A number of other issues emerged with the initial statewide training year's data. For example, the materials used for progress monitoring were permitted to vary at the local level. Although the majority of students being monitored in reading were using oral reading fluency passages from Dynamic Indicators of Basic Early Literacy Skills (DIBELS) (https://dibels.uoregon.edu) (19.6%) or AIMSweb (40.0%), a large number of students were monitored using materials from programs such as Read Naturally (2003), unknown web-based materials, or other curriculum-linked materials. In math, however, 86% of the students being monitored in math were monitored in the MBSP probes developed by Fuchs et al. (1998). Obviously, the variations in the nature of the materials used in monitoring introduced a significant confound in interpreting the resulting progress monitoring outcomes.

Another limitation to the data collection process was the fact that no direct measure of the integrity of implementation of progress monitoring was collected. Having direct observation of the degree to which teachers conducted progress monitoring as it was trained was desirable, but the feasibility of such data collection at the statewide implementation level was considered virtually impossible. Some indirect measures of integrity were provided by obtaining the actual graphs of progress monitoring for a subset of cases as well as periodic discussions with district level trained staff and teachers were obtained. Clearly, such indirect metrics limit the potential interpretation of outcomes.

Despite these issues related to the nature of the training, data collection reporting processes, integrity of implementation, and materials used for progress monitoring, GOM progress monitoring data for students in reading and mathematics were summarized and reported to the state. Data were only reported for those students identified as having Specific Learning Disabilities, which represented the largest number of students.

Second Year Training

The first year of statewide rollout provided many lessons that were used to alter the training in the second year. First, it was decided to focus only on GOM progress monitoring during training. Efforts to train SS monitoring, particularly important for those teachers teaching students with more severe and low incidence disabilities, was moved to a separate and distinct training effort independent of the statewide progress monitoring rollout. Second, a more focused data reporting requirement was established so that the nature of data being reported by teachers would be more reliable. Third, the specific materials to be used for monitoring were limited to passages from DIBELS, AIMSweb, or Read Naturally (2003). In math, only the MBSP materials were used, although only a small number of teachers reported progress monitoring of math concepts. Finally, the quality of the training delivered by the PaTTAN and IU consultants was enhanced with ongoing support from the University consultants.

Although finding a way to collect integrity of implementation was desirable, the issues of feasibility with such a wide scale implementation effort made collecting any direct integrity data impossible. Suggestions were made during training to participants for a methodology to do periodic checks of implementation integrity. Simple checklist of steps were used in conducting progress monitoring developed previously during the initial progress monitoring pilot. Teachers engage in self-monitoring, followed by peer-monitoring, and finally systematic observations were conducted by others. However, it was felt that if the outcomes of the data obtained from the progress monitoring effort statewide in the second year were similar to those collected at the end of the first year, some indirect assurance would be provided that the progress monitoring process was being implemented in ways that it had been trained. Of course, such indirect indices do not replace more direct indices of integrity but finding ways of collecting such wide scale data present substantial challenges in large scaling up efforts.

In the second year, an additional 149 districts participated, for a total of 5,742 special education teachers. Training was extended beyond special education during this year and a total of 1,196 general education teachers were also trained. A total of 24 out of 29 Intermediate Units participated in the second year of training. The changes in the second year of statewide rollout resulted in a higher quality of data reported by districts. During the first year, the data from weekly progress monitoring had to be prepared for analysis by PaTTAN and IU staff before being sent to the university consultants. An enormous amount of effort was required and long delays occurred between data submission and analysis.

To determine empirically whether a streamlined data reporting process would be equally effective, data collected during the first year on all elementary special education students in the school district of the City of Pittsburgh were examined. A comparison was made to determine whether obtaining a three-point data set (beginning, middle, end of year) would result in statistically different slope outcome than slopes generated by using the weekly progress monitoring data. Results of this analysis found no statistically significant or clinically relevant difference between slopes. As a result, a decision was made for the second year of data collection to ask teachers across the state to report only a three-point set of data with the specific dates when the data were obtained, even though teachers were collecting progress monitoring weekly.

This process greatly improved the reported data with a total of 95% of cases reported by teachers including three data points with precise indicators of the dates the data were collected. Data were reported on 1,277 (77.2%) students identified as SLD in reading and 447 (74.6%) in math computation. Students in the remaining categories of disability represented the remaining 25% of the reported sample.

Outcomes of the progress monitoring data collection process across the two years provided a clear picture of the expected rate of progress among students with SLD in reading and math computation across the year. As shown in Tables 11.4 and 11.5, data reported from the 2004–2005 training year showed that identified special education students were making progress at the levels at which they were being instructed equal to or greater than the rates expected for typical performing students at grade level, using the Fuchs et al. (1993) rates of improvement. In math computation, the outcomes were

TABLE 11.4 *Comparison of Average Rates of Gain in Reading between Fuchs et al. (1993) Study and Current Project for Instructional Level of Students Overall and those Identified as LD for 2003–2004 and 2004–2005 Data Collection Years*

Grade	Fuchs et al. (1993)	LD 2004–2005	LD 2003–2004
2	1.5	1.10	1.40
3	1.0	1.20	0.88
4	0.85	1.35	1.08
5	0.5	1.27	1.06
6	0.3	1.12	1.07

TABLE 11.5 *Comparison of Average Rates of Gain in Computation between Fuchs et al. (1993) Study and Current Project for Instructional Level of Students Overall and those Identified as LD for 2003–2004 and 2004–2005 Data Collection Years*

Grade	Fuchs et al. (1993)	LD 2004–2005	LD 2003–2004
1	n/a	0.27	0.18
2	0.3	0.32	0.56
3	0.3	0.33	0.35
4	0.70	0.27	0.56
5	0.70	0.20	0.25
6	0.45	0.22	0.58

not quite as strong compared to the Fuchs et al data, especially at grades 4 and 5. In addition, comparisons between the 2003–2004 and 2004–2005 data collection suggested that while there was some similarity, the data collected in 2004–2005 appeared to be more consistent with the Fuchs et al. and other normative outcomes (Hasbrouck & Tindal, 2005).

The outcomes of the data collection process provided strong support for the value and importance of progress monitoring. In particular, the identification of expected rates of growth for identified special education students provided teachers with an empirically supportable recommendation for goal setting (approximately 1.0 word correct per minute per week, across instructional levels in reading, and 0.25–0.35 digits correct per minute per week in math computation). Of course, no other indications of student outcomes were part of this effort. Although our data showed that the objectives of the scaling up project were successful in demonstrating that special education teachers could be trained to use the progress monitoring process, the purpose of the project was not to examine the related effect on other aspects of the instructional process. At the same time, obtaining such a wide scale implementation of progress monitoring clearly permits the opportunity for subsequent efforts focused more on instructional change.

Follow-Up Study

In fall 2005, a statewide survey was conducted to determine the full training impact of the progress monitoring initiative that was conducted between the 2003 and 2005 academic years. Surveys were sent to IU consultants who were primarily responsible for "turn-around training," that is, each IU consultant once trained was responsible for training individual districts serviced by the Intermediate Unit. The IU consultants collaborated with districts that they served to complete the survey. A total of 26 out of 29 Intermediate Units responded to the survey, representing a total of 475 Local Education Agencies (districts). Of these 475 districts, 403 (85%) indicated that their staff had attended a level 1 progress monitoring training session. A total of 58% attended as school district teams, 11% as school-wide teams, and 31% as individual teachers. Across the 403 districts who indicated that they had personnel who attended training, a total of 183 (45%) subsequently provided training for others from their local districts.

Across the 403 districts that had personnel who attended level 1 training, 135 (33%) indicated that they were implementing progress monitoring across all special education students, 188 (47%) indicated that they were implementing progress monitoring at the building or class level, and 48 (12%) indicated they were not implementing progress monitoring. The remaining 8% did not reply to this question. Clearly, the impact of the statewide effort to train progress monitoring was strong, with individuals within 80% of the districts trained indicated that they were now implementing progress monitoring at either individual student or class level.

■ Challenges and Issues in Large-Scale
Implementation of Progress Monitoring

On the positive side, a sequential method of training was developed and implemented that began with a very small, well-controlled pilot, moved to a larger statewide pilot that included a training-of-trainers model, and finally moved to statewide implementation where "turn-around" training of those receiving training was expected. In addition, the statewide implementation was conducted over a 2-year period with extensive data collection requirements that provided indirect indications both of the quality of training, quality of outcomes, and integrity of implementation. These data were used by the state to both drive improvement of the training and data collection process at each step of the process as well as to inform teachers, administrators, parents, and educational support personnel about important questions such as effective goal setting and expected levels of improvement for students with disabilities. Although there had been various studies (Deno et al., 2001; Fuchs et al., 1993) that contained similar information, the value of data coming from students within the state provided strong credibility for both the findings reported in those studies as well as the training effort itself.

Another important finding that emerged from the training process was the potential for taking training to a statewide level. When the idea of going to scale was introduced by the state, many questions were raised about the potential quality of the training when conducted at this level. However, using a trainer-of-trainers model, with sequenced implementation, ongoing support from University consultants, and frequent interaction between PaTTAN and IU consultants who served as trainers in districts, the quality of the training process was able to be maintained across time and place.

Despite these positive outcomes of the implementation process, many questions were raised regarding the statewide training effort. For example, all indicators of the quality of implementation are indirect. Data reported by teachers using specific data reporting requirements in the second year provided indirect indications that teachers were indeed conducting progress monitoring as they were trained. The high level of intact data reported, the consistency of the second and first year data, and the reported discussions with PaTTAN, IU, and district staff all suggested that the progress monitoring processes were being implemented with reasonably good integrity.

However, without some form of more direct assessment (i.e., direct observation, integrity checklists, periodic evaluations by external individuals), it is impossible to know whether the progress monitoring as trained was really implemented in the way it was supposed to have been conducted. Indeed, when on-site visits to the teachers from the original 14 districts participating in the statewide pilot were conducted two years after the pilot project ended, it was found that only 5 out of the 14 districts had continued the progress monitoring process in the same way it had been trained or extended the process beyond the originally trained staff. Only 50% of special education teachers from another 7 districts of the original pilot had continued some form of progress monitoring, and the nature of what they were doing had deviated significantly from the methods that were trained during the pilot. For example, some teachers were using reading passages from nonstandardized materials, others were using materials directly from the curriculum, or had derived their own system of progress monitoring. Adapting an innovation is a routine outcome, but it is essential to monitor that the essential components of the innovation are maintained.

What was common across all 12 districts where progress monitoring to some degree continued was that administrative support was provided to the teachers through professional development opportunities to maintain progress monitoring. Materials were purchased and made available, and contact with IU and PaTTAN consultants was offered. However, the key variable separating those five districts where progress monitoring was continued or expanded in the same way it had been trained was the presence of administrative mandate, not just support. Very simply, when school administrators (Principals and Directors of Special Education) required that progress monitoring would be used, teachers were still engaged in the same process in which they had been trained. When administrative support was present without mandate, there was a significant retreat from the progress monitoring process as it was originally trained.

Another concern is whether any "slippage" in the nature of the way progress monitoring was being conducted would have significant impact on student outcomes. Over the two years of data collection in the statewide implementation, there was no evidence suggesting such slippage was present across the sites. However, more long-term data collection and analysis of progress monitoring are needed to better assess whether this concern was a real or perceived issue. Likewise, more efforts to conduct follow-up with districts across the state are needed to determine the nature and scope of progress monitoring by those teachers who had reported the original data.

Despite these concerns, the progress monitoring initiative in Pennsylvania has been viewed by most at all levels as a large success. The primary objective of the initiative was to have special educators across the state using progress monitoring processes for all identified students. The expectation would be that progress monitoring would result in more data-based instructional decision-making. Requests for such training would diminish as teachers became increasingly comfortable with progress monitoring and outcomes would begin to appear more often in IEPs.

Although direct evidence of these outcomes has not been obtained, the most recent efforts statewide to implement a Response-to-Intervention (RTI) model, in which progress monitoring is a key component, has shown that most districts interested in establishing RTI models already have strong progress monitoring components in place within their special education programs. Moving progress monitoring into general education settings, consistent with RTI models, has shown to be fairly easy in these districts given the built-in expertise among special educators within districts.

Overall, the scaling up project described in this chapter took a well-known, science-based practice and brought it to scale through careful planning, delivery, and evaluation. Survey data from those trained suggested a large percentage of the districts were using the trained process with special education students. In addition, a substantial amount of "turn-around" training of those who attended the training was reported across districts. School administrators, teachers, and students all experienced the benefits of such planned efforts. Even further, as the state of Pennsylvania enters into a statewide initiative to implement a RTI model as one of the processes for school change as well as potential identification for students with specific learning disabilities, the presence of a well-trained, well-educated work force of special education teachers in the processes of progress monitoring will enhance the training efforts in RTI, which relies heavily on progress monitoring as one of its key components.

Despite these very positive and significant outcomes from the progress monitoring scaling up initiative, there are still many questions about the direct effect that the progress monitoring training had on schools and students. A key issue is that without direct measures of the integrity of implementation, it is very difficult to attribute changes in student performance evident from the collected progress monitoring data to the training. Although student performance showed gains over time, it is unknown if such gains were naturally occurring as a function of the instructional process or if the added components of progress monitoring itself resulted in changed student outcomes. Likewise, without ongoing integrity of implementation data, the sustainability of progress monitoring over time is impossible to determine. These concerns certainly raise important cautions in interpreting the outcomes of the scaled up initiative. Future statewide scaling up efforts need to require a method for random or periodic systematic evaluations of the integrity of implementation of the training process which need to be reported in the same way as the outcomes of the intervention impacting students are reported. Indeed, in the most recent RTI efforts in Pennsylvania, inclusion and reporting of implementation integrity data are a significant part of the process.

One area that has not been carefully studied in Pennsylvania is the effect that training of progress monitoring at the in-service level may have had on training of teachers and other school personnel at the pre-service level (see chapters in Step 6, this volume). Indeed, if future generations of teachers are trained in progress monitoring as a part of getting their teaching credentials, then it is more likely that they will enter the teaching profession viewing progress monitoring as a key element in the best practices of educating students with disabilities. Clearly, the efforts in statewide training aimed at those already practicing as teachers and educators is both logical and imperative if we are likely to have long-term change impacting future generations of educators.

Beyond the scaling up of progress monitoring, a number of general lessons were certainly learned about bringing a well-researched process to a level of statewide implementation. In particular, no matter how positive the outcome data may be, a key to sustaining the innovation was related to making sure that the administrative support for implementation was coupled by administrative mandate. Such a mandate could occur through legislative action, but the presence of a required implementation was needed to gain widespread and quick response by school professionals. Another major outcome of the statewide training was the evidence that a trainer-of-trainers model could be successful as long as support was provided at all levels of training. Finally, another general outcome of the implementation process was the recognized need for large-scale data collection of outcomes as well as integrity of implementation. All subsequent scaling up efforts involving statewide implementation must include both elements to achieve success.

Overall, the effort described in this chapter offers only one example of the way in which a well-developed, science-based process can be brought to a very large scale. More effort to fully understand the critical variables that impact effective implementation at a large-scale level are needed. Continued action research, with ongoing evaluation of integrity of implementation as well as longitudinal follow-up, is clearly needed to complete the cycle of moving from research-to-practice.

■ References

Brown-Chidsey, R. (Ed.) (2005). *Assessment for intervention: A problem-solving approach*. New York, The Guilford Press.

Deno, S. L. (1985). Curriculum-based measurement: The emerging alternative. *Exceptional Children, 52*, 219–232.

Deno, S. L. (2003a). Curriculum-based measures: Development and perspectives. *Assessment for Effective Intervention, 28*, 3–12.

Deno, S. L. (2003b). Developments in curriculum-based measurement. *Journal of Special Education, 37*, 184–192.

Deno, S. L., Fuchs, L. S., Marston, D., & Shin, J. (2001). Using curriculum-based measurement to establish growth standards for students with learning disabilities. *School Psychology Review, 30*, 507–524.

Elliott, S. N., Huai, N., & Roach, A. T. (2007). Universal and early screening for educational difficulties: Current and future approaches. *Journal of School Psychology, 45*, 137–161.

Foegen, A. (2006). Evaluating instructional effectiveness: Tools and strategies for monitoring student progress. In M. Montague & A. Jitendra (Eds.), *Teaching mathematics to middle school students with learning difficulties* (pp. 108–132). New York, The Guilford Press.

Fuchs, D., & Fuchs, L. S. (2006). Introduction to response to intervention: What, why, and how valid is it? *Reading Research Quarterly, 41*, 93–99.

Fuchs, L. S. (2004). The past, present, and future of curriculum-based measurement research. *School Psychology Review, 33*, 188–192.

Fuchs, L. S., & Deno, S. L. (1991). Paradigmatic distinctions between instructionally relevant measurement models. *Exceptional Children, 57*, 488–500.

Fuchs, L. S., Fuchs, D., & Bishop, N. (1992). Teacher planning for students with learning disabilities: Differences between general and special educators. *Learning Disabilities Research & Practice, 7*, 120–128.

Fuchs, L. S., Fuchs, D., Hamlett, C. L., & Allinder, R. M. (1991). The contribution of skills analysis to curriculum-based measurement in spelling. *Exceptional Children, 57*, 443–452.

Fuchs, L. S., Fuchs, D., Hamlett, C. L., Walz, L., & Germann, G. (1993). Formative evaluation of academic progress: How much growth can we expect? *School Psychology Review, 22*, 27–48.

Fuchs, L. S., Hamlett, C. L., & Fuchs, D. (1998). *Monitoring basic school progress—Computation black line masters.* Austin, TX, Pro-Ed.

Gickling, E. E., & Thompson, V. P. (1985). A personal view of curriculum-based assessment. *Exceptional Children, 53*, 205–218.

Glover, T. A., & Albers, C. A. (2007). Considerations for evaluating universal screening assessments. *Journal of School Psychology, 45*, 117–122.

Gravois, T. A., & Gickling, E. E. (2002). Best practices in curriculum based assessment. In A. Thomas & J. Grimes (Eds.), *Best practices in school psychology IV* (Vols. 1 and 2, pp. 885–898). Washington, DC, National Association of School Psychologists.

Grimes, J., Kurns, S., & Tilly, W. D., III. (2006). Sustainability: An enduring commitment to success. *School Psychology Review, 35*, 224–244.

Hasbrouck, J., & Tindal, G. (2005). *Oral reading fluency: 90 years of measurement.* Eugene, OR, Behavioral Research & Training, University of Oregon (Technical Report #33. Retrieved from http://brt.uoregon.edu/techreports/ORF_90Yrs_Intro_TechRpt33.pdf).

Hosp, M. K., & Hosp, J. L. (2001). Curriculum-based measurement for reading, spelling, and math: How to do it and why. *Preventing School Failure, 48*, 1–10.

Howell, K. W., & Nolet, V. (2000). *Curriculum-based evaluation: Teaching and decision making* (3rd ed.). Belmont, WA, Wadsworth.

National Center on Student Progress Monitoring. (2004). Washington, DC, American Institutes for Research (Web site). Retrieved from http://www.studentprogress.org.

Read Naturally. (2003). *Read naturally master's edition teacher's manual.* St. Paul, MN, Author.

Shapiro, E. S. (2004). *Academic skills problems: Direct assessment and intervention* (3rd ed.). New York, The Guilford Press.

Shapiro, E. S., Angello, L. M., & Eckert, T. L. (2004). Has curriculum-based assessment become a staple of school psychology practice? An update and extension of knowledge, use, and attitudes from 1990 to 2000. *School Psychology Review, 33,* 249–257.

Shapiro, E. S., Edwards, L., & Zigmond, N. (2005). Progress monitoring of mathematics among students with learning disabilities. *Assessment for Effective Intervention, 30,* 15–32.

Shinn, M. R., Habedank, L., Rossen-Nord, K., & Knutson, N. (1993). Using curriculum-based measurement to identify potential candidates for reintegration into general education. *Journal of Special Education, 27,* 202–221.

Shinn, M. R., Powell-Smith, K. A., & Good, R. H. (1996). Evaluating the effects of responsible reintegration into general education for students with mild disabilities on a case-by-case basis. *School Psychology Review, 25,* 519–536.

Shinn, M. R., Shinn, M. M., Hamilton, C., & Clarke, B. (2002). Using curriculum-based measurement in general education classrooms to promote reading success. In M. R. Shinn, H. M. Walker, & G. Stoner (Eds.), *Interventions for academic and behavior problems II: Preventive and remedial approaches* (pp. 113–142). Washington, DC, National Association of School Psychologists.

Speece, D. L., & Case, L. P. (2001). Classification in context: An alternative approach to identifying early reading disability. *Journal of Educational Psychology, 93,* 735–749.

Stoner, G., Scarpati, S. E., Phaneuf, R. L., & Hintze, J. M. (2002). Using curriculum-based measurement to evaluate intervention efficacy. *Child & Family Behavior Therapy, 24,* 101–112.

Tindal, G., Duesbery, L., & Ketterlin-Geller, L. R. (2006). Managing data for decision making: Creating knowledge from information. In S. Smith & P. K. Piele (Eds.), *School leadership: Handbook for excellence in student learning* (4th ed., pp. 380–400). Thousand Oaks, CA, Corwin Press.

Wallace, T., Espin, C. A., McMaster, K., Deno, S. L., & Foegen, A. (2007). CBM progress monitoring within a standards based system. *The Journal of Special Education, 41,* 66–67.

Wayman, M. M., Wallace, T., Wiley, H. I., Tichá, R., & Espin, C. A. (2007). Literature synthesis on curriculum-based measurement in reading. *The Journal of Special Education, 41,* 85–120.

Whinnery, K. W., & Fuchs, L. S. (1992). Implementing effective teaching strategies with learning disabled students through curriculum-based measurement. *Learning Disabilities Research & Practice, 7,* 25–30.

12. Redesigning Teacher Growth and Evaluation in a Large Urban School District

Paul Robb and Hilary Rosenfield

In 2002, a large urban public school district in the western United States began an ambitious initiative to reform its teacher evaluation policies and processes. The rationale was that the current evaluation system that determines a teacher to be either satisfactory or unsatisfactory is long on generalities and short on specifics. The process conducted as a matter of compliance lacks substance and relevance for both teachers and principals. The designers intended to replace this system with one based on teaching standards and rubrics, differentiated by experience level, and characterized by teachers focusing on their practice to increase student academic achievement. On the basis of the research of best practices in evaluation tools and philosophy, the process would encourage teacher collaboration, focus on equitable outcomes for all students, and presume continuous growth throughout the teaching career.

The project design consisted of soliciting broad-based input and involvement from school staff and principals. Educational research informed the development of the plan as well. It enabled school and district leadership to identify adaptations that needed to be made to suit the needs of varied constituencies, such as students, teachers, staff, and community. In addition to the operational challenges of the plan, implementing a system intended to support teachers' professional growth challenged the prevailing organizational culture of staff and leadership alike.

This chapter describes the context of the reform and identifies the design components (goals, tools, and targets) as well as the challenges—real and perceived—that the participants confronted throughout the project. The chapter then presents the chronology of events over a 6-year period. We then use an economic lens in theorizing what happened, and give recommendations and suggestions for similar endeavors in the future.

■ Design Components of a School Reform Intitiative

Responding to Growing Student Diversity

The student population of 46,000, though smaller than some urban school districts, is among the nation's 50 largest urban districts. Moreover, the composition and characteristics of the students are those of an urban system. Given the greater degree of complexity as well as distinctive political and economic assets and challenges, urban districts are arguably a subset of their own (Orr, 1998; Stone, 1998). The school district serves students from more than 70 countries and their families speak 129 different languages. Nearly 60% of the students are of color and more than 40% of the students are from low-income families. Student achievement varies from one school to the next and an achievement gap exists between low-income and students of color with their white, middle class counterparts throughout the system.

As in many cities, integrating the neighborhood schools has been and continues to be problematic. A recent Supreme Court decision ruled that student assignments could not use race as a deciding factor despite the fact that some schools are predominately white and others predominately serve students of color. The city's history of "redlining" neighborhoods is a contributing factor. Redlining occurs when real estate agents and bankers steer minorities from purchasing or renting homes in certain neighborhoods. As a result, the school populations often reflect their local neighborhoods. In the past, the district utilized busing to achieve a greater degree of diversity throughout the system, as did other urban districts during the 1970s and 1980s. Following the cessation of busing, school officials have not been able to maintain a consistent degree of diversity throughout the district with its student assignment policy. In fact, offering school choice has added to the complexity of the problem by exacerbating rather than mitigating the uneven distribution of students. For example, white and/or middle class students are more likely to travel beyond their neighborhood to attend a school of their preference.

Though district leaders still see diversity in the schools as an important factor in providing quality education, they realize it will not necessarily solve all the issues of equitable education. The school board and district officials recognize that at the heart of the issue is access to quality teaching and learning for all students, regardless of the student's home address, their racial/ethnic background, or their socioeconomic status. This urgent need for a systemic change in the quality of teaching and learning played a role in designing a teacher evaluation cycle that supports continuous improvement for all teachers in every school.

Change Goal: The Context

After gathering district-wide input, it became clear that district officials and teacher union representatives were in agreement over their dissatisfaction with the existing evaluation system. The current evaluation policies were extremely general; moreover, they lacked certain features that district leaders and union representatives believed important. For example, teachers lacked the opportunity to critique and monitor their own practices, or engage in collaborative dialogue with their peers. When brought to the contract bargaining table, both sides agreed to work collaboratively toward developing a new evaluation and growth process for all teachers and other certificated educational staff. The newly bargained contract authorized a joint district/ union committee charged with designing a new evaluation and professional growth system. The district and the teachers' union were each responsible for selecting their half of the 12 member committee. Furthermore, the parties agreed to pilot an initiative in a small group of schools to gather data and feedback.

Thus, the initial scale of change would begin small with the committee. The group developed a plan in which two cohorts of schools would participate in piloting the new system, successively. The committee would evaluate the pilot throughout and then make final recommendations to the teachers' membership for a vote, and finally go to the School Board for approval. If adopted, the new evaluation system and growth plan would be implemented in every school with every teacher. Both sides of the bargaining table envisioned the entire change process occurring within the five-year span of the negotiated contract.

Although everyone at the table agreed to replacing the present evaluation system and the philosophical elements of the new system, it was less clear what specific changes were to be considered and what would be required by all parties. The present evaluation had little to no impact on the quality of teaching and learning. Simply changing the evaluation procedures and forms would have little impact at the core of teaching. It would require a process that changed how teachers and administrators understood the nature of knowledge and the role of students and learning. It would effect how instruction took place, how teachers worked with their peers, and how administrators worked to support a deeper level of understanding throughout the school.

Such a change would require identifying and supporting the use of teaching standards with a laser-like focus on student achievement and equity. Teachers and administrators would need to improve the degree of collaboration that would promote a much greater level of understanding, thus changing the present core values as well as coalescing a new, shared moral commitment system-wide (Fullan, 2001). The committee members were cognizant of research findings that, despite the constant flow of change initiatives in schools throughout the country over the years, most efforts have been unsuccessful in changing the core of teaching and learning on a large scale (Elmore, 1996). However, committee members clearly recognized a potential for positive change in the system and were thus willing to dedicate a substantial amount of time in working toward a significant outcome.

Targets: Teachers and Principals

Leading up to the contract negotiations over a period of several years, a senior level administrator, who worked in the area of teacher development, cultivated a relationship with a key union officer. As they worked together, the level of trust and mutual respect grew, and so did the opportunities to discuss the benefits of developing a teacher evaluation system, among other topics. Administrators and teachers were brought into the discussions that eventually came to the bargaining table. Both sides of the bargaining table understood from their perspectives that it would be in their best interests, respectively, to identify both teachers and principals as change targets.

Clearly, with the change goal of improved teaching and learning, teachers are undeniably primary change targets. Yet, veteran teachers will point out from their personal experience that principals as instructional leaders can make a significant impacts on the effectiveness of teaching and learning in their schools. Indeed, teachers in their conversations make it clear that the effectiveness of a school is inevitably linked to the principal. Within this school district as in any large system, there are numerous examples all along the continuum of principal effectiveness. There are competent principals, who greatly enhance working conditions and job performance, as well as principals who actually make a negative impact on their teachers and schools. With plenty of room for improvement in the realm of instructional leadership, teachers who were presented with the proposed changes to the system, seemed genuinely interested in improving their working conditions through a higher quality of leadership. This sentiment by teachers is also consistently confirmed through the annual staff survey. Principals are typically considered instructional leaders and recognized as supporting school improvement.

Thus, teachers were attracted to the notion of shifting from an evaluation model, based on subjective opinions of good practice, to an evaluation model based on clear standards with the primary focus of teacher-determined growth. However, the model was predicated on administrators taking a more collaborative stance than the existing system; therefore, the administrators needed an additional set of skills and knowledge in order to make the process both meaningful and substantive. For example, principals would be expected to engage in a substantive dialogue with teachers grounded in research-based practices in content and pedagogy. Likewise, as evaluators, principals would also need to build a greater level of trust with their teachers through more collaborative efforts. It was believed that given these conditions increased student achievement throughout the system would occur.

Likewise, principals were equally attracted to the prospect of school renewal fueled in part by the ongoing process of continuous teacher growth. On the practical end, they welcomed the opportunity to support teachers based on their individual needs, rather than a one-size-fits-all model leaving little room for differentiation. Successful, experienced teachers would be more accountable to peers through their participation in collaborative teams called Professional Learning Communities (PLC) as they developed and monitored their individual growth plans during the course of the year. PLCs were expected to meet regularly during the year, and use student work to inform planning and teachers' instructional strategies. In lessening the arduous processes associated with the existing system, principals would theoretically have more time to focus on working with new teachers and intervening with struggling teachers.

On the basis of numerous conversations, principals responded positively to the prospect of a new growth and evaluation tool that could potentially raise the quality of teaching and learning in their buildings and throughout the system. Yet, when the topic was initially introduced at principal cohort meetings, their focus was often on teachers needing to improve their performance, making little to no connections with what improvements principals would need to make as well. Specifically, principals would need to learn new skills in how to be effective instructional leaders rather than simply managing personnel and resources. This would require a greater understanding of the course content, teaching pedagogy, and new skills in conducting conversations with teachers that focused on learning.

Fleshing out the details of responsibilities and commitments was the real challenge. This task could only be performed with a representative group that took into account the various perspectives and interests as agreed upon at the bargaining table. With the district's culture of placing a high value on inclusive participation, the selected committee members represented the variety of K-12 grade teachers, certificated educational support staff, building administrators, central office leadership, human resources, legal department, and union officers. The selection process also placed a priority on achieving a balance of gender representation and ethnic diversity. In a way, the committee served as a microcosm of the district, and engaged teachers and administrators in both the design and implementation process of the policy. How the committee members developed their own understanding of the issues and responded accordingly would be an essential step as well as a predictor for the district as a whole. Connecting both teachers and administrators to the change goal seemed logical since both parties were motivated with a change of policy. It also raised the likelihood of success (Schneider & Ingraham, 1993).

Tools: Learning and Capacity Building

Even though an evaluation system is implicitly mandated through the negotiated contract and by law, the district culture of site-based management suggests a collaborative approach for leveraging change in the present evaluation model. Both principals and teacher leaders, the target groups, could participate in the process of designing and implementing the new policy. Building on the assumption that staffs are capable of and willing to develop their practice, the committee believed that utilizing learning among the adults as a change strategy was a natural first step (Ostrom 1988; Ostrom, Feeny, & Picht, 1988). This also allowed the target groups to create the end goals and process for change.

Recognizing the problems of the present evaluation system, the committee worked toward understanding and agreements about what should be done. It took time to review the literature, address issues, and understand the implications of the recent school reform efforts that would predictably raise the level of conversation and promote common understandings and language. In addition to supporting learning and raising awareness, the adult learning tool strategy would also allow for experimentation in policy design as well as selecting other tools (Schneider & Ingraham, 1990). Moreover, when implemented system-wide, adult learning would continue resulting in innovative teaching and learning, a desired outcome of the teacher growth and evaluation policy.

An underlying assumption of capacity building is that teachers and principals desire to change and improve because it is the right thing to do. It empowers individuals and invests in the future. Emphasizing and modeling capacity building seemed to be both a change lever and an end result considering that the goal of teacher growth and evaluation would be a continuous developmental cycle of improvement. Capacity building also made sense in the early phase of the design stage, since few individuals were actively searching for or aware of alternative policies, despite the overwhelming dissatisfaction with the present evaluation system. It was anticipated by district leaders that the committee could discover and explore new possibilities and models when provided with information, training, and resources for rational decision-making (Schneider & Ingraham, 1990).

Constraints

At the political level, several barriers to the success of this project were apparent at the start. These barriers included a history of distrust between the central administration and the schools. Feelings of uncertainty and cynicism were prevalent as a result of the frequent change of leadership and direction over the years. In short, there was little social capital existing between the central administration and schools. A transparent process that addressed the beliefs and knowledge would be an essential starting point toward building trust.

A history of site-based management added to the intricacy of the system's organizational constraints. Ideally, in such an environment, reform structures support the increased focus on teachers' expertise and role in collaborative decision-making. Using the site-based approach at each school develops improvement plans based on the needs of students and the input from staff. Clearly, a potential for greater responsiveness, flexibility, and innovation exists that translates into raising teacher participation, morale, and student performance.

However, the promise of independence and variation also leaves open the possibility for exacerbating the inequities of the system with a wide range of student achievement and teacher effectiveness. With the advent of student performance standards, increasing the level of scrutiny, and the disaggregation of the data, it became exceedingly clear that the students' best interests were not being met as was obvious from the level of variation in achievement between schools. High stakes testing due to the No Child Left Behind legislation raised additional concerns reinforcing the need for a greater level of cohesiveness, consistency, and equity throughout the district.

The implementation of the district's elementary literacy program serves as a good illustration. Historically, instructional materials and pedagogy varied according to the particular training a teacher or school-based team had most recently completed. Though the elementary schools had two officially adopted reading programs, a review of all the schools discovered over 150 different reading programs being used in some form and in some cases, two or more within a building. An ambitious literacy initiative was rolled out over a period of seven years. Consultants were hired to give intensive training in literacy strategies. Periodic sessions were offered on Saturdays over the course of two years with each cohort.

However, despite this attempt to bring greater consistency and equity to the system, follow-up support in the schools was inconsistent, varying dramatically from one site to another. Following the initial support and enthusiasm for the literacy initiative from the district's senior leadership, the interest seemed to wane over time, or at least was frequently interrupted by other areas of concentration and concern. The sustainability of the literacy initiative was left to interested principals and teachers resulting in a wide range of practice throughout the district. This pattern of beginning new programs without consideration of how to address existing programs—or be more deliberate in marshalling long-term support to ensure sustainability—seemed to be an all too familiar pattern, regardless of the initiative. It could reasonably be asserted that the overall lack of coherence certainly contributed to teachers' sense of frustration. In general, low teacher morale and high stress existed to varying degrees throughout the district. Many teachers felt overwhelmed with the urgent sense of student needs, the variety of policies and strategies offered by the district, as well as the lack of time.

■ What Happened

Beginning the Work: Grounded in Research
and Teaching Standards

To define the policy problem, the newly formed committee agreed to review some of the research focusing specifically on the elements of effective evaluation systems and support of professional growth. The literature reviewed how effective educators were shifting their practice from a behaviorist to a more constructivist view of teaching. It also documented how teaching today was becoming increasingly more complex with frequent monitoring of student learning through formative and summative assessments, a greater focus on data, and a need for additional time for teacher reflection.

Members examined other school districts' policies and read two books by Charlotte Danielson, *Enhancing Professional Practice: A Framework for Teaching* and *Teacher Evaluation to Enhance Professional Practice* (Danielson, 1996; Danielson & McGreal, 2000). The district also commissioned her for a series of visits over a four-month period to share with the committee the documented trends in education and possible solutions. For the most part, the committee accepted the premise of the literature review suggesting that good evaluation systems supported teacher growth and development, producing more efficacious and satisfied teachers.

The committee was productive in generating concepts for the new plan. Protocols and norms within the group emphasized the importance of being inclusive and deliberate to capture both the breadth and depth of the committee's collective expertise in developing the most feasible and effective design. The deliberate nature of the process allowed members to address perceived constraints. Contributions from various members of the group lead to new possibilities in the overall design.

Yet, with each new revision to the design plan it seemed there was little movement toward an end result. Planning and revision seemed to take the place of follow-through to the next steps. For instance, on more than one occasion, the committee identified an assignment to be completed over the summer that was often left undone. As members would change, the process would begin again. It appeared that the process of generating ideas might be an end in itself.

Another complication was that even despite a number of agreements in principle among committee members, disagreements arose in the details. For instance, both administration and teachers were in favor of using teaching standards as a component of a new evaluation system. There was also general agreement on the concept of differentiation within the evaluation system according to years of teaching experience. However, when applied to teacher induction, the committee had difficulty coming to consensus upon how to differentiate or agree on what type of calibration to use.

Arriving at agreements over detailed components of an evaluation system also became more political. Research from evaluation literature and other districts indicated that teachers placed on a self-directed evaluation plan would need a more comprehensive evaluation every three to five years. Although members from the teachers' union and Human Resources agreed in principle with the recommendation, they eventually took the comprehensive evaluation off the table altogether. When compared to the present evaluation cycle that did not have a comprehensive evaluation, they realized that teachers would not view having to be comprehensively evaluated as a favorable change, so this one change could jeopardize the entire system from getting the required membership approval. The underlying tension reflected a turf mentality of the district as well as the competing needs: Here is what the research says. Here is what the voices want. Here is what the membership would ratify.

Piloting the Teacher Growth and Evaluation Plan

After four years of work, a grant-funded coordinator was hired to put together a basic plan to be piloted. Committee members understood that the pilot process would allow the individual schools to experiment with how the change would be supported. Additional time for the necessary teacher collaboration was created at the schools by altering the student arrival time on a monthly basis. This required additional resources and coordination with transportation and food services. Teacher leaders who would serve as facilitators at the department or grade level were to be paid for their additional training and preparation time. Specific components of professional development were provided to each pilot school. Principals and teacher leaders were trained in setting SMART goals that were specific, measurable, attainable, results oriented, and time bound. The goals focused on student achievement outcomes. Training also included strategies for using the teaching standards to enhance teacher growth and how to create and sustain student-learning centered professional communities. Principals were also given support in conducting learning-focused conversations that engendered growth in adults.

The intent was for departments and grade level teams to begin functioning as learning communities. Departments would shift their focus from the logistical aspects of scheduling and allocation of resources to that of student learning. Principals and teachers would learn new protocols for working together to look at student work and classroom data. They would set collective goals based on student achievement and equity. Additional resources paid for books that promoted educational reform through collaboration and changes in pedagogy. The committee presumed that in order to expect change of practice from schools and individual staff members, the district would need to provide the ongoing support of resources, time and training for the pilot schools at various stages of the implementation. The grant money that funded the pilot coordinator also provided funding for the initial pilot, with the understanding that in order to make these changes system-wide, the district would have to commit to ongoing provision of these supports.

The committee viewed the pilot as a critical step in identifying the necessary components and resources required for every school to implement the initiative successfully. The committee adopted the visual graphic of vertebrae as a metaphor to illustrate the particular components necessary to support the new system. The pilot schools would help to identify these components through the process of trial and error. The committee also recognized early in the design stage that pockets of excellence already existed within the district. Therefore, the goal of the implementation, first with a pilot and then district-wide, was to set in place structures and practices for all schools to function at a high level of proficiency.

When capacity building is used as a strategy for change, the starting point for schools and individuals vary according to the existing capacity. This proved to be a bit worrisome when variations in launching the pilot became apparent almost immediately. Clearly, this would impact the quality and substance of the work. The variation depended in part on the interests of the principal and/or the teachers despite common expectations set forth to staffs and contracts signed by the leadership within each school. In some schools, the principal was onboard and the teachers were reluctant participants at the outset. In other schools, the principal had not made the pilot a priority. In some cases, time was not set aside to allow for the essential professional development components, owing to competing requirements for the time and energy of the building. In other cases, time might have been set aside, but the training would be interrupted by other issues that took precedence. As a result, some pilot schools participated at more substantive levels than others.

The Role of Senior Leaders

Even though pilot schools were challenged with competing interests and priorities at the building level, a much greater challenge for the entire initiative existed at the central office. Recognizing a potential liability of losing focus, the committee identified early on that regular communication to achieve the buy-in of the district's senior leadership was an important goal. The committee pointed out the need to align the direction of the senior leadership, which was also challenged with competing interests and priorities at the district level.

The grant-funded pilot coordinator had been a classroom teacher, was from the committee, and also active in the union. The reassignment to the position of pilot coordinator required that she be relieved of her teaching assignment. One of her first assignments was to report to the Senior Leadership Team regarding the progress of the committee and the impending pilot launch.

The response of the team was quite positive and encouraging. They told her it all looked great to move forward with the pilot and let them know what she needed. The pilot coordinator was pleased with the initial response, but was puzzled by the lack of curiosity from the group. Aside from the Human Resources Director, no one else had questions and, in fact, departed from the room before the question and answer session started.

During the spring leading up to launching the pilot, a new Academic Superintendent was appointed to the post. The School Board directed the Academic Superintendent to bring about bold changes. The first order of business was to shake up the senior leadership team through reorganization and replacing key positions. In the throes of the reorganization and reshuffling, the creator and primary executive sponsor of the initiative as well as the teaching standards was forced to leave. The position was left unfilled for a significant period and the pilot coordinator was left without a supervisor. Responsibility for the initiative was not reassigned to another administrator, and so the senior leadership table did not include a champion or participant of the project.

Understanding the importance of aligning goals centrally, the pilot coordinator initiated several meetings with the Academic Superintendent for those purposes. It became apparent after several exchanges that the Academic Superintendent, quite familiar with an evaluation model from a previous district, was assuming this other model to be similar to this evaluation initiative. Unfortunately, they were quite different in philosophy and structure.

Other departures mattered, as well. The one remaining senior leader on the committee, representing Human Resources, who had participated in the committee process of developing understanding and capacity, left her post in the autumn. The lead grant partner, several principals, and some teacher members serving on the committee also left. After nearly 50 members had come and gone over a period of six years, only two people remained from the original group—the union leader and the teacher-turned pilot coordinator.

Beginning of the End

The first year of the pilot concluded on a bittersweet note. Despite the absence of central office administration support and the uneven start among schools, the pilot progressed remarkably well. In every case, principals and teachers implemented the new procedures for evaluation. Teams of teachers met periodically to monitor their progress by looking at student work and instructional practices. Moreover, all of the school staffs voted to continue participation in the pilot for a second year and a number of new school staff members and principals expressed interest in joining. Nevertheless, the district did not come up with funds to expand the pilot and allow for additional schools to participate. There would be enough funding remaining from the initial grant, however, to provide the initial pilot schools one more year of support at a minimal level.

The lost opportunity for pilot expansion was unfortunate on at least two accounts. Since the main beneficiaries of capacity building are those directly involved, additional schools would miss out on the potential opportunity for growth. The other benefit of capacity building is the political support gained by the participants whose beliefs and values are changed as a result of their personal involvement. Over time such a strategy for building capacity would also result in reaching the critical mass within the teacher ranks. This made political sense, since the contract eventually called for a vote of approval by the teacher association membership. What was most discouraging, however, was that the senior leaders did not support the aspect of the initiative that was the key to its long-term success—the new system requiring structural supports, or vertebrae, to work. Although the committee can make a recommendation to the teacher's education association, without the resources, practice, and leadership of those at the top, it is unlikely that the initiative would expand district-wide and become integrated into systematized practice. In addition, during the spring of the first year of the pilot as the grant funding ran low, the pilot work was not resourced. The pilot coordinator was reassigned to other central office projects so the work of pilot communications, program evaluation, and expansion was discontinued.

■ Analysis: Using an Economic Lens

Considering all the time and effort expended on the planning and collaboration of the policy, it is essential to consider what factors contributed to the eventual termination. In the following section, the critical events will be analyzed through an economic lens with a specific focus on the policy, people, and context. Economic lenses are typically used to forecast the future, but can also help analyze the past. Though analyzing educational outcomes and productivity through an economic lens is not new (Hanushek, 1997), it is not common to consider educational policy implementation with this economic approach (Loeb & McEwan, 2006). By employing the economic lens, key participants or actors' preferences are analyzed by how they impacted the decisions and actions regarding the policy. An economic lens also considers monetary and knowledge constraints that may inhibit the likelihood of implementation. A third critical factor is to consider the actors' will or desire to do something about their preferences.

Teachers and Principals

Of the original committee, the two remaining members were both teachers on special assignments—the union leader and the pilot coordinator. The phenomenon of principals' short terms on committees was an all too common occurrence within the district. Principals struggled with making long-term commitments that drew them away from the duties and responsibilities in their own buildings. Thus, it is difficult to judge the level of the principals' commitment in seeing the policy successfully implemented. As the composition of the committee changed, so did the collective knowledge of the group. Outgoing members took their level of knowledge and understanding with them. New members did not receive the same opportunities of studying the research, viewing other district's policies, or appreciating the evolution of thought from the committee's inception. In other words, some of the work of the committee to develop a collective understanding and common language was lost with the turnover of membership over time.

Nevertheless, the overall support of the committee was generally favorable, but not necessarily rock solid. It was a rare occurrence for all of the members to attend the same meeting. Though committee members agreed in principle with the need and benefit of a new evaluation system, teachers expressed concern that the new evaluation system may add to their overall work load, not a winning proposition to gain approval with the entire union membership. In other words, the teachers' preferences were for a change that would be palatable for teachers in ways that would compromise the overall plan and eventual impact on teaching and learning. This preference most probably lessened the will to take the next steps. At a significant juncture before launching the pilot, the union leader attempted to derail the next step, as the point of no return loomed imminent and the worst was most likely feared. The project creator also suggested a delaying tactic. It seemed that the effective design strategy of inclusive deliberation also provided an outlet for indecisiveness in implementation. Many other actors contributed to the committee's significant delays in progress by bringing up new plans and issues to consider when facing implementation.

Regardless, the knowledge and/or willingness to facilitate a balance between process and decision-making were/was missing in the equation. In a group composed of diverse interests, it seems inevitable that compromise would be a necessary function. Is it possible that an endless process of building capacity by designing a plan becomes an end in itself? Could this process eventually sap the momentum and be cause for procrastinating the implementation? When using such a process that one might describe as "inclusive deliberation," what is the point of diminishing returns? In other words, how inclusive and deliberate is enough? When can it be determined that the voices have been heard and the details of the plan have been determined? The tendency to delay is one of the single greatest barriers to change efforts (DuFour, 2003).

Senior Leadership

Recognizing that not all the members of the district shared the same goals, the committee correctly identified goal alignment throughout the system as an essential component. To meet the goal of informing members throughout the district, the committee devised and implemented a strategic communication plan with several important elements. The committee composed an "elevator speech" so that the message could be effectively communicated in a brief, yet consistent manner. An overview of the system design was introduced in a DVD that laid out the concepts and process. The DVD was to be viewed system-wide at a joint leadership-union representative meeting and then be brought back to each school's faculty meeting. A web site was also created as another resource and form of communication.

Although the plan specifically mentioned the importance of achieving senior leadership buy-in through meetings to inform leaders, the plan did not identify indicators of success. In other words, it was not clear what successful buy-in and alignment of these key individuals would look like. The senior leadership ultimately played a critical role in the outcome of the initiative. Their individual and collective disaffection with the project was evident by their lack of inquiry. Without knowing the underlying purpose and importance of teacher collaboration in the new system, there could not be the same level of appreciation for setting aside time and resources specifically for such a purpose. On the basis of preferences of senior leadership, the political will to support the initiative did not exist and pilot expansion was never funded. Clearly, although the committee appreciated the critical role of senior leadership as a key mediator in the policy outcome (Honig, 2006), they were not able to successfully determine the path to gain the necessary buy-in.

Committee members falsely assumed that the senior leaders had a similar level of preference and knowledge of the goals and outcomes as the committee membership. In particular, the Academic Superintendent had not experienced the same learning as the committee and possibly as a result did not share the same viewpoints such as grasping the role that teacher collaboration played in the newly proposed model. This became quite evident when the Academic Superintendent suggested that instead of piloting a few schools, the pilot could be in all schools with a few teachers participating. Rather than shifting the school culture toward collaborative work among teachers and principals, such a proposal would put the onus on individual teachers, not unlike the present system.

Also, the Academic Superintendent envisioned a teacher growth model similar to a National Board Certification process. The principal would take on a more direct role with the teacher using an intensive eight-step process. In many ways, this represented the antithesis of the plan that emphasized building capacity.

It was unclear whether the committee knew what the buy-in and alignment of goals would look like. They failed to recognize and state explicitly the degree and nature of political support, priority, time, and resources that would be required from the central leaders in order for the implementation to be successful. They either misjudged the "rules of the game" or the rules may have simply changed as a result of the senior leadership turnover. Regardless, there seemed to be little evidence of preference, knowledge, or curiosity among the central leadership that would affect their will to take action. Despite it all, the Academic Superintendent gave tacit approval to the pilot and did not overtly hinder the work of the first year. But without any senior leader to champion the initiative, there was also no level of accountability.

Nevertheless, the success of the initial pilot indicates that the overall design had great potential. Elmore makes several suggestions for getting to scale. Not unlike the evaluation initiative, teachers are more likely to experience conditions that promote continuous learning and renewal when given the opportunity to meet periodically with a small group of teachers focused on student outcomes and problems of practice. Teachers are also more likely to look outward as well as inward with the establishment of teaching standards (Elmore, 1996). It is no small irony that the recommendations describe the essence of this initiative. With such a foundation in place, the district would, in essence, have a greater capacity to support future carefully designed initiatives.

Although the district may contain "pockets of excellence," a full-scale implementation cannot take place without the political will and resources of the central office and union leadership. This alignment of goals is more likely when a common level of understanding and knowledge is achieved by all of the critical actors.

■ Recommendations

The pervasive urgency is no more apparent than in the large urban school systems as they respond to the increasing demands for all students to reach high standards. To avoid the constant swirl of initiatives and individual goals, a thoughtful, strategic response is necessary.

A common understanding and knowledge is required among the key leaders to build and sustain a strong level of political support. This entails ongoing time and effort to assess what are the common understandings and to increase the collective knowledge of key concepts and essential features that provide a rationale for the change initiative. Attention needs to be given to the alignment of goals among key individuals. Leaders must provide the district a sense of clarity and coherence that supports the improvement of instruction (Knapp, Copland, Ford, Markholt, McLaughlin, Milliken, & Talbert, 2003). The leadership of the central administration plays a critical role in the development of coherence. Indeed, without their support, it is virtually impossible to be successful. Finally, reasonable timelines need to be in place and followed to maintain the momentum, reduce the turnover of members, to turn aspirations into actions and visions into reality (DuFour, 2003).

■ References

Danielson, C. (1996). *Enhancing professional practice: A framework for teaching.* Alexandria, VA, ASCD.

Danielson, C., & McGreal, T. L. (2000). *Teacher evaluation to enhance professional practice.* Alexandria, VA, ASCD and Princeton, NJ, ETS.

DuFour, R. (2003). Procrastination can sink even the best school improvement plan. A few simple strategies can help get those projects moving forward. *Journal of Staff Development, 24,* 77–78.

Elmore, R. F. (1996). Getting to scale with good educational practice. *Harvard Education Review, 66,* 1–24.

Fullan, M. (2001). *The new meaning of educational change* (3rd ed.). New York, Teachers College Press.

Hanushek, E. (1997). Assessing the effects of school resources on student performance: An update. *Educational Evaluation and Policy Analysis, 19,* 141–164.

Honig, M. (2006). Complexity and policy implementation: Challenges and opportunities for the field. In M. I. Honig (Ed.), *New directions in education policy implementation: Confronting complexity* (pp. 1–24). Albany, NY, State University of New York Press.

Knapp, M., Copland, M., Ford, B., Markholt, A., McLaughlin, M. W., Milliken, M., & Talbert, J. (2003). *Leading for learning sourcebook: Concepts and examples.* Seattle, WA, Center for the Study of Teaching and Policy, University of Washington.

Loeb, S., & McEwan, P. (2006). An economic approach to education policy implementation. In M. I. Honig (Ed.), *New directions in education policy implementation: Confronting complexity* (pp. 169–186). Albany, NY, State University of New York Press.

Orr, M. (1998). The challenge of school reform in Baltimore: Race, jobs, and politics. In C. N. Stone (Ed.), *Changing urban education* (pp. 93–117). Lawrence, KS, University Press of Kansas.

Ostrom, E. (1988). Institutional arrangements and the commons dilemma. In F. Ostrom et al. (Eds.), *Rethinking institutional analysis and development.* San Francisco, International Center for Economic Growth.

Ostrom, V., Feeny, D., & Picht, H. (1988). *Rethinking institutional analysis and development.* San Francisco, International Center for Economic Growth.

Schneider, A., & Ingraham, H. (1990). Behavioral assumptions of policy tools. *Journal of Politics, 52,* 510–529.

Schneider, A., & Ingraham, H. (1993). Social construction of target populations: Implications for politics and policy. *American Political Science Review, 87,* 334–347.

Stone, C. N. (1998). Introduction: Urban education in political context. In C. N. Stone (Ed.), *Changing urban education* (pp 1–22). Lawrence, KS, University Press of Kansas.

13. Implementation of Instructional Consultation Teams

An Analysis of a School-University Partnership

Deborah Nelson, Kathy Aux, Michael T. Neall, and
Todd A. Gravois

■ Introduction

A consistent theme in the field of education has been the modifying, changing, or otherwise reforming of schools in order to better meet the academic and behavioral needs of students and increase student achievement. Although many innovations have been posed which address this theme, one of the greatest challenges that school systems continue to face is the successful implementation and institutionalization of educational innovations that are designed to facilitate and support the development of collaborative school cultures at a systems-level. Part of the challenge comes from innovations that necessitate changes in the norms and regulations of schools. However, without a rationale for why such changes should occur, a strategic plan for how to accomplish such changes within the context of the larger school system, and an understanding of the resources needed to sustain the innovation in a viable way, success, if attained at all, is fleeting. According to Fullan (2001), some of these challenges that need to be addressed are (a) accepting the time needed to implement innovations that result in substantive changes in student achievement; (b) scaling up innovations to accommodate the numbers of schools and districts that can benefit from the intended changes; and (c) implementing innovations in a way that facilitates school-wide and systems changes in a sustainable way.

One way to address the challenge of creating and sustaining changes in schools has been the willingness of universities and school districts to work as partners. Such partnerships maximize resources and focus efforts for the

Portions of the work described here were funded under a research grant #R305F050051, funded by the Institute for Education Sciences.

purpose of increasing the likelihood of successful implementation of a desired innovation. In some instances (e.g., Supovitz & Weinbaum, 2008), institutes of higher education have formed partnerships with school systems to facilitate the development of collaborative structures that can support the implementation and expansion of programs that are designed to improve student achievement. When effective, such partnerships marry the best of two worlds—that of research-based theories and strategies of what makes program implementation successful and that of field-based practitioners who can apply those theories and strategies for students through their daily practices in the classroom. However, the likelihood of change occurring is increased when stakeholders appreciate the nuances of the change process, how it impacts users, and how to proactively address the known challenges of bringing new practices into schools.

This chapter details and analyzes a five-year partnership between university and school district professionals. The purpose of this partnership was to implement and research a particular innovation, Instructional Consultation Teams (IC Teams; Rosenfield & Gravois, 1996). As a research-based model, IC Teams represents best practice in organizing and delivering early intervention support to teachers of struggling students. However, it is Rosenfield and Gravois's planned integration of the content knowledge of IC Teams with the necessary change actions required for its successful implementation that provided the foundation for the current partnership, and is the focus of this chapter. After providing a description of the content features of IC Teams, and the history of the partnership, the chapter will analyze the five-year partnership from the perspectives of the university trainer, the district level administrator, and a school-based implementer.

■ Instructional Consultation Teams

As a complex innovation package, IC Teams (Rosenfield & Gravois, 1996) are characterized by three features: A delivery system structured around an interdisciplinary team; a collaborative instructional consultation process; and an evaluation design to ensure that the innovation package has been implemented with integrity. The collaborative instructional consultation process is based on the original work of Rosenfield (1987, 2008) whereas the delivery system and process for implementing IC Teams is described in detail by Rosenfield and Gravois (1996); Gravois and Gickling (2008) describe the critical component of Instructional Assessment, which focuses on assessing and creating appropriate instructional conditions for students. Moreover, Rosenfield and Gravois (1996) provide a detailed description of the change process that is necessary for successful implementation of IC Teams. By integrating the extant literature related to school change, the developers provide a structured process by which to initiate, implement, and sustain IC Teams.

As described by Gravois and Rosenfield (2006),

> The primary goal of the IC Team model is to create and maintain student success within the general education environment by supporting the classroom teacher. IC Teams is theoretically grounded in, and serves as a delivery system of, instructional consultation.... By focusing both on the *content* (i.e., curriculum-based assessment, evidence-based academic and behavioral interventions) and the *process* (i.e., data collection, problem solving steps, the reflective relationship established for the classroom teacher), instructional consultation seeks to improve, enhance and increase student achievement through improving, enhancing and increasing the teachers' performance...explicit emphasis on supporting teachers' professional capacity to develop and deliver effective instruction within the general education classroom...distinguishes instructional consultation from other forms of consultation and teaming. The model is based upon the premise that quality instructional and management programming, matched to a student's assessed entry skills, increases student success, reduces behavioral difficulties, and avoids the need for special education evaluation and placement. (p. 45)

Systematic, data-based support is provided to classroom teachers via a trained team. The IC Team is composed of administrators, support personnel, and representatives from special and general education. Instead of a teacher meeting with the entire team to engage in "group problem-solving," the teacher meets one-on-one with his/her assigned team member, termed a Case Manager. In regularly scheduled meetings, it is the Case Manager's responsibility to support the teacher in engaging in a structured, data-driven problem-solving process. The IC Team Case Manager manages the process and ensures support for the teacher through each of the critical stages of problem solving. Working collaboratively, the Case Manager and teacher design and implement instructional and management practices within the classroom to address specific and measurable goals. The entire IC Team membership remains available to support the Case Manager and teacher at any point in which assistance is required or requested.

■ School-District-University Partnership

Beginning a Partnership

Although the literature on school change will outline a highly theoretical process by which change is introduced and implemented in schools, the reality is that in most instances, the start of change is not a formal process. In retrospect, the beginning of the partnership between the University of Maryland

(UMD), and PWCS for Prince William County Schools could be considered more accident than design. The second author (KA), at that time a school psychologist with the Prince William County Public Schools, had attended a national conference and heard the lead developer (S. Rosenfield) of IC Teams speak. This initial introduction to the concepts, philosophy, and structure that comprised IC Teams struck a chord in this one individual that did *not* [emphasis added] lead to immediate action on anyone's part. Instead it would be another two years before this same school psychologist, now providing site supervision for a University of Maryland intern, would meet the co-developer (T. Gravois) in a happenchance encounter and learn of a summer institute in the IC Team process. The school psychologist attended the summer training and in the midst of that training, was promoted to a supervisory position within the district.

To further illustrate the fragileness by which change occurs, it happened that at the same time the University of Maryland had been contracted to provide IC Team training with the State of Virginia. Through this statewide effort districts could apply for and participate in the IC Team training offered by the state. Interestingly, Prince William had not applied or was involved during the first round of training offered. Now in a supervisory position, KA "connected the dots" and worked to have the district considered for a second-round implementation of the IC Team model. The rest, as is often said, is history; and as with all history provides the opportunity to reflect and analyze.

Nurturing a Partnership

It is clear that personal factors created the foundation of the partnership between UMD and PWCPS. However, the growth and strength of this partnership occurred because the need for change in the district matched the relevance of the IC Team model. The district had specific needs that the university could address through the innovation and resources that potentially would fill the void.

District Readiness for Change

Prince William County Schools is the second largest school division in the state of Virginia. The student population numbers over 70,000 and represents over 100 different language groups. Over the past 20 years, Prince William County has attracted a more affluent population, has retained a highly competent administrative and instructional staff, and has the desire to be a "world class" school district providing all of its students a high-quality, competitive education.

External factors have served to increase the attention given to instruction and student achievement in districts such as this one. The President's Commission on Excellence in Special Education (2002), the No Child Left

Behind Act (2002), and most recently Individuals with Disabilities Education Improvement Act (2004) have re-emphasized the mandate for schools across the country to renew focus on accountability, student outcomes, and more substantive use of early intervening services, particularly in the area of reading. The focus of NCLB on certain disaggregated groups, such as children in poverty, English Language Learners, African American, other minority group students, or students with disabilities, has intensified the need to examine educational services provided to these groups. Specifically, processes that involve monitoring student progress, early intervening service delivery, monitoring of changes in instruction or intervention, disability identification, and special education service provision required closer scrutiny.

Internally, the school division has been highly focused on the area of instruction and has provided many professional development opportunities and requirements for its instructional staff. A division-wide strategic plan was developed with five major goal areas, two of which relate to this innovation: (a) student achievement/graduation; and (b) the provisions of targeted and quality professional development for staff. Each school and department developed individual strategic plans that were aligned with the division-wide plan. Schools furnish quarterly reports on the progress made in achieving individual goals.

A particular concern within the district centered on special education. In this district, as well as in others in the country, students with disabilities have, as a group, performed poorly on state standardized measures compared with the general population. In PWCS, this is true division-wide, as well as within individual schools. Between 2004 and 2006, three studies conducted by teams of school psychologists, social workers, and educational diagnosticians, identified flaws in the special education identification process, especially the lack of effective interventions prescribed and conducted by the problem-solving teams before referring students for special education. The review of services found that procedures that largely focused on the child as the primary factor in student learning problems had resulted in inefficient and fragmented decision-making about children and their lack of academic success (Prasse, 2006). The special education leadership within PWCS perceived a need for changing the manner in which students' learning problems were handled.

Initiating the Change

Having by-passed participation on one occasion, PWCS division was able to register one pilot school to participate in a statewide implementation of IC Teams during the 2002–2003 school year. The district was responsible for the full funding of staff (in this case, the team facilitator) and travel costs associated with the project training. These would have been shared cost had the district elected to participate in the first year of the state project.

In the year 2003–2004, the decision was made to add four additional schools in PWCS. For this implementation phase, PWCS professionals would participate within the state-sponsored training for the first half of the year and then UMD and PWCS would negotiate an independent contract for the second half of the school year. At this point, the district would assume full financial responsibility for staffing, travel, *and* training costs. An additional six schools were added during the 2004–2005 school year, bringing the total to 11 schools.

Solidifying the Partnership

The continued refinement and research of IC Teams (see Gravois & Rosenfield, 2002) allowed the program developers to compete for a national research grant funded by the Institute for Education Science, USDOE. The grant application was restricted to experimentally designed studies and had three general criteria: (a) a theoretically grounded model, (b) that could be effectively disseminated within a variety of school settings, and (c) that had sufficient research history to warrant a full-scale experimental study.

Building upon the existing partnership between UMD and PWCPS, the developers of IC Teams requested, and PWCPS agreed to expand the existing partnership to include an additional 17 IC Team project schools, bringing the total to 28 schools. In addition, another 17 PWCPS schools would be required to serve as control sites for the experimental study. At this point, a total of 45 district schools were involved in some capacity in the university-district partnership.

The strength of the partnership was evident in the school district's willingness to fully participate in the rigorous experimental research design, and to support the financial commitments of staffing an additional 17 schools. More important, the research design required that the 17 newly identified project schools be selected using randomized procedures, something that had not occurred for the original project schools. The procedure required that 34 schools be paired and a random selection process used to assign schools to either treatment or control status.

■ Analysis of a Partnership: Perspectives
   from Three Voices

Although the preceding section provides the reader the global context of the UMD and PWCPS partnership, it is the perspective of those "in the trenches" that allows for a better understanding of the trials and tribulations that accompany any change process. These analyses, through the lens of the university trainer, the district administrator, and the school-level implementer, provide a deeper and more meaningful understanding of the actions that are required on each part. The following section allows each partner to convey his or her experiences as the change process progressed from initiation to implementation and ultimately to institutionalization.

University Perspective (Voice of DN)

University Views of Initiation

Fullan (1991) defines initiation as "the process leading up to and including the decision to proceed with implementation" (p. 50). We have come to understand that initiation does not have clear starts and stops and that "it takes as long as it takes." We also discovered that initiation activities are not linear and not always evident to everyone involved. Finally, we appreciate that individual relationships seemed to promote, and at times save, the initiation process. Several instances occurred that highlight these observations.

For example, our first formal interaction with IC Teams was when KA (second author) attended the IC Team Summer Institute held at the university. It was during this time that *we informed her* [emphasis added] about the Virginia statewide IC Team initiative, which PWCPS had already passed over. From our perspective, three things started the initiation process: KA's belief in the value of the IC Team model, her own understanding of the district needs, and her recent promotion as district administrator. Although we can take credit for being available and offering information, it was KA's own efforts to bring that information to those key stakeholders that promoted further dialogue.

A second example shows the a critical role that the university played during this initiation process. Once dialogue had started between the university and the district, and additional district administrators were interested, the university negotiated on behalf of PWCPS with the state department to allow for the first school to participate. It was the university staff's perspective that the statewide coordination of IC Teams provided future benefit for sustaining the work, rather than having individual districts adopt and implement individually. From our perspective, the university effort to help the district meet its needs by joining with the statewide initiation built trust and openness. Specifically, although the district still had to finance their own staffing and travel, they received the training from the university free of charge. Although the university could have negotiated a separate contract to provide training, encouraging, and actively helping the district take advantage of state-sponsored training demonstrated the earnest effort to help the district be successful.

University Views of Implementation

The implementation of IC Teams began after the initiation tasks had occurred. Although some initiation tasks were ongoing and overlapped with implementation (i.e., ongoing staff awareness, etc.), their planning was completed before implementation was begun.

The primary goal of IC Team implementation is to train and support a group of core staff members who will function as a team in providing collaborative problem-solving support to classroom teachers in a school (Rosenfield & Gravois, 1996). A key role and support offered by the university was the delivery of professional development as outlined by the developers (see, e.g., Gravois, Knotek, & Babinski, 2001). This intensive training structure required commitment and support from all levels of the school system to assure integrity of critical components.

The university assumed a major role in helping ensure integrity of program implementation, especially in the professional development activities associated with IC Teams. For example, a key task in the implementation of IC Teams is the identification of team facilitators—those individuals who would be charged with providing training and support to a core team of individuals as they learn and apply skills with teachers in classroom settings. To fulfill the requirements of the role, it was necessary that a dedicated staff position be allotted for each school implementing the process. The university worked collaboratively to assist the district in identifying and defining the requirements of the role, including writing a specific job description for a role that previously did not exist in the district.

The university resources also allowed for some of the more intense professional development features. For example, a critical component of the IC Team training process is the coaching of new IC Team Facilitators as they engage in their first consultation case with teachers. The experience required the facilitators to audiotape their interactions with classroom teachers and receive structured feedback via an on-line coaching experience. The university was able to coordinate and provide consistent coaching experiences for the 17 facilitators.

Although the university provided leadership in the delivery of professional development to ensure integrity in the delivery of the comprehensive training package, the district remained an equal partner. For example, although previous implementations of the IC Team model used a monthly training schedule to develop IC Team Facilitator skills, the district expressed a concern that these newly identified full-time facilitators would have "down" time during the initial training phase. The legitimate fear was that without developed skills, the facilitators could quickly be subsumed into the existing school functions. In response to this concern, the district requested and the university agreed to accelerate the training schedule. This collaboration met the district's needs while ensuring integrity of program implementation.

Throughout the implementation process, additional conversations between the university and district were held, including those about how program implementation would become incorporated into the school system's dialogue with teachers, administrators, and school system officials. The moment that implementation became certain, conversations also began about how the university partner could work with school system officials to ensure that steps are taken to help the system build an infrastructure for change that included ongoing training and support, and hiring and evaluation of key implementation personnel (i.e., team facilitators).

Another major point of discussion within implementation was focused on using program evaluation as both a formative and summative tool. For example, assisting the district in organizing adequate resources to coordinate, gather, and analyze data needed to evaluate the program effectively throughout its implementation became an important point of discussion. Working closely with the system's program evaluation unit, it was important to identify the needs and concerns. This not only helped to build the collaborative relationship between the university and the school division, it also helped those responsible for program implementation to stay constantly aware of the changing conditions.

University Views of Institutionalization

Once implementation began, it was crucial to begin discussions about institutionalization. Often such discussions are delayed until implementation is well underway, or more aptly too far underway. However, preliminary discussions about how the program was to fit with long-range school system plans became important. Such discussions facilitated the development of infrastructures that would support implementation long-term, promote sustainability, and support the change processes that could enable collaborative structures to emerge.

Many veteran educators are quick to share how programs "come and go." The fate and long-term sustainability of IC Teams would not be different unless conscious efforts were made to ensure the program's institutionalization. Rather than deny the reality, the university, district and school partners confronted the challenge head on. For example, the legitimizing of the newly created IC Team Facilitator roles became an important topic of discussion. Helping the school system hire and support program staff was an example of one issue. These newly created roles, with newly created job descriptions, still required professional evaluations as mandated for all district employees. However, these roles were "nontraditional" when compared to existing positions. They were not teachers or were they administrators. Sustainability required an evaluation tool that was aligned with the new duties. Together, the university and district collaborated to develop and implement an evaluation tool that reflected the new job duties and responsibilities and recognized the unique tasks and activities to promote program implementation.

Finally, the long-term sustainability of any innovation, especially one that is grounded in professional development, requires addressing the natural attrition of staff. In the current project, the university supported the district by developing the capacity for experienced IC Team Facilitators to become skilled in delivering the necessary training for future staff. The university staff and district leaders worked collaboratively to identify a cadre of school-based facilitators who were provided additional professional development to learn how to be trainers of IC Teams.

District Perspective (Voice of KA)

District Views of Initiation

Those of us at the district level recognized that initiation was not a singular event or even limited to a set of activities. In hindsight, the initiation process of IC Teams in PWCPS seemed to "dribble" along for a couple years—first with one school, then with five more, and then five more. Each introduction of the project into schools had its own issues of initiation from the district perspective. And with such a phase-in of the project, some schools were moving into implementation while initiation activities continued at the district level. At times, then, the lines between initiation and implementation would blur.

The culmination of initiation, in the formal sense, occurred in 2005, with the prospect of conducting an experimental study involving an additional 34 district schools. The structure and outcomes required of the research study provided clear parameters and seemed to create a "higher" purpose for the existing partnership. Initially, the partnership was largely one directional—the university providing training and technical support to help the district meet its own needs. However, the research project had a different purpose, to inform the educational community at large about program effectiveness, and each partner—university, district, and individual school—had an equal and important contribution to make. In addition, our district has a highly trained and qualified office for research and program evaluation. These staff members were involved early in the planning of the research and remained members of the university-district research team.

Decisions were made collaboratively to identify and inform key stakeholders. For example, a decision was made to inform school administrators about the grant by providing an overview of the study. Before the scheduled meeting, phone calls were made to each building administrator to provide a "personal" invitation and answer any questions.

At that meeting, critical information was shared with all of those who would be potentially involved in the study in either the experimental (i.e., implementing IC Teams) or the control group, and any questions and concerns could be addressed in a central forum. Representatives from both the university research team and the school system's team jointly led the meeting. Although administrators could not be told at the outset whether they would be in the experimental or control group, they could be informed of the study, the criteria for involvement in the study, and provided with other details that would impact them and their school staff.

The working relationship that developed between the university research team and the Prince William Office of Program Evaluation was especially productive. Several meetings were held to plan how data would be collected for the grant. Although many data pieces already collected by the school system would be analyzed as part of the study (i.e., report card grades, special education data, discipline data), other data unique to the study also needed to be collected by both the control and the treatment schools. For example, the university research team developed an 80-item web-based teacher self-report survey designed to elicit teacher's perceptions on areas such as job satisfaction, instructional practices, and collaboration. Similarly, a web-based teacher report on student behavior was developed in order to get homeroom teachers' perspectives on their individual students with regard to classroom behaviors and the teacher-student relationship. Obtaining these data from 45 elementary schools required collaboration about a series of logistical details, including establishing a data collection timeline, identifying who would be responsible for each element of the data collection, and informing schools of the data to be collected, and so forth. After a plan was developed, it was co-presented to key school officials in person and via email by representatives from both the university and school system research team.

District Views of Implementation

The success of implementation seemed to center on our ability to plan collaboratively. This in itself required ongoing commitment from everyone. If anyone has ever tried to arrange a meeting with colleagues, imagine the challenge of arranging such meetings across different organizational structures. And yet, the partnership's strength was grounded in our continued belief that to achieve success, there must be joint ownership of the decisions made. The most notable examples were the careful planning of training schedules each year, selection of the quality full-time leaders of the change process in each school (Instructional Consultation facilitators), preparation, ongoing communication, and collaboration with the administrator in each school and planning for attrition of both facilitators and administrators.

District Views of Institutionalization

In these days of competing programs/processes to enhance and improve instruction and student achievement, securing funding can be challenging. Those innovations that verify implementation integrity, provide multiple measures of effectiveness, and are related directly to a school division's goals are likely to gain higher priority. Supporting IC Teams required ongoing communication of the existing database and researched results to secure funding and support. A variety of funding sources, initially for training and leadership positions and most recently for the full-time leadership positions, came from NCLB funds, Medicaid reimbursement funds and allowable special education funds for early intervening activities. It is our goal that future funding would find the full-time positions included in the School Division budget, as the IC Team Facilitator represents a staff position that cuts across almost all services and funding.

As the UMD and PWCS partnership continues, work is ongoing to develop the training and technical capacity within the school division personnel to sustain the IC Team process over time. We see IC Teams as an exemplary model of problem solving that will replace the process in all elementary schools and form the backbone for the implementation of a response to instruction process. Our next focus then is on aligning policy and budget with the services that have been created through the implementation of the IC Team model.

School Perspective (Voice of MN)

School Views of Initiation

After being in the classroom for seven years as a general and special educator, I had grown increasingly discouraged and convinced that educators needed something different in terms of support. I was frustrated with teaching. I saw increasing pressure to improve student performance, many struggling learners, and a painfully slow process to get support. Put simply, when I needed help as a teacher, I felt I had few viable options. Colleagues try to help one another, but it is not usually very effective. Informal collaboration with support personnel was difficult to maintain and the effectiveness of the child study team was not only questionable, but also its support significantly limited.

IC Teams presented a remedy for the problems that I saw, but it was a risky venture for me professionally. The classroom was a place of comfort with clearly defined roles and guidelines. I had spent time developing respect and credibility at the school as a teacher. Changing positions removed that sense of comfort and belonging. However, opportunities for professional growth did not come along often and I decided to take the opportunity to improve my own professional skills and perhaps address the concerns that I had experienced in my own classroom.

School Views of Implementation

The greatest challenge in implementing IC Teams at the school level was defining the role of IC Team Facilitator. The role was new and not defined in the same manner as other roles (i.e., teacher, school nurse, principal, etc.).

Instead, facilitators had specific responsibilities, a timeline, and specified outcomes and indicators. The responsibilities included acquiring program skills, consulting with the building principal, working collaboratively with classroom teachers, and providing professional development to IC Team members. These duties, unlike more traditional school roles, required that I structure my own day and time in order to achieve the program outcomes.

Acquisition of Skills

The acquisition of critical facilitator skills was the focus of the early implementation phases. These skills formed the foundation on which all other responsibilities were based. Skill development occurred in district-sponsored training sessions delivered by university staff. Each phase of skill development followed a similar sequence: (a) First didactic presentation, (b) then observation, (c) followed by practice with feedback, and then finally (d) being coached during application.

Although the official training program provided foundational skills, a strong peer support network of PWCS IC Team Facilitators was essential in expanding skills. The support group functioned more like a study group, allowing facilitators to problem solve together while continuing their own skill development. Problem solving occurred around real scenarios and exposed facilitators to situations that they might face in the future; the sessions helped to clarify misunderstandings, and created opportunities for constructive feedback. These discussions enhanced skills, techniques, and strategies learned during training sessions.

My own approach to learning required more than just participating in the district-sponsored training. I engaged in independent research and would often review literature that I researched independent the training, before or after training sessions. I found that the core training allowed me to find additional research that I could relate to specific cases where the consultants felt they needed more information or wanted to provide the teacher with a variety of strategies.

Building an Administrative Partnership

Since my principal was the instructional leader in the school, it was imperative that I establish an effective partnership with my administrator, one that was based on problem solving and a shared vision. Such a relationship was not usual for me and at first very uncomfortable. In nearly all school contexts, the principal is the evaluator of staff performance. Creating a partnership where the outcome was building level change at times required me to challenge the principal's beliefs. Initially, consultations with my principal were not always productive. I was still unsure of the knowledge and skills of IC Teams, and the principal was equally unsure how this process would look within the school. However, as trust built between the two of us, the consultation sessions became more productive allowing us to effectively solve problems as they arose.

Interestingly, the administrative partnership also offered the opportunity for me to provide additional support to my principal. As my principal was not able to attend all training sessions due to full schedules, the working relationship and administrative consultation helped fill the gaps by focusing on important information or skills. I found that I could also use this time to explore additional support options. For example, at times I offered to perform additional duties to secure time so that team members and teacher could consult. It was important to the implementation of the program to help foster conditions for the change to occur while at the same time maintaining the fidelity of the IC process and the facilitator's role.

Teacher Consultation

Initially, I was the only staff member trained in instructional consultation. As such, much of my time was used to model and demonstrate for staff, team members, and the principal how the new innovation would look and function. I recognized that I was setting the standard by which the entire process would be judged and that my own application of skills increased the likelihood of a positive reception from staff members.

Team Recruitment and Training

As facilitator, I was responsible for recruiting and training team members. I had to identify and recruit team members, informing them of the commitments being made (e.g., weekly team meetings). The main focus of early implementation was to ensure that team members received quality training in the IC Team core skills. Our university partner provided specific skill development on how to deliver training for team members and how to provide individual coaching, as well as offered additional support as needed.

Establishing the initial team, however, was not sufficient. It was critical to keep school personnel informed about IC Teams. Although full understanding of the IC Team process does not typically occur until most teachers use the process, it was important to keep the staff aware by providing presentations at staff meeting and publishing brief newsletters describing IC Team activities.

School Views of Institutionalization

Fulfilling the responsibilities of an IC Team facilitator was (and is) not a simple task, but one confronted with significant challenges. Changing the status quo is always a difficult chore since most people are comfortable with what they are doing and do not see a need to change. Compounding the problem of comfort is the difficulty of making the significant paradigm shift that is required in the implementation of IC Teams. The IC Team model requires individual professionals to shift their thinking from a deficit model of problem-solving to a social systems perspective of problem-solving, something that is hard considering years of habitual thinking and practice.

A major challenge confronting sustaining IC Teams is the embedding the concept of an IC Team facilitator. The role, not being clearly defined and not in the tradition of serving students directly, is open to multiple interpretations. As the idea of critically examining instructional practices can be threatening, I found that teachers frequently try to redefine my role into something with which they are comfortable—there have many times when others wanted my role to be a specialist to pull kids for remediation, an extra reading teacher, or even a substitute teacher.

I have also struggled to maintain administrative support for IC Teams. Owing to the time pressure and commitments placed on administrators (e.g., managing a budget, meetings with central office personnel, professional development, and parental issues), I often felt uncomfortable pushing for more attention to the needs of the IC Team project. At the most basic level, finding time for a 20-minute meeting one time a week with my principal was difficult. I was fortunate that my principal and I had worked together to build an open and trusting relationship that allowed us to have deep and meaningful conversations about teaching and learning within the school.

Still at other times, the IC Team facilitator role can be filled with loneliness and uncertainty. Unlike teachers who have many peers in a school, I had no one else within the building that had the same role and responsibility. The role of IC Team Facilitator filled a space between instructional staff and administrators. Not having the instructional responsibilities of teachers, the job at times appeared to others like an administrator role. However, I lacked the authority given to such a position. Lacking a peer group created a sense of loneliness and the uniqueness of the position in the school at times was unsettling.

Confronting these challenges required that I have a clear commitment to the IC Team process and the fortitude to handle conflicts constructively. There are multiple attributes that facilitators need to fulfill their duties. Most important of these are courage, self-initiative, and reflection. A courageous facilitator can confront obstacles even when faced with uncertainty. To fulfill required duties, IC Team facilitator must be able to assess their needs and organize their time efficiently and effectively. Reflection allows one to learn from situations and provides insights needed to plan for future activities.

Support Systems

Successful implementation of the IC Team process was not possible without significant support systems. The training offered by the university, the resources provided by the district, and the support given by my principal enabled the implementation and ultimate institutionalization of the IC Team process in my school. The university-sponsored coaching proved critical in my skill development and allowed a connection to other working facilitators. The coach encouraged risk-taking while at the same time ensuring that the facilitator followed the IC process.

In addition to intensive training, school division supports assisted in ensuring success. My colleague facilitators played a critical role in my skill development, and also provided emotional and moral support. Regular and planned meetings between facilitators created a larger sense of community. High levels of district support enhanced this sense of community and established the legitimacy of the IC facilitator role. Owing to the unusual stressors of the job, it was important to have a place of belonging in the district. Knowing that central office personnel legitimized the position and that a strong peer network existed created that sense of belonging.

The school-based teams were also important in creating successful conditions for the IC Team process. The team connected me to the school and established connections with grade levels that otherwise would not have formed. As my team developed, I observed my members as IC ambassadors creating additional connections within the school.

Necessary Conditions

As the IC Team process represented change on many different levels—Change in practice, skill, structure, and beliefs, after this experience I am more appreciative that change cannot be forced on individuals, and if forced will likely fail. With the support of the university and district, I have come to recognize that as change occurs it can impact others in ways that I did not anticipate. For example, as the IC Team process deepened in its implementation, teachers improved their own skills and gained confidence in their ability to help struggling students. This increase in teacher capacity often meant that they retained students that previously may have been sent to work with specialists (e.g., special educators, reading teachers, etc.). This shift in service provoked concerns by specialists, including sometimes the need to protect their domains. It made me realize that I had a role to play in supporting those individuals who might unintentionally be negatively affected by the change.

Supporting the change process and making it more accessible to teachers was the connection to the classroom and the curriculum. All assessments, strategies, and interventions grew out of the classroom environment, creating a direct connection between what students needed to know and the IC process. This not only empowered teachers and gave the process credibility, but also it created a sense of shared ownership for the instructional changes taking place. Rather than being told what to do, teachers were involved in the problem-solving process.

As the IC Team became more active, it legitimized my role as facilitator at the building level. Although a sense of ambiguity of the role still exists, it is clearer how facilitators should function and what duties we are required to fulfill.

■ Conclusion

Although we are still in the process of implementing the grant described in this chapter, the relationship between the University of Maryland and Prince William County Public Schools clearly illustrates the effectiveness of university and school system partnerships in facilitating change toward collaborative school structures. We have learned a lot in our years of work together, and have identified key elements essential for successful program implementation and institutionalization of a complex change process. There is no doubt that communication at all levels of the system is essential, as is the need to develop a common vision for program planning, implementation, and evaluation. We have seen firsthand how the change process impacts individual professionals, school building staff, and the district system itself—both positive and negative.

More important, we have seen that change is an active process; one that cannot be left alone, but instead must be guided and supported by all involved. We observed throughout the evolution of this university-district partnership a continued commitment to the work begun and a deep respect for each other's contributions. This commitment and respect has resulted in successful implementation, and with time, sustainability of the work started nearly five years ago.

■ References

Fullan, M. G. (1991). *The new meaning of educational change*. New York, Teachers College Press.

Fullan, M. G. (2001). *The new meaning of educational change* (3rd ed.). New York, Teachers College Press.

Gravois, T. A., & Gickling, E. E. (2008). Best practices in instructional assessment. In A. Thomas & J. Grimes (Eds.), *Best practices in school psychology V* (pp. 503–519). Bethesda, MD, National Association of School Psychologists.

Gravois, T. A., Knotek, S., & Babinski, L. (2001). Educating practitioners as instructional consultants: Development and implementation of the IC team consortium. *Journal of Educational and Psychological Consultation, 13*, 113–132.

Gravois, T. A., & Rosenfield, S. A. (2002). A multi-dimensional framework for evaluation of instructional consultation teams. *Journal of Applied School Psychology, 19*, 5–29.

Gravois, T. A., & Rosenfield, S. A. (2006). Impact of instructional consultation teams on the disproportionate referral and placement of minority students in special education. *Remedial and Special Education, 27,* 42–52.

Individuals with Disabilities Education Improvement Act of 2004, 20 U.S.C. § 1414.

No Child Left Behind Act of 2001, Pub. L. No. 107–110, 115 Stat. 1425 (2002).

Prasse, D. (2006). Legal supports for problem-solving systems [Electronic version]. *Remedial and Special Education, 27,* 7–15.

President's Commission on Excellence in Special Education (2002, July). *A new era: Revitalizing special education for children and their families.* Washington, DC: U.S. Department of Special Education and Rehabilitation Services.

Rosenfield, S., & Gravois, T. A. (1996). *Instructional consultation teams: Collaborating for change.* New York, The Guilford Press.

Rosenfield, S. A. (1987). *Instructional consultation.* Hillsdale, NJ, Lawrence Erlbaum Associates, Inc.

Rosenfield, S. A. (2008). Best practices in instructional consultation and instructional consultation teams. In A. Thomas & J. Grimes (Eds.), *Best practices in school psychology V* (pp. 1645–1661). Bethesda, MD, National Association of School Psychologists.

Supovitz, J. A., & Weinbaum E. H. (2008). *The implementation gap.* New York, Teachers College Press.

14. Who Can Speak for the Children? Innovations in Implementing Research-Based Practices in School Settings

Alnita Dunn and Douglas Miller

Public K-12 education in the United States has been criticized for failing to provide students with proficiency in basic academic skills (Murnane & Levy, 1996). Some progress in basic skills achievement has been made in the aftermath of legislation (Williams, Blank, Potts, & Toye, 2004). A solid foundation of evidenced-based research outlining interventions exists (see chapters on knowing the research literature in Step 1 in this book), yet there remains a gap between research and practice in field settings. In the vast majority of K-12 public schools, research-based methods of improving achievement in academics and behavior are not accomplishing goals predicted by the research. There have been situations where desired outcomes have been achieved; however, isolated success stories among schools and school districts (CASEL, 2003) have not generalized to affect significant change in public education across the United States, particularly in urban schools.

This chapter tells the story of how evidence-based literacy interventions were implemented in an urban school district serving diverse learners, many of whom lived in poverty or were not English speakers. The school psychologists (SPs) were leaders in the process, acting as intervention facilitators who executed a variety of tasks along the implementation continuum. The chapter begins with an overview of the chronology of activities. Next there is discussion of the practical realities of implementing supplementary interventions. Then, examples of how the SPs evaluated the effectiveness of the implementation of research into practice are given. The purpose was not to generate new research knowledge but rather to illustrate the importance of evaluating implementation of what worked in research to determine whether it also works for students and schools when implemented with adaptation for the school district's needs. Finally, ongoing implementations in progress and suggestions for future directions for schools to consider in implementing research into practice are discussed.

■ Process of District-Wide Translation of Research into Practice into Targeted Local Schools

The first step in the process was the realization that change was needed in how school psychology services are delivered. Concern over the growing percentage of students being placed in special education, along with the disproportionate placement of minority students, especially African Americans, led to examining the referral procedures used in the school district. The Psychological Services Department initiated steps to investigate the process as it is integrally involved in the referral and placement process. In 1999–2000 when the SPs began to search for a shift in their service delivery, special education services were often utilized as the chief method of intervening with struggling students and SPs were continually engaged in conducting initial assessments for special education services. In this district, the special education budget supports 40–90% of an SP's salary, another barrier to shifting activities. To break the referral–testing-placement cycle, the Psychological Services Department became actively involved in seeking ways to participate before referral for assessment was considered. As Walker and Shinn (2002) concluded, "School psychologists working within school and community contexts are ideally positioned to take a lead role in the systematic implementation of a multi-tiered model using evidenced-based interventions" (p. 21).

The next step was to choose which interventions and for whom. The skills necessary to achieve reading success were spelled out in the congressionally commissioned 2000 National Reading Panel's report (see Chapter 1 by McCardle and Miller in this book) as follows: (a) phonemic awareness, (b) phonics, (c) vocabulary, (d) fluency, and (e) text comprehension. In the reauthorization of the Elementary and Secondary Education Act (No Child Left Behind Act, 2001) these elements are referred to as "essential components of reading instruction" (p. 115, STATUTE 1550). Also, in the Individuals with Disabilities in Education Improvement Act (IDEIA, 2004), these elements are mentioned in the definition of specific learning disability as an exclusionary factor when "lack of appropriate instruction in reading including the essential components of reading" (p. 118, STATUTE 2706) is the contributing factor. Research is also showing the importance of orthographic awareness, handwriting, and written expression in early literacy (e.g., Berninger, Abbott, Brooksher, Lemos, Ogier, Zook, et al., 2000; Berninger, Vaughan, Abbott, Abbott, Brooks, Rogan et al., 1997) also see Chapter 2 by Hooper and colleagues in this book).

The earlier that reading problems are detected and interventions provided, the higher the probability that children will become effective readers (Kaplan & Walpole, 2005). Because these specific reading skills can be taught, it is recommended that screening and remediation for reading problems begin as early as kindergarten and first grade, with targeted instructional intervention in early literacy (Stanovich, 1993). Early writing instruction has also been shown to be beneficial and to transfer to improved reading (e.g., Berninger et al., 1997; Berninger, Rutberg, Abbott, Garcia, Anderson-Youngstrom, Brooks, et al., 2006). Thus, it was decided to focus on early intervention for reading and writing at schools with very high rates of failure to respond to beginning reading instruction.

Choosing evidence-based interventions for implementation. The Psychological Services department became interested in the research on early reading and writing conducted at the University of Washington (UW) in Seattle. The first author learned about it at a meeting of the national school psychology association where the principal investigator presented research findings supported by grants from the National Institute of Child Health and Human Development (NICHD). The findings of the studies had been translated into a set of lesson plans for teachers to implement as supplementary instruction for beginning reading, Lesson Set 1, and beginning writing, Lesson Set 3 (Berninger & Abbott, 2003).

The reading lessons contain instructional components for developing orthographic and phonological awareness, automatic spelling-phoneme correspondences in alphabetic principle, teacher-guided transfer to decoding single words, learning a self-regulated strategy for decoding during independent reading, repeated oral readings for fluency, and discussion to facilitate text comprehension. The writing lessons contain instructional components for explicit teaching of letter formation, automatic memory retrieval and production of letter forms, and transfer of handwriting to authentic composing about teacher-provided prompts and sharing one's writing with peers.

The first author invited the researcher to present the research to District SPs before the pilot implementation study and visited the University of Washington for consultation on implementation of the reading and writing interventions for the first implementation study. The researcher provided a two-day workshop at the district, which was videotaped to use in training SPs on implementation of the lessons just before the first implementation study began. Because the district is committed to evidence-based practices, at the outset the intention was to create an evaluation plan for empirical evaluation of the effectiveness of the implementation including the use of control groups. The university partners conducted the data analyses for the initial investigation, but the District has conducted analyses of effectiveness of subsequent implementations. Implementation is an ongoing process in this district as new research emerges and new implementations are considered and put into practice and evaluated for effectiveness.

TABLE 14.1   *Chronology of Activities*

School Year	Activity
Spring 1999	Discovered University of Washington (UW) evidence-based program
Nov 2001	Proposal for Pilot submitted
Spring 2002	Pilot: Using 1998 Guides for Intervention (Reading and Writing)
2002–2003	First Treatment vs. Control Group Study Process: Using research-based reading and writing lessons
	Committee meetings of special and general educators
	Investigation of other programs
2003–2004	Implementation and Training; Position paper developed
	Committee meetings of special and general educators
2004–2005	Implementation and Training
	Began including paraprofessionals in school teams
2005–2006	Implementation and Training school teams
2006–2007	Second Treatment vs. Control Group Study Process
2007–2008	Implementation and Training

Table 14.1 provides a detailed chronology of activities involved in the entire implementation process to provide the reader with an overview at a glance of the complexity of translation of research into practice. In the next section, the various challenges in applying research in the real world are discussed.

■ Realities of Initiating an Implementation of Research into Practice

Convincing school personnel that SPs might provide services other than assessment was, and is, a daunting task. One reason is that complying with special education legal mandates requires a significant amount of SPs' time, and changing that requires a genuine shift in thinking about how best to serve students who have barriers to learning and achievement. Changing perceptions regarding the service delivery of SPs has long been recognized as an important issue in professional practice (Benson & Hughes, 1985; Tilly, 2008; Ysseldyke, Dawson, Lehr, Reschly, Reynolds, & Telzro, 1997). Figure 14.1 depicts how the dynamic process of intentionally changing perceptions and attitudes of psychological services delivery was carried out in the District with involvement at many levels. The process is fluid, not hierarchial, and

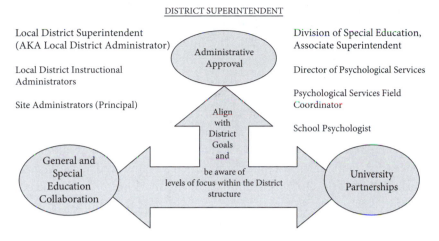

DISTRICT SUPERINTENDENT

Local District Superintendent
(AKA Local District Administrator)

Local District Instructional
Administrators

Site Administrators (Principal)

Administrative
Approval

Division of Special Education,
Associate Superintendent

Director of Psychological Services

Psychological Services Field
Coordinator

School Psychologist

Align
with
District
Goals
and

General and
Special
Education
Collaboration

be aware of
levels of focus within the District
structure

University
Partnerships

FIGURE 14.1 Precursors to Intentionally Change Attitudes of Service Delivery Models (Dunn, 2005).

subprocesses may occur simultaneously. Also the implementation plan has been modified over the years. Systems change does not occur easily or rapidly.

Administrative approval. Approval from an administrator is essential before initiating a project involving staff or students. The Director of Psychological Services (during that time period) supported the idea of SPs becoming directly involved in providing interventions, which made it possible for one of the eleven Field Services Coordinators of Psychological Services to develop the pilot proposal.

The Psychological Services Field Coordinator worked with the Psychological Services Coordinator (at the time the first author who in turn worked in Psychological Services administration) to develop and submit the pilot proposal to the Associate Superintendent of the Division of Special Education. At the same time, they also worked on obtaining approval for the pilot from school site administrators and site administrative teams. The pilot proposal was submitted to each of the 11 Local District Administrators within the larger district for deciding whether they would participate. The pilot proposal was grounded in the District's vision for improved student learning outcomes and its literacy goals related to state standards.

Approval for participation needed to be obtained from various layers of administration within special and general education almost concurrently. To illustrate, with approval of the Psychological Services Director, the Psychological Services Field Coordinator began making contacts to secure approval from school site administrators. Conversations were simultaneously carried out with the Local District Administrator's office regarding the participation of schools within the Local District. Specific contacts were made with curriculum and instruction administrators within the Local District administrative offices to ensure approval from this group who had oversight of implementing the core curriculum, *Open Court Reading* (OCR) (SRA/Open Court Reading, 2000, 2002). The Local District Administrator gave provisional approval based on obtaining cooperation and approval from the school site administrators. Finally, the pilot proposal was submitted to Local District Administrator (Local District Superintendent) and the Associate Superintendent of the Division of Special Education. Evidence of University collaboration was also a necessary component of the pilot proposal.

General and special education collaboration. The positive results for the Pilot led to a larger implementation study, which was approved by the Assistant Superintendent of the Division of Special Education. However, bridges needed to be built between the special education division and the administrative levels that govern instructional services and connect to the school site principal level. In summary, bridging the gap between special education and general education was (and remains) the major task (Dunn, 2002).

The committee was composed of a loosely formed group of central office and local district level representatives from general and special education that included SPs, teachers, and administrators. The purpose of this committee was to (a) develop a strategic understanding of prevention and early intervention; and (b) identify the factors needed to be present for an intervention program that could be successfully implemented in the District. The group met intermittently over the course of the 2002–2003 and 2003–2004 school year. Formally called meetings averaged approximately once per month during the first year and somewhat less during the second year. All during the two-year time period, the members were in constant communication (most members were housed in the same office building), including a trip to attend intervention training on another research-based intervention program (Witt, 2002). During the second year, early intervention and prevention were beginning to become conceptually entrenched among the Division of Special Education leadership.

The implementation of interventions depended on existing resources. Two essential criteria were that the interventions must be (a) easy to administer and (b) able to be implemented by a variety of trained professionals. During the first two years of implementation, SPs were the principal implementers. Later, implementation teams at participating school sites were expanded to include other members. In addition, the interventions had to be aligned with the District's core curriculum in literacy, *Open Court Reading* (OCR), which was being implemented at all elementary (K-5) schools across the District (with the exception of a very few schools that used *Success for All*). Considerable professional development aimed at obtaining widespread fidelity of (OCR) implementation was provided for teachers. Therefore, any new literacy approach, even supplemental interventions, had the potential of being viewed as a threat to fidelity of implementation of the core curriculum (*OCR*).

To allay concerns that the supplementary interventions might detract from the implementation of the core curriculum, meetings were held with central office administrators of instructional services to provide information about the program. Care was taken to communicate that the goal of the interventions was to provide assistance to students who had failed to make adequate progress in *OCR*, and that interventions would not supplant the curriculum in any way.

Universal Screening, another criterion considered by the group to be essential, was operationally defined as follows: (a) using periodic assessment data from the core curriculum to identify students who needed assistance, (b) utilizing embedded assessment tools found within the intervention program, and (c) administering other assessment tools that may be effective for screening. Finally, the group felt that an effective program should include (a) embedded progress monitoring tools and (b) interventions for both reading and writing including the essential components of reading: phonemic awareness, phonics, vocabulary, text comprehension, and fluency (NCLB, 2001).

Conducting a pilot implementation. The Psychological Field Services Coordinator initiated the implementation of the pilot by the selection of participating schools based on volunteers. Only SPs who volunteered knowing that their work load would increase, and only local school administrative teams who were enthusiastic at the prospect of utilizing their SPs in nontraditional ways, were invited to become part of the pilot. A summary of the demographic profile of the schools that participated in the pilot has been shown in Table 14.2. The pilot consisted of six schools, with one participating teacher and SP at each site. Although subsequent implementations have involved many more schools, these data illustrate the diversity within the student population of the district.

Teachers and classrooms were selected based on the cooperation level of the teachers. The participating SPs were already working at the school as part of their normal assignment; so the teachers knew them and were accustomed to collaborating with them about students. With these prior relationships already established, the SPs were perceived as offering more services and providing more assistance. Trusting interpersonal relationships are essential in bringing about system-level change (Curtis, Castillo, & Cohen, 2008). In the pilot, the interventions were carried out by the teachers and the SPs, who crafted materials for the research-based interventions outlined in *Guides for Intervention in Reading and Writing* (Berninger, 1998) and consulted with the teachers on how they should be conducted within the parameters of the research-based procedures.

SPs administered subtests to assess phonological and orthographic awareness, vocabulary, comprehension, and fluency to kindergarten students. They consulted with teachers on how to use the interventions with students identified as needing assistance, based in part on their test performance.

TABLE 14.2   *Racial, Ethnic, and English Learner Percentages in Pilot Schools 2002–2003*

	American Indian/ Alaskan Native	Asian	Filipino	Pacific Islander	African American	Hispanic	White	English Learners (EL)/Total
School S	0.3	3.8	2.2	0.3	11.8	72.5	9.1	*43.7
School A	0.6	4.4	0.4	0.0	1.2	92.5	1.0	471/1,126 = 42
School. A	0.1	2.5	3.5	0.0	0.6	92.3	1.1	1,444/1,871 = 77
School G	0.0	3.5	1.0	0.0	1.3	93.2	1.0	180/310 = 58
School N	0.0	0.1	0.5	0.0	1.0	98.3	0.1	1,463/1,690 = 86
School La	0.0	12.9	5.3	0.3	4.1	76.1	1.3	236/318 = 74
School L	0.1	7.5	2.1	0.1	0.8	89.1	0.4	1,034/1,263 = 82

*Total student population, 746,784; Total number of English Learners, 326,827.

Most of the SPs who participated in the pilot were former teachers for whom consulting with teachers on literacy interventions did not represent a steep learning curve. Even the SPs who were not former teachers demonstrated competencies in these consultation responsibilities.

The SPs benefited from the pilot by gaining first-hand knowledge of the instructional components of the learning environment for teaching students who are poor readers. Almost every time period of the instructional day in this district is scheduled to teach topics that fulfill required state content area standards, such as English Language Arts (California Department of Education, 1997), which makes finding time for supplemental instruction difficult. The structure of the learning environment was not always amenable for teachers to (a) learn different instructional strategies during the time when they were consumed with learning how to implement the core curriculum, and (b) implement the supplementary interventions in addition to keeping the pace dictated by the core curriculum. Feedback from the SPs indicated that the teachers were grateful for the strategies, and welcomed the psychologists into their classrooms. Negative reports regarding the interpersonal aspect of the consultation experiences were not reported. However, for the SPs the combined professional responsibilities of implementing interventions (i.e., acting as implementation specialists, class-wide screenings, developing materials for the lessons, teacher consultation on the lessons, and follow-up) and carrying out their day-to-day special education compliance requirements were overwhelming, inordinately time consuming, and requiring more than could be accomplished during the work day. The day-to-day SP duties invol-ved conducting counseling sessions, initial and triennial evaluations, crisis management, parent and teacher consultation, and other tasks associated with the service delivery of a SP. Frequently, the SPs involved with the pilot took work home to complete. Yet the experience left the SPs confident that they possessed the skills necessary to become intervention specialists to change the educational trajectories of children.

Follow-up feedback reports from teachers were mixed. In some cases, teachers had not utilized the lessons due to the time constraints within their classroom schedules. When strategies were used, teachers voiced satisfaction with positive student outcomes. The teacher responses were for the most part comments on their observations of students or citations of student performance on OCR unit tests. SP consultation was judged effective based on teacher receptivity and on anecdotal teacher reports of student outcomes when the strategies were used.

These preliminary analyses of the effectiveness of the pilot led to the conclusion that the implementation and the data to analyze its effectiveness needed further work. During the pilot, the SP implementers brainstormed how to overcome the time challenges. It was decided that interventions should be scheduled where there was an opening outside of the core curriculum schedule. Lessons from the pilot indicated that the following modifications were needed: (a) clearly define measurable reading achievement outcomes, (b) develop a more concise screening approach, and (c) create a training package (aimed at SPs) to explain screening, developmental literacy, intervention implementation, and to reduce concerns regarding the interventions' impact on the core curriculum. Moreover, the decision was made to implement the supplementary intervention in first grade with lesson plans for reading and writing that were based on large-scale, randomized, controlled instructional studies (Berninger & Abbott, 2003).

■ Evaluation of Effectiveness of Implementation

Evaluation of first implementation study. The reading outcomes of students who received the supplementary research-based lessons along with interventions embedded in *OCR* were compared to those of students who only received the interventions embedded in *OCR* or the *Success for All* curriculum implemented in a few district schools. This evaluation of the first large-scale implementation addressed the following questions: Will students who receive the supplementary research-based interventions show significantly higher reading achievement outcomes than students who do not receive the interventions? Does it matter if reading intervention is presented first and then writing intervention or if both reading and writing are taught concurrently?

The SPs were instructed that their schools would be considered for participation in the study only if administrative teams fully understood and were agreeable to the interventions and classrooms would be selected on the basis of the teachers' understanding and cooperation. Paraprofessionals were not used in this implementation. SPs would act as the intervention coordinators who either implemented the interventions individually, jointly with teachers, or collaborated with teachers who themselves were the implementers. The schools that were eventually selected based on the voluntary nature of the criteria were among the low performers in achievement in the district and were located in some of the most impacted socioeconomic areas. Their student populations consisted of a majority of culturally and linguistically diverse (CLD) students, which is the student population of the District.

Lesson Set 1 (beginning reading) and Lesson Set 3 (beginning writing) were used with first grade students in the treatment group. Each lesson set contained 24 lessons for reading or writing. Each lesson set contained background and general guidelines so the implementer knows the why well as what and how for implementation: (a) Unique features of the instructional approach in the lesson set and (b) a schema for each lesson set. The schema sets out the target skill, materials, and estimated time of each lesson at the subword, word, and text level. Background information also includes guidelines for how to (a) conduct progress monitoring, (b) develop or obtain other needed materials, and (c) the relevance of other research-based developmental literacy information foundational to the lessons. The SPs were given the materials implementing Lesson Set 1-reading and Lesson Set 3-writing (Berninger & Abbott, 2003): Talking Letters Student Desk Guides (phoneme sound cards), Handwriting Lessons, and Guides for Intervention (Berninger, 1998). The following materials were created and made available to the implementers (SPs and teachers) in electronic form: (a) label files with color-coded vowels in words from vocabulary word lists for creating flashcards, (b) alternative individual graphs for students to keep track of their own progress, and (c) protocol sheets of the words taught for progress monitoring in decoding. The protocol sheets were developed by the Psychological Services department. The new format significantly decreased the time needed for SPs to prepare lesson materials.

The university research partner consulted on developing the screening and progress monitoring battery (Dunn, 2002). The battery consisted of Real Word Reading and Pseudoword Decoding subtests on the Wechsler Individual Achievement Test, second edition (WIAT-II; The Psychological Corporation, 2001) and an orthographic coding subtest (Berninger, 2001) (Table 14.3).

SPs who volunteered for the study were provided an introductory training that covered assessment and instruction procedures. One of the trainings contained an overview of the OCR core curriculum. For the teachers, the lessons aligned easily with the way the alphabetic principle was taught in OCR, although there were some minor differences in the OCR sound cards and the Talking Letters Student Desk Guides (phoneme cards). The trainings were interactive including many opportunities for the attendees to participate. SPs were given a clear picture of their potential time and effort commitment and guidance for answering questions posed by school site administrators.

TABLE 14.3 *Means and Standard Deviations for Treatment and Control Groups for ANOVA with Schools as Unit of Analysis on WIAT II Real Word Reading (Reanalysis by R. Abbott, 2005, of data in Berninger et al., 2004, for individuals)*

	Pretest		Post-test	
	M	SD	M	SD
Control (*Open Court* only)	79.93	11.33	81.40	8.88
Treatment (PAL Supplementary + *Open Court*)	81.40	8.80	83.98	15.29

At three introductory meetings held in August 2002 at the beginning of the Fall 2002 semester 49 SPs attended. Three meetings were held in September and three were held in October. By the end of October the number of SPs had decreased to 38.

During the early winter of 2003, SPs screened whole first-grade classes to identify those children falling below the 25th percentile in WIAT II Real Word Reading and/or Pseudoword Decoding. Screened students who fell below this criterion were randomly assigned within the same school to the treatment group or a control group. Across schools, each treatment group was further assigned to *sequential instruction* in which the set of reading and set of writing lessons were taught sequentially or *combined* (each lesson consisted of part of the reading lesson set and part of the writing lesson set) *instruction*. Both treatment groups completed all lessons or lesson parts in Lesson Set 1 (reading) and Lesson Set 3 (writing) (Berninger & Abbott, 2003).

The intervention lessons did not encroach upon the regular reading instruction time. The *OCR* program has independent work time ("workshop time") during the regular instruction period. During this workshop time, the control group did the regular program independent work and the treatment group received supplementary reading and writing instruction; so both treatment and control groups had had the same amount of time for their regular reading instruction and the additional instruction (more intense practice with the regular program or supplementary instruction with additional reading and writing components). The treatment groups met, on average, three or four times a week for 30 or 45 minutes, depending on the school schedule during winter and spring.

The lessons were organized by instruction at the subword, word, and text levels. Implementers were encouraged to self-monitor that they were correctly following the instructions for implementation at each of these levels. However, fidelity of treatment was not assessed in a formal way.

SPs were not able to evaluate students' response to interventions in reference to a control group in five schools because general education teachers wanted to use the treatment lessons with the entire class when they saw the treatment group students responding better to core curriculum. Their data were not included in the analyses. The decision to allow this variation was based on the reality of school implementation and professional collaborations.

Ten schools completed all pretesting and all post-testing for both treatment and control groups. The total number of students participating in both the treatment and control groups was 88. Of these, 44 were girls, 43 were boys, and 1 of was of undesignated gender. With regard to ethnicity, 62 were Hispanics, 14 were African Americans, and 12 were of other or unknown ethnicity. In the control group, 21 were girls and 20 were boys. Of those, 35 were Hispanics, 5 were African Americans, and ethnicity was not reported for 1. In the treatment group, 23 were girls and 23 were boys, and gender of one student was not reported. Of these, 37 were Hispanic, 9 were African American, and ethnicity was not reported for 1. Of the treatment group, 25 received *sequential instruction* and 22 received *combined instruction.*

Previously published research (Berninger, Dunn, Lin, & Shimada, 2004) showed that the treatment group improved significantly more in reading real words and orthographic coding of written words than did the control group; both groups improved significantly in phonological decoding of pseudowords. Sequential and combined reading and writing treatment resulted in comparable improvement. Both *OCR* core curriculum and the implemented reading and writing lessons emphasize phonemic awareness, probably explaining why both control and treatment group improved in phonological decoding. However, the implemented lessons also emphasize orthographic awareness and writing, which is why they may have been relatively more effective in improving real word reading.

The initial analyses were concerned with whether individual students improved and thus used individual students as the unit of analysis to compare with other results based on curriculum-based probes and teaching probes for individual students. However, for purposes of program evaluation for reaching decisions about implementation for local schools, schools are the more appropriate unit of analysis. Such an analysis with schools as unit of analysis was subsequently performed by Robert A. Abbott, statistician on the University of Washington NICHD-literacy research projects. ANOVA with treatment and control children nested within 10 schools and schools treated as a random effect showed that children in the treatment group improved significantly more in real word reading than did those in the control group, $F(1, 9) = 5.57, p < 0.05$, thus replicating the results without taking school effects into account, but for a two-tail rather than one-tail test.

Some positive qualitative outcomes of the first implementation study were observed: (a) a change in perceptions of the role of the SP, (b) increased collaboration between general and special education, (c) consideration of other academic alternatives before referring students for special education services, and (d) an increase of enthusiasm for reading among students themselves who had been considered at risk for failure. This qualitative information came from informal discussions with SPs and teachers participating in the study and other meetings. One teacher reported that she initially had reservations that supplementary interventions would make any difference with the lowest readers in her classroom, but she was happy to report that some of her lowest readers were now some of her best, and that they could frequently be found on the rug in the library corner of the classroom.

Some challenges in implementation were observed. First, the data organization process was initially monumental until retired SPs, who supervised another retired SP, assisted with data organization; both were hired as substitutes. The data organization process required numerous meetings and daily telephone calls for SPs to submit their data. Second, a major difficulty resulted when the students began to show improvement and teachers wanted to start using the supplementary interventions immediately. Evaluating and teaching have different goals (see Chapter 19 by White in this book). The natural inclination of the teachers was to want to provide the supplementary interventions for all of their students. It would have been a public relations disaster for the Psychological Services Department if the SPs appeared uncooperative in providing the interventions for some but not all the students, even though the parameters of the study were known by all. Third, new ways to target resources were considered as an outgrowth of the study. Even with the teacher-friendly packaging of the lessons, the implementation of the interventions represented an additional amount of time to an already fully committed day in the life of an SP.

Implementation issues remain. The generalizability of the effectiveness of the implementation to other areas of the school district still needs to be explored further. It would be helpful to have a measure of the teachers'/implementers' confidence in their skills for teaching the lessons. Selecting schools based on willingness of SPs and administrative teams to incorporate supplementary intervention limits generalizability to schools with support for the implementation.

■ Subsequent Developments and Future Directions

Discussions of how SPs might expand their role to include the functions of early intervention and prevention services are ongoing (Roberts, Marshall, Nelson, & Albers, 2001). The goal is to create a match between the instructional needs of the child and the standards-based curriculum. The first implementation study led participating SPs to see themselves as part of a process that transforms perspectives, one in which the power and the possibility of creating educational opportunities for all children was embedded. Since then other implementations have been considered, implemented, and evaluated. The following overview shows that implementing research into educational practice and evaluating its effectiveness is an ongoing process, which continues without university involvement in data analysis or training.

Events during 2005–2006

What impact did the study have on implementing interventions with struggling readers in other District schools? The administrative support of the intervention program from the upper levels of the central office continued. During the fall of 2005, Psychological Services Department staff conducted trainings in the reading and writing interventions (Berninger & Abbott, 2003) for more than 90 school teams across the District, resulting in the training of more than 500 educators. These trainings represented a small component of the District's training effort to meet the requirements of Program Improvement (PI). All schools and local educational agencies (LEAs) that do not make Adequate Yearly Progress (AYP) are identified for PI under the No Child Left Behind (NCLB) Act of 2001 (NCLB, 2001). Many of the teams that participated in training represented schools that were in PI or were in danger of becoming PI. Their attendance was mandatory, which resulted in a different atmosphere than was present in the earlier voluntary trainings. The participants' feedback revealed varying levels of enthusiasm and desire to be trained. To meet the challenges of less than enthusiastic participants, the following modifications were utilized in conducting the trainings: more interactive activities, more prizes, coffee and refreshments in the morning, no cost lunch, and free parking. This set of trainings ran from August 2005 through December 2005, and the voluntary trainings resumed in January 2006.

The trainings, which continued to be organized by the Psychological Services Department, were focused on assisting struggling readers in first grade. The content of the six-hour trainings contained the same elements as described for the earlier trainings on the Reading and Writing Lesson Sets. However, participation was expanded to include a team from the school instead the SP only. School administrators were advised that team composition should include the (a) SP, (b) administrator(s), (c) general education teacher(s), (d) special education teacher(s), and (e) paraprofessionals. The team members who would be the implementers comprised most of the persons sent by the schools to be trained.

The reason for expanding training to include more than the SP involves the concept of forming lines of communication to promote wider cooperation for (a) expanding new programs and ideas, (b) evaluating school needs, and (c) charting implementation (Mayer & Ybarra, 2003). The August–December 2005 trainings also revealed that participants were more inclined to begin using the interventions immediately if all components of the lesson sets and instructional materials were provided at the time of the training. Anecdotal feedback during and after the trainings and follow-up telephone calls to schools after the trainings were helpful in developing strategies to maintain participant engagement.

Concurrently, during that year, comparisons were made between a group of students who were receiving the embedded core curriculum interventions plus the reading and writing interventions and a group of students who were only receiving interventions embedded in the core curriculum. Student learning outcomes were again measured using the WIAT II Pseudoword Decoding and Real Word Reading. The performance of both groups on the periodic *OCR* assessments was also followed. That is, both norm-referenced and curriculum-based assessment, which was linked to the actual curriculum (see Chapter 21 by Peverly in this book), were used to assess response to intervention. Preliminary evidence, gathered as part of a report submitted to the Associate Superintendent of The Division of Special Education, have not yet been statistically analyzed, but inspection of them shows that the group that received the reading and writing interventions improved in both Pseudoword and Real Word Reading. Also, the periodic *OCR* fluency assessments were also higher when compared with the group that did not receive the interventions (Dunn, 2007). These preliminary results show the effectiveness of SPs in working with the school team to implement early interventions.

Trainings of Paraprofessionals

During the trainings in 2005–2006, it was recommended that paraprofessionals also be trained as implementers. Paraprofessionals consisted of four, five, and six hour employed school aides. Some of them were students on a career ladder to becoming teachers in teacher training programs, and none were student teachers. As mentioned earlier, most classroom teachers had little time to devote to learning another research-based approach, as they were continuing to acquire skills in implementing OCR with fidelity. As the trainings progressed, more paraeducators were trained and administrators and teachers continued to have positive responses regarding students' reading progress. The paraprofessionals were responsive to the training content and enthusiastically embraced their roles as implementers in the literacy interventions.

The trainings provided an opportunity for the school teams to brainstorm and discuss a variety of options for the implementation of supplementary intervention: (a) Pull-out programs, (b) after-school programs, and (c) independent work time in the regular class. Each school developed a model that matched its particular school culture and learning environment. One of the goals of the training was to show how the interventions could be implemented utilizing existing structures and school culture.

After the trainings, in most situations, the SPs initiated the intervention program at their schools by conducting one or more small groups of five at-risk students. Their roles later expanded to coordinating implementation, conducting progress monitoring, and providing guidance to the paraprofessionals on fidelity of implementation. The model used during the 2006–2007 data gathering will be described in the next section.

Second Implementation Study: 2006–2007

The success of the interventions was incorporated into a proposal (Dunn, 2007) that resulted in supporting a more formalized data gathering process. For this evaluation, one treatment and one control school were selected. Both the treatment and the control school consisted of culturally and linguistically

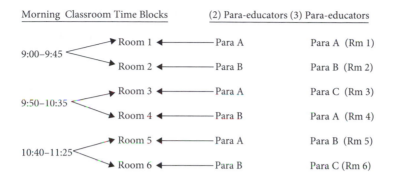

Morning Classroom Time Blocks   (2) Para-educators (3) Para-educators

FIGURE 14.2 Paraeducators Scheduling Model for Implementing Interventions.

diverse students (CLD). The treatment school was selected based on a history of enthusiastic implementation of the reading and writing interventions. The administrative leadership at the treatment school developed intentional intervention schedules that facilitated using a cadre of trained paraprofessionals. Figure 14.2 is an example of how paraeducators were scheduled for classroom interventions.

The paraprofessionals were supervised by the SP and an Intervention Coordinator, with the Intervention Coordinator developing the scheduling matrix and both the Intervention Coordinator and SP monitoring for paraprofessional attendance. During the implementation time block, there was one treatment group per classroom and each treatment group (paraprofessional and five students) was seated around a kidney-shaped table in the classroom. Sometimes, the adult worked individually with a child within the group. The rest of the class was engaged in independent work in centers, working in pairs or triads, and perhaps supervised by another roving adult. The model was flexible and can be adapted to more or fewer classrooms and paraeducators. The 45-minute block included time for the students to get seated and arrange their materials. The schedule made it possible for them to provide interventions by efficiently using the time already set aside in the morning class period for students who were not meeting target benchmarks in the OCR program, called "independent work time" or "bank time" as has been described earlier.

The demographic profiles of the treatment and control schools are found in Tables 14.4–14.6. The treatment group consisted of 117 first grade students, and 26 students from a neighboring school were in the control group. The treatment school, which had a population of 992 (54% EL), was on a year-round schedule with four tracks, and the control school with a student population of 1,086 (56% EL) was on a traditional single track calendar. These tables report other critical factors by which schools are evaluated: suspensions, expulsion referrals, percent of reclassified students, number of certificated

TABLE 14.4   *Racial Ethnic Totals in Treatment and Control Schools*

	American Indian/ Alaskan Native	Asian	Filipino	Pacific Islander	African American	Hispanic	White	Student Body Total
T	5	32	28	0	74	671	182	992
Cl	5	7	166	0	20	881	7	1,086

teachers, Title 1 school, attendance rate, and staff stability, as measured by the number of staff who have been at the school for more than 11 years. The schools appear to be fairly evenly matched, with the control school possibly having scant more factors that indicate higher achievement. For example, their reclassification percentage is somewhat higher, 22% as opposed to 15%. The reclassification process is highly impacted by achievement, and not merely facility in learning English. Both schools are Title 1 schools indicating a similarity of student/family factors that indicate the need for federal assistance. Also, at both schools more than half of the teachers have been at the school for 11 or more years.

Student performance on the *OCR* unit fluency tests formed the basis for selecting at-risk students for intervention. The *OCR* performance range consists of Intensive, Strategic, and Benchmark. Benchmark indicates that the student is performing at or above reading standards. Students who are Strategic have not yet achieved expected reading achievement standards. Intensive students are the lowest performers. The unit tests may at various times include Word Reading, Spelling, Writing, and Reading Comprehension, but always include Fluency as the constant indicator of achievement. In the first stage of the selection process teachers and literacy coaches provided input regarding students needing interventions, even if their scores were not in the Intensive range. Parent-referral information was also part of the first stage of the selection process. The pool of students was pretested with the Pseudoword Decoding and Real Word Reading subtests of the WIAT II. Students who scored below the 90 standard score level were placed in the treatment group. In some cases, students who scored above this level also received the interventions based on teacher observations of in-class performance.

No more than five students were assigned to each reading and writing intervention group. Intervention periods were scheduled for 45 minutes during the morning class period. Reading interventions conducted one day were followed by writing interventions the next day, four days each week. Post-testing was done at the end of the year. Likewise, the control group was pretested and post-tested on the WIAT II Pseudoword Decoding and Real Word Reading but only received the interventions embedded within the OCR curriculum.

TABLE 14.5 *English Learner Totals in Treatment and Control Schools*

	Armenian	Cantonese	Korean	Farsi	Filipino	Russian	Spanish	Vietnamese	Other	EL Total
T	93	0	0	1	14	5	406	0	19	538
C	0	0	2	0	70	0	533	0	5	610

Percentage of EL in student population per school: Treatment – 54%; Control – 56%

TABLE 14.6 *Critical School Characteristics in Treatment and Control Schools*

	Suspensions Average No. of Days	Expulsion Referrals	Attendance Rate	Title 1	Reclassified Students	Certificated Teachers	Staff Stability: 11 and + Years
T	1.21	0	95.41	Yes	15.02	51	27
C	1.36	0	95.9	Yes	22.03	57	33

In the initial evaluation of the second implementation, focus was on changes over time in students within the group rather than comparison between groups as had been the focus of the first implementation study. *T*-tests evaluated significant differences between paired pretest and post-test means of Pseudoword and Real Word Reading within each group—treatment and control. Within the Treatment group, significant differences occurred over time between the pretest and post-test means on Pseudoword Decoding and Real Word Reading. Within the Control group, significant differences did not occur between pretest and post-test means on Pseudoword Decoding but did between pretest and post-test means on Real Word Reading (see Table 14.7). Thus, this evaluation of an implementation resulted in gain in both real and pseudoword reading, as in the first implementation study, for the treatment group, as had been found in the first implementation study. In contrast to the first implementation study, the control group improved significantly in real word reading but not pseudoword reading.

Anecdotal reports from SPs, paraeducators, teachers, and other school site personnel indicated increased enthusiasm for reading among at-risk students. Indeed, numerous stories of students learning to read were regularly shared. One limitation of this second implementation was the lack of randomization, which may have lent more credibility when interpreting comparisons between treatment and control groups.

How do school administrators view statistical data that document achievement? The administrators, who are the instructional leaders at the schools, were interested in data that intersected with their accountability

TABLE 14.7 *T-Tests on Paired Differences between Treatment and Controls Pseudoword and Real Word Reading*

	Pretest		Post-test		t	df	Sig (two-tailed)
	M	SD	M	SD			
Treatment Group							
Pseudoword Reading	90.20	7.055	106.45	11.071	−14.469	116	0.000
Real Word Reading	94.02	9.242	102.82	11.716	−7.515	116	0.000
Control Group							
Pseudoword Reading	95.8	8.947	97.3	7.797	−0.23	25	0.539
Real Word Reading	87.7	10.129	98.3	9.457	−4.142	25	0.000

under the No Child Left Behind legislation. Although norm-referenced standardized results may be persuasive to researchers, public school administrative and teaching staffs are frequently more impressed if those data are a component of their state-required testing data systems, and if the measures are attached to the progress of their classrooms, schools, and districts. Therefore, trainings with school teams on the reading and writing interventions always included students' performance data in the core curriculum unit tests and on the state's standards mastery tests.

After the 2002–2003 implementation, the group of students who had received the interventions were monitored on their performance on OCR unit tests. These data are meaningful to school site administrators and to the Associate Superintendent. In presentations then and now, when OCR unit test data or California Standards Tests (CSTs) data are presented, the attention of the audience becomes quite keenly focused because those are the data that are attached to their daily accountabilities.

CSTs are criterion-referenced tests required as part of the 2001 No Child Left Behind legislation. These tests were developed specifically to assess students' knowledge of the California content standards in a variety of academic areas in elementary through senior high grade levels (STAR, 2004). California uses five performance levels to report student achievement in the CSTs:

1. *Advanced* performance in relation to the content standards tested,
2. *Proficient* performance in relation to the content standards tested,
3. *Basic* performance in relation to the content standards tested,
4. *Below Basic* performance in relation to the content standards tested, and
5. *Far Below Basic* performance in relation to the content standards tested.

When this chapter was written, spring 2007 CST data for the students evaluated during the 2006–2007 school year were not available Yet, results from 2005–2006 that tracked the performance of students who received the reading and writing interventions are encouraging.

How did students who received the reading and writing interventions perform in English Language Arts on the CSTs? A group of second-grade students who had received the reading and writing interventions during the 2005–2006 school year (when they were in first grade) was compared with a group of their second-grade peers who had not receive the interventions (see Figure 14.3). The students were selected based on achieving at or below the 20th percentile on the California Achievement Tests, Sixth Edition Survey (CAT/6 Survey) (STAR, 2004) in 2005–2006. Eighty percent (eight out of ten) of the students who received the reading and writing interventions earned scores in the category of Basic and Above Basic, as compared with 10% (four out of thirty-seven) in the core curriculum only interventions group. The students' performance on the CSTs support effectiveness of the reading and

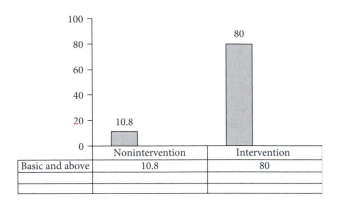

FIGURE 14.3 California Standards Test 2002–2006, Percent Scoring at Basic and Above Basic Comparison of Intervention and Nonintervention Groups, Unpublished Data. Presentation to Psychological Services Administrators (2007).

writing interventions in assisting students in their mastery of the content standards in English Language Arts. Major limitations of the above comparisons are the small sample sizes in the two groups, 10 in the group receiving the interventions and 37 in the group not receiving them, and the sample disparities. Now that more students are receiving the interventions larger sample sizes are becoming available.

An unexpected positive outcome of the trainings and implementation approaches was the effectiveness of using paraeducators as implementers. They were receptive learners and exhibited an eager willingness to implement the reading and writing interventions with fidelity. On one occasion when the first author visited one of the intervention classrooms, the paraeducator's manner and engagement of the students was such that she was mistaken for the teacher. Future investigations should measure treatment fidelity and paraeducator confidence in their ability to implement the interventions.

Bridging Gaps among General,
Special Education, and School Psychology

> Each school psychologist naturally possesses a sphere of influence,
> which includes individuals at the school level, multiple schools,
> multiple departments, and district-wide. (Johns et al., 2004, p. 723)

The need to communicate and build bridges between general and special education continues to exist, and school psychology professionals can represent the vehicle for closing this communication gap As mentioned by Johns and colleagues (2004) and Harvey & Struzziero (2000), SPs naturally interact with multiple tiers of educators. In addition, the nature of their service delivery also includes parents and community partners. Current assessment of the implementations of supplemental, research-based interventions is that (a) the supplementary interventions represent value added to students who are not making progress in the core curriculum, (b) the interventions must not in any way be implemented to detract from the emphasis of the core curriculum, and (c) students should not be pulled from the core curriculum reading period for supplementary intervention lessons. Further, trainings on the reading and writing interventions specified that core curriculum is a component of all tiers in the Three-Tier model (see Figure 14.4, adapted from the position paper, LAUSD, 2004). Literature supports that students not making expected progress in a research-based core curriculum who continue to receive the research-based core curriculum in addition to an evidence-based supplementary intervention program make significant progress in reading (Reading First, 2000). A study to determine how the interventions have affected special education referrals is currently underway. Preliminary evidence suggests that special education referrals have decreased.

The voluntary aspect of implementer/school site selection resulted in heightened enthusiasm that good outcomes were going to happen for students. It appeared that these willing SPs, cooperative school principals, and agreeable classroom teachers seemed to have an expectation that their students would experience success. The SPs served as a filter to ensure that the level of cooperation was present at a given school site, thereby raising the probability that implementation of the interventions would be received in a positive environment.

The SPs provided frequent follow-up to the classroom teachers and collaborated with them on student progress. In instances where the SPs were the implementers, they shared student progress in specific areas (e.g., segmenting,

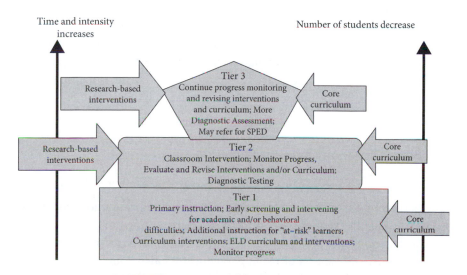

FIGURE 14.4 LAUSD Three-Tier Model for Prevention and Early Intervention.

blending, fluency, etc.) and relayed the strategies that were successful and approaches that were reinforcing with the student when teaching specific tasks. In situations where the teachers were the implementers, the SPs acted as a resource on how to implement the interventions. The SP-teacher connection extended beyond the study, with collaborations occurring on issues regarding other students not in the study. For SPs to intervene effectively with teachers some knowledge in developmental literacy was required. Without the SPs' diligence, professionalism, and dedication to data-based decision-making the study would not have been possible.

Ongoing Consideration of Research-Supported Interventions

During the time that the first investigation was being conducted, a committee was pulled together as much to communicate and gain consensus of what was occurring as to explore other potential programs for the District to investigate. The committee that was formed early in the process as we explored intervention programs considered research literature, political realities within the District, and information learned from investigating other programs. From the outset, it was known that any intervention plan must be aligned with the District's goals and vision. The Psychological Services Department organized for the committee a videoconference, which presented an evidence-based intervention program (Witt, 2003; Witt & Naquin, 2003) that resulted in a demonstration project conducted in an elementary school (Witt, 2002, 2003; Witt, Vanderheyden, & Neddenriep, 2004). Another activity involved meetings and consultation with the principal investigators of an intervention program already being implemented at some schools in the district (Haager & Windmueller, 2001). Both the demonstration project and the intervention program were based on published peer-reviewed research, and considered with regard to how intervening services should look in the District. Thus, the criteria in Figure 14.5 represent a committee consensus for an operational schema of effective early intervening services in the District. School personnel have continued to explore a variety of programs and to develop criteria for evaluating programs for future implementation (see Figure 14.5).

■ Future Directions in Implementation

Implications of the LAUSD implementation of the evidence-based intervention that may be useful to other school districts designing and evaluating research-based interventions are summarized here.

Use of paraprofessionals in implementing evidence-based interventions. First, the beneficial aspects of using paraeducators also contribute an overall burden to training needs. The inherent transience of the paraprofessional

- Uses research-based interventions
- Utilizes class-wide screening
- Easy to administer
- Addresses reading and writing
- Acknowledges student differences
- Looks at processes connected to achievement
- Targets weak areas
- Can be implemented by a variety of trained professionals
- Utilizes effective progress monitoring tools
- Aligns with content standards and core curriculum

FIGURE 14.5 Criteria for the Selection of Intervention Programs (adapted from Witt, 2001).

population at school sites requires continual training of new personnel. Currently, we are meeting the need for continual training by conducting bimonthly trainings of school teams.

Frequent changes in administrators. Similarly, the movement of administrative leadership through reassignments at school sites may result in different goals that do not include the reading and writing interventions program. Therefore, monitoring of the schools where the interventions are being conducted is necessary so that timely communications of the success of the interventions can be provided to new administrators. Administrative changes at a school where the reading and writing interventions were being effectively implemented have resulted in the interventions being discontinued or revamped (in spite of clear data which showed that the interventions were positively affecting the learning trajectories of students).

The literature on sustainability of effective interventions suggest that this issue needs to be addressed on an ongoing basis. How might schools mitigate issues related to administrator reassignment and the consequences that may incur? The changes in administrators, the numerous reasons for such changes, and their effects on successful intervention programs are relentless components of the educational landscape. Persistent education and communication are needed. We found that each connection, conversation, and training helped to prepare an environment that would be accepting of changing the way school personnel viewed the engagement between students and curriculum (which is the larger issue).

Planting seeds. Each success planted a seed for a future positive outcome, if not at the current school, then at another school. For example, although a current site administrator may discontinue the interventions, there is a good chance that the assistant administrator will initiate the interventions at his or her next assignment as principal or assistant principal at the new site. It has been our experience that as more personnel are trained and more schools participate newly assigned administrators that had been previously trained request training for teams at their new schools. Literacy coaches become assistant principals, resource specialists become assistant principals, assistant principals become principals and each job change represents a seed that may eventually bear fruit. Thus, continual training of school teams is one answer to the administrative reassignment issue.

Another component of addressing the issue of changes in administration is follow-up to schools. Follow-up by the psychological services intervention team to schools after they have been trained has reaped untold benefits in building bridges with the school site implementation teams (which includes general education personnel). These personnel in turn relate the positive student outcomes to their administrators. The eventual success of the interventions at a school site is dependent on the support of the principal, his or her administrative team, and their belief that the intervention program is helpful to students.

Informal information sharing. The word-of-mouth messages that are shared among administrators at their Administrator Staff Meetings was and is an aspect of communication that we view as essential and as worthwhile as the information that is disseminated during formal trainings. When students at a given school show positive reading success, in their OCR unit tests, in their performance on the high stakes tests (e.g., the California Standards Tests for English Language Arts), and in overall enthusiasm for reading, their school administrators share this information with peer administrators. This informal sharing of information has resulted in a continual flow of schools requesting training in the interventions.

Combining top-down and bottom-up changes in implementing research-based interventions in school districts. Change can come from the top down, which is a requirement mandating interventions as District policy, or from the bottom up, as we are attempting with our current approach (also see Chapter 8 by Knotek et al., in this book). Perhaps another way may be a combination of both the top-down and bottom-up approaches that develop district policy based on data and success that has been established in school environments.

Speaking for the children. The value of communicating the positive outcomes of the interventions within specific school sites and with parent and community stakeholders cannot be overstated. Culturally and linguistically diverse students and other students who have factors in their lives associated with poverty will likely need the additional assistance of a supplementary program if they are not able to keep pace with the core curriculum. Delivering services to students requires innovative ways to approach the use of resources. In these days of diminishing resources and increasing needs, itinerant personnel such as SPs, speech and language teachers, and school social workers can be valuable members of instructional teams. Many poor and CLD students who arrive in school do not possess the skills expected for success in kindergarten. In essence, they arrive on the scene in the position of needing to gain ground (Graves, Valles, & Rueda, 2000).

Over time they may fall further behind, and upon reaching third grade, when independent reading proficiency is expected, they too often are diagnosed as learning disabled. Early screening and intervention in literacy has been proven to successfully assist students on their path to achieving proficiency (Casey & Howe, 2002; Kaplan & Walpole, 2005; Vellutino, Scanlon, & Lyon, 2000). Targeted and explicit small group instruction is effective for ELs and their monolingual counterparts (Haager & Windmueller, 2001).

So, who can speak for the children? The voices of SPs, teachers, paraeducators, other itinerant personnel, retired SPs, parents, university partners, and administrators can collectively converge with fresh approaches. Helping children to grow into skilled readers requires that all members of the educational team "speak" or assist in the process. Our goal is to let all the voices be heard and to listen.

■   References

Benson, A. J., & Hughes, J. (1985). Perceptions of role definition processes in school psychology: A national survey. *School Psychology Review, 14*, 764–774.

Berninger, V. (1998). *Process assessment of the learner, Guides for intervention.* San Antonio, TX, The Psychological Corporation, Harcourt Brace & Company.

Berninger, V. (2001). *Process assessment of the learner; Test Battery for reading and writing.* San Antonio, TX, The Psychological Corporation.

Berninger, V., Abbott, R., Brooksher, R., Lemos, Z., Ogier, S., Zook, D., et al. (2000). A connectionist approach to making the predictability of English orthography explicit to at-risk beginning readers: Evidence for alternative, effective strategies. *Developmental Neuropsychology, 17*, 241–271.

Berninger, V., & Abbott, S. P. (2003). *Process Assessment of the Learner (PAL): Research-based reading and writing lessons.* San Antonio, TX, The Psychological Corporation (Harcourt).

Berninger, V., Dunn, A., Lin, S., & Shimada, S. (2004). School evolution: Scientist-practitioner educators creating optimal learning environments for all students. *Journal of Learning Disabilities, 37*, 500–508.

Berninger, V., Rutberg, J., Abbott, R., Garcia, N., Anderson-Youngstrom, M., Brooks, A., et al. (2006). Tier 1 and Tier 2 early intervention for handwriting and composing. *Journal of School Psychology, 44*, 3–30. [Honorable mention as one of the best research articles of the year.]

Berninger, V., Vaughan, K., Abbott, R., Abbott, S., Brooks, A., Rogan, L., et al. (1997). Treatment of handwriting fluency problems in beginning writing: Transfer from handwriting to composition. *Journal of Educational Psychology, 89,* 652–666.

California Department of Education (CDE). (1997, December). *Content Standards, English Language Arts.* Retrieved from www.cde.ca.gov.

CASEL (The Collaborative for Academic, Social, and Emotional Learning). (2003). Institute of Educational Sciences (IES), Department of Education, Mid-Atlantic Regional Educational Library.

Casey, A., & Howe, K. (2002). Best practices in early literacy skills. In A. Thomas & J. Grimes (Eds.), *Best practices in school psychology IV.* Bethesda, MD, National Association of School Psychologists.

Curtis, M. J., Castillo, J. M., & Cohen, R. M. (2008). Best practices in system-level change. In A. Thomas & J. Grimes (Eds.), *Best practices in school psychology* (5th ed., pp. 887–901). Bethesda, MD, National Association of School Psychologists.

Dunn, A. (2002, Fall). Partnership and problem solving to promote early intervention in literacy: Using the PAL. *CASP Today, Fall,* 8.

Dunn, A. (2005). *Making connections with general education: New wine in old bottles.* Presentation to WA State Association of School Psychologists.

Dunn, A. (2007). *School psychologists coordinating three-tiered interventions at school sites.* Presentation at the National Association of School Psychologists convention.

Haager, D., & Windmueller, M. (2001). Early literacy intervention for English language learners at-risk for learning disabilities: Student and teacher outcomes in an urban school. *Learning Disability Quarterly, 24,* 235–250.

Harvey, V. S., & Struzziero, J. (2000). *Effective supervision in school psychology.* Bethesda, MD, National Association of School Psychologists.

Individuals with Disabilities in Education Improvement Act, 2004. http://idea.ed.gov.

Johns, S. K., Patrick, J. A., & Rutherford, K. J. (2008). Best Practices in district-wide positive behavior support implementation. In A. Thomas & J. Grimes (Eds.), *Best practices in school psychology V* (pp. 721–733). Bethesda, MD, The National Association of School Psychologists.

Kaplan, D., & Walpole, S. (2005). A stage-sequential model of reading transitions: Evidence from the early childhood longitudinal study. *Journal of Educational Psychology, 97,* 551–563.

Los Angeles Unified School District Position Paper (LAUSD). (2004). *Early intervention and prevention of academically at-risk students.* Available online.

Mayer, G. R., & Ybarra, W. J. (2003). *Teaching alternative behaviors school-wide: A resource guide to prevent discipline problems.* Los Angeles County Office of Education.

Murnane, R. J., & Levy, F. (1996). *Teaching the new basic skills: Principles for educating children to thrive in a changing economy.* New York, The Free Press/Simon & Schuster, Inc.

National Reading Panel. (2000). *Teaching children to read: An evidence-based assessment of the scientific research literature on reading and its implications for reading instruction [on-line].* Retrieved from www.nichd.nih.gov/publications/nrp/smallbook.htm.

No Child Left Behind Act of 2001. Pub. L. No. 107–110 (Elementary and Secondary Education Act).

Presentation to Psychological Services Administrators, 2007. December 11, 2007, LAUSD.

Reading First. (2000). U.S. Department of Education. Office of Elementary and Secondary Education. CFDA Number: 84.357. Retrieved from www.ed.gov/programs/readingfirst/index.html.

Roberts, M. L., Marshall, J., Nelson, J. R., & Albers, C. A. (2001). Curriculum-based assessment procedures embedded within functional behavioral assessments: Identifying escape-motivated behaviors in a general education classroom. *School Psychology Review, 30,* 264–277.

Stanovich, K. E. (1992). Speculations on the causes and consequence s of individual differences in early reading acquisition. In P. B. Gough, L. C. Ehri, & R. Treiman (Eds.), *Reading Acquisition* (pp. 307–342). Hilldale, NJ, Lawrence Erlbaum Associates.

SRA Open Court Reading (2000, 2002). DeSoto, TX, SRA/McGraw-Hill.

Stanovich, K. E. (1993). Distinguished Educator Series: Romance and reality. *The Reading Teacher, 47,* 280–291.

STAR (Standardized Testing and Reporting) Results (2004). Retrieved from http://star.cde.ca.gov.

Success for All. Baltimore, MD, Success for All Foundation.

The Psychological Corporation (2001). *Wechsler individual test of achievement* (2nd ed.) San Antonio, TX, The Psychological Corporation, A Harcourt Brace & Company.

Tilly, D. S. (2008). The evolution of school psychology to science-based practice: Problem-solving and the three-tiered model. In A. Thomas & J. Grimes (Eds.), *Best practices in school psychology, IV* (pp. 17–36). Bethesda, MD, National Association of School Psychologists.

Vellutino, F. R., Scanlon, D. M., & Lyon, G. R. (2000). Differentiating between difficult to remediate and readily remediated poor readers: More evidence against the IQ-achievement discrepancy definition of reading disability. *Journal of Learning Disabilities, 33,* 223–238.

Walker, H. M., & Shinn, M. R. (2002). Structuring school-based interventions to achieve integrated primary, secondary, and tertiary prevention goals for safe and effective schools. In M. A. Shinn, H. M. Walker, & G. Stoner (Eds.), *Interventions for academic and behavior problems II: Preventive and remedial approaches* (pp. 1–21). Bethesda, MD, National Association of School Psychologists.

Williams, A., Blank, R. K., Potts, A., & Toye, C. (2004). *State education indicators with a focus on Title I 2000–01.* U.S. Department of Education under Contract No. ED-01-CO-0040–001, Washington, DC, Council of Chief State School Officers.

Witt, J. D. (2002). *Slide presentation and training of the Prereferral Assessment Model Program*. Baton Rouge, LA, Louisiana State University.

Witt, J. C. (2003). *Woodcrest: Report of class wide math intervention data*. Slide presentation to Psychological Services Department.

Witt, J. C., & Naquin, G. (2003). *Prereferral assessment model (PAM): A promising practice overview to schools. Fall 2002.* Presented to LAUSD school psychologists on 03–17-2003.

Witt, J. C., Vanderheyden, A., & Neddenriep, C. E. (2004). Troubleshooting behavioral interventions: A systematic process for finding and eliminating problems. *School Psychology Review, 33*, 363–383.

Ysseldyke, J., Dawson, Pl, Lehr, C., Reschly, D., Reynolds. M., & Telzro, C. (1997). *School psychology: A blueprint for training and practice*. Bethesda, MD, National Association of School Psychologists.

STEP 4

IN IMPLEMENTATION: TEACHERS PUTTING RESEARCH INTO PRACTICE

■ Introduction to Step 4

Implementing research into practice is not just a direct translation process; it is also about the practitioners who transform knowledge when implementing it into practice. The contribution of the practitioner to transforming the research to the practice setting matters!

In the first chapter in this section, Elizabeth Todd Brown, Victoria Molfese, and Mary Wagner examine what research shows about the role of the teacher and teacher practices in implementing prevention research in preschool and early childhood classrooms. Their research findings clearly show that the teacher matters, which Peverly's (Chapter 21, this volume) research review also supports. Implementing research into practice requires more than simply having research findings—practitioners have contributions to make to the implementation process through artfully and skillfully applying research to educational and clinical practice.

In the next chapter of this section, Barbara Wise, Laura Rogan, and Luann Sessions describe the implementation of Wise's creative and teacher-oriented *Linguistics Remedies* program. They document how evidence-based practices grounded in linguistic science, many based on Wise's instructional research, are tailored to the needs and knowledge of individual teachers. The profound respect for teachers as professionals that pervades this chapter serves as an important reminder that the success of the implementation of research into practice may well depend on supporting teachers to be autonomous professionals.

In the following chapter, William Nagy, an educational linguist, discusses how teachers can implement research on vocabulary and word learning in the classroom. He makes a compelling case for the critical role of vocabulary in developing literacy. For those who may think that all evidence-based instruction has to be highly teacher-directed and that intensive means boring, this chapter may open their eyes to the evidence that play with language, joy, pleasure, and engagement are also critical components of evidence-based literacy instruction that works. But teachers need a framework based on research to impart that knowledge.

The fourth and final chapter in this section tells the story of Carol Christensen and Maria Wauchope, researchers in Australia, who implemented a university-school district partnership to show how reading research could be applied to educational practice. The authors built a program based on research, and then during implementation, gathered evidence to evaluate the effectiveness of the implementation, modifying the next phase of implementation based on the findings of the initial evaluation. An interesting follow-up outcome is that the first author has left academics to work full-time on implementing research into educational practice in schools.

15. Role of Teacher Practices and Characteristics in Implementing Research in Preschool and Early Childhood Classrooms

E. Todd Brown, Victoria J. Molfese, and Mary C. Wagner

> To guide their decisions about practice, all early childhood teachers need to understand the developmental changes that typically occur in the years from birth through age 8 and beyond, variations in development that may occur, and how best to support children's learning and development during these years.
>
> Bredekamp & Copple (1997, p. 9)

The early childhood period has become a topic of special interest to the education community with the rapid growth in the population of preschool-aged children (ages birth to 5 years) and with the increase in enrollment in early childhood education programs[1] for preschool children. Indeed, nearly 7% of the total U.S. population is 5 years of age or younger; in comparison, just over 7% of the population is aged 5–9 years old (U.S. Census Bureau, 2002; Kids Count, 2000). The U.S. Census reports that in the year 2000 60% of the 3 and 4 year olds were enrolled in preschool programs, up 6% from the 1960s, and 65% of children of kindergarten age were enrolled in all day kindergarten, up 20% from the 1960s. Many states are moving toward broadening children's access to public preschool programs rather than the current practice of basing access on income eligibility or special education needs. Florida offers enrollment in public and private pre-kindergarten programs to all 4-year-olds through its Voluntary Pre-Kindergarten Program (2006) (http://www.vpkhelp.org/). Other states are expected to follow Florida's lead and it is anticipated that the increased enrollments in education-oriented preschool programs will result in more young children being ready to learn and succeed academically, socially, and emotionally when they enter kindergarten.

Along with the current and expected increases in enrollments in pre-school and pre-kindergarten programs have come changes in the perceptions of preschool programs by stakeholders—parents, educators, administrators—and the funders of preschool programs—local, state, and federal agencies as well as faith-based organization and the tuition-paying parents and caregivers. These stakeholders expect that children attending preschool programs will benefit from their preschool experiences. Defining and measuring the benefits of preschool program attendance has begun as part of a national discussion of how to accomplish the National Education Goals (1994, 1998) that by 2000 "every child will start school ready to learn." As one response to this initiative, many states began developing early learning standards to define desired learning outcomes for preschool children and the education content of curricula in preschool programs. There are expectations that early learning standards can be met through exposure of preschool children to effective instructional practices that are implemented by highly knowledgeable teachers using evidence-based curricula.

The purpose of this chapter is to describe changes in early childhood education that have led to the development of the early childhood learning standards which most states have now developed. Findings from recent studies of preschool education programs will be examined to identify what is known about teacher practices and characteristics (training, beliefs, and content knowledge) and how teacher practices and characteristics influence preschool children's learning outcomes. The specific focus of the chapter will be on teacher practices that facilitate positive-learning outcomes for preschool children in the areas of language and literacy, both of which are key skills that are linked to later academic achievement in elementary school.

■ Changes in Early Childhood Education

Studies of children in the preschool years have long emphasized the domains of social and emotional skills, fine and gross motor skills, language and communication skills, and general cognitive skills. The historical emphasis on these domains can be seen from the contents of early textbooks on child development (Goodenough, 1945), topics in child psychology (Hurlock, 1942), recommended practices in educational psychology (Thorndike, 1914), and the content of early assessments used to evaluate young children's development (Bayley Scales of Infant Development, Bayley, 1969; Denver Developmental Screening Scales, Frankenburg & Dodds, 1967; and Merrill-Palmer Scale of Mental Tests, Stutsman, 1931). Today, these skill domains and others are reflected in the early learning standards adopted by states. Through the development and publication of early learning standards, the stakeholders in these states are identifying and defining the types of skills they believe are important for young children to learn and to demonstrate through their behaviors in the preschool years.

The Early Learning Standards of several states are available for review at The National Child Care Information Center (2007) and examples of the early learning standards from several states are in Table 15.1. Shown in the table are examples of the skill domains for preschool children (e.g., language and literacy, physical development). Within the standards are concepts, skills, and behavioral indicators of a specific skill. For example, common content includes benchmark behaviors that relate to the standard (e.g., "shows interest and understanding of the basic concepts of print," "walks, runs, climbs, jumps, and hops with increased coordination, balance and control"). The early learning standards are generally written as skills that children are expected to develop during the preschool period and demonstrate at kindergarten entry. Some states also include information about the "supportive practices" of teachers and other caregivers that should be incorporated into preschool programs. These supportive practices include types of experiences, materials, and teacher practices that facilitate early learning and information about assessment tools that can be used to measure the learning outcomes of preschool children. Several states such as Kentucky also align their early learning standards to other standards, such as performance standards of national organizations or education programs (e.g., National Association for the Education of Young Children [NAEYC, 2007], Head Start) and to learning standards established for children in K-12 grades. In addition, some states provide information about the core body of knowledge that defines what teachers and other caregivers need to know and be able to demonstrate in caring for children as well as the necessary education and professional development required to garner this knowledge.

Establishing early learning standards has been important to preschool programs because, in addition to defining the expectations of how "every child will start school ready to learn" (National Education Goals, 1998), these standards also have important implications for teacher content knowledge, pedagogy, and professional development. Also, teacher beliefs and attitudes about early learning may influence instructional practices and implementation of curricula necessary to meet early learning standards in the preschool settings. However, the development and publication of early learning standards have resulted in controversies as parents, educators, researchers, administrators, and policy makers try to accommodate differences in the perceptions held by different stakeholders of what is optimal for the education of young children (Lee, 2004; Lynch, Anderson, Anderson, & Shapiro, 2006). For example, professional organizations, parent groups, and teachers have expressed concerns about the diminished role of play in the curriculum, the addition of more academically oriented content (e.g., numeracy), and the use of frequent assessments and monitoring to gauge children's progress in learning (Almon, 2004).

TABLE 15.1   *Early Learning Standards Content for Four States*

State	Domain	Document
Arizona	Social/Emotional Language and Literacy Mathematics Science Social Studies Physical Development Health and Safety Fine Arts	Arizona Department of Education, 2005
Idaho	Health Humanities Language Arts and Communication Mathematics Science Social Studies	Idaho State Department of Education, 2004
Kentucky	Arts and Humanities Health and Physical Education Language Mathematics Science Social Studies	Kentucky Department of Education, 2003
Pennsylvania	Approaches to Learning Creative Arts Language and Literacy Logical-Mathematical Personal Social Physical Health Program Partnerships Science Social Studies	Pennsylvania Department of Education and Department of Public Welfare, 2005

Expressions of these concerns and the growing reliance on research findings to provide an evidence base for educational practices and decision-making have accelerated the development of early childhood education programs. Research evidence shows that teacher-child interactions at school and parent-child interactions at home have important and long-lasting effects on the language and literacy development of young children. The experiences children have at home influence children's development of conversational skills, vocabulary, and emergent literacy skills, such as phonemic awareness, letter knowledge, and print skills (e.g., Dickinson & Tabors, 2001). Later in the chapter the influences of both home and school are examined. Current practices and research findings relevant to language and literacy development are now reviewed.

■ Language and Literacy

The domain of language is present in the early learning standards of all 28 states Scott-Little, Kagan, and Frelow (2003) studied. Examples of standards, content within standards, and behavioral skills pertaining to language and literacy for several states in different regions of the United States are shown in Table 15.2. Although the "language" label is used differently by states (e.g., in Arizona the label is "language and literacy" and in Idaho the label is "language arts and communication"), the same

TABLE 15.2 *Language and Literacy Standards, Content, and Behavioral Skills for Four States*

State	Standard	Content	Behavioral Skills
Arizona[a]	Language and Literacy	Listening and understanding	Comprehends finger-plays, rhymes, chants, poems, conversations, and stories
Idaho[b]	Language Arts and Communication	Listening	Demonstrate basic understanding of conversational vocabulary
Kentucky[c]	Language	Demonstrates general skills and strategies of the communication process	Uses nonverbal communication for a variety of purposes
Pennsylvania[d]	Language and Literacy	Develop understanding of word awareness	The child will hear and distinguish one word from another

[a] Arizona Department of Education (2005).
[b] Idaho State Department of Education (2004).
[c] Kentucky Department of Education (2003).
[d] Pennsylvania Department of Education and Department of Public Welfare (2005).

general term is implied across states. Within the language standard, various skills are described as behavioral indicators of learning. The behavioral skills described in Arizona are detailed (finger-plays, rhymes, chants, etc.) whereas those described in Kentucky are more broadly described ("uses nonverbal communication for a variety of purposes"). Cognition, physical health, and social-emotional skills are also domains common to early learning standards in most states.

The focus on early language and literacy in the standards is based on recent federal policy, which is based on research evidence linking language development and emergent literacy in the preschool years. The No Child Left Behind legislation (2001) emphasizes language development and emergent literacy skills in preschool children to enable more children to become proficient readers by third grade. Research findings are clear that the emergent literacy skills at kindergarten entry influence the development of conventional literacy skills in word decoding, reading comprehension, and spelling in the primary grades. For example, Denton and colleagues (Denton & West, 2002; West, Denton, & Germino-Hausken, 2000) reported on 22,000 children from the Early Childhood Longitudinal Study studied from kindergarten through fifth grade. They found that children who were proficient in identifying letters (alphabetic knowledge: naming upper and lower case letters, recognizing beginning and ending word sounds) at entry into kindergarten showed stronger skills at the end of kindergarten and in first grade on measures of word reading compared to children who were not proficient. Letter naming and letter sound proficiencies were specifically linked with word reading proficiency in first grade.

The development of early literacy skills involves multicomponent processes (Whitehurst & Lonigan, 1998). One component develops from the child's mastery of the links between the sounds of language and visual symbols (letters) of the language. Whitehurst and Lonigan describe these as "inside-out" skills (e.g., development of phonological awareness, and letter-sound and letter-name knowledge, writing and spelling). The "inside-out" skills are descriptive of the children's knowledge about the sound system of their language and the mapping of these sounds to visual symbols (letters) and vice versa. The second component involves the experiences that the child has that are needed to draw attention to the sounds of language and to oral and written words. These experiences are described as "outside-in" skills (e.g., language, narrative understanding, and knowledge of print conventions). McGuinness (2004) has described the interactions of "inside out" and "outside in" processes in literacy as involving children learning to listen to the phonemes (speech sounds) in language, learning to look at and write phonemes encoded as visual symbols (letters and letter combinations), and then reversing the process by using cognitive skills in decoding the sounds associated with the visual symbols to identify the meaning associated with words.

■ National Early Literacy Panel

The National Early Literacy Panel's meta-analysis of research studies published from 1934 through 2003 provides further evidence for the predictive relationships between preschool emergent literacy skills and conventional literacy skills at school age. A meta-analysis is a method used to determine the consistencies of findings across large numbers of published studies (see Chapters 1, 2, 3, and 6, this volume). By synthesizing the findings from studies, employing different experimental methods and measures of a construct (e.g., alphabetic knowledge in addition to concepts about print as measures of emergent literacy), the robustness or strength of a particular finding can be established.

For the National Early Literacy Panel meta-analysis, the criteria for inclusion of a study were as follows: child participants aged 0–5 years (or kindergarten age), the study design included specified measures of child skills and abilities, the study was published in a peer-reviewed/refereed journals, and the study involved empirical research (i.e., involved a formal systematic analysis of data). Studies were then coded for the variables included in the studies and for the results reported. The codes are then used as input for data analyses.

The National Early Literacy Panel meta-analysis (Shanahan et al., 2004) supported the conclusion, based on 234 studies, of a predictive relation between skills measured in the preschool or kindergarten period and conventional literacy outcomes (decoding, spelling, reading comprehension) measured at some time point from kindergarten forward. Early reports from this meta-analysis show small to large correlations (average $r = 0.20$–0.50 across studies) between school-age reading skills and emergent skills of *alphabetic knowledge* (e.g., identification of letter sounds and letter names), *writing* (e.g., letter and name writing), *phonological processing* (e.g., skills in blending and segmenting, and deleting phonemes in spoken words, and segmenting phonemes that make up an onset-rhyme in syllables), *rapid naming* (e.g., naming digits, letters, objects, and colors), *print concepts* (e.g., knowledge about the conventions of print), and *oral language* (e.g., vocabulary, narrative skills) in preschool. Interestingly, the early learning behavioral indicators of the state standards shown in Table 15.2 incorporate concepts similar to those found to be predictive of later reading ability by the National Early Literacy Panel.

■ Influence of the Home Environment on Early Literacy

An extensive literature shows the types of activities in the home environment that are associated with the development of emergent literacy skills. Researchers report strong correlations between language and general cognitive skills in infancy and early childhood and activities in the home involving the child, such as bedtime reading, the availability of children's books and toys/materials for learning, as well as encouragement of learning through parent-child interactions and play activities (e.g., Aylward, 1997; Bee et al., 1982; Bradley et al., 1993; Molfese & DiLalla, 1995).

The dynamics of parent-child relations in the home environment are especially important. Researchers report that children develop larger vocabularies, better reasoning skills, and more advanced emergent literacy skills in environments where conversational skills are encouraged and children engage in regular reading times (Lonigan et al., 1999; Share, Jorm, Mclean, Matthews, & Waterman, 1983). Landry and her colleagues (2000, 2002) and Assel, Landry, Swank, Smith, and Steelman (2003) report links between parents' interactive styles with their young children and the development of language and other cognitive skills. Maternal scaffolding behaviors in which the relations between objects, actions, and events are verbalized were found to result in better development of verbal and nonverbal skills in 3- to 6-year-old children. Hess, Holloway, Dickson, and Prince (1984) report that maternal expectancies, communication style, parenting practices, and affect during the preschool period are related to their children's school readiness skills at 5 and 6 years of age and their later academic achievement at school age.

Parents may influence children's learning in the home environment in ways that have to do with their own experiences. For example, parents who have reading difficulties or who do not enjoy reading activities may not model reading themselves and may not include reading as a shared activity with their children. Shared reading does impact children's emergent literacy skills (Leinonen et al., 2001; Scarborough, 1991; Scarr & Ricciuti, 1991).

■ Influence of the Teacher on Early Literacy

The environment of early childhood programs also matters. Characteristics, behaviors, and attitudes of teachers have been found to influence children's early learning. Young children benefit from early childhood programs in which instructional practices are implemented by highly knowledgeable teachers using evidence-based curricula. Teacher qualifications, characteristics, and knowledge about language and emergent literacy influence their teaching practices in preschool settings.

Basic qualifications needed by K-12 teachers are established by states, but these have recently become more stringent with the federal *No Child Left Behind* act that requires highly qualified teachers in the classroom. To receive state certification or licensure, elementary teachers are required to hold at least a bachelor's degree and successfully pass a rigorous state test (such as the Praxis) to demonstrate subject knowledge and teaching skills in reading, writing, mathematics, and other elementary curriculum basic content.

The basic qualifications are not as clearly specified for teachers in preschool programs. Forty states require no formal education beyond a high school diploma for teachers in preschool settings. Only 24 states require a bachelor's degree with courses or certification in early childhood for lead classroom teachers in state-financed pre-kindergarten programs. For example, states can mandate that personnel working as pre-kindergarten lead teachers or directors have a minimum of 120 hours of training or 6 semester hours of college credit for a Child Development Associate (CDA) credential. Some states only require that teachers have 9–12 hours of college credit from courses with early childhood content or an associate's degree with course work that includes early childhood course credits. Rhode Island is the only state that requires a bachelor's degree for all teachers in early education programs (Ackerman, 2003). Recently, however, states have begun to change their education standards for teachers in preschool programs to incorporate processes to obtain teacher's certificates in early childhood education, outline expected core content for teacher preparation programs in early childhood education, and to recommend professional development and training activities (e.g., Kentucky Department of Education, 2003). Scott-Little et al., (2003) describe the efforts made by states in the area of education standards for teachers in the preschool settings.

Although progress has been made in placing highly qualified teachers in every K-12 public classroom, many preschools still are not held to these teacher standards. Currently, it is common to find school districts with classroom teachers who have a mix of educational backgrounds, with some teachers having many years of preschool teaching experience but no college degree or preschool certification and others who are recent college graduates with preschool certification but with less teaching experience. One reason that preschool teacher education qualifications may not match those of K-12 teachers is financial. Teachers in early childhood education programs are less likely to become certified because they are paid less than half of what is paid to kindergarten and elementary teachers and teacher assistants in preschool are paid $2,000 a year less than those in K-12 classrooms (Barnett, 2003). By raising teacher educational standards and providing better compensation to teachers, the quality of preschool programs will increase and more highly qualified teachers will be remain in early childhood classrooms rather than moving to higher paying K-12 jobs or leaving the education profession.

The teacher's professional development and training in specific components of early childhood development and education, beliefs, attitudes, and educational experience are all thought to influence the learning outcomes of preschool children. Research that examines the relationships among teacher characteristics, classroom instruction, and student learning outcomes is increasing and is now reviewed.

Relationships between teacher's educational background and experience and classroom instruction. Early work reported in the National Child Care Staffing Study (Howes, Phillips, & Whitebrook, 1992) examined the relationships among formal education, specialized training, teaching experience and teacher behavior in the classroom. This study concluded that "formal education was a better predictor of teacher behavior than specialized training" (p. 413). Indeed, several studies report that teachers with a bachelor's degree or higher in early childhood provide better-quality preschool experiences for children than teachers with less education (Barnett, 2003; Bowman, Donavan, & Burns, 2001; Dunn, 1993; Helburn, 1995; Howes, et al., 1992; Whitebrook, 2003; Whitebook, Howes, & Phillips, 1990). (See Uhry and Goodman, Chapter 23, this volume, for a similar conclusion about the level of education for early literacy professional development.) The Carnegie Corporation Initiative (2002) found no factor is more important for the early childhood classroom environment than the preparedness, competence, and commitment of the teacher.

Tout, Zaslow, and Berry (2006) reviewed the research on the quality of early child care and education environments and preschool teacher qualifications and concluded that when early childhood education teachers have specialized knowledge about development in early childhood, programs are better and have more high-quality interaction between teachers and children. They noted, however, that research has not examined the threshold of education or professional development training that defines quality programs. The current preschool workforce is highly diverse with regard to educational background, experience, and ability (Whitebrook, 2003). It is also not clear what qualifications or characteristics preschool teachers need beyond the degree, certification, and professional development training to be able to facilitate children's learning outcomes and be effective practitioners in their preschool classroom.

Research based on large data sets has studied the educational levels and background knowledge of teachers in early childhood programs. Although not focused on literacy, they set the stage for examining effective early childhood teacher practices in specific content areas. An often cited study by Berk (1985), with 37 teachers in 12 centers in a Midwestern city, compared preschool teachers with high school diplomas to teachers with two years or more of college education. The teachers were observed; then detailed narrative descriptions of their behaviors were coded using an observational method developed by Prescott, Kritchevsky, and Jones (1972). Educational background was positively correlated with the teacher's commitment and with job satisfaction. College prepared preschool teachers were more responsive in their encouragement and nurturing of children's verbal skills than their counterparts with less education.

The National Child Care Staffing Study (Whitebook, Howes, & Phillips, 1990) analyzed data from 227 childcare centers in five metropolitan areas of United States. Through stratified randomized sampling of classrooms, this study looked at the characteristics of education, specialized training, and experience as predictors of teacher classroom behaviors. A total of 1,309 teaching staff were interviewed and observed. Teacher behaviors, such as verbal encouragement and the level and type of communication and interaction with children, were measured at the individual level with the Caregiver Interaction Scale (Arnett, 1989) and at the classroom level using either the Early Childhood Environment Rating Scale (ECERS; Harms & Clifford, 1980; Harms, Clifford, & Cryer, 1998) or the Infant Toddler Environmental Rating Scale (ITERS; Harms, Cryer, & Clifford, 1990). The results showed that more years of teaching experience and education were predictive of more appropriate teacher-child interactions. The teachers with more experience and education were more sensitive, more engaged, and less harsh in the classroom.

The Cost, Quality, and Outcomes Study (Helburn, 1995) and the Florida Improvement Study (Howes, Smith, & Galinsky, 1995) utilized various research methods and measures to examine adult involvement and interaction in 1,060 classrooms. These studies included interviews about teacher background and behaviors and assessments of children's verbal intelligence and pre-academic skills as well as classroom observations. The important conclusions were that teacher preparation was related to more sensitive and responsive teaching (e.g., engaging children in more verbal interactions during instructional periods). The Florida Improvement Study found teachers with a bachelor's degree in early childhood education or a child development associate certificate were more creative, engaged preschool children in a greater number of classroom activities, and had higher frequency of language activities and language play than teachers with a high school degree.

The National Center for Early Development and Learning's Multi State Pre-Kindergarten Study (Pianta et al., 2005) provided information about the features of pre-kindergarten programs, pre-kindergarten classrooms, and characteristics of teachers in 238 pre-kindergarten classrooms in six states. The study provided support for the findings of earlier research about teacher-child interactions, activities provided in centers for free choice, and quality of language interactions. Pianta et al. found that teachers' educational training (4-year college degree and teaching certificate) and years of teaching experience positively influenced the quality of the activity-centered classroom environment. The teachers were less directive and encouraged children to have a choice and voice in what the activities they selected.

The common findings in all of these studies were that the knowledge and competence of the early childhood teacher did affect the quality of the classroom activities and the interaction between teachers and students. This evidence suggests that preschool teachers' background and educational preparation are factors related to their classroom behaviors and teaching practices, such as how directive, responsive, and sensitive they are to students.

Teacher beliefs. Student learning is also influenced by a teacher's beliefs about the importance of specific early skills and abilities. As preschool programs increase their academic focus and increase their emphasis on building emergent cognitive skills, teachers' beliefs about what is developmentally appropriate for young children's learning become a factor. The link between teachers' beliefs about children's learning and classroom instructional content is supported by research (Pajares, 1992; Kowalski, Pretti-Frontczak, & Johnson, 2001; McCarty, Abbott-Shim, & Lambert, 2001), as is the relationship between measures of teacher's beliefs and the use of developmentally appropriate practice (Cassidy & Lawrence, 2000; Cassidy, Buell, Pugh-Hoese, & Russel, 1995; Charlesworth, Hart, Burts, Thommason, Mosely, & Fleege, 1993; Maxwell, McWilliam, Hemmeter, Ault, & Schuster, 2001; McMullen & Alat, 2002; Stipek & Byler, 1997; Vartuli, 1999).

However, a straightforward link between teacher beliefs and classroom instructional practices has been more difficult to document. For example, Stipek and Byler (1997) used teacher report questionnaires and teacher classroom observations to explore relations among variables that included preschool, kindergarten, and first grade teachers' beliefs about children's learning, education goals, school entry policies affecting children, testing, and grade retention. Results show that teacher beliefs about children's learning correlated with instructional practices, but Stipek and Byler noted that the goals of early childhood educators vary regarding their beliefs about whether basic skills and knowledge are appropriate curriculum content in the preschool classroom.

The challenge in examining teacher characteristics and teacher beliefs is finding empirical work on specific content areas. Brown (2005) studied teacher attitudes and beliefs about mathematics and classroom practices with a sample of 20 preschool teachers in a large urban Midwestern city. The purpose was to show that a combination of teachers' sense of their teaching efficacy and their personal beliefs about the importance of mathematics would align with observational measures of standards-based mathematics practices in the classroom. Positive correlations were found between the teachers' evaluations of their teaching efficacy and beliefs about the importance of mathematics in preschool curricula and teaching specific mathematics concepts as well as between efficacy, beliefs, and mathematics classroom practices. Brown's findings are different from Graham, Nash, and Paul (1997) who reported that preschool teachers beliefs that mathematics curricula did not mesh with observations of teachers' actual classroom behaviors that showed little mathematics instruction was occurring. These results, however, do add support to the findings of Kagan (1992), Spidell-Rusher, McGrevin, and Lambiotte (1992) and Nespor (1987) who have found that teachers' beliefs about curricula and class activities are generally related to child-centered classroom practices.

Cassidy and Lawrence (2000) studied 12 child care teachers who agreed to be videotaped in their classrooms. Three days following the videotaping the teachers viewed the videotape and participated in an unstructured interview to provide rationale for their observed behaviors. The interviews and video-tapes were coded and nine categories of child-teacher interactions emerged. The results show that 33% of the preschool teachers' interview statements and observed behaviors were focused on the socio-emotional development of the child. The authors noted a limited emphasis on general cognitive development (10%) and on language development (6%), which may indicate less teacher knowledge about or interest in these domains. Interestingly, studies investigating teacher beliefs and classroom practices have not included measures of preschool students' learning; so the impacts of teacher characteristics, beliefs, and classroom practices on student learning are not established.

Teacher characteristics and literacy instructional practices. The International Reading Association and the National Association for the Education of Young Children (IRA/NAEYC, 1998, p. 15) published a joint position statement, *Learning to Read and Write*, describing the teacher's role in children's literacy development:

> Early Childhood teachers need to understand the developmental continuum of reading and writing and be skilled in a variety of strategies to assess and support individual children's development and learning across the continuum. At that same time teachers must set developmentally appropriate goals for young children and then adapt instructional strategies for children whose learning and development are advanced or lag behind those goals. Good teachers make instructional decisions based on their knowledge of reading and writing, current research, appropriate expectations, and their knowledge of individual children's strengths and needs.

The position statement sets a high standard for teachers in early childhood education. Quality literacy instruction for early childhood and early elementary students is driven by the research findings indicating that a poor start in reading in the early grades affects student achievement in the long term (Torgesen, 1998).

The National Association for the Education of Young Children (NAEYC, 2001) and the board of the National Council for the Accreditation of Teacher Education approved five core standards for initial licensure of graduates of teacher preparation programs; and Standard 4 relates to the importance of teaching and learning and the need for teachers to relate to their students and families. By understanding the importance of the family to children's learning and gaining a sense of the knowledge students from different backgrounds bring to the classroom, teachers are better equipped to offer an array of teaching methods and strategies to meet students' learning needs. In addition to gaining a better understanding their students and families, teachers also must have strong conceptual knowledge and the desire to enable all students to learn. By acquiring and refining content skills, teachers are able to employ instructional practices that allow them to understand how the development of underlying skills results in successful student outcomes.

Although these goals and expectations are well articulated as policy, only a very limited number of studies have examined the relations between teacher education, teacher knowledge about language and literacy, and teaching practices in early childhood. Some research has examined teacher education programs for the preparation of teachers for reading instruction. Moats (1994) has written about preventing reading failure: "Contrary to expectation, teachers do not display fully explicit awareness of spoken language structure and its relationship to writing just because they themselves are literate" (p. 88). Support for Moat's statement comes from a study by Cunningham, Perry, Stanovich, and Stanovich (2004) who examined the domains of teachers' knowledge of phonics, children's literature, and regular and irregular spellings. The study was conducted with 84 kindergarten through third grade teachers. The teachers were asked to recognize popular titles of children's literature, to differentiate the phonetical structures of regular and irregular spelling patterns, to demonstrate knowledge of phonological awareness of sounds in spoken words, and to describe their core knowledge of the structure of the English language (phonology, semantics, syntax, etc.). Although Cunningham et al. viewed teachers' knowledge of a range and genre of text as a critical component of early literacy, only 10% of the teachers were familiar with titles on the list and no title was recognized by all of the teachers. Only 30% of teacher participants were able to identify at least half of the phonemes (number of sounds) in 11 different words, and only 11% of the teachers were able to identify all 11 irregularly spelled words from a list of 26 words. Thirty-seven percent of the teachers could not demonstrate the knowledge of emergent literacy skills that kindergarten students are expected to learn. Teacher participants attributed their lack of knowledge of emergent literacy skills to the lack of content in their credentialing programs.

Phelps and Schilling (2004) hypothesized that university courses are not providing teachers with the prerequisite skills necessary to teach reading to children. They designed a survey study with 1,542 elementary teachers attending 23 weeklong summer institutes to measure teachers' content knowledge about reading (i.e., what teachers need to know about reading to teach it to others). The survey contained items designed to measure knowledge of content in areas of reading comprehension and word analysis, knowledge of students and content, and knowledge of teaching and content. Phelps and Schilling found that knowledge for teaching reading is not defined by a general area of knowledge, but by several different dimensions. For example, teachers had different understandings of the content of reading that include knowledge about the reading process (decoding, fluency, and comprehension), language (semantics, syntax, and phonology), and spelling (encoding), as well as differences in understanding the specialized pedagogical content for teaching reading. The National Council on Teacher Quality (Walsh, 2001) also reported that the relations between teacher's level of literacy as measured from vocabulary scores and performance on standardized tests of reading and student achievement were stronger than the relations between student achievement and any other teacher attribute measured. Both of these studies have important implications for the breadth of content needed in college teacher preparation courses and for the importance of assuring that teachers have a good grasp of that content knowledge.

Other research has investigated the adequacy of various models of teaching and teaching strategies used in early childhood and elementary classrooms to improve reading performance. Wharton-McDonald, Pressley, and Hampston (1998) published a qualitative study of 9 first grade classrooms from four suburban districts. The classrooms were nominated by language arts coordinators as having exceptional teachers that helped their students achieve literacy or having teachers that were typical of the norm in promoting student literacy. Teachers were observed twice a month from December to June and participated in two in-depth interviews. Student data were collected on the types of books students were reading, composition writing, and active student involvement in learning activities. There were common characteristics in all nine classrooms: an assortment of teaching models, use of the writing process, and a variety of instructional student groupings.

Teachers with the highest performing students were characterized by a deliberate integrated and balanced approach to reading instruction as documented by field notes and interviews. These teachers taught explicit decoding skills, but varied the individualized instruction as well as introduced skills at different rates. The teachers were skilled at integrating multiple goals in a single lesson and scaffolding student thinking and learning through higher-level questioning. The teachers had mastery of classroom time, activities, and student interactions and were adept at making planned and impromptu decisions. The primary characteristic of the high-quality teachers was the high expectations they have for their students.

The teachers of the lower-achieving students felt their role was to provide exposure to print and build readiness, but reading was expected to occur when teachers determined that students were ready. Generally, teachers of lower-achieving students used a reading series for instruction and offered fewer opportunities for authentic reading and writing activities. Students typically read from predictable texts with limited vocabulary and writing activities were briefer and less organized. Overall, the authors concluded that the critical features for teaching reading were a strong emphasis on academics with instructional balance involving the explicit teaching of many skills, integration of reading and writing activities, and high expectations for all students.

A similar study by Taylor, Pearson, Clark, and Walpole (2000) employed quantitative and descriptive analyses to describe the effective reading instruction of primary grade teachers in 11 low-income schools throughout the country. The schools were chosen for their recent implementation of a new reading program and a reputation for obtaining higher-than-expected reading achievement among the students. School principals identified two teachers who were rated as either good or excellent teachers using an exemplary teaching rating scale. Participating teachers in kindergarten through third grade were observed for an hour once a month across a five month period, and the teachers kept a daily log of reading instructional activities for two weeks of the study and completed a questionnaire about reading instruction. Researchers compiled a school case study that included descriptions of the school and teacher factors, such as the amount of teacher-student dialogue and interaction, the frequency of instructional behaviors such as coaching and scaffolding, and nature the teacher instruction (telling or explaining). Student reading performance data were collected on a random sample of students in November and May using individually administered assessments of reading accuracy, fluency, and comprehension.

The results highlight the role of teacher characteristics in overall student success. Teachers in schools where children were higher-achieving reported reading was a priority of the teaching staff. The most effective teachers of reading included explicit instruction as well as coaching, small group instruction, independent reading time, and the use of high-level questions in text discussions plus writing activities. The collaborative school wide approach of using small groups for general reading instruction and for targeted reading intervention contributed to an average of 134 minutes a day of reading. Consistent with Wharton-McDonald et al. (1998) were the findings that student outcomes were influenced by teachers' abilities to manage student on-task time, use a balanced approach to reading instruction, and use coaching (scaffolding) as the preferred interaction style rather than primarily teacher-directed instructional styles. Unlike the Wharton-McDonald et al. study, only 16% of the K-3 grade teachers asked higher-level questions to promote student thinking.

The research generally presents evidence from different methodologies that instructional practices and teachers' abilities to provide a balanced approach to reading are related to elementary student performance. The implications of this research for preschool teachers includes realizing the depth of knowledge that is needed to implement successful instructional strategies in the early childhood classroom and the importance of knowledge of the developmental sequence of linguistic and cognitive processes associated with emergent literacy (e.g., Whitehurst & Lonigan, 1998).

Literacy Models and Teacher Training

The research on literacy instruction for emergent readers has grown in recent years. The manner in which such activities engage children in the reading process is important. Reading to children can involve just the adult reading and the child listening. In contrast, dialogic reading (Whitehurst & Lonigan, 1998) involves both the adult and child in the reading process with the adult encouraging the child to become involved in telling the story, identifying words, and asking and responding to questions about the story.

Studies have examined how interactive book readings impact children's expressive and receptive language (Elley, 1989; Hargrave & Senechal, 2000; Justice, Chow, Capellini, Flanigan, & Colton, 2003; Penno, Wilkinson, & Moore, 2002; Wasik & Bond, 2001). Some common features in the studies were the use of small groups of children in school settings, direct observations of book reading activities as part of the methodology, and the use of multiple measures to determine children's gains in expressive and receptive language. The studies differed in the role of the regular program teacher in the activities, the use of a control or comparison group, and the length of time for the book readings. In some studies, teachers introduced the vocabulary and displayed objects to represent the words before reading the book and in other studies the vocabulary was only included as a part of the book reading. Even with varied approaches, the results of these studies consistently showed greater gains in children's receptive vocabulary from exposure to interactive book readings compared to no-treatment controls. Whether dialogic book reading or shared book reading improves children's expressive vocabulary is equivocal. (See Hoskyn, Chapter 6, this volume for a different conclusion based on a recent meta-analysis, which shows that reviews of the literature may lead to different conclusions depending on which studies meet inclusion criteria.)

Teacher training was a component of several studies (Hargrave & Senechal, 2000; Wasik & Bond, 2001). For example, in the Wasik and Bond study, teacher training included defining the target vocabulary, employing questions that would move children beyond yes and no answers, and facilitating opportunities for children to be heard. The children in the Wasik and Bond study made significant gains in identifying vocabulary within the text and also on the PPVT-III (a measure of receptive vocabulary) compared to a control group. The observations of the trained teachers indicated that they had operationalized the book reading strategies into more aspects of their teaching and interaction with their students. Wasik and Bond (p. 247) noted:

> There were increased opportunities for children to talk and discuss both the story and the extension activities as well as how these educational experiences related to their lives. In turn the children were influenced by the teachers' behaviors.

Hargrave and Senechal (2000) used a video tape to train teachers and parents in dialogic reading that included role-playing and discussion. The dialogic reading techniques focused on asking "wh" questions (e.g., what, where, when, why, who, which, and how), following up children's answers with another question, and giving feedback, praise, and encouragement to guide children. The results of the study showed that teachers trained in dialogic reading asked 12 times the number of "wh" questions and praised six times more often compared to the regular teachers, but this difference in teaching practices was not statistically significant. The children in the dialogic reading condition identified new vocabulary from the text and made significant gains in receptive vocabulary as measured by the PPVT-III. The book reading and vocabulary intervention studies provide evidence that these approaches engage children in talking about the literature and understanding the vocabulary that they hear in the stories.

What emerges from the research is the need for preschool teachers to have greater expertise in specific and specialized literacy strategies and activities. The national and state focus on early learning standards will influence the knowledge that preschool teachers must have to provide the environment and pedagogy needed for the development of emergent readers and writers.

■ Discussion and Implications

Changes in early childhood education have come with the growing awareness that learning in the preschool period influences life long learning and achievement. With this growing awareness has come the development by states of early learning standards for the preschool period, changes in the preparation and credentialing of lead teachers in early childhood education programs, and the growing research literature documenting how teacher characteristics and instructional practices influence children' learning outcomes. There are now higher expectations for the benefits young children should gain from attending preschool education programs. This chapter has provided a review of early learning standards and the research evidence showing that emergent literacy skills developed in the preschool period provide the foundation upon which later reading skills are built. The important roles of the home environment and parent-child interactions were described to emphasize that learning can and should occur in settings outside as well as within the school and classroom. However, the main focus of the chapter has been the review of the literature about the influence of the teacher, including teacher qualifications, beliefs, and instructional practices, on children's literacy learning in early childhood and early primary grades.

Although the characteristics of teachers that link with good or excellent student learning outcomes have been identified, there is still the reality that many young children are not gaining the benefits from preschool and primary grades education that they should be. West, Denton, and Germino-Hausken (2000) and Zill and West (2001) report that many children, especially from low-income homes and second language learners, enter kindergarten with poorly developed emergent literacy skills despite attending preschool education programs. Others report that preschool and kindergarten children with poorly developed emergent literacy skills have difficulty catching up to children with stronger skills despite exposure to instructional programs in kindergarten and the primary grades that benefit other children (Tramontana, Hooper, & Selzer, 1988). There is still too little information about how to change the developmental trajectory of preschool children whose emergent literacy skills place them at-risk for poor reading outcomes.

In an effort to better understand the learning process, researchers have suggested ways in which children's learning outcome data can be used for instructional purposes. In the preschool years, assessments of children's skills often show that some children demonstrate large gains and some small gains in learning across the school year. For example, Molfese et al. (2006) studied 4-year-old children attending preschool programs designed for economically disadvantaged children. Changes in letter naming skills between fall and spring assessment points were compared. Within the sample of 57 children, 53% made no gains or gains of only one letter between fall and spring assessment times compared to the 47% of classmates who made gains averaging 7 letters. How can the differences between these two groups of children be evaluated? Are the gains related to the characteristics of the teacher, characteristics of the curriculum used in the classroom, characteristics of the children, or of all of these characteristics?

Identifying the source of differences in children's learning outcomes is difficult to pinpoint, but Fuchs, Fuchs, and Compton (2004) suggested that responsiveness-to-instruction (RTI) could be used to identify children with learning disabilities by examining whether their "response to generally effective instruction (i.e., instruction to which most children respond) is dramatically inferior to that of their peers" (p. 216). RTI can allow educators to determine a child's need for additional help based on his or her responses to highly structured early interventions or instruction (Reschly, 2003). If a child does not show gains in learning in the classroom with instruction that benefits most of the other children in the class, then the explanation would center on characteristics of the child, rather than on teacher or curriculum characteristics. In that case, an individual education plan for the child would be indicated. However, if neither the child nor classmates make gains, then the explanation does not lie with the child or the children. Recent research implementing the RTI approach has yielded promising results for children in the school years (e.g., O'Connor, 2000; O'Connor, Fulmer, & Harty, 2003; Vaughn, Linan-Thompson, & Hickman, 2003; Vaughn, Wanzek, Woodruff, & Linan-Thompson, 2007). Teachers in early childhood classrooms play critical roles in children's early learning, but RTI's applications to children in preschool programs who do not respond to early intervention await further investigation.

■ References

Ackerman, D. J. (2003). *States' efforts in improving the qualifications of early care and education teachers*. National Institute for Early Education Research. Retrieved, June 20, 2006, from http://epx.sagepub.com/cgi/content/abstract/18/2/311.

Almon, J. (2004). *The vital role of play in early childhood education*. Retrieved, August 1, 2006, from http://www.waldorflibrary.org/Journal_Articles/RB802.pdf#page=4.

Arizona Department of Education. (2005). *Early learning standards*. Retrieved, March 20, 2006, from www.azed.gov/earlychildhood/downloads/EarlyLearningStandards.pdf.

Arnett, J. (1989). Caregivers in day-care centers: Does training matter? *Journal of Applied Developmental Psychology, 10*, 541–552.

Assel, M. A., Landry, S. H., Swank, P., Smith, K. E., & Steelman, L. M. (2003). Precursors to mathematical skills: Examining the roles of visual-spatial skills, executive processes, and parenting factors. *Applied Developmental Science, 7*, 27–38.

Aylward, G. (1997). Environmental influences: Considerations for early assessment and intervention. In S. Dollinger & L. DiLalla (Eds.), *Prevention and intervention issues across the life span* (pp. 9–34). Mahwah, NJ, Lawrence Erlbaum Associates.

Barnett, W. S. (2003). Better teachers, better preschools: Student achievement linked to teacher qualifications. *Preschool Policy Matters, 2*, New Brunswick, NJ, NIEER.

Bayley, N. (1969). *Manual for the Bayley Scales of infant development*. New York, The Psychological Corporation.

Bee, H., Barnard, K., Eyres, S., Gray, C., Hammond, M., Spietz, A., Snyder, C., & Clark, B. (1982). Prediction of IQ and language skill from perinatal status, child performance, family characteristics, and mother-infant interaction. *Child Development, 53*, 1134–1156.

Berk, L. (1985). Relationship of caregiver education to child-oriented attitudes, job satisfaction, and behaviors toward children. *Child Care Quarterly, 14*, 103–129.

Bowman, B., Donovan, S., & Burns, M. S. (2001). *Eager to learn*. Washington, DC, National Academy Press.

Bradley, R., Whiteside, L., Caldwell, B., Casey, P., Kelleher, K., Pope, S., Swanson, M., Barrett, K., & Cross, D. (1993). Maternal IQ, the home environment, and child IQ in low birthweight, premature children. *International Journal of Behavioral Development, 16*, 61–74.

Bredekamp, S., & Copple, C. (1997). *Developmentally appropriate practice in early childhood programs. Revised edition.* Washington, DC, National Association for the Education of Young Children.

Brown, E. T. (2005). The influence of teachers' efficacy and beliefs on mathematics instruction in the early childhood classroom. *Journal of Early Childhood Teacher Education, 26,* 239–257.

Carnegie Corporation of New York. (2002). *What kids need: Today's best ideas for nurturing, teaching, and protecting young children.* Boston, Beacon Press.

Cassidy, D. J., Buell, M. J., Pugh-Hoese, S., & Russel, S. (1995). The effect of education on child care teachers' beliefs and classroom quality: Year one evaluation of the TEACH early childhood Associate degree scholarship. *Early Childhood Research Quarterly, 10,* 171–183.

Cassidy, D. J., & Lawrence, J. M. (2000). Teacher beliefs: The whys behind the how tos in child care classrooms. *Journal of Research in Childhood Education, 14,* 193–204.

Charlesworth, R., Hart, C., Burts, D., Mosely, J., & Fleege, P. (1993). Measuring the developmental appropriateness of kindergarten teachers' beliefs and practices. *Early Childhood Research Quarterly, 8,* 255–276.

Cunningham, A., Perry, K., Stanovich, K., & Stanovich, P. (2004). Disciplinary knowledge of K-3 teachers and their knowledge calibration in the domain of early literacy. *Annals of Dyslexia, 54,* 139–167.

Denton, K., & West, J. (2002). *Children's reading and mathematics achievement in kindergarten and first grade.* Washington, DC, U.S. Department of Education, National Center for Education Statistics.

Dickinson, D., & Tabors, P. (2001). *Beginning literacy with language: Young children learning at home and school.* Baltimore, MD, Brookes.

Dunn, L. S. (1993). Proximal and distal features of day care quality and children's development. *Early Childhood Research Quarterly, 8,* 167–192.

Elley, W. (1989). Vocabulary acquisition from listening to stories. *Reading Research Quarterly, 24,* 174–187.

Florida Voluntary Pre-kindergarten Program. (2006). Retrieved, August 29, 2006, from http://www.vpkhelp.org/.

Frankenburg, W. K., & Dodds, J. B. (1967). The Denver developmental screening test. *Journal of Pediatrics, 71,* 181–191.

Fuchs, D., Fuchs, L. S., & Compton, D. (2004). Identifying reading disabilities by responsiveness-to-instruction: Specifying measures and criteria. *Learning Disabilities Quarterly, 27,* 216–227.

Graham, T., Nash, C., & Paul, K. (1997). Young children's exposure to mathematics: The child care context. *Early Childhood Educational Journal, 25,* 31–38.

Goodenough, F. (1945). *Developmental psychology* (2nd ed.). New York, Appleton-Century Company.

Hargrave, A. C., & Senechal, M. (2000). Book reading intervention with preschool children who have limited vocabularies: The benefits of regular reading and dialogic reading. *Early Childhood Research Quarterly, 15,* 75–90.

Harms, T., & Clifford, R. (1980). *Early childhood environment rating scale.* New York, Teachers College Press.

Harms, T., Clifford, R., & Cryer, D. (1998). *Early Childhood Environment Rating Scale, revised edition.* New York, Teachers College Press.

Harms, T., Cryer, D., & Clifford, R. (1990). *Infant-Toddler Environment Rating Scale.* New York, Teachers College Press.

Helburn, S. W. (1995). *Cost, quality and child outcomes in child care centers. Technical report.* Denver, University of Colorado at Denver, Department of Economics, Center for Research in Economic and Social Policy.

Hess, R., Holloway, S., Dickson, P., & Prince, G. (1984). Maternal variables as predictors of children's school readiness and later achievement in vocabulary and mathematics in sixth grade. *Child Development, 55,* 1902–1912.

Howes, C., Phillips, D. A., & Whitebrook, M. (1992). Teacher characteristics and effective teaching in childcare: Findings from the national child care staffing study. *Child & Youth Care Forum, 21,* 399–414.

Howes, C., Smith, E., & Galinsky, E. (1995). *The Florida child care quality improvement study: Interim report families & work institute.* Families and Work Institute. Retrieved, October 7, 2008, from http://www.familiesandwork.org/index.asp?PageAction=VIEWPROD&ProdID=86.

Hurlock, E. (1942). *Child development.* New York, McGraw-Hill Book Company.

Idaho State Department of Education. (2004). *Idaho early learning standards resource guide.* Retrieved, October 7, 2008, from http://www.sde.idaho.gov/SpecialEd/docs/content/IdahoEarlyLearningStandards.pdf.

International Reading Association (IRA) and the National Association for the Education of Young Children (NAEYC). (1998). *Learning to read and write: Developmentally appropriate practices for young children.* Newark, DE, IRA.

Justice, L. M., Chow, S. M., Capellini, C., Flanigan, K., & Colton, S. (2003). Emergent literacy intervention for vulnerable preschoolers: Relative effects of two approaches. *American Journal of Speech-Language Pathology, 12,* 320–332.

Kagan, D. (1992). Implications of research on teacher beliefs. *Educational Psychologist, 27,* 65–90.

Kentucky Department of Education. (2003). *Kentucky's early childhood standards.* Retrieved, October 7, 2008, from https://www.kedsonline.org/Documents/AssessmentSummaryPage2004.pdf.

Kids Count. (2000). *Census Data on-line.* Retrieved, June 14, 2006, from http://www.aecf.org.

Kowalski, K., Pretti-Frontczak, K., & Johnson, L. (2001). Importance of various developmental skills and abilities. *Journal of Research in Childhood Education, 16,* 5–14.

Landry, S., Miller-Loncar, C., Smith, K., & Swank, P. (2002). The role of early parenting in children's development of executive processes. *Developmental Neuropsychology, 21,* 15–41.

Landry, S., Smith, K., Swank, P., & Miller-Loncar, C. (2000). Early maternal and child influences on children's later independent cognitive and social functioning. *Child Development, 7,* 358–375.

Lee, J. (2004). *Preschool teachers' beliefs about appropriate early literacy and mathematics education*. Doctoral dissertation, Columbia University.

Leinonen, S., Muller, K., Leppanen, P., Aro, M., Ahonen, T., & Lyytinen, H. (2001). Heterogeneity in adult dyslexic readers: Relating processing skills to the speed and accuracy of oral text reading. *Reading and Writing, 14,* 265–296.

Lonigan, C. J., Anthony, J. L., Bloomfield, B. G., Dyer, S. M., & Samwel, C. S. (1999). Effects of two shared-reading interventions on emergent literacy skills of at-risk preschoolers. *Journal of Early Intervention, 22,* 306–322.

Lynch, J., Anderson, J., Anderson, A., & Shapiro, J. (2006). Parents' beliefs about young children's literacy development and parents' literacy behaviors. *Reading Psychology, 27,* 1–20.

Maxwell, K., McWilliam, R. A., Hemmeter, M., Ault, M., & Schuster, J. (2001). Predictors of developmentally appropriate classroom practices in kindergarten through third grade. *Early Childhood Research Quarterly, 16,* 431–452.

McCarty, F., Abbott-Shim, M., & Lambert, R. (2001). The relationship between teacher beliefs and practices and Head Start classroom quality. *Early Education and Development, 12,* 225–238.

McGuinness, D. (2004). *Early reading instruction: What science really tells us about how to teaching reading*. Cambridge, MA, A Bradford Book.

McMullen, M., & Alat, K. (2002). Education matters in the nurturing of the beliefs of preschool caregivers and teachers. *Early Childhood Research & Practice* [Online], *4*. Retrieved, August 28, 2006, from http://ecrp.uiuc.edu/v4n2/mcmullen.html.

Moats, L. C. (1994). The missing foundation in teacher education: Knowledge of the structure of spoken and written language. *Annals of Dyslexia, 44,* 81–102.

Molfese, V., & DiLalla, L. (1995). Cost-effective approaches to identifying developmental delay in 4- to 7-year-old children. *Early Education and Development, 6,* 266–277.

Molfese, V., Modglin, A., Beswick, J., Neamon, J., Berg, S., Berg, J., et al. (2006). Letter knowledge, phonological processing and print awareness: Skill development in non-reading preschool children. *Journal of Learning Disabilities, 39,* 296–305.

National Association for the Education of Young Children. (2001). Retrieved, October 7, 2008, from http://www.naeyc.org/faculty/faq.asp.

National Association for the Education of Young Children. (2007). Retrieved, June 5, 2007, from http://www.naeyc.org/.

National Child Care Information Center. (2007). *Selected state early learning guidelines on the web*. Retrieved, June 5, 2007, from http://www.nccic.org/pubs/goodstart/elgwebsites.pdf.

National Education Goals 2000: Educate America Act (1994). Retrieved, June 14, 2006, from http://www.nd.edu/~rbarger/www7/goals200.html.

National Education Goals Report: Building a Nation of Learners. (1998). Washington, DC, The National Education Goals Panel.

Nespor, J. (1987). The role of beliefs in the practice of teaching. *Journal Curriculum Studies, 19,* 317–328.

No Child Left Behind. (2001). Retrieved, June 14, 2006, from http://www.ed.gov/legislation/ESEA02/.

O'Connor, R. E. (2000). Increasing the intensity of intervention in kindergarten and first grade. *Learning Disabilities Research & Practice, 15,* 43–54.

O'Connor, R. E., Fulmer, D., & Harty, K. (2003, December). *Tiers of Intervention in kindergarten through third grade.* Paper presented at the National Research Center on Learning Disabilities Responsiveness-to-Intervention Symposium, Kansas City, MO.

Pajares, M. (1992). Teacher's beliefs and educational research: Cleaning up a messy construct. *Review of Educational Research, 62,* 307–332.

Penno, J., Wilkinson, I., & Moore, D. (2002). Vocabulary acquisition from teacher explanation and repeated listening to stories: Do they overcome the Matthew effect? *Journal of Educational Psychology, 94,* 22–33.

Pennsylvania Department of Education and Department of Public Welfare. (2005). *Pennsylvania early learning standards for pre-kindergarten.* Retrieved, October 7, 2008, from http://www.pde.state.pa.us/early_child-hood/lib/early_childhood/Early_Learning_Standards_August_05.pdf.

Phelps, G., & Schilling, S. (2004). Developing measures of content knowledge for teaching reading. *The Elementary School Journal, 105,* 31–48.

Pianta, R., Howes, C., Early, D., Clifford, R., Bryant, D., & Burchinal, M. (2005). Features of pre-kindergarten programs, classrooms, and teachers: Do they predict observed classroom quality and child-teacher interactions? *Applied Developmental Science, 9,* 149–159.

Prescott, E., Kritchevsky, S., & Jones, E. (1972). *The day care environmental inventory.* Washington, DC, U.S. Department of Health, Education, and Welfare.

Reschly, R. (2003, December). *What if LD identification changed to reflect research findings?* Paper presented at the National Research Center on Learning Disabilities Responsiveness-to-Intervention Symposium, Kansas City, MO.

Scarborough, H. (1991). Antecedents to reading disability: Preschool language development and literacy experiences of children from dyslexic families. *Reading and Writing, 2,* 219–233.

Scarr, S., & Ricciuti, A. (1991). What effects do parents have on their children? In L. Okagaki & R. Sternberg (Eds.), *Directors of developmental influences on the development of children's thinking* (pp. 3–23). Hillsdale, NJ, Lawrence Erlbaum Associates.

Scott-Little, C., Kagan, S., & Frelow, V. (2003). Creating the conditions for success with early learning standards; Results from a national study of state-level standards for children's learning prior to kindergarten. *Early Childhood Research and Practice* (Online), *5.* Retrieved, August 1, 2006, from http://ecrp.uiuc.edu/v5n2/little.html.

Shanahan, T., Molfese, V., Lonigan, C., Cunningham, A., Strickland, D., & Westberg, L. (2004, December). *The National Early Literacy Panel: Findings from a synthesis of scientific research on early literacy development*. Paper presented at the National Reading Conference, San Antonio, TX.

Share, D., Jorm, A., Maclean, R., Matthews, R., & Waterman, B. (1983). Early reading achievement, oral language ability, and a child's home background. *Australian Psychologist, 18,* 75–87.

Spidell Rusher, A., McGrevin, C. Z., & Lambiotte, J. G. (1992). Belief systems of early childhood teachers and their principals regarding early childhood education. *Early Childhood Research Quarterly, 7,* 277–296.

Stipek, D., & Byler, P. (1997). Early childhood education teachers: Do they practice what they preach. *Early Childhood Research Quarterly, 12,* 305–325.

Stutsman, R. (1931). *Mental measurement of preschool children with a guide for the administration of the Merrill-Palmer Scale of mental tests*. Yonkers on Hudson, NY, Worldbook.

Taylor, B., Pearson, P., Clark, K., & Walpole, S. (2000). Effective schools and accomplished teachers: Lessons about primary-grade reading and instruction in low-income schools. *Elementary School Journal, 101,* 121–165.

Thorndike, E. (1914). *Educational psychology: Briefer course*. New York, Teachers College, Columbia University.

Torgeson, J. K. (1998). Catch them before their fall: Identification and assessment to prevent reading failure in young children. *American Educator, Spring/Summer,* 1–8.

Tout, K., Zaslow, M., & Berry, D. (2006). Quality and qualifications: Links between professional development and quality in early care and education settings. In M. Zaslow & I. Martinez-Beck (Eds.), *Critical issues in early childhood professional development* (pp. 77–110). Baltimore, MD, Brooks.

Tramontana, M., Hooper, S., & Selzer, S. (1988). Research on preschool prediction of later academic achievement: A review. *Developmental Review, 8,* 89–146.

U.S. Census Bureau. (2002). *Facts for features: Back to school*. Retrieved, June 14, 2006, from http://www.census.gov.

Vartuli, S. (1999). How early childhood teacher beliefs vary across grade level. *Early Childhood Research and Practice, 14,* 489–514.

Vaughn, S., Linan-Thompson, S., & Hickman, P. (2003). Response to instruction as a means of identifying students with reading/learning disabilities. *Journal of Exceptional Children, 69,* 391–409.

Vaughn, S., Wanzek, J., Woodruff, A. L., & Linan-Thompson, S. (2007). A three-tier model for preventing reading difficulties and early identification of students with reading disabilities. In D. H. Haagar, S. Vaughn, & J. K. Klingner (Eds.), *Validated reading practices for the three tiers of intervention*. Baltimore, MD, Brookes.

Walsh, K. (2001). *Teacher certification reconsidered: Stumbling for quality*. Baltimore, MD, Abell Foundation.

Wasik, B., & Bond, M. (2001). Beyond the pages of a book: Interactive reading and language development in preschool classrooms. *Journal of Educational Psychology, 93,* 243–250.

West, J., Denton, K., and Germino-Hausken, E. (2000). *America's Kindergartners* (NCES 2000–070). Washington, DC, National Center for Education Statistics.

Wharton-McDonald, R., Pressley, N., & Hampston, J. M. (1998). Literacy instruction in nine first-grade classrooms: Teacher characteristics and student achievement. *Elementary School Journal, 99*, 101–128.

Whitebrook, M. (2003). *Early education quality: Higher teacher qualifications for better learning environments.* Berkley, CA, Center for the Study of Child Care Employment.

Whitebrook, M., Howes, C., & Phillips, D. (1990). *The national child care staffing. Final Report: Who cares? Child care teachers and the quality of care in America.* Washington, DC, Center for the Child Care Workforce.

Whitehurst, G., & Lonigan, C. (1998). Child development and emergent literacy. *Child Development, 69*, 848–872.

Zill, N., & West, J. (2001). *Entering kindergarten: A portrait of American children when they begin school.* U.S. Department of Education, OERI, NCES 2001–35.

■ Note

1. Early childhood education encompasses the period from birth through age 8 years and involves the education of young children (National Association for the Education of Young Children). In this chapter, the focus is on educationally oriented preschool programs for children 3 years and older (e.g., pre-kindergarten programs for 4 year olds, preschool and nursery school programs for children 3–5 years old) involving teachers certified and/or trained in early childhood education. The chapter is not about child care or day care programs for children in this age range.

16. SHARING RESEARCH KNOWLEDGE WITH TEACHERS

The Story of *Linguistic Remedies*

Barbara Wise, Laura Rogan, and Luann Sessions

■ Defining Linguistic Remedies

Linguistic Remedies (LR) provides teachers with a well-organized and deep knowledge system about reading, language, and the individual needs of children (Wise, 2004a, 2004b). Just as it encourages teachers to make learning to read engaging and interesting for children, the program is engaging for teachers who want to learn this kind of teaching. To some educators, "evidence-based intervention" is synonymous with "boring," conjuring up images of stuffy schoolmarms droning out phonics rules in highly scripted lessons to bored children who parrot back rote answers in chorus. It need not be this way. We know that extensive reading for comprehension in interesting books is absolutely essential for creating independent, thoughtful, and eager readers. However, for readers who read words slowly or inaccurately, accurate

We thank the following people for contributing ideas to LR or to this paper: Joanna Stewart, Camille Hook, Debra Wilde, Denise Ensslin, Elenn Steinberg, and Irene Faivre in the Denver-Boulder area; Becky Aschbrenner and Caroline Fairchild of District 20 Colorado Springs; Jennifer Martinez, Patty Lutrell, Patte Forget, Becky Wesley, Meredith Jobe, and Bob Howell of District 11 Colorado Springs; Sarah Bender, Marsha Garrett, Caroline Nicholsen, and Jana Brucker of Colorado Springs; Deb Ingels and Lynn Doughman in northern Colorado; Phyllis Green of Denver Public Schools; Gladys Kolenovsky and Karen Avrit in Texas; and Andrea Smith, Elizabeth Sorby, Naomi Michel, Christine Billroth, and Debra Wickliff in Washington.

We thank the following agencies for supporting the research reported here: The National Institute of Health (NIH) HD11683 and HD22223 to R. Olson for the ROSS studies; NSF/IERI for REC-0115419107, to W. Kintsch; National Science Foundation (NSF) for grant IIS-0086107 to R. Cole; Institute of Education Sciences (IES), U.S. Department of Education, through Grants R305G040097 and R305A070231 to B. Wise, and NIH 5 P50 HD27802–17 to B. Wise as Project V of the Colorado Learning Disabilities Center, Olson, director. For their participation in research, we thank staff and students of these school districts: The Archdiocese of Denver, Boulder Valley, Ignacio, Strasburg and St. Vrain Valley. The opinions expressed are those of the authors and do not represent views of IES, U.S. Department of Education, NICHD, NSF or any institutions or people listed above.

and fluent word reading is required before that engaged reading can happen. We propose that word-level work can also be interesting and exciting when it includes guided discoveries of the science and history of language and reading. LR tries to communicate that excitement to teachers, parent-coaches, and students. What is unusual, though not unique, in LR is that while grounded in research and strong on all aspects of sound and word study, it is also highly engaging, with a constructive spirit of inquiry throughout the entire program.

This chapter discusses the research background for LR, and includes its core pedagogical concepts. It describes LR's basic program and supports for pacing, organization, problem solving, and communication. The chapter includes some modifications teachers have made for different children or teaching situations. The final sections discuss some patterns of successes and challenges in implementations of LR in schools, and what we have learned from those instances. The chapter aims to introduce readers to LR as an interesting example of implementing evidence-based instruction and to provide a few take home ideas for teachers to try themselves.

LR and this chapter begin from the Simple View of reading (Gough & Tunmer, 1986), which captures key instructional components.

■ Application of Research to Practice

The Simple View of Reading (Gough & Tunmer, 1986)

This view accounts for reading comprehension as the product *of the processes underlying* **word reading** *and the processes underlying* **oral language comprehension**. Language comprehension describes the ability to gain meaning and draw inferences from spoken text. Many processes underlie both word reading and language comprehension. Before we discuss these processes, let us lay out the four main categories of readers according to the simple view as Wise and Snyder (2002) also described.

The four basic profiles include children with (a) good reading (usually the largest group), (b) specific reading disabilities, (c) specific comprehension difficulties, and (4) mixed difficulties. Note that the dimensions involved are normal and continuous, with students clustering around the middle. Therefore, in a given school district, percentages depend on cut-off criteria for "difficulty," as well as on whether the district serves many English Language Learners (ELL) or children from poverty. These factors greatly impact vocabulary, the strongest predictor of language comprehension.

To clarify the four categories, we list some of the processes that underlie word reading and listening comprehension, and on which children can also vary.

Word reading is affected by at least these processes:

a. *Phoneme awareness*, the ability to identify and manipulate sounds in spoken syllables.
b. *Phonological memory and sensitivity*, the ability to repeat or judge sameness in novel words.
c. *Phonological decoding*, the ability to use letter-sound correspondences to decode print.
d. *Orthographic coding*, the ability to recognize written patterns of words.
e. *Speed of language processing*, measured by speed of naming familiar symbols.
f. *Oral Vocabulary*

Oral Language Comprehension depends on higher level linguistic and cognitive abilities including:

a. *Oral Vocabulary*
b. *Background knowledge*
c. *Morphological and syntactic abilities* for making in-text connections or bridging inferences
d. *Verbal memory or working memory*
e. *Speed of language processing*

How well does the model account for reading? In most studies, efficient word reading and oral language comprehension explain 75% of the variance in reading comprehension (Hoover & Gough, 1990). In recent behavior genetic studies, they explain everything but the error variance (Keenan et al., 2006). Whether word reading or oral language comprehension carries more weight changes with the measure used and with reading development (Catts et al., 2005; Vellutino, Tunmer, Jaccard, & Chen, 2007). Word reading impacts reading comprehension more in second grade, less in fourth, and by eighth grade oral language comprehension contributes the most. Further research may show that reading comprehension involves something beyond these measures. For instance, memory demands surely differ in reading and listening, especially if the text is available for review during a reading test (Pearson & Hamm, 2005; Swanson & Trahan, 1996). Vocabulary and naming speed affect both word reading and language comprehension (Catts, Adlof, & Weismer, 2006; Scarborough, 2001; Snow, 2002). These authors and others have found that vocabulary is the strongest predictor of language comprehension and the strongest predictor of reading comprehension, beyond word reading. Naming speed also affects both word reading and language comprehension; it also helps predict later poor reading comprehension (Cutting & Scarborough, 2006; Joshi, 2003; Scarborough, 1998a, 1998b; Wolfe, 1999).

Besides showing statistical validity, the categories can be used effectively to guide initial and general classroom instruction (even though children vary widely within the categories). One interesting computer program is finding success in making dynamic recommendations about instructional content and delivery using the simple view as a base (Connor, Morrison, Fishman, Schatschneider, & Underwood, 2007). We describe the basic profiles, variations in the patterns, and basic instructional suggestions later.

1. *Good Readers* (see Table 16.1) read words accurately and efficiently and comprehend spoken language well. When reading grade-level text, they link concepts within the text and integrate them with their background knowledge and goals, creating a "gist" of the text. Readers who have constructed a gist can summarize and make inferences from a text (Caccamise & Snyder, 2006; Kintsch, 1998). Readers with this profile usually succeed with good classroom instruction that covers the major components of reading, including at least the National Reading Panel's suggestions of Phonological Awareness, Alphabet and Phonics, Fluency, Vocabulary, and Comprehension, best presented in explicit but integrated ways (NICHD, 2000).

2. Children with *Specific Reading Difficulties* (SRD) have difficulties only on the word reading side of the model. They show problems summarizing or making inferences when *reading* a text, but not when *listening* to it (Joshi, 2003; Rayner et al., 2001). Some children with SRD misread many words. Others read words accurately, but require much time and effort to do so. This effort creates a resource bottleneck, sapping the attention needed for comprehension (Perfetti, Marron, & Foltz, 1996). Some common variations within SRD include the following:

SRD from weak phonology. Weak phonological, or speech-based, processing causes many of these word reading difficulties. Most children with SRD have a hard time with phoneme awareness, that is, becoming aware of speech sounds (phonemes) in spoken words. Compared to other children,

TABLE 16.1   *Major Profiles of Children's Reading from the Simple View*

	Low Oral Language Comprehension	High Oral Language Comprehension
High Word Reading	Specific Comprehension Difficulties (SCD)	Good Readers
Low Word Reading	Mixed Difficulties (SCD + SRD)	Specific Reading Difficulties (SRD)

they struggle to identify and manipulate sounds in spoken syllables (e.g., "Say coat without saying the sound /k/"). Without easy access to sounds in syllables, children struggle to understand the alphabetic code of how speech maps on to print (Liberman & Shankweiler, 1985). They have a hard time with decoding, getting the print to talk; reading eludes them or is loathsome. Phoneme awareness ability is reciprocal with learning to read. Thus, while children need a certain level of it to launch into reading, phoneme awareness also improves as they read (Morais et al., 1986).

Weak word reading from other causes. Word reading can also be hindered by lack of experience due to poor teaching or to high mobility. Attention deficits can impair word reading from lack of attention to teaching and to texts. About one-third of children with attention problems also have phonological problems, and vice versa (Willcutt & Pennington, 2000).

Slow word reading can also result from slow naming speed, with or without good decoding. Speeded reading practice can improve reading speed for all children with slow reading, leading to improved reading comprehension as word reading becomes easier (Stanovich, 1987). Although all children with slow word reading need work to increase reading rate, children with slow naming speed will need substantially more, and may never achieve average reading rates. Children with slow naming speeds are candidates for later help with assistive technology to compensate for slower reading rates (Elkind, Cohen, & Murray, 1993; Elkind & Elkind, 2007).

Children with weak phonology but high verbal ability in vocabulary and syntax can often read adequately from context at least into third grade, but they usually have spelling problems (Lyon, 1999; Scarborough, 1998a). Spelling turns out to be a powerful diagnostic, on a par with decoding, for identifying children at-risk for later reading problems in English and in Spanish (Arteagoitea & Howard, 2004; Hecht & Close, 2002). Their weak spelling also discourages them from writing.

To sum up, those children with SRD whose major difficulties relate *only* to slow or inaccurate word reading will need extra work in phonological awareness, decoding, encoding, and fluency. However, they should not need intensive explicit work in comprehension beyond the support from effective regular classroom instruction in vocabulary and comprehension strategies.

3. *Specific Comprehension Difficulties. (SCD):* Other children comprehend poorly despite their accurate and fluent word reading. Poor comprehenders have difficulty recalling gist and major facts of stories even when they listen to them (Nation et al., 1999; Stothard & Hulme, 1996).

SCD from environmentally weak vocabulary. The most common problem for children with SCD is a weak vocabulary due to poverty or to learning to read in a second language. Vocabulary is the strongest predictor of reading comprehension, especially among children who are not identified as struggling until fourth grade (Catts et al., 2006). Most first graders from poverty situations have weak language skills and know about four times fewer words than children with average socio-economic status (SES). Shockingly, by fourth grade, higher SES children know 14 times as many words as do the children from poverty (Biemiller, 1999)! These children need early and continuing work to enrich vocabulary, language, and concepts. They need extensive reading practice with discussions and elaborations of vocabulary and comprehension. In contrast, some higher SES ELL may only need simple vocabulary work, if they have had a richer language experience in their first language. Whatever the cause, educators must recognize and start treating vocabulary problems early (Beck & McKeown, 1991).

SCD from constitutional reasons. Some specifically poor comprehenders struggle with more than just vocabulary. They often show difficulties with abstract words and with using syntactic links like pronoun referents to make connections within and among sentences (Cain & Oakhill, 1998; Oakhill & Yuill, 1991). These children need work in vocabulary, language enrichment, engaging with text, and specific work to note and use the linguistic cues in spoken and written language to connect meaning and construct a gist.

4. *Children with Mixed Difficulties*: Children with severe mixed deficits appear to be most at-risk and require intensively delivered instruction to deal with both word reading and language comprehension issues (see Wise & Snyder, 2002). These will often include children with phonological difficulties who are also ELL or from a poverty background.

Using Response to Intervention rather than Diagnostic Labels

Many professionals now embrace a Response to Intervention (RTI) model (Vaughn & Fuchs, 2003). The model offers early identification and flexible delivery of instruction (Bradley, Danielson, & Hallahan, 2002). Most RTI implementations describe instruction in three tiers of intensity, meeting children's changing needs based on initial screening and/or on frequent measures of progress (Vaughn & Fuchs, 2003). In three-tier models, Tier 1 means good classroom instruction that covers at least these five domains: Phonological Awareness (PA), Alphabet and Phonics, Fluency, Vocabulary, and Comprehension (NICHD, 2000). Children who fail to progress in Tier 1 are assigned to Tier 2: Small group work with more intensive intervention and sometimes with a more intensive curriculum. Children who do not succeed with the small group adaptations may need some time with more intensive instruction more specifically tailored to their needs in special education or Tier 3.

Relationship of Linguistic Remedies *to the*
Simple View and RTI

LR grew out of research into causes and remedies for SRDs (Olson, Wise, Conners, & Rack, 1989; Wise & Olson, 1995), and its strategies are especially helpful for *children of all ages with SRDs and Mixed Difficulties, in Tier 2 and Tier 3 remedial settings.* Teachers learn how to teach explicit language-based strategies that especially affect word reading and vocabulary for a richer and deeper processing of words: phonological awareness, phonics, orthography, morphology, syntax, etymology, and vocabulary. It also teaches how to extend these concepts beyond competence into applied, automatic, and independent reading and writing. LR is also appropriate for *whole class Tier 1 instruction in K through second grade* for developing mastery of foundational skills in engaging yet explicit ways. Research suggests this is the most powerful time to invest in this kind of instruction, likely to help prevent later reading difficulties among many children (Fuchs et al., 2004; Torgesen, 2000).

　　Some of LR's pedagogy is helpful for children with language comprehension deficits, particularly in its expert tutoring strategies and in vocabulary. The course encourages listening to stories for interest and for the development of language, vocabulary, and comprehension. It prescribes extensive reading for meaning at the child's reading level from the earliest levels on, and it encourages good reading comprehension by engaging with the text while reading, using literature logs, and writing simple summaries. We recommend others' workshops and books that are either research validated or research compatible for more extensive coverage of engaging ways to support and teach comprehension. Among these, we find *Questioning the Author* (Beck, McKeown, Hamilton, & Kucan, 1997) and Tovani's *I Read it but I Don't Get It* (2000) to be especially helpful. Their strategies are easy and engaging for students to use, without distracting from reading the story. LR also helps teachers think about when to call in ELL and speech-language therapists for consultation or for Tier 3 treatment for students needing more in-depth treatment beyond these strategies.

Other Research Influences on Linguistic Remedies

Findings from computer-assisted intervention studies have influenced LR, and LR now also contributes to similar research. Wise and Olson's series of *Reading with ROSS* studies aimed to determine whether talking computer programs would prove powerful tools both for *remediation*, by enabling of extensive and intensive accurate practice, and for *research* about instruction, allowing comparisons of instructional treatments delivered with unbiased fidelity. Studies with real teachers in real classrooms will always be necessary to validate findings in natural settings, but computers can add unique information about what works best for which children. *After each research finding below, we italicize how LR has implemented the idea.*

In the ROSS studies, second to fifth grade children with word reading difficulties spent about 30 minutes of language arts or reading instructional time reading with ROSS in pull-out groups of 3–5 students. Each student read at his or her own computer, and a research assistant read with each child once a week. The children read interesting stories at their instructional level with speech support for any word they targeted with a mouse. ROSS tracked and supported comprehension with multiple choice main idea questions at logical breaks in the story, and it reviewed with children words they had missed. ROSS students made greater gains than similar children back in the classroom, confirming the power of talking reading programs as tools for remediation (Wise & Olson, 1995).

Specific training influenced gains. ROSS-trained children who spent their small group time and part of their computer time in phonological work made extra gains in phonological skills and untimed word reading. Other children whose small group work focused on comprehension strategies and who spent all their computer time reading accurately in context gained more on time-limited word reading (Wise & Olson, 1995). Thus, a great way to increase fluent reading is to read more, while reading accurately! The advantages from phonological work were strongest for children reading below third grade levels, and fluency advantages from more reading in context were strongest for children reading above third grade level (Wise, Ring, & Olson, 2000). *LR recommends a balance of integrated instruction that leans toward foundational skills at lower reading levels, changing to more and more reading in context as children improve in reading.*

In follow-up testing, phonologically trained children retained their advantage on phonological skills. However, with only 27–29 hours of instruction, differences between the trained groups in time-limited or untimed word reading washed out one and two years later. *For lasting gains, remediation should continue as long it takes for the child to read with self-correction and good comprehension at grade level, with established habits of independent reading of 30 minutes a day.*

Another set of ROSS studies compared different ways of teaching phonological awareness. Following a finding by Montgomery (1981) that children with SRD had difficulties tying speech-motor movements to speech sounds, one group received phonological awareness (PA) training with some speech-motor awareness, based on some of the articulatory explorations of the ADD program (Lindamood & Lindamood, 1966, 1975). Other children learned PA with a language-play base with no explicit speech-motor work. One study showed an advantage for the speech-motor version for children with the most severe deficits (Wise, Olson, Ring, & Sessions, 1997), but a second study with more subjects, but relatively fewer highly deficient readers, failed to replicate the finding (Wise, Ring, & Olson, 1999). At least the way the programs are taught, phonological awareness with speech-motor work was as helpful as with a language play base and key-word letter-sound charts. *LR teaches the speech-motor foundation for teachers' knowledge to use in pacing instruction, understanding errors, and guiding questions* as well as for developing a deep knowledge base for children's confidence and error-checking. (see Lepper et al., 1997). *LR teaches the language play methods as well, so teachers can choose the one they understand and enjoy best to teach to their students.*

In more recent research, many of LR's principles are influencing studies built on ROSS functionalities but adding an animated "Virtual Tutor" to make the program more engaging (Cole, Wise, & Van Vuuren, 2006; Wise et al., 2007). Wise and Van Vuuren's newest program (2007), Reading with RITA (Reading with Intelligent Tutoring Assistance), includes much teaching with focused hinting and covers almost the full LR sequence without the explicit speech motor work. *LR encourages using effective computer reading programs to allow teachers to work in small groups with some children, while others get needed intensive accurate reading practice.*

■ Core Concepts of Linguistic Remedies for Students and Teachers

Confidence from Competence

The concept of *confidence from competence* is pivotal in the program for both teachers and students. Teachers gain confidence as they learn more about language, reading, readers, and evaluating decisions. Students gain confidence as they learn to explore new material and check whether they are correct in reading and spelling, using their own natural speech and their scaffolding charts to check their hypotheses. Teachers' and students' confidence builds as they realize themselves as *lifelong learners who can learn anything they want to, so long as they work hard with the right tools and the support of a good team.*

Teachers as Scientists

LR encourages teachers to take *a scientific view,* grounding their teaching in research consensus and approaching the teaching situation as a scientist, observing themselves, their methods, and their children's engagement and progress to continue to refine their teaching. Teachers learn about reading research and aspects of intervention studies that make them more valid, such as control groups and random assignment to treatment and control groups. Evidence is strongest (though hard to achieve) with differently trained comparison groups. As an entrée to this literature, LR recommends review articles with varied views (Allington, 2002; Rayner et al., 2001; Simmons & Kame'enui, 1998; Wise, 2004; Wise & Snyder, 2002) and compilations of studies by research panels (NICHD, 2000; Snow, Burns, & Griffin, NRC Report, 1998). Teachers consider the bias of sources, discussing strengths and shortfalls of the "evidence" behind what is currently called evidence-based reading instruction. Evidence supports benefits for teachers (and sometimes for their students) who become well-informed about the knowledge base of reading, of language, and of intervention research (Brady & Gillis, 2006; Brady & Moats, 1997; McCutchen & Berninger, 1999; McCutchen et al., 2002).

Teaching Students to be Scientists with Focused Guided Discovery

LR helps teachers guide children's learning with *focused guided discovery.* Although Socrates is often credited with inventing this style of teaching, his dialogues are much less guided than Bruner's (1966). Bruner believed that guiding discoveries in logical sequenced ways increases the retention of material, because the child integrates new information with information already stored. He also argued that the more grounded a student was in the knowledge structures that underlie a topic, the better chance that the learning would generalize and transfer. Mayer (2003) later confirmed these expectations. Compared to unguided discovery and to expository instruction where the student is told the answer, Mayer found that guided discovery proved the most effective of the three, though it sometimes took longer than expository instruction. Lepper, Drake, and O'Donnell-Johnson (1997) found that these techniques are used by all expert effective tutors. LR adopts *guided discovery* as its central pedagogical tool. Teachers use scaffolded hints to guide students' discoveries or self-corrections about reading and language. They learn to allow *wait time* before providing a hint, to allow the child time to think and discover (Rowe, 1987; Tobin, 1987). All these help students learn to be *language scientists* who can observe, hypothesize, and check all learning, gaining knowledge, and tools for self-checking. With each success, their optimism about themselves as problem solvers grows.

To begin to learn the scaffolded hinting and wait time, teachers learn a very simple game, "*Hinting* I Spy." They use this to learn focused positive questioning and later to teach coaches and students to do this at the very start of the program. In this game "I Spy" is turned on its head. The "winner" is the coach who guides players to the right answer with the fewest focused hints. The coach always starts from agreement, avoiding "No." Coaches agree with something correct in what the learner said, and lead with a focused hint that is true about the "target" but not true about the guess (e.g., "I spy something that begins with the sound /k/." Could it be computer? "It could be 'computer' because 'computer' starts with /k/, but what I'm thinking of just tells the time.")

Using Students as Coaches

Students trade the role of scientist/explorer (team leader) and coach with each other, using the focused hinting they learned with Hinting I Spy, and providing helpful tools. The teacher is a guide they consult, who also helps set up new experiments. Setting up these teams is essential to the program. Many private therapists train parents as coaches, reducing costs and increasing chances for long-term transfer. Classroom teachers can teach concepts to small groups, while peer tutors lead other groups, a powerful way to individualize spelling, reading and automaticity practice in classrooms (Fuchs et al., 2004). When good coaching is taught and rewarded, the teacher knows that small group learning is positive and well-supported.

Scaffolding and Instructional Zones

Teachers learn about students' *comfort zone,* where they can do the work by themselves, with no need for teacher support (Berk & Winsler, 1995; Vygotsky, 1978). In the *Instructional Zone* the student feels some challenge but can discover concepts and correct errors with the support of *scaffolding* from tools and teacher or coach support. LR teaches students and teachers to feel and note the relaxed state of the body in the comfort zone and the alert and focused stance of the instructional zone. LR activities begin in comfort zone, proceed into instructional level, and always finish back in comfort zone. With this arc, when the student returns to an activity, she remembers the feeling of comfort and confidence, and returns confident, comfortable, and ready to learn more.

Ground Deeply

LR teachers ground learning deeply, so children can use their bodies, brains, abilities, new knowledge, and charts, to check or review any learned concept as needed. Confidence grows from the competence of being able to trace any new concept back to its well-grounded roots, improving the ability to transfer the concept to new situations (Bruner, 1966; Mayer, 2003).

Integrate Fully

LR teachers practice new concepts in fully integrated fashion. Most early phonics concepts are discovered first in spelling explorations. Children do not need to segment sounds to speak a word they know, so they can learn the reading patterns without having to segment the speech (Ehri & Wilce, 1987; Hecht & Close, 2002; Uhry & Shepherd, 1993). Students immediately practice any spelled pattern in reading single words. Word structure and vocabulary are integrated into these activities. Once a student has practiced a pattern to comfort level, teachers integrate its application in reading text and in dictation or composition, as discussed in the Cycles of Instruction below. Research in pedagogy (Lillard, 2005), cognitive psychology (Ehri, 1991), and neurobiology (Berninger & Richards, 2002; Richards et al., 2006) support doing word study in its full linguistic context, to develop rich, accessible representations of words.

Use of Precious Teacher-Student Time

Activities that encourage rich student-teacher interaction include lots of practice with opportunities for exploration and scaffolded hints. Other activities, such as many board games, may be high in engagement, but include more play than practice. If children love such a game, it is better used in a student center or home play as a reward than in *precious teacher-student time.*

Capture the Teaching Moment

LR encourages teachers to delight in student discoveries and *Capture the Teaching Moment.* Often a student will bring a plum question or observation. With her deepening knowledge of language and the *LR Sequence Pyramid* described later, a teacher can decide when teaching can jump to match the interest of the child, or when to praise the discovery but wait till sufficient tools are available to make the discovery straightforward.

A Playful Spirit of Inquiry

A LR class fosters an *open spirit of inquiry,* with positive support, humor, imagination, and play at its core. The whole class is a learning team, and teachers can model themselves as learners, being willing to be wrong and to check their answers with sources and with experiments. This open spirit relaxes many newer teachers once they get it, knowing that if they lead with good questions, students will often be as good at catching and correcting errors as teachers are. Games are used for practice and for rewards. They are selected for engagement and for how well they help students to ground and connect concepts in the body, the imagination, the brain, and the print. Research suggests that "embodying" concepts by aligning them with body movements aids learning, retention, and transfer (Engelkamp et al., 1994; Glenberg & Kaschak, 2002; Lillard, 2005).

■ Description of the Basic Program

The *Reading Territory* (Figure 16.1) describes the structure of the program. Teachers use it and an expansion of the *LR Sequence Pyramid* within it to

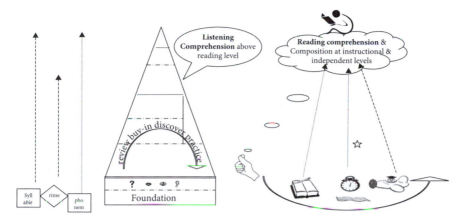

FIGURE 16.1 The Reading Territory.

motivate students, track their progress, individualize, and communicate with others working with a student, with LR or other programs. The *Cycles of Learning* reminds teachers to work on application and transfer of competent material, overlapping that work for efficiency while progressing to discovery and practice of new learning.

The Cycles of Learning

LR covers more material more quickly than many structured language programs, because teachers learn to use spiraling and overlapping *Cycles of Learning* (the curved arrows inside Figure 16.1). Teachers always start from *Review* to be sure a student knows the concepts needed to ground the new learning and check his hypotheses. Next the teacher establishes a *Buy-in*, so the student knows why the discovery is important. The teacher guides discovery of a new concept, and helps the student practice it to *Competence*, completing word work at about 80% correct with teacher or coach hints.

Some programs recommend high levels of mastery before moving to new material, but LR aims for mastery during the *Beyond Competence* activities. The Competence point is pivotal to the program. From here the student progresses in two directions. He moves up the pyramid, learning new concepts in the LR Sequence using the first part of the cycle. Within the same time period, the student takes the competent concepts into *Application* in context. With practice the new patterns become as "*Smooth as walking*," showing that the child does not need to use the scaffolds any longer. Only at this point do children with reading difficulties enjoy speeded work to hasten *Automaticity*. Speeded work done before this point is horribly frustrating. Teachers can now also assign and reward explicit examples of when students *Transfer* the new concepts to their independent work.

The Reading Territory

The *Reading Territory* Chart (Figure 16.1) illustrates how the five reading domains are linked in LR and how they are extended to independence (NICHD, 2000). Oral Language Play for phonology and morphology is suggested on the left, with suggestions for appropriate activities at all levels of reading written in on the larger version of this chart in the LR manuals. The pyramid is sketched out simply in the Territory chart. When word reading skills are below oral language levels, the talk balloons remind teachers to do Listening Comprehension and Vocabulary work with read-alouds and discussions of books at the child's language and interest level.

The thumbs-up at the center of the *Reading Territory* chart symbolizes the *Competence* or comfort pivot point of the program. After competence, the student can move vertically up the pyramid to new concepts, or horizontally to the beyond competence activities of application of a pattern in written context described above. The larger chart in the manual suggests appropriate activities to help achieve this independent use. The thought button on the right represents extensive reading comprehension and composition at independent levels.

The *Reading Territory* chart is very important for teachers and parents to grasp. Sometimes, teachers are so excited about teaching all the new content that they forget to take time to encourage children to apply the concepts and assign and reward their independent use. This chart can help them understand how to move to new skills at the same time as children practice competent concepts in context or at speeded levels. Parents and teachers can use it to grasp when to expect independent use of a pattern. Achieving competence usually takes a week or two after *buy-in, discovery,* and *practice with* a pattern in single words. *Application* in reading and writing context takes another week or two, (while also advancing to new material) and is a good time to work on smoothness and automaticity in reading. *Independent use of a concept* can be expected 5–8 weeks after introducing it, if teachers have been explicitly encouraging it and starring instances on the chart of independent use of patterns in those last few weeks. We encourage teachers of all programs to give more time to "beyond competence" activities, and to consider overlapping new learning with this work to allow their program to move faster and to include much integrated work on reading and writing whole text.

The LR Sequence Pyramid

The LR Sequence Pyramid is an expansion of the one in the Reading Territory Chart, showing all major concepts and core activities. We do not show it here in detail, because it is beyond the scope of the chapter, and the child-friendly terms would be confusing without the course. In class and with students, we underline a concept on the *Pyramid* with a yellow highlighter when it has been introduced, highlight it fully in yellow when it is learned to competence, and gradually build up a star in five strokes in another color, for major patterns or concepts that children have used completely independently, to demonstrate transfer. We describe the sequence in general terms later.

LR's sequence is based on the linguistic simplicity, consistency, and frequency of patterns used in print, as well as on the rich history of the English language. We borrowed the pyramid idea of three layers of English from the work of Marcia Henry and Bob Calfee (Anglo-Saxon, Romantic, and Greek: Henry, 1999). The *LR Pyramid* represents a multisensory exploration of four levels of instruction: First a sound awareness Foundation with consonant and vowel layers, followed by the three major levels of English word structure, each of these also partitioned.

Foundation: Ground Phonological Awareness Deeply but Quickly

The foundational level of *Linguistic Remedies*, reading, and spelling is phonological awareness. Instruction focuses on syllables, sounds, and speech. The goal of the foundational layer is for children to develop lasting phonological awareness and letter-sound correspondences, without taking too much time and drill. Instruction goes quickly to allow time for listening to and discussing great stories to develop language, vocabulary, and comprehension.

LR teachers' courses cover the speech-motor gestures that linguists use to classify phonemes, or speech sounds, in every language. Teachers learn these phoneme patterns in both adult and child-friendly terms. They can feel with their hand the "manner" how the air comes out (for instance, by *stopping* air and letting it out with a puff; by squeezing it out in a *stream*). They can close their eyes or use mirrors to focus on the "place" that is squeezed to stop air, and feel over their voice boxes whether sounds are "voiced" or "voiceless" (*whispered* or *buzzing* in child-friendly terms). Teachers and students learn a *family name* for sounds made with the same manner and highlight the air flow with blue pencil on mouth pictures. Place is highlighted in pink on the pictures, and gives the sound a *first name*. Since LR has only five *family names* for consonant manners and five places, the names are quick for most teachers and students to learn, *if they touch the pink or blue highlighting on the pictures as the say the names.* For example, the sounds /p/,/b/,/f/,/v/, and /m/ all use a *lip* placement, so their LR names are *lip stops* /p//b/(whispered or buzzed), *lip streams* /f//v/, and *lip nose* /m/.

Students learning the *mouthy* route learn these concepts with pictures, sounds, letters, names, and a glass head; with placement of letters on a map of the vocal tract (similarly to Nellie Dale, 1898). By practicing the "pony sounds" of /p//t//k//p//t//k/, they intensify their awareness of front to back placement of the stops, which they can transfer to the Lip, Tip, and Back Nose sounds. This awareness really helps feel and map the less distinct placement of vowels in the mouth.

The vowel map uses tongue position and mouth shape to describe all vowel sounds, as has been done in linguistics for hundreds of years (e.g., Ladefoged, 2000). It is usually complicated to learn, but LR simplifies it by teaching it in color-coded steps. LR starts with the "cornerstone" most extreme sounds used in every language (smiliest ee, most dropped o[] as in hot, or roundest oo). Children and teachers then learn to feel the lazy sound u[], and "set-points" of the middle smile e[] and the moving round o[]e.[1] Once the cornerstones and set-points are mastered, every vowel sound is either a smile, drop, round, or mover, and is never more than one step away from a set point or cornerstone. The mouthy pathway is easier for children to learn than for most teachers. A favorite game for children is "vowel twister," where they put a hand or foot on tongue positions on the map to match the vowel sound in each syllable in a word. Most teachers who become passionate about this program love the speech-motor part. Many describe the power that they, and their students, get from finding out that English is actually so sensible and easy to verify even at its most basic levels.

LR also teaches phonological awareness with language games and an optional keyword chart (Wise et al., 1999). The keywords all begin with the relevant sound to avoid the need to segment and co-articulation confusions, and to connect visually to the letters for better transfer. Teachers can then teach either the mouthy route, or the language-play/key-word route, or they may mix them. The key-word route is encouraged for teachers who do not like or do not feel confident with the mouth work. It is also encouraged for older students in small groups or classwork, so that they can get into the spelling and reading patterns more quickly.

Some expert teachers recommend doing the mouth-work at least with the vocal tract and the map to ground the other work. All the experts interviewed felt the embodiment of sounds in the vowel map strengthened all the later work. That is, "mouthy" children can feel the placement of vowels and go directly to the spelling pattern without the mediation step of a key-word. Teachers in several schools are using the vowel map and the key word chart together. This approach allows their students the confidence of the motor awareness, along with another tool to communicate with other teachers in the school who do not know the program.

LR sequences sounds and blends according to linguistic factors, in terms of how "visible" and salient they are, how easy they are to blend, and how close or far apart they are in speech production. This sequence and the knowledge underlying it inform teachers' practice, whether they teach the speech motor or the key word foundation. It helps them understand students' errors, such as when a child omits the nasal in spelling "send" or "camp." Their knowledge of how sounds are formed helps them scaffold and sequence instruction.

For example, the CCVC word, "flat," contains a blend that is easier to spell than is the blend in "step," because the /fl/ cluster contains continuant sounds that are more visible and are made further apart than are "step's" initial /st/ sounds. With this knowledge teachers can understand why a child might spell "dress" as "jres," and will know how to coach the child to correction or wait on that blend until more patterns are at competent levels.

Linguistic Patterns in Historic Levels

LR teaches the rich and vibrant history of English as a tool to use in confident reading and writing. LR uses this richness to make spelling meaningful, interesting, and memorable, and NOT just memorized. Although the history is hinted at early, most students study it more once they know the basic Anglo-Saxon patterns and are about to embark into the Romantic level. Young children just get the idea of a three-level house built on a sound foundation, whereas older students explore the history, the patterns, and the feeling of the levels as they apply to vocabulary, writing, and reading. The approach fosters a positive attitude in understanding English spelling and vocabulary, and it makes LR appropriate for older as well as younger students.

Most words in English have a history that harkens back to the Anglo-Saxons for strong common words like "love" and "think," to the French or Romans for more precise words like "adore" and "contemplate," or to the Greeks for technical words like "philosophize." English speakers use these words in different situations, and students learn morphological patterns unique to each layer. English spelling often intentionally breaks the patterns to mark a word from a language outside the three layers (e.g., "kangaroo, wok") or from a story (e.g., "gamut" and "shibboleth"). Learning the feeling of the layers and learning Romantic morphemes aids students' reading, spelling, and vocabulary. You know you are improving morphological awareness when a fifth grader comes to class and announces, *"Constipation* is a Romantic word!"

The Anglo-Saxon Level

The Anglo-Saxon level, the oldest level of English word origin, includes the first words students learn to say, read, and spell and the words used most frequently by all. Phonics is tied to the vowel map and/or keyword chart, grounded in the body for self-checking, and always quickly connected back to print. Students practice contrasting patterns in reading, spelling, and sound manipulation at the same time for further depth of processing.

The lowest Anglo-Saxon level consists of the fundamental letter-sound associations needed for Kindergarten to first grade, with some simple suffixes to make language more natural in the books they can use. Children *sing through the vowels* to find them in one-syllable words, minimizing segmenting issues especially in words with consonant blends. Those singing vowels become focal in all the following work. The program teaches all vowel patterns in spelling and reading simple words first without and then with blends. Even with words without blends, teachers include interesting words at appropriate age levels to build vocabulary and to let students know this is not baby work (e.g., jog, shin, case, join, muse). As soon as an early or remedial reader is competent with a pattern in single word reading and spelling, he applies it in reading confidently (e.g., *Sundance Phonics*, Sundance Publishing; *New Ways with Literature*, Steck Vaughn; *Books to Remember*, Flyleaf Publishing; and *High Noon Books* for older poor readers, Academic Therapy Press). Children learn sight words as needed for these earliest books.

Children soon discover when and when not to double letters in single syllable words, as in "feel, fell, and snarl." Students learn to be flexible with vowels flipping between short and long or the lazy sound, so they can confidently tackle books with more natural, less decodable, language. Children learn techniques for spelling tricky words, and they also discover, picture, and draw whimsical memory sentences for groups of words that break a pattern. Next they advance to the multisyllable words needed especially in second grade and higher levels. At every step, students cover the cycles from word work to shared and independent reading and writing.

Students learn that words with Anglo-Saxon histories are built differently than are words with histories from Romance languages. Anglo-Saxon words tend to be short with just one to two syllables, free roots, and compounding, reflecting their Germanic nature. However, spelling is complex with multiple ways to spell the same vowel sound and with many syllables that contain consonant clusters of two or three sounds. Also, many of the most frequently used words do not follow graphophonetic rules; they "fossilized" long before the spelling reforms of the eighteenth and nineteenth centuries, sometimes reflecting earlier pronunciations of words (e.g., said, was).

The Romantic and Greek Levels

English has the most intermingled interweaving of Germanic and Romantic word origin layers of any language because of its history. Between the years of 1066 with the Norman Conquest to around 1362, the ruling class of England actually spoke French while the poor spoke Old English. When the courts and halls of justice went back to speaking "Middle English," it was a new amalgamation of the Germanic Old English and Romantic words from French and Latin. Words with Romantic histories include the fancier words one would use when talking to the king or doing academic work, and they can pin down precise shades of meanings. They tend to have one root, either free or bound (that cannot stand on its own), with extensive use of prefixes and suffixes. Romantic words follow their own spelling patterns. They rarely use letters *k*, *oo, ee,* or *w*; and they double letters for new reasons (e.g., to mark the "chameleon" consonant endings of some prefixes such as connect, collide, commotion, correspond, all with variants of the prefix con, meaning "with or together"). In studying the Romantic layer, word structure and meaning (morphology) take center stage. Beck and McKeown (1991) and Beck, McKeown, & Kucan (2002) think words of Romantic and Greek origins are the most productive for improving vocabulary at third grade and higher levels.

Henry (1999) advocates a guided discovery approach to learning roots, where students and teacher generate many words with a root (e.g., export, import, transportation, portable, report, portapotty), intuit its meaning (to carry), check the meaning in the dictionary, and choose a key word to help remember it (e.g., "export, carry it out"). Children with reading disabilities often struggled with this approach to generate words from the root, which often occurs in the middle of a word. Therefore, LR begins by discovering meanings and spellings of about 5–8 common and clear prefixes (re, pre; con; in, ex; dis, de, pro) before overlapping that work with roots. Word finding is easier from the starts of words than the middles. To discover the meaning of a prefix, students help generate lists of words with it, hypothesize its meaning, and check their hypothesis by looking one of the words up in a good dictionary (e.g., exhale, export, exhume, extend exit. Ex = out). LR students also choose gestures to embody the meanings of prefixes and roots and make the connections easier to access and more lasting for most children with SRD or language deficits. For example, children bring their hands together for prefix "con" in all its forms; they show a bursting action with their arms for the root "rupt;" they act out pulling for "tract." (Washington teachers use American Sign Language symbols for meanings like "together, pull, or burst.")

After these discoveries, students spell and read single words, highlight the morpheme under focus, read and take dictation with sentences and paragraphs that repeat the morpheme, play games using the patterns and motions (charades, romantic dominoes), and bring back interesting words with these or other morphemes to explore with the teacher or class. Since adding the motions, not only do students retain the roots and meanings, but also they apply them more. One intermediate student thought he had forgotten the prefix meanings over the summer, until he took his hands out of his pockets, joined his hands with interlacing fingers, and exclaimed "con: with or together!" Most students now "see" the root and read it as a meaningful piece inside long words, rather than guessing from initial sounds, with better transfer to independent reading, than earlier, before LR students grounded these concepts in gestures.

Finally Greek, the top layer, extends up into sophisticated morphemes or meaning units needed to read intermediate to high school text. The Greek Layer includes scientific, medical, and technological words, like "sophisticated" and "morphemes"! Most words with Greek histories have more than one root, though they are often "bound" and cannot stand alone (e.g., *synthetic, morphology*). English marks Greek words with unique yet consistent spelling patterns (thus if a word has one ph in it, the other spelling patterns will also be Greek as in *photograph*). The roots are highly productive, so students can reuse them in other Greek words in reading, spelling, vocabulary, and games (e.g., *telephoto, graphology, photosynthesis*). Students are pleased to see how these sophisticated roots can be recombined to form many new words, usually retaining the spellings of the root even when the accent, stress, and vowel sound of the word shifts. For example, Greek words "telephone, telepathy, and telepathic" carry the spellings across the related words to reflect the meanings of the roots, not the sounds of the unstressed syllables.

■ Modifying LR for Different Teaching Situations

One strength of *Linguistic Remedies* is its scaffolded knowledge base that helps teachers make informed decisions about choosing, implementing, and modifying good programs to meet the needs of individual children. Phyllis Green, a school psychologist, says LR's flexibility allows teachers to "baby it down or grow it up," to implement it for students of different ages. This section describes just a few modifications for different groups of children.

*Examples of Variations in Program
for Younger Students (All Tiers)*

Include many large motor activities. Grounding concepts in the body is especially helpful at youngest levels. Kindergarten teachers capitalize on large muscles and movement, rolling balls, or tossing beanbags to add to some of LR's language games.

Teach phonics concepts with stories. LR uses stories to personify patterns, making them engaging, imaginative, and memorable. The stories are short and tied to the print to reinforce letter-sound concepts in a lasting way without taking too much teaching time. For example, "little" short vowels need to be protected by a consonant "babysitter" standing in the doorway at the end of a closed syllable, keeping the door closed and the short vowel safe. Students check "short vowels" in print to make sure they have consonant babysitters. Older students also use the concept of closed doors on closed syllables, but many prefer the term consonant "protectors" to the term "babysitters."

Modifications for Older Students in Tiers 2 and 3

Start with the larger view. After discussing brains, science, tools, and teamwork, older students work with the chart and the history and structure of English. By learning Linguistics, older students can learn basic skills in a sophisticated, age-appropriate manner, which protects their dignity and keeps them motivated.

Include advanced work as quickly as possible. Middle and high school struggling readers need an improved phonological foundation and strong vowel concepts with either the vowel map or the key word chart as a base. As soon as these are strong and students have a sense of the three levels of English, teachers can merge work on multisyllable Anglo-Saxon and simple Romantic words while still strengthening the more basic patterns. This inter-mingled work enriches vocabularies, writing, spelling, reading, and honors the students' intelligence. A Colorado Springs high school scheduled a lin-guistics class of one to two semesters with a teacher new to LR, with coaching from an expert one to two times a week. The novice teacher practiced some of the concepts with the students and also worked with them on fluency and comprehension. Students were highly engaged and improved reading levels significantly beyond previous efforts.

Modifications for Other Individual Differences

Teachers doing small group Tier 2 and 3 instruction adjust LR to match other individual differences. Some students with strong language comprehen-sion and low phonological skills become decent readers but awful spellers. For their early work, teachers substitute nonword for single word reading, since they read simple words well. With LR, these children's spelling usu-ally improves remarkably. Their writing now incorporates words at their high vocabulary level, and their formerly "adequate" reading comprehension usu-ally soars to the level of their vocabularies.

Even with the work of the overlapping *Cycles*, many students have par-ticular problems attaining fluent reading. A teacher can watch for this need especially among children with low naming speeds, or the teacher will also notice it if a child's fluency lags behind other students. These students can do extra automaticity practice in teams. They also benefit from repeated read-ings (Meyer & Felton, 1999) with grade-level material and specific fluency training with work on phrasing, expression, and re-reads. Text-reading soft-ware programs are recommended for older slower readers (Elkind & Elkind, 2007) to help them keep up with assigned school readings, while they still do independent careful reading with self-checking.

Teachers of children with hearing and articulation impairments appre-ciate the LR foundation to clarify vowel sounds, to learn and track sounds in words, and to improve their reading. Rather than finding pictures to match what their mouths do, these children use the pictures and map in an opposite direction: To clarify how to use their mouths to make their speech clearer. One teacher shared that the *Let's Build* sound manipulation exercise allowed several of her students to understand where words begin and end as never before, and helped many of her students understand how they were dropping sounds from words when they spoke and read.

Although LR promotes vocabulary development, some students need work beyond this, especially children with hearing impairments, ELL, and children with specific constitutional comprehension deficits. Visuals such as picture dictionaries can be very helpful with these children. ELL students like to discover how sounds from their native language are made as well and map the vowels in their own language, comparing and contrasting them with English sounds. Having two letter maps, one for their first language and one for English, allows them to see how the vowel letters represent different sounds in the two languages.

■ Examples of School Implementations: Challenges, Shortfalls, and Successes

Linguistic Remedies workshops over 14 years have taught therapists and school teachers mainly in Colorado and Washington, although the class has been taught in school and clinic settings in three other states. This section summarizes what we are learning about helping LR move from an intensive workshop to implementation in teachers' daily teaching.

Implementation among Private Therapists

Private educational therapists tend to be a passionate and highly motivated group, and implementation is strong among them. Many love the depth of knowledge and individualization LR supports. They take the courses and the "Practicum" experience, where they help in role play groups and gain more depth and practice in questioning and pacing. Many have worked out ways to watch, consult with, or be a support coach for an expert teacher, or to attend a support group to further their skills. Most of the school implementations discussed below can be traced back to someone's initial interest due to noticing the successes of students who had worked with LR therapists.

A private therapist can continue therapy until the child (a) reads independently with self-correction at 6 months above grade level, and (b) writes and edits grade level dictation, underlining incorrect but reasonably spelled words for later checking, and (c) reads 30 minutes daily outside of school. Long-term maintenance of gains is much more likely in this situation than when a teacher's program has to end with the school year, whether or not a child has achieved grade level (see Wise, 2004a, 2004b). The private therapist, however, has a harder situation than the school teacher for getting LR work integrated with schoolwork. She has to be inventive in parent training as well, to keep the home practice extensive but positive and engaging.

Implementations in Public Schools

We describe here some implementations of *Linguistic Remedies* in varied schools in Washington and Colorado where the program is being implemented well. We consider successes and challenges in these experiences, ways to help teachers who want to integrate this knowledge into their teaching, and to consider settings that are more or less likely to benefit from the course.

Examples of School Implementations in Washington

LR is implemented in many schools around the Seattle area. Situations vary from ones where only a few teachers took the course to ones where most of the staff uses the program. The focus here is on three schools that use it in systemic ways and represent very different settings.

Mid to High SES School. In this school, implementation began with a small group of teachers and grew from within. A few enthusiastic teachers took the class and started adding LR principles to what they already did that worked well, meeting with and supporting each other. Two requested on-the-job mentoring from the second author. Their students' successes inspired other teachers, and the principal helped more teachers take LR courses and practicum experience. A few became site-based experts, providing support and guidance for those newer to the approach. For example, the experienced teacher often modeled a lesson while the classroom teacher observed. A few days later, the classroom teacher delivered the same lesson or did appropriate review and practice. The experienced teacher then provided support and feedback. The school has adopted portions of LR. The Tier 1 K-fifth grade spelling program is aligned with LR, and it is the core program for remedial reading and writing at Tiers 2 and 3. LR is not used exclusively, but it structures and supplements the Tier 1 curriculum and provides a common structure and language for students receiving all three tiers of instruction with "double dosing" and extended intense work on each of the Cycles.

According to teachers, first and second grade students improved in reading, self-monitoring their reading and writing, building on their strong foundation from Kindergarten. Fourth and fifth grade students improved greatly in attention to spelling, in writing with advanced words, and with self-correction. Implementation has not been seamless. Frequent staff changes create a continuing need for new training. Different teachers incorporate more or less of the program. One positive outcome was that fewer students needed Tier 2 and 3 assistance, but that resulted in the district cutting the resource room teacher to half time. The resource teacher is now full time again, through increased enrollment as a result of new students enrolling, partly because many parents select this "choice" school based on its reputation for providing effective instruction for children with dyslexia. Teachers and therapists from around the region visit to see LR in action. The principal, teachers, and parents are committed to keeping LR a viable part of the curriculum.

Private school with students with language processing challenges. Implementation started small after one K teacher took the LR class and asked for mentoring from the second author. The kindergarten teacher incorporated LR practice, application, and transfer activities into the existing Orton-Gillingham (OG) curriculum, and later began acting as the site-based expert in her building. The preschool, first and third grade teachers, and vice principal of the school have incorporated key aspects of the *LR Sequence and Reading Territory* charts into their core OG curriculum. Some teachers have embraced LR more than others, but all are working together to create continuity for the students.

Though LR has only recently been implemented at this school, results are encouraging. The K teacher said that while she spent extra time early on teaching the mouth-sound connections, children moved beyond her traditional program well into basic Anglo-Saxon patterns including consonant blends. Implementation challenges again hinge on funding. Though known for its treatment of language processing challenges, this private school has no special education funding. As a result, students needing more intense instruction rely on outside tutors who may or may not use LR. The principal is creating a reading specialist position to help this situation.

High-risk diverse public school. Three high-risk schools in Seattle, all with 70% free or reduced lunch, hosted a year-long LR training for their teachers. The district paid for this optional training and compensated Title One teachers for their time. Training included three core classes during the school year, support sessions on implementation, training videos, and available coaching. One school stopped the program, but the other two continued. The work was fueled by the enthusiasm of three literacy coaches, especially Andrea Smith, who had previously taught LR in her classroom and had helped launch the pilot project. To conduct the training, support sessions, and create videos, the second author teamed with Smith. In coaching, Smith taught some lessons while the classroom teacher observed. Later, the teacher taught while Smith observed, with feedback and discussion of how to incorporate shortened lessons into practice and application activities in class.

Implementation was strongest in Smith's school. Numerous teachers there use the LR framework to inform their instruction, and most of the tutors, the resource room teacher, and four classroom teachers embrace it, taking the Practicum and arranging extra meetings with Smith (K, 1, 3, 4). At the end the year, DIBELS dynamic measures for all Tier 2 students had moved from at-risk to benchmark grade level. Tier 3 students from classrooms where LR was coordinated with the tutoring work increased their DIBELS scores by 50%. In classes where students received LR tutoring, but classroom work did not coordinate with it, growth occurred but less strongly. These positive trends are encouraging, but funding, staff changes, and threats of closure have impeded implementation. The district stopped supporting new or experimental programs, including LR. The current principal has found new funding and is committed to continuing with LR.

Some School Implementations in Colorado

In Colorado, LR workshops have been conducted for private therapists and school teachers, mainly in cities from Boulder to Colorado Springs. A now-retired special education coordinator in Denver Public Schools sponsored classes and paid partial tuition for volunteer teachers who took LR on their own time. Only one or two teachers took it from any school. Some still use it. A school psychologist who helped coordinate the classes would like to pursue further LR trainings for the special educators, whom she believes will need more in-depth knowledge to teach the children with the more severe needs that she expects in Tier 3 settings where RTI is implemented. She believes that administrative support and systematic mentoring, modeling, and support from experienced teachers would be essential for implementation. In Colorado Springs, five schools are systematically implementing LR. A coordinator and expert teachers from three of those schools provided the following information.

District 11 (D11) of Colorado Springs began a pilot program for RTI in 2005, and adopted LR classes as one of their training methods. D11 is the largest district in the city, with a full range of lower to higher SES schools. The Special Education Department instigated the effort and supported it for a year and a half, paying teachers' tuition for classes and giving them release time. The first author taught three introductory classes, one Intermediate, and one advanced class. Following training, the first author traveled 100 miles about once a month to visit schools and conduct support meetings for selected teachers who liked LR and used it well, to help them become trainers of trainers. At three schools with a successful new LR teacher, more teachers took the class. In one school, the literacy teacher was profoundly affected by watching the model students in class. She became an on-site expert and mastered LR and its integration in the school. The first author consulted by email and visited about once a month, sometimes watching her teach and sometimes modeling teaching, with discussion during the support meeting at the end of the day. Her school sent teachers to a class in another community, paid by the district, when the D11 class was full.

At this school, all special education, speech and literacy teachers at Tiers 2 and 3 use LR as their core program, and at Tier 1 the full-day Kindergarten teacher, both first grade teachers, and one each of the second, third, fourth, and fifth grade teachers also use it. The on-site expert and the other Tier 2 teachers support the classroom teachers, even training the other ½ time

Kindergarten teacher themselves. Many teachers there have also had some Orton-Gillingham training which they blend with LR, but all say that the vowel map and vowel chart are key to their school's teaching of phoneme awareness and phonics. The expert says, "Whenever we have a child who is not progressing, we turn to LR as the primary intervention foundation. We are anxious to see continuing ongoing impact from grade level to grade level as students continue with the program." Upper grade teachers report that students are retaining what they learned, and that LR sets a perfect foundation for other curricula such as Sitton Spelling. The expert has increased some children's time with her to increase LR and vocabulary time for very needy students in this school with a high ELL population.

Two other schools in this district each have three to five teachers well trained. In one school the two special education, two speech language teachers, and school psychologist took the full course. This school also sponsored a day and a half workshop for classroom teachers, to help them support the specialists. All the fully trained specialists use it as the core of their remedial reading and spelling program, supplemented with other programs and changing the order of concepts sometimes to match the classroom curricula, as the best of experts do. The speech teachers tag-team with severely impacted students; one concentrates more on speech work and one more on reading and spelling. They are finding great gains in reading but spelling is not as strong with primary grade-level students. Older students are making slower yet steady gains. One special education teacher is not sure whether the gains are the result of the LR she is doing or of LR in combination with other interventions for fluency and vocabulary that the students also receive; she needs more time to evaluate. The school is having a harder time integrating LR into classroom use, which the Tier 2 and 3 teachers think would increase its impact. Nevertheless, they are glad for the common language, to communicate with classroom teachers about what they can expect the students to know.

Changes in administrative levels and the recent retiring of the coordinators of the training have halted external support for the program, and called its future in the district into question. Before retiring, the coordinator met with six teachers and heard from two others who had taken the class to get their input about going forward. These teachers were optimistic that the program could work well, giving suggestions for improving its implementation. They all believe the district should support a coordinated reading effort. They seem frustrated by difficulties in coming together with regular curriculum leaders about the use of evidence-based methods in classes, RTI, and not knowing what the district plans to do to coordinate reading programs in the future.

A public school of choice in District 20. Another Colorado Springs district includes one school with an exceptional implementation of LR. Here, all the Tier 2 and 3 reading intervention specialists and speech therapists use LR, and about half the teachers have taken the Introductory class. One classroom teacher uses the program totally, three use it a good amount with half the class, and another seven use it to a lesser degree with half of their class. Similarly to the most fully implemented school in Seattle, this program was initiated at the teacher and principal level. The principal and some of the staff started this arts-based school of choice and implemented LR, having used it successfully for years in another school. Three literacy or intervention specialists brought it with them, all expert in merging the best of LR with broad knowledge about engaging students in actively reading good literature. They use decodables for beginning reading for poor readers, but choose ones with a good story arc. One expert teacher retired in Fall 06 and continued to work part-time teaching small groups and supporting teachers. As some of her children went excitedly back to class talking about her brain lesson, that teacher invited the expert to teach that lesson to her whole class. Gradually more and more teachers asked her to mentor them. The school hired another teacher for small groups and now her sole role is teacher support. She helps many teachers with preparing enough materials for small groups. She is strict about whom she will mentor beyond that. The classroom teacher must watch her teach the students and then in a few days teach that lesson or a follow-on practice lesson while the expert watches and later discusses it with her. The other master teacher believes that having on-site experts, a cooperative teaching community, and a principal committed to the teachers and the program are the only reasons it is so well implemented there.

■ Suggestions for Improving Implementation

Whether through taking classes, retaking them as practicum level students or as helpers, forming supportive teams, getting mentoring, or attending workshops, committed teachers can realize the full potential of LR. But if schools want to implement the program on a larger scale, principals or coordinators need to commit to at least a few years of intensive support for measurable impact (Brady & Gillis, 2006). Suggestions that follow are culled from experiences cited above and from interviews with teachers and coordinators. They include ideas for improving classes and materials and suggestions for ways of supporting teachers. Some ideas pertain mainly to LR or other small experimental programs, but many seem relevant to implementing other intensive reading programs.

Implementation Suggestions for Teaching the Course

Many teachers and coordinators made some of the following suggestions about classes. *Always include model students.* All teachers mentioned how this helped them grasp the value of the program and its questioning support. When this is not possible, especially in support groups, videos of children and teachers are a reasonable substitute. *Spread out the course*, allowing for practice time and support between sessions. *Allow multiple exposures to course material* for those who crave to become expert reading teachers and interventionists. *Offer a streamlined course for classroom teachers above second grade* was a suggestion from some who want the structure and the spelling patterns, but mainly want to support and coordinate with their Tier 2 and 3 colleagues. On-site experts in a district could teach these classes, hopefully while maintaining a spirit of inquiry in a streamlined class. *Provide separate classes for middle and high school teachers*, if districts have enough of these teachers to support a course. Otherwise, providing older model students, support groups, and visits from experts may help teachers see the value of the foundational work for older struggling readers.

Suggestions especially relevant to those who sponsor the classes. Other suggestions may help administrators plan training that leads to lasting growth and change. *Plan follow-on mentoring and consultation support before offering a class.* An effective way to do this is to develop on-site experts who can model and critique teaching, provide support groups, and eventually teach the classes and become trainers-of-trainers. Teachers from the schools know the issues and needs of that school better than any outside expert does. *Foster a community of collaboration.* All successful school-wide implementations have at least someone from administration, teachers, parents, and students, who have an ongoing commitment to sustaining it. Examples of collaborative support ran the gamut from modeling, mentoring, and critiques and informal problem solving or review sessions to more formal workshops designed to help classroom teachers modify their curriculum to integrate key LR concepts into classroom curricula. *Provide materials*: Teachers need to have extensive materials for reading, including engaging decodables for beginning reading and then a wide variety of interesting literature at gradually increasing reading levels. Teachers want time to create materials, or access to other supplementary materials. *Provide software*: The D20 expert mentioned the software support and the mentoring of the on-site expert as the two most important factors for LRs successful implementation at her school. For LR software that supports good practice in word-learning skills, teachers mentioned *My Reading Coach* for children with severe difficulties, *Lexia Learning Systems* for children with mild-to-moderate problems, and *Success-Maker* for older poor readers. *WYNN* or *Kurzweil* were mentioned as text readers for middle and high school students with slow reading speeds. These teachers said the programs were not as effective as their 1:1 teaching, but that they allowed the children to get extensive accurate practice with immediate feedback, and freed the teacher to do small group work with other children. The Summer 2007 *Perspectives* issue focuses on factors to look for in evaluating software for children with reading disabilities and improving implementation (Wise & Raskind, 2007).

■ Conclusion

Linguistic Remedies is a small program that helps teachers understand evidence-based reading instruction, implement it with children with different needs, and deepen their knowledge for solving problems. All teachers interviewed mentioned the breadth and depth of the knowledge imparted to teachers. LR is not a boxed scripted program but a well-guided problem-solving approach that encourages a spirit of inquiry and confidence from competence among teachers and students. Support teams or coaching of some kind seem essential to help novices become self-sustaining teachers. With all schools, LR was most easily implemented in remedial settings for all ages and in whole classes at K and first grade. Most third and fourth grade whole class teachers prefer LR as a word study and spelling supplement rather than as a core reading program.

Becky Aschbrenner, who helped create the arts-based school of choice made this statement:

> Before I took Linguistic Remedies, I didn't know why I needed it.
> Once I took it, I couldn't imagine how I taught reading without it.
> When teachers ask me how to become good teachers of reading, I
> tell them the most important thing they can do is to take this class.

Of course, not everyone who takes the class shares Aschbrenner's enthusiasm and the class is frankly not for all teachers. In districts with very high turnover, it is likely to be useful mainly for specialists to help with problem-solving and for dealing with students with high needs. Voluntary participation in core schools, inspired by others' successes, seems the way to go for a course like LR. Without some kind of structure for sharing the load of creating materials, small experimental programs such as LR are unlikely to scale to many schools. Therefore, finding ways to share effort or provide materials is worthwhile. However, some of LR's successes may also be tied to its small size, individualization, and willingness to share.

Becoming an expert reading teacher is a long trek. Interviewed teachers made it clear that the journey can be enjoyable and that attaining the summit is certain if the individual *wants it, works at it,* and *finds support and guidance.* Most said that LR is the class to take if one wants to become an expert reading teacher, and that experts should take the class more than once. Perhaps LR can become easier to implement in whole classrooms by creating a separate strand of streamlined classes for nonexperts, and by providing more materials or more explicit links to outside materials tied directly to the LR Sequence. It remains to be seen whether public schools can have the administrative stability, resources, and time to sustain and scale intensive intervention programs like LR.

■ Disclosure

All the authors have used LR in private practices where they teach children and teachers. Wise and Rogan provide Teaching Manuals and Activities Manuals included in the teachers' classes. Wise owns a company, Remedies for Reading Disabilities, Inc., which provides (a) educational therapy for students and their parents; (b) teachers' classes; and (c) consultation with schools and companies (some of whose software is named in the chapter). For further information on LR training and procedures, contact the authors at the provided addresses.

■ References

Allington, R. (2002). *Big Brother and the National Reading Curriculum: How ideology trumped evidence.* Portsmouth, NH, Heinemann.

Arteagoitea, I., & Howard, E. (June, 2004). *Spelling v decoding as a predictor of reading comprehension in English and Spanish.* Paper presented at the annual meeting of the Society for the Scientific Study of Reading, Amsterdam, The Netherlands.

Beck, I., & McKeown, M. (1991). Conditions of vocabulary acquisition. In R. Barr, M. Kamil, P. Mosenthal, & P. Pearson (Eds.), *Handbook of reading research* (Vol II, pp. 789–814). NY, Longman.

Beck, I., McKeown, M., Hamilton, R., & Kucan, L. (1997). *Questioning the author: An approach for enhancing student engagement with text.* Delaware, International Reading Association.

Beck, I. L., McKeown, M. G., & Kucan, L. (2002). *Bringing words to life: Robust vocabulary instruction.* New York, The Guilford Press.

Beimiller, A. (1999). *Language and reading success.* Newton, MA, Brookline Books.

Berk, L. E., & Winsler, A. (1995). *Scaffolding children's learning: Vygotsky and early childhood education.* Washington, DC, NAEYC.

Berninger, V., & Richards, T. (2002). *Brain literacy for educators and psychologists.* New York, Academic Press.

Bradley, R., Danielson, L., & Hallahan, D. P. (2002). *Identification of learning disabilities: Research to practice.* Mahwah, NJ, Lawrence Erlbaum Assoc.

Brady, S., & Gillis, M. (November, 2006). *Mastering reading instruction: A professional development project with first grade teachers.* Paper presented in symposium on Preparing and Supporting Teachers of Reading: What's wrong, what's right, what's needed now? At 57th meeting of the International Dyslexia Association, Indianapolis, IN.

Brady, S., & Moats, L. (1997). *Informed instruction for reading success: Foundations for teacher preparation.* Position paper. Baltimore, MD, International Dyslexia Association.

Bruner, J. (1966). *The process of education.* Cambridge, Harvard University Press.

Caccamise, D., & Snyder, L. (2006). Theory and pedagogical practices of text comprehension. *Topics in Language Disorders, 25,* 5–20.

Cain, K., & Oakhill, J. (1998). Comprehension skill and inference-making ability: Issues of causality. In C. Hulme & R. Joshi (Eds.), *Reading and spelling: Development and disorders.* Mahwah, NJ, Lawrence Erlbaum Associates.

Catts, H., Adlof, S., & Weismer, S. (2006). Language deficits in poor comprehenders: A case for the simple view of reading. *Journal of Speech, Language, & Hearing Research, 49,* 278–293.

Catts, H., Hogan, T., & Adlof, S. (2005). Development changes in reading and reading disabilities. In H. Catts & A. Kamhi (Eds.), *Connections between language and reading disabilities* (pp. 25–40). Mahwah, NJ, Lawrence Erlbaum Associates.

Cole, R., Wise, B., & Van Vuuren, S. (2006). How Marni teaches children to read. *Educational Technology, 47,* 14–18.

Connor, C., Morrison, F., Fishman, B., Schatschneider, C., & Underwood, P. (2007). The early years: Algorithm guided reading instruction. *Science, 315,* 464–465.

Cutting, L., & Scarborough, H. (2006) Prediction of reading comprehension: Relative contributions of word recognition, language proficiency, and other cognitive skills can depend on how comprehension is measured. *Scientific Studies of Reading, 10,* 277–299.

Dale, N. (1898). *On the teaching of English reading.* London, J.M. Dent and Co.

Ehri, L. C. (1991). Development of the ability to read words. In R. Barr, M. L. Kamil, P. Mosenthal, & P. D. Pearson (Eds.), *Handbook of reading research* (pp. 383–417). New York, Longman.

Ehri, L. C., & Wilce, L. S. (1987). Does learning to spell help beginners learn to read words? *Reading Research Quarterly, 22,* 47–65.

Elkind, J., Cohen, K., & Murray, C. (1993). Using computer-based readers to improve reading comprehension of students with dyslexia. *Annals of Dyslexia, 42,* 238–259.

Elkind, K., & Elkind, J. (2007). Text to speech software to aid reading and writing. *Perspectives, 33,* 11–16.

Engelkamp, J., Zimmer, H. D., Mohr, G., & Sellen, O. (1994) Memory of self-performed tasks: Self-performing during recognition. *Memory & Cognition, 22,* 34–39.

Fuchs, D., Fuchs, L., McMaster, K., Yen, L., & Svenson, E. (2004) Nonresponders: How to find them? How to help them? What do they mean for special education? *Teaching Exceptional Children, Sept/Oct,* 72–77.

Glenberg, A., & Kaschak, M. P. (2002). Grounding language in action. *Psychonomic Bulletin & Review, 9,* 558–565.

Gough, P., & Tunmer, W. (1986). Decoding, reading, and reading disability. *Remedial & Special Education, 7,* 6–10.

Hecht, S. A., & Close, L. (2002) Emergent literacy skills and training time uniquely predict variability in responses to phonemic awareness training in disadvantaged kindergartners. *Journal of Experimental Child Psychology, 82,* 93–115.

Henry, M. (1999) A short history of the English Language. In J. Birsch (Ed.), *Multisensory Teaching of Basic Language Skills.* Baltimore, Paul H. Brooks Publishing.

Hoover, W., & Gough, P. (1990). The simple view of reading. *Reading & Writing, 2*, 127–160.

Joshi, M. (2003). Diagnosis and remediation of dyslexia: A pragmatic solution. In M. Joshi (Ed.), *Our mission to literacy commemorative booklet* (pp. 13–19). Baltimore, IDA.

Keenan, J., Betjemann, R., Wadsworth, S., DeFries, J., & Olson. (2006). Genetic and environmental influences on reading and listening comprehension. *Journal of Research in Reading, 29*, 75–91.

Kintsch, W. (1998). *Comprehension: A paradigm for cognition.* Cambridge, UK, Cambridge University Press.

Ladefoged, P. (2000). *A course in phonetics* (4th ed.). Fort Worth, TX, Harcourt Brace.

Lepper, M., Drake, M., & O'Donnell-Johnson, T. (1997). Scaffolding techniques of expert human tutors. In Hogan, K. & Pressley, M. (Eds.), *Scaffolding student learning: Instructional approaches and issues.* Cambridge, MA, Brookline.

Liberman, I. Y., & Shankweiler, D. (1985). Phonology and the problems of learning to read and write. *Remedial & Special Education, 6*, 8–17.

Lillard, A. (2005). *Montessori: The science behind the genius* (pp. 38–79). New York, Oxford University Press.

Lindamood, C., & Lindamood, P. (1966, 1975). *Auditory Discrimination in Depth (A.D.D.).* Allen, TX, DLM Teaching Resources.

Lyon, G. R. (1999). Reading development, reading disorders, and reading instruction: Research-based findings. *Language, Learning, & Education, 6*, 8–16.

Mayer, R. E. (2003). *Learning and instruction.* Upper Saddle River, NJ, Pearson Education, Inc.

McCutchen, D., Abbott, R. D., Green, L. B., Beretvas, S. N., Cox, S., Potter, N. S., et al. (2002). Beginning literacy: Links among teacher knowledge, teacher practice, and student learning. *Journal of Learning Disabilities, 35*, 69–86.

McCutchen, D., & Berninger, G. (1999). Those who know teach well: Helping teachers master literacy-related subject matter knowledge. *Learning Disabilities Research and Practice, 14*, 215–226.

Meyer, M., & Felton, R. (1999). Repeated reading to enhance fluency: Old approaches and new directions. *Annals of Dyslexia, 49*, 283–306.

Montgomery, D. (1981). Do dyslexics have difficulty accessing articulatory information? *Psychological Research, 43*, 235–243.

Morais, J., Bertelson, P., Cary, L., & Alegria, J. (1986). Literacy training and speech segmentation. *Cognition, 24*, 45–64.

Nation, K., Adams, Bowyer-Crane, N., & Snowling, M. (1999). Working memory deficits in poor comprehenders reflect underlying language impairments. *Journal of Experimental Child Psychology, 73*, 139–158.

National Institute of Child Health and Development. (2000). *Report of the National Reading Panel. Teaching Children to Read* (NIH 00–4754). Washington, DC, NICHD.

Oakhill, J., & Yuill, N. (1991). *Children's problems in text comprehension: An experimental study.* Cambridge, UK, Cambridge University Press.

Olson, R. K., Wise, B., Conners, F., & Rack, J. (1989). Specific deficits in component reading and language skills: Genetic and environmental influences. *Journal of Learning Disabilities, 22,* 339–348.

Pearson, D., & Hamm, D. (2005). The assessment of reading comprehension: A review of practices past present and future. In S. Paris & S. Stahl (Eds.), *Children's reading comprehension and assessment* (pp. 13–69). Mahwah, NJ, Lawrence Erlbaum Associates.

Perfetti, C. A., Marron, M. A., & Foltz, P. W. (1996). Sources of comprehension failure: Theoretical perspectives and case studies. In C. Cornoldi & J. Oakhill (Eds.), *Reading comprehension difficulties: Processes and remediation* (pp. 137–165). Mahwah, NJ, Lawrence Erlbaum Associates Inc.

Rayner, K., Foorman, B., Perfetti, C., Pesetsky, D., & Seidenberg, M. (2001). How psychological science informs the teaching of reading. *Psychological Science in the Public Interest, 2,* 31–74.

Richards, T., Aylward, E., Raskind, W., Abbott, R., Field, K., Parsons, A., et al. (2006). Converging evidence for triple word form theory in children with dyslexia. *Developmental Neuropsychology, 30,* 547–589.

Rowe, M. B. (1987). Wait time: Slowing down may be a way of speeding up. *American Educator, 11,* 38–43.

Scarborough, H. (1998a). Predicting the future achievement of second graders with reading disabilities: Contributions of phonemic awareness, verbal memory, rapid naming, and IQ. *Annals of Dyslexia, 48,* 115–136.

Scarborough, H. (1998b, April). *What underlies rapid serial naming?* Presentation at the Society for the Scientific Study of Reading, San Diego, CA.

Scarborough, H. (2001). Connecting early language and literacy to later reading (dis) abilities: Evidence, theory, and practice. In S. Neuman & D. Dickinson (Eds.), *Handbook for early literacy research.* New York, The Guilford Press.

Simmons, D. C., & Kame'enui, E. J. (1998). *What research tells us about children with diverse learning needs.* Mahwah, NJ, Lawrence Erlbaum Associates.

Snow, C. (2002). *The influence of early oral language skills on the acquisition of literacy.* Paper presented at the Katherine Butler Symposium on Child Language Development and Disorders, San Jose, CA, March 2002.

Snow, C., Burns, M. S., & Griffin. (1998). *Preventing reading difficulties in young children: A report of the National Research Council (NRC).* Washington, DC, National Academy Press.

Stanovich, K. (1987). The impact of automaticity. *Journal of Learning Disabilities, 20,* 167–168.

Stothard, S., & Hulme, C. (1996). A comparison of reading comprehension decoding difficulties in children. In Cornoldi, C. & Oakhill, J. (Eds.),

Reading comprehension & difficulties: Processes & intervention (pp. 93–112). Mahwah, NJ, Lawrence Erlbaum Associates.

Swanson, H., & Trahan, M. (1996) Working memory in skilled and less skilled readers. *Journal of Abnormal Psychology, 17*, 145–156.

Tobin, K. (1987). The role of wait time in higher cognitive level learning. *Review of Educational Research, 57*, 69–95.

Torgesen, J. (2000). Individual responses in response to early intervention in reading: The lingering problem of treatment resisters. *Learning Disabilities Research & Practice, 15*, 55–64.

Tovani, C. (2000). *I Read It but I Don't Get It*. Portland, ME, Stenhouse Publishers.

Uhry, J., & Shephard, M. (1993) Segmentation/spelling instruction as part of a first-grade reading program. *Reading Research Quarterly, 28*, 218–233.

Vaughn, S., & Fuchs, L. (2003). Redefining learning disabilities as inadequate response to instruction, *Learning Disabilities Research & Practice, 18*, 137–146.

Vellutino, F., Tunmer, W., Jaccard, J., & Chen, R. (2007) Components of reading ability: Multivariate evidence for a model of reading development. *Scientific Studies of Reading, 11*, 3–32.

Vygotsky, L. (1978). *Mind in society* (Trans. M. Cole). Cambridge, MA, Harvard University Press.

Willcutt, E. G., & Pennington, B. F. (2000). Comorbidity of reading disability and attention-deficit/hyperactivity disorder: Differences by gender and subtype. *Journal of Learning Disabilities, 33*, 179–191.

Wise, B. (2001). The indomitable dinosaur builder (and how she overcame her phonological deficit and learned to read instructions, and other things). *Journal of Special Education, 35*, 134–144.

Wise, B. (2004a). *Linguistic remedies for reading disabilities*. Boulder, CO, RRD, Inc.

Wise, B. (2004b). *Advanced linguistic remedies: Morphology and phonology in advanced reading, spelling, and writing*. Boulder, CO, RRD, Inc.

Wise, B., Cole, R., van Vuuren, S., Schwartz, S., Snyder, L., Ngampatipatpong, N., et al. (2007). Learning to read with a virtual tutor. In C. Kinzer & L. Verhoeven (Eds.), *Interactive literacy education* (pp. 31–76). New York: Lawrence Erlbaum Associates, Taylor & Francis Group.

Wise, B., & Olson, R. K. (1995). Computer-based phonological awareness and reading instruction. *Annals of Dyslexia, 45*, 99–122.

Wise, B., & Raskind, M. (2007). Technology and reading difficulties. *Perspectives, 33*, 7–8.

Wise, B., Ring, J., & Olson, R. K. (1999). Phonological awareness training with and without explicit attention to articulation. *Journal of Experimental Child Psychology, 72*, 271–304.

Wise, B., Ring, J., & Olson, R. K. (2000). Individual differences in benefits from computer-assisted remedial reading. *Journal of Experimental Child Psychology, 77*, 197–235.

Wise, B., Ring, J., Sessions, L., & Olson, R. (1997). Phonological awareness with and without articulation: A preliminary study. *Learning Disabilities Quarterly, 20,* 211–225.

Wise, B., & Snyder, L. (2002). Clinical judgments in language-based learning disabilities. In R. Bradley, L. Danielson, & D. Hallahan (Eds.), *Identification of learning disabilities: Research to practice.* Mahwah, NJ, Lawrence Erlbaum Associates.

Wise, B., & Van Vuuren, S. (2007) Choosing software gems to improve children's reading. *Perspectives, 33,* 34–42.

Wolfe, M. (1999). What time may tell: Towards a new conceptualization of developmental dyslexia. *Annals of Dyslexia, 49,* 3–28.

■ Note

1. We have a convention of using [] to represent a consonant placeholder; thus o[] is short sound of "o," which only happens when the syllable is closed by a consonant, and o[]e is long "o" with a magic e or silent e following some consonant.

17. UNDERSTANDING WORDS AND WORD LEARNING

Putting Research on Vocabulary

into Classroom Practice

William Nagy

Vocabulary size—how many word meanings a student knows—is, not surprisingly, one of the strongest predictors of reading comprehension (Anderson & Freebody, 1981; Cromley & Azevedo, 2007; Davis, 1944; Snow, Burns, & Griffin, 1998). Adequate decoding skills and fluency are of course essential for proficient reading, but they are not sufficient. Once students have decoded words, their ability to understand text depends on whether they know the meanings of these words, and how well they know these meanings.

Vocabulary research is one of the oldest subfields in the domain of reading research. By the end of the 1940s, significant work had already been performed on word frequencies (e.g., Thorndike & Lorge, 1944), on the role of vocabulary knowledge in reading comprehension (e.g., Davis, 1944), on individual differences in vocabulary knowledge (e.g., Seashore & Eckerson, 1940), and on vocabulary assessment (e.g., Sims, 1929). Though the topic of vocabulary has come in and out of fashion over the decades, the past 30 years have seen sustained efforts by numerous individual scholars and teams of researchers trying to understand the sources of, and the best means for promoting, vocabulary learning. A single best method of vocabulary instruction has yet to be identified (NICHD, 2000; Petty, Herold, & Stoll, 1968); however, we have gained substantial knowledge about the nature of our language and about principles of vocabulary instruction that can have a profound impact on the effectiveness of instructional practice (cf., Aitchison, 2003; Carlisle & Rice, 2002; Graves, 2006; Nagy & Anderson, 1984; Stahl & Nagy, 2006).

Above all else, effective instruction depends on knowledgeable teachers. Hundreds of books, articles, and Web sites offer a wealth of interesting and engaging ways to teach word meanings. But the help offered will be truly effective only if it is applied wisely—for the right words, for the right purposes, for the right amount of time. Effective vocabulary instruction depends on insight into the nature of words and the process of word learning. In this chapter, what research tells us about effective instruction is organized in terms of five key insights: Teachers need to understand that words are *powerful*, *innumerable*, *complex*, *heterogeneous*, and *fascinating*.

■ Words Are Powerful

Words are extremely powerful, in at least two ways. First, vocabulary knowledge is strongly related to indicators of academic success and risk for academic failure. Second, effective word choice—the appropriate use of a large vocabulary—is one of the most powerful communicative tools in written language. These two points could be summed up in one phrase: Words play a key role in the language of power.

Vocabulary knowledge is strongly correlated with socioeconomic status (SES) (White, Graves, & Slater, 1990); children with parents of low SES may have less opportunity to learn academic vocabulary (Hart & Risley, 1995). Acquiring sufficient command of academic vocabulary is also one of the most serious challenges facing English Language Learners (Carlo, August, McLaughlin, Snow, Dressler, Lippman, Lively, & White, 2004). Because academic risk factors are so often associated with differences in vocabulary knowledge, students at-risk can be helped by promoting their vocabulary growth in terms of both breadth and depth of word knowledge (Ordóñez, Carlo, Snow, & McLaughlin, 2002; Vermeer, 2001; White, Graves, & Slater, 1990).

Language is our primary tool of communication, and words, though not the whole of language, are its essential building blocks. There are other contexts in which children have to rely on verbal skills, but school requires, if not a higher level, certainly different kinds of verbal skills than children are likely to need elsewhere. It is important for teachers to understand that words have a unique power in written language, and a role that is qualitatively different from the role words play in the patterns of oral communication that are likely to be most familiar to children (see Chapter 4 by Silliman and Scott, this volume).

Comparisons of written and oral language have shown that the vocabulary of conversation is impoverished compared with the vocabulary of written language (Chafe & Danielewicz, 1987; Hayes, 1988; Hayes & Ahrens, 1988). One reason is that face-to-face conversation has other important channels for conveying information—facial expression, gesture and body language, intonation, and the possibility of referring to the immediate physical environment. Furthermore, the possibility of feedback makes precision of expression less necessary in conversation than in writing: In a conversation, if the speaker does not make something clear enough the first time, he or she will find out from the response (or the facial expression) of the listener, and can try again.

The limited vocabulary of conversation can also be traced back to the word frequency effect—the fact that it takes more time to access a word in memory that is less frequently used in the language (Anderson & Bower, 1972; Gerhand & Barry, 1999; Gilhooly & Logie, 1980). In conversation, this makes it easier to use a more common word, perhaps with a hedge (e.g., "sort of green"), whereas in writing, one can take time to think of the precise word such as *chartreuse* or *turquoise*, which would typically have a much lower frequency and take longer to access in memory (Chafe & Danielewicz, 1987).

Another factor impacting the role of words in different types of communication is the role of shared knowledge. In face-to-face conversation, one can often evoke shared knowledge with relatively few words (e.g., referring to someone as "you know who"). In fact, in conversation, verbal elaboration and intimacy are often at odds with each other: If you have to explain something clearly, it suggests that the person who needs the explanation is not a part of your group. The language of in-group status is allusion, not explanation. However, in much written language, and especially in the language of text, explicit explanation is often the goal, and the means is careful and precise choice of words. Thus, the communicative strategies and language skills that make one an effective conversationalist are quite different from those that make one an effective writer or an effective interpreter of academic text.

Because of these profound differences between oral and written language, conversational proficiency is not an adequate basis for literacy. The vocabulary of commercial television, another potentially large source of verbal input, is not much richer than that of face-to-face conversation (Hayes, 1988; Hayes & Ahrens, 1988). Nor does experience with written language guarantee familiarity with literate language; e-mail and text-messaging are in many respects more like conversation than like traditional written language. Hence, the language of textbooks is to some extent a foreign language, not just for English Language Learners, but for many students from English-speaking homes as well.

This is not to say that conversations with adults cannot be a source of vocabulary knowledge for children. On the contrary, the amount of time that children spend talking with adults is a powerful predictor of their vocabulary size (Hart & Risley, 1995). However, the degree to which children benefit from conversations with adults depends in part on the quality of those conversations. Children benefit more from talking with adults if the adult speech they hear has some of the attributes of text, for example, extended talk about nonpresent topics (Beals, 2001) and use of richer vocabulary (Tabors, Beals, & Weizman, 2001). Children also gain more from conversations with adults if the adults interact with them in a way that requires more extended language on the part of the children—for example, by using more open-ended questions (McKeown & Beck, 2003; Wasik, Hindman, & Bond, 2006). Consider the following two excerpts from a conversation between an adult and a four-year-old boy. In the first, the adult and child are playing with Legos, and their attention is focused completely on the situation at hand:

> Child: This is me and that's you.
> Adult: Okay
> Child: No, This is me and that's you and that's me.
> Adult: No, No. That's me. Wait. That's me?
> Child: Yeah.
> Adult: All right.

However, when the focus on the conversation changes—when the adult asks a question inviting the child to talk about a nonpresent topic—the nature of the language changes as well:

> Adult: Where did you find out about Star Wars?
> Child: I dreamed that I was in Star Wars and I saw this strange pack of ooie and I saw mud.
> Adult: You saw a strange pack of ooie?
> Child: I saw a big pack of stinky, ooie garbage. He lives in there, in a stinking pack of garbage.
> Adult: Who does?
> Child: Jabba!

In the first segment, the syntax was extremely simple, and as for vocabulary, there were hardly any content words. In the second segment, on the other hand, the child used adjectives, prepositional phrases, and subordinate clauses, and the vocabulary includes some rather vivid and rare words (the word *stinking* occurs less than once in a million words of text), not to mention made-up words (*ooie*).

To recap this first insight, words are powerful, and they are especially powerful in varieties of language which may be unfamiliar to children whose language experience has primarily been in conversation, television, and forms of written language such as email and text messaging which share many of the communicative dynamics of conversation. Adults fluent in both conversational and academic English are often unaware of how different these language varieties are, and in particular, how greatly the role of word choice depends on which variety of language one is using. There are at least five specific instructional practices that follow from the understanding that words are powerful.

Model the use of rich vocabulary. Teachers can increase the vividness and specificity of the vocabulary in their own speech—for example, saying "it's uncomfortably chilly here on the playground" rather than "it's cold out." The use of richer vocabulary by teachers contributes to students' vocabulary growth in at least two ways. First, it provides children encounters with new words, and hence more opportunities for incidental learning of new meanings.

Second, and perhaps even more important, it helps children gain familiarity with the rich, descriptive language that is typical of the written register. They begin to learn not only specific words, but new ways that words can be used. Teacher modeling of adept diction is recommended by vocabulary researchers (e.g., Graves, 2006) and is one part of a language development intervention shown to have significant impact on the receptive and expressive vocabulary knowledge of Head Start children (Wasik et al., 2006—see below).

Draw students' attention to powerful and effective use of words. The most important way to encourage students to use rich language in their own writing is to call their attention to examples of rich language. Students will learn the power of words by seeing them used skillfully and powerfully. In addition to selecting reading or read-aloud materials that make effective use of language, teachers should point out especially well-crafted sentences or phrases, and encourage students to collect their own examples. One of the ways you can ask students to respond to what they have read, is to suggest, in the words of one expert teacher (quoted in Johnston, 2004, p. 16), that they "write down a line you wish you had written."

Encouraging students to use more vivid and precise language. Simply asking more open-ended questions can lead to richer oral language use and vocabulary growth on the part of students (Wasik et al., 2006). There are also a variety of ways to encourage students to use richer language in their own writing. The examples of vivid language students collect from their reading can be used as models (Scott & Nagy, 2004). A simple "word jail" poster can serve as a reminder for students to replace overused words and expressions with more colorful and vivid language.

Encourage students to see themselves as writers. For students to truly understand the power of words, they have to see themselves as participants in arenas in which words have power. Teachers should encourage students to see themselves in roles in which effective use of language is essential—to see themselves as writers, poets, teachers, and advocates for causes. Peter Johnston's book *Choice Words* (2004) describes how simple but strategic use of language by teachers—for example, referring to students as poets or writers—can have a powerful impact on students' ability to try on these identities.

Talk with students about language variation. Children may implicitly understand that people speak and write differently for different audiences, situations, and purposes, but it is important to make variation in language use a topic of explicit and thoughtful classroom discussion. One reason for this is that bringing language variation to the table robs it of some of its potentially destructive power. There are strong emotions and widespread prejudice associated with linguistic differences. The attitudes associated with linguistic differences constitute an additional obstacle to the academic success of students from homes where languages other than English, or varieties of English other than Standard English, are spoken. Students and teachers need to understand that different varieties of language are suitable for different situations and purposes. At the same time, it is also important for students to become fully aware of the language attitudes of the society in which they live (Delpit, 2006). These attitudes are another reason why words are powerful, and why mastery of the academic register is an essential tool for survival.

■ Words Are Innumerable

For teachers to deal effectively with vocabulary, they have to have an accurate assessment of the overall size of the task—the number of words that students will encounter while reading, and the number of words that students need to learn. In both cases, the numbers are extremely large. For all practical purposes, one can assume that words are innumerable. There are too many words in the materials that students will read to teach them all these words; and most students add words to their vocabularies at a rate that exceeds what they could be explicitly taught.

It is beyond question that the number of words in the English language is extremely large. *Webster's Third New International Dictionary of the English Language* (1981), for example, has over 200,000 main entries. According to Nagy and Anderson (1984), the number of distinct word families in printed school English (i.e., the books, magazines, and other printed materials that students are likely to encounter in grades 3 through 9), is roughly 90,000. This estimate would be doubled if one included proper names. Although the bulk of any text is made up of high frequency words, the distribution of words in the language is such that in any corpus of written material one reads, no matter how small or large, a substantial number of the word types in that corpus will occur only once. Hence, a comprehensive program for promoting vocabulary growth must necessarily include teaching students strategies for dealing with the unfamiliar words they will encounter while reading (Graves, 2000, 2006).

The number of words children actually learn, or need to learn, is of course much smaller than the number of words they will encounter in print. Some new words are defined or explained in the text; some are not crucial for understanding the text, and some occur so infrequently that they are simply not worth the trouble to learn. (According to Carroll, Davies, & Richman [1971], about half the words in English occur less than once in ten million words of text.)

However, the number of words that children do learn is substantial. There is of course some disagreement among researchers as to what the exact numbers are. The most conservative estimates are that during the school years, average children added about 1,000 root words a year to their reading vocabularies (Anglin, 1993; Biemiller, 1999; D'Anna, Zechmeister, & Hall,

1991; Goulden, Nation, & Read, 1990). Other estimates are closer to 3,000 words per year (Beck & McKeown, 1991; Bloom, 2000; Nagy & Herman, 1987; White, Graves, & Slater, 1990). But even the low-end estimate of 1,000 words learned per year is a large number.

Furthermore, the lower estimates are underestimates of the amount of word learning by average students in several respects (Anderson & Nagy, 1992). First, most estimates of vocabulary size ignore multiple meanings. High frequency words usually have several meanings, and multiple meanings can be especially problematic for second-language learners (Nagy, 1997). Second, most estimates also exclude proper names. In the study by Goulden et al. (1990), for example, proper names were operationalized as words listed as capitalized in the dictionary, including words such as *Tuesday, Chicago,* or *Islam.* Whether or not these words should be counted as "general vocabulary," it is certain that knowing their meanings will sometimes be crucial to understanding the point of a text. Third, most estimates of annual growth are in terms of root words. The assumption is that if the student learns the root word, prefixed and suffixed versions of the word can be learned with little additional effort. To some extent this is true; once you have learned the word *spoil,* the words *unspoiled* or *spoilage* should not present too much of an additional learning burden. However, morphological awareness—the ability to recognize relationships among words related by prefixation, suffixation, or compounding—is highly correlated with vocabulary size (Nagy, Berninger, & Abbott, 2006; Nagy, Berninger, Abbott, Vaughn, & Vermeulen, 2003). Thus, the students with the smallest vocabularies are least likely to make the generalization from the root word to its prefixed and suffixed relatives. In effect, unless their ability to recognize morphological relationships is improved, the students with smaller vocabularies face a bigger task than the students with larger vocabularies, as the students with smaller vocabularies are less likely to be able to capitalize on relationships among words.

One final way that estimates of average annual vocabulary growth underestimate the size of the task facing a teacher is that the students who need the most help with vocabularies need to catch up, and not just keep up. Differences in absolute vocabulary size in elementary school involve thousands of words. Some second graders would have to add twice the number of words learned by average students to their reading vocabulary each year to catch up with those students by the time they reach middle school. Even if you accept the most conservative estimates of annual average vocabulary growth, this is a daunting task.

The important point is that the number of new words students encounter and the number of words students should learn every year far exceeds the number of words that students could be taught. The situation is not hopeless, but teachers need to have a realistic understanding of the size of the task in order to be effective in promoting vocabulary growth in their students.

Recognizing that words are innumerable has a number of implications for how one addresses the goal of promoting students' vocabulary growth:

Be strategic in selecting words for instruction. Because students will encounter far more new words than you can possibly teach them, you cannot, nor do you need to, teach all of them. Words should be taught if they are of high utility—especially important for a unit, or for the understanding of a text, and likely to be encountered repeatedly by students (Beck, McKeown, & Kucan, 2005; Biemiller, 2005; Hiebert, 2005). Being strategic in selecting words for instruction also means that you have the freedom not to teach some of the words that might be unfamiliar to students.

Teach students word-learning strategies. It has been shown that students can be taught to be more effective in using morphology (word parts) and context clues in figuring out the meanings of new words (Baumann, Edwards, Boland, Olejnik, & Kame'enui, 2003; Fukkink & de Glopper, 1998; Goerss, Beck, & McKeown, 1999; Nunes & Bryant, 2006). Many effective reading comprehension interventions include strategies for dealing with breakdowns in comprehension, which are often the result of unknown words—for example, the "clunk" component of Collaborative Strategic Reading (Klingner & Vaughn, 1999) or the clarification component of Reciprocal Teaching (Palincsar & Brown, 1984; Rosenshine & Meister, 1994).

Saturating the school day with word-learning opportunities. Because there are so many words to learn, teachers need to do all they can to make their classroom a word-rich environment, and to make learning about words a natural and pervasive part of the school day. It is especially important for students to feel comfortable asking questions about the meanings of words.

The quality of classroom discourse plays an important role in language development. Observational and correlational studies (e.g., Dickinson & Smith, 1994, Dickinson & Tabors, 2001) have given us a consistent picture of the attributes of adult talk that promote language acquisition in children. Children's rate of vocabulary growth depends on both the quantity and quality of their verbal interactions with adults. Hart and Risley's (1995) study is often cited as a demonstration that volume of adult input is an important factor in children's vocabulary development. However, their results also confirm much of what has long been known about the importance of the quality of input as well. For example, their results show that children's vocabularies grow faster if adults are responsive to children—that is, if adults pick up on and comment or elaborate on something the child has said. Conversely, children's vocabularies grow more slowly to the extent that conversations with adults are driven by the adults' agendas. Children's vocabularies also grow more quickly if the adult language they hear is richer in adjectives and adverbs, and in verbs in the past tense (which indicates the discussion of nonpresent topics). Questions by adults are associated with greater vocabulary growth, whereas imperatives (commands) by adults are associated with less vocabulary growth.

It has also been shown that shown that adults can learn to increase their use of such patterns of interaction, and that children's vocabularies grow as a result. The *What Works Clearinghouse* review of research in early childhood education (Institute of Education Sciences, 2007) lists Dialogic Reading (as exemplified by Lonigan & Whitehurst, 1998; Lonigan, Anthony, Bloomfield, Dyer, & Samwel, 1999; Wasik & Bond, 2001; Whitehurst, Arnold, Epstein, Angell, Smith, & Fischel, 1994) as the only early childhood intervention that has been shown to have a positive impact on children's language development. One of the most recent interventions in this area of research is described by Wasik et al. (2006). In their study, Head Start preschool teachers were trained to use several patterns of verbal interaction with children associated with increased language development. These included responsiveness to utterances by children, use of richer and more descriptive language, and open-ended questions. At the end of the 9-month intervention, children in the 10 treatment classrooms showed significantly greater growth than children in 6 control classrooms on measures of both receptive vocabulary as measured by the PPVT-III (Dunn & Dunn, 1997) and expressive vocabulary as measured by the EOWPVT-III (Brownell, 2000).

Increasing the amount of student reading. To learn words in large numbers, students must be immersed in rich language. There is no more powerful way to increase one's reading vocabulary than by lots of reading. A somewhat controversial (e.g., Krashen, 2001) finding of the National Reading Panel was that there is no solid evidence documenting the claim that independent silent reading increases either vocabulary knowledge or reading fluency (NICHD, 2000). However, the position of the National Reading Panel is not that independent reading has been found to be ineffective, but rather that it has not yet been documented to be effective. Given the strong correlational findings linking volume of reading to vocabulary growth and numerous other benefits (Cunningham & Stanovich, 1991; Stanovich & Cunningham, 1992, 1993; Stanovich, West, & Harrison, 1995), it is reasonable for teachers to do what they can to increase the amount of time students spend reading, to the extent that this can be performed without cutting into time devoted to effective instruction. Teachers can also increase the effectiveness of time spent reading by supporting students in finding and choosing books of interest to them, and at an appropriate reading level.

■ Words Are Complex

Another essential insight into the nature of words is that words are complex. This complexity may be painfully obvious when we are dealing with words at the growing edges of our own vocabularies, but when it comes to teaching words to others, we are often in danger of underestimating the complexity of word knowledge. Some seductive oversimplifications are that what one needs to know about a word is captured in its definition, and that when one understands the definition, one knows the word. A related oversimplification is to assume that students usually understand definitions—an assumption called into question by studies that have actually examined children's ability to use definitions (McKeown, 1993; Miller & Gildea, 1987; Scott & Nagy, 1997).

A little reflection should be enough to make it clear that knowing a word is more than knowing its definition. Knowing a word is more like knowing how to use a tool, like a chisel or a paintbrush, than it is like being able to recite a memorized fact. Knowing a word includes knowing how it can function in a sentence, what other words it is commonly used with, how it is related in meaning and form to other words, and what styles of language for which it is appropriate.

Numerous Web sites report literal translations or mistranslations that travelers may encounter. When China prepared for the Olympic games, for example, there was a major effort to remove signs such as "the slippery are very crafty," apparently meaning something like "caution: slippery surface." Such errors, a source of humor for tourists and embarrassment for the government, make it clear that one needs far more than the dictionary meaning of a word to use it successfully. However, one does not need to go abroad to find evidence that definitional knowledge is not sufficient. When English-speaking children are given definitions of new words and asked to write sentences, the result makes the same point with equal or greater force (Miller & Gildea, 1987). In addition, research on vocabulary instruction has demonstrated that learning only the definitions of new words is not sufficient to improve students' comprehension of text containing those words (e.g., McKeown, Beck, Omanson, & Pople, 1985; Stahl & Fairbanks, 1986).

Instructional implications of complexity. One important implication of the complexity of word knowledge is that vocabulary instruction must seek to establish rich connections between the word being learned and the knowledge and concepts students already have (Stahl & Fairbanks, 1986). Although such connections can be established within a program of rich vocabulary instruction, encouraging connections outside of the vocabulary instruction, for example, by asking students to report back when they encounter the instructed words outside of school, also increases depth of word learning (McKeown, Beck, Omanson, & Pople, 1985).

Another implication of the complexity of word knowledge is the incremental nature of word learning—that word learning normally involves a large number of small steps (Nagy & Scott, 2000). Even with the most engaging and meaningful instructional activities, multiple encounters with a word are necessary before it is learned to the point of ownership. In many classrooms, it would be rare to find as many as four instructional encounters with a word being learned; and yet in McKeown, Omanson, and Pople's (1985) study, four encounters with a word, even when they involved high-quality instruction, were not sufficient to reliably increase comprehension of text containing the instructed words. In the research by Beck, McKeown, and their colleagues, 12 was the smallest number of instructional encounters to produce reliable gains in comprehension (Beck, Perfetti, & McKeown, 1982; McKeown, Beck, Omanson, & Perfetti, 1983; McKeown, Beck, Omanson, & Pople, 1985).

Because words are complex, rich, intensive instruction is necessary if teachers want students to learn words to the point of ownership. Such instruction must provide multiple types of information about words, provide multiple instructional encounters with each word, and include activities that require mental effort and creativity from students (Beck, McKeown, & Kucan, 2002; McKeown, Beck, Omanson, & Pople, 1985; Stahl, 1986). Because rich vocabulary instruction is time-intensive for both teachers and students, teachers must be strategic in choosing which words are to be instructed in that depth, and in deciding when it is appropriate simply to help students take one or two steps forward in the process of learning a given word. (See below for a little more discussion about selecting words for this kind of instruction.)

There is also another dimension to the complexity of word knowledge that is not always addressed in discussions of vocabulary instruction: The fact that words often have multiple meanings. In a large dictionary, you can find large numbers of words that have only a single meaning—but these tend to be words that are used so rarely that they have not had the opportunity to make themselves at home in the language. For words that are widely used, polysemy (multiplicity of meaning) is the rule rather than the exception. One implication of the fact that words tend to have more than one meaning is that any instruction in dictionary use must include selection of the appropriate meaning as an essential skill. However, an awareness that words invariably take on shades of meaning, and sometimes substantially different meanings, should inform all vocabulary instruction. Books such as the Amelia Bedelia series (e.g., Parish, 1963) make it clear that polysemy can be approached in an entertaining way.

The complexity of word knowledge also has implications for how one should teach word-learning strategies to students. As word knowledge is complex, it follows that any one source of information about a word—whether a dictionary definition, the parts of the word, or the context in which it is encountered—can at best only provide partial information about that word. This does not mean that such sources of information are not useful; but it does mean that they must be used strategically, cautiously, and in combination with each other. Because word-learning strategies are in fact complex and cognitively demanding, they must be taught in ways that reflect what we know about effective strategy instruction. For example, such instruction often begins with a clear explanation of how, when, and why to use a strategy. Effective strategy instruction also includes modeling of the strategy by the teacher, gradual transfer of responsibility to students, and calling students' attention to opportunities to apply the strategies across the curriculum.

■ Words Are Heterogeneous

A fourth important insight into the nature of words and word learning is that words are heterogeneous. Different kinds of words place different demands on the learner. Furthermore, there are a number of dimensions along which words may differ from each other, such as stylistic level, frequency in the language, conceptual difficulty, and part of speech. Words also differ in the role they play in a text, and in their relative importance to a given topic or unit of study.

Because there are different kinds of words, teachers must be strategic in choosing instruction that is appropriate for the specific needs and challenges of the words to be taught. Some words need to be taught intensively; others could be taught briefly and opportunistically, and others might not need to be taught at all. The word *ubiquitous*, for example, is itself not at all ubiquitous; it occurs about once in two million words of text, which means that even a student who is an avid reader might encounter it once a year or less. Good children's authors often sprinkle their writing with vivid, exotic, and even completely made-up words, but prior knowledge of the meanings of these words is often unnecessary for comprehending the text. For example, though *trogglehumper* is an exceedingly low-frequency word, and its meaning is not inferable on the basis of its parts, one would hardly recommend preteaching it as preparation for reading Dahl's *The BFG* (Dahl, 1982). Likewise, in *Charlotte's Web*, the description of a barn includes a list of "all sorts of things that you find in barns: Ladders, grindstones, pitch forks, monkey wrenches, scythes, lawn mowers, snow shovels, ax handles, milk pails, water buckets, empty grain sacks, and rusty rat traps" (White, 1952, p. 14). Knowing what a scythe is may enhance one's appreciation of the text and make the image even more vivid, but is not crucial to comprehension. Nor is *scythe* a word that one would expect students to use in their own writing. For such words, a passing explanation is often adequate, and even that is not always necessary.

On the other hand, there are some words that do need to be learned, and learned well. But even among words that students need to learn well, there are important distinctions that teachers need to make. One obvious but sometimes overlooked distinction is between words already in students' oral vocabularies that they need to learn to recognize in print, and words for which students need to learn the meaning. Both are important, but what constitutes the most effective instruction for one purpose is clearly not the best for the other. Helping a student learn to recognize a word in print is quite different from helping a student learn the meaning of a new word.

Even when consideration is narrowed to learning new word meanings, and to words that need to be learned thoroughly, there are important distinctions to be made. There are three types of words which require thorough instruction but which pose quite different challenges to the teacher and to the learner: high frequency words, general academic vocabulary, and key content area terms.

High frequency words. There is a relatively small set of words that make up the bulk of words normally encountered in text. For example, the 100 most frequent words in the language make up about half of the running words (tokens) in text, and the thousand most frequent words make up about three quarters (Nation, 2001). Knowing the most frequent words in the language is essential for reading, and conversely, not knowing some of them can pose problems for both fluency and comprehension.

There are a number of places where one can find lists of high frequency words. A list of the thousand most frequent words in the language can be found in Fry's (2004) *The Vocabulary Teacher's Book of Lists*. West's (1953) General Service List, which covers 2,284 high frequency words, can be found on the Internet, as can Coxhead's Academic Word List, which adds another 570 high utility academic word families to the General Service List. More recent frequency data are available (e.g., Zeno, Ivens, Millard, & Duvvuri, 1995), but the frequencies of the most common words in the language are relatively stable, so older lists are not very much out of date.

Since these words are so commonly used, one can assume that most of them will be known by most students. However, given the increasing diversity of our student population, one cannot take anything for granted. There may be unexpected gaps in students' knowledge of even these high frequency words—especially among English Language Learners, but possibly among other students as well. For example, one eight-year-old who recently immigrated to the U.S. from Mexico easily learned to decode the word *orange*, but asked the school psychologist who was working with him, "But what is *orange?*"

The high frequency of these words makes them important for students to know, but also raises a variety of problems for the teacher. First of all, there is the fact that most students already know the meaning of any word in this category, so that instruction would have to be carefully targeted to those students who actually needed it. But these words pose other problems as well. Since they are so frequent, it is unlikely that they can be defined easily without using words that are less frequent than the word being explained. High frequency words also tend to have large numbers of meanings. They are also less likely to have simple one-to-one relationships with words in other languages. Most instructional encounters with the word should therefore include at least a brief context. Since the primary focus of instruction will be on fluency and on familiarity with the form of the word, repetition and review are especially important for this type of word.

General academic vocabulary. This phrase describes approximately the same set of words that Beck, McKeown, and their colleagues would refer to as Tier 2 words (Beck, McKeown, & Kucan, 2002). These are words that might not be common in conversation, but which are frequently used in text across a variety of disciplines, and which teachers would probably like students to be able to use in their own writing. Because they are not specific to a particular domain or subject area, the concepts represented by these words are likely to be explainable in terms of words already familiar to the students, so that definitions can serve as one part, though certainly not the bulk, of the instruction. In the section on complexity earlier, the characteristics of instruction recommended by Stahl (1986) and Beck, McKeown, and their colleagues (e.g., Beck, McKeown, & Kucan, 2002) are outlined for helping students learn such words to the point of ownership.

Key content area terms. Some of the words it is important for students to learn are key content area terminology—words that represent concepts specific to a particular domain. Such words differ from the previous two categories primarily in their conceptual difficulty. That is, in this case learning the new word involves learning a concept that goes beyond the students' existing knowledge and experiences. For this reason, a definition is less likely to serve as an appropriate starting point, though it may be effective to have students construct a definition as a summarizing activity after the concept has been thoroughly taught.

Furthermore, the concept is likely to be part of an interrelated set of new concepts, many of which will be new to the student. For example, learning the word *photosynthesis* involves grasping the relationships among a set of terms and concepts which might include *respiration, oxygen,* and *carbon dioxide.* Teaching new concepts requires making connections with students' existing knowledge, but activating background knowledge can become a two-edged sword, evoking misconceptions as well as points of meaningful contact.

Because relationships among concepts are so important, teaching key content area terms is an arena in which graphic organizers are often helpful. Schwartz and Raphael's (1985) Concept of Definition map, available in several forms on the Web (e.g., http://www.readingquest.org/strat/cdmap.html), is a generic map that will work for a variety of concepts. However, as the nature of the relationships among concepts differs from one domain to another, one should take care to choose a graphic organizer that works well for the specific concepts being taught. In teaching new concepts, applying the concept by distinguishing examples from nonexamples is also often helpful.

The preceding three categories represented types of words that might require relatively intensive instruction, although what constitutes effective instruction would be quite different for each of these categories. For most new words, however, less intensive instruction may be appropriate. Words differ in how much they contribute to understanding a given text, and in how likely they are to be used in writing; hence, different words deserve different levels of instruction. The important thing is to make sure your expectations for students are commensurate with the intensity of your instruction: If you want students to be able to use words, you will have to take the time to teach those words thoroughly.

Only a limited amount of classroom time could be devoted to rich, intensive vocabulary instruction. However, attention to word learning should be a pervasive characteristic of the classroom, and questions and discussions about words and their meaning should be frequent, and welcomed. Answering a question about a word by sending a student to the dictionary is not recommended—the primary result would probably be to decrease the number of questions students ask about words. It would be better to capitalize on such a question as a learning opportunity for the whole class, or to go to the dictionary with the student and model both dictionary skills and the fact that you, too, are a word learner.

In summary, because words are *heterogeneous* both in themselves, and in the role they play in a text, teachers need to distinguish between the different types of learning demands that different words present to children, and adapt instruction to the nature of the word being taught, the role it plays in the text or lesson, and the purpose for which it is being learned.

■ Words Are Fascinating

The fifth key insight about words is that they are fascinating. If students are to be motivated to learn words, teachers must have a passion for words, and, more generally, a love of language. Jane Yolen once said "If you want to write and you're not in love with your language, you shouldn't be writing" (1973). What she says about writing could be said about teaching; as much as anything else, teachers are teachers of language. Teachers, therefore, need to find ways to cultivate their own love of language, so that they can communicate that love to their students.

One way to cultivate one's love of language is to keep learning new things about words. There are numerous and varied resources which can supply fascinating information about words. Blachowicz and Fisher (2004) and Johnson, Johnson, and Schlichting (2004), for example, provide an assortment of activities and resources related to various aspects of wordplay. Likewise, books on etymology (word histories) such as John Ayto's *Dictionary of Word Origins* (1990) can provide intriguing details about the past lives of seemingly familiar words. Few students are likely to know, for example, that the word *burly* originally meant something closer to "bowerly," that is, "fit to frequent a lady's apartment" (Ayto, 1990, p. 87).

Beyond doubt, teachers should do all they can to convey a delight in, and playfulness with, language, and wordplay of various kinds is an important means of doing so. A certain amount of completely frivolous "word trivia" can thus be appropriate. However, though not wanting to put a damper on anyone's sheer delight in the language, I would add that whenever possible wordplay should be used to help students gain insight into their language. For example, word histories can be used as ways of explaining why particular words currently have the spellings and meanings that they do. The fact that the word *carriage* is derived from *carry* not only explains something about the spelling, but also provides a basis for understanding why it has come to have seemingly quite distinct meanings such as "wheeled vehicle" and "manner of holding the body." Knowing why a word behaves like it does is a powerful aid to memory. It is also a boost to motivation—it is reassuring to know that the odd collection of meanings a word may have today is not simply a random assortment, but rather a family with resemblances that are discernable when one knows from where the word comes.

Word histories also give us more than just explanations for otherwise inexplicable spellings and meanings of particular words. They can illustrate essential understandings about the nature of language: that word meanings are conventional; that they change over time; that one generation's errors can become the next generation's standard; that meaning is context-dependent; and that concrete meanings have frequently served as metaphors to convey abstract concepts. Studying how words have changed in meaning over time also provides students with a foundation for understanding how authors use figurative language to extend word meanings in fresh ways.

In summary, because words are fascinating, teachers should continue to deepen their own awareness of and appreciation for words and language, and to communicate a delight in words to their students. Teachers should model being word learners, locating resources that provide them and their students with intriguing as well as useful information about words. As much as possible, word play should aim for insight rather than merely entertainment; intriguing information about words should be used to help students gain a better understanding of how their language works, and how language changes.

■ What Teachers Need to Know about Words, Students Need to Know Too

In this chapter, basic understandings of words and word learning have been presented which are necessary for making effective decisions about instructional practice relating to students' vocabulary growth. These understandings are grouped under five key insights—that words are powerful, innumerable, complex, heterogeneous, and fascinating.

Although the focus has been on what teachers need to know about words and word learning, it has also covered what students need to know well. In vocabulary growth as in other areas, it is essential that students take increasing responsibility for their own learning. Such responsibility presupposes metacognitive knowledge and awareness appropriate to the domain of study. Hence, one final implication of these key insights to stress is that vocabulary instruction, in all its various forms, should have as a goal to impart to students not just knowledge of specific words, but also the insights, strategies, and dispositions that foster word learning.

■ References

Aitchison, J. (2003). *Words in the mind: An introduction to the mental lexicon* (3rd ed.). Oxford, UK, Blackwell.

Anderson, J. R., & Bower, G. H. (1972). Recognition and retrieval processes in free recall. *Psychological Review, 79*, 97–123.

Anderson, R. C., & Freebody, P. (1981). Vocabulary knowledge. In J. Guthrie (Ed.), *Comprehension and teaching: Research reviews* (pp. 77–117). Newark, DE, International Reading Association.

Anderson, R. C., & Nagy, W. (1992). The vocabulary conundrum. *American Educator, 16*, 14–18, 44–47.

Anglin, J. M. (1993). Vocabulary development: A morphological analysis, *Monographs of the Society of research in Child Development 58*, Serial #238.

Ayto, J. (1990). *Dictionary of word origins.* New York, Arcade.

Baumann, J. F., Edwards, E. C., Boland, E. M., Olejnik, S., & Kame'enui, E. (2003). Vocabulary tricks: Effects of instruction in morphology and context on fifth-grade students' ability to derive and infer word meanings. *American Educational Research Journal, 40*, 447–494.

Beals, D. E. (2001). Eating and reading. In D. Dickinson & P. Tabors (Eds.), *Beginning literacy with language* (pp. 75–92). Baltimore, MD, Brookes.

Beck, I., & McKeown, M. (1991). Conditions of vocabulary acquisition. In R. Barr, M. Kamil, P. Mosenthal, & P. D. Pearson (Eds.), *Handbook of reading research* (Vol. II, pp. 789–814). New York, Longman.

Beck, I., McKeown, M., & Kucan, L. (2002). *Bringing words to life.* New York, The Guilford.

Beck, I., McKeown, M., & Kucan, L. (2005). Choosing words to teach. In E. Hiebert & M. Kamil (Eds.), *Teaching and learning vocabulary: Bringing research to practice* (pp. 207–222). Mahwah, NJ, Lawrence Erlbaum Associates.

Beck, I., Perfetti, C., & McKeown, M. (1982). Effects of long-term vocabulary instruction on lexical access and reading comprehension. *Journal of Educational Psychology, 74*, 506–521.

Biemiller, A. (1999). *Language and reading success.* Cambridge, MA, Brookline Books.

Biemiller, A. (2005). Size and sequence in vocabulary development: Implications for choosing words for primary grade vocabulary instruction. In E. Hiebert & M. Kamil (Eds.), *Teaching and learning vocabulary: Bringing research to practice* (pp. 223–242). Mahwah, NJ, Lawrence Erlbaum Associates.

Blachowicz, C., & Fisher, P. (2004). Keeping the "fun" in fundamental: Encouraging word awareness and incidental word learning in the classroom through word play. In J. Baumann & E. Kame'enui (Eds.), *Vocabulary instruction: Research to practice* (pp. 218–237). New York, The Guilford Press.

Bloom, P. (2000). *How children learn the meanings of words.* Cambridge, MA, MIT Press.

Brownell, R. (2000). *Expressive one-word picture vocabulary test, third edition.* Novato, CA, Academic Therapy Publications.

Carlisle, J., & Rice, M. (2002). *Improving reading comprehension: Research-based principles and practices.* Baltimore, MD, York Press.

Carlo, M., August, D., McLaughlin, B., Snow, C., Dressler, C., Lippman, D., Lively, T., & White, C. (2004). Closing the gap: Addressing the vocabulary needs of English-language learners in bilingual and mainstream classrooms. *Reading Research Quarterly, 39*, 188–215.

Carroll, J. B., Davies, P., & Richman, R. (1971). *The American Heritage word frequency book.* Boston, Houghton Mifflin.

Chafe, W., & Danielewicz, J. (1987). Properties of spoken and written language. In R. Horowitz & S. J. Samuels (Eds.), *Comprehending oral and written language* (pp. 83–113). San Diego, CA, Academic Press.

Coxhead, A. (2000). A new academic word list. *TESOL Quarterly, 34*, 213–238.

Cromley, J. G., & Azevedo, R. (2007). Testing and refining the direct and inferential mediation model of reading comprehension. *Journal of Educational Psychology, 99*, 311–325.

Cunningham, A. E., & Stanovich, K. E. (1991). Tracking the unique effects of print exposure in children: Associations with vocabulary, general knowledge, and spelling. *Journal of Educational Psychology, 83*, 264–274.

Dahl, R. (1982). *The BFG.* New York, Penguin.

D'Anna, C. A., Zechmeister, E. B., & Hall, J. W. (1991). Toward a meaningful definition of vocabulary size. *Journal of Reading Behavior, 23*, 109–122.

Davis, F. B. (1944). Fundamental factors of comprehension in reading. *Psychometrika, 9*, 185–197.

Delpit, L. (2006). *Other people's children: Cultural conflict in the classroom.* New York, The New Press.

Dickinson D., & Smith, M. (1994). Long-term effects of preschool teachers' book readings on low-income children's vocabulary and story comprehension. *Reading Research Quarterly, 29*, 104–122.

Dickinson, D. K., & Tabors, P. O. (Eds.) (2001). *Beginning literacy with language.* Baltimore, MD, Brookes.

Dunn, L. M., & Dunn, L. M. (1997). *Peabody picture vocabulary test, third edition.* Bloomington, MN, Pearson Assessments.

Fry, E. (2004). *The vocabulary teacher's book of lists.* San Francisco, Wiley.

Fukkink, R. G., & de Glopper, K. (1998). Effects of instruction in deriving word meaning from context: A meta-analysis. *Review of Educational Research, 68*, 450–469.

Gerhand, S., & Barry, C. (1999). Age of acquisition, word frequency, and the role of phonology in the lexical decision task. *Memory & Cognition, 27,* 592–602.

Gilhooly, K. J., & Logie, R. H. (1980). Age of acquisition, imagery, concreteness, familiarity, and ambiguity measures for 1,944 words. *Behavior Research Methods & Instrumentation, 12,* 395–427.

Goerss, B., Beck, I., & McKeown, M. (1999). Increasing remedial students' ability to derive word meaning from context. *Reading Psychology, 20,* 151–175.

Goulden, R., Nation, P., & Read, J. (1990). How large can a receptive vocabulary be? *Applied Linguistics, 11,* 341–363.

Graves, M. (2000). A vocabulary program to complement and bolster a middle-grade comprehension program. In B. Taylor, M. Graves, & P. van den Broek (Eds.), *Reading for meaning: Fostering comprehension in the middle grades* (pp. 116–135). Newark, DE, International Reading Association.

Graves, M. (2006). *The vocabulary book.* New York, Teachers College Press.

Hart, B., & Risley, T. (1995). *Meaningful differences in the everyday lives of young American children.* Baltimore, Brookes.

Hayes, D. P. (1988). Speaking and writing: Distinct patterns of word choice. *Journal of Memory and Language, 27,* 572–585.

Hayes, D. P., & Ahrens, M. (1988). Vocabulary simplification for children: A special case of 'motherese.' *Journal of Child Language, 15,* 395–410.

Hiebert, E. (2005). In pursuit of an effective, efficient vocabulary curriculum for elementary students. In E. Hiebert & M. Kamil (Eds.), *Teaching and learning vocabulary: Bringing research to practice* (pp. 243–263). Mahwah, NJ, Lawrence Erlbaum Associates.

Institute of Education Sciences. (2007). *What Works Clearinghouse.* Retrieved, July 5, 2007, from http://www.whatworks.ed.gov.

Johnson, D. D., Von Hoff Johnson, B., & Schlichting, K. (2004). Logology: Word and language play. In J. Baumann & E. Kame'enui (Eds.), *Vocabulary instruction: Research to practice* (pp. 179–200). New York, The Guilford Press.

Johnston, P. (2004). *Choice words: How our language affects children's learning.* Portland, ME, Stenhouse.

Klingner, J., & Vaughn, S. (1999). Promoting reading comprehension, content learning, and English acquisition through Collaborative Strategic Reading (CSR). *The Reading Teacher, 52,* 738–747.

Krashen, S. (2001). More smoke and mirrors: A critique of the National Reading Panel report on fluency. *Phi Delta Kappan, 83,* 119–123.

Lonigan, C. J., Anthony, J. L., Bloomfield, B. G., Dyer, S. M., & Samwel, C. S. (1999). Effects of two shared-reading interventions on emergent literacy skills of at-risk preschoolers. *Journal of Early Intervention, 22,* 306–322.

Lonigan, C. J., & Whitehurst, G. J. (1998). Relative efficacy of parent and teacher involvement in a shared-reading intervention for preschool children from low-income backgrounds. *Early Childhood Research Quarterly, 13,* 263–290.

McKeown, M. (1993). Creating definitions for young word learners. *Reading Research Quarterly, 28,* 16–33.

McKeown, M., & Beck, I. (2003). Taking advantage of read-alouds to help children make sense of decontextualized language. In A. van Kleeck, S. Stahl, & E. Bauer (Eds.), *On reading books to children* (pp. 159–176). Mahwah, NJ, Lawrence Erlbaum Associates.

McKeown, M., Beck, I., Omanson, R., & Perfetti, C. (1983). The effects of long-term vocabulary instruction on reading comprehension: A replication. *Journal of Reading Behavior, 15,* 3–18.

McKeown, M. G., Beck, I. L., Omanson, R. C., & Pople, M. T. (1985). Some effects of the nature and frequency of vocabulary instruction on the knowledge and use of words. *Reading Research Quarterly, 20,* 522–535.

Miller, G., & Gildea, P. (1987). How children learn words. *Scientific American, 257,* 94–99.

Nagy, W. (1997). On the role of context in first- and second-language vocabulary learning. In N. Schmitt & M. McCarthy (Eds.), *Vocabulary: Description, acquisition and pedagogy* (pp. 64–83). Cambridge, Cambridge University Press.

Nagy, W., & Anderson, R. C. (1984). How many words are there in printed school English? *Reading Research Quarterly, 19,* 304–330.

Nagy, W., Berninger, V., & Abbott, R. (2006). Contributions of morphology beyond phonology to literacy outcomes of upper elementary and middle school students. *Journal of Educational Psychology, 98,* 134–147.

Nagy, W., Berninger, V., Abbott, R., Vaughan, K., & Vermeulen, K. (2003). Relationship of morphology and other language skills to literacy skills in at-risk second grade readers and at-risk fourth grade writers. *Journal of Educational Psychology, 95,* 730–742.

Nagy, W., & Herman, P. A. (1987). Breadth and depth of vocabulary knowledge: Implications for acquisition and instruction. In M. McKeown & M. Curtis (Eds.), *The nature of vocabulary acquisition* (pp. 19–59). Hillsdale, NJ, Lawrence Erlbaum Associates.

Nagy, W. E., & Scott, J. A. (2000). Vocabulary processes. In M. L. Kamil, P. B. Mosenthal, P. D. Pearson, & R. Barr (Eds.), *Handbook of reading research* (Vol. III, pp. 269–284). Mahwah, NJ, Lawrence Erlbaum Associates.

Nation, I. S. P. (2001). *Learning vocabulary in another language.* Cambridge, Cambridge University Press.

National Institute of Child Health and Human Development (NICHD). (2000). *Teaching children to read: An evidence-based assessment of the scientific research literature on reading and its implications for reading instruction: Reports of the subgroups* (NIH Publication No. 00–4754). Washington, DC, U.S. Government Printing Office. Available on-line: http://www.nichd.nih. gov/publications/nrp/upload/report_pdf.pdf.

Nunes, T., & Bryant, P. (2006). *Improving literacy by teaching morphemes.* New York, Routledge.

Ordóñez, C. L., Carlo, M. S., Snow, C. E., & McLaughlin, B. (2002). Depth and breadth of vocabulary in two languages: Which vocabulary skills transfer? *Journal of Educational Psychology, 94*, 719–728.

Palincsar, A. S., & Brown, A. L. (1984). Reciprocal teaching of comprehension-fostering and comprehension-monitoring activities. *Cognition and Instruction, 1*, 117–175.

Parish, M. (1963). *Amelia bedelia*. New York, HarperCollins.

Petty, W. T., Herold, C. P., & Stoll, E. (1968). *The state of knowledge about the teaching of vocabulary.* Champaign, IL, National Council of Teachers of English.

Rosenshine, B., & Meister, C. (1994). Reciprocal teaching: A review of the research. *Review of Educational Research, 64*, 479–530.

Schwartz, R. M., & Raphael, T. E. (1985). Concept of definition: A key to improving students' vocabulary. *The Reading Teacher, 39*, 198–205.

Scott, J, & Nagy, W. (1997). Understanding the definitions of unfamiliar verbs. *Reading research Quarterly, 32*, 184–200.

Scott, J. A., & Nagy, W. (2004). Developing word consciousness. In J. Baumann & E. Kame'enui (Eds.), *Vocabulary instruction: Research to practice* (pp. 201–217). New York, The Guilford Press.

Seashore, R. H., & Eckerson, L. D. (1940). The measurement of individual differences in general English vocabularies. *Journal of Educational Psychology, 31*, 14–38.

Sims, V. M. (1929). The reliability and validity of four types of vocabulary test. *Journal of Educational Research, 20*, 91–96.

Snow, C., Burns, M. S., & Griffin, P. (1998). *Preventing reading difficulties in young children.* Washington, DC, National Academy Press.

Stahl, S. (1986). Three principles of effective vocabulary instruction. *Journal of Reading, 29*, 662–668.

Stahl, S., & Fairbanks, M. (1986). The effects of vocabulary instruction: A model-based meta-analysis. *Review of Educational Research, 56*, 72–110.

Stahl, S., & Nagy, W. (2006). *Teaching word meanings.* Mahwah, NJ, Lawrence Erlbaum Associates.

Stanovich, K. E., & Cunningham, A. E. (1992). Studying the consequences of literacy within a literate society: The cognitive correlates of print exposure. *Memory & Cognition, 20*, 51–68.

Stanovich, K. E., & Cunningham, A. E. (1993). Where does knowledge come from? Specific associations between print exposure and information acquisition. *Journal of Educational Psychology, 85*, 211–229.

Stanovich, K. E., West, R. F., & Harrison, M. (1995). Knowledge growth and maintenance across the life span: The role of print exposure. *Developmental Psychology, 31*, 811–826.

Tabors, P. O., Beals, D. E., and Weizman, Z. (2001). You know what oxygen is? Learning new words at home. In D. Dickinson & P. Tabors (Eds.), *Beginning literacy with language* (pp. 93–110). Baltimore, MD, Brookes.

Thorndike, E. L., & Lorge, I. (1944). *The teacher's word book of 30,000 words.* New York, Teachers College Press.

Vermeer, A. (2001). Breadth and depth of vocabulary in relation to L1/L2 acquisition and frequency of input. *Applied Psycholinguistics, 22*, 217–234.

Wasik, B. A., & Bond, M. A. (2001). Beyond the pages of a book: Interactive book reading and language development in preschool classrooms. *Journal of Educational Psychology, 93*, 243–250.

Wasik, B., Bond, M., & Hindman, A. (2006). The effects of a language and literacy intervention on Head Start children and teachers. *Journal of Educational Psychology, 98*, 63–74.

Webster's Third New International Dictionary. (1981). Springfield, MA, Merriam-Webster.

West, M. (1953). *A general service list of English words.* Longman, London.

White, E. B. (1952). *Charlotte's web.* New York, Harper & Row.

White, T., Graves, M., & Slater, W. (1990). Growth of reading vocabulary in diverse elementary schools: Decoding and word meaning. *Journal of Educational Psychology, 82*, 281–290.

Whitehurst, G. J., Arnold, D. H., Epstein, J. N., Angell, A. L., Smith, M., & Fischel, J. E. (1994). A picture book reading intervention in daycare and home for children from low-income families. *Developmental Psychology, 30*, 679–689.

Yolen, J. (1973). *Writing books for children.* Boston, The Writer, Inc.

Zeno, S. M., Ivens, S. H., Millard, R. T. K., & Duvvuri, R. (1995). *The educator's word frequency guide.* New York, Touchstone Applied Science Associates, Inc.

18. WHOLE SCHOOL LITERACY

Using Research to Create Programs that Build Universal High Levels of Literate Competence

Carol A. Christensen and Maria Wauchope

W hen the first author was approached by a principal of a secondary school in Queensland, Australia, who asked if she could assist in developing a literacy program, she was aware that no secondary teacher had the background or expertise to teach basic reading and writing. Their lack of preparation to teach skills normally mastered during primary education presented a major challenge in transforming student literacy in the school. Secondary schools in the state cater to students who range in age from approximately 12 to 17 years. Teachers focus on disciplinary areas rather than teaching basic literacy. Nevertheless, she accepted the challenge and in this chapter shares how she approached the task and created whole school literacy (WSL) programs at the secondary level and what she found. To begin, the research that informed this approach to practice is briefly reviewed.

■ The Research Basis

The Role of Background Knowledge

Research has consistently shown that domain-specific knowledge is central to the development of expertise (Bereiter & Scandamalia, 1993; Chi, 1978; Chi, Feltovich, & Glaser, 1981; Snyder, 2000). Experts' knowledge structures are distinguished by large, complex networks of concepts and ideas and deep understanding of the content domain (Bransford, Brown, & Cocking, 2000). Students who have extensive background knowledge find it easier to comprehend new ideas embedded within the text. Both knowledge of word-meanings and domain-specific knowledge related to the topic are strong predictors of reading comprehension (Cain et al., 2004). For example, Stahl, Chou-Hare, Sinatra, and Gregory (1991) found that prior knowledge as well as vocabulary predicted high school students' ability to recall details of story elements from a passage of text. Recht and Leslie (1988) found that extensive knowledge about baseball enabled students to compensate for poor reading skills when students were assessed on their understanding of a text on baseball. Students who knew a lot about baseball but had poor reading skills performed better on measures to assess understanding of the text than students who had good reading skills but limited knowledge of baseball. In fact, poor readers who knew a lot about baseball performed almost as well as good readers who knew a lot about baseball. Teachers in the WSL programs are encouraged to scrutinize text for essential prerequisite knowledge and either build students' knowledge or modify texts so that they better match student existing knowledge or the demands made by the text.

Attention and Automaticity

Attention is a scarce cognitive resource (Anderson, 1981; Lesgold, Rubison, Feltovich, Glaser, Klopfet, & Wang, 1988). Processing that is automatic does not require attention (LaBerge & Samuels, 1974) but is quick, accurate, and effortless (Schneider & Shriffrin, 1977). To the extent low-level aspects of tasks are automatic, more attentional resources are available for higher-order, comprehension, and thinking tasks (Bransford et al., 2000) because cognitive load is reduced (Sweller, 1988) and attention can be devoted to the most complex and demanding aspects of tasks (Sweller & Cooper, 1985). Practice is the path to automaticity. Therefore, WSL programs sequence curriculum so that lower-level skills, such as decoding, are automated through practice regimes.

Cognitive and Metacognitive Strategies

Flavell (1979) defined *metacognition* as the control and awareness of cognitive processes. Students who have *metacognitive strategies* are aware of their thinking processes and can exert deliberate control to regulate those processes and, consequently, have much higher levels of learning (Zimmerman, 1990). *Rehearsal strategies* include written and oral repetition such as written verbatim notes, underlining, or highlighting. *Organizational strategies* involve restructuring of information so that new connections are created among the concepts and ideas embedded in the text (e.g., outlining key points or creating a hierarchy). *Elaboration strategies* go beyond the information given, to link new content to existing knowledge and include paraphrasing, and creating images, rhymes, stories, analogies, metaphors, models, and diagrams (Weinstein & Mayer, 1986). A key feature of WSL programs is that students are encouraged to invent and use sophisticated cognitive and metacognitive strategies.

Literacy Curriculum

An effective literacy program must cover a broad range of competencies. For example, Cain, Oakhill, and Bryant (2004) found that both lower-level skills, such as accuracy and speed of decoding, and higher-level capabilities, such as sensitivity to anomalies, inference making, and awareness of text structure, contributed separate and unique variance to children's reading comprehension. The curriculum in the WSL programs is therefore comprehensive, covering all facets of literacy from oral language, phonological awareness, and decoding to comprehension and use of sophisticated cognitive and metacognitive strategies to learn from text.

Students from different cultural and social backgrounds can have dramatically different opportunities to develop oral language skills (Hart & Risley, 1995), which are the foundation on which reading is built (Storch & Whitehurst, 2002). Both oral and written language can be analyzed at different levels: phonological, morphemic, syntactic, semantic, and pragmatic.

Phonological level refers to the speech sounds that make-up language.

Morphemic level refers to the smallest unit that conveys meaning. Words or parts of words that have regular meaning (e.g., "*un*" or "*re*") are morphemes.

Syntactic level refers to the structural elements of language (i.e., grammar).

Semantic level refers to the meaningful content of language; the concepts and ideas that are conveyed through language.

Pragmatic level refers to the communicative component of language.

All students in WSL programs engage in oral language activities each week that cover all levels of oral language. For example, phonological awareness activities are used with students reading at lower elementary level; word games based on synonyms are designed to build students' vocabularies; higher achieving students engage in activities such as debates and simulations.

Phonological awareness. Phonological awareness refers to the ability to analyze and manipulate the sound structure of oral language and plays a fundamental role in learning to read (Stanovich, 1986). Within WSL Programs, students are screened for sensitivity to rhyme and initial sounds and if found to lack that sensitivity participate in activities to develop phonological awareness.

Decoding. The process of translating letters and words on a page into spoken language is referred to as decoding, which is an essential component of reading instruction, especially at the beginning stages (Adams, 1990; National Reading Panel, 2000; Yuill & Oakhill, 1991). However, simple accuracy in decoding is not sufficient for high levels of comprehension (Stahl & Hiebert, 2005). If students' decoding skills are accurate but slow and deliberate, their cognitive resources are consumed in the decoding process so that they do not have sufficient attention available to focus on the meaning of the text (LaBerge & Samuels, 1974). WSL reading programs at the secondary level for students who lack proficiency in basic reading, WSL programs build decoding skills through a carefully sequenced and structured approach that teaches students to use letter-sound correspondences to work out unfamiliar words. It also teaches sight word recognition and uses sequenced readers to encourage students to use their skills by reading extended text (Christensen, 2005; Christensen & Bowey, 2005).

Comprehension. The ability to understand, analyze, and use text for learning is a fundamental goal of reading. For very young readers, there is a very strong relationship between comprehension and lower-level decoding skills (Juel, Griffith, & Gough, 1986; Swanson & Berninger, 1995) as well as vocabulary knowledge (Cain et al., 2004; Stahl & Hiebert, 2005). However, higher-order processes such as inference making, sensitivity to anomalies, and comprehension monitoring are more strongly related to literacy achievement for older readers (Hannon & Daneman, 2001; Saarnio, Oka, & Paris, 1990). Instructional strategies, which are discussed next, that facilitate and enhance comprehension form a key component of WSL programs.

Comprehension monitoring and sensitivity to anomalies. Comprehension monitoring refers to the process whereby individuals actively monitor their understanding of the text, identify errors or breakdowns in comprehension if they occur, and employ fix-up strategies to resolve ambiguity or inaccuracies. Ability to monitor understanding is strongly related to reading comprehension and achievement (August, Flavell, & Clift, 1984; Brown, Bransford, Ferrara, & Campione, 1983). Oakhill, Hartt, and Samols (2005) compared the ability of good and poor comprehenders to detect inconsistent information or anomalies in sentences. They found that good comprehenders were consistently better at detecting anomalies than poor comprehenders. However, the difference was particularly marked when the anomalous information was contained in sentences located in separate sections of the text rather than when located in adjacent sentences. Rubman and Waters (2000) used storyboards to assist a group of children to represent the information in a story. Other children were given text only. They found that storyboards increased children's ability to detect anomalous information. This effect was particularly marked for less-skilled readers.

The most frequently used and evaluated technique to enhance children's ability to monitor comprehension, Reciprocal Teaching (Palincsar and Brown, 1984) involves four processes to enhance their ability to work with text. First, the teacher demonstrates each process and then students model the teacher's activity. The processes that are taught include the ability to predict, summarize, clarify, and ask questions. Extensive research has demonstrated that Reciprocal Teaching is a very efficacious intervention that enhances children's comprehension monitoring as well as their basic understanding of text

(Rosenshine & Meister, 1994). Reciprocal Teaching to build comprehension monitoring is a core element in WSL programs designed for students reading at upper elementary and secondary levels.

Inferential thinking. Making inferences allows the reader to go beyond a literal interpretation of the text to develop a more coherent and accurate understanding of the text. An inference is an understanding that is not explicitly mentioned in the text and can be generated only by connecting discrete elements within the text (Royer, Carlo, Dufresne, & Mestre, 1996). The first step in the ability to create inferences appears to depend on the integration of information in the text. Readers may need to integrate information from different sentences in the text to construct coherent representations (Graesser, Singer, & Trabasso, 1994). Readers may also need to integrate their existing knowledge with new information contained in the text (Cain et al., 2004). Thus, integration is dependent in part on rich prior knowledge structures (Trabasso & Magliano, 1996). Ozgungor and Guthrie (2004) found that elaborative interrogation enhanced students' ability on three measures of learning from text—inference-making, recall of information, and construction of coherent representations for the information in the text. Elaborative interrogation involves higher-order questioning focusing on asking "why." The ability to make inferences is also improved by teaching students to focus on key words (Yuill & Joscelyne, 1988). Working with Grade 6 students, Carr, Dewitz, and Patberg (1983) increased students' inferential comprehension by using structured overviews to activate background knowledge, cloze activities to integrate prior knowledge with new information, and a self-monitoring checklist. Dewitz, Carr, and Patberg (1987) found that cloze activities improved fifth grade students' ability to integrate information from the text with their existing knowledge and showed stronger gains in comprehension and metacognitive control than teaching students to use structured overviews or a control group program. Yuill and Oakhill (1988) compared three interventions for children with poor comprehension and found that the most effective one encouraged lexical inferences, generating questions about the text, and generating predictions about information that was not available in the text. The WSL programs include clarifying, predicting, summarizing, cloze, elaborative questioning, inferential questioning, and sensitivity to anomalies activities.

Mental representations. In order for readers to learn and remember information from text, they must construct an internal mental representation that corresponds to the concepts and ideas embedded in the text. Craik (1943) described mental models as representations within the mind that parallel the individual's experience of the external natural and social worlds. Johnson-Laird (1983) argued that mental models are structured in a way that corresponds to the structure of the phenomena that they represent, and may include images (based either on observation or imagination), linguistic representations, and other abstractions. Instruction to prompt students' ability to create images is one effective approach to enhancing the ability to build mental models (Hibbing & Rankin-Erickson, 2003; Pressley, Johnson, Symons, McGoldrick, & Kurita, 1989). For example, working with junior high school students who were above and below grade level in reading, Peters and Levin (1986) compared the performance of students taught a mnemonic imagery strategy with a control group. Students reading at both above and below grade level performed better in the mnemonic imagery condition than control group students. The WSL programs use a sequence of experiences, based on quick sketches, to encourage students to create mental images that correspond to ideas in text. This component of the program is used with students reading at upper elementary and secondary levels.

Teaching for Universal High Levels of Achievement

The WSL programs are driven by the belief that all students can achieve high levels of literate competence. The idea that all students could experience high levels of achievement was developed by Bloom (1976, 1984). In 1963, Carroll suggested that the key factor in determining the level of student achievement was time; some students needed a great deal of time to master specific content, while others required less time. Bloom formulated a system he referred to as *"Mastery Learning,"* which enabled him to translate ideas developed by Carroll into practices that could be implemented in classroom environments. He argued that if all students were provided with the amount of time they needed, then all students could achieve at levels which previously characterized the achievement of only the top few students. He suggested that by sequencing instruction and linking outcomes to prerequisite knowledge, all students could experience success in learning.

Early studies found that a key variable in instruction that led to higher student outcomes was time (Rosenshine, 1997). Berliner and his colleagues (Berliner, 1990; Fisher, Berliner, Filby, Marliave, Cahen, & Dishaw, 1980) found that students could be doing many things that impacted on their learning during the time that was allocated to instruction. A more important variable he identified as *"engaged time."* This variable was the amount of time that students spent attending to the assigned task. Fisher et al. (1980) identified a third even more potent variable, *"academic learning time."* This variable was the amount of time that students spent actually learning. They found that optimal learning occurred when students were engaged in tasks where they experienced success more than 85% of the time. Rosenshine, in a seminal paper in 1984, reviewed the extensive literature on effective instruction. He suggested that effective teaching was direct and explicit and maximized academic learning time if it proceeded in a series of phases: The first stage was review, where the teachers reviewed previous work. Next, new content was presented. This was followed by guided practice, which led to independent practice. During the practice phase of the lesson, effective teachers analyzed errors and provided corrective feedback.

Thus, WSL programs are grounded in the belief that all students can learn. Academic learning time is maximized by ensuring that students work at a level at which they can achieve continual success. Tasks are sequenced and linked so that students acquire essential prerequisite knowledge for each skill as they move through the program.

■ Implementation

WSL programs do not rely on a set recipe or prescriptive package. Rather they are developed through negotiation with each individual school-site based on the specific context of the school and a set of underlying principles.

Principle 1: All Students Must Experience Continual Success in Learning

The first principle is that every student must work at a level where he or she can experience continual success. This is very difficult to achieve in highly diverse classroom environments where students' literacy attainments may range from kindergarten to Grade 12 level. To attain universal high levels of achievement, significant reorganization of school structures was and is necessary. Homogeneous grouping is used to manage diversity in current student achievement. In this way, instruction becomes manageable and groups of students, working at a similar level, can work through the curriculum sequence based on their existing knowledge. This approach means that each of our schools needs to restructure the timetable to accommodate the organizational arrangements necessary to administer the program.

Principle 2: Curriculum and Instructional Activities Must Have Demonstrated Efficacy in Published Research that Includes Control Groups

The WSL programs curriculum framework is provided in Figure 18.1 and is developed from the research on effective practices in teaching literacy. The curriculum consists of teaching eight essential skills.

Prerequisite skills. Three areas are considered to be essential prerequisite knowledge for learning to read: oral language, phonological awareness, and letter knowledge. In particular, students must demonstrate mastery of phonological awareness before decoding is introduced.

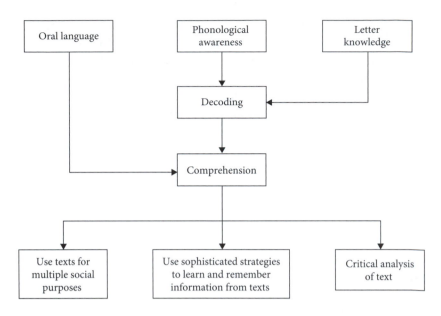

FIGURE 18.1 Overview of Curriculum for Whole School Literacy Programs.

Decoding. If beginning readers can demonstrate competence in the prerequisite skills, particularly phonological awareness, they must learn to decode text to a level of automaticity. A commercially available program titled Reading LINK-Decoding (Christensen, 2005) is used. It takes a sequenced and structured approach to teaching students to use letter-sounds to work out unfamiliar, regular words. It also builds a sight word vocabulary of irregular words and has extended text for students to practice their word-attack skills in context and to provide some of the foundation skills in comprehension. The structure of the program emerged from research carried out by Christensen and Bowey (2005).

Comprehension. If students can decode the text proficiently, they go into a program that focuses on their ability to comprehend the text. Comprehension activities revolve around reciprocal teaching (Palincsar & Brown, 1984), facilitation of students' ability to engage in ideas and enhancing students' ability to build mental models. Reciprocal teaching is designed to encourage students' ability to monitor their comprehension. It requires students to predict, clarify unfamiliar terms and concepts, summarize key points, and ask questions about the text. Activities that promote students' ability to engage in ideas include use of puzzles, jokes, codes, and riddles; integrating concepts located in various parts of the text; engaging in elaborative interrogation and inferential question asking and answering; and completing cloze activities.

Development of mental models is promoted through a sequence of lessons that encourage students to create mental images. The sequence begins with simple concrete objects, and moves on to more complex concrete objects. It then works with pictures and finally texts. Initially short, simple descriptive texts involving familiar objects and ideas are used. However, they gradually become more complex, abstract, and unfamiliar. Students are taught to "create a picture in the mind" and then asked to quickly sketch the object or idea. They are given only 20–30 seconds to create an image. Once they have created a sketch, they reflect on what they have done. Reflection is prompted by asking students to discuss their efforts in small groups followed by each group reporting to the whole class.

Use of texts. Once students can decode and understand the text, they need to be able to use the information in the text for multiple social purposes. The underlying philosophy of the program is that the most important purpose of engaging with text is personal pleasure and enjoyment. Students are encouraged to read for pleasure as part of their daily lives.

Cognitive and metacognitive strategies. One of the aims of the program is to provide students with the literacy skills to enhance their achievement in all content areas across the curriculum. This aspect of the program is based on research showing that the ability to use sophisticated cognitive and metacognitive strategies results in higher levels of achievement. A distinctive feature of our approach is that rather than explicitly teaching strategies, students are encouraged to invent and use their own strategies. The taxonomy developed by Weinstein and Mayer (1986) is used as a framework for analyzing strategies. Students are encouraged to invent and use a range of organizational and elaboration strategies depending on the information they are learning in conjunction with their own existing knowledge and personal preferences.

In addition to encouraging students to invent cognitive strategies, metacognition is promoted through reflection. Initially, students work in small groups to discuss how they learn particular content. Later, they use reflective journals to record the processes they use to learn. Reflection promotes metacognition in two ways (McCrindle & Christensen, 1995). First, it develops students' awareness of their learning processes. Second, this awareness facilitates their ability to exercise deliberate control over their learning.

Critical literacy teaches students to scrutinize text for political and ideological content. Political analyses are essentially about the exercise of power—the ways in which individuals or groups of individuals seek to exercise influence over others. Thus, critical literacy examines the ways in which texts are used to influence the reader. Issues of social justice and equity become central to this analysis.

Steps in Implementing the Program

Building teacher expertise. In many secondary schools, no teacher has had professional education in teaching literacy. Therefore, teachers are provided with a comprehensive program of professional development. There are a total of eight 1/12-hour presentations provided to schools which cover:

- Research and theory on human learning
- Overview of the literacy program
- Teaching decoding to beginning readers
- Teaching reading comprehension
- Teaching students to invent and use sophisticated strategies to learn from text
- Critical literacy
- Writing skills (two sessions)

In addition to presentations, demonstrations of teaching techniques are given, for example, in reciprocal teaching. The university consultant spends approximately three hours consulting with each school to develop a schedule of activities for each program strand.

School sites also develop ongoing professional dialogue around the literacy program. Literacy coordinators, administrators, and key teachers across schools meet regularly during the year to share ideas, materials, and successes. They discuss emerging problems and jointly problem-solve solutions. They also hold regular open meetings where schools can discuss ideas and collaboratively problem-solve. Finally, annual conferences allow schools to showcase their achievements, and share experiences and teaching activities.

Each school site decides how many literacy lessons are timetabled each week and how long each lesson will last. They also decide the mechanism to create space in the timetable to accommodate the program. Literacy coordinator(s) are appointed to organize and manage the day-to-day implementation of the program. They oversee testing, assign students and teachers to class groups, and assist in the development of activities and materials.

Identifying individual levels of achievement. To provide a program where each student experiences success in learning, it is necessary to identify the current level of achievement of all students. Although teachers were aware that students were failing to learn because of low levels of literacy, they were unaware of students' precise level of literacy achievement. A standardized measure, with established validity and reliability, was used to assess students' current level of reading comprehension. A commercially available spelling test and a battery of other assessment measures that we have specifically designed for the WSL programs were also administered. These include measures of critical literacy, cognitive strategy use, and quality of written text.

Allocation of students to program strands. On the basis of students' reading comprehension age, the student cohort is devoted into three broad program strands based on the curriculum sequence described in Figure 18.1 (Decoding, Comprehension, and Strategies). A fourth strand referred to as

Transition consists of students who undertake some decoding activities and some comprehension:

- Students who are reading at lower elementary level (K-Grade 2) are assigned to a strand that focuses on building decoding skills (Decoding Strand).
- Students who are reading at mid-elementary level (Grades 3–4) are assigned to Transition Strand.
- Students who are reading at upper-elementary level (Grades 5–6) are assigned to a program that focuses on developing comprehension (Comprehension Strand).
- Students reading at secondary level are assigned to a program that focuses on invention and use of cognitive and metacognitive strategies, and critical analysis of text (Strategy Strand).

Schedule of activities. The curriculum depicted in Figure 18.1 is translated into a set of day-to-day classroom activities. First, a schedule of activities is created for every strand and each lesson of the week. Table 18.1 provides an illustration of a schedule of activities. Generally, each lesson consists of two activities. One of the activities usually relates to the focus of the strand (decoding, comprehension, or strategies). The other encourages reading for enjoyment.

Students in the lower-elementary strand work on decoding skills-in-isolation in every lesson. Their schedule also covers oral language and student reading of sequenced books that correspond to the decoding skills program (readers). The low level of these students' reading skills means that they could not access complex text independently. Thus, there is a teacher read-aloud component where the teacher reads highly engaging books to the class. Some schools also include written language and handwriting, while others choose to focus on reading.

Students in the upper-elementary group have a program that focuses on comprehension. Their schedule includes reciprocal teaching, activities to encourage engagement in ideas, and the creation of mental models through imagery. This strand also covers oral language, silent sustained reading, teacher read-aloud, and written language.

Transition Strand is for those students who are reading at mid-elementary level. In our early programs, these students were assigned to a Comprehension Strand along with upper-elementary students. However, while they have some basic decoding skills, they frequently lacked automaticity in decoding and this continued to impact on their ability to comprehend text. Thus, these students are now provided with a composite of the decoding and comprehension programs. They do some skills-in-isolation, as well as reciprocal teaching, engagement in ideas, and mental models. They also read sequenced books as well as participate in silent sustained reading. As with the other strands, they have oral language and teacher read-aloud every week.

TABLE 18.1 *Illustrative Schedule of Activities for Program with Five Lessons per Week, Each 35 Minutes*

Strand	Day 1	Day 2	Day 3	Day 4	Day 5
Decoding	Decoding Skills Teacher Read-Aloud	Decoding Skills Student Oral Reading from Readers	Decoding Skills Oral Language	Decoding Skills Teacher Read-Aloud	Decoding Skills Student Oral Reading from Readers
Transition	Decoding Skills Student Silent Reading	Reciprocal Teaching Teacher Read-Aloud	Decoding Skills Oral Language	Engagement in Ideas Student Oral Reading from Readers	Decoding Skills Teacher Read-Aloud
Comprehension	Reciprocal Teaching Student Silent Reading	Engagement in Ideas Teacher Read-Aloud	Building Mental Models Student Silent Reading	Oral Language Teacher Read-Aloud	Writing
Strategy	Reciprocal Teaching Oral Language	Cognitive Strategies Student Silent Reading	Critical Literacy Teacher Read-Aloud	Engagement in Ideas/ Mental Models Student Silent Reading	Writing

Students reading at Grades 7–12 participate in a program that focuses on the invention and use of sophisticated cognitive strategies to conceptualize, learn, and remember information from text. This is combined with reflection to enhance their awareness and control of learning (metacognition). There is also a focus on critical literacy and written language. Initially, comprehension-fostering activities were not included in Strategies Strand. However, Comprehension Strand students frequently made more gains than Strategies students. Thus, reciprocal teaching, engagement in ideas, and creation of mental models were all added to Strategies Strand, although they are not covered as frequently as for Comprehension Strand students. As with other program strands, students participate in oral language activities, silent sustained reading, and teacher read-aloud.

Initially, it was thought that silent reading and teacher read-aloud were not appropriate to these students. However, many students, even those achieving at high levels, simply do not read for pleasure. Thus, the silent reading and read-aloud components are designed to engage and encourage life-long habits of reading for pleasure.

Creating Organizational Structures to Deliver the Program

After students have been assigned to curriculum strands, homogenous groups are constructed within each strand. Students reading at Grades K-2 level have experienced many years of failure in learning to read. They are reading between 5 and 12 years below grade level. They require very small class groups. The limit is set at a maximum of eight students. However, some schools reduce class sizes further for these students, assigning no more than four students to a group who are reading at kindergarten level, six for Grade 1 readers, and eight for Grade 2 readers. Students in Transition Strand have groups of no more than 12; Comprehension Strand has no more than 15. Groups in Strategies Strand are larger, up to 28.

The homogenous nature of the grouping runs counter to much research that suggests that low-achieving students are strongly disadvantaged by streaming (Harlm & Malcolm, 1999; Ireson & Hallam, 1999). However, that occurs when streaming is accompanied by a lock-step system of grade progression—students in Grade 7E progress to Grade 8E and then to Grade 9E. The WSL homogenous grouping is predicated on the assumption that students will move through achievement levels—students in Decoding are expected to move into Comprehension Strand and then into a program that focuses on developing the skills required for college study. Homogenous grouping in this case is not a condemnation to persistent failure but a mechanism to deliver instruction that will resolve failure.

■ Outcomes

Regular assessment of student progress has generated different kinds of data from each school. Individual schools decide when to commence their programs, structural arrangements around the number of lessons per week and the length of each lesson, resource allocation in terms of coordinator time, the assignment of teachers, and the final size of class groups. Table 18.2 provides the means and standard deviations for reading comprehension grades at pretest and post-test for schools that recently commenced the program throughout the school year. The data vary as schools commenced the program at various times during the year and ran it for different periods before they assessed students at the end of the year. Nevertheless, the data

TABLE 18.2   *Pretest and Post-Test Means and Standard Deviations for Reading Comprehension Grades for Schools in First Year of Implementation of Whole School Literacy Program*

School	Length of Program	Pretest		Post-Test		Improvement (Years)
		Mean	SD	Mean	SD	
1	5 weeks	7.5[a]	(3.0)	8.9	(3.1)	1.4
2	8 weeks	4.7	(3.6)	5.8	(3.6)	1.1
3	12 weeks	8.1	(3.1)	9.7	(2.8)	1.6
4	12 weeks	7.8	(2.9)	8.7	(3.1)	0.9
5	12 weeks	7.3	(2.8)	8.8	(3.0)	1.5
6	18 weeks	5.9	(3.0)	7.4	(3.1)	1.5

[a] Reading Comprehension Grade.

show that dramatic gains were made by students in all schools. If these rates of improvement were sustained for a school year (approximately 40 weeks), then gains of between 3 and 12 years would have been made.

Only one school has included a control group in their monitoring of performance. Because the program runs on a minimum of a full grade cohort of students, the school assessed Grade 8 students who were not participating in the program. These students acted as a control group. Students in Grade 7 participated in the literacy program and are regarded as the experimental group. Means and standard deviations for the reading comprehension assessment before the implementation of the program (Time 1), after the first year of implementation (Time 2), and after the second year of the program (Time 3) are reported in Table 18.3.

Data are reported for students who completed assessment at all three data collection points. A two-way analysis of variance was conducted with time and group as the independent variables and reading age as the dependent variable. Analyses were conducted on raw scores. However, results are reported in terms of reading comprehension grade equivalents for ease of interpretation. Main effects for both independent variables were significant (Time, $F_{(1, 379)} = 20.46$, $p < 0.001$; Group, $F_{(1,379)} = 10.86$, $p = 0.001$). However, these effects were not surprising as students could be expected to change over time and the control group would be different from the experimental group as they were older. The significant interaction, time $\times$ group indicated the impact of the program over time ($F_{(1, 379)} = 71.63$, $p = <0.001$).

At the time of the initial assessment, before the implementation of the program, the mean reading age for the nonparticipating students was 2.6 years ahead of the participating students. The control group was significantly better than the experimental students at post-test 1 but not post-test 2 (see Table 18.3).

TABLE 18.3   *Reading Comprehension Age Means and Standard Deviations for Participating and Nonparticipating Groups at Each Assessment Point Across Two Years*

	Control		Experimental		Difference	*F*	*p*
	Mean	SD	Mean	SD			
Pretest	13.9[a]	(3.3)	11.3	(2.8)	−2.6	67.1	<0.001
Post-test 1	13.3	(3.2)	12.3	(2.9)	−1	12.2	<0.001
Post-test 2	12.3	(3.1)	13.0	(3.0)	0.7		<0.001

[a] Reading age in years.

Even though the nonparticipating, control students were older than the participating students, the experimental students eventually outperformed them.

At the end of the first year, the nonparticipating students continued to have higher reading comprehension scores. However, the difference had been reduced from 2.6 to 1 year. By the end of the second year, the difference had been reversed. Students who had participated in the literacy program were 0.7 of a year better in reading comprehension than students who were chronologically a year older. Thus, over the two years, the students in the WSL program had a gain of 3.3 years in reading comprehension over a group of students in the same school who did not participate in the program.

Impact on individual students. Although significant differences in mean scores indicate the superiority of achievement of Experimental group compared with Control group, means may mask the impact of the program across individual students. Diversity of impacts was examined in terms of the percent of students making various gains across the two years (see Table 18.4).

Overall, reading comprehension scores decreased for 60% of students in the Control group compared with 6% in the Experimental group. In contrast, 48% in Experimental group made gains in excess of the duration of the program (three or more years), while only 7% of control students made similar gains. No Control group student made five or more years improvement over the two years, while 17% of Experimental group made five or more years improvement.

Differences can be seen in all strands. In the Decoding Strand, 10% of students not participating in the program compared with 3% of participating students performed more poorly at post-test than pretest. The most marked differences were seen for Comprehension Strand. Seventy-two percent of Control Strand declined in performance. No student in the group increased by two or more years. In contrast, only 4% of Experimental students declined and 71% made two or more years improvement. Most notably, 11% of Experimental students gained a remarkable six or more years in reading comprehension and a further 16% gained five to six years.

TABLE 18.4   *Percent of Students Making Gains in Control (Ctl) Compared with Experimental (Exp) Groups Across Two Years*

Improvement	Group							
	Decoding		Comprehension		Strategies		Total	
	Ctl	Exp	Ctl	Exp	Ctl	Exp	Ctl	Exp
Decline	10[a]	4	72	4	69	22	60	6
0–1 yrs	20	19	20	19	16	6	18	15
1–2 yrs	30	6	8	8	3	10	9	11
2–3 yrs	20	17	0	17	3	14	5	18
3–4 yrs	0	19	0	19	3	26	1	20
4–5 yrs	20	8	0	8	6	21	6	11
5–6 yrs	0	16	0	16	0	0	0	10
6 & more yrs	0	11	0	11	0	0	0	7

[a] Percent of students.

Gains for Strategies were compromised by ceiling effects. Forty-two percent of Control and six percent of Experimental students were reading at Year 12 level at pretest. These students could not demonstrate gains over the two years. Nevertheless, a pattern similar to Comprehension Strand can be seen in gains for Strategy Strand students. Sixty percent of nonparticipating students showed a decline in scores, while only 7% showed more than three years improvement. Only 6% of students in the Experimental group showed a reduction in reading comprehension and 48% improved by three years or more.

The impact of the program on individual performance can be seen in Table 18.5, which provides the frequency distribution for both the Control and Experimental students. The percentage of students in Control group who were reading at lower elementary level remained stable over the first year and increased slightly in the second. In contrast, the number of students participating in the literacy program who were reading at this very low level showed a marked decrease. The number more than halved from 16% to 7% of the total group. It should be noted that these students were reading from five to eight years below grade level. Yet, many of them made excellent gains in reading comprehension.

There was a similar pattern for students who commenced the program at upper elementary level. The number of Control students reading below grade-level nearly doubled over the two years. However, the proportion of students in the literacy program reading below grade-level halved from 43% to 20%.

There was a steady incremental increase in students participating in the program reading at secondary level; from 41% before the implementation of the program to 65% after two years. Before implementation of the program only 19% of students were reading one year or more above grade level.

TABLE 18.5   *Percentage of Students in Control and Experimental Groups Reading Across Time*

Reading Grade Level	Control			Experimental		
	Time 1	Time 2	Time 3	Time 1	Time 2	Time 3
1	1.5	1.5	1.5	2.8	0.4	0.4
2	2.3	3.8	3.8	4.3	2.8	2.0
3	4.5	3.0	6.8	8.7	4.7	4.3
% Lower elementary	8.3	8.3	12.1	15.8	7.9	6.7
4	5.3	4.5	6.8	13.0	7.1	5.5
5	3.8	4.5	12.9	16.6	15.8	8.3
6	6.1	12.9	10.6	13.8	17.0	14.2
% Upper elementary	15.2	21.9	30.3	43.4	39.9	20
7	6.8	13.6	14.4	10.3	11.1	11.9
8	12.9	9.8	12.1	11.1	7.1	10.7
9	3.8	6.8	4.5	6.7	8.3	7.1
10	3.0	2.3	4.5	1.6	3.2	1.6
11	8.3	9.1	6.8	4.7	9.9	9.5
12	41.7	28.0	15.5	6.3	12.6	24.5
% Secondary	76.5	69.6	57.8	40.7	52.2	65.3

However, after two years, 36% of students were reading one year or more above grade level.

Limitations on growth in achievement. Although the difference between the two groups at Time 3 was statistically significant, it was not as dramatic an improvement as observed in other schools which commenced programs during the school year. There seems to be a number of issues that contributed to the outcomes for this school.

First, it is clear that Control group actually decreased in performance across the two years. This result appears to be a reflection of trends across the state and other states across the country. Similar trends were identified in data from a large longitudinal study in the same state (Lingard, Ladwig, Mills, Hayes, Bahr, Christie, Gore, & Luke, 2002) as well as data from other states (Centre for Applied Educational Research, 2001). Thus, it appears that Control group reflected a realistic expectation of achievement trends in the absence of the literacy intervention.

The second issue of concern was the relatively smaller gains made by the participating students in relation to other schools in the first year of the implementation of the program. There appears to be two factors that contribute to the difference between this cohort of students and others.

Performance within strands. One of these factors related to the progression paths that students took at the end of the first year of the program. In addition to analysis of overall levels of achievement, gains in reading comprehension in each strand were examined. Tables 18.6–18.8 show the means and standard deviations as well as significance tests for both participating and nonparticipating students in each program strand.

TABLE 18.6   *Reading Comprehension Age Means and Standard Deviations for Participating and Nonparticipating Groups in Decoding Strand*

	Control		Experimental		Difference	F	p
	Mean	SD	Mean	SD			
Pretest	7.6[a]	(0.8)	7.6	(0.8)	0	0.2	0.898
Post-test 1	8.3	(1.4)	9.6	(2.1)	1.3	4.1	0.048
Post-test 2	8.9	(1.7)	9.6	(2.1)	0.7	0.9	0.354

[a] Reading grade.

TABLE 18.7   *Reading Comprehension Age Means and Standard Deviations for Participating and Nonparticipating Groups in Comprehension Strand*

	Control		Experimental		Difference	F	p
	Mean	SD	Mean	SD			
Pretest	13.9[a]	(3.3)	11.3	(2.8)	−2.6	67.1	<0.001
Post-test 1	13.3	(3.2)	12.3	(2.9)	−1	12.2	<0.001
Post-test 2	12.3	(3.1)	13.0	(3.0)	0.7		<0.001

[a] Reading grade.

TABLE 18.8   *Reading Comprehension Age Means and Standard Deviations for Participating and Nonparticipating Groups in Strategies Strand*

	Control		Experimental		Difference	F	p
	Mean	SD	Mean	SD			
Pretest	17.0[a]	(1.8)	15.3	(1.7)	1.7	33.2	<0.001
Post-test 1	15.3	(2.5)	15.6	(2.1)	0.3	0.44	0.507
Post-test 2	13.6	(2.6)	17.0	(2.1)	3.4	54.2	<0.001

[a] Reading grade.

Before the implementation of the program, there was no difference between Experimental and Control groups in Decoding and Comprehension Strands. However, significant differences began to emerge after the first year of the program. In the case of Decoding, both Control and Experimental groups improved after the first year. However, Experimental students were significantly better in reading comprehension, scoring nearly two years ahead of Control students. This difference was not sustained after the second year of the program where there was a nonsignificant difference between groups of 0.7 years.

The lack of continuing progress for participating students who commenced at Decoding level was examined by analyzing the performance according to destination group in Year 2. Students who began the program in the Decoding Strand in Year 1 could either remain in Decoding or progress into Comprehension Strand in Year 2. Dramatic differences seem to occur depending on the progression paths of students. Students who progressed to Comprehension in Year 2 made much larger gains in Year 1 compared with students who remained in Decoding. Students who progressed to Comprehension increased their reading comprehension age from 7.6 years to 10 years in the first year of the program (see Table 18.9). Students who remained in Decoding showed much smaller gains, from 7.3 years to 7.6 years.

However, the picture was quite different in Year 2. Students who remained in the Decoding Strand continued to make modest but steady gains. Their reading comprehension age improved by 4.8 months from 7.6 to 8 years. In contrast, students who progressed to Comprehension Strand scored lower in Year 2 than in Year 1. Their reading age at the end of Year 1 was 10 years. This declined to 9.6 years at the end of Year 2.

The same pattern was repeated for students who commenced the program in Comprehension Strand (see Table 18.10). Students, who remained

TABLE 18.9   *Means and Standard Deviations According to Destination for Students Who Were Located in the Decoding Strand in Year 1*

	Remained in Decoding Year 2		Moved to Comprehension Year 2	
	Mean	SD	Mean	SD
Pretest	7.3[a]	(0.86)	7.6	(0.59)
Post-test 1	7.6	(0.53)	10.0	(1.9)
Post-test 2	8.0	(1)	9.6	(2.0)

[a] Reading grade.

TABLE 18.10   *Means and Standard Deviations According to Destination for Students Who Were Located in Comprehension Strand in Year 1*

	Remained in Comprehension Year 2		Moved to Strategies Year 2	
	Mean	SD	Mean	SD
Pretest	9.6[a]	(1.2)	10.6	(1.6)
Post-test 1	10.6	(1.4)	15.3	(2.6)
Post-test 2	12.0	(2.3)	14.6	(2.6)

[a] Reading grade.

in Comprehension Strand in Year 2, went from a reading age of 9.6 years at pretest to 10.6 years at the end of Year 1, and 12 years at the end of Year 2; an overall gain of 2.4 years. In comparison, students who were promoted from Comprehension to Strategies Strand commenced the program with the same reading age of 10.6 years. Their mean reading comprehension age was 15.3 at the end of Year 1. This represents an improvement of 4.7 years. However, their mean reading comprehension age declined to 14.6 years in the second year of the program.

There could be a number of reasons for this apparent decline in the performance of those students who moved up into a more demanding strand. Stability or decline in test scores could simply be the result of a plateau effect. These students made such large gains in the first year of the program that they could not be expected to continue to improve in the second year. Alternatively, although these students had made good gains in Year 1, they possibly still required some of the experiences provided to the lower-level strands. In other words, students who commenced in Decoding Strand still needed to build decoding skills in Year 2 while students who commenced in Comprehension would continue to benefit from comprehension activities in Year 2.

The WSL programs are continually evolving. As a result of the lack of improvement demonstrated by students who progressed from one strand to the next, we have modified the program. Students moving from Decoding to Comprehension Strands have a transition program in the second year, which has elements of both decoding and comprehension. They do some skills in isolation as well as the comprehension activities. Similarly, students in Strategies Strand spend some time on comprehension activities, including comprehension monitoring, engagement in ideas, and building mental models as well as the core activities for Strategies Strand. The results of this modification are not yet available but initial impressions suggest that it is an effective amendment.

Impact of individual teachers. It appears that there are strong teacher effects that impact on student performance. Some teachers seem to have had very large gains in student achievement while others had relatively small, or no gains. For example, in the second year, one class in Decoding Strand had a mean improvement of 2.5 years, while another had reading comprehension scores that dropped by 0.7 of a year. Similar large differences were recorded across classes in Comprehension Strand. In Year 2, the largest gain in a Comprehension Strand class was 3 years. The smallest gain was 0.2 of a year.

The program has been modified in four ways to address differences in teacher effectiveness. First, more support has been given to individual teachers in terms of materials, resources, and activities. Second, processes of teacher monitoring were instituted. Schedules of activities were provided to each teacher so that they had clear guidelines on what range of activities should be undertaken and the duration of various activities. Third, a program of enhanced professional development and peer collaboration within the school was implemented. A literacy coordinator was given time to visit each classroom to review how each of the activities were being taught. Outstanding teachers were identified. Teachers who were having difficulty in implementing aspects of the program visited the classrooms of expert practitioners to observe model lessons. Regular presentations and discussions were held where teaching techniques, resources, and materials were discussed. The emphasis of these sessions was both to provide teachers with the practical skills to deliver the program and to ensure that they had an understanding of the theoretical underpinnings of the program; the purposes of the activities and the nature of the outcomes they should expect from students. Fourth, accountability procedures were put in place where each teacher was interviewed by a senior administrator and performance of the students in his or her class was discussed. Teachers who were effective in promoting the achievement of the students were recognized and congratulated but equally teachers whose students were not gaining from the program were asked to account for the lack of progress being demonstrated by students. These measures have only recently been implemented so that final results are not yet available.

■ Research in Practice: Lessons Learned

Researchers and practitioners have different perspectives, goals, and agendas. Researchers are concerned with issues such as methodological precision, empirical rigor, and theoretical coherence. Practitioners are often concerned with day-to-day practicalities of working with children and adolescents: how to survive 9E English until the 11 o'clock break.

For research to be able to have a major impact on school practice, not only must teachers value what research has to offer but researchers need to appreciate the day-to-day realities of life in schools. The schools in which we implement programs are diverse, ranging from as few as 350 students to as many as 2000. Their locations vary from urban and suburban to regional and rural areas. Some schools cater for students from middle-income families which others are located in indigenous communities, others have students with low socioeconomic backgrounds, large numbers of refugee students, and students who speak English as a second language. A program that can be effectively implemented across this diversity needs to be flexible, allowing for the unique social, cultural, and professional context of each school.

It is clear that translating research findings into effective programs and practical outcomes for students is a complex and multifaceted undertaking. Our programs are based on a range of research findings on effective practices. Yet, as WSL programs are implemented, new challenges and unanticipated hurdles to student achievement will be encountered and need to be problem-solved.

Translating research into practice must take into account the complex social, cultural, and administrative environments of schools. The largest school implementing our programs has over 2,000 students. Timetabling for a WSL program alone is a massive undertaking. When dealing with such a large number of students, the requirements for initial and ongoing assessment, teacher education, program development, and the creation of resources and materials are enormous. In contrast, implementing programs with schools with as few as 250 students presents an entirely different set of challenges. For example, creating a number of small, homogeneous groups is far more difficult with a limited number of students and teachers.

In the vast majority of the schools, student gains have been nothing short of remarkable. Yet, the need to continually revise and renew practice will be ongoing; to learn from mistakes and search for better, more effective practices is both the challenge and the reward.

■ References

Adams, M. J. (1990). *Beginning to read: Thinking and learning about print.* Cambridge, MA, Bolt, Beranek, and Newman.

Anderson, J. R. (1981). *Cognitive skills and their acquisition.* Hillsdale, NJ, Lawrence Erlbaum Associates.

August, D. L., Flavell, J. H., & Clift, R. (1984). Comparison of comprehension monitoring of skilled and less-skilled readers. *Reading Research Quarterly, 20,* 39–53.

Bereiter, C., & Scandamalia, M. (1993). *Surpassing ourselves: An inquiry into the nature and implications of expertise.* Chicago, Open Court.

Berliner, D. C. (1990). What's all the fuss about instructional time? In M. Ben-Peretz & R. Bromme (Eds.), *The nature of time in schools* (pp. 3–35). New York, Teachers College Press.

Bloom, B. S. (1976). *Human characteristics and school learning.* New York, McGraw-Hill.

Bloom, B. S. (1984). The 2 sigma problem: The search for methods of group instruction as effective as one-to-one tutoring. *Educational Researcher, 13,* 4–16.

Bransford, J. D., Brown, A. L., & Cocking, R. R. (2000). *How people learn: Brain, mind, experience, and school.* Washington, DC, National Academy Press.

Brown, A. L., Bransford, J. D., Ferrara, R. A., & Campione, J. C. (1983). Learning, remembering and understanding. In J. H. Flavell & E. H. Markman (Eds.), *Handbook of child psychology: Cognitive development* (Vol. 3, pp. 77–166). NY, Wiley.

Cain, K., Oakhill, J., & Bryant, P. (2004). Children's reading comprehension ability: Concurrent prediction by working memory, verbal ability, and component skills. *Journal of Educational Psychology, 96,* 31–42.

Carr, E. M., Dewitz, P., & Patberg, J. P. (1983). The effects of inference training on children's comprehension of expository text. *Journal of Reading Behavior, 15,* 1–18.

Carroll, J. B. (1963). A model of school learning. *Teachers College Record, 64,* 723–733.

Centre for Applied Educational Research. (2001). *Middle years research and development project: Final report.* Melbourne, Victorian Department of Education and Training.

Chi, M. (1978). Knowledge structures and memory development. In R. Seigler (Ed.), *Children's thinking: What develops* (pp. 75–96). Hillsdale, NJ, Lawrence Erlbaum Associates.

Chi, M., Feltovich, P., & Glaser, R. (1981). Categorization and representation of physics problems by experts and novices. *Cognitive Science, 5,* 121–152.

Christensen, C. A. (2005). *Reading LINK-decoding.* Brisbane, Knowledge Books and Software.

Christensen, C. A., & Bowey, J. (2005). The efficacy of grapheme-phoneme correspondence, rime and whole language approaches to teaching decoding skills. *Scientific Studies of Reading, 9,* 327–349.

Craik, K. (1943). *The nature of explanation.* Cambridge, UK, Cambridge University Press.

Davidson, M. J., Dove, L., & Weltz, J. (2007). *Mental models and usability.* Retrieved from http://www.lauradove.info/reports/mentalmodels%20 models.html.

Dewitz, P., Carr, E. M., & Patberg, J. P. (1987). Effects of inference training on comprehension and comprehension monitoring. *Reading Research Quarterly, 22,* 99–121.

Fisher, C. W., Berliner, D. C., Filby, N. N., Marliave, R. S., Cahen, L. S., & Dishaw, M. M. (1980). Teaching behaviors, academic learning time and student achievement: An overview. In C. Denham & A. Lieberman (Eds.), *Time to learn* (pp. 7–32). Washington, DC, U.S. Department of Education, National Institute of Education.

Flavell, J. H. (1979). Metacognition and cognitive monitoring: A new area of cognitive-developmental inquiry. *American Psychologist, 34*, 906–911.

Graesser, A. C., Singer, M., & Trabasso, T. (1994). Constructing inferences during narrative text comprehension. *Psychological Review, 101*, 371–395.

Hannon, B., & Daneman, M. (2001). A new tool for measuring and understanding individual differences in the component processes of reading comprehension. *Journal of Educational Psychology, 93*, 103–138.

Harlm, W., & Malcolm, H. (1999). *Setting and streaming: A review of research.* Edinburgh, UK, The Scottish Council for Research in Education.

Hart, B., & Risley, T. R. (1995). *Meaningful differences in everyday experience of young American children.* Baltimore, MD, Brookes.

Hibbing, A., & Rankin-Erickson, J. L. (2003). A picture is worth a thousand words: Using visual images to improve comprehension for middle school readers. *The Reading Teacher, 56*, 756–770.

Ireson, J., & Hallam, S. (1999). Raising standards: Is ability grouping the answer? *Oxford Review of Education, 25*, 343–358.

Johnson-Laird, P. N. (1983). *Mental models: Towards a cognitive science of language, inference, and consciousness.* Cambridge, MA, Harvard University Press. Cambridge, England, Cambridge University Press.

Juel, C., Griffith, P. L., & Gough, P. B. (1986). Acquisition of literacy: A longitudinal student of children in first and second grade. *Journal of Educational Psychology, 78*, 243–255.

LaBerge, D., & Samuels, S. J. (1974). Toward a theory of automatic information processing in reading. *Cognitive Psychology, 6*, 293–323.

Lesgold, A. M., Rubison, H., Feltovich, P., Glaser, R., Klopfet, D., & Wang, Y. (1988). Expertise in a complex skill: Diagnosing x-ray pictures. In M. T. Chi, R. Glaser, & M. Farr (Eds.), *The nature of expertise* (pp. 311–342). Hillsdale, NJ, Lawrence Erlbaum Associates.

Lingard, R., Ladwig, J., Mills, M., Hayes, D., Bahr, M., Christie, P., Gore, J., & Luke, A. (2002). *The Queensland school reform study: Final report.* Brisbane, The Queensland Department of Education.

McCrindle, A. R., & Christensen, C. A. (1995). The impact of learning journals on metacognitive and cognitive processes and learning performance. *Learning and instruction, 5*, 167–185.

National Reading Panel. (2000). *Teaching children to read.* Retrieved from http://www.nationalreadingpanel.org/Publications/summary.htm.

Oakhill, J., Hartt, J., & Samols, D. (2005). Levels of comprehension monitoring and working memory in good and poor comprehenders. *Reading and Writing, 18*, 657–686.

Ozgungor, S., & Guthrie, J. T. (2004). Interactions among elaborative interrogation, knowledge, and interest in the process of constructing knowledge from text. *Journal of Educational Psychology, 96*, 437–443.

Palincsar, A. S. & Brown, A. (1984). Reciprocal teaching of comprehension-fostering and comprehension-monitoring activities. *Cognition and Instruction, 1*, 117–175.

Peters, E. E., & Levin, J. R. (1986). Effects of a mnemonic imagery strategy on good and poor readers' prose recall. *Reading Research Quarterly, 21,* 179–192.

Pressley, M., Johnson, C., Symons, S., McGoldrick, J., & Kurita, J. (1989). Strategies that improve children's memory and comprehension of text. *The Elementary School Journal, 90,* 3–32.

Recht, D., & Leslie, L. (1988). Effect of prior knowledge on good and poor readers' memory of text. *Journal of Educational Psychology, 80,* 16–20.

Rosenshine, B., & Meister, C. (1994). Reciprocal teaching: A review of the research. *Review of Educational Research, 64,* 479–530.

Rosenshine, B. V. (1997). Advances in Research on Instruction. In J. W. Lloyd, E. J. Kameenui, & D. Chard (Eds.), *Issues in educating students with disabilities* (pp. 197–221). Mahwah, NJ, Lawrence Erlbaum Associates.

Royer, J., Carlo, M., Dufresne, R., & Mestre, J. (1996). The assessment of levels of domain expertise while reading. *Cognition and Instruction, 14,* 373–408.

Rubman, C., & Waters, H. (2000). The role of constructive processes in children's comprehension monitoring. *Journal of Educational Psychology, 92,* 503–514.

Saarnio, D. A., Oka, E. R., & Paris, S. G. (1990). Developmental predictors of children's reading comprehension. In T. H. Carr & B. A. Levy (Eds.), *Reading and its development: Component skills approaches* (pp. 57–79). New York, Academic Press.

Schneider, W., & Shriffrin, R. M. (1977). Controlled and automatic human information processing: Detection, search and attention. *Psychological Review, 84,* 1–66.

Snyder, J. L. (2000). An investigation of the knowledge structures of experts, intermediates, and novices in physics. *International Journal of Science Education, 22,* 979–992.

Stahl, S. A., Chou-Hare, V., Sinatra, R., & Gregory, J. F. (1991). Defining the role of prior knowledge and vocabulary in teaching comprehension: The retiring of number 41. *Journal of Reading behavior, 23,* 487–508.

Stahl, S. A., & Hiebert, E. H. (2005). The "word factors": A problem for reading comprehension assessment. In S. Paris & S. Stahl (Eds.), *Children's reading comprehension and assessment* (pp. 161–186). Mahwah, NJ, LEA.

Stanovich, K. E. (1986). Matthew effects in reading: Some consequences of individuals differences in the acquisition of literacy. *Reading Research Quarterly, 21,* 360–407.

Storch, S., & Whitehurst, G. (2002). Oral language and code-related precursors to reading: Evidence from a longitudinal structural model. *Developmental Psychology, 38,* 934–947.

Swanson, H. L., & Berninger, V. (1995). The role of working memory in skilled and less skilled readers' comprehension. *Intelligence, 21,* 83–108.

Sweller, J. (1988). Cognitive load during problem solving: Effects on learning. *Cognitive Science, 12,* 257–285.

Sweller, J., & Cooper, G. A. (1985). The use of worked examples as a substitute for problem solving in learning algebra. *Cognition and Instruction, 2,* 59–89.

Trabasso, T., & Magliano, J. P. (1996). Conscious understanding during comprehension. *Discourse Processes, 21,* 255–287.

Weinstein, C. E., & Mayer, R. E. (1986). The teaching of learning strategies. In M. Wittrock (Eds.), *Handbook of research on teaching* (3rd ed., pp. 315–327). NY, Macmillan.

Yuill, N., & Joscelyne, T. (1988). Effects of organizational cues and strategies on good and poor comprehenders' story understanding. *Journal of Educational Psychology, 80,* 152–158.

Yuill, N., & Oakhill, J. (1988). Effects of inference training on poor reading comprehension. *Journal of Applied Cognitive Psychology, 2,* 33–45.

Yuill, N., & Oakhill, J. (1991). *Children's problems in text comprehension: An experimental investigation.* Cambridge, UK, Cambridge University Press.

Zimmerman, B. J. (1990). Self-regulated learning and academic achievement: An overview. *Educational Psychologist, 25,* 3–17.

STEP 5

IN IMPLEMENTATION: ASSESSING EFFECTIVENESS DURING AND AFTER IMPLEMENTATION

■ Introduction to Step 5

In evaluating effectiveness of implementations, we need to move beyond the parochial, narrow view that one kind of data or statistical analysis is superior to another. That is why chapters were included on both single subject designs for generalizing conclusions to individual students, the chapter by Owen White, and program evaluation for generalizing conclusions to students in general in classrooms, schools, districts, or states, the chapter by Sam Stringfield.

As we move to the two chapters on evaluation, it is clear that multimodal evidence is needed to evaluate the effectiveness of implementations at different levels. Owen White, widely known for his work on single subject design and precision teaching, focuses in this chapter on how a teacher can conduct and evaluate assessments for the purpose of making instructional decisions. After critiquing the response to intervention (RTI) assessment approach, he makes a compelling case for an emphasis on frequent and multiple assessments within conditions in order to have reliable measures of a student's performance. With multiple examples, he provides evidence for how misleading infrequent assessments can be in judging the impact of a program on a student. His call for examining unusual results is a good reminder about the importance of really exploring the data, and he provides strategies for doing that. He closes with a set of guidelines for how to apply a small N research approach to changes in a student's instructional program. Given that no evidence-based instruction will work for all students, the assessment approach described in this chapter is a valuable guide to accurate assessment for classroom decision-making.

In the next chapter, Sam Stringfield shares with the reader his extensive experience as a program evaluator of large-scale research implementations. After reviewing the current standards for scientific research and program evaluation, he looks at the differences in world views of the major players in this field and concludes with a set of observations about program evaluation, particularly the pitfalls to avoid. Among his key observations are the recognition of the co-construction of innovations as they are implemented and acknowledgment of the complex relationship among developers, implementers, and evaluators. As he and others have found, no two implementations of research programs are identical. He raises interesting challenges to how we define integrity of implementation.

Stephen Peverly has thought long and hard about the need for meaningfully integrating assessment of curriculum, teacher knowledge and practices, and student knowledge and characteristics, which he refers to as school-based assessment. He exposes the flaws in focusing exclusively on student characteristics and discusses the limits of curriculum-based assessments. To justify his critique, he provides a review of the literature on the impact of both curriculum and teacher knowledge and practices on student outcomes. He concludes with a description of a school-based model that integrates his three assessment targets. This model converges nicely with the consultee-centered consultation described in Step 2 (see Chapter 8 by Knotek et al.) and Step 3 (the Chapter 13 by Nelson, Aux, Neal, and Gravois).

19. A Focus on the Individual

Single-Subject Evaluations of

Response to Intervention

Owen R. White

"Response to intervention" (RTI) evaluations seek to identify pupils who are not making acceptable progress under existing conditions, and bring to bear increasingly individualized resources to correct that problem. However, the frequency of assessment recommended for RTI evaluations is often too low to facilitate truly timely decisions about an individual's RTIs. The chapter begins with a brief overview of the most generally recommended approach to RTI evaluations, then seeks to explain the elements of pupil performance and progress evaluations, identify fundamental weaknesses in most RTI systems for identifying individual needs, and discuss the role teachers can play in achieving the individualized goals of RTI at the classroom level. The focus is on how a *teacher* should conduct and evaluate assessments to make timely instructional decisions. "Group distributions" at the class level are discussed because teachers are interested in their classes as a group; but individual progress over time is emphasized because it is the progress of each pupil in the class that should interest the teacher most.

■ A Brief Review of RTI Evaluations

RTI is usually implemented as a multitiered system beginning with the application of uniform, scientifically supported curricula, instructional methods, and "high-efficiency" assessments for all pupils in a state, district, or school. Pupils who fail to perform or progress adequately under those "core" conditions are targeted for increasingly individualized and more frequent assessments of special needs and alternative interventions to address those needs.

Table 19.1 provides an overview of a three-tiered RTI system as typically recommended in the professional literature. In that table, **Performance** refers to a pupil's overall *level* of demonstrated skill in an established curricular

TABLE 19.1 A Three-Tiered RTI System

	Target Pupils	Expected Success Rate	Assessment		Instruction & Intervention
			Method	Frequency	
Tier 1: Core Interventions	All pupils in system are initially targeted for Tier 1 intervention and assessments	80%–90% of all pupils are likely to be successful at this level	Uniform "high-efficiency" assessments of core curricula	3/year (once every 3 months)	*Uniformly Applied Interventions*: scientifically supported curricula, materials, and instructional methods in all core curricula, uniformly applied to all pupils. *Note*: Actions taken at ALL levels of the system should be scientifically supported
Tier 2: Strategic Interventions	Pupils not demonstrating adequate performance or progress in Tier 1	If they require additional help, 5–10% of all pupils will be successful at this level	Uniform "high efficiency" assessments of core curricula + additional individualized assessments as necessary	2/month (every 2 weeks)	*Standard Protocol Interventions*: Alternative curricula, materials, and/or instructional methods that were preselected as potentially effective "next step" approaches for pupils experiencing difficulties in Tier 1 and/or *Initial Individualized Interventions*: Specialized plans to meet the unique needs of the individual
Tier 3: Intensive Individualized Interventions	Pupils not demonstrating adequate performance or progress even with Tier 2 interventions	If they require help beyond that offered in Tier 2, 1–5% of all pupils are likely to be successful at this level	Assessments focusing on the pupil's immediate instructional goals. Core curricula assessments are also likely to be continued	1/week, usually on the same day each week	*Highly Individualized Interventions*: Individually tailored curricula, materials, and/or instructional methods based on a more extensive assessment of the special needs of the pupil. A special team of educators and other concerned people usually conducts the evaluations and develops these interventions. A similar team might also be involved in planning Tier 2 interventions

area. If a pupil's performance meets or exceeds the performance standards established for that skill, the pupil is considered to have demonstrated "success" in that skill, and instructional attention can be re-focused on a different, perhaps more advanced skill. If a pupil's performances fail to meet established standards, but still fall within the range of expected performances for most children at that time of the year, the program is likely to be continued without change. If the pupil's performance falls well below most of her peers, the judgment of success within the pupil's current tier of the RTI program will depend on the pupil's demonstrated *rate of progress toward* performance standards.

Progress refers to the *systematic change* in pupil's performance *over time*. A pupil is considered to be making "successful progress" as long as the rate of systematic change in performance is sufficient to predict skill mastery within allowable time. The interventions used with a pupil and the RTI tier to which the pupil is assigned usually remain unchanged as long as the pupil continues to make acceptable progress.

Standards for Success for performance and/or progress can be established in several different ways. "Norms" and "criterion-based" standards are the most common. *Norm-* or *peer-referenced* standards are based on what is typically accomplished by students of the same age. *Criterion-referenced* standards are based on whether specified benchmarks are achieved. Presumably, those benchmarks reflect the level of skill necessary for the successful application of the skill, regardless of what might be considered "typical." Those standards can be broadly developed at the national or state level, as when evaluating whether a school or district is meeting the requirements of *No Child Left Behind* Act of 2001 (NCLB, Public Law 107–110), or "locally" developed and applied at the district, building, class, or program level. They can also be modified or adapted to account for individual differences (White, 1984b, 1985a, 1985b, 1985c).

High-Efficiency Assessments. Whenever assessments are conducted with a large number of pupils, it is important to employ methods that take as little time as possible, cost as little as possible, and still yield valid information for making effective educational decisions.

Scientifically Supported procedures must be used with pupils whenever possible. That includes curricula, materials, instructional methods, assessment protocols, and even grouping and placement procedures. Because nothing will work all the time with all pupils; however, we must be prepared to replace or augment one scientifically supported practice with another when an intervention fails to help a pupil achieve adequate performance or progress. Prioritizing the sequence of interventions we try is usually a matter of evaluating the *strength* of the scientific evidence (i.e., which approach appears to produce the greatest gains in the most pupils), the *similarity* between previous research subjects and our own pupils, and the *efficiency* with which the intervention can be applied. It is also important to implement each intervention with good *fidelity*, that is, in the same manner with which the intervention was applied during the supporting research. However, situations will arise when a pupil's special needs require modifications of an intervention or the application of a completely new intervention for which there is little or no formal research support. In those cases, it is particularly important to evaluate the effects of the modified or new intervention in a way that clearly demonstrates its effectiveness.

■ How Often Should We Assess a Pupil?

How many assessments do we need before we can have confidence in our estimate of a pupil's performance or progress over time? Most educators advocate RTI evaluations three times a year at Tier 1, two times per month for Tier 2, and weekly for Tier 3 (see Table 19.1). However, as pupils who are at-risk of failure are identified, the frequency of at least *some* assessments should be increased dramatically, especially if they are to be useful to teachers in making truly informed and timely decisions about individuals in their class.

Most questions concerning the impact of an education program boil down to whether we believe a "reliable/believable difference" exists between an actual outcome and what we expected or desired: Is there a difference between a pupil's performance and the standard we want the pupil to achieve? Is a pupil progressing rapidly enough to reach our curricular goal in a reasonable time? Do pupils perform at higher levels and/or progress more rapidly with one instructional approach than with another? Answering those and similar questions requires more than a comparison of two numbers. We need *multiple* assessments *within* conditions before we can reasonably make comparisons *across* conditions.

Evaluating Levels of Performance

Figure 19.1 presents two sets of data. Panel A shows the class means for two teachers—Teacher 1 is applying a program for the first time, and Teacher 2 has had a year's experience in applying the program. Unexpectedly, Teacher 2's mean is *lower* than Teacher 1's mean. Does that suggest that experience actually makes a teacher *less* effective? Panel B shows two assessments of how often a pupil appropriately raised her hand to offer an answer to a question posed by the teacher during group discussion. The first assessment was completed during "baseline," before a special program was implemented to improve hand-raising; the second assessment was completed after an intervention was implemented to improve the pupil's behavior. The proportion

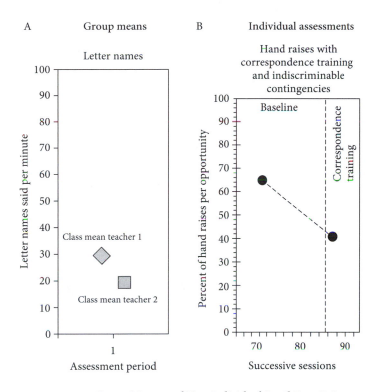

FIGURE 19.1 Group Means and Two Individual Pupil Data Points.

of appropriate hand-raising goes *down* after the new intervention is implemented. Does that mean that the new program was a bad idea?

The answer to both of those questions is, "we can't tell," at least with the data presented. We need more information before we can draw reasonable conclusions about the effects of teacher experience. It is quite possible that single assessments of performance in each condition (i.e., the class mean for each teacher, or a single assessment in each phase of the hand-raising program) are misleading. To place those assessments in perspective, we need *within-condition estimates of variance—multiple* assessments of performances *in each condition.*

Figure 19.2A shows us the results of additional assessments in the two classrooms we were using to evaluate the impact of teacher experience. Now we have assessment information for each of the 20 pupils in each teacher's classroom.

After adding assessment results for each pupil in each classroom, we can see that there is a great deal of overlap among the individuals in the class distributions—the *within class variance* is large compared with the difference *between class averages.* The scores for the pupils in Teacher 1's class (the teacher with no previous experience in the program) do range higher than the individual scores for Teacher 2, but there are also a lot of

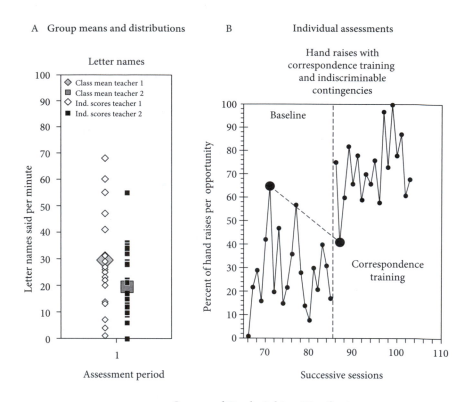

FIGURE 19.2 Group and Single-Subject Distributions.

pupils in Teacher 2's class who are performing better than many pupils in Teacher 1's class.

Figure 19.2B shows the results of 20 assessments in *baseline* (before a new program was implemented) and 18 assessments during the *intervention* (after the new program was implemented) (Guevremont, Osnes, & Stokes, 1986). It is now clear that the single assessment in each condition we used in our earlier analysis (indicated by the large dots on this chart) misrepresented the pupil's overall levels of performance before and after the intervention (White, 1987). When *all* the assessment data are examined, it is clear that the new program produced a relatively large and positive impact on appropriate hand-raising with this pupil.

There are at least **two lesson***s* to be learned from these discussions. One is relatively straightforward, the other a little more difficult to learn.

First, before we can speak with any confidence about the difference *between* conditions (between the classes of two teachers or between two phases of an individual child's program) we need to have good estimates of variance *within* each condition. We can only get those estimates through multiple within-condition assessments; and the greater the number of those assessments, the greater our confidence when judging the impact of any difference or change in conditions.

Second, remember that we were only able to make reasonable judgments about the impact of a program on an *individual pupil* when we assessed that pupil multiple times in each condition (see Figure 19.2B). Now look again at Figure 19.2A. We might be reasonably confident in judging differences in the *classes as a whole* (for which we have multiple measures), but really cannot say anything with confidence about any *individual within the class* (because we have only one assessment for any given individual).

That should serve as a warning about making important educational decisions on the basis of a single assessment. Simply put, if a single assessment of pupil performance on "core" curricula conducted in the fall of each year shows the student is performing comfortably above established standards, then fine, leave her program alone. However, if that assessment suggests a deficit in performance, we should reassess the pupil *multiple times* before asserting that a fundamental change in the pupil's program is warranted. Fortunately, most RTI program guidelines explicitly state that no important decisions should be made without multiple assessments, with either the same or different instruments or procedures (cf. OSPI, June 2006).

Evaluating Progress

The issue of *performance*—the overall level of behavior for a group or individual—is important in RTI evaluations when it comes to comparing a pupil's achievement with standards or aims, but if an individual has not yet reached a performance aim, we need to consider the pupil's progress *toward* that aim.

The entire data set for our hand-raising program provides a useful example (see Figure 19.3). The heavy solid lines drawn through each phase of 3 summarize the pupil's progress during baseline and intervention. We get a picture of "no substantial gain" in performances over the course of the baseline. The "bounce" in the data from one day to the next is pretty large, but there is little systematic up or down progress over the course of the phase as a whole. When the new program is implemented, there is a "step up" in general performance (a relatively quick change in performance level), and the pupil begins to make noticeable systematic progress in the right direction ("up"). Those changes in performance level and rate of progress are reasonably clear and suggest the new program is effective in helping the pupil develop appropriate hand-raising behavior. We might wonder, however, whether estimates of performance and progress using fewer assessments would have yielded the same results.

To address that question the National Research Center on Learning Disabilities (NRCLD, 2005) reviewed several studies and concluded that

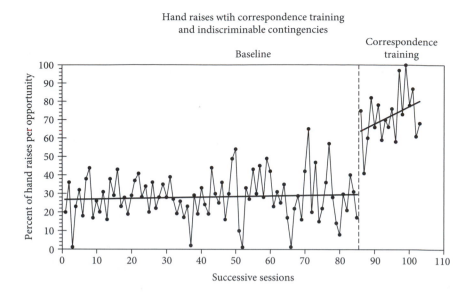

FIGURE 19.3 The Entire Data Set for Hand-Raising with an Individual Pupil.

5 weekly assessments could adequately predict pupil progress over the course of 9 weeks when curriculum-based measurements (CBM) were used—repeated assessments of pupil performance using materials that closely approximate the local curriculum. However, most CBM researchers recommend a minimum of *9 or 10 weekly assessments* before making a decision concerning the adequacy of a pupil's progress (cf. Jenkins et al., 2007; NCRLD, 2005). In general, our predictions of a pupil's progress become more accurate as more assessments are included (cf. Koënig, 1972; Silberglitt et al., 2007; White, 1971). The results of these studies are not entirely comforting, however, for at least two reasons. First, errors in judging overall progress are high in a large proportion of cases. This is especially troublesome if expected progress is relatively low, as with pupils who are "at risk" of learning difficulties under core interventions. Because of those problems, several investigators have suggested that using progress estimates as an indicator for learning difficulties might be ill advised, especially with small numbers of assessments (cf. Silberglitt & Hintz, 2007; Jenkins, personal communication, September 2007). Second, based on the assumption that data collected more frequently than once per week will interfere with instruction or be perceived as too burdensome by teachers (cf. Jenkins et al., 2006; Jenkins et al., 2007; Fuchs et al., 2006), most studies of the predictive validity of progress estimates have been based on weekly data or data collected even less frequently. But studies dating from the early 1970s (Koënig, 1972; White, 1971) suggest that the key to reasonably accurate predictions of progress may be the *number* of assessments, not how closely those assessments fall in time.

Using Multiple, but Infrequent Assessments

Individual patterns of progress are especially subject to error. Since any given assessment might be subject to transient conditions (e.g., a pupil might be ill on the assessment day), it's usually unwise to base estimates of progress on only a few repeated assessments, as might be the case with Tier 1 or Tier 2 RTI assessments (cf. Silberglitt & Hintze, 2007). Even with Tier 3 weekly assessments, it would likely take 9 or more weeks before a reasonable estimate of individual pupil progress can be established with any confidence. If estimates of progress are to be a part of a timely decision making process, it will probably be necessary to collect data more frequently.

I will explore the advisability and implications of more frequent assessments in the remainder of this chapter. Please note, however, that I am not proposing a replacement for the sorts of assessments recommended for existing RTI systems, but rather, an extension to such systems to better meet the immediate needs of teachers and their pupils.

■ Spotting "Unusual" Results

A large part of the reason we need many assessments to estimate a pupil's performance or progress lies in the inherent instability of any given assessment. There are usually many little (or not-so-little) ups-and-downs in a pupil's assessment results from one day or one week to the next, and we need lots of information to see whatever underlying systematic progress a pupil might be making. It will help if we can identify unusual results and minimize their influence on our judgments. A few strategies for doing so follow.

Be Aware that Many Things Can Influence a Measure

All RTI procedures depend on the *validity* of the assessments we conduct; that is, the degree to which assessment results tell us what we need to know. For example, if an individual performs poorly on an assessment, we often assume that the poor performance was due to the individual's lack of skill relative to the assessment target, and that a decision to implement alternative instructional methods would be appropriate. Unfortunately, lots of other things can also affect assessment results. A child could be ill or distracted; the assessment materials might not be culturally appropriate; or perhaps we simply made an error in recording the results of the assessment. When a pupil appears to perform poorly, or something else about the assessment results is unexpected, it is important to ask "why?"

There is often little we can do to avoid "unusual days" that produce "unusual results," but there are a few things we can do to help us decide whether an assessment result might be suspect and improve our chances of identifying *why* that might be so.

Evaluate Assessment Data As Soon As They Are Collected

If we wait too long to evaluate our data, it will be more difficult to track down the answers to questions concerning unusual results. For example, several months after the data were collected for a study of inclusion, one researcher noted that a pupil had gained 69 percentile points on standardized test over the course of a single year. That is more than a bit unusual. When he examined the data more closely he found that the pupil had an extremely low "pretest" score. Perhaps the pupil really started with virtually no knowledge of the skills being assessed, but it is more likely he was ill or simply confused on the day of the pretest, and was feeling better by the time of the post-test. Unfortunately, by the time the data were evaluated, it was too late to find out what had happened at the time of the pretest.

Some statistical guidelines suggest that the researcher should remove the suspect data completely from the analyses so that it will not affect the study's overall results, but doing so without any direct evidence as to *why* the assessment might be invalid is never a comfortable thing to do. Having no idea about the possible reasons for suspect data is even more troublesome for a teacher who has to make ongoing decisions about the pupil's educational program.

Lesson: Evaluate data as soon as it is collected, when there is still a chance to identify unexpected conditions that might have influenced the results.

CHART the Data, Do Not Just Look at Numbers

Unusual data or patterns in the data are often hard to spot when looking at a column of numbers, but easily detected when looking at a chart of the data. Chart the data as soon as they are collected. If we evaluate a program daily, we should update the chart daily. It is often a great idea to have pupils keep their own charts, with only an occasional "reliability check" from the teacher. The pupil will then feel they "own" their progress records, and teachers will be relieved of a daily task. Of course, both the pupil and the teacher should review the chart after every new assessment is recorded and try to identify any conditions that might have produced unusual results. Table 19.2 and Figure 19.4 adapted from Guevremont, Osnes, & Stokes (1986, pp. 215–219) provide an example of the benefits of daily charting.

Scanning the data shown in Table 19.2 does not help us much. Perhaps the "nonzero" values in baseline are out of line, since all the other values are zero; and conversely, the zero results during intervention seem odd, as most

TABLE 19.2   *Tabled Data for an Intervention Designed to Time-on-Task in Class*

Baseline (No Contingency)		Intervention (Percentile Criteria)			
Session	Time in Seconds	Session	Time in Seconds	Session	Time in Seconds
1	0	9	36	33	215
2	0	10	219	34	238
3	0	11	0	35	200
4	0	12	52	36	244
5	12	13	83	37	218
6	22	14	0	38	233
7	0	15	159	39	209
8	0	16	45	40	208
		17	175	41	261
		18	32	42	252
		19	0	43	260
		20	211	44	188
		21	206	45	222
		22	207	46	134
		23	233	47	121
		24	188	48	222
		25	179	49	250
		26	162	50	248
		27	218	51	264
		28	183	52	247
		29	241	53	257
		30	210	54	251
		31	241	55	254
		32	243	56	259

of the other numbers in that phase of instruction are pretty large. Should we remove those values from our evaluations of performance and progress? The chart shown in Figure 19.4 presents a clearer picture of results. Compared to the overall "bounce" or variability in the entire data set, the nonzero values during baseline *do not* look all that unusual. Similarly, the zero values during intervention now appear to be simple extensions of a period of high-bounce (large variability) extending from the first day of intervention through session 19. We might simply call those sessions a "transition" or "familiarization" period associated with the introduction of a new program. We should probably segregate all the data in that transition period from any overall estimate of progress or performance we ultimately attribute to intervention, not just the "low" values. Segregating the transition period from the rest of the data has a

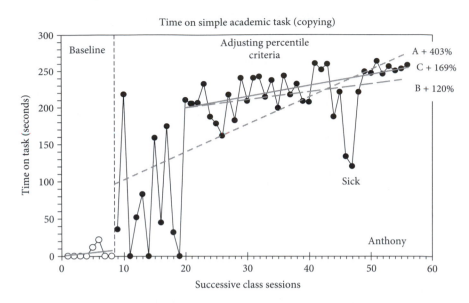

FIGURE 19.4 Effects of Eliminating "Unusual" Data from Progress Estimates. Line "A" Is Based on All the Data during Intervention; Line "B" Is Based on All the Data Following the Initial "Transition" Period (Sessions 20 Through 57); Line "C" Is Based on the Data Following the Transition Period after the "Sick Days" Have Been Removed from Consideration.

dramatic impact on our estimate of the pupil's systematic progress over time. Line "A" in Figure 19.4 is based on all the data collected during intervention and yields an overall progress improvement estimate of 403% over baseline, but when the transition period (sessions 1 through 19) is removed from the progress estimate (line "B"), the improvement in systematic progress drops to only 120%.

Once the transition period has passed, the performances during intervention demonstrate far less day-to-day bounce or variability and there appears to be a pattern of gradual upward progress throughout the remainder of the intervention period—with some exceptions. Two sessions, corresponding to sessions 44 and 45, and perhaps a few sessions before and after that period, produce assessment results noticeably lower than surrounding data. The investigator helpfully noted that the pupil was sick on those days (Guevremont, Osnes, & Stokes, 1986). We should definitely segregate those assessment results from our summary of the pupil's overall performance and progress. Doing so has the interesting result of producing an estimate of systematic progress (labeled "C" in Figure 19.4) of 169%—falling between the estimate of progress based on all the data (line "A") and all the data following the transition period (line "B"). This last estimate is, quite probably, our best estimate as to overall impact of the intervention on the systematic progress of the pupil.

Keep a Log or Diary

Evaluating and charting data as soon as they are collected might be difficult if the RTI procedures involve scoring by some other person or at some remote site. However, most RTI systems employ assessments that are administered and at least recorded (if not scored) by a pupil's teacher or a teaching assistant. If so, encourage that person to take a moment at the end of an assessment to ponder whether the pupil seemed "OK" and performed as expected. If something seems awry, have them jot down a word or two of caution (e.g., "Susan seemed under the weather today") and pass it on to the person responsible for interpreting the results. Even if the persons making those notes are going to interpret the results themselves, it will help to have those observations in writing to jog their memory.

If the assessment is "group administered," have the proctor take a moment to glance around the room to see if any pupil is behaving in an unusual manner (is someone asleep?). Before submitting the group's work for scoring, check the class list to see who was absent, not just on the day of the test, but for a day or two before the test. Illness can have lingering effects. The same sort of note would be helpful when interpreting the assessments of a pupil who spent the morning in the principal's office for discipline problems, or returned late to the class after a break. In other words, *keep a diary* to help identify and explain suspect results. Diaries are a mainstay of any good research or evaluation project. Without them, we can be stuck scratching our heads and wondering how a pupil improved or worsened by an incredible amount from one assessment to the next.

Look for Individuals or Groups of Individuals
Who Are Not Behaving According to "Type"

Rightly or wrongly we often have expectations of an individual or group based on "classifications," "types," or "precedent." We expect pupils with disabilities will perform and progress at lower levels than typically developing pupils (cf. Deno et al., 2001); one pupil might generally be "very stable" in performances from day-to-day, while we have observed another pupil to be "highly erratic." If a pupil or a group of pupils deviates from those expectations, we should take note. Often the deviation signals something important. For example, the daily up-and-down bounce shown by the pupil in Figure 19.3 is pretty consistent and predictable during baseline. There are 4–6 exceptions on the low side, however, and a similar number of "high" days that seem out of place. What happened on those days? The answers could help us to avoid low-days and improve the frequency of high-days. Unfortunately, the investigator in that study did not keep a diary of unusual events and circumstances, or at least did not share those observations.

At the group level, Figure 19.5 shows the overall annual gains of pupils in the two classes we studied before. Some interesting patterns emerge that might explain why the experienced teacher started with a lower class mean than the less experienced teacher, and why that discrepancy disappeared over time. It turns out that the more experienced teacher (teacher 2) had 4 English Language Learners (ELL) in her class. The less experienced teacher (teacher 1) had no such pupils. We often expect ELL pupils to perform at lower levels than native-speaking pupils, and it would appear our expectations are fulfilled—all four of the ELL pupils fall at or near the bottom of the first performance assessment (their assessments are indicated on Figure 19.4 by x's and the change in their performance over the year is indicated by dotted lines). That might explain, at least in part, why the more experienced teacher's class had a lower overall mean performance than the less experienced teacher's class at the beginning of the year.

Typical expectations are confounded when we look at *progress* between the first and last assessments. Instead of having more difficulty in making progress, all four of the ELL pupils make gains *equal to or greater than* the overall class average. That could help explain why the more experienced teacher's class caught up with the average of the less experienced teacher's class over the course of the year. It is also easy to see that more of Teacher 2's pupils started at lower levels than Teacher 1's pupils, overall; but pupil *progress* in the more experienced teacher's class is surprisingly uniform—all pupils are improving, and most at rates very similar to the overall class mean over time. Pupils in the less experienced teacher's class, on the other hand, vary considerably in their patterns of change over time. Some are progressing

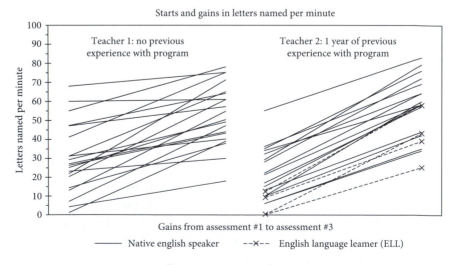

FIGURE 19.5 Overall Gains in Pupil Performance in Two Classes.

nicely, others are relatively "flat." To complicate the picture even more, there does not seem to be any easy way to predict which pupils in teacher 1's class are progressing nicely and which are not—some high and some low pupils are making good progress; some high and some low pupils are making virtually no progress.

We might draw two conclusions from these "true to form" and "break from expected" patterns of progress within and across classes. First, ELL pupils perform "true to type" by demonstrating relatively poor performances at the beginning of the year, but "break from the expected" by making good progress over time. Second, the more experienced teacher appears more adept at meeting the individual needs of pupils regardless of a pupil's initial performance than the teacher with less experience. Of course, whether we can attribute those apparent differences with confidence to "experience" is a matter that would require more information. For now, suffice it to say that searching for unusual or unexpected patterns in performance or progress can be very informative.

More About Segregating Unusual Data

If we spot "unusual" or "suspect" data they should probably be segregated from our analyses of overall performances or patterns of progress. For example, if we segregate the ELL pupils in the more experienced teacher's classroom from the rest of the pupils in our analyses of performance and progress, we find that there are no longer any "statistically reliable" differences between her class and the less experienced teacher's class, and that her class is slightly superior, overall, to the less experienced teacher's class by the end of the year. The ELL pupils, on the other hand, are generally worse than the typically developing pupils in either class at the beginning of the year, but make gains during the course of the year that are equal to or superior to most of their classmates. Segregation by "pupil type" can alter our perceptions of what is going on.

Segregating unusual subsets of the data might not always substantially alter overall results, but they can still raise interesting questions. For example, removing the "unusually high" days in the hand-raising program from our summary analyses will not substantially change our estimates of overall performance or progress during baseline—there are just too many "regular" days to offset the relatively rare "unusual" days. Nevertheless, had we been keeping a diary so we could pinpoint special circumstances associated with those days, we might have discovered a "natural intervention" that could be used to our advantage. Would it not be interesting if, whenever "Charlie" sat next to the "cute little red-haired girl" in class, he just happened to behave more appropriately?

Lesson: In order to see the general impact of a program it is sometimes a good idea to segregate unusual data from analyses of overall patterns.

But do not ignore unusual data.

Although it is often a good idea to "segregate" unusual or suspect data, we should not disregard it. Although some formal statistical guidelines suggest the complete elimination of suspect data from the data set before analyses (cf. Ross, 2003), unless there is clear evidence that the data were improperly collected or recorded, we should *chart* all the data we have. Unusual data might be segregated from some statistical analyses, like when calculating means or lines of progress, but those data often have very important lessons to teach us. Pupils might experience a transition period before the effects of a new program take hold, but even if a pupil is ill for a few days, their performances might *still* be better under the new program than they were before (cf. Figure 19.3). It is important to tell teachers that ELL pupils might experience performance deficits early in the year, but that with good instruction, they can *still* progress as well or better than other pupils in the class (see Figure 19.5).

Lesson: Do not ignore or throw away unusual data. Highlight them, point to them with arrows, try to identify the reasons they might be unusual, and put notes directly on the chart. Learn as much as you can from those data. Of course, that involves some guesswork. To pin down the "real" story behind a data point, it would be necessary to recreate and replicate the circumstances and see what happens.

Deciding When to Change

If a pupil demonstrates unusually low performance on a "core" assessment at Tier 1, most RTI systems call for continued monitoring to determine whether the pupil is able to make acceptable progress toward adequate performance while remaining within the Tier 1 instructional system. If progress is deemed acceptable, the pupil remains in Tier 1; if progress is too slow to enable the pupil to reach acceptable levels of performance within a reasonable period, the pupil is moved to Tier 2 and instruction is modified in an attempt to improve performances and/or progress. Unfortunately, the frequency of assessments at Tier 1 of most RTI systems is so low (once every 3 months) that estimating progress with any degree of confidence can take a year or even longer; and the frequency of assessments at Tier 2 (twice monthly) might still require 3 or 4 months of assessment data before reasonable estimates of progress can be made. Later in this chapter I will address some things a teacher can do to evaluate progress in a more timely manner. Even so, however, judging "acceptable performance and/or progress" can be a tricky business.

To judge "acceptable performance" and "acceptable progress" we need clear standards against which a pupil's assessments can be judged.

Unfortunately, those standards are often referenced to "normal" or "typical" performance and progress, rather than established criteria that have some demonstrated connection with successful learning and skill "mastery." In Washington State, for example, "low performance" is defined as meeting one or more of the following criteria: (a) Falling at or below the 7th percentile on grade-level material (i.e., having a score equal to or lower than the lowest 7% of the pupils completing the assessment); (b) falling below the 16th percentile on material taken from the *previous* grade-level; (c) falling 1.75 or more standard deviations below grade-level means on the assessment; (d) having a performance equal to or less than half the median performance of their peers on grade-level material; or (e) having a performance level that is 2 or more grade-levels below his or her grade-level placement. Similarly, "modest" through "ambitious" standards for rates of progress have been suggested ranging from a low of 0.5 (1/2) words per minute growth per week to a high of 3.0 words per minute growth per week—all based on normative studies of how rapidly age-matched peers typically progress.

Washington State's standards are all geared toward performance—focusing on the discrepancy between a pupil's performance and the performance of his or her peers. However, most research on CBM-based RTI systems focuses on *progress* standards, or how fast deficient performers should progress from one week to the next to overcome any performance deficit. Although a strong case can be made for individualized performance and progress standards (cf. White, 1984b, 1985a, 1985b, 1985c), the standards usually recommended for CBM assessment systems are based on "high, moderate, and low" averages for typically developing peers (Deno, Fuchs, Marton, & Shin, 2001). As an alternative, several researchers have studied the use of progress aim-lines describing how rapidly a pupil *must* progress to move from their present level of performance to a desired level of performance within the allowable time, regardless of how quickly typically developing peers usually progress (cf. Bohannon, 1975; Liberty, 1972; Mirkin, 1978; White & Haring, 1980).

Regardless of the approach employed to set the progress standard, the decision rule for identifying when actual progress is unacceptably below desired progress is usually based on a comparison of assessment results to the progress standard—whenever three consecutive assessments fall below the line, a change in instruction is implemented, or at least considered. Procedures for making such decisions have been described in detail elsewhere (cf. White, 1985d, 1986; White & Haring, 1980), and an example will be provided later in this chapter.

Regardless of whether we use performance, progress, or a combination of factors to determine when a pupil's program should be changed, we will undoubtedly want to evaluate the impact of an intervention in terms of both performance and progress.

■ Applying Single-Subject Research Designs to the
Evaluation of Ongoing Educational Programs

We are admonished to employ only "scientifically supported practices" in the
education we provide our pupils (IDEA, 2004), but we cannot always depend
on the relevant research to have already been completed. Often it is not necessary to make major reforms in a pupil's instructional program to remediate a deficit, but rather, to simply adjust one small aspect of the program,
or add some bit of extra assistance to an otherwise good program. An extra
five minutes of reading practice before an assessment, for example, or the
chance to earn a sticker for a performance on or above a progress aim-line.
Not all such changes will have been adequately researched with the curricula we employ or the types of pupils we serve, but our experience indicates
that those small interventions could have dramatic positive effects. Does that
mean that teachers should do sound experimental research whenever they
make any unproven adjustment in a pupil's program? Sometimes that might
be possible, but it is not always desirable, if a teacher is to make timely and
effective instructional decisions.

Teaching and research have different goals. The **goal of teaching** and
other "helping professions" is very pragmatic: *Do whatever is possible as
soon as possible to facilitate good performance and learning in our pupils or
clients.* If a pupil is performing well and learning rapidly, then great, keep
doing whatever is being done. If a pupil's performance falls short of what is
necessary and is not progressing quickly enough to reach good performance
goals in the time available, then change something *now* to try and correct the
problem. The teacher should not care so much *why* a child is learning, only
that she *is* learning.

The **goal of research**, on the other hand, is to gather convincing evidence
that a particular curriculum, instructional method, or some other "intervention" was probably *responsible* for changes in performance and learning. To
get that evidence, the researcher must compare one program or approach with
another, repeatedly, and show that performance and/or learning is greater
with the "recommended" program than with the alternative. That means,
essentially, that the researcher must expose a child, or different children, not
only to the program we think will work *better*, but also to a program we think
will *not work as well*. That raises serious ethical concerns. Is it fair for us to
spend a pupil's time in activities we do not believe are as effective as other
activities? No. There's a conflict of purpose between the goals of teaching and
the goals of research. Among other things, that is why formal research must
usually be reviewed by "human subjects research committees" to make sure
we are not violating the rights of the pupil.

Nevertheless, there are at least three conditions under which teachers might justify structuring programs to meet at least some of the requirements for formal research:

1. *If we really do not know what to do and we need to select carefully from alternatives.*
   Instead of choosing blindly and devoting extensive time to testing one of the alternatives virtually at random, there are some research designs that will allow us to test alternatives quickly, and then select the most promising alternative for long-term implementation.

2. *If we need to make a program change anyway, and practical considerations suggest that doing so within the context of a reasonable research design would be OK.*
   When we decide to make a change in several programs, it is often a good idea to stagger the implementation of those changes—applying the change to one program, waiting a while, then applying the change to another, and so on, until all the programs have been converted to the new procedure. That approach allows us to devote more resources to the individual programs where changes are currently being made, and the results of earlier changes can help us decide whether it is a good idea to use the same intervention with the other programs. This sort of "one-at-a-time" change schedule is actually a particular type of research protocol called a mult*iple baseline design*, and can provide very powerful evidence of program effectiveness.

3. *If the overall risk to the pupil for imposing research designs on a part of the instructional program is small, and the possible gain in useful knowledge is great.*
   Sometimes, the implications of making a poor program choice are great. Perhaps the new program will be very expensive in terms of time or other resources, and if the program does not work as well as we hope, the pupil might suffer an undesirable setback. In those situations, the risk to the pupil when we carefully test alternatives (e.g., the loss of some instructional time) is outweighed by the possible gain (identifying a program that will really meet the needs of the pupil) and a "formal" research design to aid us in making the right long-term decision might be justified.

Space does not permit even a cursory discussion of *all* basic single-subject research designs that might meet the conditions outlined above, so I will focus on three designs that are most likely to prove amenable to the conditions under which teachers and practitioners must work. They vary in sophistication from simple "demonstrations" to "formal experimental research," all quite within the grasp of teachers and other practitioners.

Pre-Experimental ABC... "Demonstration" Designs

"**AB**" or "**ABC...**" or "demonstration designs" involve the assessment of performance and learning under a series of different program options. In such designs, each option is usually only tried once until we find something that "works." Such approaches to program evaluation are considered "pre-experimental" because they do not control adequately for all the different things that might contribute to a learner's progress other than the program we want to study. To identify which changes in condition are probably responsible for changes in performance and learning, we would need to try each intervention more than once and, preferably, at different times, under different circumstances, and/or with different pupils. An ABC... design does not do that in any systematic way. It simply documents what happens to performance and learning when we make program changes. However, although those evaluations are not convincing "experimentally," they come closest to addressing the primary goal of a teacher—making whatever program changes seem reasonable as soon as the need for a change is recognized, and to keep making changes until the pupil *learns*.

Many of the charts shown earlier in this chapter illustrate this sort of design (e.g., Figure 19.3 and Figure 19.4), although each of those figures represent only individual elements of more extensive designs published in the research literature. Figure 19.6 provides an example of a program actually conducted by a classroom teacher as part of her ongoing instruction. Rather than "proving" that her instructional prowess was responsible for a pupil's growth, she simply made successive changes in the program until the pupil reached his performance aim within the available time.

To monitor her pupil's progress from day to day, Ms. Munson conducted one-minute timings of Brad's oral reading from a list of Dolch words. She used a "Standard Celeration Chart" to display the results, and it might be helpful to describe a little about that chart.

The Standard Celeration Chart was developed by O. R. Lindsley and Carl Koënig in the late 1960s specifically for use in classrooms. Behaviors can be charted that occur as infrequently as once per day, or as rapidly as 1,000 times per minute—essentially the entire range of human behavior we might want to monitor. By having one chart that can be used to display all sorts of behaviors, we do not have to change charts and their scales as our attention shifts from one behavior to another; and using the same chart for all our projects allows us to gain familiarity and expectations that make interpretation of the data much quicker and easier. We can develop a sense for what "good progress" will look like, and how "bouncy" the data might be from day to day and still be considered acceptable and, in turn, those expectations make it easier to spot "unusual data."

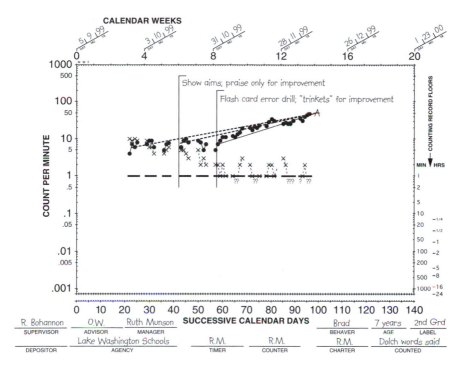

FIGURE 19.6 Classroom Project Using a Standard Celeration Chart.

Space does not permit a complete description of the Standard Celeration Chart and the conventions for its use, but suffice it to say that "acceleration targets" (behaviors that we want to increase) are charted with "dots", and "deceleration targets" (behaviors we want to decrease) are charted with "x's." We can tell at a glance, therefore, whether behaviors are moving in the right direction and make decisions accordingly. The dashed line across the chart at the "1" line represents the assessment time (here, one minute), and any frequencies falling below that line are essentially "zero" (or in Standard Chart parlance, "no count"). For further information about the Standard Celeration Chart, the reader can consult Graf and Lindsley (2002), Pennypacker, Gutierrez, and Lindsley (2003), or White (2003).

For the program shown in Figure 19.6 the performance aim and aim-date are indicated by the "A" on the chart (just to the right of the data, at a level of about 50 words per minute). The first dotted line on the chart (extending from the first week of data to the "A") represents how fast Brad must progress from day-to-day from the beginning of the program in order to reach the performance aim in time. When his correct performances fall below that line for several days in a row, Ruth changes the program. It was a modest change, involving only an effort to point out his daily performance aims (adjusted, now, to reflect his current performances, and shown on the chart as second dotted line), and making sure only to provide special praise when his performances fall on or above that line. That first program change did not improve his performance or progress (he fell below the second aim-line for 3 days in a row), so Ruth made another change—this time using a one-minute flash card drill over the errors he made the previous day, and giving him little "trinkets" for each day his correct performance falls on or above his new progress aim-line (represented by the solid line on the chart leading the "A"). This time his progress improves dramatically, he meets or exceeds his daily progress aim on most days, and he reaches his performance aim a few days early.

Is this an example of "good teaching?" Yes. Ruth did not wait the recommended nine weeks to see if Brad would demonstrate adequate progress on weekly assessments. She monitored performances daily and reacted *quickly* when Brad's progress seemed to falter. Is this good "research?" Not in the formal sense of the word. Ruth did not employ one of the accepted research designs to support the notion that the intervention "caused" Brad's improvement. However, those data *do* demonstrate that Brad learned what he was supposed to learn within the time available; and along the way, Ruth gathered information that strongly suggests what helps Brad to learn.

Lesson: Children can make good progress when we carefully pinpoint desired behaviors, set explicit performance and progress aims, monitor daily progress, and make timely decisions based on that progress, even if those data do not meet the criteria of "experimental research."

Practical Experimental Designs

"True" experimental designs attempt to control conditions in a way that allows us to narrow the range of factors that might have contributed to the pupil's success. To illustrate the experimental designs most amenable to applied classroom circumstances, we will look at two examples drawn from the "traditional" research literature. Each was published in a refereed journal devoted to applied behavior analysis, and each demonstrates research strategies well within the reach of teachers and other applied practitioners.

An **alternating treatments design** switches rapidly (usually session-by-session) among two or more conditions to see if one of them consistently produces higher or lower performances. The advantage to this sort of design is that it can replicate effects by introducing and withdrawing a condition several times quickly, *without* keeping the pupil in an inferior condition for any extended period. That minimizes ethical concerns about purposefully using what we might believe are less powerful interventions with a pupil simply to prove that something else is better. However, since the pupil is only exposed to a condition for brief periods, this design does not work very well if it takes a protracted period for a pupil to adapt to condition changes.

Figure 19.7 provides an example of such a design employed by Gortmaker et al. (2007) in a two-part study to identify effective and efficient strategies for parental tutoring. In the first part of the study, an alternating treatment design was employed to identify which of several tutoring strategies might be most effective when applied by a teacher.

Notice that the most effective strategy for a given pupil is not necessarily most effective with the other pupils. Rachel responded best to "reward+instruction," but Angel and Misty responded best to instruction without reward. The last condition tested for each pupil was the application of the previously demonstrated most effective strategy, but implemented by the parents. The parents did as well or better than the teacher. The results of those alternating treatment assessments were then subjected to a more extensive analysis using a multiple baseline design.

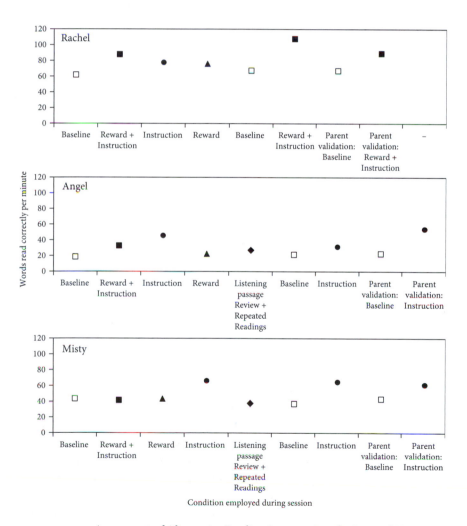

FIGURE 19.7 Assessment of Alternative Reading Interventions for Parental Tutoring.

A **multiple baseline design** begins by establishing several concurrent baselines of preintervention performance and progress. The different baselines could represent several different behaviors of the same pupil (e.g., different spelling lists), several different conditions or environments for the same behavior (e.g., putting on a coat before recess and then again before going home in the afternoon), or different pupils with the same behavior under the same or similar conditions. After stable or predictable performances have been established for each behavior, the new program is introduced for *one* of the baselines, whereas preintervention conditions are maintained with the other baselines. At staggered intervals, the intervention is applied to the remaining baselines, one at a time, until the intervention has been applied to all the baselines. Clear changes in performance or progress that occurs only when intervention is applied are taken as evidence that the new program is responsible for that change, rather than some coincidental event.

The advantage of the multiple baseline design is that if an intervention appears to help the pupil, it is not necessary to terminate or remove the intervention just to "prove" it was the intervention and not some coincidental event that led to and sustained improvement. A potential ethical problem exists, however, in the fact that what we believe will be an effective intervention is delayed for longer and longer periods with each successive baseline in the series. If the baselines are relatively short, overall, or if there is some practical reason we must delay intervention with some of the baselines (perhaps it is not possible to deal with all the interventions at the same time anyway), then multiple baseline studies are generally considered among most ethical designs we can use in applied situations.

During the second part of the Gortmaker et al. (2007) study, a multiple baseline design was employed with each pupil to provide a more extensive evaluation the effectiveness of parental tutoring using four "high-word-overlap" passages and four "low-word-overlap" passages. Figure 19.8 presents the data collected on Rachel's reading.

Although there is some progress in Rachel's reading fluency during each of the four baselines (during which Rachel's reading was assessed by her parents, but no explicit instruction was provided), there is a noticeable "jump" in performance and an improvement in Rachel's rate of progress when the intervention was introduced (and *only* when the intervention was introduced). It seems reasonable to conclude, therefore, that it was the intervention that contributed to Rachel's improvement, and not some other, coincidental event. To complete their evaluation, the researchers decided to remove the intervention for each passage in staggered intervals and enter a "maintenance" phase. Strictly speaking, withdrawal of intervention (as in the maintenance phase) is not necessary to the scientific validity of a multiple baseline design. Since maintenance is an important outcome in education, however, the addition of that phase gives us confidence that we have produced a "permanent change" in the pupil's skill. There is a slight dip in performance in the maintenance

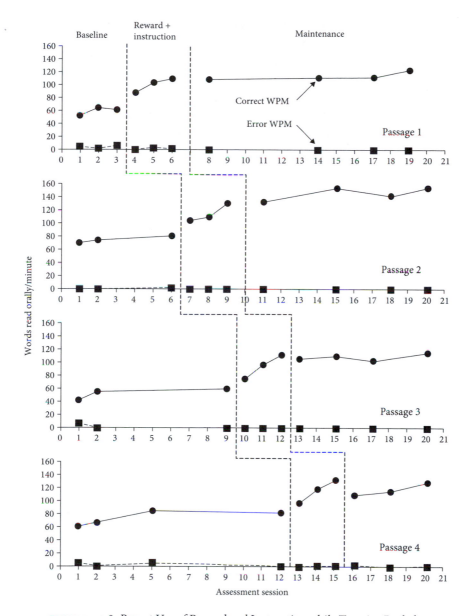

FIGURE 19.8 Parent Use of Reward and Instruction while Tutoring Rachel.

phase, but Rachel demonstrates a good continuing level of performance, so we can be pleased with the overall outcome of parental tutoring.

■ Summary and Recommendations

We can learn a lot from teachers collecting data about how they deal with real problems in real situations with real pupils. The movement toward RTI systems of evaluation offers great potential for meeting the individual needs of all our pupils. There is a compromise, however, between the usefulness of RTI evaluations in meeting "global" needs and "individual" needs. Tier 1 RTI systems focus on "core curricula" and the effectiveness of "core interventions" or systems of instruction. Individuals at-risk of failure will be identified with those evaluations, but possibly only after months or years of less-than-satisfactory progress. Tier 2 RTI systems offer more potential for meeting individual needs quickly, but often still rely on "standard protocols" for intervention and only modest efforts to truly individualize instruction. A reliance on those standard procedures certainly makes sense from the standpoint of giving well-researched and validated interventions a chance to work, but it can still take weeks or months before a need for further individualization is recognized. Finally, even in Tier 3 of an RTI system, most protocols require only weekly assessments of pupil progress and recommend treatment cycles of 9–12 weeks (minimum) before concluding whether an intervention is working.

The frequency of evaluations in many RTI systems is too low to be truly responsive to changing pupil needs. Practitioners should implement more frequent, preferably *daily* evaluations of pupil progress whenever possible. That will enable them to make timelier and potentially more effective decisions than the typical RTI system enables. *Precision Teaching* is one approach to RTI that offers practical approaches for collecting, organizing, and using daily assessment data for decision-making (e.g., Graf, 1999; Lindsley, 1997; McGreevy, 1983; White, 1986; White & Haring, 1980). Single-subject research can be both a source of information about "scientifically supported practices" and a method for teachers and other practitioners to validate their own practices (e.g., Horner et al., 2005; White, 1984a). It is particularly important for us to employ single-subject research designs in RTI systems where, presumably, the focus is on identifying pupils with individual needs and the development of programs to meet those needs in the most efficient and effective manner possible.

■ References

Bohannon, R. M. (1975). *Direct and daily measurement procedures in the identification and treatment of reading behaviors of children in special education.* Unpublished doctoral dissertation. Education, Special Education, University of Washington, Seattle, Washington.

Deno, S. L., Fuchs, L. S., Marston, D., & Shin, J. (2001). Using curriculum-based measurement to establish growth standards for pupils with learning disabilities. *School Psychology Review, 30,* 507–524.

Fuchs, D. F., Compton, D. L., Fuchs, L. S., & Bryant, J. D. (2006, February). *The prevention and identification of reading disability.* Paper presented at the Pacific Coast Research Conference, San Diego, CA.

Gortmaker, V. J., Daly, E. J., III, McCurdy, M., Persampieri, M. J., & Hergenrader, M. (2007). Improving reading outcomes for children with learning disabilities: Using brief experimental analysis to develop parent-tutoring interventions. *Journal of Applied Behavior Analysis, 40,* 203.

Graf, S., & Lindsley, O. R. (2002). *Standard Celeration Charting 2002.* Poland, OH, Graf Implements (7770 Lee Run Rd, Portland, OH 44514–2510).

Graf, S. A. (1999). *Monitoring behavior: An introduction to psychology.* Edition 5.1. Poland, OH, Graf Implements.

Guevremont, D. C., Osnes, P. G., & Stokes, T. F. (1986). Programming maintenance after correspondence training interventions with children. *Journal of Applied Behavior Analysis, 19,* 215–219.

Horner, R. H., Carr, E. G., Halle, J., McGee, G., Odom, S., & Wolery, M. (2005). The use of single-subject research to identify evidence-based practice in special education. *Exceptional Children, 71,* 165–179.

IDEA (2004). *Individuals with Disabilities Education Act.* Regulations published August 3, 2006.

Jenkins, J. R., Graff, J. J., & Miglioretti, D. L. (2006, February). *How often must we measure to estimate oral reading growth?* Paper presented at the Pacific Coast Research Conference, San Diego, CA.

Jenkins, J. R., Graff, J. J., & Miglioretti, D. L. (2007, October). *Estimating reading growth with intermittent CBM progress monitoring.* University of Washington.

Koënig, C. H. (1972). *Charting the future course of behavior.* Unpublished Doctoral Dissertation, University of Kansas, Lawrence.

Liberty, K. A. (1972). *Decide for progress: Dynamic aims and data decisions.* Working Paper, Regional Resource Center for Handicapped Children, Eugene, OR.

Lindsley, O. R. (1997). Precise instructional design: Guidelines from Precision Teaching. In C. R. Dills & A. J. Romiszowski (Eds.), *Instructional development paradigms* (pp. 537–554). Englewood Cliffs, NJ, Educational Technology Publications.

Pennypacker, H. S., Gutierrez, A., & Lindsley, O. R. (2003). *Handbook of the Standard Celeration Chart.* Gainsville, FL, Zerographics, Inc.

McGreevy, P. (1983). *Teaching and learning in plain English.* Plain English Publications.

Mirkin, P. K. (1978). *A comparison of the effects of three formative evaluation strategies and contingent consequences of reading performance.* Unpublished doctoral dissertation, University of Minnesota.

NCLB. (2001). U.S. Department of Education Web site. Retrieved October 9, 2008, from http://www.ed.gov/policy/elsec/leg/esea02/index.html.

NCRLD. (2005). *Topical Forum I: Applying Responsiveness to Intervention (RTI) to specific learning disability (SLD) determination decisions research findings.* A topical conference hosted by the National Research Center on Learning Disabilities (NRCLD), Kansas City, MO. September 29 and 30, 2005.

OSPI. (June 2006). *Using Response to Intervention (RTI) for Washington's Pupils.* Olympia, WA, Office of the State Superintendent of Public Instruction.

Ross, S. M. (2003). Peirce's criterion for the elimination of suspect experimental data. *Journal of Engineering Technology,* 20, 38.

Silberglitt, B., & Hintze, J. M. (2007). How much growth can we expect? A conditional analysis of R-CBM growth rates by level of performance. *Exceptional Children,* 74, 71–84.

White, O. R. (1971). *A pragmatic approach to the description of progress in the single case.* Unpublished doctoral dissertation, University of Oregon, College of Education, Department of Special Education.

White, O. R. (1984a). Selected issues in evaluation: Arguments for the individual. In B. Keogh (Ed.), *Advances in special education, Vol. 4: Evaluating program impact* (pp. 69–121). Greenwich, CT, JAI Press.

White, O. R. (1984b). Aim*star wars (setting aims that compete): Episode I. *Journal of Precision Teaching,* 5, 55–63.

White, O. R. (1985a). Aim*star wars (setting aims that compete): Episodes II and III. *Journal of Precision Teaching,* 5, 86–94.

White, O. R. (1985b). Aim*star wars (setting aims that compete): Episode IV. *Journal of Precision Teaching,* 6, 7–13.

White, O. R. (1985c). Aim*star wars (setting aims that compete): Episode V. *Journal of Precision Teaching,* 6, 30–34.

White, O. R. (1985d). Decisions, Decisions,… *B.C. Journal of Special Education,* 9, 305–320.

White, O. R. (1986). Precision teaching/precision learning. In B. Algozzine and Maheady (Eds.), *Exceptional children (Special issue): In search of excellence: Instruction that works in special education classrooms,* Reston, VA. *Council for Exceptional Children,* 52, 522–534.

White, O. R. (1987). Some comments concerning "The Quantitative Synthesis of Single-Subject Research." *Remedial and Special Education,* 8, 34–39.

White, O. R. (2003). *The Finder book.* Available for downloading as a PDF file from a class Web site: http//courses.wasington.edu/edspe510/, under the "Readings" tab.

White, O. R., & Haring, N. G. (1980). *Exceptional teaching.* Columbus, OH, Charles Merrill.

20. Application of Program Evaluation Tools for Large-Scale Research Implementation

Sam Stringfield

A former senior executive in the Government Accounting Office (GAO) once observed that, after 20 years of testifying before Congressional committees she was convinced that Congresspersons want two things from a GAO study. First, they want "the data," by which they mean large-n statistics on the issue at hand. Second, "they want a story." The story both allows the member of Congress to connect to the data, and—as importantly—provides a mechanism for helping the folks back home understand why the Congressperson voted as s/he did. People—congresspersons, school board members, and everyone in between—who must make tough, practical decisions want to know the general, "scientific" trend, and real-world stories that allow connection of quantitative data to "the data" of human experience.

This chapter presents an exploration of methods for providing the information that decision makers need. The chapter presents general and specific concerns related to large-scale research and evaluation efforts to determine the effectiveness of various educational interventions. By large scale, I mean efforts involving 10 or more schools, often in multiple districts and states.

The chapter proceeds through four areas. The first two set frames for planning and interpreting research and evaluation efforts: A brief overview of the nature of "scientific" research in education, and a review of program evaluation standards. The third and fourth topics address more day-to-day pragmatic topics. The third topic addresses implications of the differing lives of district evaluation offices and those of university and/or private research shop researchers. Fourth, in an effort to "keep it real," I provide observations from my quarter-century-plus of gathering data in relatively large-scale educational "effects" projects.

One note is necessary before proceeding: There are many fine texts on research design and program evaluation (e.g., Shadish, Cook, & Campbell, 2002; Tashakkori & Teddlie, 1998), and valuable, practical, "how to" manuals for evaluating local reform efforts (e.g., Aldersebaes, Railsback, Shaughnessy, & Speth, n.d.). My goal is not to condense these excellent reference volumes, but to provide a broad overview and to add several practical observations that might supplement one's efforts to conduct rigorous, useful, large-scale investigations in schools.

■ Scientific Research in Education

Over the past several decades, educational research has swung from almost an obsession with defining "research" in a logical positivist framework (with the careful counting of highly specified, low-inference behaviors, great concern for the internal validity of studies, etc.) to an era of almost anything goes,[1] to the current, multimethod but more constrained notions of "science." Seeking a defensible scholarly ground, the National Academy of Sciences' National Research Center (NRC) created a commission to try to determine what was *Scientific Research in Education* (Shavelson & Towne, 2002). The committee "concluded that six guiding principles underlie all scientific inquiry." These six form an overarching canopy for any rigorous discussion of educational research and evaluation, and hence are critical to this chapter:

1. Science poses significant questions that can be answered empirically.
2. Science links research to relevant theory.
3. Science uses methods that permit direct investigation of the question.
4. Science provides coherent, explicit chains of reasoning.
5. Science allows for replication and generalization across studies.
6. Science requires that researchers disclose their work to encourage professional scrutiny and critique (Shavelson & Towne, 2002, pp. 3–5).

The NRC team made several additional observations, six of which are particularly relevant to this volume. The committee observed that progress in science is "jagged," and characterized much more by self-correction than an historic or current requirement to get things exactly right the first time. Second, values and politics both play central roles in the education enterprise. In education, there are sometimes "main effects" and often unintended effects, both positive and negative. Sometimes the unintended effects are more powerful than the intended, and a researcher must be alert to such possibilities. This leads to a third observation: There are strong public and professional interests in educational research, and these require any evaluator to put a premium on ethical considerations in all of his or her work.

Fourth, unlike research in the "hard" sciences, educational research must cope with issues generated by human volition (see, e.g., Rosnow & Rosenthal, 1997). We are humans, not chemicals in beakers; we exert will, and we enjoy exerting it. This produces infinite variability in educational programs as implemented, and in their effects.

A second component of volition in education is that the great major-ity of professional educators are constantly working to change and improve their classrooms and schools, regardless of externally defined or mandated "reforms." As Tyack and Cuban (1996) observed, in the history of American education, efforts at reform are not the exceptions; they are and have been the near-universal norm. Research in schools necessarily focuses on complex, moving targets.

Fifth, the organization of education in the United States is tremendously complicated and uneven. Our 50 states, 15,000 school districts, and 90,000 schools vary on almost every imaginable dimension from funding mecha-nisms to teacher and student demographics and evaluation systems. Finally, for all of the discussion of the potentially positive roles of science in educa-tion, the enterprise of educational research is dramatically underfunded. Less than 1% of the U.S. Department of Education's budget is allocated to research and assessment, and no state exceeds 1%. One of the early findings from the federally funded "What Works Clearinghouse" was how few rigorous (typ-ically expensive) studies had been completed on what does—or does not—work. Research is not free. No aspect of a modern society's economy moves forward without a substantially greater investment in research and develop-ment.[2] Federal funding for educational research has never been adequate to the task of rapidly advancing American education.

■ Program Evaluation Standards

With such a high bar for "science," such a complex space for gathering data, and with modest funding, how should a field attempt to progress? A group of 16 national associations, ranging from the American Educational Research Association and the American Psychological Association to the National School Boards Association and the Council of Great City Schools, has worked to find agreement on evaluation standards. *The Program Evaluation Standards, 2nd edition* (Joint Committee on Standards for Educational Evaluation, 1994) eventually agreed on 4 overarching and 50 specific evalua-tion standards. These can be viewed as a second valuable frame for designing or examining large-scale efforts at understanding the complex enterprise of education.

In the judgment of the committee, the first set of standards must be concerned with *utility*. Would the potential evaluation serve the information needs of the intended users? The group of standards under utility includes stakeholder identification, evaluator credibility, information scope and selec-tion, values identification, report clarity, report timeliness and dissemina-tion, and evaluation impact. It is interesting that the very prestigious, skilled, NRC group began with a premise that could be paraphrased, "If it isn't rig-orous science, it can't be useful." An equally prestigious group working on the evaluation standards insisted, in effect, that "If it can't be made useful, it doesn't matter whether the design was rigorous." Research-informed education moves forward when these two potentially very different perspectives can be coaxed into marching together.

The Joint Committee on Standards for Educational Evaluation concluded that the second set of standards to be considered relate to *feasibility*. Feasibility standards include practical procedures, political viability, and cost effectiveness. An intervention that cannot be replicated in the practical, often messy world of American education is of extremely limited value, regardless of its findings.

The third set of evaluation standards is *proprietary standards*. These include service orientation, formal agreements, rights of human subjects, respect for human dignity in all interactions, complete and fair assessment, full disclosure of findings, dealing openly with any conflicts of interest, and fiscal responsibility. If a study cannot be conducted in the full light of day, with clear agreements among all involved, then it should not be conducted. The Joint Committee did not require that none of those involved in a study have any conceivable conflicts of interest. Rather, they suggested that any potential conflict be fully revealed in advance.

Accuracy standards concern a range of topics including (a) program documentation; (b) context analysis; (c) clear description of purposes and procedures, using defensible information sources; (d) obtaining valid, reliable, systematic information; (e) appropriate analyses of data; (f) clear justification of conclusions; (g) impartial reporting; and (h) a final evaluation of the evaluation itself, so that stakeholders can examine a study's strengths and weaknesses. Both in the original standards and in the second edition, the committee made clear that the final set of standards, "Accuracy" (the major focus of the NRC report), while very important, should only be considered after issues of utility, feasibility, and propriety have been fully addressed.

Taken together, the NRC's *Scientific Research in Education* and the Joint Committee's *Program Evaluation Standards* provide invaluable frames through which to consider issues in large-scale evaluation. The two sets of standards are not mutually exclusive; rather they focus on different, critical aspects of a very important set of tasks. They do, however, place substantial demands on any group considering conducting large-scale educational research.

It is unlikely that there has ever been a study that lived up to the purest definitions of "science" and the evaluation standards represented above. I have worked with dozens of state and local evaluation units, and with several of the more highly regarded research centers and organizations in American, European, Australian, and Asian education. Almost all of those groups have laudable strengths, and each group has worked to achieve high scientific and ethical standards. But studies are designed and conducted by—and agencies are products of—human beings.[3] Most of us strive for excellence, while acknowledging our inevitable imperfections. This chapter now turns toward "real world" considerations in large-scale studies that seem to be underdiscussed in education.

■ Different Organizational Contexts and Processes

For 30 years I have had the privilege of participating in studies that involved, in various degrees and times, district and state research and evaluation (R & E) offices, university-based research teams, and independent for-profit and not-for-profit research organizations. Any effort to overstate the differences among them would involve quite a challenge. Because almost any large-scale study involves at least two of those three groups, it is important to have an appreciation of their similarities and differences.

The first thing to note about local Education Authorities' (LEAs') R & E offices is that most LEAs do not have one at all. Of the 15,000+ LEAs in America, perhaps 1,000 have one or more full-time professionals with advanced training whose jobs are focused exclusively on research, evaluation, and assessment. Those LEAs that do have R & E offices tend to be larger districts and those near a research-intensive university. Large districts typically have diverse specialists focused on testing, data warehousing, statistical analyses, and the conduct of specific evaluation studies. Where R & E offices exist, the professionals in them tend to be pulled in many directions, and underfunded to achieve the evaluation tasks requested by their LEA.[4] Hence, local evaluations, of whatever scale, are typically conducted either by whomever is available at the time regardless of professional qualifications or by overburdened R & E professionals. Neither is a prescription for consistent excellence. Still, LEAs often produce reports that, if they make their way to national distribution through presentations at national conferences or—less often—through publication in scholarly journals, are valuable contributions to the field.

The second group is university professors. The obvious strengths of university-based researchers are their specialized skills and knowledge bases. They are often nationally recognized experts in specific fields. They are the more likely to conduct thorough literature reviews in preparation for a study, and are the most likely to spend extended periods of time pondering findings. However, they, too, have limitations. They typically know their department and university at much greater detail than the LEA with which they work, and know the LEA in greater detail than their state and nation. Second, they often lack the broad knowledge of "how education systems work," which is the daily bread of LEA-based R & E staff.[5] They tend to want to analyze all data, regardless of source, through techniques that they have used before. Flexibility is not a universal trait in academia.

Third are independent research organizations. These may be large regional laboratories (e.g., Northwest Regional Educational Laboratory, McREL), for-profit and not-for-profit organizations (e.g., Westat, Abt Associates, Policy Studies Associates), or small, one-person shops. They are typically staffed by research generalists who are quite skilled at research design and data analysis, and typically write rapidly and well. Almost by definition, they know little about a local context, and often know little about a specific content area, such as early reading or career and technical education. They are continuously under pressure to finish the current contract and move on to the next one, so as to maintain robust funding streams.

For the purposes of large-scale research, a typical team includes a combination of at least two of the above three groups. It is virtually impossible to conduct studies without the facilitation of the local R & E apparatus, however sophisticated it may be. University people have valuable expertise and perspectives, but are often woeful at the logistics required to "get the troops into the field." Most research shops are too busy surviving and getting the next research grant to get their findings into wide distribution, and thus help become the shoulders on which the next generation of scientists can stand. When teams can be built across the groups, valuable research is more often possible.

One laudable example of the potential for cross-boundary collaboration is the Consortium on Chicago School Research (Roderick & Easton, 2007). The consortium, now in its second decade, is a successful collaboration between a very large district, teachers' and administrators' organizations, the University of Chicago, Northwestern University, and several other colleges and universities. This group has produced a regular supply of evaluations and policy analyses for the district, and has also published research that has influenced both theory and practice nationwide.

■ Additional Notes from Thirty Years of Multisite R & E Experience

Experienced large-scale evaluators will regard nearly all of the above as well-established "givens" in the work. These are relatively accessible to any would-be research or evaluation teams. The 11 points that follow are more nearly of the, "things that teams learn through (often sad) experience" variety, and can potentially help guide future studies in avoiding pitfalls of the past efforts. Most of them relate to avoiding mistakes "before the beginning," so as to not create, in essence, irreparable initial damage to expensive studies. Others range through the studies proper to the importance of longitudinal follow up and contributing to the larger field.

*1. The Research Team Must Thoroughly Understand
the "It" Being Studied*

Before making initial inquiries as to possible samples, a research team should understand the reform as envisioned by its developers. Research teams that go into the field without all team members first reading multiple sources and then conducting detailed discussions with the authors of those sources about the reform are hobbled and will, at best, reinvent several wheels.

Reports from others who previously studied the practicalities of a reform are invaluable. By the end of almost any study, the research team knows more than it can write for publication. For that reason, it is often valuable for members of a prospective research team to interview previous authors and ask them whether there are specific signs of success or failure about which the new team should be particularly attentive.

*2. The Research Design Should Replicate Key
Aspects of the Reform Design*

Some reform designs are targeted more at the district and/or school levels (America's Choice, see e.g., Ross, Sanders, Wright, Stringfield, Wang, & Alberg, 2001; Rothman, 1997), while others are targeted to the classroom with the school or higher levels as representing the necessary glue to hold key components in place (e.g., Direct Instruction, see Borman, Hewes, Overman, & Brown, 2003, for over 20 studies involving DI). All reform designs are almost by definition unique. These will require different strategies regarding research-team resource allocation. The team should go primarily where the "it" is most intended to work. The Core Knowledge curriculum (Hirsch, 1995) and Success for All (Slavin & Madden, 2000) should be visible in classrooms every day. America's Choice may be more visible at the district level.

Virtually all educational reforms assume a multiyear implementation, and seek long-term effects. Although this issue is discussed more in the next point, it is important in the design phase to note that a one year study of almost any school reform is at best a study of implementation. At worst—and far more likely—such a study risks being so ill-matched to the reform process as to be misleading.

*3. Find, or, If Necessary, Develop Measures of Key
Components of the Reform(s) Being Studied*

If studying the Coalition of Essential Schools (Sizer, 1992), a research team must have measures of teacher teaming and teacher-teams' understanding of the Coalition's basic principles. In contrast, a team studying Direct Instruction must have classroom-level measures of phonics instruction.

Over the past two decades various research teams have developed reasonable measures of the key components of, for example, Success for All (Slavin & Madden, 2000). Tools to measure less well-known reforms are also available. Wherever possible, teams are well advised to use existing instruments over inventing and refining tools.

The equally large point is that it is possible to go into a study of a specific reform and conclude that "principal leadership" and "professional development" are what matters, regardless of the reform. Those things do matter, but how they matter varies by reform, and unless the team is studying school effectiveness generally (e.g., Teddlie & Reynolds, 2000; Teddlie & Stringfield, 1993), then it is good to keep gathering data on the key components of the specific reform.

4. Sampling Is Destiny

It is almost impossible to overstate this point. If the intent of the research is to study relatively sturdy implementations of the "it," the team should make at least one and perhaps several visits to any given site before including the site in the study. If a study does not include multiple relatively high implementing sites, the study and its authors will be severely criticized for not "getting" the reform. Similarly, if a study does not include some relatively "typical" sites, its authors risk misinforming readers as to likely pitfalls involved in reform implementation.[6]

During 15 years of multisite studies of school reform, the Center for Social Organization of Schools team with which I worked gathered over 300 mixed-method, multiyear case studies of schools in over a dozen studies. Two of the clear findings drawn from a cross-study, cross-site analysis of those cases were that variance in level and quality of implementation were universal and that in many of the cases, the reform to be studied had, in fact, been dead on—or very soon after—arrival. In many instances, some in sites recommended by the developers of the reforms themselves, the reform in specific locations was little more than a name on a tombstone in a largely forgotten graveyard of discarded ideas. A related finding across studies and reforms was that at least one-third of the schools implementing "it" discontinued implementation within two-to-four years of implementation. Hence, having examples in a sample of indifferent or discontinued implementations is easily achieved. Having universally high implementers of a reform borders on being an unachievable goal. Having a balance of very strong and more typical implementations is a strength that most studies lack, in part through lack of attention to initial sampling considerations.

5. Agreement among All Parties in Advance Is Critical

The Joint Committee's proprietary standards of formal agreement and respect for human dignity in all interactions can hardly be overemphasized. Not covered by the Joint Committee, but very important in practice, is a point that one would think might be obvious but that causes problems in practice: A promise of anonymity for the sites team must be respected absolutely. Funders often seek the names of implementation sites, especially very successful sites. The funders typically mean no harm and often want to trumpet a school's successes. However, negotiated agreements between researchers and schools almost always include a guarantee of anonymity. In our experience, all sides would eventually allow the research team to inform the sites themselves that the funders would like to know who they are, but also to reassure the sites that whether they self-identified to the funder and others was their business, not ours. Successful schools almost always agree to forward word of their schools' successes. The research team must know its obligations and its boundaries, as must the local school district, the schools and teachers involved in the studies.

6. Local Testiness about Testing

Throughout my decades of multisite, multidistrict school research, a constant has been LEA- and school-level reticence on additional testing of students. Research teams either have to commit to making near-heroic efforts to convince LEAs, schools, and often individual parents to allow additional testing (often with implications for the external validity of a study), or to accept local measures. Given that any state's testing program may be insensitive to the specific intended outcomes of a reform, this causes a tough series of choices, but they must be resolved in advance of a study. During deliberations between a funder and a research team, both parties are well advised to assume that adding one or more student-level measures will greatly increase sampling challenges.

The next four observations relate to the in-the-field work of large-scale research and evaluation.

7. If a Visiting Team Cannot See "It" and/or Teachers Cannot Describe "It," It Is Not Happening

For example, in a study of five different reforms, Datnow, Borman, Stringfield, Rachuba and Castellano (2003) visited a school that the central administration and principal declared to be a leading example of a particular reform. In over a dozen classroom observations, the research team could not point to specific teacher behaviors or attitudes that would seem unique to the reform. In two subsequent teacher focus groups, the large majority of teachers were unaware that the school was implementing the specific reform, and none could describe a unique characteristic of the reform. The fact that the school produced mediocre achievement gains did not demonstrate that the reform *when well implemented* had no effects, but it did constitute a cautionary note on the implementability of the reform.

*8. In Practice, All Reforms are "Co-Constructed" or They
Are Not Implemented*

Berman and McLaughlin (1978) concluded that in the intersection of reform design and school, either was "mutual adaptation" or no meaningful implementation. After an additional 20 years of research, Datnow and Stringfield (2000) described essentially the same finding as "co-construction" and declared that local educators "co-construct" the reform, or it does not happen. Across the 300+ aforementioned multiyear case studies, the Hopkins team never saw a "pure" implementation of any school reform design. Rather, we were consistently presented with local educators actively co-constructing reform components that they perceived to be necessary to make the design work in their specific environment. We have never seen, for example, two identical implementations of Success for All or Direct Instruction.

For a research team, it is important to remember that co-construction is not the abandonment or negation of a design. Rather it is similar to an architect designing a building and then engineers and carpenters making site- and condition-specific modifications as the building is being constructed. The overall design can remain the same, but inevitably carpenters will need to move a beam or a window due to an unanticipated feature of the land or a supplier's inability to provide a specified component in a timely fashion. In the end it matters that the architect's vision, the engineer's and carpenter's sense of the possible, and the purchaser all have a building with which they are pleased to identify.

*9. Sustainability I: The Initial Buy-in and Long-Term Co-Construction
Must Happen at Multiple Levels If Sustained Student-Level Effects
Are to be Achieved*

In the 300+ aforementioned multiyear case studies, the Hopkins team saw no examples of either teacher[s] or district administrators being able to create and sustain reform without multilevel cooperation. Superintendents can force principals and teachers to pay lip service to a reform, but not to implement it at a level that will affect change in student learning. Teachers can implement a reform but cannot sustain it long-term without principal- and usually system-level support. Principals change positions with increasing frequency. Colleagues and I are involved currently in a study in which, over a 3.5-year time period, five of five LEA superintendencies have seen changes in personnel, as have almost all of the 17 principalships. One high poverty school has had six principals and acting principals in three years. In some schools, the teacher leadership teams have experienced 100% turnover. In annual interviews of a wide range of district staffs, we have found no one who regards these levels of transition as extreme in the modern world. For a research team to understand the challenges facing those wishing to create and stabilize reform, it is necessary to study the reform at multiple interconnected levels, and to follow all levels over time. This makes implementation integrity hard to sustain, and means that the co-construction itself will vary over the long haul.

10. Sustainability II: The Long Haul

In their meta-analysis of comprehensive school reform and student achievement, Borman, Hewes, Overman, and Brown (2003) found modest effects for reforms (regardless of reform type) during studies' first four years, and increasingly larger effects for longer-term studies. Two longer-term studies not referenced in Borman et al. illustrate the point.

In the *Perry Preschool Study*, initial effects of participation in the project (contrasting randomly assigned experimental vs. control preschoolers) were encouraging but not exceptional. However, follow-up data when the former preschoolers reached age 19 (Schweinhart, Barnes, & Weikart, 1993) indicated that there were dramatic differences favoring those who had attended the Perry preschool. Perry graduates were less than half as likely to have required special education services, had higher grades and test scores throughout school, and were significantly more likely to have graduated from high school. An additional follow-up at age 27 (e.g., more than 20 years post-preschool-participation) found that the Perry students were much less likely to have been arrested for dealing drugs or to have had multiple arrests on any charges. Former Perry students had higher mean incomes and were more than three times as likely to own their own homes (Parks, 2000). We would not know of these dramatic long-term gains had the research team not created databases that were themselves sustainable.

Following research from diverse fields on efforts to create unusually highly reliable organizations, Reynolds, Stringfield, and Schaffer (2006) spent three years assisting secondary schools in three British LEAs in attempting to become more nearly High Reliability Organizations (HROs). The results were seen as significant. For example, in a Welsh district with 10 nonsectarian secondary schools, at the end of three years of "High Reliability Schools (HRS)" implementation, the 10 HRS schools' mean gain on the British age 16 national exam was nearly double the Welsh average gain. This was seen as impressive, but in the five subsequent years, the mean gain for the High Reliability schools was fully triple the Welsh national average gain (Stringfield, Reynolds, & Schaffer, 2008).

Combining the meta-analytic finding with observations from two unusually long-term, proactive studies invites one to wonder if almost all educational reform studies are of insufficient duration. At the least, the studies suggest that the authors of any school reform study should create data sets and circumstances such that long-term follow-up studies—of students and/or of schools—are possible.

11. Contributing to Future Research and Research Syntheses

In *Toward reform of program evaluation*, Cronbach et al. (1981) proposed that the solution to the intractable imperfection of any one study was the triangulation of findings across diverse, often relatively humble evaluations. In this way, the imperfections of each study were most likely to cancel each other out. For subsequent researchers and reviewers of research to make progress, those of us in the field must put our work in places that are subsequently accessible. We must provide the shoulders on which subsequent generations of researchers can stand.

The field of scientific reviewing of previous research is rapidly gaining in sophistication and policy importance (Cooper & Hedges, 1994; Cooper, Hedges, & Valentine, in press). The Cochran Collaboration (2007) in medicine, the Campbell Collaboration (2007) in education and the social sciences are drawing increasingly well-respected conclusions in their respective fields. The federally supported "What Works Clearinghouse" (www.whatworks. ed.gov) receives millions of "hits" and is regarded in some circles as the definitive (and free) source for information on effort-worthy reforms. These resources are completely dependent on the release of research by scholars from around the world on a broad range of topics. We all have a professional obligation to release our research to the larger community, so that, over time, it can become part of a very large, coherent summary of what can work in education, where, and under what conditions.

■ Summary

In this chapter, I have drawn from decades of my own and others' research and evaluation experience in an effort to drive home several practical points of value for future large-scale evaluators and researchers. The first point is that what we do often matters. Rigorous evaluation research often impacts the creation of national laws, the choices of directions for local schools, and everything in between. Decades of observation of policy change indicate that our work is more likely to have impact if it combines large quantitative data bases with more qualitative attention to the practical workings of individual schools and classrooms.

A related point is that something approaching a commonsense consensus exists as to what should count as "science" in educational research. The National Academy of Science deserves much credit for bringing together such a consensus (Shavelson & Towne, 2002). Further, the Joint Committee on

Standards for Educational Evaluation provides clear guidance for the practical, ethical conduct of both research and evaluation activities. The field has a strong foundation from which to build.

Virtually every group of participants in the educational research and evaluation field brings strengths to the table, and each brings limitations. Groups like the Consortium on Chicago School Research provide examples of ways through which the strengths of each specialized group can be used to maximum benefit while each group's limitations are being addressed through the strengths of others.

The second half of the chapter focused on practical observations from one who has participated in large-scale educational reform evaluations for over a quarter century. Although hopefully encouraging of future efforts, my goal is to provide an at least partial road map so that others may move forward more effectively and more rapidly. The first cluster of observations is intended to reduce the probability that a study will be predestined to provide no useful information. Research and evaluation teams must thoroughly understand the "it" before going into the field. Much has been written and much more known about various reform efforts, and would-be evaluators are well advised to learn as much as possible about specific reforms as a first step in study designs. The designs themselves should map on to key characteristics of reforms (including multiyear implementation timelines), and should use instruments that are sensitive to specific aspects of the reforms being studied.

In studies of school reform, it is critical to understand that sampling is destiny. Both funders and the research teams invariably are anxious to get into "the field." However, this laudable desire must be tempered with a patient examination of all sites being nominated for study. Similarly, clear agreements between research teams and local schools and districts must be worked out in advance. These must include understandings of the levels of intrusion that will be required for the study. Any additional testing must be agreed to in advance, and the research team must understand that the greater demands they place on schools, the greater their chance of ending up with a nonrepresentative sample of schools agreeing to participate.

Research teams should understand that reforms as implemented are invariably "co-constructed." This does not mean that specific aspects of various reforms have no value or should be ignored. It does mean that local educational professionals will not abandon their own decades of observations of "what can work here, how and why." Sometimes locals' adaptations are eventually picked up by the design teams and integrated into subsequent versions of the reform. Sometimes the locals' adaptations simply do not work and are—or should be—dropped. But it is important for research teams to understand that in all fields practicing professionals make adaptations in response to what they see as conditions "on the ground." Those adaptations should be documented, understood, and reported. Reforms that are not adapted to local realities invariably disappear over time. Those that do adapt have opportunities to become increasingly effective.

Finally, it is important to report results from diverse studies, and to report out on methodological successes and failures in addition to reporting on the effects of the reforms themselves. Through those processes, both the work of education and the work of studying education can continue improving.

■ References

Aldersebaes, I., Railsback, J., Shaughnessy, J., & Speth, T. (n.d.). *Evaluating whole-school reform efforts: A guide for district and school staff* (128 pp.). Portland, Northwest Regional Educational Laboratory.

Berman, P., & McLaughlin, M. (1978). *Federal programs supporting educational change. Vol. VIII, Implementing and sustaining innovations.* Santa Monica, CA, RAND.

Borman, G., Hewes, G., Overman, L., & Brown, S. (2003). Comprehensive school reform and achievement: A meta-analysis. *Review of Educational Research, 73,* 125–230.

Campbell Collaboration. (2007). Retrieved, December 10, 2007, from http://www.campbellcollaboration.org/.

Cochran Collaboration. (2007). Retrieved, December 10, 2007, from http://www.cochrane.org/.

Cooper, H., & Hedges, L. (1994). *The handbook of research synthesis.* New York, Russell Sage Foundation.

Cooper, H., Hedges, L., & Valentine, J. (in press). *The handbook of research synthesis* (2nd ed.). New York, Russell Sage Foundation.

Cronbach, L., Ambron, S., Dornbusch, S., Hess, R., Hornik, R., Phillips, D., Walker, D., & Weiner, S. (1981). *Toward reform of program evaluation.* San Francisco, Jossey-Bass.

Datnow, A., Borman, G., Stringfield, S., Rachuba, L., & Castellano, M. (2003). Comprehensive school reform in culturally and linguistically diverse contexts: Implementation and outcomes from a four-year study. *Educational Evaluation and Policy Analysis, 25,* 143–170.

Datnow, A., & Stringfield, S. (2000). Working together for reliable school reform. *Journal of Education for Students Placed At Risk, 5,* 183–204.

Hirsch, E. D., Jr. (1995). *Core knowledge sequence.* Charlottesville, VA, Core Knowledge Foundation.

The Joint Committee on Standards for Educational Evaluation. (1994). *The program evaluation standards* (2nd ed.). Thousand Oaks, CA, Sage.

Parks, G. (2000). The High-Scope/Perry Preschool Project. *Juvenile Justice Bulletin,* 1–4.

Reynolds, D., Stringfield, S., & Schaffer, E. (2006). The High Reliability Schools Project: Some preliminary results and analyses. In J. Chrispeels & A. Harris

(Eds.), *School improvement: International perspectives* (pp. 56–76). London, Routledge.

Roderick, M., & Easton, J. (2007, July 16). *Developing new roles for research in new policy environments: The Consortium on Chicago School Research.* Chicago, Unpublished Manuscript.

Rosnow, R., & Rosenthal, R. (1997). *People studying people: Artifacts and ethics in behavioral research.* New York, Freeman.

Ross, S., Sanders, W., Wright, P., Stringfield, S., Wang, L., & Alberg, M. (2001). Two- and three-year achievement results from the Memphis Restructuring Initiative. *School Effectiveness and School Improvement, 12,* 323–346.

Rothman, R. (1997). Reform at all levels: National Alliance for Restructuring Education. In S. Stringfield, S. Ross, & L. Smith (Eds.), *Bold plans for school restructuring.* Mahwah, NJ, Lawrence Erlbaum Associates.

Schweinhart, L., Barnes, H., & Wiekart, D. (1993). *Significant benefits: The high/scope perry preschool study through age 27.* Ypsilanti, MI, High/Scope Press.

Shadish, W. R., Cook, T. D., & Campbell, D. T. (2002). *Experimental and quasi-experimental designs for generalized causal inference.* New York, Houghton Mifflin.

Shavelson, R., & Towne, L. (Eds.) (2002). *Scientific research in education.* Washington, DC, National Academy of Science.

Sizer, T. R. (1992). *Horace's school: Redesigning the American high school.* New York, Houghton Mifflin.

Slavin, R., & Madden, N. (2000). *One million children: Success for all.* Thousand Oaks, CA, Corwin.

Stringfield, S., Reynolds, D., & Schaffer, G. (2008). Improving secondary students' academic achievement through a focus on reform reliability: The first five years of The High Reliability Schools Project. *School Effectiveness and School Improvement, 19,* 409–428.

Tashakkori, A., & Teddlie, C. (1998*). Mixed methodology.* Thousand Oaks, CA, Sage.

Teddlie, C., & Reynolds, D. (2000). *The international handbook of school effectiveness research.* London, Falmer.

Teddlie, C., & Stringfield, S. (1993). *School matters: Lessons learned from a 10-year study of school effects.* New York, Teachers College Press.

Tyack, D., & Cuban, L. (1996). *Tinkering toward Utopia.* Cambridge, Harvard.

What Works Clearinghouse. Retrieved, August 30, 2007, from www.whatworks. ed.gov.

■ Notes

1. As one example, for several years the annual meeting of the American Educational Research Association program planning documents specifically invited "interpretive dance" as a method of educational research.

2. For comparison purposes, the readers are invited to imagine Google or Honda or Boeing trying to move forward while spending less than 1% of their annual budgets on research.

3. Our imperfections do not free us from the ethical requirements of our field. Some things, such as full information to and willing participation by all participants in studies must be guarded vigorously and absolutely; hence, the existence of review boards at all universities and districts.

4. For example, in a typical year between 2002 and 2005, the Baltimore City Public Schools' R & E office was asked to conduct 50+ evaluations and administer, sort, and report results from over a million tests of one type or another per year.

5. I have been struck repeatedly with how genuinely surprised a full professor is upon learning that the typical elementary reading lesson (for example) is mediocre, or that many teachers in very high poverty contexts have no training and few skills in classroom management.

6. Viewed in isolation, success looks natural and simple. When a professional golfer swings a three wood and the struck ball travels 250 yards and stops 20 feet from the hole, or when a Boeing 777 safely lands 250 passengers after flying across the Atlantic, we think very little of it. In fact, in the case of the golfer, we are watching a remarkable athlete make a shot s/he has practiced thousands of times. The commercial pilot has sat in simulators and landed theoretical planes hundreds of times, then served for years as a co-pilot on this one aircraft type. In contrast, a school implementing a reform is doing "it" for the first time, and typically implementing it in virtual isolation. Most of us would refuse to board a commercial aircraft if we knew that the pilot had never previously flown a plane of this type, and had no experienced co-pilot. To miss the variance—and the causes of variance—in reform implementations is to fundamentally misunderstand American school reform.

21. BEYOND THE MONITORING OF STUDENTS' PROGRESS IN CLASSROOMS

The Assessment of Students, Curricula, and Teachers

Stephen T. Peverly

All approaches to educational and psychoeducational assessment focus on students and almost all of them focus on students exclusively. In this chapter, a case will be made for why that is insufficient and why there is a need to focus more widely on two critical aspects of the instructional delivery system: The curriculum and the teacher.

■ Definitions of CBA/CBM Models

The term curriculum-based assessment (CBA) refers to a group of methods that assess elementary school students' progress in the local curriculum, typically in the areas of reading, spelling, mathematics, and writing, for the purpose of making instructional and curriculum modifications for struggling students (Deno, 1985; Hintze, Christ, & Methe, 2006; Shapiro, 2004). With the exception of curriculum-based measurement (CBM), which uses standardized measures to monitor students' progress in a curriculum, all other forms of CBA measure students academic skills directly, since they test what is taught, rather than indirectly, such as in norm-based assessment, which uses items (e.g., passages, word lists) that may or may not correspond to those in the local curriculum.

There are several different models of CBA. Criterion-referenced-CBA (CR-CBA; e.g., Blankenship, 1985; Idol, Nevin, & Paolucci-Whitcomb, 1999) focuses on the measurement of a student's mastery of hierarchically ordered objectives (from the easiest to the most difficult) derived from the classroom curriculum. Assessment is followed by teaching deficient skills to mastery.

The behavioral assessment of academic skills model of CBA (BAAS; e.g., Shapiro, 1987, 1989, 1990, 2004), unlike some other methods, addresses the adequacy of children's performance in the curriculum *and* of the instructional environment via a four-step process: Assessing the instructional environment, assessing students' placement in the curriculum, creating instructional modifications to maximize students' success in the curriculum, and progress monitoring.

CBA for instructional design (CBA-ID; e.g., Gickling & Rosenfield, 1995; Gickling & Thompson, 1985; Gravios & Gickling, 2002, in press) conducts assessments in phases. In Phase I the assessor attempts to create a "comfort zone" between students' skill and knowledge levels and the level of the curriculum, to maximize students' opportunity for success. Assessment is used to identify classroom instructional materials that are at students' instructional level, the optimal level for teaching and learning, both for comprehension (93–97% known information) and for rehearsal and practice (70–85% known information). In Phase II, using the instructional level materials identified in Phase I, assessments are conducted to identify students' strengths and weaknesses in the academic skills that formed the basis of the referral, and to develop appropriate approaches to instruction. In Phase III, teachers focus on teaching the skills and strategies identified in Phase II, monitoring growth, and determining whether adjustments are needed to ensure students' continued progress. Mastery learning is emphasized so that all students can learn materials to a comparable level.

There are two other points of note regarding CBA-ID. Recently, Gravois and Gickling (2008) changed the name of their model from CBA-ID to Instructional Assessment (IA) to emphasize that the principles that underlie effective assessment and effective teaching are the same (e.g., activating students' background knowledge; linking new to known information; establishing appropriate instructional levels). Also, CBA-ID (or IA) is a central component of Instruction Consultation Teams (IC-Teams; Gickling & Rosenfield, 1995), which will be discussed later in this paper. Briefly, teachers and IC-Team members work together to develop procedures to implement the phases of CBA-ID into classroom routines. In that way, as the change in name to IA denotes, assessment is an integral part of instruction.

Curriculum-based evaluation (CBE; e.g., Howell, Fox, & Morehead, 1993; Howell, Kurns, & Antil, 2002; Howell & Nolet, 2000) is a hierarchical assessment system that consists of screenings, more in-depth assessments if needed, task and error analyses, probes, direct observation and trial teaching, among other activities, to identify students' academic strengths and weaknesses in basic skills. The purpose is to provide teachers with as much information as possible for instruction. For example, an assessment of decoding (which has already been task analyzed) would begin with a survey to determine whether there is a problem. If a problem is detected, then the evaluator uses follow-up assessments to determine causes (e.g., poor understanding of sound and print concepts; sufficient opportunity for practice, appropriate levels of self-monitoring) and to test the efficacy of different teaching methods, to provide teachers with information sufficient to make decisions about instruction.

CBM (e.g., Deno, 1985; Shinn, 2002) differs from the other forms of CBA in several critical ways. First, it was designed to monitor students' progress in the curriculum, not to propose intervention strategies. Second, unlike all of the other forms of CBA, it focuses on long-term instructional goals (e.g., oral reading fluency) that can be measured frequently throughout the year to assess students' progress in the curriculum. It does not assess specific sub-skills (e.g., symbol/sound association) that may contribute to the development of the goals. Finally, it uses standardized measures of basic skills with demonstrated reliability and validity.

■ Purpose

The purpose of this chapter is to update an article Kay Kitzen and I (Peverly & Kitzen, 1998) wrote many years ago on our reservations about CBA. In that paper, we used a research-based analysis of the cognitive skills that underlie the development of reading to argue two points primarily. First, CBAs of reading were not cognitive enough and were not structured to assess all of the cognitive skills related to learning how to read well. Thus, they could not always provide all of the information needed to remedy reading problems effectively. Second, CBAs did not focus on the quality of reading curricula. Decades of research indicate that reading programs that do not provide explicit instruction in the alphabetic code and language and comprehension skills can cause reading problems in some children (Adams, 1990; Foorman, 1995; National Reading Council, 2000; Vellutino, Fletcher, Snowling, & Scanlon, 2004). Thus, to prevent the development of reading problems, CBAs of reading skill must also evaluate how well classroom reading curricula enable the teaching of these skills. If instruction in the alphabetic code and comprehension are not sufficient, the curriculum should be changed to one that does for all children, not only those experiencing problems learning to read.

■ Has CBA Changed?

Since Peverly and Kitzen (1998), there has been good progress on our first point—many of the cognitive skills related to the ability to read are now covered in most forms of CBA. I will not focus on this further. The purpose of this article is to focus on the second point raised in our earlier article, the quality of the curriculum used to teach students how to read, and by extension, the quality of the teachers who teach the curriculum in their classrooms. I have chosen to focus on these because of (a) the attention given to evidence-based practices by the federal government through legislation (e.g., the No Child Left Behind Act) and the money allocated by them to synthesize research on best practices (Slavin, 2008) and (b) the curriculum-based alternative to IQ-Achievement discrepancies in the diagnosis of a learning disability— response to intervention (RTI). Briefly, many researchers and practitioners have argued that the discrepancy-based approach is limited: (a) It does not help us distinguish between the two primary causes of reading difficulties: cognitive deficits (e.g., constitutionally based deficits in phonological awareness) and experience (poor instruction and/or poor early home environment) (Fletcher, Francis, Morris, & Lyon, 2005; Vellutino et al., 1996); (b) there is little empirical justification for the distinction between poor readers who meet the IQ-Ach discrepancy criterion and those who do not; that is, both groups have deficits in skills related to reading difficulties (e.g., phonological knowledge, naming speed; Stanovich & Siegel, 1994; Stuebing et al., 2002) and both respond similarly to instruction (Vellutino, Scanlon, & Jaccard, 2003); and (c) the discrepancy approach is not inherently helpful in planning remediation (Fletcher et al., 1994, 2005; Foorman, Francis, Fletcher, & Lynn, 1996; Stuebing et al., 2002; Vellutino et al., 1996; Vellutino, Scanlon, & Tanzman, 1998). As a result of changes in special education law, some school systems have begun to use RTI as the basis for the determination of a reading disability.

RTI is typically administered in three phases (Fuchs & Vaughn, 2005). In Phase I, students' rate of growth in reading in the regular classroom is tracked using a form of CBA. For this stage to be valid, most students must be progressing adequately in the curriculum as it is being instructed by the classroom teacher, to ensure that instruction is sufficient to foster growth in reading. The second phase focuses on identifying students whose level of performance and rate of improvement are well below most of the other students in the class. Instructional adaptations are introduced and students' responsiveness, using CBA, is measured. Students' responsiveness determines whether the instructional modifications improved students' performance to a level consonant with that of most of the other children in the classroom. If students' performance does not improve adequately, special education services are considered in Phase III of RTI.

It should be noted that there are two general approaches to intervention in Phase II (Fletcher et al., 2005; Fuchs & Fuchs, 2006; Fuchs & Vaughn, 2005): problem-solving and standard protocol. In the problem-solving approach, typically preferred by practitioners (Fuchs & Vaughn, 2005), instructional modifications are made and evaluated on a student by student basis. In the standard protocol approach, favored by researchers, all students get the same remedial protocol (e.g., Vellutino et al., 1996). In either case, CBA or CBM is typically used to measure students' outcomes.

One of the purported advantages of CBA is that it is based on the curriculum used to teach children how to read in the classroom (Shapiro, 2004). However, it is rare that the curriculum in the regular education classroom is evaluated using evidence on best practices, to determine whether children's difficulties in reading might be due to the classroom curriculum. One notable exception is the Instructional Consultation (IC) model (Rosenfield, 2002) mentioned earlier. Rosenfield argues that curricula, in addition to students and instruction, should be a focus of assessment. In fact, Rosenfield (1987) describes some students with reading problems as "curriculum casualties" (see also, Cramer & Rosenfield, 2008).

Although RTI implicitly seems to assume that reading curricula are important to learning outcomes, since the purpose of Phase I is to ensure that the teacher is providing a "generally nurturing instructional environment" (Fuchs & Vaughn, 2005), in actuality very little attention is paid to evaluating curriculum and its implementation in the RTI process. In other words, a "generally nurturing curriculum" does not necessarily mean that the curriculum is entirely adequate. If students come to school prepared to learn, most children can learn how to read well regardless of the method of reading instruction used in the classroom—phonics or whole language. It is my guess that approximately 75–80% of children can learn to read no matter what form of instruction is used. My estimate is based on estimates of the percentage of children that have literacy difficulties, which may be as high as 20% (Lyon, 1995; Shaywitz, Fletcher, & Shaywitz, 1994), and the persistent finding in reviews of research (e.g., Adams, 1990; Bond & Dykstra, 1967; Chall, 1967, 1983) that a reasonably high percentage of students can profit from instruction in reading no matter how they are taught.

However, students who have deficits in the cognitive processes that underlie word recognition and/or the language skills that underlie comprehension (Berninger et al., 2002; Nation, 2005; Sabatini, Chapter 10, this volume; Wise et al., Chapter 16, this volume) or students from some urban schools, with high percentages of poor ethnic and linguistic minorities, who often have very, very high rates of reading failure, need a curriculum with a strong and explicit emphasis on phonics, language skills, and comprehension to learn how to read well (Foorman, Francis, Fletcher, Schatschneider, & Mehta, 1998). For example, in screening first-grade children who were at-risk for a reading disability, Vellutino et al. (1996) identified 9% of the total sample that were having difficulty learning to read, based on teachers' ratings of children's progress in reading and a modified discrepancy formula [an IQ of 90 or above on either the Verbal or Performance Scales of the Wechsler Intelligence Scale for Children-Revised (Wechsler, 1974) and a score at or below the 15th percentile on either the Word Attack or the Word Identification subtests of the Woodcock Reading Mastery Tests-Revised (Woodcock, 1987)]. After the conclusion of the intervention (daily individual tutoring for 30 minutes outside of the regular classroom), which included both a phonics-based and whole-word approach to word recognition, instruction on comprehension, among a variety of other activities, only 3% needed further remedial help in reading. In other words, the classroom curriculum may have been contributing to the development of a reading disability in some children.

Thus, instead of focusing all of our evaluation efforts on monitoring children's progress in the curriculum and on individual children judged to be at-risk because of insufficient progress in the curriculum, we should also be engaged in a school-wide effort of evaluating reading curricula using research on the efficacy of the curricula (Berninger, 1998, 2007). If curricula are not empirically sound, they should be replaced with ones that are empirically sound before the first phase of RTI is implemented. In addition, we should evaluate the effectiveness of the teachers who communicate the curriculum to children. If their teaching is not adequate, for example, the students in their classes consistently perform below those in other classes, they should receive professional development and monitoring of their teaching to improve their performance. The remainder of this article reviews research related to the quality of curricula and teachers to argue for school-based assessment (SBA), a comprehensive school-wide approach to assessment that focuses on curricula and teachers, as well as children (Peverly, 2004). The reader should note that I referred to SBA previously as instruction-based assessment (IBA; Peverly, 2004). However, to avoid confusion with IA, the new name for CBA-ID, I changed the name to SBA.

In the following sections, I review research on the impact of curricula and teachers on students' educational outcomes.

■ The Impact of Reading Curricula on Students' Educational Outcomes

The primary function of beginning reading programs is to teach children to read words accurately and quickly and comprehend what they read. The "great debate" among reading researchers, educators, and teachers has been about the best way to achieve this outcome: A systematic emphasis on phonics or whole-word or whole-language approaches. Chall (1967, 1983), in *Learning to Read: The Great Debate*, and Bond and Dykstra (1967) both came to the conclusion that systematic approaches to teaching phonics produced better results than nonsystematic approaches during the primary grades and that ample opportunities for connected reading with instruction in language skills and comprehension, in addition to phonics, produced even better outcomes. Later, Adams (1990) came to a similar conclusion. She found that students in programs with a systematic emphasis on phonics had better word recognition and spelling skills and comprehension skills that were comparable to students in programs that did not place an emphasis on phonics. Students in programs that combined a systematic emphasis on phonics, language instruction, and connected reading produced the best results of all.

In a more recent evaluation of research on the relative efficacy of systematic instruction in phonics and whole-word approaches in early reading instruction, Ehri, Nunes, Stahl, and Willows (2001) found that systematic instruction in phonics produced better outcomes than whole word approaches. Younger readers (kindergarten and first grade) exposed to phonics produced better outcomes than those exposed to whole language on all outcome measures: decoding regular and pseudowords, reading miscellaneous words, spelling, reading text orally, and comprehension of text. Positive effects of phonics-based curricula were also found for older readers (second through the sixth grade), although significant effects were found for only some outcome measures with this age group (decoding regular and pseudowords, reading miscellaneous words, and oral reading) and the effects sizes were generally not as large. Significant effects in favor of phonics-based programs were also found for young at-risk and normal readers, and older normal and reading-disabled students. The only group that did not seem to benefit were the second through sixth grade low-achieving readers (students not classified as reading disabled).

In conclusion, systematic instruction in the association of symbol to sound produces a decided advantage in learning how to read well for many students. That, combined with instruction in language and comprehension and the opportunity to read connected text, seems to produce even more favorable outcomes, especially for those with word recognition and/or language deficits. If a child does not learn how to read well, then the impact may well be felt beyond the task of reading itself. Over the years, poor reading can lead to a diminution of other cognitive skills (e.g., vocabulary, verbal IQ) and to decreases in motivation for learning (Perfetti, 1985; Stanovich, 1986). Thus, in the context of assessment, it is absolutely essential that we evaluate the quality of reading curricula. If they do not place a sufficient emphasis on phonics (especially), language and reading comprehension, and provide children with the opportunity to read connected text, they should be replaced.

■ Teacher Quality and Student Outcomes

As one would expect, research generally indicates that teacher quality is significantly and positively related to student academic outcomes (Mitchell, Robinson, Plake, & Knowles, 2001; see Hanushek, 1996, for an opposing point of view). The size of the impact, however, is a matter of debate. In this section, we focus on both reading and mathematics outcomes given the paucity of research on the relationship of teacher quality to students' skill in reading alone.

Scheerens and Bosker (1997) in a review of research on the effects of teachers, students, and schools on student achievement found that 15–20% of the variance lies among schools, 15–20% lies among classrooms (i.e., teachers), and 60–70% lies among students. Nye, Konstantopoulos, and Hedges (2004), as a part of Project STAR in Tennessee (a project designed to evaluate the effects of class size—small, medium, and large—on student achievement), which randomly assigned teachers and students to classrooms in kindergarten and grades 1, 2, and 3, enabled the researchers to evaluate the contribution of teachers without the biases that often result from the assignment procedures typically used in schools. The percent of variance accounted for by teachers was 6–7% in reading and 12–14% in math. Overall, these data suggest that individual differences in students account for more of the variance in student outcomes than individual differences in teachers.

Although the estimates of teachers' effects on students are relatively small compared to those in Scheerens and Bosker (1997), it is worth noting their effects on student achievement, as presented by Nye et al. (2004).

> If teacher effects are normally distributed, these findings suggest the difference in achievement gains between having a 25th percentile teacher (a not so effective teacher) and a 75th percentile teacher (an effective teacher) is over a third of a standard deviation (0.34) in reading and almost half a standard deviation (0.48) in mathematics. Similarly, the difference in achievement gains between having a 50th percentile teacher (an average teacher) and a 90th percentile teacher (a very effective teacher) is about one third of a standard deviation (0.33) in reading and somewhat smaller than half a standard deviation (0.46) in mathematics. In Kindergarten the effects are comparable, but larger for reading. For example, the difference in achievement status in kindergarten between having a 50th percentile teacher and a 90th percentile teacher is about 0.40 standard deviations in reading and 0.43 standard deviations in mathematics. (p. 253)

Rowan, Correnti, and Miller (2002) used three approaches to analyze data from *Prospects: The Congressionally Mandated Study of Educational Growth and Opportunity 1991–1994*. They contended that a primary determinant of the size of the effect of teachers on students is how data are analyzed. First, they used a variance decomposition approach which characterizes student achievement as a point in time. In this model, achievement is decomposed into variance lying among schools, within schools among classrooms, and within classrooms among students. All of the studies reviewed by Scheerens and Bosker (1997) used this approach. Rowan et al. found that between 12% and 23% of the variance of students' performance lies among classrooms for reading and 18–28% for math, findings similar to those of Scheerens and Bosker (1997). Next, they used a value-added model, which uses students' growth in achievement over the year and attempts to control for prior learning and other student background characteristics better than variance decomposition models. Rowan et al. found that the estimates of teachers' effects on reading (4–16%) and math (8–18%) declined, although they were still significant. This approach is similar to the one used by Nye et al. (2004). However, when Rowan et al. used HLM techniques that model students' growth more accurately, teachers accounted for 60–61% of students' growth in reading and 52–72% of students' growth in math.

Sanders and Rivers (1996), evaluated data from the Tennessee Value-Added Assessment System (TVAAS), which contains statewide data from the Tennessee Comprehensive Assessment Program Achievement Tests, on second through eighth grade students' achievement in the areas of mathematics, reading, and science. The purpose was to quantify the effects of teachers on students' achievement in mathematics in grades 3 through 5. In the analyses, teachers from two metropolitan areas (systems A and B) were grouped into quintiles based on their effectiveness in producing gains in mathematics among low-achieving students, holding second grade achievement constant (Q1 = lowest; Q5 = highest). Students with Q1 teachers were compared to students with Q5 teachers in both systems. Although complete and specific descriptions of the sample, data, measures, and analyses have not yet been published (see Kupermintz, Shepard, & Linn, 2001), the authors reported that in system A, students with Q1 teachers were at the 44th percentile in fifth grade; students with Q5 teachers were at the 96th percentile. In system B, students with Q1 teachers were at the 29th percentile in the fifth grade; students with Q5 teachers were at the 83rd percentile.

In summary, no matter how data are analyzed, teacher quality is significantly related to student academic outcomes. Even if the percentage of variance accounted for by teachers is relatively small, its impact on students' achievement is substantial (e.g., Nye et al., 2004). According to Darling-Hammond and Ball (1999) teachers' knowledge and skills affect all the core tasks of teaching and help students master the curriculum.

If teachers are to be the focus of assessment, however, the question becomes, "how do we define teacher quality?" One possible way of defining teacher quality is teacher knowledge. One might hypothesize that no matter how good the curriculum is, teachers who are not sufficiently knowledgeable about the world in general, the topic(s) they are teaching, and students, cannot help students learn material as well as teachers who are more knowledgeable. Shulman's (1986, 1987) model of teachers' knowledge suggests that teachers' knowledge consists of three components: subject matter knowledge (SMK), pedagogical content knowledge (PCK—How teachers represent and formulate knowledge to make it comprehensible to others), and general pedagogical knowledge (GPK—Knowledge of learners, knowledge of principles and techniques of classroom behavior and management, knowledge of the essential components of effective instruction, etc.). I add a fourth, teachers' general world knowledge (GWK). It may be that teacher quality is defined not only by SMK, PCK, and GPK but by their knowledge of the world/culture that surrounds them and their ability to communicate that knowledge to students. The remainder of this section focuses on evidence from the domains of reading and mathematics, and not reading alone, because of the relative paucity of data in the area of reading.

General World Knowledge

Using teacher certification test scores or college admissions scores, a number of researchers have evaluated the relationship between teachers' GWK (assuming such tests are a proxy for general world knowledge) and student educational outcomes. Greenwald, Hedges, and Laine (1996), in a review of the literature, found that teachers' ability, which they do not define, and students' achievement were strongly related. Ferguson (1991) evaluated the relationship between the Texas Examination of Current Administrators and Teachers (TECAT) scores, which measure reading, language, and vocabulary primarily, and student achievement. Average TECAT scores were strong predictors of the variation among districts' reading and math scores. Ferguson and Ladd (1996) found essentially the same results in Alabama among third and fourth grade students using teachers' college entrance ACT scores.

Ferguson and Brown (2000), using data from the 1986 administration of the TECAT and district-wide average math scores for grades 1, 3, 5, 7, 9, and 11, evaluated whether there was a relationship between teacher quality and student achievement. To do this, they identified districts in Texas in which teachers performed above or below the average on the TECAT (one standard deviation above or below district level means) and districts in which students performed above or below the average (by more than one-half a standard deviation) on standardized math and reading achievement tests, and categorized them into one of four categories: (a) Teachers with TECAT scores one standard deviation above the mean and students with high first and third grade math scores ($N = 37$); the numbers presented here represent districts; also, Ferguson and Brown (2000) point out that it is often very difficult to find districts where there is a mismatch between the quality of teachers and the quality of students; (b) TECAT scores one standard deviation above the mean and low first and third grade math scores ($N = 3$); (c) TECAT scores one standard deviation below the mean and low first and third grade math scores ($N = 25$); and (d) TECAT scores one standard deviation below the mean and high first and third grade math scores ($N = 4$). They reasoned that if skilled teachers are important and their impact accumulates over time, then teachers with unusually high or low average TECAT scores should influence students' scores over time, positively or negatively (respectively). They found that those districts that performed the best over the long run, regardless of whether students were above or below the mean in achievement, were those that had teachers with high TECAT scores. Indeed, the math scores of students in districts with high-quality teachers, regardless of the starting point of the students (high or low math scores) were comparable by the eleventh grade. The authors reported that the outcomes for reading were similar to the outcomes reported for math but they did not provide the data.

Subject Matter Knowledge

In this section, I will discuss the effects of teachers' SMK on student achievement, by skill domain.

Reading and Writing. Research has shown that many teachers' knowledge of speech sounds, their identity in words, the correspondence between sounds and symbols, concepts of language, and the presence of morphemic units in words is not typically well developed (McCutchen, Abbott, et al., 2002; McCutchen, Harry, et al., 2002; Moats, 1995; Moats & Lyon, 1996). In addition, Moats and Foorman (2003) found a significant albeit modest relationship between teachers' linguistic knowledge and third and fourth grade students' achievement in reading.

McCutchen and colleagues (McCutchen, Abbott, et al., 2002; McCutchen & Berninger, 1999) set up a teacher training program to help in-service kindergarten and first grade teachers develop the kinds of linguistic knowledge needed to help children learn how to read and write. The program consisted of (a) a 2-week summer institute that taught teachers the knowledge needed to teach reading (e.g., orthographic, phonological, morphological awareness) and writing skills (e.g., transcription and composing). All participating teachers were part of the experimental group; waitlisted teachers acted as the control group; (b) 3 one-day follow-up sessions in November, February, and May; and (c) regular visits to classrooms for consultation. The dependent variables were teachers' knowledge, as measured by a pretest and post-test given immediately before and after the summer institute, classroom practices, and student learning outcomes. Results indicated that experimental teachers' linguistic knowledge increased significantly from pretest to post-test but control group teachers' knowledge did not; experimental kindergarten teachers spent considerably more time on teaching the alphabetic principle; and both groups spent a considerable amount of time on orthography (primarily letter knowledge). There were no significant differences between the first grade experimental and control groups on the time spent on phonological or orthographic activities; however, experimental first grade teachers spent more time on explicit comprehension instruction.

In analyzing the effects of experimental condition on student outcomes, the researchers evaluated kindergarten and first grade students three times a year on phonological awareness, orthographic fluency, word reading, and listening comprehension. Among kindergarten students, the effect of experimental condition was significant only for orthographic fluency. Among first grade students, however, McCutchen, Abbott, et al. (2002) found that compared to children in the control group, children in the experimental group, based on an HLM analysis of growth curves, evidenced an increase of 36% in phonological awareness, 60% in reading comprehension, 29% in vocabulary, 37% in spelling, and 100% in orthographic fluency.

Mathematics. Zhou, Peverly, and Xin (2006) studied Chinese and American third grade teachers' knowledge of the fractions they teach in their classrooms using a 13-item test that assessed basic fraction concepts, computations, and word problems. The between group differences were highly significant. Across all 13 items, the Chinese teachers averaged 95% correct while the U.S. teachers averaged 32% correct, despite substantial differences in favor of U.S. teachers in years of education. Among the U.S. teachers ($N = 90$), 3 had a Ph.D., 57 had a masters degree, 28 had a bachelors degree, and 2 had an associates degree. Among the Chinese teachers ($N = 70$), 3 had a bachelors degree, 34 had an associates degree, and 33 had completed high school (with a focus on teacher training). Moreover, there was no effect of teaching experience for either the Chinese or the U.S. teachers.

Ma (1999) compared American and Chinese elementary school teachers' knowledge of mathematics (SMK) in four areas: subtraction with regrouping, multidigit multiplication, division by fractions, and the relationship between perimeter and area. She found that Chinese teachers had a significantly deeper understanding of these concepts than American teachers. Although Ma (1999) and Zhou et al. (2006) did not evaluate the relationship of teachers' knowledge to student performance, the implication is that teachers' knowledge may be one reason for Chinese students' superior performance, compared to U.S. students, on international tests of mathematics knowledge.

Unfortunately, there is very little research on the relationship of teachers' knowledge to students' achievement in mathematics. In the country of Belize, Mullens, Murnane, and Willett (1996) evaluated the relationship between three possible indicators of teachers' effectiveness—whether or not teachers had completed a three-year pedagogical program, whether they had completed high school, and whether their mathematics knowledge, as measured by their score on the primary-school-leaving examination, taken by all students who wanted to go to high school, was related to third grade students' performance on a test of basic and advanced mathematics concepts. None of the three teacher variables was related to students' *basic concept* knowledge. For *advanced concepts*, however, teachers' mathematics knowledge was related to students' math performance but teachers' pedagogic training was not. Completion of high school was important only if the teacher had not taken the math exam. For similar results from rural Brazil, see Harbison and Hanushek (1992).

Hill, Rowan, and Ball (2005) evaluated the relationship of first and third grade teachers' knowledge of the mathematics they taught to student achievement in math. They found that teachers' knowledge was not correlated with the number of mathematics methods and content courses they had, whether or not they were certified, or years of experience. The only significant predictors for both, grades were teachers' knowledge, students' initial math scores, and students' SES.

Before leaving this section, the reader should note that some researchers have used proxies for teachers' mathematics knowledge such as the number of mathematics courses taken as an undergraduate, in an attempt to evaluate the relationship between teachers' knowledge and student performance. Although the number of math courses sometimes makes a difference, their contribution to student outcomes is often small (Begle, 1979; cited in Ball, Lubienski, & Mewborn, 2001; Monk, 1994). Research also indicates, however, that the number of mathematics courses does not necessary equal useable knowledge. Ball and colleagues (Ball, 1990; Ball et al., 2001) found that elementary and secondary teachers (the latter are typically math majors) often have very poor mathematical knowledge for teaching (i.e., PCK, which is discussed in the next section). That is, they may get the correct answers but they often have great difficulty explaining the meaning of their answers to others.

Pedagogical Content Knowledge

Reading/Writing. For kindergarten students, McCutchen, Abbott et al. (2002) found (a) teachers use of phonological awareness strategies in the classroom was significantly related to students' growth in phonological awareness and end of the year word reading; and (b) teachers emphasis on orthographic activities was significantly related to student growth in alphabetic fluency (alphabet letter production).

Mathematics. Stigler and Hiebert (1999) focused on how teachers' mathematical knowledge was incorporated in the classroom. They compared the instructional practices of teachers in eighth grade mathematics classrooms in Japan, Germany, and the United States. They found that the Japanese teachers presented the most conceptually and procedurally demanding problems, and they allowed their students a reasonable measure of freedom in inventing their own solution procedures. In comparison, the German teachers were more concerned with technique, that is, the rationale for and the precise execution of the procedures used to solve problems. The U.S. teachers' course content was the weakest of the three countries and they placed more of an emphasis than did teachers in the other countries on the memorization and practice of problem-solving procedures.

Zhou et al. (2006) found U.S. and Chinese teachers were comparable in their understanding of the difficulties their students would encounter in learning, and in how they would address those difficulties. The Chinese teachers were superior to the American teachers in three areas: identifying which concepts to include in instruction, teachers' understanding of students' instruction-relevant knowledge, and how teachers could ensure students' thorough understanding of the concepts presented in instruction.

In an earlier cross-national study, Zhou and Peverly (2004) found that an in-school mentoring program in China called Teaching-Regulated Ability (TRA) had a very positive effect on PCK. Specifically, Zhou and Peverly (2004) examined the effects of socioeconomic status (rural = low SES; urban = average SES) and quality of instruction (experimental—teachers who were trained in TRA; traditional—more of an emphasis on computation and memorization) on first, third, and fifth grade Chinese students' understanding of distance, time, and speed. These results were compared to those of a sample of average SES students from the U.S. taken from a previous study by Zhou, Peverly, Boehm, and Chongde (2000).

In TRA, teachers are trained by experts from Beijing Normal University in TRA theory and by expert teachers, selected from schools in the same school district to (a) construct lesson plans, (b) evaluate their own teaching, (c) modify their activities based on their own self-evaluations and the evaluations of BNU experts and expert teachers, and (d) develop students' thinking using Lin's "Five Traits of Thinking" model (Lin, 1992). The latter includes instruction that promotes the following: depth (analysis and synthesis of relationships between number and quantity), flexibility (divergent thinking), creativity (creating unique solutions to existing problems), self-criticism (evaluating arguments and proofs), and fluency (speed and accuracy in using the most efficient problem solutions). The results indicated that students in the urban Chinese schools performed better than those in the rural traditional schools but that there were no significant differences between the students in the urban and rural experimental schools. Both the urban and rural experimental Chinese students performed better than the U.S. students. There were no significant differences between the rural Chinese students in traditional schools and the U.S. students.

General Pedagogical Knowledge

Brophy and Good's (1986) review of the literature suggests that it is not instructional time that matters per se, but what teachers do during that time. In this regard, Rosenshine (1995; Rosenshine & Stevens, 1986), based on a review of the literature on direct instruction or teacher-directed instruction (not to be confused with Direct Instruction, i.e., Distar) outlined the instructional variables that separate teachers who consistently produced better academic outcomes from those who do not. Good teachers more consistently do the following: (a) Review previous learning and homework; (b) present new concepts by stating the lesson's goals, teaching in increments, modeling, providing instructions, descriptions, and explanations that are clear and detailed, using examples, and checking for understanding; (c) provide a high level of guided and independent practice with feedback and re-teaching if necessary; and (d) review material weekly and monthly.

Berliner's (1994; see also Hogan, Rabinowitz, & Craven, 2003) analysis of the literature yielded several propositions with regard to the behaviors of expert teachers in classrooms (see Berhart, 1987; Calderhead, 1983; Carter, Cushing, Sabers, Stein, & Berliner, 1988; Carter, Sabers, Cushing, Pinnegar, & Berliner, 1987; Leinhardt & Greeno, 1986; Leinhardt, Putnam, Stein, & Baxter, 1991; Leinhardt & Smith, 1985). Expert teachers (a) rapidly recognize and represent problems encountered in classrooms in qualitatively different ways than novices, (b) are more sensitive to task demands and social situations when solving problems (i.e., novices cannot always make sense of what they experience and solve problems more slowly), (c) apply repetitive operations needed to accomplish their goals automatically, and (d) are more opportunistic and flexible in their teaching than novices.

Summary

Research clearly indicates that teachers matter and some evidence indicates that teacher quality, as defined by GWK, SMK, PCK, and GPK, is related to better academic outcomes. Although there is a need for a great deal more research in each of these areas, the evidence indicates that teachers, like curricula, should be considered as a variable that significantly effects students' learning.

■ School-Based Assessment

Despite all of the differences between CBM and most forms of CBA (CBA-ID being the notable exception) and other forms of assessment (norm-based, criterion-based, portfolios, etc.), there is one characteristic they all have in common—the focus of the assessment is typically the child, not the curriculum or the teacher. Since evidence indicates that teacher skill and curriculum quality substantially affect students' educational outcomes, it does not make sense to evaluate children outside of the context of teachers and curricula.

SBA and CBA-ID (or IA), in contrast, assume that learning is contextual (Bransford, 1979; Bransford, Brown, & Cocking, 1999; Gravois & Gickling, 2008; Rosenfield, 2008) and that many variables can have an impact on students' performance in classrooms: The quality of the curriculum, the quality of the teacher, and the skills and competencies of the child. Unlike CBA-ID, however, SBA argues that curricula and teachers should be assessed independently of the child.

SBA also assumes, like RTI, that a child should not be referred for a special education evaluation unless other variables have been ruled out. Thus, monitoring students' progress in SBA would proceed somewhat differently within the RTI framework. Although children's progress would be monitored continually, school districts would also have the responsibility of monitoring the quality of their curricula and teachers, to help prevent academic difficulties. SBA has six potential components: selecting evidence-based curricula, evaluating teachers, monitoring students' progress, modifications in the regular classroom, psychoeducational assessment, and determining placement. Again, reading is used as an example.

Selecting Evidence-based Curricula. Rather than determining whether an existing curriculum is providing a "generally nurturing instructional environment" through an evaluation of children's progress in the curriculum, districts would determine whether the elementary school reading curriculum is evidenced-based. That is, does it have a strong, consistent emphasis on the phonological, orthographic, and morphological skills needed to learn how to read words accurately and quickly and on language and comprehension strategies (e.g., teaching students how to generate inferences) needed to comprehend effectively (Otaiba, Kosanovich-Grek, Torgesen, Hassler, & Wahl, 2005). As discussed previously, a number of reading programs have been tested over the years and proven to be more effective than alternatives (e.g., whole language curricula) in promoting reading growth among students. In this view, if the curriculum is not supported by research, the curriculum would be eliminated and the district would replace it with one that is research based. All of this should be done *prior* to monitoring students' progress in the curriculum, the first step in RTI and CBA/CBM.

Evaluating Teachers. Since research indicates that student outcomes are strongly influenced by teachers' skill in the classroom (Ferguson & Brown, 2000; Rowan et al., 2002; Sanders & Rivers, 1996), which in turn seems to be related to teachers' GWK (Greenwald et al., 1996; Rowan et al., 2002), SMK (McCutchen & Berninger, 1999; Zhou et al., 2006), PCK (McCutchen, Abbott, et al., 2002; Stigler & Hiebert, 1999), and GPK (Rosenshine, 1995; Rosenshine & Stevens, 1986), the second component would focus on teacher quality. This component would be carried out in four phases. First, all teachers would be monitored to determine which teachers consistently produce better student outcomes than others (controlling of course for student and other kinds of variables that could vary among classrooms) and whether the students of the poorest performing teachers are falling below a predetermined cut-off for poor student performance. This could be done by applying the progress monitoring procedures of RTI school-wide or through the use of the school-wide or statewide standardized testing programs used by schools and states to measure students' educational progress.

Second, for teachers who consistently fall below expectation, teachers' implementation of the curriculum would be evaluated. Research indicates that not all teachers implement all of the components of the curriculum, or implement them well, which can have a negative impact on student outcomes (Wang, Peverly, & Randolph, 1984). The evaluation of teachers' implementation would be carried out by expert teachers or other school personnel. The purpose would be to improve implementation integrity, which would be done in Phase III.

Phase III would focus on providing mandatory help for struggling teachers. This could be done in several ways. Districts could establish mentoring programs for teachers whose skills are not found to be sufficient. Mentoring would provide them with the support they need to deal with the stressors of the classroom and to help them learn the skills they need to teach reading (or any other content) effectively. The mentoring program should not bear any resemblance to the typical type of in-service education provided in schools, the one or two day workshop. These are largely ineffective (Fullan, 2001), since they (a) do not focus sufficiently on teacher performance, (b) are not based in a model or theory of teacher development, (c) typically do not include any kind of follow-up to in-service activities, and (d) often include activities that teachers' perceive as irrelevant (Miller & Ellsworth, 1985). In my view, the mentoring program should be similar to Teacher Regulated Ability (TRA), the program used in China to support math teachers (discussed earlier), or the in-service education model used by McCutchen and Berninger (1999) to update teachers on recent developments in the prevention and remediation of learning difficulties.

Another approach would to establish professional learning communities among teachers (Fullan, 2001). They have the advantage of not being limited in time and they are an active and integral part of teachers' daily lives in schools. One approach is "lesson study," a process used by Japanese teachers to develop and critically evaluate their own teaching (Fernandez, 2002; Fernandez, Cannon, & Chokshi, 2003; Fernandez, & Chokshi, 2002). The practice of lesson study begins with a goal (e.g., student transfer of knowledge) and a content area (e.g., the mapping of students' understanding of discrete representations of fractions, with continuous representations). The goals teachers establish are based on the outcomes they want students to achieve and their perceptions of students' weaknesses and how these might prevent students from achieving the outcomes. Then teachers develop a detailed lesson plan to achieve the goal, one of the members of the group teaches the lesson to his/her class and is observed by the other teachers, and the teachers reassemble to discuss their observations. They then either revise and re-teach the lesson (the most common outcome), or go on to another lesson plan if they are satisfied with the outcome.

A final possibility is consultee-centered consultation (e.g., Rosenfield, 1987, 2008; Rosenfield & Gravois, 1996). As discussed previously, Rosenfield and colleagues have developed IC-Teams for the purpose of improving student and staff performance. When teachers request assistance because of problems with students' classroom performance, IC-Team members, who are trained in school change, problem solving and communication skills, assessment, and instructional interventions, help teachers assess students' difficulties, design evidence-based interventions, and monitor students' responsiveness. Research indicates that IC-Teams have been effective in reducing referrals to and placements in special education (Gravois & Rosenfield, 2002, 2006).

Monitoring Student Progress: The third component of SBA, which corresponds to the first component of RTI, is monitoring students' progress for the purpose of identifying students who are doing poorly. In monitoring the development of students' reading skills in the early elementary grades, both word fluency and comprehension should be evaluated, as is done in some forms of CBA. Word fluency is necessary (but not sufficient) for skilled comprehension, as it is typically correlated quite highly with comprehension (approximately 0.7). However, there are always outliers, and in most situations you will find students who read words quickly with poor comprehension and those who read words slowly with good comprehension (Cramer & Rosenfield, 2008; Nation, 2005).

The assessment of comprehension should be theoretically based. One suggestion is to create questions that are based in Kintsch's (1998) construction-integration model of comprehension. There are two ways to do this: (a) Use text implicit (inference) and text explicit (memory) questions to measure the situation model and the text base, respectively (these can be multiple choice questions; see Peverly, Brobst, Graham, & Shaw, 2003); or (b) construct questions that measure Kintsch's macrorules: main idea questions that test information stated directly in text, main idea questions that require students to construct inferences to answer them correctly, and superordination questions that test students ability to classify information. Any kind of question that asks students to generate an inference is preferable, since inference questions covary more strongly with individual difference variables such as reading ability and background knowledge, than memory questions do (Peverly et al., 2003).

Modifications in the Regular Classroom. If the classroom reading curriculum is not sufficient for some children, the fourth component would focus on using CBA to develop a more detailed portrait of the child's deficits in reading and the reasons for those deficits. Then, in-class instructional modifications implemented by the teacher, a teacher' assistant, or school-based consultant would be tested to see whether the curriculum can be changed to increase students' growth in reading in the regular classroom. As indicated by Fuchs and Fuchs (2006), the modifications should be more intense than regular instruction. By intense they mean, for example, instruction that is more explicit and systematic and more frequent and longer in duration.

Individual Psychoeducational Assessment: The fifth component would consist of a psychoeducational evaluation for those children who still do not respond sufficiently to the modifications implemented in component four (Berninger, 2006; Fiorello, Hale, & Snyder, 2006; Fletcher et al., 2005). The purpose would be to identify the reason or reasons not identified in previous steps—cognitive, linguistic, behavioral, and/or emotional variables—that might be causing or contributing to a child's difficulty in reading.

Determining Placement. The results of a psychoeducational assessment could lead to further modifications in the regular classroom, and to an assessment of their efficacy. If the modifications work, the child can remain in the regular classroom. If they do not, the child should be placed in special education or other more intensive interventions.

■ Summary

In this chapter, I have reviewed research on curriculum and teacher quality to argue that both can have a substantial impact on student performance. On the basis of that review I proposed an assessment system called SBA that would focus concurrently on all three sources of potential variance to students' academic outcomes: students, teachers, and curricula. Schools would have the responsibility of monitoring the quality of their curricula and teachers, and the progress of their students. Schools would make changes or modifications in curricula as needed, provide ongoing support for teachers through mentoring programs and professional development communities, and help students by providing them with the modifications and assistance they need to perform well academically.

■ References

Adams, M. J. (1990). *Beginning to read*. Cambridge, MA, MIT Press.

Ball, D. L. (1990). The mathematical understandings that prospective teachers bring to teacher education. *The Elementary School Journal, 90*, 449–466.

Ball, D. L., Lubienski, S., & Mewborn, D. (2001). Research on teaching mathematics: The unsolved problem of teachers' mathematical knowledge. In V. Richardson (Ed.), *Handbook of research on teaching* (4th ed., pp. 433–456). New York, Macmillan.

Begle, E. G. (1979). *Critical variables in mathematics education: Findings from a survey of the empirical literature*. Washington, DC, Mathematical Association of American and National Council of Teachers of Mathematics.

Berhart, D. C. (1987). Ways of thinking about students and classrooms by more and less experienced teachers. In J. Calderhead (Ed.), *Exploring teachers' thinking* (pp. 60–83). London, Cassell Educational Limited.

Berliner, D. C. (1994). Expertise: The wonder of exemplary performances. In J. N. Mangieri and C. C. Block (Eds.), *Creating powerful thinking in teachers and students* (pp. 161–186). Ft. Worth, TX, Holt, Rinehart & Winston.

Berninger, V. W. (1998). *Process Assessment of the Learner (PAL). Guides for intervention: Reading and writing.* San Antonio, TX, Harcourt/PsyCorp.

Berninger, V. W. (2006). Research supported ideas for implementing reauthorized IDEA with intelligent professional psychological services. *Psychology in the Schools, 43,* 781–796.

Berninger, V. W. (2007). *Process assessment of the Learner II User's guide.* San Antonio, TX, Harcourt/PsyCorp.

Berninger, V. W., Abbott, R., Vermeulen, K., Ogier, S., Brooksher, R., Zook, D., & Lemos, Z. (2002). Comprehension of faster and slower responders to early intervention in reading: Differentiating features of the language profiles. *Learning Disability Quarterly, 25,* 59–76.

Blankenship, C. S. (1985). Using curriculum-based assessment data to make instructional management decisions. *Exceptional Children, 52,* 233–238.

Bond, G. L., & Dykstra, R. (1967). The cooperative research program in first-grade reading instruction. *Reading Research Quarterly, 2,* 5–142.

Bransford, J. D. (1979). *Human cognition: Learning, remembering and understanding.* Belmont, CA, Wadsworth.

Bransford, J. D., Brown, A. L., & Cocking, K. (1999). *How people learn: Bridging research and practice.* Washington, DC, National Academy Press.

Brophy, J. E., & Good, T. (1986). Teacher behavior and student achievement. In M. C. Wittrock (Ed.), *Handbook of research on teaching* (3rd ed., pp. 328–375). New York, Macmillan.

Calderhead, J. (1983, April). *Research into teachers' and student teachers' cognitions: Exploring the nature of classroom practice.* Paper presented at the annual meeting of the American Educational Research Association, Montreal, Canada.

Carter, K., Cushing, K., Sabers, D., Stein, P., & Berliner, D. (1988). Expert-novice differences in perceiving and processing visual classroom stimuli. *Journal of Teacher Education, 19,* 25–31.

Carter, K., Sabers, D., Cushing, K., Pinnegar, S., & Berliner, D. (1987). Processing and using information about students: A study of expert, novice and postulant teachers. *Teaching and Teacher Education, 3,* 147–157.

Chall, J. S. (1967). *Learning to read: The great debate.* New York, McGraw-Hill.

Chall, J. S. (1983). *Learning to read: The great debate* (Updated ed.). New York, McGraw-Hill.

Cramer, K., & Rosenfield, S. (2008). Effect of degree of challenge on reading performance. *Reading and Writing Quarterly, 24,* 1–19.

Darling-Hammond, L., & Ball, D. (1999). *Teaching for high standards: What policymakers need to know and be able to do.* Philadelphia, CPRE, National Commission on Teaching for America's Future.

Deno, S. L. (1985). Curriculum-based measurement: The emerging alternative. *Exceptional Children, 52,* 219–232.

Ehri, L. C., Nunes, S., Stahl, S., & Willows, D. (2001). Systematic phonics instruction helps students learn to read: Evidence from the National Reading Panel's meta-analysis. *Review of Educational Research, 71,* 393–447.

Ferguson, R. F. (1991). Paying for public education: New evidence on how and why money matters. *Harvard Journal on Legislation, 28,* 465–498.

Ferguson, R. F., & Brown, J. (2000). Certification test scores, teacher quality, and student achievement. In D. W. Grissmer & J. M. Ross (Eds.), *Analytic issues in the assessment of student achievement* (pp. 133–156). Washington, DC, U.S. Department of Education.

Ferguson, R. F., & Ladd, H. F. (1996). How and why money matters: An analysis of Alabama schools. In H. F. Ladd (Ed.), *Holding schools accountable: Performance based reform in education* (pp. 265–298). Washington, DC, Brookings Institution Press.

Fernandez, C. (2002). Learning from Japanese approaches to professional development: The case of lesson study. *Journal of Teacher Education, 53,* 393–405.

Fernandez, C., Cannon, J., & Chokshi, S. (2003). A US-Japan lesson study collaboration reveals critical lenses for examining practice. *Teaching and Teacher Education, 19,* 171–185.

Fernandez, C., & Chokshi, S. (2002). A practical guide to translating lesson study for a U.S. setting. *Phi Delta Kappan, 84,* 128–134.

Fiorello, C. A., Hale, J. B., & Snyder, L. E. (2006). Cognitive hypothesis testing and response to intervention for children with reading problems. *Psychology in the Schools, 43,* 835–853.

Fletcher, J. M., Francis, D. J., Morris, R. D., & Lyon, G. R. (2005). Evidence-based assessment of learning disabilities in children and adolescents. *Journal of Clinical Child and Adolescent Psychology, 34,* 506–522.

Fletcher, J. M., Shaywitz, E. E., Shankweiler, D. P., Katz, L., Liberman, I. Y., Steubing, K. K., Francis, D. J., Fowler, A. E., & Shaywitz, B. A. (1994). Cognitive profiles of reading disability: Comparisons of discrepancy and low achievement definitions. *Journal of Educational Psychology, 86,* 6–23.

Foorman, B. R. (1995). Research on "The Great Debate": Code-oriented versus whole language approaches to reading instruction. *School Psychology Review, 24,* 376–392.

Foorman, B. R., Francis, D. J., Fletcher, J. M., & Lynn, A. (1996). Relation of phonological and orthographic processing to early reading: Comparing two approaches to regression-based, reading-level matched designs. *Journal of Educational Psychology, 88,* 619–652.

Foorman, B. R., Francis, D. J., Fletcher, J. M., Schatschneider, C., & Mehta, P. (1998). The role of instruction in learning to read: Preventing reading failure in at-risk children. *Journal of Educational Psychology, 90,* 37–55.

Fuchs, D., & Fuchs, L. S. (2006). Introduction to response to intervention: What, why, and how valid is it? *Reading Research Quarterly, 41,* 93–99.

Fuchs, L. S., & Vaughn, S. R. (2005). Response to intervention as a framework for the identification of learning disabilities, *NASP Communique, 34*, pp. 1, 4–6.

Fullan, M. G. (2001). *The new meaning of educational change* (3rd ed.). New York, Teachers College Press.

Gickling, E. E., & Rosenfield, S. (1995). Best practices in curriculum-based assessment. In A. Thomas and J. Grimes (Eds.), *Best practices in school psychology III* (pp. 587–595). Washington, DC, National Association of School Psychologists.

Gickling, E. E., & Thompson, V. P. (1985). A personal view of curriculum-based assessment. *Exceptional Children, 52*, 205–218.

Gravois, T. A., & Gickling, E. E. (2002). Best practices in curriculum-based assessment. In A. Thomas and J. Grimes (Eds.), *Best practices in school psychology IV* (pp. 885–898). Washington, DC, National Association of School Psychologists.

Gravois, T. A., & Gickling, E. E. (2008). Best practices in instructional assessment. In A. Thomas & J. Grimes (Eds.), *Best practices in school psychology V* (pp. 503–518). Washington, DC, National Association of School Psychologists.

Gravois, T. A., & Rosenfield, S. A. (2002). A multidimensional framework for evaluation of instructional consultation teams. *Journal of Applied School Psychology, 19*, 5–29.

Gravois, T. A., & Rosenfield, S. A. (2006). Impact of instructional consultation teams on the disproportionate referral and placement of minority students in special education. *Remedial and Special Education, 27*, 42–52.

Greenwald, R., Hedges, L. V., & Laine, R. D. (1996). The effect of school resources on school achievement. *Review of Educational Research, 66*, 397–409.

Hanushek, E. A. (1996). A more complete picture of school resource policies. *Review of Educational Research, 66*, 411–416.

Harbison, R. W., & Hanushek, E. A. (1992). *Educational performance of the poor: Lessons from rural northeast Brazil.* New York, Oxford University Press.

Hill, H. C., Rowan, B., & Ball, D. L. (2005). Effects of teachers' mathematical knowledge for teaching on student achievement. *American Educational Research Journal, 42*, 371–406.

Hintz, J. M., Christ, T. J., & Methe, S. A. (2006). Curriculum-based assessment. *Psychology in the Schools, 43*, 45–56.

Hogan, T., Rabinowitz, M., & Craven, J. A. (2003). Representation in teaching: Inferences from research of expert and novice teachers. *Educational Psychologist, 38*, 235–247.

Howell, K. W., Fox, S. L., & Morehead, M. K. (1993). *Curriculum-based evaluation: Teaching and decision making* (2nd ed.). Pacific Grove, CA, Brooks/Cole.

Howell, K. W., Kurns, S., & Antil, A. (2002). Best practices in curriculum-based evaluation. In A. Thomas & J. Grimes (Eds.), *Best practices in school psychology IV* (pp. 753–771). Washington, DC, National Association of School Psychologists.

Howell, K. W., & Nolet, V. (2000). *Curriculum-based evaluation: Teaching and decision-making* (3rd ed.). Belmont, CA, Wadsworth.

Idol, L., Nevin, A., & Paolucci-Whitcomb, P. (1999). *Models of curriculum-based assessment: A blueprint for learning.* Austin, TX, Pro Ed.

Kintsch, W. (1998). *Comprehension: A paradigm for cognition.* Cambridge, Cambridge University Press.

Kupermintz, H., Shepard, L., & Linn, R. (2001, April). *Teacher effects as a measure of teacher effectiveness: Construct validity considerations in TVAAS (Tennessee Value Added Assessment System).* Paper presented in D. Koretz (Chair), New Work on the Evaluation of High-Stakes Testing Programs. Symposium at the National Council on Measurement in Education (NCME) Annual Meeting, Seattle, WA.

Leinhardt, G., & Greeno, J. G. (1986). The cognitive skill of teaching. *Journal of Educational Psychology, 78,* 75–95.

Leinhardt, G., Putnam, R. T., Stein, M. K., & Baxter, J. (1991). Where subject knowledge matters. In J. Brophy (Ed.), *Advances in research on teaching: Vol. II. Teachers' knowledge of subject matter as it relates to their teaching practice* (pp. 87–114). Greenwich, CT, JAI Press Inc.

Leinhardt, G., & Smith, D. A. (1985). Expertise in mathematics instruction: Subject matter knowledge. *Journal of Educational Psychology, 77,* 247–271.

Lin, C. (1992). *Xuexi yu fazhan* [Learning and developing]. Beijing Education Publisher.

Lyon, G. R. (1995). Toward a definition of dyslexia. *Annals of Dyslexia, 45,* 3–27.

Ma, L.-P. (1999). *Knowing and teaching mathematics: Teachers' understanding of fundamental mathematics in China and the United States.* NJ, Lawrence Erlbaum Associates.

McCutchen, D., Abbott, R. D., Green, L. B., Beretvas, N., Cox, S., Potter, N. S., Quiroga, T., & Gray, A. L. (2002). Beginning literacy: Links among teacher knowledge, teacher practice, and student learning. *Journal of Learning Disabilities, 35,* 69–86.

McCutchen, D., & Berninger, V. W. (1999). Those who know, teach well: Helping teachers master literacy-related subject-matter knowledge. *Learning Disabilities Research and Practice, 14,* 215–226.

McCutchen, D., Harry, D. R., Cunningham, A. E., Cox, S., Sidman, S., & Covill, A. E. (2002). Reading teachers' knowledge of children's literature and English phonology. *Annals of Dyslexia, 52,* 207–228.

Miller, J. W., & Ellsworth, R. (1985). The evaluation of a two-year program to improve teacher effectiveness in reading instruction. *The Elementary School Journal, 85,* 485–495.

Mitchell, K. J., Robinson, D. Z., Plake, B. S., & Knowles, K. T. (Eds.) (2001). *Testing teacher candidates: The role of licensure tests in improving teacher quality.* Washington, DC, National Academy Press.

Moats, L. C. (1995). Knowledge about the structure of the language: The missing foundation in teacher education, *Annals of Dyslexia, 44,* 81–102.

Moats, L. C., & Foorman, B. R. (2003). Measuring teachers' content knowledge of language and reading. *Annals of Dyslexia, 53,* 23–45.

Moats, L. C., & Lyon, G. R. (1996). Wanted: Teachers with knowledge of language. *Topics in Language Disorders, 16,* 73–81.

Monk, D. H. (1994). Subject area preparation of secondary mathematics and science teachers and student achievement. *Economics of Education Review, 40,* 139–157.

Mullens, J. E., Murnane, R. J., & Willet, J. B. (1996). The contribution of training and subject matter knowledge to teaching effectiveness: A multilevel analysis of longitudinal evidence from Belize. *Comparative Education Review, 40,* 139–157.

Nation, K. (2005). Children's reading comprehension difficulties. In M. J. Snowling & C. Hulme (Eds.), *The science of reading* (pp. 248–265). Malden, MA, Blackwell Publishing.

National Reading Panel. (2000). *Teaching children to read: An evidence-based assessment of the scientific literature on reading and its implications for reading instruction.* Washington, DC, National Institute for Child Health and Human Development.

Nye, B., Konstantopoulos, S., & Hedges, L. V. (2004). How large are teacher effects? *Educational Evaluation and Policy Analysis, 26,* 217–236.

Otaiba, S., Kosanovich-Grek, M. L., Torgesen, J. K., Hassler, L., & Wahl, M. (2005). Reviewing core kindergarten and first-grade reading program in light of No Child Left Behind: An exploratory study. *Reading and Writing Quarterly, 21,* 377–400.

Perfetti, C. A. (1985). *Reading ability.* New York, Oxford University Press.

Peverly, S. T. (2004, August). *Evolution of curriculum-based measurement (CBM) to instruction-based assessment (IBA): Rethinking identification and prevention of learning disability.* Symposium presented at the annual meeting of the American Psychological Association, Honolulu, Hawaii.

Peverly, S. T., Brobst, K., Graham, M., & Shaw, R. (2003). College adults are not good at self-regulation: A study on the relationship of self-regulation, note-taking, and test-taking. *Journal of Educational Psychology, 95,* 335–346.

Peverly, S. T., & Kitzen, K. R. (1998). Curriculum-based assessment of reading skills: Considerations and caveats for school psychologists. *Psychology in the Schools, 35,* 29–47.

Rosenfield, S. A. (1987). *Instructional consultation.* Hillsdale, NJ, Lawrence Erlbaum Associates.

Rosenfield, S. A. (2008). Best practices in instructional consultation. In A. Thomas & J. Grimes (Eds.), *Best practices in school psychology IV* (Vol. 1, pp. 1645–1660). Bethesda, MD, National Association of School Psychologists.

Rosenfield, S. A., & Gravois, T. A. (1996). *Instructional consultation teams.* New York, The Guilford Press.

Rosenshine, B. (1995). Advances in research on instruction. *Journal of Educational Research*, *88*, 262–268.

Rosenshine, B., & Stevens, R. (1986). Teaching functions. In M. C. Wittrock (Ed.), *The handbook of research on teaching* (pp. 376–391). New York, Macmillan.

Rowan, B., Correnti, R., & Miller, R. J. (2002). What large-scale, survey research tells us about teacher effects on student achievement: Insights from the *Prospects* study of elementary schools. *Teachers College Record*, *104*, 1525–1567.

Sanders, W. L., & Rivers, J. C. (1996). *Cumulative and residual effects of teachers on future student academic achievement*. Unpublished manuscript, University of Tennessee Value-Added Research and Assessment Center.

Scheerens, J., & Bosker, R. (1997). *The foundations of educational effectiveness*. New York, Pergamon.

Shapiro, E. S. (1987). *Behavioral assessment in school psychology*. Hillsdale, NJ, Lawrence Erlbaum Associates.

Shapiro, E. S. (1989). *Academic skills problems: Direct assessment and intervention*. New York, The Guilford Press.

Shapiro, E. S. (1990). An integrated model for curriculum-based assessment. *School Psychology Review*, *19*, 331–349.

Shapiro, E. S. (2004). *Academic skills problems: Direct assessment and intervention* (3rd ed.). New York, The Guilford Press.

Shaywitz, S. E., Fletcher, J. M., & Shaywitz, B. A. (1994). Issues in the definition and classification of attention deficit disorder. *Topics in Language Disabilities*, *14*, 1–25.

Shinn, M. (2002). Best practices in curriculum-based measurement in a problem solving model. In A. Thomas & J. Grimes (Eds.), *Best practices in school psychology IV* (pp. 671–697). Washington, DC, National Association of School Psychologists.

Shulman, L. S. (1986). Those who understand: Knowledge growth in teaching. *Educational Researcher*, *15*, 4–14.

Shulman, L. S. (1987). Knowledge and teaching: Foundations of the new reform. *Harvard Educational Review*, *57*, 1–22.

Slavin, R. E. (2008). What works? Issues in synthesizing educational program evaluations. *Educational Researcher*, *37*, 5–14.

Stanovich, K. E. (1986). Matthew effects in reading: Some consequences of individual differences in the acquisition of literacy. *Reading Research Quarterly*, *21*, 360–406.

Stanovich, K. E., & Siegel, L. S. (1994). Phenotypic performance profile of children with reading disabilities: A regression-based test of the phonological-core variable-difference model. *Journal of Educational Psychology*, *86*, 24–53.

Stigler, J. W., & Hiebert, J. (1999). *The teaching gap: Best ideas from the world's teachers for improving education in the classroom*. New York, The Free Press.

Stuebing, K. K., Fletcher, J. M., LeDoux, J. M., Lyon, G. R., Shaywitz, S. E., & Shaywitz, B. A. (2002). Validity of discrepancy classifications of reading disabilities: A meta-analysis. *American Educational Research Journal, 39,* 469–518.

Vellutino, F. R., Fletcher, J. M., Snowling, M. J., & Scanlon, D. M. (2004). Specific reading disability (dyslexia): What have we learned in the past four decades? *Journal of Child Psychology and Psychiatry, 45,* 2–40.

Vellutino, F. R., Scanlon, D. M., & Jaccard, J. (2003). Toward distinguishing between cognitive and experiential deficits as primary sources of difficulty in learning to read: A two year follow-up of difficult remediate and readily remediate poor readers. In B. R. Foorman (Ed.), *Preventing and remediating reading difficulties: Bringing science to scale* (pp. 73–120). Baltimore, York.

Vellutino, F. R., Scanlon, D. M., Sipay, E. R., Small, S. G., Pratt, A., Chen, R., & Denckla, M. B. (1996). Cognitive profiles of difficult-to-remediate and readily remediated poor readers: Early intervention as a vehicle for distinguishing between cognitive and experiential deficits as basic causes of specific reading disability. *Journal of Educational Psychology, 88,* 601–638.

Vellutino, F. R., Scanlon, D. M., & Tanzman, M. S. (1998). The case for early intervention in diagnosing specific learning disability. *Journal of School Psychology, 36,* 367–397.

Wang, M. C., Peverly, S. T., & Randolph, R. F. (1984). An investigation of the implementation and effects of a full-time mainstreaming program. *Journal of Special and Remedial Education, 5,* 21–32.

Wechsler, D. (1974). *Wechsler Intelligence Scale for Children-Revised.* New York, Psychological Corporation.

Woodcock, R. W. (1987). *Woodcock Reading Mastery Tests-Revised.* Circle Pines, MN, American Guidance Services.

Zhou, Z., Peverly, S. Boehm, A., & Chongde, L. (2000). American and Chinese children's understanding of distance, time, and speed interrelations. *Cognitive Development, 15,* 215–240.

Zhou, Z., & Peverly, S. T. (2004). Within- and across cultural variations in children's understanding of distance, time, and speed interrelations: A follow-up study. *Journal of Genetic Psychology, 165,* 5–27.

Zhou, Z., Peverly, S. T., & Xin, T. (2006). Knowing and teaching fractions: A cross-cultural study of American and Chinese mathematics teachers. *Contemporary Educational Psychology, 31,* 438–457.

STEP 6

IN IMPLEMENTATION: PROFESSIONAL DEVELOPMENT OF TEACHERS AND PSYCHOLOGISTS TO IMPLEMENT RESEARCH INTO PRACTICE

■ Introduction to Step 6

In this final step, we actually come back to the beginning point, that of professional preparation and continuing professional development, critical to the process of knowing both what current research knowledge is and how to translate it into educational practice. In this section, chapters focus on two professions for whom knowledge in this domain is critical: teachers and school psychologists.

Malatesha Joshi, who has been a leader in evidence-based practices in preservice education of teachers, and colleagues Emily Binks, Marty Hougen, Emily Dean, Lori Graham and Dennie Smith report, in the first chapter in this section, the results of empirical surveys of knowledge of university instructors in teacher education programs (most of whom have Ph.D.s) that are relevant to evidence-based teaching practices for reading. Of concern, few of these teacher educators had the requisite declarative (factual) knowledge and overall they had more knowledge of phonological awareness than of phonics or morphological awareness, which are also essential, according to research, in learning (and presumably teaching) reading. Moreover, these coauthors surveyed the major textbooks used in teaching preservice teachers and found them to be lacking in or having misleading information about the linguistic aspects of teaching reading. Future research of this nature should also investigate whether the teacher education instructors or textbooks present adequate knowledge of how to teach oral language along with written language to students who are struggling as well as those with language learning disability (see Chapter 4 by Silliman and Scott).

Professional education does not end when students graduate from their preservice programs. Joanna Uhry, who is also a leader in evidence-based practices in preservice education of teachers, and Nina Goodman conducted a study that compared inservice teachers who concurrently received graduate coursework and supervised practicum experience in tutoring students in the schools, to three kinds of controls: (a) Other graduate students who received only coursework in evidence-based practices and no supervised practicum experience in tutoring; (b) preservice students who received coursework in evidence-based practices; and (c) preservice students who received coursework in practices for which no research shows efficacy. Results demonstrated that only the group that received supervision in teaching along with coursework in evidence-based practices improved significantly, based on a survey of teacher knowledge (compared to the three control groups above) and student learning outcomes, (compared to another control group of students in the school who were tested but not tutored). This empirical study provides important evidence that learning to teach effectively requires both supervised procedural knowledge in how to teach (putting knowledge into practice) and declarative knowledge of what the research says about teaching.

Two other chapters focus on training of school psychologists. Susan Forman, who is also a member of the Task Force on Evidence-Based Intervention in School Psychology (Task Force) and co-chair of the Task Force's Research to Practice Committee, describes a unique course developed for a doctoral leadership program in school psychology. She recognizes the complexity of the implementation and change processes, and the need for training. Forman's innovative, leading-edge program includes preparing pre-service students in the change process, and developing the knowledge and skills needed to implement evidence-based programs in schools and evaluate their effectiveness. With these skills, she empowers the future school psychologists to be change agents and leaders in the schools.

Three graduate students in a NASP-approved program in school psychology, Nicole Alston-Abel, Erin Olsen, and Kelly Cutler Kirk, coauthored the final chapter that describes the evidence-based projects they conducted as part of their specialist-level certification internship. They were required to draw upon research in designing the intervention and to gather data to evaluate whether the intervention as implemented was effective. Future research might address whether such data-based decision-making during pre-certification training, as required in the NASP standards for training programs, increases the probability that later, as certified practicing school psychologists, they will continue to engage in data-based decision-making.

22. The Role of Teacher Education Programs in Preparing Teachers for Implementing Evidence-Based Reading Practices

R. Malatesha Joshi, Emily Binks, Martha C. Hougen,
Emily Ocker Dean, Lori Graham, and Dennie L. Smith

■ Unmet Needs in Literacy

According to the reports by the National Assessment of Educational Progress (NAEP, 2005) and National Center for Educational Statistics (NCES, 1999), approximately 25% (or 70 million) individuals in the United States have reading difficulties. An increasing number of adults are unable to read a newspaper or bus schedule; one-third of fourth graders are unable to read simple books with clarity and fluency. This percentage may go as high as 60% among students from minority groups. Furthermore, 38% of the fourth graders are reading below the Basic level and 29% of the eighth graders are reading below the Basic level, which means that these students cannot perform at the minimum academic expectations.

Because of the concerns with reading, the Congressional Hearing on Measuring Success: Using Assessments and Accountability (Lyon, 2001) declared illiteracy a public health issue. As evidence, statistics were cited that 75% of the students who drop out of high school have reading problems and at least half of the adolescents with criminal problems and about half of the individuals with a history of substance abuse also have reading problems. Various reasons have been proposed for the reading problems: poor oral language development (Hart & Risley, 1995; Moats, 2001), number of books available at home (Chiu & McBride-Chang, 2006), genetics linked to reading disabilities (Pennington & Olson, 2005), and poor classroom instruction, especially at the early primary grades (Foorman, Francis, Shaywitz, Shaywitz,

& Fletcher, 1997; Torgesen, 2005; Vellutino, Scanlon, & Jaccard, 2003). Snow, Burns, and Griffin (1998) conclude, based on a review of the literature, that "quality classroom instruction in kindergarten and the primary grades is the single best weapon against reading failure" (p. 343).

■ What Are Evidence-Based or Scientifically Based Reading Practices?

Evidence-based reading practices are synonymous with Scientifically Supported Reading Instruction (SSRI), which refers to application of rigorous, systematic research of reading instruction (Fletcher & Francis, 2004). According to the Reading Excellence Act (1998), SSRI can draw on observation or experiment, involve rigorous data analyses, and is been accepted by a peer-reviewed journal has undergone other rigorous, scientific review.

In 1998, the federal government created the National Reading Panel (NRP) to review such studies and determine the most effective reading instructional practices. The Panel performed a meta-analysis and outlined the findings that had been repeatedly replicated. According to the National Reading Panel (NICHD, 2000), the five essential components of reading based on scientifically based reading research include explicit, systematic instruction in phonemic awareness, phonics, fluency, vocabulary, and comprehension. (For further discussion of the evidence that not all students are reading as well as they should, science-based reading instruction, and the National Reading Panel findings, see McCardle and Miller, Chapter 1, this volume.)

■ Do Teachers Know What Evidence-Based Reading Instruction Is?

Recent reports on effective reading instruction have stressed the importance of teachers' knowledge in breaking the code to develop literacy skills (Brady & Moats, 1997; Darling-Hammond, 2006; McCardle & Chhabra, 2004; NICHD, 2000). Unfortunately, many studies have shown that teachers are not familiar with the required linguistic knowledge necessary to teach reading and spelling. In one of the earliest studies of the teachers' knowledge of linguistic concepts necessary to teach literacy skills, Moats (1994) administered a questionnaire to 89 subjects consisting mainly of reading teachers, special education teachers, and speech-language pathologists. The items included in the survey were related to locating or giving examples of phonic, syllabic, and morphemic units in written words as well as analyzing words into speech sounds, syllables, and morphemes. Responses on the survey indicated an inadequate understanding of language concepts needed for direct, language-focused reading instruction, such as the ability to count phonemes and to identify phonic relationships. Hardly anyone could identify a consonant digraph[1] and very few participants could explain where "ck" is used in spelling[2] or the number of sounds in the word "ox."[3] Since the initial study by Moats, several other studies have produced similar results with preservice and inservice teachers (Bos, Mather, Dickson, Podhajski, & Chard, 2001; Cunningham, Perry, Stanovich, & Stanovich, 2004; Fielding-Barnsley & Purdie, 2005; Mather, Bos, & Babur, 2001; Spear-Swerling & Brucker, 2003; also see Uhry, Chapter 23, this volume).

However, when teachers were trained in explicit instruction in the linguistic knowledge and applied such knowledge to their instructional practices, their students performed better on reading tasks (McCutchen, Abbott, et al., 2002a; McCutchen & Berninger, 1999; Moats & Foorman, 2003; Spear-Swerling & Brucker, 2004). McCutchen et al. (2002a) found correlated relationships among teachers' knowledge of basic linguistic skills, classroom reading instruction, and student reading achievement. McCutchen, Harry, Cunningham, Cox, Sidman, & Covill (2002b) indicated a correlated relationship between teachers' knowledge of basic linguistic skills and classroom reading instruction, as well as teachers' knowledge of basic linguistic skills and their students' reading achievement. Moats and Foorman (2003) established a predictive relationship among teachers' knowledge of basic linguistic skills, classroom reading instruction, and student reading achievement. Finally, Spear-Swerling and Brucker (2004) established significant correlations between teachers' knowledge of basic linguistic skills and students' reading achievement.

Components of basic linguistic knowledge that contribute to improved classroom reading instruction and hence improved student reading achievement are outlined by Moats (1994):

1. Knowledge of the psychology of reading and reading development including basic facts about reading, the characteristics of poor and novice readers, and how reading and spelling develop;
2. Language as the foundation for reading instruction including the knowledge of language structure and application to teaching phonetics, phonology, morphology, orthography, semantics, and syntax and text structure;
3. Practical skills of instruction in a comprehensive reading program; and
4. Assessment of classroom reading and writing skills.

Through scientifically based reading research, it has been shown that the direct teaching of linguistic structure concepts is of great importance to both beginning and struggling readers (Moats, 1994) and that this linguistic structure should include phonological awareness (Fielding-Barnsley & Purdie, 2005) and orthographic awareness (Adams, 1990). Research also shows that early, systematic instruction in phonics improves the reading and spelling skills of struggling readers and reduces the number of them reading below grade level (Bos, Mather, Dickson, Podhajski, & Chard, 2001). Phonics instruction in English requires teacher guidance through the multilayered, complex, and variable correspondences among spelling, sound (at the phoneme and syllable levels), and morphemes (units of meaning) (Moats & Foorman, 2003). This knowledge is necessary for developing accurate, automatic word recognition, which is needed for fluent reading. Teachers' knowledge of morphology and historical changes in English helps inform vocabulary instruction, which requires a systematic understanding of the relationships among word structure, syntax, and meaning, all of which contributes to reading comprehension (Moats & Foorman).

The National Council on Teacher Quality (Walsh, Glaser, & Wilcox, 2006) concluded that many schools of education may not be teaching their preservice teachers the basic knowledge required to teach linguistic skills. For example, despite a large number of studies that have shown the importance of phonemic awareness in becoming a good reader not only in English but also in other alphabetic languages (Ball & Blachman, 1991; Bertelson, 1987; Blachman, 1988; Cossu, Shankweiler, Liberman, Tola, & Katz, 1988; Defior, Martos, & Cary, 2002; Lundberg, Frost, & Petersen, 1988), this knowledge may not be disseminated to preservice teachers sufficiently well that they can implement it in practice when they begin teaching. McCardle and Chhabra (2004) asked a fundamentally important question, "Why is it that the colleges of education do not arm teachers with this vital information before they enter the classroom to teach our children?" To answer that question, the following hypotheses were tested: (a) Teacher educators themselves may not be knowledgeable about the linguistic constructs and/or (b) the textbooks used in the reading education classes may not be providing the information about evidence-based reading instruction.

Linguistic knowledge of teacher educators. To measure linguistic knowledge, a questionnaire was constructed that consisted of 68 items based on questionnaires developed by other researchers (McCutchen et al., 2002a; Moats, 1994) in the field. The items[4] on the questionnaire, which is in the Appendix, included questions like how well the teacher educators felt prepared to teach normal readers and struggling readers of elementary age the skills of phonological awareness and decoding (Items # 4–5). Other items asked for definition of terms such as phoneme[5] (Item # 9) and morpheme[6] (Item # 37), as well as identification of the number of speech sounds in words such as box[7] and moon[8] (Item # 12) or of the number of morphemes in words such as observer[9] and heaven[10] (Item # 19). In the questionnaires administered by previous researchers, the items mainly referred to decoding and children's literature. In contrast, items relating to teaching vocabulary and comprehension were also included. The internal consistency reliability of the instrument, based on Cronbach's α, was 0.918.

The questionnaire was administered to 66 (40 females and 26 males) teacher educators of elementary reading education, 58 of whom had a doctorate and 8 of whom were working on their doctoral degree. All had previously taught in elementary schools. The teacher educators were currently teaching two to four courses in reading education at the university level to preservice elementary teachers and were from approximately 30 different universities and community colleges in the southwestern part of the United States. They were teacher educators in various departments, including Educational Psychology, Curriculum and Instruction, Special Education, ESL and Bilingual Education, Reading, Educational Administration, and Educational Leadership. Their number of years of experience with teacher education ranged from 1 to 20 years. All teacher educators reported that they believed that they were well prepared to teach reading.

The questionnaire was administered to approximately 20 participants per group as they were attending a workshop and sufficient precaution was taken to ensure that participants did not discuss the questions among themselves. The experimenters walked around the room observing the participants to ensure that they did not discuss or look up answers. They were instructed that their responses would remain anonymous and no form of identification of the participants was obtained. They were specifically requested not to write their names. There was no time limit, but most of the participants completed the questionnaire within 45 minutes. Each content item was scored as right or wrong, and the total number of correct items was recorded for final analysis.

The items were grouped into phonological-based, phonics-based, morphological-based, and comprehension (including vocabulary)-based categories. For instance, "how many speech sounds are there?" is an example of a phonological-based item (Item # 12 on the questionnaire); a combination of two or three consonants pronounced so that each letter keeps its own identity (Item # 11 on the questionnaire) is an example of a phonics-based item; the number of morphemes in a word (Item # 19) is an example of a morphological-based item; and the components of reciprocal teaching (Item # 31) is an example of a comprehension-based item.[11] There were 22 items in the phonological-based category; 11 items in the phonics-based category; 16 items in the morphological-based category; and 11 items in the comprehension-based category but some of the items can fit in more than one category.

The items were further classified into declarative knowledge-based (knowledge that) ($n = 26$) and procedural knowledge-based (knowledge how) items ($n = 34$). An example of a declarative knowledge-based item is recognizing the definition of a phoneme (Item # 9), and an example of an procedural knowledge-based item is counting the number of speech sounds in a word (Item # 12).

Results. The mean percentages of correct responses along with the standard deviations in each category are in Table 22.1. A paired *t*-test evaluated

TABLE 22.1   *Mean Percentage Phonological-, Phonics-, Morphological-, and Comprehension-based Items (Standard Deviations in Parentheses)*

Category of Items	Mean Percent of Items Correct (Standard Deviation)
Phonological-based	78.97% (13.24)
Phonics-based	56.47% (19.67)
Morphological-based	34.36% (12.63)
Comprehension-based	57.5% (19.50)

whether the means were significantly different among the four types of items. Means were significantly different between the phonological- and phonics-based items ($t_{(1, 65)} = 7.422, p < 0.0001$; Cohen's $d = 1.3421$), between phonics-based and morphological-based items ($t_{(1, 65)} = 8.084, p < 0.0001$; Cohen's $d = 1.3379$), and between phonological-based and morphological-based items ($t_{(1, 65)} = 11.509, p < 0.0001$; Cohen's $d = 3.4485$).

For none of the language concepts relevant to teaching reading were all the professors knowledgeable. They were most knowledgeable about phonological awareness, which is a reason for optimism, given the national effort to implement this knowledge into practice through federal initiatives (see McCardle & Miller, Chapter 1, this volume). However, implementation efforts need to continue. Overall performance was lower on phonemic-only items: 70.24% (13.14) than other phonological-based items (91.15%). Of concern, they were significantly less knowledgeable about phonics and morphology, which are also relevant to teaching reading. Many participants did not know the definition of phonemic awareness,[12] although most knew the definition of phoneme. Only 50% of the participants could correctly recognize the principle governing the use of the letter "c" for /k/ at the initial position (see questionnaire Item # 34: "c" is used for /k/ in the initial position before a, o, u, or any consonant {as in cat, coal, cute, and clock}) and only 21% of the participants could correctly identify the principle governing the use of the letter "k" for /k/ (see questionnaire Item # 35: "k" is used for /k/ before e, i, or y {as in key, kite, and sky}). The performance on morphological-based items was significantly worse than both the phonological-based and phonics-based items (see Table 22.1). Also, only 38% of teacher educators were able to correctly identify the components of reciprocal teaching.

The mean percentages of correct responses for declarative knowledge-based versus procedural knowledge-based items, along with the standard deviations in each category, are shown in Table 22.2. Compared to an earlier study the teacher educators did not differ significantly between these two kinds of knowledge as preservice teachers, who had greater knowledge of procedural than declarative phonological knowledge did (Joshi, Binks, Dean,

TABLE 22.2   *Mean Percentage Correct on Declarative Knowledge-Based and Procedural Knowledge-Based Items (Standard Deviations in Parentheses)*

Category of Items	Average Percent of Items Correct (Standard Deviation)
Declarative Knowledge-based	63.80% (18)
Procedural Knowledge-based	72.34% (23.17)

Hougen, & Graham, 2006). However, the less than optimal level of either kind of knowledge (Table 22.2) raises the issue of whether they can prepare future teachers for the kind of explicit instruction in phonological and phonics skills that many children require (Liberman & Liberman, 1990).

At the same time, teacher educators performed well in certain areas of knowledge: 90% defined and counted the number of syllables correctly, 98% correctly recognized the definition of a phoneme, and 92% correctly recognized that "chef" and "shoe" begin with the same sound. Moderate weaknesses were observed in syllable awareness: 65% correctly recognized a word with two closed syllables (napkin), 56% correctly recognized a word with an open syllable (bacon), 58% correctly recognized the definition of phonological awareness, 54% correctly recognized the definition of phonemic awareness, 63% correctly counted speech sounds in "through," and 67% correctly recognized the definition of a morpheme. The most severe weaknesses appeared when phonological and orthographic knowledge had to be coordinated: 42% correctly counted the correct speech sounds in "box," 27% correctly recognized a word with a final stable syllable (paddle), 50% correctly recognized the rule that governs the use of "c" in the initial position for /k/, and 21% correctly recognized the rule that governs the use of "k" in the initial position for /k/. Clearly, counting the number of syllables in words seems to pose little problem compared to counting the number of morphemes (see Table 22.3).

Analysis of the textbooks used in the reading education classes. The recent report entitled *What Education Schools Aren't Teaching About Reading and What Elementary Teachers Aren't Learning* by the National Council on Teacher Quality (NCTQ; Walsh, Glaser, & Wilcox, 2006) analyzed the textbooks used in reading education courses and concluded that "The quality of almost all the reading texts is poor. Their content includes little to no hard science and in far too many cases the content is inaccurate and misleading" (p. 33). This conclusion was arrived at after 226 textbooks were examined by three "literacy experts" established by NCTQ as to whether the textbook is acceptable either as core or as supplemental, nonacceptable as core or as supplemental, or not relevant.

For the purpose of the present study, five well-known reading textbooks publishers were contacted and the titles and authors of their most popularly

TABLE 22.3   *Percentage of Teacher Educators Correctly Identifying the Number of Syllables and Morphemes in Given Words*

	No. of syllables correctly identified	No. of morphemes correctly identified
Heaven	92%	40%
Observer	96%	25%
Teacher	92%	48%
Frogs	88%	29%
Spinster	90%	17%

adopted books in reading education classes were requested; the research team was given names for 17 textbooks. Two of the co-authors independently examined three items: (a) Whether *at least* the five instructional components recommended by the National Reading Panel (phonemic awareness, phonics, fluency, vocabulary, and comprehension) (see McCardle & Miller, Chapter 1, this volume) were included in the textbook; (b) whether the definitions provided in the text matched that of the NRP definition; and (c) how much of the text was devoted to those components. The amount covered in the text was computed by dividing the number of pages[13] devoted to the five components of reading recommended by NRP by the total number of pages of the text excluding the references, appendices, and glossaries and multiplying by 100 to obtain the percentage of the content covered.

The analyses of the above three items showed that 13 out of the 17 most popularly adopted textbooks included all five components recommended by the NRP and 10 textbooks had correctly defined each component. The percentage of total NRP content covered ranged from 4% to 60%. Some noteworthy findings were that four textbooks did not cover the topics of phonemic awareness and phonics, which are considered basic building blocks of reading acquisition. One of the textbooks adopted by 84 universities devoted only 10% of the entire volume to the five components of reading and another textbook adopted by 91 universities did not cover phonemic awareness, fluency, and comprehension. Nine textbooks devoted one-third of the textbook to the five components. These findings are similar to the findings of NCTQ in that we also found very few textbooks that met scientifically based reading research (SBRR) and NRP criteria.

■ Role of Teacher Education Programs

According to the National Center for Education Statistics report (Donahue, Finnegan, Lutkus, Allen, & Campbell, 2001), schools of education are turning out more than 125,000 teachers each year. Undoubtedly, the two main sources of information from which preservice teachers obtain such knowledge are (a) the teacher educators who are the instructors in the reading education courses and (b) the textbooks used in the reading education courses. Teacher education programs should, therefore, ensure (a) the teacher educators are knowledgeable in scientifically based research on reading instruction and learning to read; and (b) the textbooks are giving sufficient coverage to current scientific research on reading for which a consensus exists, and how all of this evidence-based knowledge can be translated to practice. College deans pay careful attention to the selection of reading education faculty knowledgeable in these areas when hiring faculty. *Knowledge to Support the Teaching of Reading: Preparing Teachers for a Changing World* (Snow, Griffin, & Burns, 2005) specifically outlines critical knowledge for preservice teachers about the development, acquisition, and teaching of language, literacy, and reading, as part of a larger initiative by the National Academy of Education in creating a core knowledge base for teacher education. This resource could serve as one potential guide for administrators of teacher and reading education programs (i.e., deans, department heads, and reading education faculty members) for hiring knowledgeable reading education faculty members. Reading education faculty themselves should also take more responsibility in coordinating and collaborating with one another so that their courses and textbook selection are current with regard to SSRI for reading.

Teacher educators must also educate and encourage authors and publishers to write and publish reading education textbooks based on *scientific research* and use such textbooks in their courses. According to Walsh, Glaser, and Wilcox (2006), the current list of "acceptable" textbooks aligned with SSRI has few titles. Other textbooks analyzed by NCTQ, although acceptable for teaching one or some components, did not contain information on all components of the science of reading. Most textbooks were classified as "unacceptable" for "either omitting the science entirely or conveying it inadequately or inaccurately, but some for being openly derisive of the science of reading" (Walsh et al., 2006).

Supporting teacher educators through ongoing professional development. Creating highly qualified teachers is the responsibility of teacher education preparation programs and necessitates faculty who have in-depth knowledge of the science of teaching reading. Snow (2005) raised a fundamentally important implementation issue: If the role of the teacher educator in reading education is to make "abstruse knowledge potentially usable," who is ensuring that the teacher educator has a solid grasp of the most relevant, sometimes "abstruse," and often controversial research?

In light of the critical responsibility facing teacher educators of reading education, who strive to improve the reading achievement of all students but often do not have an in-depth knowledge of how to teach struggling readers, the Texas Reading First Higher Education Collaborative (HEC) was established. The Texas HEC was formed in 2000 to support teacher educators of reading education throughout the state in integrating SSRI into their teacher preparation courses. The HEC began with 15 members from 5 institutions that certify teachers. Currently, the HEC consists of approximately 300 members representing over 100 institutions. The HEC provides ongoing professional development and collaborative opportunities for teacher educators and educational administration faculty representing traditional university undergraduate teacher preparation programs, post-baccalaureate programs, community colleges, and alternative certification programs. The successful implementation of the HEC is evidence that teacher educators do enthusiastically welcome opportunities to learn more about teaching reading, and that they thrive on collaborating with their colleagues. The HEC is open for any teacher educator in reading in Texas, and participation requires a certain amount of self-motivation on the part of the teacher educator.

The HEC serves this purpose by ensuring that teacher educators have knowledge of evidence-based research in the field of reading and have support when integrating this knowledge into their teacher preparation courses. Rather than relying on how they were initially taught, or what they intuitively think is effective in teaching struggling students, teacher educators of the HEC are provided with knowledge and practices validated by SBRR and scientifically based reading instruction (SBRI).

Typically, it is up to individual teacher educators to stay abreast of the research, join organizations, attend conferences, and study the literature. For some individuals, these activities are difficult to pursue. Institutions of higher education do not have the funds to support travel or memberships, and often the teacher educators teach so many classes that there is little time or energy left to delve into current research. The HEC provides the financial support for members to attend seminars and a means to collaborate with colleagues. In addition, an online forum, HEC Online, facilitates collaboration, communication, and sharing among the HEC members. Research reports, sample syllabi, and other information are posted online. Members can participate in a running dialogue regarding issues of concern, as well as participate in special features such as conversing with a reading expert on the "Ask an Expert" feature. HEC members share journal articles; discuss textbook selection, student assignments and activities; and collaborate on research and publications. Participants may request an HEC staff member, as well as other HEC members, to model lessons, review syllabi, assist with course content alignment, and make presentations for students and faculty at their respective institutions.

Evidence of effectiveness of the HEC includes the following: an increase from 15 members in the year 2000, to almost 300 active members in the year 2007; a 175% increase in the integration of SBRI in teacher educators' syllabi; and a 25–75% increase in scores on knowledge surveys following attendance at seminars.

Members have reported that there are six activities that are most useful to them:

1. Dissemination of research-based materials for use in the college classroom;
2. Online support and collaborative opportunities;
3. Opportunities to attend seminars and dialogue with experts and colleagues in the field;
4. Opportunities to present and disseminate their own research and effective teaching strategies;
5. Sharing syllabi that integrate research and instruction; and
6. Review of syllabi by HEC staff and members and the provision of feedback to further integrate current research.

Some members felt trepidation initially upon joining the HEC, anticipating a mandate to teach a certain way and to accept particular beliefs. Many of these teacher educators taught whole language as the only approach to reading instruction. However, as a result of the HEC, members are aware of the current research, have discussed the data with the experts, and have received answers they value. The active HEC members are incorporating SSRI into their course-work and are open to learning about the latest research in their field. Their practices have changed, not because they were "forced" to change, but because they have had the opportunity to learn about the current research in the field and have support to integrate the new research into their classes. These teacher educators want to provide their preservice teacher candidates, and ultimately school-age students, with the most effective research-based teaching strategies. Hence, when they become aware of the most efficacious practices, HEC members willingly and eagerly integrate this new knowledge into their syllabi and courses according to preservice teacher reports. Formal analyses of their teaching of preservice teachers are currently under investigation.

At this time, there are no other forums available that systematically and consistently provide ongoing professional development and collaborative opportunities for teacher educators. The HEC has demonstrated that, when provided with the necessary support, teacher educators enthusiastically continue their own learning. Members are hopeful and optimistic that the HEC will remain a viable, responsive collaborative. This is a promising outcome of the Reading First Initiative and one that has the potential to sustain efforts to improve reading instruction.

A combination of knowledgeable teacher educators and research-based textbooks with good teaching and ample practice should most effectively prepare preservice teachers with the knowledge and skills they need to promote reading success in their future classrooms. Cunningham, Perry, Stanovich, and Stanovich (2004) concluded, *"We should continue to turn our attention toward improving teacher preparation and teacher development in the area of early literacy by highlighting the direction that reading education for both preservice and in-service teachers might take"* (*italics added*, p. 161). We cannot expect teachers to learn the essential components of reading instruction through field/teaching experience, reading programs, screening tests, or even individual pursuit. Rather, we must improve preservice coursework, which has been proven to increase teachers' reading knowledge and ability when such courses provide explicit instruction and ample practice in each component (Moats & Foorman, 2003; Spear-Swerling & Brucker, 2004). In order for reading education coursework to be improved, an increase of teacher educators' knowledge and quality of textbooks in these critical components of reading is needed.

■ Conclusions

Reading is a basic skill for survival and those who have reading difficulties in early grades continue to struggle in school and in life. However, evidence-based reading practices are available (see components of good reading instruction identified by the National Reading Panel, NICHD, 2000), but, unfortunately, classroom teachers are not provided with this information at many colleges of education. The results reported in this chapter showed that many teacher educators are not knowledgeable in several of the basic linguistic constructs needed for literacy development and many of the textbooks used in reading education courses in colleges are not providing the evidence-based reading instruction programs. These results further highlight the *strong need* for increased preparation of preservice teachers to teach the linguistic components of the English language through (a) teacher training programs that explicitly teach the interdependence of these components in effective reading instruction and (b) textbooks used in preservice reading education courses that are carefully selected to include all components of scientifically based reading research. These results support Spear-Swerling and Brucker's conclusions (2003) that teacher education must include information about English word structure for educators who will teach reading. They also support the conclusion that more research is needed on what it will take to prepare future teacher educators who can prepare the next generation of teachers to implement evidence-based reading knowledge in classroom practice.

■ References

Adams, M. J. (1990). *Beginning to read: Thinking and learning about print.* Cambridge, MA, MIT Press.

Ball, E. W., & Blachman, B. A. (1991). Does phoneme awareness training in kindergarten make a difference in early word recognition and developmental spelling? *Reading Research Quarterly, 26,* 49–66.

Bertelson, P. (1987). *The onset of literacy: Cognitive processes in reading acquisition*. Cambridge, MA, MIT Press.

Blachman, B. (1988). An alternative classroom reading program for learning-disabled and other low achieving children. In W. Ellis (Ed.), *Intimacy with language: A forgotten basic in teacher education* (pp. 49–55). Baltimore, MD, The Orton Dyslexia Society.

Bos, C., Mather, N., Dickson, S., Podhajski, B., & Chard, D. (2001). Perceptions and knowledge of preservice and inservice educators about early reading instruction. *Annals of Dyslexia, 51,* 97–120.

Brady, S., & Moats, L. C. (1997). *Informed instruction for reading success— Foundations for teacher preparation.* A position paper of the International Dyslexia Association, Baltimore, MD, International Dyslexia Association.

Chiu, M. M., & McBride-Chang, C. (2006). Gender, context, and reading: A comparison of students in 43 countries. *Scientific Studies of Reading, 10,* 331–362.

Cossu, G., Shankweiler, D., Liberman, I. Y., Tola, G., & Katz, L. (1988). Awareness of phonological segments and reading ability in Italian children. *Applied Psycholinguistics, 9,* 1–6.

Cunningham, A. E., Perry, K. E., Stanovich, K. E., & Stanovich, P. J. (2004). Disciplinary knowledge of K-3 teachers and their knowledge calibration in the domain of early literacy. *Annals of Dyslexia, 54,* 139–167.

Darling-Hammond, L. (2006). 21st-Century Teacher Education. *Journal of Teacher Education, 57,* 300–314.

Defior, S., Martos, F., & Cary, L. (2002). Differences in reading acquisition development in two shallow orthographies: Portuguese and Spanish. *Applied Psycholinguistics, 23,* 135–148.

Donahue, P. L., Finnegan, R. J., Lutkus, A. D., Allen, N. L., & Campbell, J. R. (2001). *The nation's report card: Fourth-grade reading 2000, NCES 2001-499.* Washington, DC, U.S. Department of Education, Office of Educational Research and Improvement, National Center for Education Statistics (NCES).

Fielding-Barnsley, R., & Purdie, N. (2005). Teacher's attitude to and knowledge of metalinguistics in the process of learning to read. *Asia-Pacific Journal of Teacher Education, 33,* 1–12.

Foorman, B. R., Francis, D. J., Shaywitz, S. E., Shaywitz, B. A., & Fletcher, J. M. (1997). The case for early reading interventions. In B. Blachman (Ed.), *Foundations of reading acquisition and dyslexia: Implications for early intervention* (pp. 243–264). Mahwah, NJ, Lawrence Erlbaum Associates.

Fletcher, J. M., & Francis, D. J. (2004). Scientifically based educational research. In P. McCardle & V. Chhabra (Eds.), *The voice of evidence in reading research* (pp. 59–80). Baltimore, MD, Brookes.

Hart, B., & Risley, T. R (1995). *Meaningful differences in the everyday experience of young American children.* Baltimore, MD, Brookes.

Joshi, R. M., Binks, E., Dean, E. O., Hougen, M., & Graham, L. (2006). *Roadblocks to reading acquisition: Is teacher knowledge one of them?* Paper presented at the annual meeting of the International Dyslexia Association, Indianapolis, IN.

Liberman, I. Y., & Liberman, A. M. (1990). Whole language versus code emphasis: Underlying assumptions and their implications for reading instruction. *Annals of Dyslexia, 40,* 51–78.

Lundberg, I., Frost, J., & Petersen, O. P. (1988). Effectiveness of an extensive program for stimulating phonological awareness in preschool children. *Reading Research Quarterly, 23,* 263–284.

Lyon, G. R. (2001). *Measuring success: Using assessments and accountability to raise student achievement.* Hearing before the Subcommittee on Education Reform, Committee on Education and the Workforce, U.S. House of Representatives; March 8, 2001.

Mather, N., Bos, C., & Babur, N. (2001). Perceptions and knowledge of preservice and inservice teachers about early literacy instruction. *Journal of Learning Disabilities, 34,* 472–482.

McCardle, P., & Chhabra, V. (Eds.) (2004). *The voice of evidence in reading research.* Baltimore, MD, Brookes.

McCutchen, D., Abbott, R. D., Green, L. B., Beretvas, S. N., Cox, S., Potter, N. S., Quiroga, T., & Gray, A. L. (2002). Beginning literacy: Links among teacher knowledge, teacher practice, and student learning. *Journal of Learning Disabilities, 35,* 69–86.

McCutchen, D., & Berninger, V. (1999). Those who know, teach well: Helping teachers master literacy-related subject-matter knowledge. *Learning Disabilities Research & Practice, 14,* 215–226.

McCutchen, D., Harry, D. R., Cunningham, A. E., Cox, S., Sidman, S., & Covill, A. E. (2002). Reading teachers' knowledge of children's literature and English phonology. *Annals of Dyslexia, 52,* 207–225.

Moats, L. C. (1994). The missing foundation in teacher education: Knowledge of the structure of spoken and written language. *Annals of Dyslexia, 44,* 81–102.

Moats, L. C., & Foorman, B. R. (2003). Measuring teachers' content knowledge of language and reading. *Annals of Dyslexia, 53,* 23–45.

National Assessment of Educational Progress (NAEP). (2005). *The Nation's Report Card: Reading 2005.* Washington, DC, National Center for Educational Statistics.

National Center for Educational Statistics (NCES). (1999). *Condition of Education.* Washington, DC, U.S. Department of Education, Office of Educational Research and Reform.

National Institute of Child Health and Human Development (NICHD). (2000). Report of the National Reading Panel. *Teaching children to read: An evidence-based assessment of the scientific research literature on reading and its implications for reading instruction: Reports of the subgroups* (NIH Publication No. 00–4754). Washington, DC, U.S. Government Printing Office.

Pennington, B. F., & Olson, R. K. (2005). Genetics of dyslexia. In M. J. Snowling & C. Humle (Eds.), *The science of reading* (pp. 453–472). London, Blackwell.

Reading Excellence Act of 1998, Pub. L. No. 105–277, div. A, Sec. 101(f) (title VIII), 112 Stat. 2681–337, 2681–391 et. seq. United States Department of Education, 2003. *The reading excellence act.*

Snow, C. E., Burns, M. S., & Griffin, P. (Eds.) (1998). *Preventing reading difficulties in young children.* Washington, DC, National Academy.

Snow, C. E., Griffin, P., & Burns, M. S. (Eds.) (2005). *Knowledge to support the teaching of reading: Preparing teachers for a changing world.* San Francisco, Jossey Bass.

Spear-Swerling, L., & Brucker, P. O. (2003). Teachers' acquisition of knowledge about English word structure. *Annals of Dyslexia, 53,* 72–103.

Spear-Swerling, L., & Brucker, P. O. (2004). Preparing novice teachers to develop basic reading and spelling skills in children. *Annals of Dyslexia, 54,* 332–364.

Torgesen, J. K. (2005). Recent discoveries on remedial intervention for children with dyslexia. In M. J. Snowling & C. Hulme (Eds.), *The science of reading: A handbook* (pp. 521–537). Oxford, UK, Blackwell.

Vellutino, F. R., Scanlon, D. M., & Jaccard, J. (2003). Toward distinguishing between cognitive and experiential deficits as primary sources of difficulty in learning to read: A two-year follow-up of difficult to remediate and readily remediated poor readers. In B. R. Foorman (Ed.), *Preventing and remediating reading difficulties: Bringing science to scale* (pp. 73–120). Baltimore, York Press.

Walsh, K., Glaser, D., & Wilcox, D. D. (2006). *What education schools aren't teaching about reading and what elementary teachers aren't learning.* National Council on Teacher Quality (NCTQ).

■ Notes

1. Consonant digraphs: When two consonant letters make one sound, like 'sh' in "short" or 'ch' in "chair."
2. "ck" is used in the final position in a single syllable word following a short vowel sound, like in "back" and "sack." English words do not begin with "ck."
3. "ox" has three sounds; "x" makes two sounds: /k/ and /s/.
4. Although questions are numbered 1–27 when choices on multiple choice questions are considered, there are more items that are used for different classification schemes for different analyses.
5. A single speech sound.
6. A single unit of meaning.
7. Four: /b/ /o/ /k/ /s/
8. Three: /m/ /oo/ /n/
9. Three: "ob" "serve" and "er"
10. One: "heaven"
11. *Note:* The authors recognize that the item categorization could be subjective at times, i.e., counting speech sounds was considered a phonological task,

although participants actually had to read the words and therefore it was not purely spoken language, as a true "phonological" task would be.

12. The ability to break down and manipulate the individual sounds in spoken language.

13. The amount on the page may be one or 25 sentences but would still count as "one" page in this calculation as long as the component was included on the page.

■ Appendix

Please complete the following questions. **Please be honest, as this survey is completely anonymous**.

1. Please list previous work experience (i.e., teacher, administrator, business, etc.):

2. Please list the courses in teaching reading and language arts you teach (including level):

3. Please list any certifications you have (i.e., reading specialist, etc.):

How well do you feel prepared to teach normal and struggling readers of elementary age:

4. Instruction in explicit phonics
   a. MINIMAL   b. MODERATE   c. VERY GOOD   d. EXPERT

5. Providing students with structured practice in phonemic awareness
   a. MINIMAL   b. MODERATE   c. VERY GOOD   d. EXPERT

6. Knowledge of children's literature
   a. MINIMAL   b. MODERATE   c. VERY GOOD   d. EXPERT

7. Teaching K-3 English language linguistic skills to English language learners (ELLs)
   a. MINIMAL   b. MODERATE   c. VERY GOOD   d. EXPERT

8. Using assessment data to inform reading instruction
   a. MINIMAL   b. MODERATE   c. VERY GOOD   d. EXPERT

Please answer the following questions:

9. A phoneme refers to
   a. a single letter   b. *a single speech sound   c. a single unit of meaning
   d. a grapheme   e. no idea

10. If *tife* is a word, the letter "i" would probably sound like the "i" in:
    a. if   b. beautiful   c. *find   d. ceiling   e. sing   f. no idea

11. A combination of two or three consonants pronounced so that each letter keeps its own identity is called:
    a. silent consonant   b. *consonant digraph   c. diphthong
    d. consonant blend   f. no idea

12. How many speech sounds are in the following words? For example, the word "cat" has 3 speech sounds "k"-"a"-"t". Speech sounds do not necessarily equal the number of letters.
    a. Box (4)
    b. Grass (4)
    c. Ship (3)
    d. Moon (3)
    e. Brush (4)
    f. Knee (2)
    g. Through (3)

13. What type of task would the following be? "Say the word 'cat.' Now say the word without the /k/ sound."
    a. blending   b. rhyming   c. segmentation   d. *deletion
    e. no idea

14. A soft "*c*" is in the word:
    a. Chicago   b. cat   c. chair   d. *city   e. none of the above
    f. no idea

15. Identify the pair of words that begin with the same sound:
    a. joke-goat   b. *chef-shoe   c. quiet-giant   d. chip-chemist
    e. no idea

(The next two items involve saying a word and then reversing the order of the sounds. For example, the word "back" would be "cab.")

16. If you say the word, and then reverse the order of the sounds, *ice* would be:
    a. easy   b. sea   c. size   d. *sigh   e. no idea

17. If you say the word, and then reverse the order of the sounds, *enough* would be:
    a. fun   b. phone   c. *funny   d. one   e. no idea

18. All of the following nonsense words have a silent letter, except:
    a. bamb   b. wrin   c. shipe   d. knam   e. *phop   f. no idea

19. For each of the words on the left, determine the number of syllables and the number of morphemes. (Please be sure to give both the number of syllables and the number of morphemes, even though it may be the same number.)

	No. of syllables	No. of morphemes
a. disassemble	(4)	(3)
b. heaven	(2)	(1)
c. observer	(3)	(3)
d. spinster	(2)	(2)
e. pedestal	(3)	(2)
f. frogs	(1)	(2)
g. teacher	(2)	(2)

20. Which of the following words has an example of a final stable syllable?
    a. wave   b. bacon   c. *paddle   d. napkin   e. none of the above
    f. no idea

21. Which of the following words has two closed syllables?
    a. wave   b. bacon   c. paddle   d. *napkin   e. none of the above
    f. no idea

22. Which of the following words contains an open syllable?
    a. wave   b. *bacon   c. paddle   d. napkin   e. none of the above
    f. no idea

23. Phonological awareness is:
    a. the ability to use letter-sound correspondences to decode.
    b. *the understanding of how spoken language is broken down and manipulated.
    c. a teaching method for decoding skills.
    d. the same as phonics.
    e. No idea

24. Phonemic awareness is:
    a. the same as phonological awareness.
    b. the understanding of how letters and sounds are put together to form words.
    c. *the ability to break down and manipulate the individual sounds in spoken language.
    d. the ability to use sound-symbol correspondences to spell new words.
    e. No idea

25. Morphemic analysis is:
    a. an instructional approach that involves evaluation of meaning based on multiple senses.
    b. an understanding of the meaning of letters and their sounds.
    c. *studying the structure, functions, and relations of meaningful linguistic units occurring in language.
    d. classifying and recording of individual speech sounds.
    e. no idea

26. Etymology is:
    a. not really connected to the development of reading skills.
    b. *the study of the history and development of the structures and meaning of words.
    c. the study of the causes of disabilities
    d. the study of human groups through first-hand observation
    e. no idea

27. Reading a text and answering questions based on explicit information found within the text describes:
    a. inferential comprehension

b. *literal comprehension
c. summarization
d. question generating
e. no idea

28. Questions that combine background knowledge and text information to create a response describes which of the following:
    a. *inferential comprehension
    b. literal comprehension
    c. morphemic analysis
    d. reciprocal teaching
    e. no idea

29. Moving beyond the text, questioning, and understanding the relationship that exists between the author and the reader describes:
    a. inferential comprehension
    b. reciprocal teaching
    c. etymology
    d. *critical reading
    e. no idea

30. Which of the following is a phonemic awareness activity?
    a. *having a student segment the sounds in the word cat orally
    b. having a student spell the word cat aloud
    c. having a student sound out the word cat
    d. having a student recite all the words that they can think of that rhyme with cat
    e. no idea

31. Which of the following is **not** a reciprocal teaching activity?
    a. summarization
    b. question-generating
    c. *using graphic organizers
    d. clarifying
    e. no idea

32. Which of the following is a semantic mapping activity?
    a. concept of definition word web
    b. hinks pinks
    c. *writing a brief definition of different terms
    d. predicting
    e. no idea

33. According to the National Reading Panel, instruction in summarizing will contribute to all of the following **except**:
    a. readers more accurately identify main ideas
    b. summarizing improves memory for what is read
    c. ability to recall and answer questions improves

    d. *enhances student generation of inferential questions

    e. no idea

34. What is the rule that governs the use of "c" in the initial position for /k/?

    a. "c" is used for /k/ in the initial position before e, i, or y

    b. the use of "c" for /k/ in the initial position is random and must be memorized

    c. *"c" is used for /k/ in the initial position before a, o, u, or any consonant

    d. none of the above

    e. no idea

35. What is the rule that governs the use of "k" in the initial position for /k/?

    a. *"k" is used for /k/ in the initial position before e, i, or y

    b. the use of "k" for /k/ in the initial position is random and must be memorized

    c. "k" is used for /k/ in the initial position before a, o, u, or any consonant

    d. none of the above

    e. no idea

36. Which answer **best** describes the reason for an *older* student's misspelling of the following words?

    hav (for have)   luv (for love)

    a. the student spelled the word phonetically

    b. *the student has not been taught that English words do not end in v

    c. the student is using invented spelling

    d. the student must memorize the spellings of these irregular words

    e. no idea

37. A morpheme refers to:

    a. a single letter.

    b. a single speech sound.

    c. *a single unit of meaning.

    d. a grapheme.

    e. no idea

38. What is the root in the word audience?

    a. *aud

    b. ience

    c. no root in the word audience

    d. audible

    e. no idea

39. For each of the words on the left, please list the prefix, root, and suffix. (You may use a dash to represent "none." If two fall under one category, please list both.)

	Prefix	Root	Suffix
a. undetermined	(un)	(determine)	(ed)
b. uniform	(uni)	(form)	

c. under		(under)	
d. unknowingly	(un)	(know)	(ing) (ly)
e. conductor	(con)	(duct)	(or)
f. disruption	(dis)	(rupt)	(ion)
g. immaterial	(im)	(mater)	(ial)

40. Question answering and question generation have been found in scientific research to improve all of the following skills **except**:
    a. guide and monitor reading comprehension skills
    b. *instruction of specific word meanings with vocabulary practice
    c. integrating and identifying main ideas through summarizing
    d. some improvement in general reading comprehension on standardized comprehension tests
    e. no idea

41. Story structure could best be taught using which of the following:
    a. *the use of questions and graphic organizers such as story maps
    b. the focus should be on the characters in the story and less about the setting and things that happen in the story
    c. repeated readings
    d. simultaneous oral reading
    e. relying specifically on a child's background knowledge

42. Comprehension monitoring would be considered similar to or the same as:
    a. *metacognitive awareness
    b. examples and comparisons used to develop an understanding of an abstract idea
    c. relating two or more sets of ideas
    d. schema theory
    e. no idea

43. Cooperative learning has been determined to be relevant in the area of instruction. This type of learning is described effectively in which of the following scenarios:
    a. Students create individual travel posters to share with the classroom and "sell" them on the idea of traveling to their respective states and/or countries.
    b. Each student generates vocabulary words as they look over their upcoming story for the following week and the teacher follows with a comprehensive list of their collection of words as a group.
    c. *Students are assigned to planet groups and generate reports and demonstrations about their particular planet.
    d. I do not know how to effectively use cooperative learning.

* indicates correct answer.

23. University-School Partnerships in Urban Classrooms

Professional Development in Applying

Reading Research to Practice

Joanna K. Uhry and Nina E. Goodman

Although some of the earliest research on phonemic awareness (PA) and its relationship with beginning reading is over 35 years old (e.g., Liberman, 1973), it is only in the past few years that PA has become a common curriculum component. The implementation process—from generation of the knowledge to putting it into practice—typically takes a long time. Although *Reading First* has been responsible for more widespread use of scientifically supported early reading curriculum (see McCardle & Miller, Chapter 1, this volume), many university-based preservice or inservice teacher-education programs still do not include teacher preparation in understanding the research evidence for teaching phonological awareness or phonics or practical methods and guidelines for doing so. Many teachers do not have the linguistic knowledge and/or pedagogical skills necessary to plan and implement appropriate instruction involving PA and phonics (e.g., Moats, 1994; Moats & Foorman, 2003). An important part of the implementation of research knowledge in school settings is overcoming this disconnect between the knowledge base of the scientific research community and that utilized by teacher educators and teachers working with children.

The authors wish to acknowledge the critically important role played in this project by the Hello Friend/Ennis William Cosby Foundation. Tuition for university coursework in *Young Readers at Risk: The Ennis William Cosby Graduate Certificate Program* was funded by the Foundation, and the content of the program itself was a collaboration between the University and the Foundation. We also acknowledge the support provided by the principal and first grade teachers in our partner school. Margaret Jo Shepherd has made important contributions to both the PD program and the manuscript. Most of all we wish to acknowledge the tutors and their dedication, stamina, and thoughtful teaching of their young readers.

Overcoming this disconnect will require new approaches to teacher education at both the undergraduate and graduate levels that offer professional development for future teacher educators and current teachers, respectively. This chapter reports on a research project involving a university-based professional development (PD) program with university-based coursework and a yearlong supervised tutoring practicum in the field. One goal of this PD program, which is uniquely designed to improve the implementation process of applying research knowledge to practice, was to provide certified, practicing teachers with additional knowledge and skills grounded in research-based instruction. The research reported in this chapter explored the effects of the program on 28 certified teachers who came from 19 schools across several districts, and on the 28 first-grade children they tutored after school in a local partner school.

This particular ongoing project was originally conceptualized as a way to use research results (e.g., National Reading Panel, 2000; Snow, Burns, & Griffin, 1998) to improve teaching practice and thus corresponds exactly with the theme of this book on implementing evidence-based instruction. Reading, discussing, and practicing researched methods were expected to increase the knowledge and skills of the 28 participating teachers. However, before the project ended it became apparent that there might be benefits to the partner school as well, beyond the benefits to the 28 tutored children. Although data on the effect of the project on the school, and especially on its five first-grade teachers, were not collected in any formal sense, the chapter ends with a discussion of possible benefits to teachers working at schools involved in research.

■ The Role of Phonemic Awareness and Phonics in Beginning Reading

The role of code-based reading instruction as a component of teaching beginning reading has been widely studied, and there is massive evidence that direct, systematic instruction in phonological awareness (PA) and phonics is highly beneficial (e.g., Adams, 1990; National Reading Panel, 2000; Snow, Burns, & Griffin, 1998). Although the studies reported in these analyses do not indicate that PA and phonics should be the only reading instruction provided to beginning readers, the evidence they report is extensive and converging in its argument that these areas should be included in the curriculum. For a review of the scientific research literature on PA and phonics instruction, see Chapter 1 by McCardle and Miller in this volume. The PA- and phonics-related findings reported by the National Reading Panel (2000) relevant to this study are reviewed next.

Young Children Struggling with Word Reading

Instruction in PA and phonics is especially beneficial for young children struggling with word reading, including those children with special needs and from low socioeconomic status (SES) backgrounds (National Reading Panel, 2000). This finding was foundational to the study reported in this chapter because knowledge and skills related to early intervention in word reading constituted the instructional goal of the university's PD program, which prepares teachers to work with Title 1 children in urban schools.

The National Reading Panel (2000) also reported that systematic, direct phonics instruction in first grade has a significantly stronger effect on comprehension growth than indirect phonics or nonphonics instruction. Implications of this finding ran counter to the meaning-based curriculum used in the university's partner school at the onset of the yearlong tutoring project. That is, while the school valued comprehension as the outcome of instruction, the instruction utilized in the early grades in the school was not a good match for this goal because it did not include classroom-based direct instruction in PA, phonics, and word reading.

Tutoring Programs: Research into Practice

Two recent studies of tutoring programs for struggling young readers have provided examples of positive effects for tutoring in PA and phonics (Blachman et al., 2004; Ehri, Dreyer, Flugman, & Gross, 2007; Shaywitz et al., 2004). Blachman et al.'s intervention was delivered by teachers certified in either reading or special education, almost all of whom had a Master's degree. Each teacher provided individual tutoring to three to four low-achieving second and third graders five days a week for 50 minutes a day from September to June. Tutor training was ongoing. Each lesson contained a core of five activities: (a) Letter-sound cards with consonants in black and vowels in red; (b) phoneme blending and analysis using letter cards or tiles (e.g., "change *fan* to *fat* to *sat* to *sag*" [p. 449]); (c) rapid, timed reading of phonetically regular as well as sight words on flash cards for fluency; (d) reading of both decodable text and narrative and expository text in trade books; and (e) dictation of words taught earlier in the lesson to include both single words and sentences. Two effects can be attributed to this tutoring program. First, tutored children outperformed controls in terms of gains on multiple measures of reading at the end of the year. Second, as reported by Shaywitz et al. (2004) in a second study involving these same children, participants in the intervention group showed changes in fMRIs from pretest to post-test, indicating more efficient processing during reading compared with children who did not have tutoring in phonological processing.

The second example of a tutoring program, *Reading Rescue* (Hoover, 1995), comes from a first-grade intervention used with low-SES language-minority first graders in urban public schools. Ehri and her colleagues (2007) carried out an independent evaluation of Hoover's program. Tutoring in Reading Rescue was delivered by paraprofessionals as well as by certified teachers during the first-grade school year, with training ongoing, as with Blachman's (2004) program. Reading Rescue also has five components in each session but the list differs a little from Blachman et al.'s: (a) Familiar books are timed as they are re-read for fluency; (b) instructional-level books are read under tutor observations and are used for planning next steps; (c) multisensory instruction of PA and word study with a phonics sequence is aligned with *Ready Readers* decodable text; (d) writing is aimed at both PA and comprehension; and (e) comprehension and oral vocabulary are taught through reading a new book. By post-test, Ehri et al. reported advantages for the Reading Rescue children in comparison with controls on multiple literacy measures. They also reported that children tutored by paraprofessionals made gains equal to those made by children tutored by certified teachers, but that the paraprofessionals utilized more tutoring sessions to achieve these gains. Thus, the academic preparation of teachers is relevant to their effectiveness as teachers.

Both of these studies of tutoring curricula provided ongoing training for the tutors. Both programs worked from systematic instructional sequences but relied on tutors to make instructional decisions based on informal, ongoing assessment. That is, neither program was scripted; both programs relied on teachers' skills and knowledge in planning for individual children.

The Role of Teacher Education in the Development of Teachers' Linguistic Skills

Although there are hundreds of studies on the effect of curriculum on children's beginning reading abilities, relatively few look at the role played by teachers who use this effective curriculum. One underlying assumption of the studies that do exist is that children's skills in PA and phonics are dependent on the linguistic knowledge and skills of their teachers. Teacher knowledge of linguistics (see Chapter 22 by Joshi et al., this volume) is important for a number of reasons. Moats (1994) described the following five instructional advantages for teachers who understand the phonetic and orthographic structure of English: (a) Planning based on error analysis, (b) choosing teaching examples, (c) sequencing instruction, (d) using morphology to teach spelling, and (e) integrating word study into other aspects of balanced literacy instruction. This approach implies a shift in fundamental attitude from teachers playing an indirect role in instruction to that of teachers playing a more direct, critical role in the delivery of instruction. This approach does not imply that the curriculum has to be "teacher proof" (e.g., Brady & Moats, 1997; McCutchen & Berninger, 1999; Moats, 1994).

Teachers' Linguistic Skills

Moats (1994) was among the first researchers to point out that many teachers who work with beginning readers are lacking in critical linguistic skills themselves (see Joshi et al., Chapter 22, this volume). Her seminal study of experienced teachers involved the development of a frequently cited measure for assessing the code-related linguistic knowledge and skills of teachers. Her measure, the *Informal Survey of Linguistic Knowledge*, uses items such as "How many speech sounds are in the word *ox*?" and "What are the six common syllable types in English?" Moats reported that her instrument demonstrated an "insufficient grasp of spoken and written language" (p. 93) in many teachers. She attributed this finding to several causes. First, she cited Lindamood (1993) who found that many adults have weak PA skills. Second, she cited Ehri (1984) who found that experienced readers tend to count letters in words rather than sounds during PA exercises.

Other researchers using other test item formats have replicated Moats' (1994) finding that many adults are weak in word structure knowledge (e.g., Scarborough, Ehri, Olson, & Fowler, 1998). Bos and Mather developed a multiple choice measure of teacher linguistic knowledge in order to look at the relationships among linguistic knowledge, teaching experience, and sense of self-efficacy in large numbers of preservice and inservice teachers. Teachers with the most experience (11+ years) earned significantly higher knowledge scores than novice teachers (1–5 years), and special education teachers earned higher knowledge scores than regular education teachers (Bos, Mather, Dickson, Podhajski, & Chard, 2001; Mather, Bos, & Babur, 2001). However, even experienced teachers scored well below ceiling in these studies.

Spear-Swerling, Brucker, and Alfano (2005) also looked at relationships among teachers' linguistic knowledge, teaching experience, academic preparation, and self-perceptions. Tasks included one modeled on Scarborough, Ehri, Olson, and Fowler's (1998) graphophonemic task. Although the ability on this task was strongly correlated with preparation, teaching experience, and both perceived and actual ability in phonemic knowledge, even the best prepared of these 132 teachers struggled with many of the graphophonemic items.

Teacher Linguistic Knowledge with
and without Practical Experience

In two earlier studies, Spear-Swerling and Brucker (2003, 2004) reported on special education teacher candidates in university courses with and without tutoring practica. Although post-test scores at the end of the course demonstrated significant growth for all of the teacher candidates, those with opportunities to practice what they were learning about linguistics made more progress, consistent with Bos et al.'s (2001) finding (see above) that more-experienced teachers were better at linguistic skills. Teachers appear to need to put this knowledge into practice in order to understand it thoroughly.

Teacher Linguistic Knowledge and Student Outcomes

Another measure of the quality of teacher linguistic knowledge and skill lies in students' reading outcomes. To claim a logical connection between teacher training and student outcomes, both teachers and their students must be significantly stronger than controls at post-test. For example, Bos, Mather, Friedman Narr, and Babur (1999) reported positive effects for a PD project (i.e., *Reading Instructional Methods of Efficacy* or RIME) involving a two-week summer institute plus follow-up classroom-based support with 11 K-2 teachers in two schools. The RIME teachers made significant growth on Bos et al.'s test of teacher linguistic skills, while controls did not. In addition, the K-2 students of RIME teachers were stronger in spelling in comparison with the students of control teachers.

■ Urban University-School Partnership in Teacher Professional Development

Innovative Approach to Professional Development

Although supervised tutoring has been reported as a successful component of preservice education (e.g., Al Otaiba, 2005; Spear-Swerling & Brucker, 2003, 2004), it is less commonly used as a model for inservice PD. Uhry and Shepherd (1997) reported on a tutoring program that was a component of a master's degree in learning disabilities for both preservice and inservice students, but the data were collected on the children's rather than the teachers' growth. Supervised tutoring has two advantages over supervised classroom visits: (a) The tutors can watch each other work and share ideas, and (b) supervision can be carried out often and intensively.

Research questions. The present study followed the growth of 28 certified teachers through a funded PD sequence that included tutoring 28 first graders for seven months. Following are the questions addressed in this study:

1. Does university training in PA and phonics education, in combination with a supervised tutoring practicum, result in an advantage for trained teachers on a test of teacher knowledge and skill in comparison with

untrained controls? Does university training alone provide an advantage, or is the advantage associated with supervised practice?

2. Do children tutored by teachers involved in this PD have an advantage in PA and word reading over children in an after-school program with general homework help? Is this advantage associated with an advantage in reading and understanding stories as well?

Method. Two sets of contrasts were carried out in this seven-month study. In the first, four groups of teachers, who were trained under several different instructional conditions, were compared using a measure of linguistic knowledge before and after training. Although all were enrolled at the same university in one of four separate sections of the same beginning reading class, some received direct instruction in teaching PA and phonics while others did not, and some practiced this knowledge under supervision as after-school tutors and some did not. In the second set of contrasts, first-grade children, who were tutored in PA and phonics by one of the above groups of teachers trained in linguistic knowledge and skills, were compared to first graders in the same school who received after-school homework help but received no direct instruction in PA and phonics.

Settings. There were two settings for this study: (a) A university classroom where 81 teachers took master's level literacy courses, and (b) a high-needs, urban school where 28 of these teachers tutored 28 first-grade children in a seven-month reading practicum.

The university classroom. The university is situated in a large city on the east coast of the United States. Its graduate school offers master's degrees at both the preservice and inservice levels. The university has an historical commitment to working in low-income urban neighborhoods and the PD program was designed to provide in-depth instruction in reading education for teachers working in high-needs schools with young children at-risk for reading difficulties.

Partner school as practicum site. The second setting was a local elementary school that served as a site for the supervised tutoring practicum. This school already served as a university partner in multiple capacities. For instance, student teachers from the university's preservice programs were routinely placed with cooperating teachers here. Several of the lower-grade classroom teachers were graduates of the PD program.

Although poverty and home language status made many of the children in this school at-risk for reading difficulties, the school was high functioning and supportive of its children and teachers. It met most of Edmunds' (1979) criteria for successful schools (i.e., positive principal leadership, high expectations for student outcomes, and an orderly environment) as evidenced through an outside quality review by the school's district office describing the principal as a strong leader who managed the school well, and the students as behaving well and as having positive attitudes toward learning. The principal was in her second year in this school at the time of the study and was interested in working toward Edmund's remaining criteria: (a) Focus on basic skills such as reading, and (b) ongoing planning-based evaluation.

Teacher participants. Four groups of teachers participated in the study, the group of 28 in the PD program, and three other groups of university students who served as controls. As shown in Table 23.1, all four groups were enrolled in university literacy courses over the academic year in which the study took

TABLE 23.1   *Outline of Teacher Education Experiences for Groups 1–4*

	Group 1	Group 2	Group 3	Group 4
Group size	$n = 28$	$n = 19$	$n = 15$	$n = 19$
State certification	Yes	Yes	No	No
Level of teaching experience by the end of study	Inservice 1—17 years	Inservice 1—14 years	Preservice 1 year of student teaching	Preservice 1 year of student teaching
Ethnicity	14 Cauc. 10 AA 3 Hispanic 1 Arabic	17 Cauc. 1 AA 1 Hispanic	15 Cauc.	17 Cauc. 2 AA
Number of university literacy courses at the master's level taken before the end of the study	4	4–8	5	4
Beginning reading course	Yes	Yes	Yes	Yes
Beginning reading course with direct instruction in PA and phonics education	Yes	No	Yes	No
Classroom experiences including university-assigned case studies	Yes	Yes	Yes	Yes
Supervised tutoring experiences with supervisor knowledgeable in PA and phonics	Yes	No	No	No

Note: Cauc. = Caucasian; AA = African American.

place. All met the university's criteria for entrance to master's level study (i.e., strong references, BA degree with GPA of 3.0 or higher, strong essay).

Teacher experimental group (Group 1). The 28 inservice teachers who participated in the funded PD program were drawn from 31 who originally were enrolled. One teacher withdrew from the program at midyear with family issues, and two others were excluded from the study because the children they tutored withdrew from the school and their replacement tutees received only 2–3 months of tutoring. As shown in Table 23.1, these 28 participants' years of teaching ranged from 1 to 17, with a mean of 5.0 years. Two of the 28 were men and 26 were women. Half were from ethnic groups underrepresented in the local teaching force (i.e., African American, Hispanic, Arabic). They taught in 19 elementary schools in the large city school district in which the university was located. Almost all served as K-2 classroom teachers. Exceptions included a Grade 3 teacher, a K-2 teacher of English as a second language, and a Grade 4 special education contained-classroom teacher. Some of the K-2 classrooms were team-taught and included children with individualized education plans (IEPs). The average number of children in their classrooms was 24. Close to 100% of the children were African American, Hispanic, Chinese, and/or English language learners (ELL). With entitlement to free or reduced lunch as the criterion, 91% of the children taught by these teachers could be described as coming from families with low-SES. Four of the schools were classified as "schools under review" by the state, indicating such poor student outcomes that the state had oversight.

Teacher control groups (Groups 2, 3, and 4). Three control groups participated as intact university classes. These groups were invited to participate in the study because they were enrolled in other sections of the same beginning reading class taken by Group 1. As shown in Table 23.1, an initial difference between experimental and control participants involved differences in ethnicities, with much more diversity in Group 1 than in Groups 2–4. A second difference was that all of the 28 teachers in Group 1 taught children in low-SES neighborhoods, while the 53 teachers in Groups 2–4 taught or student taught across a much wider range of SES. Other group characteristics are described as follows.

Group 2: Inservice controls without linguistic instruction. Group 2 was made up of certified, experienced teachers seeking master's degrees as literacy specialists. Although some taught in high-needs schools, about half worked with middle-class children, with some working in suburban rather than urban schools. All of the 19 students were women. This control group was used to compare experienced teachers who did and did not receive systematic linguistic instruction. Their instructor focused on meaning-based beginning reading strategies.

Group 3: Preservice controls with linguistic instruction. As shown in Table 23.1, these teacher candidates were student teachers. Their program placed and supervised them in urban classrooms for state-certification-mandated experiences with both low- and middle-SES children. Some of them actually student taught at the school that served as a tutoring site, but did not work with first graders. Two of the 15 students were men. As with Group 1, their instructor was the first author and their coursework included the same instruction in linguistic knowledge included in the PD program section of the course. Groups 3 and 4 were included to compare preservice teachers across both instructional groups and teaching experiences.

Group 4: Preservice controls without linguistic instruction. These 19 teacher candidates were similar to Group 3 except that they were all women and they took their beginning reading course from an instructor who focused on meaning-based reading instruction.

Child participants. The tutored children participating in this study and their untutored controls attended an urban public school near the university in which the tutors received their training. The school offers a universal free lunch program demonstrating its very high percentage of students qualifying for Title 1 services. The school's Web site reports its student population as diverse and as reflecting the school's neighborhood. The ethnicity of its students is reported on the Web site to be 47% Hispanic, 29% African American, 20% Caucasian, and 4% other. The children described below reflected this pattern of diversity.

Child experimental group. The first-grade children who were tutored after school by teachers in the experimental group were all in the lowest quartile of their class on a screening consisting of invented spelling and had been recommended for tutoring by their teachers. Their mean score at pretest on the invented spelling measure was 49.4.

Child control group. A control group was constructed from the next-lowest Grade 1 spellers and from children on the original list whose parents did not wish them to be tutored. Their mean score at pretest on the invented spelling measure was 55.3, which was higher, but not significantly higher, in comparison with the experimental group's mean score.

University instruction for teachers. Table 23.1 provides a brief overview of group experiences in teacher instruction. All four groups were engaged in a master's level course in beginning reading at the start of the study in the fall semester. Course content for all sections included using ongoing assessment for planning instruction, shared and guided reading, the relationship between early writing and reading acquisition, and classroom organization focused on small group work. All four groups were assigned a case study documenting assessment, planning, and teaching a beginning or struggling reader in their classroom as a final project. As outlined in Table 23.1, Groups 1 and 3 also received direct instruction in PA and phonics, while Groups 2 and 4 did not. The following elaborates on this and other curricular differences in groups.

Professional development for teachers in experimental group (Group 1). The experimental PD program consisted of six graduate courses (18 credits) in literacy. One of the six courses was the tutoring practicum. Four of the courses had been taken by the time that the post-test for tutored children was administered. The first course in the program was a two-week summer institute with speakers and discussions of the focus of the program: The neurology of dyslexia, the importance of instruction focused on PA, phonics, and fluency in the early grades, and the assessment and instruction of children with cultural and linguistic differences. The second and third were the fall beginning reading course, and the yearlong tutoring practicum. The fourth, before the tutoring intervention ended, was a spring semester course on connections between oral and written language focused on vocabulary and discourse comprehension.

University instruction in PA and phonics (i.e., the beginning reading course) involved research (e.g., Blachman, Tangel, Ball, Black, & McGraw, 1999; Bradley & Bryant, 1983), research syntheses and reviews (i.e., National Reading Panel, 2000; Snow, Burns, & Griffin, 1998; Uhry & Clark, 2005), and research-into-practice curricula (e.g., Adams, Foorman, Lundberg, & Beeler, 1998; Blachman, Ball, Black, & Tangel, 2000; O'Connor, Notari-Syverson, & Vadasy, 1998). Each of these levels of study was followed by application-based discussions and theory-to-practice demonstrations (e.g., using cards with letters and key word pictures for learning letter sounds, practicing phoneme segmentation using puppets). Group 1 practiced these techniques during tutoring under the supervision of mentors who were graduates of the PD program. The instructor for this group and for Group 3 was the first author.

Professional development for teachers in control group 2. The inservice control group was enrolled in a 36-credit master's degree. Their required entry-level courses, which were completed before post-test, included a two-semester sequence focusing on the theoretical underpinnings of the linguistic, cognitive, sociocultural, and developmental dimensions of literacy. The third course for this noncohort group was either an assessment course or a summer institute focused on meaning-based instruction (not the institute taken by Group 1). These three courses plus the beginning reading course had all been completed at the time of post-testing. Although a practicum was the final course for Group 2, this was not scheduled until after the research ended. As outlined in Table 23.1, their instructor in beginning reading did not focus on PA or phonics or on direct instruction.

Professional development for teachers in control groups 3 and 4. These two preservice groups were enrolled in a yearlong, full-time, 36-credit master's level initial certification program. The curriculum included five literacy and language courses and a year of student teaching, three days a week in the fall, and five days a week in the spring. Case studies were assigned in both fall and spring, each for a specific literacy course, involving planning assessment-based instruction and reporting on the evidence of progress made during instruction. Field-based supervision did not include specific support for using

PA and phonics in this assignment, and for the most part, teacher candidates did not observe modeling of this instruction by their cooperating teacher. Group differences in preservice experiences are reported as follows.

As outlined in Table 23.1, the first author taught Group 3 their fall semester course in beginning reading. It included PA and phonics instruction as described under Group 1 earlier. The first author also taught a spring semester course in which the second case study was assigned (i.e., reading across the curriculum). This cohort group began the program during the summer and at the time of post-test had completed all five literacy courses: (a) Foundations in language and literacy, (b) Multicultural children's literature, (c) Beginning reading, (d) Teaching reading across the curriculum, and (e) Teaching reading to children for whom English is a second language.

An instructor with a strong preference for meaning-based instruction taught Group 4. She taught both the fall beginning reading course and the spring curriculum course. Unlike Group 3, this group did not receive instruction in PA or phonics in their beginning reading course. Another difference is that Group 4 did not begin the program until the fall semester and did not take the fifth course listed above until after post-test.

Classroom instruction for all children. The year of this study coincided with the first year of a new district curriculum mandate for meaning-based literacy instruction supplemented with an implicit, unsystematic phonics program. Daily literacy instruction for first grade typically began with 15-minute whole-group phonics activities, often based on the children's names. This was followed by 75-minute blocks including, for example, genre discussions, guided reading groups, and writing centers with individualized teacher-child writing conferences.

Experimental group for tutored children. The tutoring intervention involved an hour of one-to-one instruction two afternoons a week. It was embedded in a 3:00–5:30 p.m. after-school program that also included a snack, outdoor play, homework help, and special projects. Tutoring took the place of homework help for the 28 children who were tutored by the teachers in the PD program.

The introduction of new material was systematic but not scripted. Tutors were expected to be able to make instructional decisions about introducing new material based on ongoing informal assessment. Each tutoring session was structured around a daily sequence of activities. Table 23.2 outlines a lesson format (Format 1) for children learning letter names. Identification of 22–26 letters by name was our criterion for moving children on to Format 2. The first three of Adams' (1990) five levels of PA (i.e., sensitivity to rhyme, onset segmentation, and blending) were taught in Lesson Format 1, as were conventions of print.

Once children knew how to read and write most letters, they moved into Lesson Format 2 (Table 23.3), which was based on lessons developed for

TABLE 23.2 *Tutoring Session Framework 1 for Children Learning Letter Names and Phonemic Awareness*

Targeted Outcome	Instructional Activity
Sensitivity to rhyme	Shared reading—listening and joining in with rhyming words
Letter names	Shared reading and finger-point reading with looking for letters pointed out by tutor
Letter names	Reading letter flash cards with key word pictures
Letter forms	Writing letters from spoken letter names
Blending phonemes	Tutor says phonemes in two-phoneme words and child blends
Onset segmentation	Tutor says word from story and child says first phoneme
Phoneme segmentation	Mrs. Magic Mouth (Elkonin Task) with two-phoneme words
Comprehension	Listening to stories and responding orally

TABLE 23.3 *Tutoring Session Framework 2 for Children Who Know Letter Names*

Targeted Outcome	Instructional Activity
Text fluency	Finger-point reading or re-reading familiar text from the prior lesson
Letter sound fluency	Letter-sound flash cards with key word pictures
Phoneme segmentation	Mrs. Magic Mouth (Elkonin Task)
Developmental spelling	Spelling dictation of decodable words
Reading decodable words	Flash cards with words using current letter-sounds
Reading sight words	Flash cards with sight words and prior decodable words
Decoding strategies	Guided reading of decodable text
Multiple reading strategies	Guided reading of partially decodable, meaning-based text
Comprehension and writing	Responding to literature orally, in pictures, and in writing

an earlier study by Uhry and Shepherd (1997) and had a number of components in common with programs designed by Blachman et al. (2004) and by Hoover (1998).

Lesson Format 2 began with a rereading of an old book to practice fluency and to see what the child remembered from the previous lesson (Clay, 1993). This also provided an opportunity for the tutor to use running records to practice taking notes on miscues in order to plan future lessons. Next, a new letter-sound was taught very explicitly with a short lesson focused on the new sound alone and the sound in words (e.g., "The children in this picture are having fun. Say *fun*. The sound of the letter *f* is /f/. Does *fun* start with /f/? Does *fat* start with *f*? Does *sat* start with *f*?"). Once the new sound was taught, it was practiced embedded in a review of all previous letter sound cards. The cards were reviewed for speed and each new letter was practiced for automaticity and speed before another new letter was added. See the sequence for introducing letter sounds and syllable types in Table 23.4.

One distinguishing feature of the intervention tutoring is the consistency with which each new letter-sound pattern was practiced throughout all lesson sections. New letter-sound patterns were practiced in isolation, in spelling practice with decodable words on flash cards, and in decodable text. The final sections of each lesson involved reading these new words in simple storybooks with predictable, repetitive text that contained the target pattern but were not completely decodable. For example, a decodable text that focused on short *a* and simple consonants read, "Mac had a pal" (Makar, 1995). This activity was followed, for example, by a storybook that read, "I am Dan, the flying man. Catch me, catch me if you can" (Cowley, 1990). Children were encouraged to

TABLE 23.4   *Order of Letter-Sounds and Syllable Structures Introduced once Children Know Letter Names*

Order of Letter Sounds Introduced

Simple and common consonants: m, s, p, t, l, f, hard c, d, n, b, r, j, k, v, z, hard g

Short vowels: a, i, o, e, u

Less frequent, more complex consonants: h, w, x, y, h, qu, soft g, soft c

Consonant digraphs: sh, ch, th (unvoiced), th (voiced), ph

Long vowels with simple vowel teams: oa, ai, ea, ee

Long vowels with silent *e*

*Order of Syllable Structures Introduced**

Closed, vowel teams, silent *e*

---

*Note: Most children did not move beyond silent *e* syllables to open, *r*-controlled, or consonant-*l*-*e* syllables but all were taught to the tutors. We taught open and vowel team syllables first to establish the left-to-right, letter-by-letter (or letter team) strategy before introducing silent e.

identify words geared to a sounding-out strategy (i.e., *Dan, man, can*) and those geared toward use of pictures ("Look at the picture. How did he get up in the air? Right, he's flying. He's a flying man"). This strategy prepared children for the transition from decodable text to storybooks. Although the National Reading Panel reported a paucity of research on decodable text, Jenkins, Peyton, Sanders, and Vadasy (2004) have provided evidence that decodable text is no more effective than meaning-based text. As in Blachman et al. (2004), both text types were used in every lesson here.

Children were taught to identify syllable types that were within their repertoire, in this case, closed syllable words with short vowels and final consonants. It is a premise of metacognitive theory that knowing when to use which strategy is important. By the end of tutoring, most children could also identify and read syllables with vowel-teams and silent-e.

A second distinguishing feature of the experimental intervention is that it was considered an instructional frame rather than a scripted lesson. In collaboration with a tutoring *mentor*, decisions were made about the amount of time devoted to each activity, time for moving to the next sound in a sequence (see Table 23.4), and materials used. Teachers gradually moved from this mentoring support and a set frame for the lesson to a more individualized frame based on ongoing assessment. This model of mentoring is consistent with Snow, Griffin, and Burns' (2005) stages in teacher development from concrete, situated *declarative knowledge*, which is typical of preservice or new teachers, through stages of *expert, adaptive knowledge*, which is demonstrated by experienced teachers who become more flexible and able to apply new learning. As Spear-Swerling and Brucker (2004) point out, learning to administer assessments, interpret the results, and implement assessment-based instruction is a highly complex process. Most of the 28 teachers in the PD program had carried out classroom-based, district-mandated informal assessments as a requirement of their positions, but few had felt comfortable interpreting results and implementing assessment-based instruction at the onset of the PD program.

Control group for untutored children (homework help). The untutored children received homework help from after-school staff in small, informal groups. Reading homework typically consisted of reading aloud from a small collection of books selected weekly by each child's teacher for practice after school and at home. Books were routinely sent back and forth in the children's backpacks for all first grade children. The untutored and tutored children had comparable classroom experiences (neither group had direct instruction in PA or phonics in the classroom) and comparable amounts of after-school time engaged in reading activities, but the untutored group received no PA or phonics tutoring.

Assessment instruments for teachers. Teachers in the experimental PD program were assessed at pretest and post-test using an instrument based on Moats' (1994) *Informal Survey of Linguistic Knowledge.* We used the 70 items in 10 of her original 15 sections of the test. Five sections were dropped because they seemed more appropriate to teachers of older children (e.g., the rule for adding a suffix to words ending in *Y*, recognition of words with Greek origins). This survey was designed to measure linguistics knowledge with a focus on knowledge of the elements of the sound structure of English (i.e., PA and phonics). Sample items were (a) "How many speech sounds are in the following words?" (*boil* [3], *ox* [3], *precious* [6]); (b) "(*first, pumpkin, scratch*)"; and (c) "What are the six common syllable types in English?" (closed, vowel teams, silent *e*, *r*-controlled, open, consonant-*l-e*) (pp. 89–90). The format for this assessment was open-ended response.

Assessment measures for children. Invented spelling was used at pretest as a screening to identify children who might be appropriate for tutoring support in reading. A number of literacy measures were used at post-test to demonstrate positive outcomes in the areas analyzed by the National Reading Panel (2000).

A measure of *invented spelling* with a developmental scoring system was used at pretest for identifying candidates for the tutoring program and for establishing the general level of emergent literacy for both experimental and control groups. Because it combines phonological awareness and letter knowledge, invented spelling in kindergarten and early first grade is a strong predictor of later reading ability (Mann, Tobin, & Wilson, 1987; Morris & Perney, 1984). Uhry (1999, 2002) found that at both mid- and end-of-kindergarten, developmental spelling accounted for significantly more unique variance in finger-point reading and word reading than measures of letter knowledge and phonological awareness combined. Invented spelling was measured in the present study using existing data from a beginning-of-year screening administered by classroom teachers. The classroom teachers dictated 35 words. The protocols were rescored using a developmental scoring system described by Morris (1999) to score uniformly across classes of children with a scoring system that recognizes nuances of literacy development before the acquisition of word reading. In this system, one point of credit is given for a reasonable initial letter (e.g., K for CAT), two points for initial and final letters (e.g., KT for CAT), three points for representing every phoneme in a word (e.g., JRAS for DRESS), four points for orthographic features (e.g., PEKING for peeking), and five for a word correctly spelled. This measure was used at pretest, together with teachers' recommendations, to select children for the tutoring program. It was also used at post-test to measure growth.

Phonemic awareness. Rosner's (1975) Test of Auditory Analysis Skills (TAAS) provided a second measure of post-test PA. The TAAS asks children to repeat back a word without one of the syllables or phonemes. The first of the 13 items is, "Say *sunshine*. Now say it again, but don't say *shine*." The final item is "Say *smack*. Now say it again but don't say /m/" (p. 47). Grade level performance from K-3 is provided based on raw scores.

Fluency. A measure of phonics fluency was administered at post-test. The Voyager Benchmark Nonword Fluency Test (Voyager Expanded Learning, 2004) is part of the Voyager Passport B instructional system. The test measures the number of letter-sounds in decodable nonwords that a child can read within 60 seconds from a list of 60 words. Children are credited for reading either individual letter sounds or the whole words aloud (i.e., two points for reading either /u/-/k/ or "uk" and three points for either /v/-/i/-/z/ or "viz"). Passport B's Benchmark 3 form was used at post-test.

Reading words in lists. The Word Identification (WID) subtest from the Woodcock Reading Mastery Tests (Woodcock, 1987) was administered at post-test. This norm-referenced test presents progressively more difficult words for children to read in lists. It allows up to 5 seconds to read each word. All children were asked to begin reading with the easiest items and to read through the designated ceiling of six consecutive failed responses at the end of a section. Raw scores represent words read correctly up to the designated ceiling and were used here for analysis of group differences. Standard scores and percentiles can be calculated from raw scores. The publisher reports the split-half reliability coefficient as 0.98.

Reading words in stories. In addition to the Woodcock WID (1987), a storybook word-reading measure with leveled passages (i.e., leveled from easier to harder) was used. The passages also provided text for listening and reading comprehension as outlined below. In an earlier study (Uhry, 2000), the validity of this storybook word-reading measure was established through its strong correlation ($r = 0.91$) with the Woodcock WID (Woodcock, 1987). The three-passage measure begins with 106 words from *The Wobbly Tooth* (Jordan, 1989), which is at roughly early first-grade level. This passage was followed by 94 words from pages 14–16 of *Wagon Wheels* (Brenner, 1978), which is mid second-grade level, and 128 words from pages 2–3 of *The Courage of Sarah Noble* (Dalgliesh, 1954), which is roughly mid third-grade level. As with the Woodcock WID, up to 5 seconds per word were allowed. After 5 seconds, the word was provided for the child who was encouraged to move on to the next word. Children who missed roughly one-third of the words at one level were not asked to read the subsequent level. The score was derived from the total number of words read in all three stories out of a possible 328 words.

Listening comprehension. Because ability to listen and understand a story is, together with decoding words, considered critical to skilled reading comprehension (Gough & Tunmer, 1986), a measure of listening comprehension was included. Whether or not they struggled to read the first two leveled books, all children were asked to listen to the first 130 words of *The Courage of Sarah Noble* (Dalgliesh, 1954) while looking at an illustration. Note that this task preceded the third reading comprehension task, which is described below. The first author developed eight listening comprehension questions including an open-ended first question: "*Who* is this story about and *what* are they doing?" Other questions involved additional plot points, vocabulary, predictions, and comparison with the previous story. Acceptable answers were scripted following a pilot period during which the first author and doctoral student research assistants transcribed answers and compared scoring using criteria for consistency. Listening comprehension is not an area that was expected to be responsive to training in PA or phonics.

Reading comprehension. The three oral reading passages used to measure word decoding in passages were used to assess reading comprehension at each of the three reading levels. Eight questions at each level were developed following the format for listening comprehension as outlined above. As above, criteria for scoring were developed with the research assistants who administered the measure.

Selection of tutoring site. A tutoring site was selected that was less than two miles from the university so that access would be easy for both students and university faculty. The school had an existing after-school program that provided the administrative support needed for the supervised tutoring, specifically, caring for the children during the time gap between school dismissal and the arrival of tutors and dismissing children after tutoring.

Although there is disagreement on criteria for partner or PD schools[1] (Murray, 1993), several themes re-occur in the literature: (a) Bridging the gap between the ivory tower culture of the university and the hands-on culture of the school; and (b) mutual interest in inquiry around school reform (Winitsky, Stoddart, & O'Keefe, 1992). Both of these themes were considered in initial conversations with the principal of the chosen school. Both school and university wanted to be collaborative, sharing partners in improving both teacher PD and instruction for children.

Pretesting and selection of children to be tutored. Classroom teachers sent home consent forms in both English and Spanish. From the pool of 105 returned forms, the lowest-scoring children were identified for tutoring using several sources of information, including the developmental scoring from the invented spelling screening described earlier as well as teacher recommendations. Not all recommended children's parents gave permission for tutoring; some gave permission for data collection as controls but not for tutoring.

Tutoring schedule. The children were tutored twice a week after school from late October through the first week in June. Each of the twice-weekly tutoring sessions lasted 1 hour. The total tutoring time for children with 100% attendance was 54 hours. Tutoring records indicated a range of participation from 46 to 54 hours. Tutoring was carried out in six classrooms. Each classroom housed 4–5 tutoring pairs (i.e., a child and his or her tutor) plus one of our six tutoring mentors. A doctoral student who coordinated the attendance served as liaison between the children's tutors, who arrived at the school at 4:15, and the classroom teachers, who usually left for the day before 4:15. Another role involved temporary matching of children with tutors when absences left one or the other without a partner for the day.

Supervision. The mentors, who were graduates of the program, were selected on the basis of successful acquisition of the components of the program as demonstrated through end-of-program scores on the Moats (1994) measure during the previous spring, and on their leadership skills as demonstrated during small-group coursework. The mentors were trained and supervised by a doctoral student (the second author) who coordinated the tutoring program. The mentors observed the same tutors each week and provided both individual and group feedback on a once-a-week basis. In addition to the mentors, the tutoring course instructor, who was the second author, regularly observed the tutors and children and made suggestions to both the mentors and the tutors.

Post-testing of children. A team of additional doctoral students who were not connected to the tutoring and did not know which children were in which group carried out post-testing in May and early June. The entire first grade was tested to make these data available to the elementary school first-grade teachers who expressed interest in seeing scores for children who had not participated in the study as well as for those who had.

Post-testing of teachers. Teachers in the PD program and in the three control groups were readministered the Moats (1994) measure of linguistic knowledge and skills in early May. Testing was administered during class time for Groups 1, 3, and 4. Not all of the teachers in Group 2 were taking the same course in the spring semester, so they were contacted individually and tested in small groups.

Feedback to the partner school. A meeting was scheduled for all staff involved in support for first grade reading. Both the tutoring program and the end-of-program assessment tools were described. General findings were reported in terms of group differences. This group meeting was followed by a meeting with each of the classroom teachers to share children's reading scores and to talk about the children's needs. Scores were shared for all first graders, not just those in the research project.

Results

Results for teachers. To measure effect of the different kinds of PD on teacher growth in linguistic knowledge, t-tests were used to evaluate change in means for the four groups from pretest and post-test. As shown in Table 23.5, only the inservice group that tutored children under university supervision (Group 1) changed significantly from pretest to post-test on the Moats (1994) Informal Survey of Teacher Knowledge. None of the three other groups demonstrated

TABLE 23.5   *Teachers' Means, Standard Deviations, and Significant Differences across Time on the Informal Survey of Linguistic Knowledge (Moats, 1994; Range 0–70)*

Time 1	Time 2	Significant Difference
Group 1 (Inservice Experimental with PA instruction and tutoring, $n = 28$)		
33.6 (8.24)	45.5 (8.51)	<0.001
Group 2 (Inservice Control with no PA Instruction and no tutoring, $n = 19$)		
34.2 (7.00)	33.1 (7.29)	ns
Group 3 (Preservice Control with PA Instruction but no tutoring, $n = 15$)		
25.7 (6.71)	28.3 (5.89)	ns
Group 4 (Preservice Control with no PA instruction and no tutoring, $n = 19$)		
22.5 (6.42)	25.9 (7.16)	ns

significant change over the seven-month period of time. The other inservice group (Group 2) had post-test scores that were lower than their pretest scores. Whether or not they had received explicit instruction in linguistic knowledge, the preservice teachers did not improve. University learning without supervised practice in implementing PA and phonics may not be enough for significant change in teacher linguistic knowledge.

Teachers in Group 1 were also compared on selected items on the Moats (1994) survey specific to PA and phonics. Because the sections vary in number of items, the means as well as change scores were transformed by dividing the item totals by the number of items in the section to allow comparison of change scores across sections. As shown in Table 23.6, teachers improved significantly in knowledge of syllables, blends, and phonemes, but the amount of the change, expressed by proportion of items answered correctly was greatest for syllable knowledge.

Results for children. As shown in Table 23.7, the tutored group improved significantly more than the untutored control group on the spelling measure (e.g., Morris & Perney, 1984; Uhry, 1999) given at pretest and post-test. They had not differed significantly at pretest. Although no pretest data are available for measures of PA, phonics, and reading to compare change over the seven months of tutoring, these measures were given at post-test. At post-test (see Table 23.7) the tutored children were significantly stronger than the controls on PA (elision task), phonological decoding (nonword fluency), real word reading on lists (word identification) and in context (story words), and reading comprehension (story comprehension). The only skill on which they were not different was listening comprehension, which had not been a focus of the tutoring.

TABLE 23.6 *Comparisons of Pretest and Post-test Mean Item Scores* (with Standard Deviations) and across Item Changes from PA and Phonics Sections of the Informal Survey of Linguistic Knowledge (Moats, 1994)*

Section	Pretest	Post-test	Change	Significance
Name 6 syllable types (six items)	0.30 (0.30)	0.70 (0.30)	0.40 (0.31)	<0.001
			>0.001	
Identify cons. blends (seven items)	0.46 (0.16)	0.62 (0.17)	0.17 (.14)	<0.001
			ns	
Count phonemes (10 items)	0.54 (0.17)	0.65 (0.15)	0.11 (0.16)	<0.01

*Note: The term "item score" means the total score for a section, divided by the number of items in the section. For example, in the first item, there were 10 phoneme-counting items, so the mean score for phoneme counting was divided by 10. This was done to compare means across sections.

TABLE 23.7 *Means, Standard Deviations, and t-Test Results for Scores of Tutored and Nontutored Low-Achieving Students Before and After Treatment*

	Group 1 Children	Group 2 Children	
	Tutored ($n = 28$)	Untutored ($n = 28$)	Significant Difference
Pretest (October)			
Inv. Spell-1 (PA)	49.4 (29.11)	55.3 (33.76)	ns
Post-test (May)			
Invented Spell-2 (PA)	150.3 (16.41)	108.6 (57.42)	<0.01
TAAS (PA: elision)	8.7 (2.26)	6.4 (1.93)	<0.001
Nonword fluency	58.1 (27.50)	33.8 (15.61)	<0.001
WRMT Word ID	34.7 (12.22)	22.1 (14.07)	<0.01
Story Words	213.5 (89.13)	140.9 (90.96)	<0.01
Story Comp	13.9 (4.94)	9.0 (5.22)	<0.01
Listening Comp	4.2 (1.92)	3.3 (1.59)	ns

Note: Raw scores were analyzed. WRMT Word Identification were also converted to percentiles. The mean reading score for the tutored children in Group 1 was at roughly the 48th percentile while that for the untutored children was at roughly the 18th percentile.

■ Significance of Findings for Teacher
Linguistic Knowledge

Two kinds of evidence were used to evaluate the effectiveness of the PD model
for developing teachers' linguistic knowledge for teaching reading: (a) Change
in teacher's responses on a paper and pencil survey of linguistic knowledge and
(b) Change in student performance on a spelling task sensitive to PA and phonics knowledge following teacher implementation of PA and phonics knowledge during supervised tutoring. Both kinds of evidence showed that the
inservice PD model that combined academic preparation in language processes
related to reading and opportunity to implement that knowledge in practice was
effective. Findings are consistent with earlier studies showing that (a) Inservice
teachers are stronger in linguistic knowledge and skills than preservice teachers (e.g., Mather, Bos, & Babur, 2001); (b) Training in linguistic skills raises
teachers' scores, especially if the training is associated with supervised practice
(e.g., Spear-Swerling & Brucker, 2003, 2004); and (c) Many teachers of young
children lack skills and knowledge in PA and phonics (e.g., Bos et al., 1999,
2001; Moats, 1994; Scarborough et al., 1998; Spear-Swerling et al., 2005).

The major contribution of this study is in defining the conditions under
which teachers in the PD program appear to have an advantage over controls
in their knowledge and skills in PA and phonics. As is reported in other studies (e.g., Bos et al., 2001) both groups of experienced teachers here outperformed inexperienced teachers at pretest in terms of linguistic knowledge.
Both groups of inservice teachers in this study had taught for an average of 5–6
years at pretest and were significantly stronger in linguistic knowledge and
skills than the preservice teachers who were just beginning to teach students.
Teaching experience, then, is one attribute of the teacher who is better able
to implement research knowledge in practice. Training involving supervision
is another attribute. Significant growth in these areas over the seven-month
course of the study was associated here with both university-based, instruction and with linguistically focused supervision of practical experiences.

Note that both inservice and preservice teachers (Groups 1 and 3) received instruction with the first author as university instructor, but only the
inservice teachers (Group 1) received practicum-site supervision focused
on linguistic knowledge and skills (e.g., consulting, modeling, small group
discussion of case studies). The researchers had been optimistic about the
possibility of making a difference in preservice preparation in this area, but
apparently university-based instruction is not sufficient for this. There was no
significant difference in preservice teachers (Groups 3 and 4) with and without
linguistically focused instruction. Results are consistent with Spear-Swerling
and Brucker's (2003) finding that a group of preservice teachers with linguistically based university instruction plus supervised tutoring learned more
than a second university-taught group without this supervised tutoring.

Multiple pieces of evidence point to a successful experience in the PD program for the 28 participating teachers, including (a) their own growth in linguistic skills and their advantage over other teachers serving as controls; and (b) the growth and academic advantage of the children they tutored. Exactly how did the supervised tutoring help these experienced teachers learn more about linguistic skills and their application to instruction? As stated by one PD program teacher in her end-of-program portfolio:

> In tutoring I got a chance to put into practice what I was learning.
> I improved my own PA. We were constantly assessing our tutoring child and my mentor has given me strategies to use with my struggling students.

■ Limitations, Strengths, and Future Directions

Limitations. One limitation of this research is that neither the teacher nor the student groups were formed through random assignment. The school felt strongly that the lowest scoring children should be given preference for tutoring. Children in the experimental group, while lower scoring at pretest, might have had parents who were more supportive; theirs were the parents who signed up for the program whereas the control group contained three children whose parents did not wish them to be tutored. However, children of parents who returned no form at all were not included in either the experimental or control groups. Another drawback is that only one measure was taken at pretest because the teachers did not want the children taken from the room so early in the year for additional testing. Additional data on observing the teaching process would have been helpful. No data were collected on children's reading outcomes in 28 tutor's own classrooms.

Strengths. Two kinds of converging evidence resulted that showed learning to teach well benefits from a combination of coursework and supervision in applied situations. University classroom exposure to knowledge is not enough, even for experienced teachers. Intensive supervision in a time-consuming after-school practicum was both effective and valued by the teachers. This finding is consistent with literature reporting the value of supportive classroom visits (e.g., Bos, Mather, Friedman Narr, & Babur, 1999) and supervised tutoring (e.g., Spear-Swerling & Brucker, 2003, 2004). It is also consistent with Snow, Griffen, and Burns' (2005) model of professional growth in which teachers become more and more flexible in terms of applying and synthesizing knowledge in more and more contexts. Snow et al. describe five levels of teacher knowledge: "declarative, situated, stable, expert, (and) reflective" (p. 210). They argue that experienced teachers grow in terms of the amount of knowledge they have, as well as in use of that knowledge at the "expert-adaptive-reflective end of the continuum" (p. 208). That is, over time, and with support, they are able to move from knowledge of how to follow a prescribed protocol to the successful problem solving involved in designing assessment-based protocols that continue to be adapted during actual use. For teachers to be able to move beyond the declarative knowledge often provided in university coursework and in single-workshop PD experiences, they need the kind of ongoing support provided by mentors or coaches in inservice practicum experiences, and the mentors or coaches need to be proficient in linguistic knowledge themselves.

Future directions. Being able to provide valued data to the partner-school classroom teachers was an opportunity to bridge the research-practice gap. Over the course of the tutoring and data collection, the researchers began to conceptualize the research audience as both the scientific community and the children's school community. End-of-year reading and spelling data were shared with the classroom teachers in the partner school through a process in which data for all first graders were shared with individual teachers as well as at a grade-level meeting including teachers, the literacy coach, and the principal. Conversation focused on individual children's progress as well as on group differences. McCutchen, Abbott, et al., in discussing a similar university-school conversation, made a good point when they advised, "grounding...discussions in terms of *student knowledge* rather than philosophical orientations" (2002, p. 81). Keep in mind that at the time of the present study both the school and the district were committed to meaning-based instruction. The focus of our presentation was on individualizing instruction based on what children already knew rather than on a particular orientation.

Another strategy for engaging teachers in the findings was the use of high-quality children's literature in assessing both word reading and comprehension. Although word lists could have been used as the only word reading measure, a storybook word-reading measure with leveled passages was also used. Some classroom teachers tend to consider reading words in passages as more authentic and relevant than reading words in isolation. Measures of word reading and comprehension based on literature were highly correlated with the Woodcock WID (1987), a word-reading measure that is widely used and trusted by researchers. Using both the Woodcock and the more contextualized literature measure, which teachers consider more authentic, provided connections for teachers between the values of the scientific community and the values of the classroom. Unfortunately, systematic data documenting possible changes in first grade teacher's literacy orientations were not collected, but anecdotal evidence suggested that the school shifted toward a more scientifically researched curriculum. On the basis of their own observations of growth in particular children, as well as on the shared data, the school decided to invest in a systematic phonics program to supplement its meaning-based curriculum. Toward the end of the year following this study, Wilson's (2002) *Fundations* program was implemented with K-2 children who appeared to be at risk.

A recent report, "Educating School Teachers" (Levine, 2006, p. 106), recommended that schools of education partner with K-12 schools just as medical schools partner with hospitals for residencies because schools provide a "superb laboratory for education schools to experiment with initiatives designed to improve student achievement." The teacher-training agendas of most partner schools are clearer than their research agendas. Partnering around research could benefit all involved. Future research could document changes in teacher literacy orientation as well as teacher knowledge, changes in curriculum, and changes in student outcomes associated with research situated in schools. The present study suggests the benefit of school-based practica for inservice teachers learning to implement research in real-world classrooms.

■ References

Adams, M. J. (1990). *Beginning to read: Thinking and learning about print.* Cambridge, MA, The MIT Press.

Adams, M. J., Foorman, B. R., Lundberg, I., & Beeler, T. (1998). *Phonemic awareness in young children.* Baltimore, MD, Brookes.

Al Otaiba, S. (2005). How effective is code-based reading tutoring in English for English learners and preservice teacher-tutors? *Remedial and Special Education, 26,* 245–254.

Blachman, B., Tangel, D., Ball, E., Black, R., & McGraw, D. (1999). Developing phonological awareness and word recognition skills: A two-year intervention with low-income, inner city children. *Reading and Writing: An Interdisciplinary Journal, 11,* 239–273.

Blachman, B. A., Ball, E. W., Black, R., & Tangel, D. M. (2000). *Road to the code: A phonological awareness program for young children.* Baltimore, MD, Brookes.

Blachman, B. A., Fletcher, J. M., Schatschneider, C., Francis, D. J., Clonan, S. M., Shaywitz, B. A., & Shaywitz, S. E. (2004). Effects of intensive reading remediation for second and third graders and a 1-year follow-up. *Journal of Educational Psychology, 96,* 444–461.

Bos, C., Mather, N., Dickson, S., Podhajski, B., & Chard, D. (2001). Perceptions and knowledge of preservice and inservice educators about reading instruction. *Annals of Dyslexia, 51,* 97–120.

Bos, C. S., Mather, N., Friedman Narr, R., & Babur, N. (1999). Interactive, collaborative professional development in early literacy instruction: Supporting the balancing act. *Learning Disabilities Research and Practice, 14,* 227–238.

Bradley, L., & Bryant, P. E. (1983). Categorizing sounds and learning to read—a causal connection. *Nature, 301*, 419–421.

Brady, S., & Moats, L. (1997). *Informed instruction for reading success: Foundations to teacher preparation.* A position paper of The International Dyslexia Association. Baltimore, MD, The International Dyslexia Association.

Brenner, B. (1978). *Wagon wheels.* New York, Harper Trophy.

Clay, M. (1993). *An observation survey of early literacy achievement.* Portsmouth, NH, Heinemann.

Cowley, J. (1990). *Dan, the Flying Man.* New York, The Wright Group.

Dalgliesh, A. (1954). *The courage of Sarah Noble.* New York, Macmillan.

Edmunds, R. (1979). Some schools work and more can. *Social Policy, 9*, 28–32.

Ehri, L. C. (1984). How orthography alters spoken language competencies in children learning to read and spell. In J. Downing and R. Valtin (Eds.), *Language awareness and learning to read* (pp. 119–147). New York, Springer-Verlag.

Ehri, L. C., Dreyer, L. G., Flugman, B., & Gross, A. (2007). Reading Rescue: An effective tutoring intervention model for language-minority students who are struggling readers in first grade. *American Educational Research Journal, 44*, 414–448.

Gough, P. B., & Tunmer, W. E. (1986). Decoding, reading and reading disability. *Remedial and Special Education, 7*, 6–10.

Hoover, N. (1995). *Reading Rescue for elementary readers: An early intervention program 1994–1995 end-of-second year report on student progress at Interlachen Elementary School, Putnam County, Florida* (Tech. Report No. 2). Gainesville, FL, University of Florida.

Jenkins, J. R., Peyton, J. A., Sanders, E. A., & Vadasy, P. F. (2004). Effects of reading decodable texts in supplemental first-grade tutoring. *Scientific Studies of Reading, 8*, 53–85.

Jordan, S. (1989). *The wobbly tooth.* Crystal Lake, IL, Rigby.

Levine, A. (2006). *Educating school teachers.* Washington, DC, The Education Schools Project.

Liberman, I. Y. (1973). Segmentation of the spoken word and reading acquisition. *Bulletin of the Orton Society, 23*, 65–77.

Lindamood, P. (1993). Issues in researching the link between phonological awareness, learning disabilities, and spelling. In G. R. Lyon (Ed.), *Frames of reference for the assessment of learning disabilities: New views on measurement issues.* Baltimore, MD, Brookes.

Makar, B. W. (1985). *Mac and Tab primary phonics series.* Cambridge, MA, Educators Publishing Service.

Mann, V. A., Tobin, P., & Wilson, R. (1987). Measuring phonological awareness through the invented spellings of kindergarten children. *Merrill-Palmer Quarterly, 33*, 365–391.

Mather, N., Bos, C., & Babur, N. (2001). Perceptions and knowledge of preservice and inservice teachers about early literacy instruction. *Journal of Learning Disabilities, 34*, 472–482.

McCutchen, D., Abbott, R. D., Green, L. B., Beretvas, N., Cox, S., Potter, N. S., Quiroga, T., & Gray, A. L. (2002). Beginning literacy: Links among teacher knowledge, teacher practice, and student learning. *Journal of Learning Disabilities, 35*, 69–86.

McCutchen, D., & Berninger, V. W. (1999). Those who know, teach well: Helping teachers master literacy-related subject matter knowledge. *Learning Disabilities Research and Practice, 14*, 215–226.

Moats, L. C. (1994). The missing foundation in teacher education: Knowledge of the structure of spoken and written language. *Annals of Dyslexia, 44*, 81–102.

Moats, L. C., & Foorman, B. R. (2003). Measuring teachers' content knowledge of language and reading. *Annals of Dyslexia, 53*, 23–45.

Morris, D. (1999). *Case studies in teaching beginning readers: The Howard Street tutoring manual.* New York, NY, The Guilford Press.

Morris, D., & Perney, J. (1984). Developmental spelling as a predictor of first-grade reading achievement. *The Elementary School Journal, 84*, 441–457.

Murray, F. (1993). "All or none" criteria for professional development schools. *Educational Policy, 7*, 61–73.

National Reading Panel. (2000). *Report of the National Reading Panel: Teaching children to read: An evidence-based assessment of the scientific research literature on reading and its implications for reading instruction.* Washington, DC, National Institute of Child Health and Human Development (NIH Publication No. 00–4769).

O'Connor, R. E., Notari-Syverson, A., & Vadasy, P. F. (1998). *Ladders to literacy: A kindergarten activity book.* Baltimore, MD, Brookes.

Rosner, J. (1975). Test of auditory analysis skills. In J. Rosner (Ed.), *Helping children overcome learning difficulties.* New York, Walker & Co.

Scarborough, H., Ehri, L. C., Olson, R. K., & Fowler, A. (1998). The fate of phonemic awareness beyond the elementary years. *Scientific Studies of Reading, 2*, 115–142.

Shaywitz, B. A., Shaywitz, S. E., Blachman, B. A., Pugh, K. R., Fulbright, R. K., Skudlarski, P., Mencl, W. E., Constable, R. T., Holahan, J. M., Marchione, K. E., Fletcher, J. M., Lyon, G. R., & Gore, J. C. (2004). Development of left occipitotemporal systems for skilled reading in children after a phonologically-based intervention. *Biological Psychiatry, 55*, 926–933.

Snow, C. E., Burns, M. S., & Griffin, P. (Eds.). (1998). *Preventing reading difficulties in young children.* Washington, DC, National Academy Press.

Snow, C. E., Griffin, P., & Burns, M. S. (Eds.) (2005). *Knowledge to support the teaching of reading: Preparing teachers for a changing world.* San Francisco, Jossey-Bass.

Spear-Swerling, L., & Brucker, P. O. (2003). Teachers' acquisition of knowledge about English word structure. *Annals of Dyslexia, 53*, 72–102.

Spear-Swerling, L., & Brucker, P. O. (2004). Preparing novice teachers to develop basic reading and spelling skills in children. *Annals of Dyslexia, 54*, 332–359.

Spear-Swerling, L., Brucker, P. O., & Alfano, M. P. (2005). Teachers' literacy-related knowledge and self-perceptions in relation to preparation and experience. *Annals of Dyslexia, 55,* 266–296.

Uhry, J. K. (1999). Invented spelling in kindergarten: The relationship with finger-point reading. *Reading and Writing: An Interdisciplinary Journal, 11,* 441–464.

Uhry, J. K. (2000, June). *Reading accuracy, rate and comprehension in grades one through three.* Paper presented at the annual meeting of the Society for the Scientific Study of Reading in Stockholm.

Uhry, J. K. (2002). Finger-point reading in kindergarten: The role of phonemic awareness, one-to-one correspondence, and rapid serial naming. *Scientific Studies of Reading, 6,* 319–342.

Uhry, J. K., & Clark, D. B. (2005). *Dyslexia: Theory and practice of instruction* (3rd ed.). Baltimore, MD, York Press.

Uhry, J. K., & Shepherd, M. J. (1997). Teaching phonological recoding to young children with dyslexia: The effect on sight vocabulary acquisition. *Learning Disabilities Quarterly, 20,* 104–125.

Voyager Expanded Learning. (2004). *Voyager Passport.* Dallas, TX, Author.

Wilson, B. A. (2002). *Fundations Teacher's Manual, Levels K-1.* Millbury, MA, Wilson Language Training Corporation.

Winitsky, N., Stoddart, T., & O'Keefe, P. (1992). Great expectations: Emergent professional development schools. *Journal of Teacher Education, 43,* 3–18.

Woodcock, R. (1987). *Woodcock Reading Mastery Tests—Revised.* Circle Pines, MN, American Guidance.

■ Note

1. These terms are differentiated by a more formal relationship between university and school in the professional development school (PDS), often involving a written contract. Several professional organizations provide formal criteria for the PDS (e.g., The Holmes Partnership, the National Council for Accreditation of Teacher Education).

24. INNOVATION IMPLEMENTATION

Developing Leadership for

Evidence-Based Practice

Susan G. Forman

■ Evidence-Based Practice and the
  Importance of Implementation

A substantial body of knowledge has been developed showing how academic, behavioral, social, and emotional functioning of children and adolescents can be improved and how school student development in these areas can be supported (Osher, Dwyer, & Jackson, 2004). Programs, practices, and procedures based on that knowledge are called evidence-based interventions. Evidence-based interventions are empirically supported with findings in the research literature that they are likely to produce predictable, beneficial, and effective results. Appropriate contemporary professional practice in school psychology, special education, and related professions calls for use of evidence-based interventions in schools (Forman & Burke, 2008). In order for evidence-based interventions to yield positive outcomes for students, they must be implemented successfully (Fixsen, Naoom, Blasé, Friedman, & Wallace, 2005).

Unfortunately, there is increasing documentation that although our knowledge concerning effective practices and programs for students has increased, the frequency of implementation of evidence-based interventions in school settings is undesirably low. Several major reports have highlighted the gap between our knowledge of effective interventions and the services currently being received by students (Schoenwald & Hoagwood, 2001). For example, the report of the President's Commission on Excellence in Special Education (2002) indicated that schools frequently do not implement evidence-based practices and that bridging the gap between research and practice will be a continuing challenge. A recent evaluation of drug use prevention

This work was supported in part by U.S. Department of Education grant no. H325D060002–07. Opinions expressed do not reflect the opinions of the sponsor.

practices in 1,795 schools indicated that more than 80% of school districts implemented some type of drug use prevention program, but only 17% of schools used efficacious methods to deliver the program, and only 14% used efficacious program content (Ennett et al., 2003).

Engaging in use of evidence-based practice involves two major tasks for the school professional: (a) Developing knowledge and skill in the content and methods of evidence-based interventions; and (b) developing knowledge and skill in the process of implementation. In the recent past, implementation was thought to be an event that would happen automatically when information was made available about a practice or program of good quality. However, literature now informs us that implementation is a complex process in which a practice or program is put into use within a particular context for a particular population.

■ The Need for Education and Training in Implementation

For many years, literature on the training of school psychologists has called for developing an understanding of the change agent role and of a systems orientation to service delivery (Magary, 1967; Sarason, 1971). Recently, a variety of articles and book chapters continue the call for "practitioner training in the implementation and sustainability of innovations at multiple setting or systems levels" (Schaughency & Ervin, 2006, p. 163) to bridge the research to practice gap (Elias, Zins, Graczyk, & Weissberg, 2003). In addition, in the most recent *Blueprint for Training and Practice* the National Association of School Psychologists specified "systems-based service delivery" as a primary domain of competence for training and practice in school psychology (Ysseldyke et al., 2006). This document also points to the current disconnect between educational research and practice, indicating that although the availability of research-based practices is greater than ever before, the availability of positive outcomes data on school interventions will not by itself lead to improved practice.

Despite continuous calls over the long term in the literature for education and training in this area, it is not widespread. A recent survey of school psychology training programs indicated that most programs are not providing training in evidence-based interventions and practices, and that when such training is provided, it tends to be didactic in nature, focusing on the content of the practice or program, and failing to address implementation issues (Shernoff, Kratochwill, & Stoiber, 2003). The manner in which this education and training should occur has not been specifically and comprehensively delineated. What knowledge and skills do practitioners' need in order to understand and successfully work with the systems that impact the successful delivery of evidence-based interventions to students?

Researchers know much more about the efficacy of interventions than they do about effectiveness. Empirical studies have established that in controlled studies and circumstances, a variety of interventions yield positive outcomes with children and adolescents, yet implementation attempts in the "real world" of schools frequently do not yield the same positive outcomes that are found in efficacy studies. However, across a variety of human sciences, literature on the science and technology of implementation has appeared. A great deal of this literature focuses on the importance of working within context and systems. On the other hand, the current training of school psychologists and other educational professionals has focused on individuals and individual differences, while the understanding of context and systems issues tends to be less widespread. The remainder of this chapter describes a graduate course designed to address the implementation process for doctoral level school psychology graduate students and related professionals in training.

■ Course Goals and Objectives

The course, entitled "Implementing Innovations in Educational and Human Service Organizations: Research to Practice," addresses current knowledge about theory and research on implementing innovations in schools and other organizational settings, emphasizing the process of bringing psychological and educational research to professional practice. Designed to be taken by advanced (third year) doctoral students, the course seeks to develop skills in methods and practices of effective innovation implementation, with an emphasis on the implementation of evidence-based interventions. The course was developed in conjunction with a U.S. Department of Education, Office of Special Education Programs, Preparation of Leadership Personnel Grant. This grant supports the development of a School Psychology Program Concentration in Psychological and Systems Support for Learning in which students focus on knowledge and skills related to implementation of evidence-based school interventions.

The knowledge base for this course is cross-disciplinary, as it is drawn from many disciplines in addition to psychology and education including public health, sociology, anthropology, communications, marketing, management, and political science. The relevant knowledge base includes theory and research regarding the manner in which the process of implementation proceeds through a number of different stages, and the individual, group, and organizational factors that influence implementation success at these various stages. Critical to student mastery of this knowledge base is the understanding that potential implementers of evidence-based interventions operate within a context of social and organizational systems that influence their attitudes, beliefs, and behaviors about interventions, and that a successful plan for implementation will address the various systems that may impact potential implementers.

Course objectives include increasing student understanding of (a) the stages of implementation; (b) the role of innovation characteristics in implementation; (c) the role of implementer characteristics, attitudes, and beliefs in implementation; (d) the impact of peer attitudes, beliefs, and behaviors on the implementer; (e) the impact of organizational factors on innovation implementation; (f) the role of the organization's external environment in the implementation process; and (g) issues related to fidelity and reinvention in the implementation process. In addition, the course seeks to develop student understanding of the purposes and methods of implementation research and evaluation as a methodological framework for working in the area of innovation implementation. In this respect, it is hoped that students will develop an understanding of how a specific implementation process can be evaluated to provide practical information to implementers, administrators, and policymakers regarding implementation success and potential improvement, as well as how new knowledge about the process of implementation can be created.

In addition to developing student knowledge, the course also seeks to develop skills deemed necessary to support successful implementation of evidence-based interventions. These skills include the ability to (a) develop strategies for building positive implementer and stakeholder attitudes and beliefs about an evidence-based intervention; (b) develop programs and procedures for appropriate provision of training and technical assistance related to an evidence-based intervention; (c) develop strategies for financially supporting an evidence-based intervention including obtaining external financial resources through grant funds; (d) develop strategies for building an organizational structure and climate that supports implementation of an innovation; and (e) develop a plan for evaluating the implementation process for an evidence-based intervention and utilizing the implementation evaluation data.

■ Course Structure

This three credit course is taught within a traditional semester time frame of one meeting of approximately three hours per week for 15 weeks. Instructional methods used in the course include lecture, discussion, examination of case studies of implementation, interviews with school and other human service professionals who have experience with innovation implementation, and development of innovation implementation plans.

Three major texts are used for the course, along with a number of journal articles and book chapters. One of the texts for the course provides an interdisciplinary overview of theory and research on innovation diffusion (Rogers, 2003). The second text provides an overview of the state of implementation research, with an emphasis on schools (Fixsen et al., 2005). The third text provide a series of case studies on education reform, with an emphasis on the process of implementation, sustainability, and scale-up (Glennan, Bodilly, Galegher, & Kerr, 2004). The references in the following sections, which describe the content base of the course sessions, form the basis for the course reading list.

During most class sessions, in addition to traditional lecture/discussion about the topics described in the following sections, students participate in an analysis of a case study from Glennan et al. (2004) on efforts to scale up interventions. These interventions have a variety of targets for change, including individual teachers, groups of teachers within a school teaching a specific subject, whole schools, and school systems. The case studies describe the intervention developers' experiences in attempting to implement, sustain, and scale-up the interventions. The purpose of the case study analysis is to supplement information about the theory and research on implementation provided in course lectures and readings, and to provide an opportunity for students to use this information in thinking about "real world" implementation attempts. The instructor leads the first case study analysis, and a student leads each subsequent case study analysis, with every student leading at least one discussion during the course. The discussions focus on identifying implementation strategies, implementation barriers, and potential responses to these barriers. Students are provided with an Implementation Case Study Discussion Guide, which can be found in Table 24.1, to provide a structure for this activity.

Interviews conducted by the class during some of the class sessions also provide students with "lessons from the field" from professionals who have substantial experience in efforts to implement evidence-based interventions and other innovations in education and human service organizations. For example, during one semester, students interviewed four individuals who had

TABLE 24.1   *Implementation Case Study Analysis Discussion Guide*

Briefly describe the intervention.

Briefly describe the organizational setting for implementation.

What was the reason for implementing the intervention?

Who were the stakeholders?

Who was opposed to implementation?

What implementation strategies did the intervention developer use?

Why did they use those strategies?

What alternative or additional strategies could they have used?

What were the implementation outcomes?

What were the implementation challenges?

What were the implementation failures? What was the response to these failures?

From your perspective, what is the most important "lesson learned" from this case study?

---

experience with innovation implementation at different types of organizations, including a superintendent of a local school district, an assistant commissioner of the state department of education, a program director from a private foundation, and the director of a state funded project that focuses on assisting schools to effectively implement and sustain evidence-based programs in the areas of substance use and violence prevention. Some of the interviews are conducted in the classroom, and for some the class travels to the office of the interviewee. Although partially a matter of convenience for the interviewees, travel outside of the classroom emphasizes the importance of direct interface with the individuals and systems that may impact implementation. Each interviewee is invited through a letter from the instructor which outlines the issues that will be of relevance to speak about with the class. For example, the school district superintendent was asked to talk about his experiences in attempting to implement new practices and programs in schools; the strategies he used to develop support and capacity for the practices and/or programs; the barriers to implementation he encountered; and how he responded to those barriers. The assistant commissioner of the state department of education was asked to speak about the new practices and programs the state department of education is encouraging in schools districts; how they go about doing this; what grant funding is available for innovation in schools; and how schools access these funds. In the class session before the interview, students develop additional questions that will form the basis of the interview.

In addition to participating in traditional class sessions, the interview sessions described earlier, and completing readings, students in this course develop an Innovation Implementation Plan for an evidence-based intervention in an educational or human service setting. The Innovation Implementation Plan is a primary means of assessing student learning in the course. The Innovation Implementation Plan (described in more detail later) is based on course content which outlines the issues that need to be addressed in planning for successful implementation of an innovation in an education or human service setting.

The following sections describe the rationale for and scope of the content of each of the major areas addressed in this course. Each of the course sessions addresses an area of literature that forms the knowledge base for a technology of implementation. This knowledge base should help course participants develop effective means of supporting implementation efforts in schools and related settings.

■ Why Focus on Innovation Implementation?

The course begins with a discussion of why innovation implementation is important, the definition of relevant terms, and a discussion of stages of implementation. An innovation is defined as an idea, practice, or object that is perceived as new. Thus, a practice, procedure, or program attempted for the first time by school personnel, such as an evidence-based intervention, can be viewed as an innovation. It does not matter if the intervention is not objectively new as measured by time since its development. If the intervention seems new to the individual, it is an innovation.

Implementation is an effort to incorporate an innovation at the organizational, group, or individual level. Implementation has been defined as a "specified set of activities designed to put into practice an activity or program of known dimensions" (Fixsen et al., 2005, p. 5). No matter how good, innovations, such as evidence-based interventions, will not result in positive outcomes for students unless they are implemented successfully. Understanding the process of successful implementation of innovations is presented as essential to bridging the current gap that exists between research and professional practice in schools.

In addition to beginning the course by exploring the meaning of innovation and the meaning of implementation, the degrees of implementation described by Hernandez and Hodges (2003) provides a helpful way of viewing potential variations in depth of implementation and the effects of these on clients. These degrees of implementation include (a) paper implementation—new policies and procedures are developed, but paperwork, forms, and manuals are not the same as putting an innovation into practice; (b) process implementation—new operating procedures are begun such as training workshops, consultation, use of new reporting forms, although the innovation is not yet being implemented with clients; and (c) performance implementation—involves developing and using new procedures and process, as well as implementing the components of an innovation with clients. Fixsen and colleagues (2005) point out that in many circumstances schools develop the trappings of evidence-based interventions through paper or process implementation, but only performance implementation can yield positive outcomes for students.

■ Stages of Implementation

It is important for students to understand that implementation is a process that takes place over time, and that implementation activities during the various stages of implementation will probably differ. The work of Rogers (2003) and Fixsen et al. (2005) provide useful frameworks for understanding implementation stages and issues that will need to be planned for and addressed at each stage.

Rogers (2003) describes an innovation-decision process in which an individual or group seeks and processes information to reduce uncertainty about the advantages and disadvantages of the innovation. In the knowledge stage, an individual or group learns about the existence of an innovation and how it works. In the persuasion stage, a favorable or unfavorable attitude is formed toward the innovation. In the decision stage, a decision to adopt or reject is made by learning the advantages and disadvantages to the individual or group's own situation. In the implementation stage, the innovation is put to use. In the confirmation stage, reinforcement is sought for the decision that has been made. Relevant to school-based practice, Rogers (2003) indicates that the innovation-decision process in organizations is more complex, typically involving both champions and opponents of the new idea. He also points out that implementation involves mutual adaptation in which the innovation and the organization change.

Concurring with this view of the innovation implementation process in organizations, Glennan et al. (2004), as a result of a review of case studies of implementation of educational reform, point out that implementation is a process of interaction, feedback, and adaptation among program providers, teachers, and school, district, and state administrators. They contend that implementation sites are not solely being acted upon, but are active participants in an iterative process.

Although Rogers (2003) presents the innovation process from the point of view of the adopting and implementing individual, group, or organization, Fixsen et al. (2005) describe six stages of implementation that focus on the innovation. During the exploration and adoption stage, the potential match between individual and/or organizational needs and resources and those of the innovation are assessed, and a decision is made about proceeding. During program installation, necessary structural supports and resources are put into place. During initial implementation, implementers and stakeholders deal with the difficulties of doing something new. During full operation, the innovation is fully carried out with clients. During the innovation phase, there may be opportunities to refine the innovation. Finally, during the sustainability phase the innovation is implemented in subsequent years with issues of long-term survival such as changing staff and leadership, funding, program requirements, social problems, and so forth.

Through examination of literature on the stages of implementation, students learn that different issues will assume importance at different stages in the implementation process. Thus, implementation activities at the various stages should be purposeful and based on current knowledge about events, implementer needs and concerns, and potential barriers and facilitators at each stage of implementation.

■ Leadership for Implementation

The course continues with a session devoted to leadership issues. There are several reasons for addressing leadership in this course. First, many graduate students think of themselves as learners rather than leaders, as they have been in the habit of looking to faculty and supervisors to teach them how to think, what to think, and how to engage in professional behaviors. Second, many school psychologists do not think of themselves as potential leaders because they are not in formal positions of power such as school administrative positions. Third, the emphasis on collaboration in school psychology training and practice may at times preclude graduate students and practitioners from viewing themselves in leadership roles, because to some, leadership may imply imposing unwanted practices on others. This may be viewed by some as especially undesirable when the school psychologist functions as part of a decision-making team. Finally, leadership is necessary for successful implementation and sustainability of innovation. As described here, innovation implementation includes development, coordination, and follow-through on long-term plans for multiple individuals within an organization, social influence, and engaging in the roles of champion for an innovation and change agent.

There are a great variety of views of leadership, but all definitions share the perspective that leadership involves the process of influencing one or more followers. The definition of leadership presented by Vroom and Jago (2007) is especially relevant to innovation implementation and to this course. They state, "We see leadership as a process of motivating people to work together collaboratively to accomplish great things" (p. 18). In this section of the course, we review a variety of conceptions of leadership that have been developed over the years, and then focus on Sternberg's (2007) recent WICS model of leadership that views leadership as a matter of how an individual formulates, makes, and acts on decisions.

In the WICS model, a synthesis of wisdom, intelligence, and creativity is seen as containing the key components of leadership. Creativity is defined as having the skills and dispositions needed for generating ideas and products that are novel, of high quality, and appropriate for the context. Intelligence means having the skills and dispositions needed to succeed in life. Wisdom is the use of successful intelligence, creativity, and knowledge mediated by values to seek to reach a common good. This model views these attributes as modifiable skills that can be taught and learned. The course proceeds with further discussion of the issue of leadership and values, methods of leadership for changing beliefs and behaviors, and of course participants' beliefs about the benefits and drawbacks of leading innovation implementation.

Finally, the change agent role in innovation implementation is discussed within the context of leadership. In school psychology literature, practitioners have been advised to become change agents for a variety of innovations in school settings (Merrell, Ervin, & Gimpel, 2006). One role of a change agent is to facilitate the flow of an innovation from the innovation developer to potential clients, or to bring research to practice. The tasks and behaviors involved in this role are presented and discussed.

■ Implementation Evaluation and Research

The course proceeds with an examination of implementation evaluation and research. Implementation evaluation and research is concerned with the questions "What is happening and why?" whereas the questions of interest in outcomes evaluation are "What are the effects of the intervention and why?" An understanding of how to conduct implementation evaluation and research is valuable because successful implementation requires continual monitoring so that implementation strategies can be adjusted, if necessary, as the implementation process proceeds. This area is important for practitioners interested in tracking the implementation process as a means of yielding positive outcomes for clients. Implementation evaluation can also provide relatively rapid feedback to program managers and policymakers so that operations can be adjusted when necessary to improve client outcomes. It is also important for scholars who are interested in increasing knowledge about the implementation process. Training in school psychology and related areas typically addresses outcomes research and evaluation, whereas little attention is typically given to implementation evaluation and research issues that are essential to the understanding of the innovation implementation process.

Implementation evaluation and research examines what is happening in intervention implementation efforts, whether what is happening is what is expected or desired, and why particular implementation activities or trends are occurring. Some of the questions that implementation evaluation and research seeks to answer include (Werner, 2004):

1. What is the theoretical and practical basis of the intervention? Are they sound? Do they match the needs of the target population?
2. What are the resource requirements of the intervention, and does the implementing organization have these in place?
3. Is the intervention suited to its environment? How has the environment influenced implementation?
4. Are intervention processes and systems operating as planned? How and why are they not operating as planned? How can they be improved?
5. Is the intervention reaching the intended target population with the intended activities and services?
6. Is the intervention achieving desired outcomes? If not, how and why? How can intervention performance be improved? If an intervention is unsuccessful in achieving desired outcomes, the intervention's design, resources, relation to the environment, administrative structure, policies, and/or procedures may be questioned.

Within the context of these questions, assessment methods, and data collection procedures are addressed. A variety of methods are included such as key informant interviews, focus groups with stakeholders, observation of intervention activities and processes, surveys, records review, and review of organizational documents. The goal of collecting this information is to "tell the story" of the intervention (Werner, 2004, p. 81). Data related to implementation of the intervention is compared with some set of expectations such as the initial program model, federal or state performance standards, professional standards, descriptions of exemplary programs, the evaluator's professional experience and judgment, and/or opinions of stakeholders to evaluate and explain results.

■ Innovation Characteristics

Characteristics of innovations that may influence implementation success are examined next. In an extensive cross-disciplinary review of the literature on diffusion of innovations, Rogers (2003) found that five characteristics of innovations influence adoption rates.

1. Relative advantage is the degree to which an innovation is perceived to be better than what is currently used. An intervention that is perceived as being better than current educational practices has a greater chance of adoption.
2. Compatibility is the degree to which an innovation is compatible with the current state of the individual or organization. An intervention that is compatible with current school needs, practices, programs, policies, and philosophy has a greater chance of adoption.
3. Complexity is the degree to which an innovation is perceived as difficult to understand and use. Interventions that are simpler to understand are more likely to be adopted.
4. Trialability is the degree to which an innovation may be implemented on a limited or "trial" basis. New practices or programs that can be tried initially on a limited basis will generally be adopted more quickly.
5. Observability is the degree to which an individual can see or "observe" the results of an innovation. Interventions that result in visible improvements have a greater chance of adoption.

Risk and task issues have also been found to influence adoption (Greenhalgh, Robert, Mcfarlane, Bate, & Kyriakidou, 2004). If an intervention is perceived as risky, it is less likely to be adopted. If the intervention is seen as relevant to the performance of the implementer's work and as improving that performance, it is more likely to be adopted.

Thus, the nature of an innovation should be considered relative to the context of stakeholders. Course participants learn that those working to increase implementation success will need to highlight intervention characteristics that will increase the likelihood of adoption and implementation.

■ Adopter and Implementer Characteristics

Rogers (2003) also points out that characteristics of potential adopters and implementers can influence implementation success. He contends that individuals can be categorized on the basis of innovativeness, the timeframe within which individuals or groups adopt new ideas relative to others. Rogers (2003) delineates five categories of adopters (innovators, early adopters, early majority, late majority, laggards) that have been found to have different personality variables and communication patterns. Course participants learn that these differences imply that different approaches can be used with individuals or groups in different adopter categories to facilitate the implementation process.

Implementers' beliefs about their self-efficacy have also been found to influence implementation. Teacher self-efficacy beliefs are judgments about their own capability to affect students' behavior and performance. Teachers who perceive themselves as efficacious are likely to produce enough effort to implement new practices and to persist despite setbacks (Gusky, 1988). Thus, positive self-efficacy is presented as an important characteristic to consider when selecting implementers for a new evidence-based intervention.

■ Attitudes and Beliefs

Individuals may judge the attributes or characteristics of an innovation differently from one another; what is easy for one person to use may be difficult for another person to use. In addition, the meaning attached to an innovation is not necessarily fixed, but can be reframed through discourse (Greenhalgh et al., 2004). Perceptions, attitudes, and beliefs related to evidence-based interventions will have a strong influence on the success of their implementation. Course participants learn that a major task for school psychologists will be to establish perceptions, attitudes, and beliefs in implementers and other stakeholders that will be supportive of implementation success through presentations, workshops, formal and informal discussion, and consultation. Here, an understanding of the research on treatment acceptability (Eckert & Hintze, 2000) as well as literature on decision making (Plous, 1993) is useful.

The innovation-decision process (Rogers, 2003) discussed at the beginning of the course is a helpful conceptual framework for understanding and working with attitudes and beliefs related to innovation implementation. Through this process a series of choices is made over time. The new idea is evaluated and decisions are made concerning whether or not to incorporate it into ongoing practice. The uncertainty related to newness is a key aspect of this type of decision making, as well as the relevance of the innovation to the individual's particular situation and needs. Rogers (2003) emphasizes the fact that diffusion of innovations is a very social process, and that most people make decisions about innovations based on their knowledge of what others like themselves think about the innovation. The process provides guidance about the nature of information, and how and to whom it should be provided in order to support successful implementation.

■ Developing Teacher, Administrator, and other Stakeholder Support

Identification of potential stakeholders is an important beginning step in planning for successful implementation. This includes determining who is going to deliver the innovative intervention and which other individuals will have an interest in the intervention. Evidence-based interventions typically have primary and secondary implementers. The primary implementer delivers the main components of the intervention, whereas secondary implementers are individuals in the environment of the target children or adolescents who can engage in behaviors, such as prompting use of newly learned skills, which support the intervention. As stated earlier, innovation diffusion is a social process, with innovation decision-making frequently based on opinions of peers. Therefore, in addition to working with implementers, it is essential to work with individuals who have relationships with implementers. These individuals may influence the perceptions, attitudes, beliefs, and behaviors of implementers, and thus influence implementation effectiveness.

Within the school setting, the primary implementers for many evidence-based interventions are teachers. Therefore, teacher "buy-in" is critical to successful implementation. In this segment of the course, we address the importance of making the effectiveness of the innovation observable to teachers, involving teachers in the selection process, the concept of critical mass and how it can be developed, and how peers and opinions leaders influence the decisions of potential teacher implementers.

Strong support for the innovation on the part of school principals is a critical component of successful implementation. Therefore, the roles and behaviors of principals in support of innovative practices are also examined in the course. School leaders are responsible for creating a culture, climate, and structure that supports positive change. Some studies have found that principal support is necessary to produce intervention effects (Kam, Greenberg, & Walls, 2003).

Two models for developing stakeholder support are presented. The Participatory Intervention Model (Nastasi et al., 2000) is an iterative process with a focus on the involvement, ownership, and empowerment of stakeholders who are responsible for implementing and sustaining an innovative intervention. Using this model, interventionists or consultants are partners with stakeholders in continuous data collection to ensure acceptability and cultural specificity of the intervention, to adapt the intervention to the demands of the context, and to monitor change toward program goals. Thus, the intervention consultant and the stakeholders together design the intervention, monitor its implementation, and evaluate its effectiveness. Collaborative Strategic Planning (Stollar, Poth, Curtis, & Cohen, 2006) is a second model for integrating an innovative intervention and the culture of a specific school. It uses a team-based planning and problem-solving approach to address student and system-level issues. A school-based planning team composed of a variety of stakeholders directs the Collaborative Strategic Planning process in a school, collecting and using student outcome data to construct and maintain a three-tiered model of student support, providing universal, selected, and indicated interventions.

■ Developing Knowledge: Training and Technical Assistance

Developing knowledge of potential implementers and other stakeholders about the content and processes of a new intervention is essential for successful implementation. Knowledge related to the innovative intervention will impact attitudes and beliefs as described earlier, as well as skill in delivering the intervention. Implementation of innovative practices and programs requires behavior change from implementers. Training and technical assistance are the principle ways in which this behavior change can be brought about.

On the issue of training, the course addresses the fact that it is important for all innovation stakeholders to have general knowledge of the rationale, content, and methods of the innovative intervention, as well as the potential outcomes of the intervention and risks of not implementing. Primary implementers of the intervention will need more intensive training. In preservice and inservice training sessions, information can be presented on the theory, philosophy, and values associated with the intervention, the rationale and components for key practices, acceptable forms of flexibility and adaptation, and potential outcomes of the intervention. The literature on good training and professional development practices tells us that training should be multisession, and include written materials, goal setting, modeling, practice, feedback, and follow-up booster sessions and/or technical assistance (Joyce & Showers, 2002).

Most skills can be introduced in training, but they must be learned further on-the-job with the help of a consultant/coach/technical assistance provider. Ongoing, intensive support has been found to strongly affect the level of implementation and the likelihood of continuation of educational as well as other types of innovations. Ideally, a facilitator will be available who will work closely with primary implementers to model innovation components, and to provide coaching and feedback regarding implementation of the new intervention (Noell, 2008). In addition to such technical assistance designed to increase the implementer's skill with the new intervention, implementers need training and feedback on how to adapt the intervention to the needs of their specific setting, which in the case of a teacher implementer will most probably be a classroom.

■ Organizational Characteristics and Structures

The structure of a social system can help or hinder implementation of an innovative intervention. This part of the course explores organizational variables that have been found to impact the innovativeness of organizations and thus may affect attempts to implement evidence-based interventions. These variables include leader characteristics, internal structural characteristics, organizational climate, and characteristics of the external environment in which the organization operates. Organizational climates in which staff members perceive that the innovation is rewarded, supported, and expected support effective implementation (Klein & Sorra, 1996). Interestingly, certain organizational structures may facilitate adoption of innovations, while others may facilitate implementation of innovations. Thus, students in the course learn that certain types of schools may tend to be successful at adopting innovations, but not at implementing those innovations when power and control are not centralized and rules and procedures are not formalized. They also learn that some of the organizational variables that impact implementation are amenable to change.

When organizations successfully adopt and implement innovations, one or more champions for the innovation have typically emerged. Champions work to make implementation a success by overcoming indifference or resistance to the innovation within the organization. The organizational position and personal characteristics of an individual can influence their success as a champion for innovation. It is not necessary for an innovation champion to be in a position of power, but he or she is usually especially good at dealing with people and skillful in persuasion and negotiation (Rogers, 2003). A school psychologist might play the role of a champion, or may be instrumental in identifying and encouraging another individual to be the champion for an evidence-based intervention.

Course participants also learn that both the innovation and the organization usually change in the innovation implementation process. This occurs because an innovation almost never fits perfectly with an organization. Therefore, a great deal of planning and activity are required to avoid or overcome misalignments between the innovation and the organization.

■ Policy

As indicated earlier, an organization's external environment will impact the implementation of an innovation. For schools, the policy context in place during an attempted implementation of an evidence-based intervention is likely to affect success. In most schools, public policy shapes their interest in interventions leading to improved teaching and learning. Conflicting mandates and policies at the federal, state, and/or district levels may lead to implementation problems. These conflicts occur because policymakers are responding to diverse constituencies with competing interests. Unfortunately, this may result in unsuccessful implementation and/or sustainability of many interventions.

It is therefore important for students to understand how public policy may influence their implementation efforts. In this section of the course, students examine policies of the U.S. Department of Education and the Department of Health and Human Services that have had an impact on the implementation of evidence-based interventions in schools, specifically with regard to child and adolescent social and emotional well-being. Legislations, policies, guidelines, regulations, standards, and funded initiatives from these federal agencies, as well as from states and local entities need to be understood as influential to school organizational behavior.

■ Financing Innovation

Finding and maintaining financial support is one of the major tasks before those who wish to implement innovative evidence-based interventions in schools. Issues related to program and service finance are rarely addressed in school psychology training programs, although the availability of funds significantly impacts the delivery of educational programs and services to children and adolescents in schools. If a professional is interested in launching and sustaining a new program or practice, it is essential to be able to identify and procure the financial resources for this endeavor. These financial resources may be needed for such items as program materials, supplies, equipment, staffing, professional development expenses, and/or consultant fees.

We begin this section of the course by discussing resource allocation in schools and school districts. What does a school budget look like and where is one likely to find funds in a school or district budget to support the implementation of innovative interventions? Use of school district local funds, state general funds, state special education funds, funding from IDEA, and Medicaid reimbursement are discussed as potential means of funding implementation of evidence-based interventions in schools.

In addition, a portion of this course addresses how to develop external financial resources through grant writing. Grant writing is a major method of obtaining financial support for programs for which schools do not have internal budgetary support. It is a significant means of funding implementation of innovative programs and therefore is a necessary skill for any education professional with an interest in being a catalyst for useful change in schools. Grant writing provides an answer to the question, "Where will we get the funds to do this new program that we think will lead to positive outcomes for our students?"

We begin our examination of grant writing by discussing potential funding sources for the types of programs likely to be of interest to those working in schools, and to school psychologists in particular. These include federal government, state government, private foundations, private industry, and professional organizations. We proceed with an exploration of how to develop proposal ideas and how to write a grant proposal. Typical proposal formats for the funding sources cited earlier are addressed.

■ Reinvention vs. Fidelity

Reinvention is the degree to which an innovation is changed by a user in the process of implementation (Rogers, 2003). Implementation fidelity, also called treatment integrity, refers to how well the intervention is implemented in comparison with the original design as used in efficacy studies. Many researchers believe that positive outcomes should be expected only if effective practices are fully implemented as intended by the program developer (Fixsen et al., 2005). Yet, some researchers have also found that a higher degree of reinvention can lead to faster adoption and a higher degree of sustainability (Rogers, 2003). The tension between these two points of view is explored, as well as means of measuring and promoting fidelity (Gresham, 1989) while allowing for some degree of reinvention. Course participants learn that in attempting to resolve this tension, those working to effectively implement evidence-based interventions should ensure that the core values, assumptions, and components of the program are not violated in adaptations that may be necessary for particular populations, environments, or political or funding circumstances (Dane & Schneider, 1998).

■ Sustainability

As the course concludes, the issue of sustainability is addressed. Sustainability is defined as the degree to which the innovative intervention continues to be used after its first implementation. Participation and reinvention have been identified as significant factors in sustainable innovations in an organization (Rogers, 2003). Participation and the importance of involving all stakeholders has been a theme throughout the course in discussions of successful implementation practices. When many members of an organization, such as a school, participate in designing, discussing, and implementing an innovation, its sustainability is more likely. In addition, implementers must be able to adapt the new intervention to changing classroom, school, and district needs so that there continues to be a fit between the intervention and the organizational context.

■ Implementation Plans and Related Skills Practice

As indicated earlier, development of an Innovation Implementation Plan is a significant component of the course requirements and means of evaluating student performance. Course participants produce a written document that outlines a plan for implementation of an evidence-based intervention in an organizational setting, with which they are familiar, such as a school. The plan should provide a blueprint for action regarding issues that must be addressed in the implementation process. The plan requires the development of information and strategies in the following areas: (a) Description of the intervention, its core properties, evidence base, and relationship to needs of the target population; (b) intervention resource requirements; (c) organizational fit; (d) identification of primary implementers and their attributes; (e) identification of other stakeholders; (f) strategies for bringing about the adoption decision; (g) external resource development plans; (h) strategies for ensuring effective implementation including training, technical assistance, and use of social influence; (i) strategies for developing administrator support; (j) strategies for developing a champion for the intervention; (k) dealing with the impact of policy; (l) implementation evaluation; and (m) strategies to enhance sustainability. Table 24.2 shows the outline provided to students to be used in organizing and writing their plans. This plan provides a way for students to consider implementation issues within the context of a real organization, target population, and evidence-based intervention, and to demonstrate their learning regarding planning for implementation.

Practicum placements that provide opportunities for students to gain experience with implementation and systems issues have also been developed. Students are placed in field experiences with administrators in local school districts, nonprofit organizations working with schools, and at the state department of education. In these practicum placements, students are involved in activities related to efforts to initiate evidence-based practices and programs.

TABLE 24.2 *Innovation Implementation Plan*

In this Innovation Implementation Plan you will describe how you would plan for implementation and sustainability of a specific evidence-based intervention in an organization with which you are familiar. Your plan should be written in APA style, using references, where appropriate. Your plan should be about 20 pages in length.

1. Description and Rationale for Use of the Innovation

Include the theory base for the intervention, core assumptions, core components, and summary of the evidence base. Does the intervention match the needs of the target population? How do you know this?

2. Resource and Infrastructure Requirements

Include staffing, equipment, materials, supplies, space, professional development activities, financial requirements, and any other requirements. Does the implementing organization have these in place?

3. Organizational Fit

Describe the organization in which this intervention will be implemented. Describe the organizational characteristics that make for a good intervention/ organization fit in this case.

4. Identification of Primary Implementers

Who will the primary implementers be? What existing personal characteristics are likely to make these individuals effective implementers? What attributes will you try to develop? How will you do this?

5. Identification of other Stakeholders

Identify secondary implementers and other stakeholders for this intervention. Describe what their interest will be in the delivery of the intervention or the outcome.

6. Adoption Decision

What methods will you use to bring about a decision to adopt the intervention by implementers and stakeholders? Describe formal and informal meetings and discussions and identify participants. Describe any training activities and who will be involved. Describe how you will address the characteristics of the intervention in these meetings, discussions, and/or training activities. Who will oppose this innovation? How will you deal with this opposition?

7. External Resource Development

What federal, state, local, private foundation, corporate foundation, or professional association grant program(s) might serve as a source of funds for implementation of the innovation? Describe the purpose of the grant program. Describe your rationale for requesting funds from this program. For what purpose will you ask for funds and how much money will you ask for?

(*continued*)

TABLE 24.2   *Continued*

8. Implementation

Describe training and technical assistance activities including participants, content, methods. Describe other types of meetings and discussions that may take place. Describe your strategies for dealing with social influence. How will you address issues of re-invention and fidelity?

9. Administrator Support

From which administrators will you need support? What strategies will you use to develop this support? How will you ask them to demonstrate their support for the intervention?

10. Innovation Champion

Who might serve as a champion for this intervention? Why have you selected this individual? How will you develop and maintain their support?

11. Organizational Structures

What organizational structures need to be changed or developed in order to support this intervention? How will you bring this about?

12. Policy

How is federal, state, and/or local policy likely to impact implementation? What strategies can you use to overcome policy barriers and utilize policy facilitators?

13. Implementation Evaluation

Describe the instruments and methods you will use to obtain information about fidelity and the success of implementation process. Describe what you will do with this information

14. Sustainability

What strategies will you use to sustain this intervention after the first complete implementation? How will you maintain the support of implementers and other stakeholders?

■ A Final Note

This course combined with the specialized practicum provides students with opportunities for learning theory and research, as well as practicing new skills related to innovation implementation. Such training should provide a knowledge and skill base from which future professionals can later draw on in their efforts to one day successfully implement evidence-based interventions in schools.

■ References

Dane, A. V., & Schneider, B. H. (1998). Program integrity in primary and early secondary prevention: Are implementation effects out of control? *Clinical Psychology Review, 18*, 23–45.

Eckert, T. L., & Hintze, J. M. (2000). Behavioral conceptions and applications of acceptability: Issues related to service delivery and research methodology. *School Psychology Quarterly, 15*, 123–148.

Elias, M. J., Zins, J. E., Graczyk, P. A., & Weissberg, R. P. (2003). Implementation, sustainability, and scaling-up of social-emotional and academic innovations in public schools. *School Psychology Review, 32*, 303–319.

Ennett, S. T., Ringwalt, C. L., Thorne, J., Rohrbach, L. A., Vincus, A., Simons-Rudolph, A., & Jones, S. (2003). A comparison of current practice in school-based substance use prevention programs with meta-analysis findings. *Prevention Science, 4*, 1–14.

Fixsen, D. L., Naoom, S. F., Blasé, K. A., Friedman, R. M., & Wallace, F. (2005). *Implementation research: A synthesis of the literature.* Tampa, FL, University of South Florida.

Forman, S. G., & Burke, C. R. (2008). Best practices in selecting and implementing evidence-based school interventions. In A. Thomas & G. Grimes (Eds.), *Best practices in school psychology V* (pp. 799–812). Washington, DC, National Association of School Psychologists.

Glennan, T. K., Bodilly, S. J., Galegher, J. R., & Kerr, K. A. (2004). *Expanding the reach of education reforms: Perspectives from leaders in the scale-up of educational interventions.* Santa Monica, CA, Rand Corporation.

Greenhalgh, T., Robert, G., Macfarlane, F., Bate, P., & Kyriakidou, O. (2004). Diffusion of innovations in service organizations: Systematic review and recommendations. *The Milbank Quarterly, 82*, 581–629.

Gresham, F. M. (1989). Assessment of treatment integrity in school consultation and prereferral intervention. *School Psychology Review, 18*, 37–50.

Gusky, T. R. (1988). Teacher efficacy, self-concept, and attitudes toward the implementation of instructional innovation. *Teaching and Teacher Education, 4*, 63–69.

Hernandez, M., & Hodges, S. (2003). Building upon the theory of change for systems of care. *Journal of Emotional and Behavioral Disorders, 11*, 19–26.

Joyce, B., & Showers, B. (2002). *Student achievement through staff development* (3rd ed.). Alexandria, VA, Association for Supervision and Curriculum Development.

Kam, C., Greenberg, M. T., & Walls, C. T. (2003). Examining the role of implementation quality in school-based prevention using the PATHS curriculum. *Prevention Science, 4*, 55–63.

Klein, K. J., & Sorra, J. S. (1996). The challenge of innovation implementation. *Academy of Management Review, 21*, 1055–1080.

Magary, J. F. (1967). *School psychological services.* Englewood Cliffs, NJ, Prentice Hall.

Merrell, K. W., Ervin, R. A., & Gimpel, G. A. (2006). *School psychology for the 21st century*. New York, The Guilford Press.

Nastasi, B. K., Vargas, K., Schensul, S. L., Silva, K. T., Schensul, J. J., & Ratnayake, P. (2000). The participatory intervention model: A framework for conceptualizing and promoting intervention acceptability. *School Psychology Quarterly, 15*, 207–232.

Noell, G. (2008). Research examining the relationships among consultation process, treatment integrity, and outcomes. In W. P. Erchul & S. M. Sheridan (Eds.), *Handbook of research in school consultation: Empirical foundations for the field* (pp. 467–483). Mahwah, NJ, Lawrence Erlbaum Associates.

Osher, D., Dwyer, K., & Jackson, S. (2004). *Safe, supportive and successful schools*. Longmont, CO, Sopris West.

Plous, S. (1993). *The psychology of judgement and decision making*. Philadelphia, Temple University Press.

President's Commission on Excellence in Special Education. (2002). *A new era: Revitalizing special education for children and their families*. Available On-line at www.ed.gov/inits/commissionsboards/whspecialeducation.

Sarason, S. B. (1971). *The culture of the school and the problem of change*. Boston, Allyn and Bacon.

Schaughency, E., & Ervin, R. (2006). Building capacity to implement and sustain effective practices to better serve children. *School Psychology Review, 35*, 155–166.

Schoenwald, S. K., & Hoagwood, K. (2001). Effectiveness, transportability, and dissemination of interventions: What matters when? *Psychiatric Services, 52*, 1190–1197.

Shernoff, E. S., Kratochwill, T. R., & Stoiber, K. C. (2003). Training in evidence-based interventions: What are school psychology programs teaching? *Journal of School Psychology, 41*, 467–483.

Sternberg, R. J. (2007). A systems model of leadership: WICS. *American Psychologist, 62*, 34–42.

Stollar, S. A., Poth, R. L., Curtis, M. J., & Cohen, R. M. (2006). Collaborative strategic planning as illustration of the principles of systems change. *School Psychology Review, 35*, 181–197.

Rogers, E. M. (2003). *Diffusion of innovations*. New York, The Free Press.

Vroom, V. H., & Jago, A. G. (2007). The role of the situation in leadership. *American Psychologist, 62*, 17–24.

Werner, A. (2004). *A guide to implementation research*. Washington, DC, The Urban Institute Press.

Ysseldyke, J., Burns, M., Dawson, P., Kelly, B., Morrison, D., Ortiz, S., et al. (2006). *School psychology: A blueprint for training and practice*. Bethesda, MD, National Association of School Psychologists.

25. Evaluating Student Response to Implementations of Evidence-Based Interventions

Nicole Alston-Abel, Erin M. Olson, and Kelly Cutler Kirk

The purpose of this chapter is two-fold. First, we explain the relevance of the University of Washington School Psychology Internship program requirement for an evidence-based intervention project to the theme of this book. On the one hand, it is important to draw upon research findings that provide evidence that validates (a) theoretical constructs relevant to various interventions, and (b) specific kinds of interventions that have been effective under certain controlled research conditions. On the other hand, it is also important to evaluate the effectiveness of those same interventions when implemented with specific students in specific school settings. What worked in research with a sample, which may or may not reflect the characteristics of students receiving intervention in a specific school setting or the conditions under which the intervention is delivered, may not replicate in or generalize to other samples and situations. Thus, we need evidence not only from research studies but also from implementations of applications of research findings. Second, the role of preservice school psychology internships in introducing future school psychologists to evidence-based practices in applying research to practice is emphasized. If interns learn to draw on research to design interventions and then evaluate the effectiveness of implementing the interventions, then they are more likely to use evidence-based practices throughout their careers as school psychologists. That is why school psychology interns at the University of Washington are required to complete a project on evidence-based intervention and evidence-based evaluation of the implementation of that intervention.

For purposes of this evidence-based intervention project, the intern is asked to draw on conceptual frameworks, general principles, and instructional or intervention procedures in published research to design an intervention and choose instructional or intervention materials. As part of their pre-internship coursework, they are introduced to such research in reading, writing, and math (see Chapters 1, 2, 3, 4, 5, and 6 in Step 1 in Implementation, this volume) and in behavioral and mental health interventions for school age children and youth. The intern is also asked to gather data to evaluate whether the implementation of that research-based intervention is effective for the individuals and/or group of students for whom it is implemented during the internship year (see Chapters 17, 18, 19, 20, and 21 in Step 4 in Implementation, this volume).

The internship director encouraged the interns to plan, implement, and evaluate interventions for students who were not meeting benchmark standards in one or more academic skills. The purpose of this assignment was not to generate new research knowledge but rather to have novice school psychologists at the beginning of their professional careers adopt and apply an evidence-based approach to not only choosing interventions but also evaluating how the interventions are implemented. The scientist-practitioner model, in which this training program is grounded, emphasizes gathering and evaluating evidence for these purposes at both the individual student level for the purpose of evaluating effectiveness of an intervention for an individual student and at the group level for purposes of program evaluation when multiple students receive the intervention in a group. At issue is whether a particular instructional intervention is effective in meeting the needs of diverse learners in a small instructional group that provides the same supplementary reading instruction for all identified at-risk students (see Vadasy, Sanders, & Peyton, 2005).

Many of the schools where interns are placed already have in place curriculum-based progress monitoring of response to instruction (RTI) (see Chapters 11 and 21 by Shapiro and Peverly, respectively, this volume) but they are not tied to specific interventions. All students in the school receive the same progress monitoring tool regardless of specific supplementary interventions they may be receiving; the goal is simply to assess whether students are responding to whatever instruction they may be receiving. Such an approach is not designed to evaluate the effectiveness of specific supplementary interventions, which may vary across students. Also, the RTI assessment is not necessarily yoked to the nature of the interventions. For example, the intervention may be designed to teach accurate application of multiple, explicit, flexible strategies for word reading but the RTI measures may only assess rate of reading. Although there is a myth that only curriculum-based rate measures can be used to assess response to instruction, using both norm-referenced and curriculum-based assessment of response to intervention (multimodal approach to assessment; Berninger, 1998a) provides stronger, possibly converging, evidence that the school implemented appropriate research-supported instruction and used appropriate research-supported assessment tools in monitoring the progress. Also, research has identified a number of processes that identify students at-risk for reading or writing problems and that have been validated for response to intervention. Showing that students improve on these measures, which have also been validated for relationship to biological risk factors (genetic and brain based), also indicates the degree to which students may be overcoming biological risk factors as a function of participating in the instructional treatment program.

In this chapter, three evidence-based projects are described that were based on instructional research and implemented during the 2005–2006 academic year when the authors were interns working on their school psychology certification. The order in which the interventions are presented illustrates how in the primary grades supplementary instruction in writing (not just reading) may be needed and may be effective (first study), how in the intermediate grades supplementary reading instruction may still be needed (second study), and how some children require interventions with both academic and mental health goals (third study). See Berninger (2006) for another example in which the intern conducted a successful evidence-based intervention that included both academic and mental health goals. The order of authorship is not the same as the order of presentation of the studies because the first two authors assumed the major responsibility for writing the chapter and the first author, who was trained in both individual subject data analyses and program evaluation of group data, helped the third author, who is no longer at the university, in analyzing the data for the purposes of this chapter. All interventions were delivered by the school psychology interns who varied in prior teaching experience from none to several years.

During the internship year, each of the interns worked closely with their field internship supervisors to design an implementation that was both based on research learned during the pre-internship graduate courses and also suited to the individual students and the school setting in which the struggling students were being served. With on-site supervision from the field supervisor, but not the off-site university internship supervisor, each intern also created a progress monitoring plan to collect data to evaluate whether the implementation was effective for individual students and, if the intervention was implemented in a small group, for that group as a whole. Both individual and group analyses were performed so that the intern and supervisor could provide feedback, respectively, to parents of individual students about their child and to the building principals who requested evidence that the supplementary intervention program was effective in general and justified taking multiple students out of the regular program.

Before implementation, the interns had to present their plans for the evidence-based intervention project to their peers in a weekly seminar led by the university-based internship supervisor. The purpose of presenting the plans at the university before implementing them was to receive peer and faculty input to share with the internship supervisor before the intervention was implemented. Otherwise, the school-based interventions were conducted by the intern under the supervision of the field supervisor without university input. Then at the end of the internship year, the results of the evaluation of the implementation were presented to the university-based internship supervisor and peers in the weekly seminar at the university. Thus, in keeping with the theme of this volume, the intern first drew on research learned in the program to design an intervention tailored to the students at the internship site. Before implementing it, the intern did receive consultation from peers and university supervisor. After implementing it, the intern presented the evidence gathered to evaluate the effectiveness of the implementation of the intervention to peers and university supervisor, as well as to parents of individual students and building teachers and principals.

■ Intervention 1: Writing Intervention for First and Second Grade Students

Purpose

This intervention was designed based on the recent research showing that some students have been adversely affected by the current de-emphasis on teaching handwriting and spelling, which are perceived to be merely mechanical, and primary focus on the authentic communication of meaningful writing products (Troia, 2002). As a result, students often receive less explicit instruction in handwriting and spelling (Graham & Harris, 1994, 2000), both of which are critical for the development of written expression (Graham, Berninger, Abbott, Abbott, & Whitaker, 1997). Unfortunately, struggling writers frequently have trouble with the transcription skills (handwriting and spelling) involved in translating content into written text (Troia & Graham, 2003), which are not always taught or practiced to the level of mastery. Struggling writers require explicit and individualized instruction to develop lower-level transcription skills as well as higher-level composing strategies (Troia & Graham, 2003). Thus, the purpose of the first intervention was to develop writing skills in first and second grade students in handwriting automaticity, orthographic and phonological awareness, alphabetic principle, and spelling. The goal was not only to prevent more severe writing problems (Berninger & Amtmann, 2003) but also to help students pass the high-stakes tests in writing that not only Washington State but also many other states now require (Jenkins, Johnson, & Hileman, 2004).

Participants

The participants were 11 first and second grade students attending a public elementary school in a rural school system in the Pacific Northwest. First and second grade teachers volunteered their classes to be screened for participation. Informed consent, as is required by the state and local school districts, was sent home with each student for his or her parents to sign and return. The students whose parents returned the written permission forms were then screened with writing and writing-related subtests from the *Wechsler Individual Achievement Test-Second Edition* (WIAT II) (Psychological Corporation, 2002) and the *Process Assessment of the Learner (PAL) Test Battery for Reading and Writing* (Berninger, 2001). The spelling subtest and five-minute writing prompt were administered to groups, but the rest of the subtests were given individually either in a quiet place in the hall or in the back of a classroom during a quiet time.

Once all the students had completed the pretest measures, the scores were tabulated. According to the *PAL Reading and Writing Test* manual (Berninger, 2001) available at the time of this intervention,[1] scores at the 40th decile or lower were considered at-risk or deficient on each subtest. A decile is like a stanine but divided into ten intervals rather than nine; it is like a percentile but only for multiples of ten—scores cannot be interpreted for percentiles that fall within multiples of ten. Students who had three or more subtest scores that were at the 40th decile or lower and did not receive special education services were invited to join the writing club. All students who were identified to be eligible for the writing club received intervention.

Eleven students qualified for the writing intervention. The first grade group consisted of three boys and two girls. The second grade group contained four boys and two girls. Children were told that there was only space to invite a few children so they should feel honored to be in the writing club. They were also told that when the clubs were completed there would be a celebration with games and snacks.

Instructional Materials and Procedures

The instruction provided during writing clubs was based on randomized, controlled research on handwriting with first graders (Berninger, Vaughan, Abbott, Abbott, Brooks, Rogan, et al., 1997) and spelling with second graders (Berninger, Vaughan, Abbott, Brooks, Abbott, Reed, et al., 1998). Because this research was funded by NIH and investigators are required to make the results of research available to the public, these instructional interventions were translated into teacher-friendly lesson plans for handwriting (Berninger, 1998b; Berninger & Abbott, 2003, Lesson Set 3) and spelling (Berninger, 1998a, Phonological Lessons; Berninger & Abbott, 2003, Lesson Set 4).

Each writing club met twice a week for 30 minutes for 8 weeks or 10 weeks, depending on when individual children qualified for participation. Tuesdays were devoted to handwriting and composing (Lesson Set 3, Berninger & Abbott, 2003). In each handwriting lesson, the 26 letters of the alphabet were practiced by studying numbered arrow cues, covering the letters, writing the letters from memory, and comparing the written letters with the models and revising if necessary. Following handwriting practice, children wrote a 5-minute composition based on a writing-prompt. Children shared compositions by reading them to each other. In controlled research, this handwriting and composing practice improved both handwriting and authentic composing (Berninger et al., 1997).

Thursdays were devoted to spelling. Children played four *sound games* (see Phonological Lessons, Berninger, 1998a) in which they listened for *phonemes* (the smallest sound that makes a difference in meaning and that corresponds to a 1- or 2-letter spelling unit), decided which phoneme had been deleted from a word, said words without deleted phonemes, and substituted phonemes for designated ones in words. They also played these four games with *syllables*. In addition, they played *looking games* (Berninger, 1998a) in which they carefully looked at all the letters in a written word that was shown briefly and then covered. The children were asked to spell back all the letters or said or wrote the letter (e.g., first, last, third) or letter group (first two or last two or third and fourth) in a designated position in the word. They also practiced saying and looking at *Talking Letters* (Berninger & Abbott, 2003, Lesson Set 4) in the *sound-to-letter(s) direction* and in writing spelled words in the lesson plans as well as words they brought to the clubs that they were working on in their regular classes. Research has shown that phonological awareness (phoneme) games and orthographic (looking) games (Berninger & Traweek, 1991) and teaching alphabetic principle in the phoneme-to-grapheme direction (Berninger et al., 1998) improves spelling. Flash cards for spelling grade-appropriate words (Berninger & Abbott, 2003, Lesson Set 4) were created out of regular copy paper that was then laminated to increase durability. Students were taught how to apply alphabetic principle to spelling real words.

All students had a 4 × 6 note card on which they wrote their name. During the intervention, when the students were quietly working and on-task, the group leader (school psychology intern) would stamp the card with a self-inking stamp. At completion of the writing clubs, students were congratulated on their progress and had a session where each group ate cookies and popcorn while they played hangman.

Evaluation Plan

The screening scores served as the pretest scores for the progress monitoring plan. Many of the same subtests were readministered after the intervention was implemented to evaluate progress and the effectiveness of the intervention. Owing to an oversight, the spelling test and composition prompt given at screening (pretest) were not readministered at post-test. The effectiveness of the implementation was evaluated on the basis of whether students improved significantly from pretest to post-test as individuals and as a group on handwriting measures and spelling-related measures.

Results

First, results for individual children were compared to evaluate whether individuals had a higher score at post-test than at pretest. If so, that is evidence that individual students had responded to the instructional intervention as implemented. Next, inferential statistics were used to compare means of the group at pretest and at post-test to evaluate the program for the children in general. If the group improved on the average, then that is evidence that the program was generally effective. The purpose was not to generalize to a population of children in general but rather to evaluate whether this implementation in this school setting had been generally effective for the students in this school receiving the supplementary intervention. Thus, approaches used in individual subject design *and* program evaluation were combined to provide multimodal evidence in evaluating the effectiveness of this small-scale, relatively brief implementation of evidence-based writing instruction.

The first and second graders were combined for the group analyses since they received the same intervention. One of the four first graders did not have complete data on each measure so the group analyses were based on a sample size of 9. The children varied greatly in which writing or writing-related skills they were impaired at pretest and in which ones improved in response to intervention. This finding replicated prior research showing normal variation in how children respond to the same instructional intervention (Abbott, Reed, Abbott, & Berninger, 1997; Berninger & Abbott, 1992).

Individual analyses. The normed scores for the individual analyses are reported in deciles (percentiles with a band of 10). Of the *four first graders* with pretest and post-test data on Alphabet Writing (number correct in first 15 seconds), an index of automatic letter writing from memory, all improved (from 30th to 70th, 50th to 90th, 30th to 50th, and 30th to 80th). Likewise, all four improved in receptive orthographic coding (from 40th to 60th, 50th to 80th, 90th to 100th, and 70th to 100th). Also, three improved in Rapid Automatic Naming (RAN) for letters (from 50th to 70th, 30th to 70th, and 80th to 100th). Three improved in syllable awareness (from 40th to 70th, 20th to 40th, and 10th to 20th). Two improved in phoneme awareness (from 70th to 90th, 60th to 90th). Three improved in phonological decoding of pseudowords (90th to 100th, 60th to 90th, and 60th to 80th).

Of the *six second graders*, three improved in Alphabet Writing (first 15 seconds, an index of automaticity) (from 20th to 100th, 40th to 80th, or 80th to 90th). Four improved in receptive orthographic coding (from 70th to 100th, 90th to 100th, 60th to 90th, or also 60th to 90th). Five improved in RAN letters (from 30th to 50th, 20th to 60th, 20th to 40th, 40th to 50th, and

20th to 80th). One improved in syllable awareness (from 20th to 60th). Three improved in phoneme awareness (from 60th to 70th, 20th to 60th, and 50th to 60th). Five improved in phonological decoding of pseudowords (from 60th to 80th, 40th to 60th, 40th to 50th, 50th to 60th, and 40th to 50th).

Group analyses. Because means and standard deviations for grade are reported in the PAL test manual, z-scores (mean = 0, SD = 1) for grade can also be calculated from raw scores. Means and standard deviations for z-scores for the pretest and post-test measures are reported in Table 25.1. Table 25.2 reports the results of the pairwise t-tests used to compare the statistical significance of the difference in means for pretest and post-test measures on the same subtest. Although two-tail tests are typically considered conventional levels of statistical significance, in intervention research results that are significant for a one-tail test ($p < 0.10$) are also noted because they are relevant to improvement in the upper tail of the distribution. One-tail tests are also reported to avoid type 2 errors (failing to note gains, especially when individual participants in an instructional group may have shown improvement).

As shown in Tables 25.1 and 25.2, students made significant improvement (based on a two-tail statistical test) on receptive orthographic coding, which uniquely predicts handwriting (e.g., Abbott & Berninger, 1993), and pseudoword decoding, which discriminates good, average, and poor spellers in second, fourth, and sixth grades (Garcia, 2007). They made significant improvement

TABLE 25.1   *Descriptive Statistics for Group Analyses (z-Scores for Grade) for N = 9*

	Mean	Standard Deviation
Alphabet Writing Pretest	−0.03	0.81
Alphabet Writing Post-test	0.68	0.62
Receptive Coding Pretest	0.51	0.43
Receptive Coding Post-test	1.16	0.59
RAN—Letters Pretest	0.04	0.52
RAN—Letters Post-test	−0.28	0.38
Syllables Pretest	−0.97	0.97
Syllables Post-test	−0.50	0.94
Phonemes Pretest	0.06	0.85
Phonemes Post-test	0.34	0.83
Pseudoword Pretest	−0.14	0.56
Pseudoword Post-test	0.37	0.65

Note: For Ran—z is faster.

TABLE 25.2   *Paired Samples t-Test (Change in Mean z-Score from Pretest to Post-test)*

	t	df	Sig. (two-tailed)
Alphabet Writing Pre-Post	−2.079	8	0.071
Receptive Coding Pre-Post	−5.093	8	0.001*
RAN—Letters Pre-Post	2.063	8	0.073
Syllables Pre-Post	−1.972	8	0.084
Phonemes Pre-Post	−1.480	8	0.177
Pseudoword Decoding Pre-Post	−3.861	8	0.005*

(based on a one-tail directional hypothesis) on Alphabet Writing (handwriting automaticity), RAN letters, and syllable awareness. Orthographic coding was taught through looking games. Decoding may have improved as a result of the orthographic, phonological, and handwriting training; research shows that each of these may contribute to the improvement of decoding or real word reading skills (Berninger et al., 1997, 2000; Berninger, Rutberg, Abbott, Garcia, Anderson-Youngstrom, Brooks, et al., 2006).

This evidence-based project illustrates the importance of focusing not only on reading but also writing in the early grades. All too often early intervention focuses only on reading and not on writing (see Chapter 14 by Dunn & Miller, this volume, for importance of providing early intervention in reading and writing).

Reflections of the School Psychology Intern in Final Report

Having learned in coursework on research-supported academic intervention that identifying and treating writing skill deficits early in the child's school career may prevent later writing problems (for review of evidence, see Berninger & Amtmann, 2003; see Chapter 2 by Hooper et al., this volume), she used her internship opportunity to target assessment and treatment of handwriting and spelling because research has shown that these transcription skills are significantly related to compositional fluency (Berninger, Yates, Cartwright, Rutberg, Remy, & Abbott, 1992) and training these transcription skills generalizes to improved compositional fluency (e.g., Berninger et al., 1997, 1998). Because of an oversight the screening measures for compositional fluency and spelling given at pretest were not given again at post-test; thus, it was not possible to test whether these research-supported findings replicated in the school implementation. For practitioners who try to implement research-supported instruction and are focused on the day to day implementation of that instruction, it is easy to forget the essentials of collecting sufficient data to evaluate the effects of the intervention, but the intern recognized the importance of doing so in future school psychology practice.

However, the individual results showed that during the time the writing clubs met, all first graders and three of the six second graders improved significantly on automatic letter writing on the Alphabet Writing Task from pretest to post-test. Given the relationship between automatic letter writing and compositional fluency, the children who improved are likely to write more in the classroom, as teachers reported some of these treated children were. The intern also noted that future evaluations of implementations should systematically collect teacher observations of changes in classroom performance as a result of receiving early intervention services. Despite the lack of a post-test measure of spelling, both individual and group results show that children improved on skills research has shown are significantly related to spelling: receptive orthographic coding (Abbott & Berninger, 1993; Garcia, 2007) and phonological decoding of pseudowords (Garcia, 2007). All four first graders and four of the six second graders improved significantly in receptive orthographic coding. Three of the four first graders and five of the six second graders improved on phonological decoding of pseudowords. A brief intervention of 8–10 weeks may only be sufficient for students to begin to respond to supplementary instruction but not to increase writing skills substantially or sustain improved writing over large stretches of time. Substantial and sustained writing improvement may require a longer, more sustained supplementary instruction program.

■ Intervention 2: Reading Skills Intervention for Fourth Grade Students

Purpose

Children do not always receive explicit, systematic instruction in reading after the first three grades. Although many children learn to read sufficiently well during these grades and move on to the next developmental stage of reading to learn (Chall, 1983), many do not and require additional systematic reading instruction. This intervention addressed both word decoding and reading comprehension skill deficits in fourth graders identified as at-risk for failing the statewide reading assessment. Passing that test is now required for high school graduation in Washington State and schools are eager to start early to prevent school drop out and nongraduation.

Participants

Participants were nine fourth grade students in a suburban elementary school serving an ethnically diverse student body. These students were selected from a pool of 15 students identified by their classroom teachers as having reading problems. The teachers secured consent from parents to screen students during end of trimester conferences for participation in a special reading group. Once all the students were screened, students with standard scores below 95 in one or more areas were considered eligible. All the students were then rank ordered to determine which 10 were in greatest need of extra help and would be selected to participate in the group. One of the students moved less than one week after the intervention began. This student was replaced by the next student on the list. A second student moved eight weeks into the intervention. This student was not replaced.

Two students in the study were identified as having speech and language problems and were receiving special education services in this area. One of these students and two additional students were considered English language learner students, and were receiving additional services in this area. None of the students in this study was receiving special education services for reading, writing, or math. Thus, general education students who are not qualified for special education are a diverse group who may share common as well as unique instructional needs, posing challenges for implementing research-supported instruction in the classroom. Samples in published research studies may have different kinds or mixes of diversity than students receiving intervention in schools.

Materials

Instructional materials and lessons were drawn from *PAL Reading and Writing Lessons* (Berninger & Abbot, 2003), *Words* (Henry, 1990), and *Reasoning and Reading* (Carlisle, 2003). Each is based on research on different aspects of reading. The intervention plan created an intervention that integrated all the relevant aspects in a comprehensive manner and that was grade-appropriate for these fourth grade struggling readers.

Procedures for Assessment and Intervention

At pretest, before the supplementary intervention began, selected subtests from the *Woodcock Johnson, Tests of Achievement, Third Edition (WJ III) Form A* (Woodcock, McGrew, & Mather, 2001) were given. See Table 25.4 for seven subtests that were administered.

Once participants were selected, they were also given the pretest from the *Words* (Henry, 1990) program in order to get a criterion-referenced baseline of student knowledge of applying letter-sound knowledge and morphemes to decoding and recognizing syllable patterns. A critical thinking exercise from *Reading and Reasoning* (Carlisle, 2003) was also administered to gauge student reading comprehension on a curriculum-based measure linked to the instructional materials. Thus, multiple modes of assessment—standardized and curriculum-based—were used for progress monitoring.

Once baselines were established, the intervention began. The reading group met three days per week, for 40 minutes per session. Children were told that the theme of the reading group was "Word Study" and that they would be asked to study words, their parts, and their meaning.

Each session consisted of two parts. The first part used instructional activities for phonological and orthographic awareness from *PAL Research-Supported Reading and Writing Lessons* (Reproducibles for Lesson Set 12) (Berninger & Abbott, 2003). These lessons are based on the dissertation research of a doctoral student in the same school psychology program (Abbott & Berninger, 1999). Participants were also systematically taught automatic correspondences between phoneme sounds and their orthographic representations (1- and 2-letter spelling units). Syllable types were also taught. Then students were asked to apply what they had learned about letter-sound relationships and syllable types to decode unfamiliar words.

The second part focused on comprehension skills using lessons in *Reasoning and Reading* (Carlisle, 2003). Students completed (a) word-level vocabulary activities (e.g., synonyms and antonyms), (b) sentence-level activities (interpreting sentence meaning), and (c) discourse-level activities (e.g., main idea, cause and effect). Comprehension exercises were explained and practiced in class and then sent home as homework. Over the course of the implementation, students were given incentives for completing and returning homework. Sitting at the head of the conference table was used as a privilege. Students who answered questions correctly were moved to the "Head of the Table." To remain in that position, they were required to continue answering questions correctly. Students earned "passes" for turning in homework, which allowed them to pass on questions and remain at the *"Head of the Table."*

At post-test, after the supplementary intervention was completed, the same seven subtests from the *WJ III Tests of Achievement* were readministered but *Form B* rather than *Form A* was given. Analyses were conducted of pretest–post-test change for both individuals and the group.

To facilitate home-school communication and collaboration, which can become constrained when older students are not succeeding in basic skills such as reading, parents were sent a letter when the intervention was completed. This letter contained a summary of the student's performance on pretest and post-test measures so that parents could see where progress was made. Parents were also given suggestions to assist their child in further developing their child's reading skills with activities in the home or with strategies for helping the child complete school assignments.

Results

Individual analyses. Table 25.3 summarizes the pretest and post-test scores for each of the standardized measures. Of the nine children, post-test scores were higher than pretest scores for seven on reading real words (WI) and reading pseudowords (WA), for eight on reading comprehension (PC) and spelling sounds, that is, pseudowords (SS), for six on reading fluency (FLU) and vocabulary (VOC), and for four on real word spelling (SP).

Group analyses. Table 25.4 reports means and standard deviations for pretest and post-test measures for the group and Table 25.5 provides the results of paired *t*-tests for evaluating whether the means were significantly different from pretest to post-test on each measure. These analyses are relevant to program evaluation for a specific implementation of a research-based instructional intervention in a specific school setting rather than to generation of new knowledge based on research designed to generalize to the population of fourth grade struggling readers in general.

As shown in Table 25.4, the students in the reading intervention group were as a group below the population mean on all measures at pretest in a school setting where the average achievement is at or above the population mean. As shown in Table 25.5, the group as a whole showed significant improvement on a two-tailed test in word identification, word decoding, comprehension, and spelling of pseudowords. The first two skills were taught while the last finding may reflect transfer from a taught skill to a related nonreading skill. Although mean scores increased in each of these skills, only phonological decoding (WA) was above the population mean at post-test. These findings, which are based on program evaluation of the implementation of an intervention based on research on teaching word decoding and word-, sentence-, and discourse-level comprehension skills, show that the implementation was effective for the group in general. This conclusion is consistent with the results of the individual student analyses as well.

Gains in vocabulary, which was taught, were significant on a one-tailed, directional test. The average score for spelling real words, which were not taught, showed a slight decline between pretest and post-test measures. Ability to spelling real words is highly influenced by word-specific knowledge, which was not the focus of the intervention that emphasized rule-governed learning and associations in time.

*Reflections of the School Psychology Intern
in the Final Report*

Each student in this intervention had previously received supplemental instruction through Title 1 services, but continued to struggle with basic word reading and comprehension skills in fourth grade. Although not every student

TABLE 25.3 *Comparison of Pretest and Post-test Standard Scores for Age for Individual Students (See Table 25.4 for Names of WJ III Subtests.)*

S	WID pre	WID post	WA pre	WA post	FLU pre	FLU post	PC pre	PC post	VOC pre	VOC post	SP pre	SP post	SS pre	SS post
1	97	98	99	112	91	93	91	90	96	92	92	105	96	93
2	91	93	90	103	96	95	81	88	80	86	97	98	90	93
3	97	104	95	107	101	98	99	103	97	112	98	96	91	95
4	99	101	96	106	101	113	88	97	103	98	106	108	93	111
5	98	103	104	101	103	106	88	94	96	96	95	89	96	97
6	91	91	96	100	90	88	91	97	93	104	98	92	93	97
7	86	88	84	94	88	92	84	87	84	88	93	86	84	106
8	89	88	91	97	90	97	93	95	93	96	83	82	96	99
9	91	94	95	94	91	96	91	92	100	110	91	92	96	102

TABLE 25.4　*Descriptive Statistics for Group Analyses (Standard Scores for Age) for N = 9*

	Mean	Standard Deviation
WI Letter-Word ID Pretest	93.22	4.60
WI Letter-Word ID Post-test	95.56	6.19
WA Word Attack Pretest	94.44	5.68
WA Word Attack Post-test	101.56	6.11
FLU Read Fluency Pretest	94.56	5.77
FLU Read Fluency Post-test	97.56	7.60
PC Comprehension Pretest	89.56	5.20
PC Comprehension Post-test	93.67	5.05
VOC Read Vocab Pretest	93.56	7.33
VOC Read Vocab Post-test	98.00	9.11
SP Spelling Pretest	94.78	6.28
SP Spelling Post-test	94.22	8.50
SS Spelling Sounds Pretest	92.78	4.02
SS Spelling Sounds Post-test	99.22	6.10

TABLE 25.5　*Paired Samples t-Test (Changes in Mean Standard Score for Age from Pretest to Post-test)*

	t	df	Sig. (two-tailed)
Letter-Word Identification	−2.86	8	0.021*
Word Attack	−3.55	8	0.008*
Reading Fluency	−1.90	8	0.094
Passage Comprehension	−3.88	8	0.005*
Reading Vocabulary	−1.96	8	0.086
Spelling (Real Words)	0.27	8	0.792
Spelling of Sounds (Pseudowords)	−0.24	8	0.045*

in the reading intervention made progress in every skill assessed, all students made progress in at least one skill and typically many skills and the psychometric normed tests were sensitive to student response to instruction. It appeared that once the "holes" in some of these students' foundational reading skills were addressed, they were able to better apply these learned skills to the act of reading familiar and unfamiliar words and to the comprehension of text.

Similar to many experienced teachers, this school psychology intern decided to integrate several research-based instructional materials to achieve the instructional goals for decoding *and* reading comprehension rather than to use a standard script (protocol) that is implemented in a standard way and focused on only one of these goals. Such an integrated approach is research-supported (Berninger, Vermeulen, Abbott, McCutchen, Cotton, Cude, et al., 2003). In her past professional work as a teacher, this school psychology intern had used teacher-designed assessment to evaluate student response to instruction. However, she thought that systematically collecting multiple, norm-referenced measures before and after supplementary instruction was valuable because it focused her attention on evaluating evidence as to whether the student has made relative gains (compared to age peers). In addition, she used multimodal assessment. She examined the criterion-referenced baseline and curriculum-based measures described earlier and noted upward trends.

She was most gratified that the children's regular teachers reported that they were doing better in the classroom. Most importantly, student and teacher comments suggested that both students themselves and teachers who had given up hope that these children could become better readers seemed to have renewed confidence that these children could learn to read. See Chapter 16 by Wise et al., this volume, for the importance of gaining confidence in reading competence as a motivator for continuing to work to achieve reading success and to teach struggling readers effectively.

■ Intervention 3: Improving School Attitude, Motivation, and Writing

Purpose

This intervention had the goal of improving school attitude, motivation, and writing skills of a third-grade student with multiple exceptionalities. The intervention planning, implementation method, and pre/post-test assessment for response to instruction took into account the student's background as well as existing research.

Student Background

Students identified as twice exceptional are at-risk for school failure, poor self-esteem, and lack of academic motivation (Robinson, 1999). Twice exceptional students have cognitive abilities and academic skill in at least one area within the superior to gifted ranges, and also exhibit specific learning disabilities in reading, writing, or mathematics. At an elementary school with many high-achieving students due to the gifted programming, the needs of twice-exceptional students were increasingly unmet. Some referred students did not meet special education qualification requirements, whereas others were viewed as lazy and/or disruptive and were not referred at all or were referred for behavioral rather than learning issues. The school psychologist intern recognized a trend in referrals of gifted third-grade boys for both writing difficulties and behavior that often did not result in special education placement under the IQ-Achievement discrepancy model. To address this trend of underidentifying and underserving students with both high IQs and learning disabilities and to model for teachers how such students might benefit from differentiated instruction in general education, the school psychology intern designed and piloted a cognitive-behavioral writing intervention for one third-grade boy. He was selected to participate based on the need to address his multiple exceptionalities and behavior issues.

Trevor (name changed to protect the student's identity) resided in an intact, affluent family. In Kindergarten, Trevor qualified for enrichment and displayed strong reading and math skills. During Kindergarten, he was also diagnosed with sensorineural hearing loss. His level of hearing loss resulted in an inability to discriminate several speech sounds. It was estimated that he was missing anywhere from 25% to 75% of classroom discussion and lecture. This hearing loss appeared to affect speech development and clarity, as well. Owing to his refusal to wear hearing aids, he qualified for a 504 plan in second grade that specified accommodations for the general education setting. This 504 plan required the use of sound fields within the classroom such that speakers were installed and teachers used a microphone during lecture to amplify their voices.

The sudden onset of the hearing loss was of great concern for Trevor's parents who had not noticed signs of the deficit before Kindergarten. His parents had him evaluated by a pediatrician, an otolaryngologist, a neurologist, an audiologist, an occupational therapist, a speech and language pathologist, and a psychologist. These evaluations resulted in diagnoses of Attention Deficit Hyperactivity Disorder (ADHD), Hearing Deficit, and Motor Planning Difficulties. At the time of this intervention, Trevor was receiving private individual counseling and occupational therapy weekly.

Pretest Results

Previous occupational therapy reports indicated that Trevor was unable to recall letter formation and his teachers reported that his handwriting was illegible. During pretest, Trevor attained scores falling within the deficient range on the Alphabet and Copying tasks from the *Process Assessment for the Learner, Test Battery for Reading and Writing* (PAL-RW; Berninger, 2001). Therefore, primary intervention goals focused on developing automatic letter recognition and reproduction as well as handwriting improvement in his written work.

In addition, based on parent and teacher report, Trevor exhibited a negative attitude toward school, was not completing his work, and appeared to lack motivation. *Behavior Assessment System for Children, Second Edition, Self-Report Form* (BASC-2-SRP; Reynolds & Kamphaus, 2004) results also indicated attitude toward school subscale scores within the clinically significant range. On the basis of this information, a second goal of the intervention was to improve attitude toward school and motivation. Other areas falling within the clinically significant or at-risk ranges, such as depression, parent-child relationship, attention difficulties, and self-reliance, were followed-up with brief counseling with the student and conversations with both his parents and the school psychologist.

Finally, writing samples from the general education classroom and special education resource room were also collected. The samples confirmed Trevor's handwriting often showed (a) distortion of the relative proportion of component strokes, for example, the left most vertical line in n and h were the same height, and (b) illegibility—others could not decipher which letter was intended. In addition, several writing samples reflected his attitude toward school and lack of engagement. For example, when instructed to write for 20 minutes on a topic of his choice, the student wrote two pages of, "I like cheese! Cheese! Cheese! Cheese!...Cheesy Cheese!" accompanied by illustrations of cheese wedges. This type of work completion was common throughout Trevor's coursework. His teachers described him negatively using terms such as "lazy." Trevor's enrichment teacher indicated that she felt he did not belong in her class and did not deserve to receive enrichment services because of his misbehavior and lack of engagement in the enrichment activities provided.

Procedures

Intervention sessions were scheduled once a week for approximately 40 minutes. Each session began with a brief, 5- to 10-minute handwriting practice that consisted of looking at a sample letter written in cursive, saying the letter, and copying it from memory three times (adapted from Berninger, 1998a). In each session, he completed this practice for three lowercase and three uppercase letters. Trevor was then instructed to evaluate his handwriting, which was followed by a brief discussion of his evaluation and how he could improve each letter. In addition, cognitive-behavioral techniques were used to address the student's thoughts regarding the writing process, how he could effectively share information, and why legibility was important.

The rest of each session was devoted to in-depth project work based on the project approach by Katz and Chard (1989). As suggested by Winebrenner (2003) for children who are both gifted and learning disabled, the project work was based on both classroom activities and Trevor's individual interests. The third-grade classrooms had just begun publishing a newspaper and students were learning how to write various articles. Trevor had indicated a strong interest in robotics. Therefore, it was hypothesized that if Trevor could combine his personal interest with the writing task and preview robotics within higher education, he would not only adequately complete the writing assignment with improved writing quality, but also develop an educational goal and increase his academic motivation.

The school psychology intern contacted a University of Washington robotics laboratory and found a graduate student in the lab who agreed to meet with Trevor and give him a tour. On the basis of this opportunity, Trevor decided to write an interview article about the lab tour for the third-grade newspaper. The project consisted of researching robotics, visiting the university robotics laboratory, and interviewing the graduate student who was giving the tour. Then, based on his research, Trevor developed interview questions, practiced taking notes, and prepared for the interview by writing his questions on individual note cards.

Trevor was held accountable for following through on each step of the project. It was his responsibility to determine and meet deadlines within the time allotted for this class assignment. Resistance was encountered when Trevor was required, as homework, to write his interview questions on note cards. He did not complete this task for two consecutive weeks. Trevor's resistance was addressed directly with him to explore his cognitions about the writing task and lack of motivation to complete it. In addition, a consequence was established. The robotics lab tour was contingent upon Trevor's work completion; both Trevor and his parents were informed that if he did not complete the task by the following meeting, the tour would be cancelled. Fortunately, with the support of his parents and the incentive of the tour of the robotics lab as a motivator, Trevor was able to complete the note cards.

Following the robotics laboratory tour, and interview, Trevor wrote an initial draft of the interview article using the computer. The draft was edited during an intervention session, which Trevor then revised and submitted for publication *three days prior to the class deadline.*

Post-test Results

Following 10 intervention sessions and the field trip, Trevor was reassessed using the *PAL-RW* Alphabet Writing, Copy A, and Copy B tasks. During post-test, Trevor wrote seven of seven letters correctly on the Alphabet Task, which was completed at the same rate as at the pretest, but with markedly improved letter formation. On both of the Copy Tasks, Trevor's writing rate had improved. For example, he completed the Copy Task A sentence in cursive within 78 seconds during pretest and within 47 seconds during post-test. In addition, Trevor's handwriting in both print and cursive had improved in legibility and his letters were proportionate.

See Figures 25.1 and 25.2 for a comparison of the pretest and post-test samples. When asked to compare his pretest and post-test Copy B writing samples, Trevor described the post-test sample as "under control."

Trevor also completed a follow-up *BASC-2-SRP*. These results did not indicate improvement in attitude toward school, depression, attention difficulties, or the parent-child relationship, each of which still fell within the at-risk and clinically significant ranges. He made some changes in his ratings of other areas. During post-test, his feelings of self-efficacy increased and fell

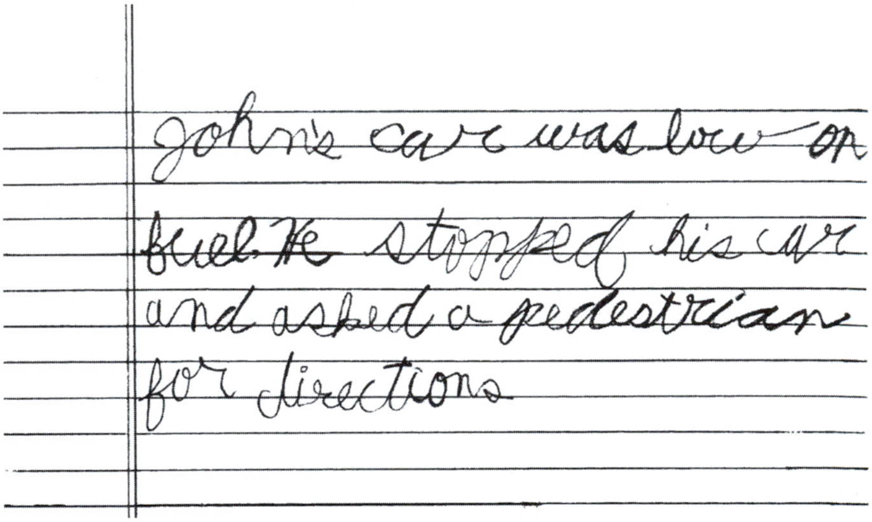

FIGURE 25.1 Pretest Copy Task B.

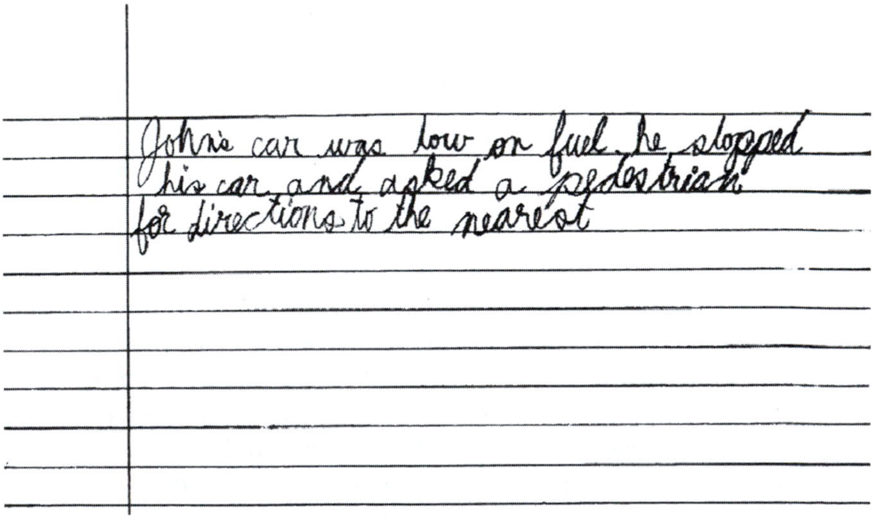

FIGURE 25.2 Post-test Copy Task B.

within the normal range; however, his self-esteem was now rated within the at-risk range. Ratings regarding Trevor's attitude toward teachers, feelings of being controlled by others, and social stress also fell within the at-risk range. These concerning results were again discussed with the student and his parents. These ratings appeared to be a reflection of the increased accountability required of Trevor by both his parents and teachers and the implementation of consistent discipline, each of which had resulted in dramatic behavioral changes at home and school over the course of the school year. Trevor's therapist was informed of these issues for which Trevor continues to receive ongoing treatment.

On the other hand, Trevor made comments such as "Third grade is the best year for me. I'm finally learning." He had stated a goal of applying to and attending a prestigious private school during middle and high school, and was completing his work. His teachers commented on his improved attitude within class and the increased quality of his written work. Finally, Trevor's interview article was not only well-written, it was completed, and turned in prior to the deadline.

Reflections of the School Psychology
Intern in Final Report

In evaluating the effectiveness of the intervention, which had goals of improving academic skills and social emotional goals that are relevant to the practice of school psychology, the school psychology intern used multiple modes of assessment, including norm-referenced tests, rating scales, and clinical observation. Overall, this intervention was successful in improving handwriting and motivation. By increasing self-awareness and positive encouragement through cognitive-behavioral therapy, implementing brief letter writing practice with self-evaluation, and finding an engaging subject matter, the student's handwriting and written expression improved. His work completion, development of an educational goal, and positive comments from teachers were evidence of his increased academic motivation. In addition, the positive experience during the robotics tour and interview may have also facilitated his goal development and increased motivation to complete academic work.

Unfortunately, standardized assessment did not reflect changes in Trevor's attitude toward school and, in fact, post-test results demonstrated increased social/emotional problems. These results may reflect the overall changes in structure and accountability Trevor experienced throughout the year and the need for further positive school experiences within his interest areas. Fortunately, Trevor has support from his family, teachers, and therapists. His attitude toward school and social emotional difficulties may improve with continued counseling and positive school experiences.

■ Summary and Discussion

These three studies illustrate two aspects of evidence-based implementations with which practitioners must be concerned: (a) What published research shows is effective in controlled research studies; and (b) What the progress monitoring data show is effective for the specific implementation of that research in a specific school setting for a specific child or children. These evidence-based projects, which were required during the school psychology internship in a NASP-approved School Psychology Program, demonstrate the importance of not only using evidence-based practices but also collecting evidence to evaluate whether, based on comparing one student at a time before and after the supplementary instruction, individual students improve in response to instruction and whether, based on group means, the students in general improve in response to the supplementary intervention program. The evidence used for evaluating the implementation is generalized only to the individual at hand or the instructional group at hand—not to the population in general as published research studies typically do. In evaluating these interventions pretest–post-test designs without control groups were used. That is another reason the results should be generalized only to the children receiving the intervention. For examples of randomized, controlled evaluations of implementations by school psychologists in partnership with teachers, see Dunn and Miller (Chapter 14, this volume) or Nelson et al. (Chapter 13, this volume).

The first project illustrated the evidence-based implementation approach for writing early in schooling. The second intervention illustrated the evidence-based implementation approach for reading in older, intermediate grade students in word decoding and comprehension. The third intervention, which was the most individualized, provided positive results for a student that was both gifted and learning disabled, or "twice exceptional." These projects also provide evidence to support the expanded role of the school psychologist, beyond assessment for special education, toward becoming a resource for teachers in implementing evidence-based, research-supported academic interventions and then evaluating, with evidence, student responses to intervention. Also, see Dunn and Miller (Chapter 14, this volume) on the expanding role of the school psychologist beyond assessment for special education placement (e.g., Marston, 2005; Tilly, Reschley, & Grimes, 1999).

The results show that school psychology interns, at the dawn of their professional careers as psychologists, can design interventions based on scientific research, implement them, and collect evidence about their effectiveness. Regardless of amount of prior teaching experience, these school psychology interns were able to show, with evidence, that the supplemental instruction benefited each student in at least some ways. Including such evidence-based project requirements in preservice training programs may better prepare school psychologists for planning evidence-based interventions and evidence-based evaluations of implementations of those interventions during their future careers as school psychologists. Future research might investigate whether preservice experience with evaluating, on the basis of evidence, implementations of instructional interventions based on prior research, results in a higher probability of using evidence-based practices throughout one's career as a school psychologist.

■ References

Abbott, R., & Berninger, V. (1993). Structural equation modeling of relationships among developmental skills and writing skills in primary and intermediate grade writers. *Journal of Educational Psychology, 85*, 478–508.

Abbott, S., & Berninger, V. (1999). It's never too late to remediate: A developmental approach to teaching word recognition. *Annals of Dyslexia, 49*, 223–250.

Abbott, S., Reed, L., Abbott, R., & Berninger, V. (1997). Year-long balanced reading/writing tutorial: A design experiment used for dynamic assessment. *Learning Disability Quarterly, 20*, 249–263.

Berninger, V. (2006). Research-supported ideas for implementing reauthorized IDEA with intelligent and professional psychological services. *Psychology in the Schools, 43*, 781–797.

Berninger, V. (2007). *Process Assessment of the Learner, 2nd Edition. Diagnostic for Reading and Writing (PAL-II RW). Process Assessment of the Learner Diagnostic for Math (PAL II-M). PAL II User Guide (CD) for Tier 1, Tier 2, and Tier 3 assessment-instruction links and downloadable instructional tools*. San Antonio, TX, The Psychological Corporation.

Berninger, V., & Abbott, R. (1992). Unit of analysis and constructive processes of the learner: Key concepts for educational neuropsychology. *Educational Psychologist, 27*, 223–242.

Berninger, V., Abbott, R., Brooksher, R., Lemos, Z., Ogier, S., Zook, D., et al. (2000). A connectionist approach to making the predictability of English orthography explicit to at-risk beginning readers: Evidence for alternative, effective strategies. *Developmental Neuropsychology, 17*, 241–271.

Berninger, V., & Abbott, S. (2003). *PAL research-supported reading and writing lessons*. San Antonio, TX, Harcourt.

Berninger, V., & Amtmann, D. (2003). Preventing written expression disabilities through early and continuing assessment and intervention for handwriting and/or spelling problems: Research into Practice. In H. L. Swanson, K. Harris, & S. Graham (Eds.), *Handbook of Learning Disabilities* (pp. 345–363). New York, The Guilford Press.

Berninger, V., Rutberg, J., Abbott, R., Garcia, N., Anderson-Youngstrom, M., Brooks, A., et al. (2006). Tier 1 and tier 2 early intervention for handwriting and composing. *Journal of School Psychology, 44*, 3–30.

Berninger, V., & Traweek, D. (1991). Effects of two-phase reading intervention on three orthographic-phonological code connections. *Learning and Individual Differences, 3,* 323–338.

Berninger, V., Vaughan, K., Abbott, R., Abbott, S., Brooks, A., Rogan, L., et al. (1997). Treatment of handwriting fluency problems in beginning writing: Transfer from handwriting to composition. *Journal of Educational Psychology, 89,* 652–666.

Berninger, V., Vaughan, K., Abbott, R., Brooks, A., Abbott, S., Reed, et al. (1998). Early intervention for spelling problems: Teaching spelling units of varying size within a multiple connections framework. *Journal of Educational Psychology, 90,* 587–605.

Berninger, V., Vermeulen, K., Abbott, R., McCutchen, D., Cotton, S., Cude, J., et al. (2003). Comparison of three approaches to supplementary reading instruction for low achieving second grade readers. *Language, Speech, and Hearing Services in Schools, 34,* 101–116.

Berninger, V., Yates, C., Cartwright, A., Rutberg, J., Remy, E., & Abbott, R. (1992). Lower-level developmental skills in beginning writing. *Reading and Writing. An Interdisciplinary Journal, 4,* 257–280.

Berninger, V. W. (1998a). *Guides for intervention: Reading, writing.* San Antonio, TX, The Psychological Corporation.

Berninger, V. W. (1998b). *PAL handwriting lessons.* San Antonio, TX, The Psychological Corporation.

Berninger, V. W. (2001). *Process assessment of the learner: Test battery for reading and writing.* San Antonio, TX, The Psychological Corporation.

Carlisle, J. (2003). *Reasoning and reading.* Cambridge, MA, Educators Publishing Service.

Chall, J. (1983). *Stages of reading development.* New York, McGraw-Hill.

Garcia, N. (2007, December). *Phonological, orthographic, and morphological contributions to the spelling development of good, average, and poor spellers.* Ph.D. Dissertation, University of Washington.

Graham, S., Berninger, V., Abbott, R., Abbott, S., & Whitaker, D. (1997). The role of mechanics in composing of elementary school students: A new methodological approach. *Journal of Educational Psychology, 89,* 170–182.

Graham, S., & Harris, K. R. (1994). Implications of constructivism for teaching writing to students with special needs. *Journal of Special Education, 28,* 275–289.

Graham, S., & Harris, K. R. (2000). The role of self-regulation and transcription skills in writing and writing development. *Educational Psychologist, 35,* 3–12.

Henry, M. (1990). *Words.* Austin, TX, Pro-Ed Inc.

Jenkins, J., Johnson, E., & Hileman, J. (2004). When reading is also writing: Sources of individual differences on the new reading performance assessments. *Scientific Studies in Reading, 8,* 125–151.

Katz, L., & Chard, S. C. (1989). *Engaging children's minds: The project approach.* Norwood, NJ, Ablex Publishing Corp.

Marston, D. (2005). Tiers of intervention in responsiveness to intervention: Prevention outcomes and learning disabilities identification patterns. *Journal of Learning Disabilities, 38*, 539–544.

Psychological Corporation. (2002). *Wechsler Individual Achievement Test* (2nd ed.). San Antonio, TX, The Psychological Corporation.

Reynolds, C. R., & Kamphaus, R. W. (2004). *Behavior assessment scale for children* (2nd ed.). Bloomington, MN, Pearson Assessments.

Robinson, S. M. (1999). Meeting the needs of students who are gifted and have learning disabilities. *Intervention in Schools and Clinic, 34*, 194–204.

Tilly, W. D., Reschly, D. J., & Grimes, J. (1999). Disability determination in problem-solving systems: Conceptual foundations and critical components. In D. Reschly, W. D. Tilly, & J. Grimes (Eds.), *Special education in transition: Functional assessment and noncategorical programming* (pp. 285–321). Longmont, CO, Sopris West.

Troia, G. (2002). Teaching writing strategies to children with disabilities: Setting generalization as the goal. *Exceptionality, 10*, 249–269.

Troia, G., & Graham, S. (2003). Effective writing instruction across the grades: What every consultant should know. *Journal of Educational and Psychological Consultation, 14*, 75–89.

Vadasy, P., Sanders, E., & Peyton, J. (2005). Relative effectiveness of reading practice or word-level instruction in supplemental tutoring. *Journal of Learning Disabilities, 38*, 364–380.

Winebrenner, S. (2003). Teaching strategies for twice-exceptional students. *Intervention in Schools and Clinic, 38*, 131–137.

Woodcock, R., McGrew, K., & Mather, N. (2001). *Woodcock-Johnson III—Tests of Achievement.* Rolling Meadows, IL, Riverside.

■ Note

1. The current version of PAL (PAL II; Berninger, 2007) has scaled scores with a mean of 10 and SD of 3.

Epilogue: State of the Science and Art in Implementation of Evidence-Based Academic Interventions

Sylvia Rosenfield and Virginia Berninger

In native culture in North America, the lowest person on the totem pole is the most important person because that person is closest to the ground where the action is that makes a difference on earth. The teachers, most especially, and also the psychologists, speech and language specialists, administrators, and other educational professionals are the ones that are directly in the position to make a difference in the learning and behavioral and mental health of individual students. That difference is ultimately the purpose of implementing interventions in support of student academic development. We conclude with guarded optimism that effective implementation of evidence-based intervention will make a positive difference, but also offer some cautions as educators, psychologists, and other school-based specialists confront the challenges of evidence-based practice.

■ The Nature of Evidence

In reading the research, one is reminded of Senator Proxmire's complaint about the need for a one-handed researcher. He demanded straightforward answers to tough questions, rather than having researchers present their "on the one hand, and on the other hand" caveats and complexities. In reviewing the chapters in this book, it becomes clear that the concepts of evidence and interventions are not as simple as those with policy and practice responsibilities would like. Many of the studies that provide the evidence have been conducted under experimental conditions and it is not at all clear how they would work in the school environment or for whom under what conditions. There is a need for more studies of effectiveness, and procedures for scaling up interventions with an evidence base. Ensuring access to skills in small N research designs for evaluating effectiveness in individual students, as described by

White (Chapter 19, this volume), and program evaluation, as described by Stringfield (Chapter 20, this volume), remains essential for both educators and psychologists working in schools. Further, both Peverly (Chapter 21, this volume) and Nelson et al. (Chapter 13, this volume) remind us that it is important to assess curriculum and instruction as well as individual students.

Science is an evolving process, and reviews of literature are also not written in stone (or gold). For example, meta-analyses on the same topic can differ, as there is selectivity in which studies are selected; some questions, approached differently, can lead to different conclusions, and to whom the studies apply, students in regular or special education, can also lead to different outcomes. Variability in effect size for the same intervention in different circumstances has been reported as well (see, e.g., Hoskyn, Chapter 6, this volume).

Across the reading (Chapter 1, this volume), writing (Chapter 2, this volume), and math (Chapter 3, this volume) domains, research has supported the benefits of explicit instruction and strategy instruction. Much remains, however, to be learned about how to best teach domain-specific cognitive skills at specific stages of reading, writing, and math development. We know more about the developmental milestones for motor and language skills than we do for reading, writing, and math and how these are relevant to classroom instruction and assessment practices. For students with learning difficulties, a combination of explicit instruction and strategy instruction provided a general evidence-based instructional heuristic for improving academic performance (effect sizes >0.80) in children with learning difficulties. It has been suggested that intensity and explicitness of the instructional design is what differentiates instruction along the continuum of learners.

On the other hand, the importance of language in academic development is one significant area that may be underappreciated in the schools (see Chapter 4, this volume). For example, one important finding is that a broad-based, everyday, oral language register in preschool, and not just phonological awareness, directly related to alphabetic knowledge in grade 1 and reading comprehension in grade 3. A second finding was that oral language capability played a central role in how children learned the academic languages of instruction (e.g., for math, science, language arts). Children who had acquired a rich, everyday oral language register were more likely to be successful in acquiring the more specialized academic language register that then allowed them to meet academic discourse demands in grades 1–3. The importance of all levels of language development, as well as the academic and oral register of language, goes against the widespread devotion of instructional time in early grades to phonics. Of course, with the national and international increases in language diversity within schools, including dialect differences within the mainstream language (see Chapter 5, this volume), implementation of research into educational practice also needs to consider how to adapt evidence-based practices for students who speak a different language at home than the language of school instruction.

Chapter 6 provides an overview of a small but growing body of research evidence on prevention science for academic, language, and social competence skills. The rest of the book (see Chapters 7–25, this volume) provides a comprehensive overview of not only the complexities, barriers, and unresolved issues in dealing with how to apply research to educational practice but also the initial small-scale successes that give hope as educational science-practitioners try earnestly to implement evidence-based practices in classrooms, schools, districts, state, and the nation.

■ Lessons from the Classroom

In Lipsky's (1980) classic work on street-level bureaucracy, he reminds us that policy is delivered through workers, such as teachers, who interact directly with their clients, in this case students, and "who have substantial discretion in the execution of their work" (p. 3). As with other such workers, teachers are expected to both follow policy and, "to a degree…be capable of responding flexibly to unique situations and to be able to treat people in terms of their individual circumstances…Teachers are expected to be interested in the individual child." (p. 105). The one-size fit all implementation of evidence-based interventions will not deal adequately with the individual differences among learners that are normal and expected. Intervention programs such as those described by authors in Steps 2, 3, and 4 are examples, at multiple levels, of processes being used to implement practices with a research base.

Teachers need to know more than how to implement evidence-based lessons, which may or may not be scripted. They also need to know how to respond to students in the moment of instruction, assess who needs help, understand why they need help and what kind of help they need, and evaluate whether they are making reasonable progress. As one graduate student in school psychology wrote on a recent reflection paper, "as a teacher for eight years I was taught how to deliver two of the evidence-based instructional programs on the What Works list, but not until I came to the University of Washington school psychology program did I learn why." Teachers need to learn how lesson plans, which are just *plans* reviewed before teaching begins, can be adapted to individual students and their response to instruction. In an era when educational professionals are being asked to implement research-supported intervention, we also need research-supported assessment tools to identify who need which kinds of intervention for early intervention and prevention as well as for more general academic development goals and data-based decision-making.

Efforts to disseminate research widely through national top-down efforts, such as Reading First, have left the unfortunate impression among many educational practitioners that what is being implemented is science-supported educational practice. Yet more than one educational practitioner has expressed skepticism that this evidence-based practice movement is largely an effort to get schools to purchase specific textbooks or assessment tools (e.g., on the What Works List). Attention is needed to making sure that practitioners have access to the scientific findings apart from commercial products and have professional autonomy to assess how these findings can be translated into their practice. According to a guide for practitioners published by the Department of Education (Coalition for Evidence-Based Policy, 2003, December), practitioners need the tools to identify evidence-based interventions, which may then "spark major improvements in their schools and, collectively, in American education" (p. 5). The guide provides an excellent source of information for practitioners on how to understand the quality of evidence.

However, selecting evidence-based programs is not enough. In their study of the quality of school-based prevention practices, Gottfredson and Gottfredson (2002) found that prevention practices resembling those effective in research were not implemented with integrity in the schools in their sample. They suggested more attention to the implementation of the programs, and recommended "that schools increase their emphasis on the quality of prevention activities" (p. 27).

In the process of turning to science for the validation of concepts that are relevant to educational practice, educational professionals should not lose sight of the importance of their professional autonomy and judgment in implementing research into practice. As a school psychology student remarked at the end of her consultation courses, "I thought it was the packaged program that I needed to find, and now I am looking for the instructional principles that need to be implemented after the problem has been identified." However, with autonomy comes the responsibility to be held accountable for the implementation and the outcomes. It is critical to ensure that those professionals in practice settings have the skills in both the evidence-based principles, an understanding of the critical importance of implementation quality, and accountability procedures.

■ Response to Instruction

The role of instructional principles in moving students forward academically is a consistent theme of this book. As the Assistant Secretary of Special Education stated during a visit to the University of Washington just before the implementation of IDEIA (2004) went into effect, reauthorization is really about bridging the gap between general and special education to implement more evidence-based practices in general education. Many of the instructional principles seem to be effective whether implemented in general or special education settings.

However, many practicing school psychologists are caught up in a debate about the appropriate way to assess students for special education eligibility, as if substituting one measurement (response to intervention) for another (using psychometric measures exclusively) will resolve the identification conundrum. This fixation on assessment misses the whole point of the conclusion of the Commission on Excellence in Special Education (see Chapter 1 by McCardle and Miller, this volume). That commission recommended putting more emphasis on the nature of the intervention and ensuring that the children who need specialized or differentiated instruction are identified very early in the process—even before they fail to respond to tier one core curriculum. In addition, emphasis on the quality of the implementation of the intervention needs to be addressed.

School psychologists have to go beyond being assessment only specialists and work more actively to learn about evidence-based instructional interventions tailored to individual students with learning differences that will bridge the gap between general and special education. We strongly believe that school psychologists need to know who needs help, why they need help, what kind of help they need, and if they get better (and if not, conceptual frameworks for how to plan another instructional approach). Increasing the knowledge base of school psychologists on both academic interventions (as described in Step 1) and delivery systems, such as consultee-centered consultation (see Knotek et al., Chapter 8, and also Nelson et al., Chapter 13, this volume) should improve student-learning outcomes.

■ University-School Relationships

The university-school relationship has several layers, and examples were presented in chapters about training at preservice to inservice levels, as well as collaboration on research, as in Chapter 13 (this volume). Shernoff, Kratochwill, and Stoiber (2003) provide a compelling case for school psychologists "to enter the workforce...trained in interventions with demonstrable efficacy" (p. 468), enabling them to be more accountable and better prepared to improve outcomes for students. Although they surveyed school psychology program directors for their knowledge of EBIs related to social-emotional and behavioral interventions, the status of knowledge among program faculty on academic EBIs remains a question. Research reported in Chapter 22 showed that teacher educators often lack linguistic knowledge needed to use scientifically supported reading instruction in the classroom and that the textbooks they use in preservice teacher education do not provide sufficient background knowledge for teachers about these linguistic concepts. Research reported in Chapter 23 added the evidence that lecture and textbook knowledge may be necessary but it is not sufficient—mentoring of teachers by university faculty familiar with the evidence is also needed. Clearly teachers need to be introduced to what research has found that is relevant to educational practice at the preservice level before they face the realities of the classroom. However, they may also benefit from continued professional development (see Chapters 11–18, this volume). Both preservice and inservice professional development should prepare educational professionals for evaluating the effectiveness of the interventions for individuals (see Chapter 19, this volume) and groups (classrooms, schools, districts, states, see Chapter 20, this volume). Not only the students but also the teachers and curriculum should be evaluated in considering the effectiveness of an implementation (see Chapter 21, this volume). Not only teachers but also psychologists have an important role to play in translating research into practice (see Chapters 9, 13, and 25, this volume).

Even less is known about how school-based professionals are learning about implementation issues. Just as science is an evolving process, so is becoming a scientist-practitioner. Chapter 24 provides insight into the content and skills needed for practitioners and researcher/developers alike. Chapter 25 shows that school psychology interns can begin to apply research to educational practice and evaluate their evidence-based implementations. There needs to be additional attention paid both to an understanding of implementation issues and research on how to increase the use of EBIs in school practice.

■ Just a Beginning Step

We undertook the challenge of this book with an understanding that implementation is emerging as an equal challenge to researching and disseminating EBIs. Effective implementation requires that educational professionals have deep conceptual understanding of the research (theoretical questions addressed, methodology used to answer the questions, and the findings). Improving the implementation process requires a more focused examination of the realities of the school environment and the lived experiences of those who reside at the service delivery level. The voices of the authors in these chapters are a resource for improving the implementation quality of evidence-based practices in schools in the United States and other countries, with the potential to improve student learning outcomes. We hope that this book has provided a better sense of what the challenges are, stimulated thinking about the issues that need to be resolved, and encouraged readers who conduct successful EBIs to share their stories as inspiration for other educational professionals.

■ References

Coalition for Evidence-Based Policy. (2003, December). *Identifying and implementing educational practices supported by rigorous evidence: A user friendly guide*. Washington, DC, Department of Education.

Gottfredson, D. C., & Gottfredson, G. D. (2002). Quality of school-based prevention programs: Results from a national survey. *Journal of Research in Crime and Delinquency, 39*, 3–35.

Lipsky, M. (1980). *Street-level bureaucracy: Dilemmas of the individual in public services*. NY, Russell Sage Foundation.

Shernoff, E. S., Kratochwill, T. R., & Stoiber, K. C. (2003). Training in evidence-based interventions (EBIs): What are school psychology programs teaching? *Journal of School Psychology, 41*, 467–483.

Index